Reading for Thinking

Eighth Edition

Laraine E. Flemming

Dina Stewart Levitre
Community College of Rhode Island
Contributing Writer and Consultant

"The point here is to see and reflect on what sorts of things you need to add to the language to gain clarity: what sorts of inferences or guesses you need to make; what knowledge you need to bring to bear . . ."

—*How to Do Discourse Analysis: A Toolkit,* James Paul Gee

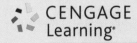 CENGAGE
Learning·

Australia • Brazil • Mexico • Singapore • United Kingdom • United States

CENGAGE
Learning®

Reading for Thinking, Eighth Edition
Laraine Flemming

Product Director: Annie Todd

Senior Product Manager: Shani Fisher

Managing Content Developer: Megan Garvey

Development Editor: Maggie Barbieri

Content Coordinator: Erin Nixon

Marketing Brand Manager: Lydia LeStar

Senior Content Project Manager:
  Aimee Chevrette Bear

Art Director: Faith Brosnan

Manufacturing Planner: Betsy Donaghey

Rights Acquisition Specialist: Ann Hoffman

Production Service: Books By Design, Inc.

Text Designer: Books By Design, Inc.

Cover Designer: Saizon Design

Cover Image: shutterstock.com
  © Fedor Selivanov

Compositor: S4Carlisle Publishing Services

Library of Congress Control Number: 2013941274

ISBN-13: 978-1-285-43046-1
ISBN-10: 1-285-43046-8

Cengage Learning
200 First Stamford Place, 4th Floor
Stamford, CT 06902
USA

Cengage Learning is a leading provider of customized learning solutions with office locations around the globe, including Singapore, the United Kingdom, Australia, Mexico, Brazil and Japan. Locate your local office at **international.cengage.com/region.**

Cengage Learning products are represented in Canada by Nelson Education, Ltd.

For your course and learning solutions, visit **www.cengage.com**.

Purchase any of our products at your local college store or at our preferred online store **www.cengagebrain.com**.

Instructors: Please visit **login.cengage.com** and log in to access instructor-specific resources.

Printed in the United States of America
1 2 3 4 5 6 7 17 16 15 14 13

Contents

2 Vocabulary Building for College Reading 66

3 Reviewing Paragraph Essentials 110

4   Identifying and Learning from Organizational Patterns   181

5   Understanding, Outlining, and Summarizing Longer Readings   256

8   Understanding the Difference Between *Fact* and *Opinion*   487

9 Analyzing Arguments 537

10 Evaluating Arguments 610

Putting It All Together 654

A Word from Laraine Flemming

"The ideal teacher functions as a model of comprehension-fostering-and-monitoring activities. . . ."

—From *Instructing Comprehension: Fostering Activities in Interactive Learning Situations* by Ann L. Brown, Annemarie Sullivan Palinscar, and Bonnie B. Armbruster

Much of what I do in my books—focus on explaining skills and concepts in as clear and as concrete a way as possible—comes from what I have learned over the course of thirty-five years as a classroom instructor teaching reading and writing to very diverse student populations—from eight-year-olds struggling to master phonics and the mysteries of English spelling to my current class of poetry students, whose ages range from 78 to 96. Without illustrations that model the process of both reading and composing, students are likely to get confused, thus my consistent emphasis on showing them how to think their way through a text, whether they are reading it or writing it.

My more formal training includes a Bachelor of Science in English Education with a secondary reading certification, a Master of Arts in Victorian Literature, and a Ph.D. in American literature, all of which have also contributed to how I think about language and learning and the role they should play in teaching both reading and writing.

Still, it's definitely been the classroom that has forged my ideas about how to improve students' reading and writing. What you see in my books are classroom-tested, research-based explanations and exercises that have worked for me, as well as the many instructors who have generously helped me revise and refine them over the years. As always, my hope is that they will work for you just as well.

Preface

Laraine Flemming unlocks the mystery of critical reading in the Eighth Edition of *Reading for Thinking,* the most advanced text in her three-book series.

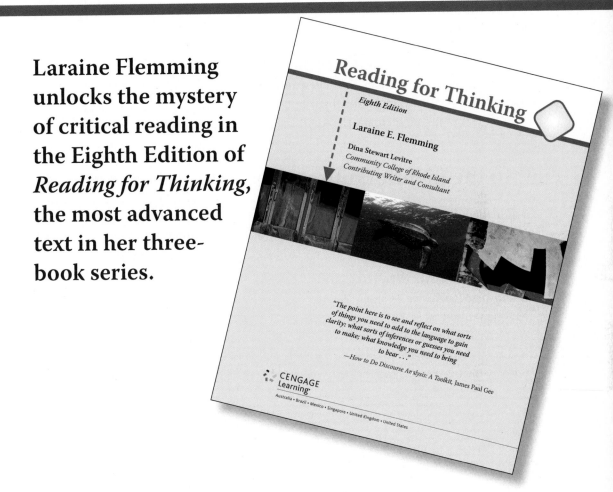

Reading for Thinking

Eighth Edition

Laraine E. Flemming

Dina Stewart Levitre
Community College of Rhode Island
Contributing Writer and Consultant

"The point here is to see and reflect on what sorts of things you need to add to the language to gain clarity: what sorts of inferences or guesses you need to make; what knowledge you need to bring to bear . . ."
—*How to Do Discourse Analysis: A Toolkit,* James Paul Gee

CENGAGE Learning·

Australia · Brazil · Mexico · Singapore · United Kingdom · United States

"The strength of this edition is Laraine's writing style."

—Michelle Hollitz, Borough of Manhattan Community College

"One strength about this book is its clear and simple explanation of the skills and concepts. . . . The many exercises allow students to practice and reinforce the skills and knowledge."

—Danhua Wang, Indiana University of Pennsylvania

Unlike other textbooks that assume critical reading requires an entire set of new and different skills, *Reading for Thinking* shows students step by step how to broaden and deepen their idea of comprehension until it includes the analysis of a writer's language, logic, tone, and evidence.

Using high-interest readings from textbooks, magazines, and newspapers, the author goes beyond asking students to analyze the ideas of others and encourages them to express strong opinions of their own. They then have to explain and defend those opinions by using the analytical tools identified in her text. As always, this new edition features Laraine Flemming's trademark clear writing style and engaging tone.

New to the Eighth Edition

While the book's much praised style and approach remain the same, the eighth edition of *Reading for Thinking* includes a number of new and important features.

◆ Connecting Writing to Reading

Brand-new *Reviewing Through Writing* assignments follow up explanations of reading techniques, so that students better understand how writers and readers work together. As soon as students have learned what a writer does to help readers focus on key words and get the point of a text, they are asked to switch roles. They become the writers, who provide the necessary clues that help readers re-create their intended message.

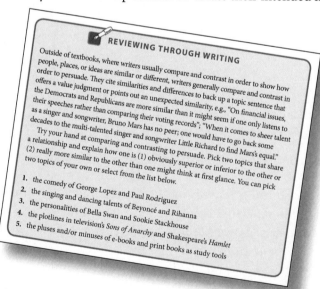

REVIEWING THROUGH WRITING

Outside of textbooks, where writers usually compare and contrast in order to show how people, places, or ideas are similar or different, writers generally compare and contrast in order to persuade. They cite similarities and differences to back up a topic sentence that offers a value judgment or points out an unexpected similarity, e.g., "On financial issues, the Democrats and Republicans are more similar than it might seem if one only listens to their speeches rather than comparing their voting records"; "When it comes to sheer talent as a singer and songwriter, Bruno Mars has no peer; one would have to go back some decades to the multi-talented singer and songwriter Little Richard to find Mars's equal."

Try your hand at comparing and contrasting to persuade. Pick two topics that share a relationship and explain how one is (1) obviously superior or inferior to the other or (2) really more similar to the other than one might think at first glance. You can pick two topics of your own or select from the list below.

1. the comedy of George Lopez and Paul Rodriguez
2. the singing and dancing talents of Beyoncé and Rihanna
3. the personalities of Bella Swan and Sookie Stackhouse
4. the plotlines in television's *Sons of Anarchy* and Shakespeare's *Hamlet*
5. the pluses and/or minuses of e-books and print books as study tools

◆ Marginal Think Alouds Model Expert Reading

Drawing on the research of Annemarie Palinscar, Ann L. Brown, and P. David Pearson, all of whom emphasize the importance of consistent and explicit instruction in comprehension strategies, Flemming has included marginal annotations—*Think Alouds*—that show students how to use clues from the text to determine the writer's main idea and store it in their long-term memory.

> The opening sentence already suggests this idea will be challenged.
>
> Sentence 2 intensifies the shift away from the opening point. Sentence 3 hones in on the real point of the reading.
>
> Sentence 4 identifies the basic difference and the remaining sentences alternate illustrating the two types of rules.

[1]In casual conversation, we are likely to treat the words *morals* and *ethics* as synonyms. [2]But they aren't really synonymous. [3]Morals and ethics differ in subtle but important ways. [4]***Morals*** are personal rules about good or virtuous behavior, and they can contradict or undermine ***ethics***, which are rules defined by the larger group or society to which an individual belongs. [5]For instance, an attorney is ethically bound to defend a client to the best of his or her ability. [6]Yet that attorney, upon discovering that the client is actually guilty of a horrific crime, may feel immoral about providing the client with a good defense. [7]Similarly, the pharmacist who refuses to fill a prescription for a birth control pill is ignoring professional ethics in favor of obeying what are considered moral rules. [8]On an individual level, moral rules are also less subject to change than ethical rules are. [9]For instance, people who believe it's immoral to eat the flesh of animals don't usually change their mind about that belief, even if they resume eating meat. [10]Both morals and ethics, however, are strongly influenced by the cultural context. [11]While an American might consider it both moral and ethical to keep a secret revealed by a friend or relative, someone in Afghanistan might feel morally and ethically bound to reveal the secrets if they involved the betrayal of family honor.

◆ New Material About Reading on the Web

The Eighth Edition includes many more practical tips on how experienced readers respond to writing created specifically for the Web. A brand-new section identifies the specific differences between writing for print and writing for an online audience.

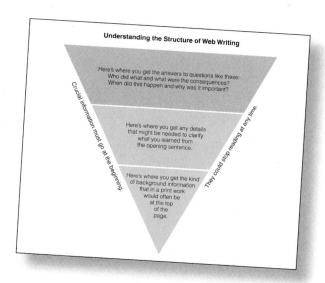

◆ Writing Exercises Test Web Expertise

The Eighth Edition also provides original exercises that encourage students to apply what they know about the differences between print and Web-based texts to create print text ready for viewing online.

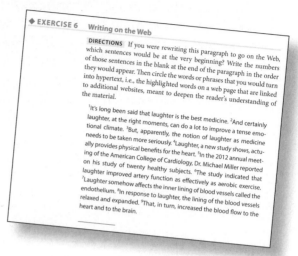

◆ EXERCISE 6   Writing on the Web

DIRECTIONS If you were rewriting this paragraph to go on the Web, which sentences would be at the very beginning? Write the numbers of those sentences in the blank at the end of the paragraph in the order they would appear. Then circle the words or phrases that you would turn into hypertext, i.e., the highlighted words on a web page that are linked to additional websites, meant to deepen the reader's understanding of the material.

[1]It's long been said that laughter is the best medicine. [2]And certainly laughter, at the right moments, can do a lot to improve a tense emotional climate. [3]But, apparently, the notion of laughter as medicine needs to be taken more seriously. [4]Laughter, a new study shows, actually provides physical benefits for the heart. [5]In the 2012 annual meeting of the American College of Cardiology, Dr. Michael Miller reported on his study of twenty healthy subjects. [6]The study indicated that laughter improved artery function as effectively as aerobic exercise. [7]Laughter somehow affects the inner lining of blood vessels called the endothelium. [8]In response to laughter, the lining of the blood vessels relaxed and expanded. [9]That, in turn, increased the blood flow to the heart and to the brain.

◆ New Tips on Evaluating Websites

Despite the media hype about students being digital natives, research on Web use indicates that students vary widely in their ability to use the Web with many of them unsure about how to go about gathering and evaluating information. *Reading for Thinking* now provides specific tips designed to help students critically evaluate online information.

◆ More Visuals to Please the Brain

The latest cognitive research on learning indicates that information is stored in different ways in different regions of the brain. In response to that research, this edition makes heavier use of diagrams and photos that echo the message of the text, thereby doubling the chances that students will store it in long-term memory.

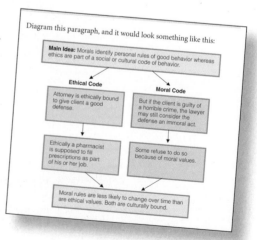

Diagram this paragraph, and it would look something like this:

Main Idea: Morals identify personal rules of good behavior whereas ethics are part of a social or cultural code of behavior.

Ethical Code

Attorney is ethically bound to give client a good defense.

Moral Code

But if the client is guilty of a horrible crime, the lawyer may still consider the defense an immoral act.

Ethically a pharmacist is supposed to fill prescriptions as part of his or her job.

Some refuse to do so because of moral values.

Moral rules are less likely to change over time than are ethical values. Both are culturally bound.

◆ Revised and Expanded Discussion of Summarizing

The new edition of *Reading for Thinking* gives summarizing more attention than ever before. Chapter 1, **Acquiring the Keys to Academic Success**, shows students how to create summary sheets for note-taking. Chapter 5, **Underlining, Outlining, and Summarizing Longer Readings**, offers a revised series of pointers on how to construct a useful summary, showing students how text-specific questions can help them decide which details go into a summary and which ones can be left out.

> Who or what was involved?
> When did these events happen?
> Who or what caused them?
> What was attempted or accomplished?
> What was the outcome?
> Where did events take place?
> What was the time frame?
> How were the people or events involved related?
> What's the underlying organizational pattern?

◆ More Practice with Paraphrasing

Like summarizing, paraphrasing is a crucial academic skill. In recognition of this, the Eighth Edition of *Reading for Thinking* offers a revised list of paraphrasing pointers in the opening chapter, **Acquiring the Keys to Academic Success**, and expands throughout the number of exercises asking students to paraphrase main ideas and brief excerpts.

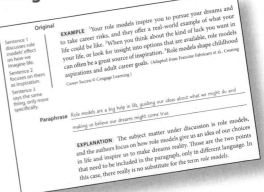

Original

Sentence 1 discusses role models' effect on how we imagine life.

Sentence 2 focuses on them as inspiration.

Sentence 3 says the same thing, only more specifically.

EXAMPLE [1]Your role models inspire you to pursue your dreams and to take career risks, and they offer a real-world example of what your life could be like. [2]When you think about the kind of luck you want in your life, or look for insight into options that are available, role models can often be a great source of inspiration. [3]Role models shape childhood aspirations and adult career goals. (Adapted from Francine Fabricant et al., *Creating Career Success* © Cengage Learning.)

Paraphrase Role models are a big help in life, guiding our ideas about what we might do and making us believe our dreams might come true.

EXPLANATION The subject matter under discussion is role models, and the authors focus on how role models give us an idea of our choices in life and inspire us to make dreams reality. Those are the two points that need to be included in the paragraph, only in different language. In this case, there really is no substitute for the term *role models*.

> *"The first chapter is also a strength—it's nice to start with study strategies before starting into other content."*
>
> —Michelle Hollitz, Borough of Manhattan Community College

> *"Paraphrasing is very helpful to the students."*
>
> —Cathy Hunsicker, Dalton State College

◆ More Questions That Encourage Personal Engagement

Appearing throughout the chapters are *What Do You Think?* questions designed to stimulate discussion of ideas introduced in the readings. The questions help students recognize, early on, that the title *Reading for Thinking* refers not just to the thinking of others but also to their own ability to form opinions on critical issues.

"I love using Reading for Thinking. *The comprehension skills are presented in a friendly, casual way, and the readings are interesting, so the comprehension issue is very well addressed."*

—Dina Levitre, Community College of Rhode Island

◆ Revised Discussion of Bias

Identifying bias in a reading passage can be challenging, so Chapter 10, **Evaluating Arguments**, offers a revised discussion of the topic with many new examples that illustrate the difference between acceptable and unacceptable bias. Chapter 10 also describes four key characteristics of a bias that has gone overboard to become so excessive readers need to look elsewhere for information.

1. Does the author use a tone that is heavy with outrage, sarcasm, or irony?
2. Does the author insist that an opposing point of view is not possible for anyone who has common sense?
3. Does the author claim that the opposing point of view has no merit without explaining *why* the opposition does not have a leg to stand on?
4. Does the author spend more time insulting the opposition than supporting his or her point of view?

"I love this textbook. I chose it because it has targeted skill development that builds and then is assessed in longer readings. . . . Flemming does an excellent job of providing readings that spark discussion."

—Michele Forbis, North Central Texas College

Copyright © Cengage Learning. All rights reserved.

◆ Revised End-of-Chapter Format Allows for More Comprehensive Reviews

Titled *Taking Stock*, the end-of-chapter readings cover a wide range of topics from the environmental importance of the alligator to the evolutionary significance of romantic infatuation. In completing each *Taking Stock* selection, students review what they have learned not just from the chapter just completed but also from the chapters that came before. The majority of the *Taking Stock* readings are drawn from college textbooks.

◆ Double the Number of Textbook Selections

The Eighth Edition of *Reading for Thinking* includes more textbook selections than ever before. But like all the readings in a Flemming text, the textbook excerpts included focus on topics and issues that will stimulate student interest; among them are discussions of children raised by animals, the origin and function of romantic love, the mysterious "white nose syndrome" that threatens the existence of bats, and the influence of optimism on human survival.

◆ New Thematically Linked Readings in *Putting It All Together*

Four out of the five end-of-book readings are new and focus on the way culture shapes consciousness. Readings range from media researcher Sherry Turkle's contention that our ability to interact with others is shrinking as we increasingly rely on digital communication to sociologist Jim Henslin's argument that our personal interactions are what make us human. Because the readings are now thematically linked, students get additional chances to compare and synthesize different positions on the same topic.

◆ A New Format for *Putting It All Together*

All the end-of-book readings include marginal annotations that guide the reader's attention while questions on the readings are divided into two parts. *Taking a Closer Look* offers a review of specific comprehension skills while *Reading with a Critical Eye* encourages students to use the critical reading tools introduced in the second half of the book.

Putting It All Together

© Ulrich Flemming

The readings that follow let you apply everything you have learned about understanding and evaluating a writer's explanation or argument. However, these readings are meant to serve another purpose as well. Because they explore issues of past and current importance for our culture, you should try to determine your own personal perspective on the issues discussed. As the preface of *Reading for Thinking* points out, the goal of this textbook was always twofold: to help you analyze the thoughts of others while hammering out your own position on topics relevant to your life, if not right now, then very soon.

654

And Some Things Never Change

In its latest edition, *Reading for Thinking* still offers

- an incremental approach with each new skill building upon the previous one.

- lively readings that encourage student motivation.

- numerous and varied exercises.

- clear, comprehensive, and concrete explanations.

- *Check Your Understanding* reviews that help students and instructors assess learning.

- a variety of test and practice questions that go beyond testing content to teach students how to think their way through a text.

- vocabulary reviews concluding Chapters 3 through 10.

Additional Resources

◆ For Students

Aplia for Developmental Reading, an online reading and learning solution, helps students become better readers by motivating them with compelling material, interactive assignments, and detailed explanations. In-text vocabulary features new and challenging words. Students receive immediate, detailed explanations for every answer, and grades are automatically recorded in the instructor's Aplia gradebook.

Aplia's chapter specific problem sets ensure that students are learning course concepts and practicing their application on a regular basis. With this text you may also have your students use an Individualized Study Path (ISP). ISP is an alternative course format for Developmental English. Based on diagnostic performance data, an ISP creates a unique list of assignments in Aplia for each student. For more information visit www.aplia.com/developmentalenglish.

◆ For Instructors

The Instructor's Resource Manual and Test Bank offers suggestions for teaching each chapter and supplementary exercises for skills introduced in *Reading for Thinking*. These suggestions and exercises are great for the new instructor looking for support or the more experienced teacher looking for ideas. The Instructor's Resource Manual also provides a list of all the vocabulary words introduced in the book, along with a sample midterm and final, and glossary of key terms.

Cengage Learning Testing Powered by Cognero® is a flexible, online system that allows instructors to author, edit, and manage text-specific test-bank content. Instructors can create their own questions or edit existing ones using the online system. Content can be delivered through an LMS with no special installs or downloads required.

The Instructor Companion Website features a wide variety of teaching aids, including chapter-specific PowerPoint presentations, the Instructor's Manual, and more. Instructors who want to use the companion website should go to login.cengage.com. Faculty who have not set up a username and password can create an account on this site.

Acknowledgments

As always, I relied heavily on reviewers' suggestions to guide this revision, and once again, my reviewers came through with ideas for improvements that were thoughtful, imaginative, and practical, a more complicated, three-part mix than one might think. The following reviewers were definitely up to the challenge. Many thanks to Rita Alonso-Sheldon, Palm Beach State College; Wendy Crader, Alamo Colleges Northeast Lakeview; Michele Forbis, North Central Texas College; Carol Friend, Mercer County Community College; Laura Hamilton, Oregon County Community College; Michelle Hollitz, Borough of Manhattan Community College; Cathy Hunsicker, Dalton State College; Dina Levitre, Community College of Rhode Island; Donalyn Lott, Nunez Community College; and Danhua Wang, Indiana University of Pennsylvania.

In addition to my reviewers, I want to thank my editor Shani Fisher for her almost superhuman patience and support as well as her smart revision suggestions, which shaped my thinking about what would improve the book; Maggie Barbieri, whose remarkable talents as a writer and a human being helped me meet tight deadlines; Nancy Benjamin of Books By Design, whose two decades of work as the packager of my books have been invaluable to me and a major reason why the books have been successful; Mary Schnabel, whose proofreading and design suggestions have always made the pages of my books better than they were when they left my desk; Karyn Morrison, whose endless patience tracking down the permission rights for my readings never ran out, and last but never least, to Ulrich Flemming, whose gorgeous photographs continue to light up the pages of my books.

Acquiring the Keys to Academic Success

1

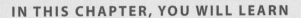

IN THIS CHAPTER, YOU WILL LEARN

- how to use a five-step method for comprehending text-book assignments.
- how annotating and underlining aid both comprehension and memory.
- why paraphrasing while reading is critical to academic success.
- how to use the Web to prepare for reading assignments.
- how to adapt your learning strategies to reading on the Web.

"Studying requires a double or split mental focus. On the one hand, you need to be focused on the material itself. At the same time, however, you need to be constantly checking to see that you are actually performing those mental operations that produce learning."
—E. A. Locke, *A Guide to Effective Study*

By the time you finish this textbook, you'll possess all the reading and learning strategies you need to succeed in college. However, like most of us, you probably don't want to wait. You'd prefer more immediate results. The good news is that you can get those quick results by consistently putting into practice all the learning techniques and study habits introduced in this chapter. Start using them now, and refine them as you go along.

 ## Have a Method for Completing Textbook Assignments

If you are reading a novel purely for your own pleasure, it's fine to just open the book and start reading. You don't need to make an effort to focus or distribute your attention selectively. But if you do the same thing with a textbook assignment, it's easy to pay too much attention to details that don't matter and miss the ones that do. Effective textbook reading requires a method.

SQ3R Is Worth the Effort

One of the most popular and time-tested methods for study reading was created by psychology instructor Francis Robinson. The method is called SQ3R, and it reflects Robinson's understanding of how the mind works. Robinson knew, for instance, that the rate of forgetting is highest immediately after new information is learned. For that reason, SQ3R includes a recall step that you do as soon as you finish reading a chapter section. Doing the recall step right after reading a chapter section slows down the rate of forgetting.

Robinson also knew that good reading comprehension relies heavily on the mind's ability to make and confirm predictions about how a writer's ideas will develop. Thus, SQ3R starts with a survey, or preview, step that provides a basis for making predictions. Those predictions are then confirmed or contradicted through the actual reading of the text.

Using a Different System

Since Robinson created SQ3R, other systems have come along, most of them quite similar and distinguished only by the acronym[†] or the initials used to create the name. If you are familiar with one of those systems and think it works, then by all means continue using it. But if you don't already have a method for reading textbooks and tend to read them the same way you might read an article in *USA Today*, consider learning, adapting, and applying the following steps in SQ3R.

S: Survey

"A quick overview orients the reader and allows him to comprehend at least partially what is to come."

—Francis Robinson, *Effective Study*[†]

To survey, or preview, a chapter takes a few minutes—ten or fifteen—to get a general sense of the chapter's contents and organization. The elements of the chapter you cover during a survey will vary with the textbook format. Still, you should always read any portions of text titled *introduction, preview, summary,* or *review*. Then skim the remaining pages, looking for the kinds of clues to significance listed in the following box.

[†]Others you might consider are PQRST (Preview, Question, Read, Self-Recitation, Test) and REAP (Read, Encode, Annotate, Ponder). I suggest trying two or three different methods and figuring out which one suits you best.
[†]All quotations attributed to Robinson in this section come from the fourth edition of Robinson's book, *Effective Study*, published by Harper and Row in 1961.

Textbook Clues to Significance ♦	1. Titles, major and minor headings
	2. Marginal notes on key terms and concepts
	3. Questions appearing between or at the start of chapter sections
	4. Pictures, cartoons, graphs, tables, and charts, including captions
	5. Words printed in boldface, colored ink, or italics
	6. Icons, or symbols, like checkmarks, asterisks, or boxes used to highlight information in the text
	7. Boxed statements or lists of any kind

A Note on Being a Flexible Reader

Experienced readers are **flexible readers**. They know that one reading strategy does not suit all texts. Thus they are always ready to try something different if their first approach doesn't produce results. If, for instance, trying to visualize the author's meaning doesn't work because the concepts, or ideas, being explained are too abstract, or lacking in physical form, flexible readers try to **paraphrase**, or re-state, the author's ideas using their own words. Similarly, if you've read the introduction and summary page plus glanced at all the clues listed above, yet still have no idea what direction the chapter will take, read the opening sentence of every paragraph. Still struggling? Then try reading the first and last sentence of every paragraph.

Q: Question

"The use of a question at the beginning of each section gives . . . a core idea around which to organize the material [that] follows."[†]

—Francis Robinson

Raising and answering questions while you read will help you stay motivated. Each time you answer a question, you'll feel a sense of accomplishment. Questions will also help you zero in on the most important elements of the chapter section. But there is an additional bonus as well.

Posing questions based on the title, headings, photos, illustrations, and other visual aids helps you distribute your attention while you read. That's because the purpose of headings and visual aids is to highlight, emphasize, and sometimes elaborate on key information. Guided by

---

[†]Robinson's method, if consistently applied, can really boost your comprehension, but no one would ever claim he was a stylish writer.

these verbal and visual signals, you are bound to focus on what the author considered important.

Take, for instance, this picture of Thomas J. "Stonewall" Jackson, which appears in an American history book. Based on the caption, you might well ask the question: What made this man a hero?

Thomas J. "Stonewall" Jackson was widely viewed as the hero who saved the South in the Battle of Bull Run.

The Corcoran Gallery of Art/Corbis Museum/Corbis

Now read to find the answer:

In the first Battle of Bull Run,[†] Union soldiers were met by a Confederate force of 22,000 under the command of General Beauregard, recently arrived from Charleston. The Union general, McDowell, attacked immediately, guessing the Confederate left flank to be the weakest point in the line. Although McDowell's troops were shocked by the ferocity of the musket fire that greeted them, they almost cracked the southern line. Had it cracked, the war might have been over in the upper

[†]There were two battles at the same location, a stream known as Bull Run. In the South, the battles were called the battles of Manassas, a town in Virginia.

South. At the critical moment, however, 9,000 Virginians commanded by Confederate general Joseph E. Johnston arrived on the field after a frantic train ride from the Shenandoah Valley. At the same time, a brigade under the command of Thomas J. Jackson, a thirty-seven-year-old mathematics instructor at Virginia Military, shored up the sagging Confederate left. The Union soldiers fell back and broke in hysteria, fleeing for Washington. (Adapted from Joseph Conlin, *The American Past*, vol.1, 9e, © Cengage Learning.)

The caption accompanying the picture identified Jackson as a hero because he helped turn the tide in the first Battle of Bull Run. A reader not armed with a question based on the caption might have missed how important Jackson was to the South during the Civil War. In contrast, readers who had looked closely at the photo and the caption would never have missed Jackson's importance.

R-1: Read

As soon as you start your reading assignment, see if the opening sentences give you a sense of the **main idea**, or general point, the author intends to develop. Then read to confirm or revise your prediction. For instance, here is the opening sentence of a textbook selection about marriage. What does this sentence suggest?

In the discussion of the status and vitality of marriage, we often hear that a retreat from marriage has taken place in the United States in recent decades. (Bryan Strong et al., *The Marriage and Family Experience* 10e, © Cengage Learning.)

The sentence suggests that the author is going to challenge what "we often hear." It suggests that interpretation because this is a **textbook template**, or explanatory pattern, academic writers—actually writers of all kinds but textbook authors in particular—commonly use. They tell their readers that some idea has been repeated often, commonly believed, or thought to be true in the past. Then they go on to challenge that traditional or common sense point of view.

To illustrate, here's that opening sentence again. Now it's followed by the rest of the paragraph. Notice that by the end, the authors have revised their opening point.

After the word *yet* suggests a reversal is coming up, the authors make their real point: A retreat from marriage is not taking place in all social groups.

[1]In the discussion of the status and vitality of marriage, we often hear that a retreat from marriage has taken place in the United States in recent decades. [2]R. S. Oropesa and Nancy Landale (2004) describe the retreat from marriage as evident in a number of recent and ongoing trends: "historic" delays in the age at which women and men first marry, nearly "unprecedented" proportions of the population never marrying, "dramatic" increases in cohabitation and nonmarital births, and continued high divorce rates. [3]Yet, closer inspection indicates that the retreat from marriage has not occurred among all social groups. [4]Instead both racial and economic differences can be identified.

Whenever you are doing study reading, it pays to start each new section of a chapter with an idea about what's ahead. It doesn't matter if your predictions or expectations are wrong. It's the mental preparation that helps both concentration and remembering, even when you have to revise your initial predictions.

Be Alert to Common Textbook Patterns

Textbook writing, like other kinds of writing, makes use of common explanatory patterns or templates that provide a framework for communicating information. In your role as reader, you can benefit from becoming aware of these common patterns. Your pattern awareness will help you decide what's really important in a paragraph and allow you to focus your attention selectively. For instance, in the example above on marriage, experienced readers would finish reading that first sentence and immediately be on the lookout for an opposing point of view.

As you begin to notice typical ways writers present their ideas, pay close attention to explanatory patterns that turn up repeatedly. Use them in your own writing. Make note of them in your textbooks. Then when you see a familiar type of opening phrase or sentence, you are likely to know automatically how the author's train of thought will proceed. You'll know because you are familiar with the verbal patterns common to academic language.

Reading in Chunks

In addition to looking for clues that help you shape your expectations of what's to come, remember to break your assignments into manageable pieces. Don't assume you are going to read the entire chapter in a sitting. Plan on reading ten or fifteen pages per study session, even less if the material is difficult and unfamiliar.

Read with an Outline

Some expert readers make an outline based on chapter headings before they start reading (more on outlining on page 271). Each time they finish reading a chapter section, they jot down what they've learned from reading it. Here, for example, is the outline of a chapter section created during pre-reading.

Main Point Social Media Can Help Your Career

Major Headings 1. Facebook

2. Twitter

3. Pinterest

4. LinkedIn

5. YouTube

Here is the outline again after a first reading:

Social Media Can Help Your Career

1. Facebook

   a. "Liking" company news source on Facebook gets company updates into your newsfeed

2. Twitter

   a. Following a company will help you stay up-to-date on what's going on

   b. Tweets include easy-to-access articles about the company

3. Pinterest

   a. Best for highly visual fields like fashion, design, photography

4. LinkedIn

   a. Join groups in the industry you hope to work in

   b. Good for networking to make connections

   c. For a fee, you can get job postings

5. YouTube

    a. Companies post videos that tell a lot about company direction

    b. Good for videos about how to do well in interviews

    c. Excellent source of information about skills essential to medical, legal, and academic work

R-2: Recall

When Robinson first devised the SQ3R system, the second *R* meant *Recite*. At the time, Robinson thought students should look away and briefly recite answers to the questions they had initially posed, as soon as they finished a chapter section. For him, recitation was a way of **monitoring**, or checking, comprehension so that students wouldn't trick themselves into thinking they had understood a passage they actually needed to re-read.

Because Robinson himself was inclined to modify this step, suggesting, for instance, that students write out the answers to clarify fuzzy thinking, more modern versions of SQ3R have broadened the meaning of the second *R*, which now almost always means *Recall*.

Given the substitution of the more general term, there are a number of different ways to complete this step. As Robinson initially suggested, you can look away from the text and try to recite the key points in the passage. You can also write out answers to your original questions. You might even ask a friend or roommate to prompt you with a few key words while you respond with ideas linked to those words. You can also use the outline mentioned above and fill in whatever you remember about the chapter section. Whatever method you choose, the goal is to see how much you can recall from what you've just read. If it turns out you can recall very little, then mark the chapter section for a second reading (2X or RR).

Use Summary Sheets for Key Reviews

For courses that are particularly important or particularly difficult, consider making **summary sheets** that reduce the original text to its bare bones. You can create summary sheets on paper or in an online notebook.[†] Wherever or however you use summary sheets, they need to include labels for the three key elements of a text: (1) the **topic** or subject being discussed,

---

[†]My favorite online notebook is Evernote, because it makes organizing information into groups or categories fairly straightforward. It also allows you to clip web pages to your notes and easily send both notes and images via email. But there are others to choose from. Type the phrase "online notebooks" into your search engine to get a selection.

(2) the **main idea** or message, and (3) two or three **key details** that explain the author's general point. To illustrate, here is a section from a psychology text followed by a summary sheet filled in as part of the recall step in SQ3R:

Sample Summary Sheet

Short-Term Memory

The heading and repetition of the phrase "short-term memory" identify the topic.

Extended discussion of selective attention suggests it's essential to storing information in long-term memory.

Opening question focuses the reader's attention on how short-term memories are stored—by sound rather than image.

Paragraph 3 emphasizes again that short-term memory can hold on to only small amounts of information. The repetition suggests the importance of the idea.

1 Not everything we see or hear stays in memory. Imagine that a radio is playing in the background as your friend reads her shopping list. Will you remember what the announcer says too? Probably not. Because *selective attention* (focusing on a selected portion of sensory input) controls what information moves on to short-term memory. Short-term memory (STM) holds small amounts of information in conscious awareness for a dozen seconds or so. By paying attention to your friend, you will place her shopping list in short-term memory (while you ignore the voice on the radio saying "Buy Burpo Butter").

2 *How are short-term memories stored?* Short-term memories can be stored as images. But more often they are stored phonetically (by sound), especially in recalling words and letters. If you are introduced to Tim at a party and you forget his name, you are more likely to call him by a name that sounds like Tim (Jim, Kim, or Slim, for instance), rather than a name that sounds different, such as Bob or Miles.

3 Short-term memory briefly stores small amounts of information. When you dial a phone number or briefly remember a shopping list, you are using STM. Notice that unless you rehearse information (say it over and over to yourself), it's quickly "dumped" from STM and forever lost. Short-term memory prevents our minds from storing useless names, dates, telephone numbers, and other trivia. (Adapted from Dennis Coon and John O. Mitterer, *Introduction to Psychology* 12e, © Cengage Learning.)

Sample Summary Sheet

Topic Short-Term Memory

Main Message Short-term memory holds new information for a few seconds, then dumps it.

Key Details 1. Entries get stored more by sounds than images. 2. Forgetting is STM's response to interruptions. 3. STM holds small amounts of information for a short time.

The summary sheets you complete for the recall stage of your reading are unlikely to be very detailed. They are not supposed to be. At this stage, you are only using them to recall the basics of what you've read. However, as you review for exams or learn more about the topic, you may want to add details.

R-3: Review

After you finish reading the entire chapter, take a few minutes to review everything you have read. You can do this in any number of ways. For instance, you can list the chapter headings and then jot down a few key points about each one. You can also ask a friend or your roommate to pose questions based on the headings while you provide the answers. Consider as well making a concept, or idea, map linked to the headings in the chapter.

Here is an example of a concept map that shows the ideas introduced by some of the headings in the Taking Stock reading on pages 50–52.

Concept Map Highlighting Content and Relationships

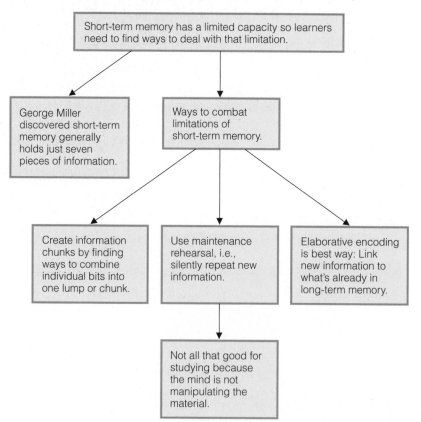

CHECK YOUR UNDERSTANDING

Monitor your comprehension of this chapter section by answering the following questions.

1. *True* or *False*. The Survey step in SQ3R requires you to skim the entire chapter from beginning to end.

2. *True* or *False*. The questions you pose as part of SQ3R should all be brief ones that require only a *yes* or *no* answer.

3. *True* or *False*. Textbook reading assignments should usually be completed in one sitting.

4. *True* or *False*. The only way to complete the second *R* in SQ3R is to recite aloud the key points of each chapter section.

5. *True* or *False*. There is no set way to review a chapter once you complete it. The method of review changes with the student and the material.

◆ **EXERCISE 1** **Surveying Reading Selections**

DIRECTIONS Survey the following selection using the steps listed in the box below. When you finish surveying, answer the questions in Part A. When you finish Part A, read the selection and answer the questions in Part B.

Survey Steps
◆

1. Read the title. Use it to make predictions and ask questions about the reading.

2. Read the first paragraph to see if it confirms your prediction about the reading or suggests a different idea.

3. Read the headings and turn them into questions.

4. Read the first sentence of every paragraph.

5. Read the last paragraph.

6. Ask yourself what you might already know or have learned about the need for achievement.

How the Need for Achievement Spurs Motivation

1 Many athletes who hold world records still train intensely; many people who have built multimillion-dollar businesses still work fourteen-hour days. What motivates these people? A possible answer is a motive called *need achievement*. People with a high need for achievement seek to master tasks—such as sports, business ventures, intellectual puzzles, or artistic creations—and feel intense satisfaction from doing so. They work hard at striving for excellence, enjoy themselves in the process, take great pride in achieving at a high level, and often experience success.

2 **Individual Differences** How do people with strong achievement motivation differ from others? To find out, researchers gave children a test to measure their need for achievement and then asked them to play a ring-toss game. Children scoring low on the need-for-achievement test usually stood so close or so far away from the ring-toss target that they either could not fail or could not succeed. In contrast, children scoring high on the need-for-achievement test stood at a moderate distance from the target, making the game challenging but not impossible.

3 **Characteristics of People with High Achievement Needs** Experiments with adults and children suggest that people with high achievement needs tend to set challenging, but realistic, goals. They actively seek success, take risks as needed, and are intensely satisfied with success. Yet, if they feel they have tried their best, people with high achievement motivation are not too upset by failure. Those with low achievement motivation also like to succeed, but success tends to bring them not joy but relief at having avoided failure (Winter, 1996).

4 People with strong achievement motivation tend to be preoccupied with their performance and level of ability (Harackiewicz & Elliot, 1993). They select tasks with clear outcomes, and they prefer feedback from a harsh but competent critic rather than from one who is friendlier but less

competent (Klich & Feldman, 1992). They like to struggle with a problem rather than get help. They can wait for delayed rewards, and they make careful plans for the future (F. S. Mayer & Sutton, 1996). In contrast, people who are less motivated to achieve are less likely to seek or enjoy feedback, and they tend to quit in response to failure (Graham & Weiner, 1996).

5　**Development of Achievement Motivation**　Achievement motivation tends to be learned in early childhood, especially from parents. For example, in one study young boys were given a very hard task, at which they were sure to fail. Fathers whose sons scored low on achievement motivation tests often became annoyed as they watched their boys work on the task, discouraged them from continuing, and interfered or even completed the task themselves (B. C. Rosen & D'Andrade, 1959). A different pattern of behavior emerged among parents of children who scored high on tests of achievement motivation. Those parents tended to (1) encourage the child to try difficult tasks, especially new ones; (2) give praise and other rewards for success; (3) encourage the child to find ways to succeed rather than merely complaining about failure; and (4) prompt the child to go on to the next, more difficult challenge (McClelland, 1985).

6　**Role of Cultural Influences**　Cultural influences also affect achievement motivation. Subtle messages about a culture's view of the importance of achievement often appear in the books children read and the stories they hear. Does the story's main character work hard and overcome obstacles, thus creating expectations of a payoff for persistence? Or does the main character loaf around and then win the lottery, suggesting that rewards come randomly, regardless of effort? And if the main character succeeds, is it the result of personal initiative, as is typical of stories in individualist cultures? Or is success based on ties to a cooperative and supportive group, as is typical of stories in collectivist cultures? Such themes appear to act as blueprints for reaching one's goals. It is not surprising, then, that ideas about achievement motivation differ from culture to culture. In one study, individuals from Saudi Arabia and from the United States were asked to comment on short stories describing people succeeding at various tasks. Saudis tended to see the people in the stories as having succeeded because of the help they got from others, whereas Americans tended to attribute success to the internal characteristics of each story's main character (Zahrani & Kaplowitz, 1993).

7 **Increasing Achievement Motivation**   Achievement motivation can be increased in people whose cultural training did not encourage it in childhood (McClelland, 1985). For example, high school and college students with low achievement motivation were helped to develop fantasies about their own success. They imagined setting goals that were difficult but not impossible. Then they imagined themselves concentrating on breaking a complex problem into small, manageable steps. They fantasized about working hard, failing but not being discouraged, continuing to work, and finally feeling great about achieving success. Afterward, the students' grades and academic success improved, suggesting an increase in their achievement motivation (McClelland, 1985). In short, achievement motivation is strongly influenced by social and cultural learning experiences and by the beliefs about oneself that these experiences help to create. People who come to believe in their ability to achieve are more likely to do so than those who expect to fail (Butler, 1998; Dweck, 1998; Wigfield & Eccles, 2000). (Adapted from Douglas Bernstein and Peggy Nash, *Essentials of Psychology* 2e, © Cengage Learning.)

Part A: Surveying

1. Throughout the reading, what question is the author trying to answer?

_____

2. *True* or *False*. Everyone has the same need for achievement, but not everyone is aware of it.

3. *True* or *False*. People with high achievement needs tend to set themselves impossible goals.

4. *True* or *False*. Achievement motivation is learned during adolescence.

5. *True* or *False*. Culture affects achievement motivation.

6. *True* or *False*. Once established, a person's level or degree of achievement motivation cannot be changed or altered in any way.

Part B: Reading

DIRECTIONS Answer the following questions by filling in the blanks or circling the letter of the correct response.

7. How do people with high achievement motivation respond to failure?
   a. They get outraged and give up.
   b. They criticize the person in charge for causing their failure.
   c. If they've tried their best, they don't get too upset by failure.
   d. They refuse to quit even when everything is against them.

8. Which of the following does *not* characterize people with high achievement motivation?
   a. They prefer to get feedback from someone who won't hurt their feelings.
   b. They like to struggle with a problem.
   c. They tend to make careful plans for the future.
   d. They select tasks with clear outcomes.

9. What was the difference when individuals from Saudi Arabia and the United States were asked to comment about people in stories succeeding at various tasks?

   _____

   _____

10. *True* or *False*. People who believe in their ability to achieve are more likely to succeed than people who expect to fail.

Write While You Read

The desire to leave textbooks without a mark on them is understandable. You probably want to sell them at the end of the semester. Unfortunately, that short-term goal may interfere with your long-term goal of leaving school a more informed and professionally prepared person. Although the research varies as to what kinds of marks on a text are most valuable,[†] most studies of writing and learning agree that marking pages consciously and selectively will help you comprehend and remember.

Mindless highlighting appears to do absolutely nothing for your comprehension or your memory. Similarly, underlining without thinking about why you are marking a particular sentence or phrase will not improve your comprehension. Likewise, marginal comments like *Boring*, *Whatever*, and *Who Cares* are not going to advance your college career. What will advance it is applying the following pointers for thoughtful annotation and selective marking of pages.

Annotating and Marking Textbook Pages
♦

1. Underline (or highlight) sparingly, marking only those words and phrases essential to the author's meaning.

2. If an entire sentence seems important, don't underline the whole sentence. Paraphrase it in the margins using your own words to express the author's ideas. (More on paraphrasing on pages 20–23.)

3. Make mini-diagrams in the margins of your textbook. For instance, draw arrows to show connections between cause and effect, generalization, and example, or claim and proof. Use chains of boxes or circles to describe a sequence or chain of events; e.g., Heavy tax collection 1786 → Shays' Rebellion 1787.

4. Paraphrase the main, or central, points of chapter sections, along with one or two examples, details, studies, or statistics used to explain the key points; e.g., "Amphibia suggest environmental threat; e.g., three-legged frogs."

5. Identify possible test questions; e.g., TQ : "Explain the purpose of *The Federalist Papers*."

6. Record ideas for term papers; e.g., TP : "In a very short period of time, J. Robert Oppenheimer went from hero to outcast."

7. Make marginal notes, **synthesizing**, or combining, what you learned from lectures and outside readings with what you are

---

[†]Some studies suggest underlining works; others come out on the side of diagramming, while very few support the most popular method—highlighting with a colored marker.

discovering from the chapter; e.g., "Baylin is like Zinn in his emphasis on the economic basis for the colonists' rebellion against the British." (More on synthesizing in Chapter 7 on pages 433–456.)

8. Compare and contrast the author's point of view with those of writers who agree or disagree.

9. Circle vocabulary words that seem central to the subject under discussion. Jot down brief definitions in the margin. You can also double underline the actual textbook definitions.

10. Make personal connections to movies you might have seen or novels you might have read dealing with the same or similar subjects; e.g., "Movie *Bad Day at Black Rock* good example of author's thinking."

11. Check your underlining at the end of each chapter section to see if reading just the underlined words and phrases makes enough sense for you.

12. If you are reading a particularly difficult chapter, it's a good idea to underline in pencil first. Use pen only on the second reading.

13. Create your own personal index. Every time you see a word or an idea that you think is central to the author's explanation, list it along with the page number on a blank page or an inside cover. When you are through reading, go back and add definitions.

14. Use the space at the top of the page to create general categories or headings that sum up portions of the text; e.g., "Causes of the Revolutionary War"; "Characteristics of Minerals"; "Effects of Acid Rain."

Symbols for Underlining and Annotating

The following chart lists symbols for underlining and annotating pages. Feel free to adapt the symbols listed here so that they work for you. You can even make up your own symbols. Whichever symbols you choose, though, be sure to use them consistently. That way you will remember what they represent.

<table>
<tr><td rowspan="15">Symbols for
Marking
Textbook
Pages
♦</td></tr>
</table>

Symbols for Marking Textbook Pages ♦

Arrows to identify cause and effect relationships

Boxes to highlight names you need to remember

Charles Darwin

Cause and effect diagrams to indicate relationships

Coercive Acts → Revolutionary War

Circles to highlight key points, specialized vocabulary, key terms, statistics, dates, and unfamiliar words

(1830)

Colon to signal the simpler or more specific restatement of a complex or general thought.

:

By 1960, parts of Great Lakes polluted: contamination by bacteria and industrial chemicals.

Cross-reference notes to compare closely related statements in the text

See p. 27 *or* Compare p. 27

Double underlining to highlight the main idea of the entire reading

═ ═ ═

Equals sign to signal a definition

=

Exclamation points to indicate your surprise at the author's statements

!

Mini-outlines to indicate relationships

Issei want to prove loyalty
　　buy war bonds
　　become superpatriots

Numbers to itemize and separate a series of statistics, studies, reasons, etc.

1, 2, 3, 4

Question marks to indicate confusion

?

Quotation marks to remind about quotes that might be effective in term papers

" "

Star to identify a crucial piece of information

★

Single underlining to highlight key ideas in paragraphs

— — —

Initials to identify ideas for term papers, possible sources of test questions, or passages in need of a second reading

TP, TQ, RR

Vertical lines to emphasize key passages longer than a sentence or two

‖

To illustrate what the pages of your textbook should look like when you finish underlining and annotating, here's an example of a page that's been thoroughly annotated for maximum understanding.

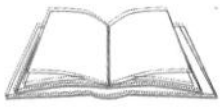

The Internment of Japanese-Americans

1   Far more than any other minority in the United States, Japanese-Americans suffered grievously during World War II. The internment of about thirty-seven thousand first-generation immigrants (Issei)** and nearly seventy-five thousand native-born Japanese-American citizens of the United States (Nisei)** in "relocation centers" guarded by military police was a tragic reminder of the fragility of civil liberties in wartime.

2   The internment of Japanese-Americans reflected forty years of anti-Japanese sentiment on the West Coast, rooted in racial prejudice and economic rivalry. Those who wanted Japanese-American land and businesses had long decried "the yellow peril." Following the attack on Pearl Harbor, anti-Japanese fervor grew among white Californians. Patriotic associations and many newspapers demanded the evacuation of Japanese-Americans. They were aided by the pronouncement of Jon De Witt, the Army general in charge of the Western Defense Command, who proclaimed, "It makes no difference whether he is an American citizen or not. . . . I don't want any of them."

3   In February 1942, President Roosevelt gave in to the pressure and issued Executive Order 9066, authorizing the removal from military areas of anyone deemed a threat. Although not a single Japanese-American was apprehended for spying or aiding the enemy and no evidence of any disloyal behavior by Japanese-Americans, the military ordered the eviction of all first-generation Japanese immigrants and native-born Japanese-American citizens of the United States from the West Coast.

Margin annotations:

Japanese-Americans got the worst treatment of all minorities.

Greed, not spying, was the real cause.

Openly racist

Executive Order 9066 = military rounded up and imprisoned Japanese-Americans with no evidence of wrongdoing.

Hawaii had no internment policy, but nothing bad happened as a result.

Only Hawaii was excepted. Despite the far larger number of Hawaiians of Japanese ancestry, as well as of Japanese living in Hawaii, no internment policy was implemented there, and no sabotage occurred. (Adapted from Paul Boyer et al., *The Enduring Vision* 6e, © Cengage Learning.)

While Japanese-American civilians living stateside were being treated as traitors, Japanese-American soldiers fighting overseas were winning medals for their bravery.

AP Photo/U.S. Army Signal Corps.

 ## Paraphrase to Check Comprehension

"Paraphrasing can serve as a form of note taking, allowing you to preserve the writer's exact meaning in those terms you understand best."

—Charles Bazerman, *The Informed Writer*

The term *paraphrasing* is probably familiar to you from writing courses. You know, for instance, that if you want to sum up an author's ideas in a term paper, you have to paraphrase them, using your words to make or explain the same point. If you don't paraphrase, you can easily end up with several pages of tacked-together quotations—almost the worst thing you could hand in to your instructor. Even worse, though, you could accidentally end up plagiarizing an author's words by picking them up directly. To avoid this mistake, it is extremely important to know how to paraphrase in writing.

Paraphrasing while reading, though, is different from paraphrasing for a term paper. A reading paraphrase requires you to be accurate. However, it doesn't require you to be especially complete or grammatically correct. Compare, for instance, two different paraphrases of the original text shown below. The first paraphrase is for a paper. The second is a reading paraphrase, created solely for the purposes of monitoring comprehension or taking marginal notes.

Original ◆
The word *irony* derives from "Eiron," one of the core characters in classical Greek drama. Eiron is a trickster who likes making fun of boastful, self-important people. By pretending he is ignorant and asking naïve questions, Eiron provokes the overly proud into revealing their ignorance. Eiron's technique, however, was not confined to the stage. In his lectures to students, the Greek philosopher Socrates used a similar strategy: He would pretend complete ignorance when asking a question such as "What is truth?" His goal was to provoke the person answering into revealing ignorance or lack of depth. This technique is known as "Socratic irony."

Paraphrase for a Paper ◆
Eiron was one of the staple characters in early Greek drama. He was a trickster, who acted as if he knew nothing while encouraging others to give explanations that revealed their ignorance. The Greek philosopher Socrates used a similar device. He would pose seemingly naïve questions like "What is truth?" and pretend he didn't know the answer. When the person questioned responded, Socrates would make it clear that the person's answer was poorly thought out. This pretense of ignorance to uncover a lack of knowledge or depth is called "Socratic irony."

Reading Paraphrase ◆
Word *irony* comes from Eiron, trickster in Greek plays, who asked dumb questions to reveal ignorance. "Socratic irony" uses similar method, pretending ignorance to uncover superficial thinking.

As the above examples show, paraphrasing to check reading comprehension or take notes doesn't require recalling every detail of the original. You just need to answer two basic questions: (1) What does the author say about some person, practice, idea, place, or event? (2) How did the author clarify, illustrate, or prove that point?

Be aware, though, that more difficult or unfamiliar material may require you to ask additional and more specific questions. If the text revolves around events happening over time, you may need to ask

"What chain of events is the author describing, and why?" "What do they lead to or result from?" If the passage points out similarities and differences between two topics, ask yourself what the point of the comparisons is. Whatever the questions—and they should always be formulated in response to the material—the goal is always the same: to uncover the core elements of the passage.

Paraphrase in Marginal Notes

For another illustration of a reading paraphrase, study the passage and marginal notes that follow. The passage is the original text; the notes are the reader's paraphrase of that text.

Many students cope with stress by asking for pets in the classroom.

Officials unsure when pets medical necessity.

Across the country, a growing number of students are seeking permission to bring "psychiatric service" animals into college classrooms and dormitories. The students say the animals, which range from cats and dogs to snakes, rats, and even tarantulas, help them cope with the stress of college life. But the law is unclear on whether colleges must accommodate such animals, and many colleges have struggled with how to distinguish a student with a true need from one who simply does not want to be separated from Fluffy or Spot.

As they should, the marginal notes identify the author's general point: Students are asking to bring pets into classrooms to alleviate stress. Notice, too, that the first marginal note tells you not just who's doing what but also why they are doing it: Students want to bring animals into the classroom because they want help coping with stress.

The second marginal note answers the question "What are the consequences or results?" Apparently college administrators are unsure as to where they should draw the line when it comes to allowing animals in the classroom.

These two brief notes, one of them not even a grammatically correct sentence, are all a reader would need to paraphrase for a comprehension check and memory aid. As the examples show, paraphrasing while reading doesn't require the same precision or completeness paraphrasing for a paper does. Each kind of paraphrasing has a different purpose.

Pointers on Paraphrasing While Reading

The more you get into the habit of paraphrasing while you read, the better you will be at it. Here are some pointers to get you started.

1. **Paraphrase only the basics.** When paraphrasing for marginal notes, your goal is to sum up in your own words the main idea or message of the passage, along with one or two details used to explain or prove the author's central thought.

2. **Use questions to focus your paraphrase.** If you finish a chapter section and have only a foggy notion of its content, don't get discouraged. Force yourself to answer questions like these: What person, event, or idea does the writer focus on? Is the author talking about a particular time frame? What happens in the reading? Is there someone who performs an action? Are there events that have big consequences? Your answers can provide the basis for your paraphrase.

3. **Be ready to re-read.** If you pose any of the questions above without getting an answer, mark the passage you wanted to paraphrase for a second reading. Good readers know that difficult texts sometimes require a second, *even a third*, reading.

4. **Don't get hung up on individual words.** There will be lots of times when you paraphrase a sentence and can't, without spending too much time, find a good substitute for a word. If it's only one word out of the original text, don't worry about it. Use the original word. The time to worry is when one word grows into six. That's a sign that you've started copying the original text rather than paraphrasing it.

5. **Look away from the page while paraphrasing.** If you look at the paragraph while you paraphrase it, you are likely to think you understand the material better than you do. Looking at the original text while paraphrasing encourages you to use the author's words and forget about finding your own. That defeats the purpose of paraphrasing.

6. **Make the underlying relationships part of the paraphrase.** If you are reading about how Alexander Hamilton and Thomas Jefferson differed on the role federal government should play in society—Jefferson mistrusted it; Hamilton promoted it—your paraphrase shouldn't sum up Jefferson and Hamilton's points of view individually. Those paraphrased points of view need to show the relationship explained in the passage: The two men <u>differed</u> in their attitude toward government.

CHECK YOUR UNDERSTANDING

1. In your own words, why should you paraphrase while reading?

   _____

   _____

2. When you paraphrase you need to understand the _____ along with the words.

◆ **EXERCISE 2**   **Practice with Paraphrasing**

DIRECTIONS   Read each passage. Then select the letter of the reading paraphrase that would be most useful as notes on the material.

EXAMPLE   For the milk industry, yogurt drinks, soymilk, and vitamin waters have all been a disaster. Gone are the days when kids walked around with milk moustaches. Nowadays they are more likely to be drinking a yogurt smoothie through a straw. In short, the milk industry is in a crisis. As the consumption of other dairy products has gone up, the consumption of milk as a drink has gone down. Since 1975, per capita consumption of milk in the United States has dropped by 30% according to the U.S. Department of Agriculture.

Reading Paraphrase

a. Milk business is in trouble. Too much competition from soy products.

b. Milk business is in serious trouble with a 30% drop in consumption since 1975.

c. Kids don't drink milk anymore, leaving milk industry in a shambles and trying to compete.

EXPLANATION   Answer *a* misrepresents the original meaning since it isn't just soy products that are giving the milk industry a headache. Answer *b* is correct because it doesn't change the meaning and gives a reason why the industry is anxious. Answer *c* misrepresents the original statement by suggesting that kids don't drink milk at all when the original suggests that, where kids are concerned, milk has competition.

Original **1.** Erik Erikson's theory of developmental tasks appropriate to different stages of life has profoundly influenced the way many psychologists think. Yet because research on Erikson's stages of development would require extensive and costly long-range studies, his ideas have not been scientifically proven. (Adapted from Barbara Engler, *Personality Theories* 7e, © Cengage Learning. All Rights Reserved.)

Reading
Paraphrase

a. Theory of stages and tasks very influential among medical doctors but no longitudinal studies to prove it.

b. Erik Erikson's theory of developmental stages is very influential despite lack of long-term studies.

c. Erik Erikson has had a big influence on how we see ourselves and our lives. No longitudinal studies have been done. Too expensive.

Original **2.** Coal is the single biggest air polluter in coal-burning nations, and burning coal accounts for at least one-fourth of the world's annual CO_2 emissions. To a growing number of scientists and economists, the burning of coal is one of the most serious environmental problems of the twenty-first century. (G. Tyler Miller and Scott E. Spoolman, *Sustaining the Earth* 9e, © Cengage Learning.)

Reading
Paraphrase

a. Big coal-burning power plants have major impact on environment in industrialized countries.

b. Coal is the biggest polluter among coal-burning nations, and the rate coal-burning is increasing has scientists worried.

c. Because coal is biggest polluter in coal-burning countries, many scientists think burning coal a huge environmental threat due to CO_2 produced.

Original **3.** Technology can make workers more accountable by gathering information about their performance. However, it can also contribute to worker error. In a recent study of a popular hospital computer system, researchers found several ways that the computerized drug-ordering program endangered the health of patients. For instance, the software program warned of a patient's drug allergy *after* the drug was ordered. (Adapted from Linda Mooney et al., *Understanding Social Problems* 8e, © Cengage Learning.)

<table>
<tr>
<td>Reading
Paraphrase</td>
<td>a. While technology can help monitor workers' behavior, it can also encourage workers to make deadly mistakes. Hospitals are particularly likely to show computer errors with patients getting the wrong drugs because of drug-ordering software.</td>
</tr>
<tr>
<td></td>
<td>b. Despite its benefits, technology in workplace can encourage mistakes. One hospital study found errors in drug-ordering software, for instance allergy notification coming after drug was ordered.</td>
</tr>
<tr>
<td></td>
<td>c. In recent studies of popular hospital software, researchers found major errors. Patient health was endangered because software didn't notify about allergy-related reactions.</td>
</tr>
</table>

◆ EXERCISE 3   Paraphrasing with Accuracy

DIRECTIONS   Read each brief passage. Then write what you consider to be an accurate paraphrase of the original.

Original

Sentence 1 discusses role models' effect on how we imagine life.

Sentence 2 focuses on them as inspiration.

Sentence 3 says the same thing, only more specifically.

EXAMPLE [1]Your role models inspire you to pursue your dreams and to take career risks, and they offer a real-world example of what your life could be like. [2]When you think about the kind of luck you want in your life, or look for insight into options that are available, role models can often be a great source of inspiration. [3]Role models shape childhood aspirations and adult career goals. (Adapted from Francine Fabricant et al., *Creating Career Success* © Cengage Learning.)

Paraphrase   Role models are a big help in life, guiding our ideas about what we might do and making us believe our dreams might come true.

EXPLANATION   The subject matter under discussion is role models, and the authors focus on how role models give us an idea of our choices in life and inspire us to make dreams reality. Those are the two points that need to be included in the paragraph, only in different language. In this case, there really is no substitute for the term *role models*.

Those aren't trees in the background; they are the clouds of dust that swirled over the Great Plains in the 1930s.

1. The dust storms that roared over the Great Plains of the United States during the 1930s were like nothing anyone had ever seen before. The ground dried up and cracked, the air went black with dust, and nothing would grow. While few had an answer to what had caused this environmental disaster, Hugh Hammond Bennett, a soil conservationist, did. He pointed an accusing finger at the U.S. Department of Agriculture, which had claimed that soil was the one resource that could not be exhausted and encouraged farmers to grow the same crop on the same soil for decades. As a result, the soil was depleted of necessary nutrients and turned to dust.

Paraphrase

_____

_____

_____

_____

_____

2. William Carlos Williams's book of poems *By Word of Mouth* is a tribute to his Spanish ancestry. Williams's mother was of Dutch and Spanish descent, and his father of English and Puerto Rican ancestry. The family spoke Spanish and English in the home, and Williams thought of his family as uniquely American in what he called its

"mingling" of ancestry and language. In *By Word of Mouth*, he translated famous poems by Spanish-speaking poets into English and displayed the poems, in both languages, side by side, a symbol of how he imagined his life.

Paraphrase _____

_____

_____

_____

_____

 # Use the Web to Build Background Knowledge

> "The . . . Web is a marvelous resource, but it also has some drawbacks. One is that it has the tendency to promote the rapid spread of misinformation. All one has to do is to put up some sloppily researched and/or incorrect data, and this will be picked up on by other persons who have no reason to believe otherwise, and who don't have the time or inclination to check their facts."
>
> —From the unofficial Stephen Jay Gould Archive, www .stephenjaygould.org

For more than three decades research on reading has consistently come to the same conclusion: The more background knowledge readers have about the topic under discussion, the easier it is to follow the writer's train of thought. On tests of reading comprehension, the people with the most knowledge about the topic consistently get the highest scores.

When evidence for the importance of background knowledge began to emerge, it was hardly cause for joy among college students. After all, if you were a student trying to master a chapter on the theory of continental drift,[†] background knowledge on the subject was not especially easy to acquire. The Internet, however, has changed all that. Now you can get the background knowledge you need by logging on to the Web.

Looking for Background Knowledge on the Web

Imagine that you are reading a chapter in your biology book titled "Mendel, Genes, and Inheritance." Although the words *genes* and *inheritance* might well mean something to you, if you didn't take a biology course in high school, you might draw a blank on the name *Mendel*. In addition, you might not have any idea about Mendel's role in our understanding of genes and inheritance.

_____

[†]continental drift: theory that explains how the continents were once combined and split apart due to the movement of plates that cover the Earth's surface.

Two decades ago, you'd have to scurry around looking for the right reference book to answer these questions: (1) Who was Mendel? (2) What did he have to do with the theory of genetic inheritance? Today, however, you can use the Web to get background about the topics addressed in your textbooks. All you need is a precise search term that will get you, as quickly as possible, to a solid source. Often, and this is true in this case, you can take a chapter heading for your search term. Chapter headings will usually be precise enough to get you the information you need. If you type a chapter heading like "Mendel, Genes, and Inheritance" into a search-engine box, in this case, Google's, up would come a list like this:

One or more of these sites is likely to give you precisely the background knowledge you want for the assignment. The problem is that you don't have time to look at them all, so you have to be selective about which ones you actually view.

Selecting the Right Sites to View

To avoid spending a lot of time finding the right website you need for background knowledge, you should have some strategies in mind to help identify the most promising sites for review.

Start by Using the Process of Elimination

The first thing you need to know is this: Search engines don't list websites by quality. The first site that comes up is *not* necessarily the best written, best organized, or most complete. Instead of automatically clicking on the first site that comes up or choosing a website too quickly, start your search by eliminating those that suggest they won't be useful. These are the websites that

1. seem to go beyond basic background information, for instance site number 7.

2. tell you to "jump" to another web page, for example, sites 2 and 6.

3. appear to offer mainly outlines, key terms, or flash cards, for example, site 5.

4. are written in highly technical language (none of the websites on our sample is that technical).

After applying these criteria, or standards, you have three websites to choose from. The first one you look at should be the one with the clearest caption language. In this case, that's site number 1, where you will find this explanation of Mendel, Genes, and Inheritance:

Mendel's Genetics

For thousands of years farmers and herders have been selectively breeding their plants and animals to produce more useful <u>hybrids</u> 🦋. It was somewhat of a hit or miss process since the actual mechanisms governing inheritance were unknown. Knowledge of these genetic mechanisms finally came as a result of careful laboratory breeding experiments carried out over the last century and a half.

Gregor Mendel
1822-1884

By the 1890s, the invention of better microscopes allowed biologists to discover the basic facts of cell division and sexual reproduction. The focus of <u>genetics</u> 🦋 research then shifted to understanding what really happens in the transmission of hereditary traits from parents to children. A number of hypotheses were suggested to explain heredity, but Gregor Mendel 🦋, a little known Central European monk, was the only one who got it more or less right. His ideas had been published in 1866 but largely went unrecognized until 1900, which was long after his death. His early adult life was spent in relative obscurity doing basic genetics research and teaching high school mathematics, physics, and Greek in Brno (now in the Czech Republic). In his later years, he became the abbot of his monastery and put aside his scientific work.

While Mendel's research was with plants, the basic underlying principles of heredity 🦋 that he discovered also apply to people and other animals because the mechanisms of heredity are essentially the same for all complex life forms.

Through the selective cross-breeding of common pea plants (*Pisum sativum*) over many generations, Mendel discovered that certain traits show up in offspring without any blending of parent characteristics. For instance, the pea flowers are either purple or white—intermediate colors do not appear in the offspring of <u>cross-pollinated</u> pea plants. Mendel observed seven traits that are easily recognized and apparently only occur in one of two forms:

Common edible peas

1. flower color is purple or white
2. flower position is axil or terminal
3. stem length is long or short
4. seed shape is round or wrinkled
5. seed color is yellow or green
6. pod shape is inflated or constricted
7. pod color is yellow or green

This observation that these traits do not show up in offspring plants with intermediate forms was critically important because the leading theory in biology at the time was that inherited traits blend from generation to generation. Most of the leading scientists in the 19th century accepted this "blending theory." Charles Darwin proposed another equally wrong theory known as "pangenesis" 🦋. This held that hereditary "particles" in our bodies are affected by the things we do during our lifetime. These modified particles were thought to migrate via blood to the reproductive cells and subsequently could be inherited by the next generation. This was essentially a variation of Lamarck's incorrect idea of the "inheritance of acquired characteristics."

Based on this website,[1] we can answer the two questions posed earlier: Who was Mendel and what did he have to do with genes and inheritance? Mendel was a late-nineteenth-century monk who figured out the principles of heredity. In particular, he figured out that certain traits are not a blend of parental characteristics but instead are inherited

---

[1]The URL for this website includes the letters *edu*: http://anthro.palomar.edu/mendel/ mendel_1.htm. That means it's maintained by an educational institution. Thus you don't automatically have to compare it to the contents of another website for accuracy, even though it's good practice to do so.

individually, a discovery that contradicted the existing wisdom of the day. This is the kind of background knowledge that can give you a general framework for reading a discussion of Mendel's role in explaining the relationship between genes and inheritance. As this example illustrates, background knowledge is at your fingertips when you use the right search term and then evaluate carefully the websites that your search term calls up.

Creating Effective Search Terms

1. **Brief phrases are usually better than single words.** If, for instance, you're reading about Harry Truman's use of loyalty oaths[†] to evaluate applications for government jobs, don't type just "Truman" or even just "loyalty oath" into the search-engine box. Instead, create a phrase like "Truman's loyalty oath." Phrases like this one narrow the number of websites a search engine brings up. And that's a good thing.

2. **Don't stick with search terms that fail to get results.** If using your textbook headings for search terms doesn't get you the information you need, change the wording of your search term to make it even more specific. If the heading of the chapter section is "César Chávez," and the list of sites that comes up in response to Chávez's name is both long and not obviously useful for the subject you are interested in—his role as a union leader—modify your search term by adding a related word or words, making your search term "César Chávez's leadership United Farm Workers."

3. **Consider using the word *AND* to focus your search term.** If you are researching the effect poverty has on psychological depression and can't use any of the headings in your textbook and no specific phrase comes to mind, try linking words together using "AND." Typing "depression AND poverty" into your search box will call up documents that contain both the word *poverty* and the word *depression*. In addition, the search engine will provide more focused and fewer results.

4. **If the order of the words is important, put quotation marks around the search term.** Sometimes the words in your search term require a specific order. When word order is important, put quotation marks

---

[†]The Democrats were being attacked for being "soft" on communism. To prove that they weren't, Truman, a Democrat, made loyalty oaths a requirement for federal employees, who had to swear loyalty to the United States and disavow any connections to groups critical of the government. No oath meant no job.

around the term to indicate the exact phrase you want the search engine to bring up, for instance "adjustable rate mortgages." That tells the search engine to return only those websites that discuss the entire phrase used in your search term.

Pointers for Picking a Website

1. **Don't just start at the top.** The first website on the list that comes up on your screen is not necessarily the one most appropriate to your needs. Hold off on looking at any one website until you have looked over all the items on the screen.

2. **Keep your purpose in mind.** If your goal is to get some overall background knowledge, then you don't need to look at websites that suggest the author is focusing on some very specific aspect of your topic. If you are reading a chapter passage on the Pony Express, and either the name or caption of a website focuses on Louise "Lou" McCloud, a female Pony Express rider who managed to disguise her gender and get a job galloping cross country, hold off and read about Lou some other time.

   For your purpose, a website with more general information is what's needed. However, you might want to engage in what web researchers call "squirreling." Bookmark the website to read at a later time, say when you are trying to come up with an idea for a paper. That's when having more specialized information about your assignments may do you some real good.

3. **Read the captions carefully.** The caption describing a website's contents can help you determine what's actually on the site. If the caption seems off target from what you need to know, the website probably is too. Don't click on it.

4. **Pay particular attention to sites with a URL, or web address, ending in .edu.** This indicates that the site is related to an educational institution, which means the information on it is probably accurate. It's also likely to have been double-checked by more than one person. That's not to rule out personal or organizational websites ending in *.com* or *.org*. But with these, you should check the information against two, even three, other websites to authenticate the website's accuracy.

5. **Hold off on using personal websites and blogs.** Like blogs, personal websites can be terrific sources of information, hosted by people deeply interested in their subject matter and enthusiastic about sharing their knowledge. Unfortunately, they can also be hosted by crackpots who believe that U.S. astronauts never made a moon landing or aliens are set to invade from outer space. It takes some time to sift through personal websites and evaluate their information by checking them against other sources, so leave them for a later date.

6. **Avoid websites expressing a strong bias.** Expressing a **bias**, or personal favoritism, is hard to avoid. Even when we don't mean to, we often reveal, through the language we use or the selection of details, how we feel about someone or something. Thus, it should come as no surprise that web writing can favor one viewpoint over another. As long as the bias doesn't distort the facts, there's nothing wrong with that.

   However, if you are just getting acquainted with a new topic or issue, you may not know when the author's bias has become excessive and tends toward factual distortion. For that reason, you should avoid websites that express a strong bias for or against some person or idea.

7. **Pick a website with a neutral tone.** When the word **tone** is used in the context of writing, it refers to the feeling, emotion, or attitude toward both subject matter and audience that emerges from the writer's words, imagery, and selection of details. Writers choose their words carefully to create a tone they think most appropriate to their **purpose**, or reason for writing. Writers whose **primary**, or main, purpose is to **inform**, i.e., give their readers information without including a personal point of view, are going to keep their tone fairly neutral as it is here:

   > In April 2012, seven-year-old Emily "Emma" Whitehead suffered her second leukemia relapse. With no other way to fight the disease at that point, the seven-year-old's parents and her doctors turned to an unlikely source to save the young girl's life—the HIV virus that causes AIDS. Emma underwent an experimental procedure involving a disabled form of virus being injected into her T-cells, which in turn fought the cancer cells in her body. The treatment, pioneered at The Children's Hospital of Philadelphia, seems to have worked, and it is similar to therapies being developed at other cancer centers around the United States.

In contrast, writers whose central purpose is to **persuade** want to convince you to share or at least consider their point of view. To that end, they are very likely to infuse their tone with feeling, as this writer has done:

> In April 2012, seven-year-old Emily "Emma" Whitehead suffered her second leukemia relapse. Desperate to fight the disease that was taking their young daughter's life, the seven-year-old's parents and her doctors turned to an unlikely source to save the child—the HIV virus that causes AIDS. Emma underwent an extraordinary experimental procedure involving a disabled form of virus being injected into her T-cells, which in turn fought the cancer cells in her body. The treatment, which was pioneered at The Children's Hospital of Philadelphia, seems to have worked. It is one of similar promising therapies being developed at other cancer centers around the United States, and researchers are excited about its possibilities.

Here you can see how words like *promising*, *extraordinary*, and *excited* give an excerpt with almost the exact same information a more enthusiastic tone. Read the first excerpt and you know a new therapy is in the works. Read the second, and you are likely to think a big breakthrough in cancer research is on the way. Given the effect a writer's tone can have on the information conveyed, it's a good idea to avoid websites where the tone is obvious. Perhaps more precisely, you should avoid them when you are first developing some general background knowledge. As with bias, you need to be on solid ground with your understanding of the information before you let someone else's opinion influence you.

Warning Signs That Signal Untrustworthy Websites

In addition to being distorted by bias or influenced by tone, information on the Web is sometimes purposely misleading and totally inaccurate. As Farhad Manjoo illustrates in his book *True Enough*, some statements and images on the Web lack any shred of credibility:

> During the 2004 presidential campaign, a skilled Photoshopper swiped a 1971 shot of John Kerry at an antiwar rally in Mineola, New York, from the Website of Corbis, a photo agency, and stitched it seamlessly with a 1972 image of Jane Fonda at a rally in Miami Beach,

Florida.[†] The composite photo shows a thoughtful, appreciative Kerry next to an agitated Fonda. It was given a border, a headline, a caption, and an Associated Press credit and was made to look like an authentic newspaper clipping that *proved* Kerry's close association with a reviled Hanoi Jane. (Farhad Manjoo, *True Enough*, Hoboken: N.J.: Wiley Publishing, 2008, p. 82.)

But an awareness of how the Web is used to spread misinformation does not mean that you should stop using it. It does mean you should use it with great care, critically evaluating any websites you visit. To help you in that task, here's a list of website warning signs.

There's Little or No Indication of Who Is Responsible for Content

A trustworthy website will have a page describing the credentials of the person or group responsible for the content and currency of the website. This information will usually be linked to labels like "About Us," "Home," or "My Background." If there is no description of the person or group who maintains the website or the information provided about the person or group is very sketchy, like the example shown below, look elsewhere.

> I am a physicist who has written many books on the subject of alien invasion, but must keep my identity a secret for fear of government reprisals.

References to Evidence and Experts Are Vague

Watch out when the web author repeatedly cites "research" or "studies" that are never explicitly named, for instance:

> Numerous studies have shown that students understand more when they are working with interactive e-books than with print on paper.

Trustworthy websites created to offer or explain a specific point of view will not only cite specific statements or studies by experts, they will also provide hypertext links to the evidence that underlies their claims.

[†]John Kerry was running for president at the time. Jana Fonda had made enemies during the Vietnam War (1964–1975) when she publicly supported the North Vietnamese over the United States. Linking Kerry to Fonda was someone's attempt to discredit Kerry as a candidate. Fonda got her nickname because Hanoi was the capital of North Vietnam.

Generalizations Never Get Specific

If the writing on the website generalizes, or draws conclusions, about large numbers of people (see the example below) without citing at least a few representative individuals, groups, or institutions by name, you probably need to look elsewhere for information.

> The Left has always claimed that the Rosenbergs were not guilty, even in the face of overwhelming evidence that they were.

Rhetorical Questions Function as Proof

If the web author is overly fond of rhetorical questions† that assume your agreement and thereby avoid the pesky need for evidence, this is not the website for you.

> Before playing in the World Series, baseball player Shoeless Joe Jackson told the owner, Charles Comiskey, that a fix was in play and asked to be benched. *Does that sound like a man who is guilty of cheating and should therefore be banned from Baseball's Hall of Fame?* Now that you know the facts, please write the Commissioner of Baseball and ask that Joe Jackson be admitted to the Hall of Fame.

An Absence of Evidence Is Considered Proof

If the text of the website suggests that the lack of evidence to the contrary proves the author's claim, then you know for sure that the website is not going to provide you with credible information.

> The government, however, does not want to make the populace aware of the possible tragedy that awaits them. For that reason, there is no mention of how the predictions of Nostradamus and the Mayan calendar coincide to make 2012 the year of the apocalypse.* No government-affiliated scientific organization even mentions this looming catastrophe because a conspiracy of silence is in place.

There Are No Outside Sources

If you click the hypertext on a web page, and it links you to other pages on the same site or other articles by the same author, turn to another

---

†Rhetorical questions are those that assume an answer so obvious, the writer doesn't need to provide one, e.g., "Would you want your child answering the emails of a convicted sex offender?"
*apocalypse: total devastation, an earth-shattering disaster.

website for information. A writer who can only cite him- or herself for clarification or proof is probably not a good source of information.

The Outside Sources Make a Bad Impression

The outside sources an author considers important enough to turn into hypertext are like character references. If the websites that come up when you click on their links seem crudely written and lack concrete information, that says a lot about the site on which you found them.

The Bandwagon Appeal Makes an Appearance

When a website promotes a point of view without offering anything resembling specific reasons, studies, statistics, or facts, you're likely to encounter phrases like "As every American knows," "We all believe," and "Everyone agrees." These phrases signal that the author is employing what's called the **bandwagon appeal**. He or she is telling you to believe what's being said because everyone else does. That's hardly an appeal to logic since no one can know what everyone else thinks, and, historically, the majority has sometimes been dead wrong. If a web author tells you to believe or think something because everyone else does, you need to look for background knowledge on another website.

> The current attempt to ban citizen ownership of assault rifles will fail in the same way other attempts in the past have. Americans are not stupid. Every school child knows that the Second Amendment of the Constitution[†] guarantees us the right to own a gun.

The Photos Express a Bias

Bias doesn't turn up just in language. If you were researching the courtroom battle between Holocaust denier David Irving and his arch critic Deborah Lipstadt, author of *Denying the Holocaust: The Growing Assault on Truth and Memory,* you would need to be wary of a website that offers cheery photos of Irving with his family right next to photos of Lipstadt in court looking grim. Photographs can be as biased as language, so pay close attention to which ones are used on a website.

[†]Actually the Second Amendment grants the right to bear arms to members of a militia, or military civilian force, not to individual citizens.

◆ **EXERCISE 4**   **Evaluating Websites**

DIRECTIONS   Cut and paste or type the following URLs into a search engine and read the pages that come up. Check off the box that fits your response, and write a brief explanation of what you found was good or bad about the website.

1. In terms of the warning signs described above, how would you label the following website: www.truthism.com.

   ☐ trustworthy   ☐ not trustworthy

   Briefly describe the basis for your decision:

   _____

   _____

   _____

   _____

2. In terms of the warning signs described above, how would you label the following website: www.elizabethbaron.com.

   ☐ trustworthy   ☐ not trustworthy

   Briefly describe the basis for your decision:

   _____

   _____

   _____

3. In terms of the warning signs described above, how would you label the following website: http://skeptoid.com/blog/2012/05/20/skeptic-vs-psychic/?

   ☐ trustworthy   ☐ not trustworthy

   Briefly describe the basis for your decision:

   _____

   _____

   _____

Think Twice About Using Wikipedia

Wikipedia is an **open-source database**, meaning volunteers write and edit the entries that appear on the site, relying on a free source code to post, revise, or add information. At one time the entries on *Wikipedia* went largely unedited except by volunteers. However, after a few entries were found to contain inaccurate information, site administrators became much stricter about overseeing the information that made it onto the site.

But is there still a chance you might end up with information that is factually inaccurate? Yes, there is. However, in general, it's not a huge one, as mistakes on the site usually get corrected in time.[†] A bigger concern is the amount of information in each entry, as people interested in a particular subject add more and more detail. When your goal is to get a general idea about a person, idea, or event, *Wikipedia* is likely to overwhelm you with more information than you need at that point.

In addition, *Wikipedia* entries are filled with **hypertext**, or links to additional websites. Thus it's easy to get distracted from the purpose of your original search. If you are going to use *Wikipedia*, you're better off doing so after you have completed your assignment and want to flesh out your understanding of some key terms or names.

To get good, credible background knowledge on a particular topic, websites maintained by the Internet Public Library, the Public Broadcasting Service, *Time* magazine, and the *New York Times* might serve you far better. The discussions are likely to be briefer, the language more lively, and the information fact-checked prior to posting.

◆ EXERCISE 5   Finding the Right Search Term

DIRECTIONS For each question, write down a search term that you think would get you the information you need in the shortest amount of time. Then use that search term to find an answer on the Web. Feel free to change search terms if you need to. Just make sure to indicate in the blank provided how you revised your original search term.

[†]Some writers and researchers have also complained that *Wikipedia*, because it is largely staffed by volunteers, who are bound by strict editorial rules, often doesn't have access to the most up-to-date information on a subject and deletes entries that are factually accurate but express ideas that are relatively new. For an example, see www .npr.org/2012/02/22/147261659/gauging-the-reliability-of-facts-on-wikipedia.

1. The novelist James Baldwin[†] played an influential role in the civil rights movement. In his attitude toward civil rights, who did Baldwin resemble more, Malcolm X or Martin Luther King Jr.?

   What would be a good search term to use to answer this question in the shortest amount of time?

   _____

   _____

   What's the answer to the question?

   _____

   _____

   _____

   Did you have to revise your search term to get the answer? If so, how did you change it?

   _____

2. As the result of her death, singer Amy Winehouse belongs to what tragic club?

   What would be a good search term to use to answer this question in the shortest amount of time?

   _____

   What's the answer to the question?

   _____

   _____

   _____

[†]James Baldwin (1924–1987): Baldwin was a novelist, poet, essayist, and political activist, whose writing called attention to prejudice and racism in the United States. His novel *Go Tell It on the Mountain* is largely autobiographical and describes growing up poor and black in an urban setting.

Did you have to revise your search term to get the answer? If so, how did you change it?

_____

3. Did Jane Fonda ever apologize for visiting North Vietnam while the United States was at war with the North Vietnamese?

What would be a good search term to use to answer this question in the shortest amount of time?

_____

What's the answer to the question?

_____

_____

Did you have to revise your search term to get the answer? If so, how did you change it?

_____

✔ CHECK YOUR UNDERSTANDING

1. _True_ or _False_. Personal blogs are a good source of information for developing background knowledge about chapter content. Please explain.

_____

_____

2. What can you expect to find on a web page labeled "About Us"?

_____

3. If you went to a website and saw this text, what should be your response and why?

Study after study shows that students in public schools are victims of left-brain training that leaves them without the intellectual resources to do creative thinking.

_____

4. If you find the following text on a website, what should follow in its wake?

   Feminists have consistently underrated the importance of family in the lives of women. They thought work could replace the satisfaction families provide, and that has been the movement's undoing.

   _____

   _____

5. Imagine that you visit a website arguing that children who spend two or more years in day care tend to have learning difficulties in school. When you hit the hypertext links on the web page, they all go to other articles by the same author. What will you do and why?

   _____

   _____

 # Writing and Reading on the Web

"Readers [on the Web] fixate or focus on the content at the top of a page."

—Kara Pernice Coyne, Web usability researcher

As web expert Jakob Nielsen,[†] among others, has repeatedly pointed out, people who read on the Web are inclined to look closely at the beginnings of pages but then scan for individual words and phrases at the beginnings of sentences rather than reading closely. By the middle of the page, if they haven't found what they want, they tend to give up and go to a different page or website. Most web page creators are aware of this pattern (Nielsen calls it the "F-Shaped pattern"), and their awareness has influenced their writing.

For one thing, web writing[††] frequently resembles newspaper writing in that the author of the web text relies on what's called the inverted pyramid format of conveying information. With the inverted pyramid, the author starts with the main idea, follows with the supporting illustrations, statistics, or reasons, and then provides background, making the shape of the text look like this:

[†]Jakob Nielsen: Nielsen is an engineer who has written extensively about web usability and reading on the Internet.
[††]Web writing is writing created specifically for the Web. If what comes up on a website is actually a textbook chapter that's been posted for web use, then key points will probably vary in location.

Understanding the Structure of Web Writing

Crucial information must go at the beginning.

They could stop reading at any time.

Here's where you get the answers to questions like these:
Who did what and what were the consequences?
When did this happen and why was it important?

Here's where you get any details
that might be needed to clarify
what you learned from
the opening sentence.

Here's where you get the kind
of background information
that in a print work
would often be
at the top
of the
page.

The web page that appears on page 31 neatly illustrates this inverted pyramid pattern. The most important information comes at the beginning of the text, with information of decreasing importance completing the paragraph.

Paragraph opens → ¹By the 1890s, the invention of better microscopes allowed
with a large   biologists to discover the basic facts of cell division and sexual
general point   reproduction. ²The focus of genetics research then shifted to ← Sentence 2
about the 1890s.   understanding what really happens in the transmission of   narrows down
                           hereditary traits from parents to children. ³A number of   the focus.
                           hypotheses were suggested to explain heredity, but Gregor
                           Mendel, a little known Central European monk, was the only
Sentence 3 ——→ one who got it more or less right. ⁴His ideas had been
zeroes in on the   published in 1866 but largely went unrecognized until 1900,
key point.   which was long after his death. ⁵His early adult life was spent
                           in relative obscurity doing basic genetics research and   Background
                           teaching high school mathematics, physics, and Greek in Brno   about Mendel
                           (now in the Czech Republic). ⁶In his later years, he became ← comes at the
                           the abbot of his monastery and put aside his scientific work.   very end.

Notice how the information about Mendel's life appears at the end? In a textbook, that information would very likely appear at the beginning of a paragraph, where it would be used as an introduction. Web writing, in general, doesn't place as heavy an emphasis on introductions, especially not long introductions that provide basic background. Even web writers who include introductory material usually limit the introduction to a sentence or two.

In response, savvy web readers give headings and paragraph openings extra-special attention. Before reading entire paragraphs, they skim the last three or four sentences to evaluate them. They look to see if the remaining content is still central to the writer's opening thought or if it has turned to less-essential background information. If they decide the writer has used the inverted pyramid approach, they move on to the next heading. While this might not be the best approach for delving deeply into a topic to get a thorough understanding of it, it's absolutely perfect when you are in pursuit of basic background knowledge.

◆ EXERCISE 6   Writing on the Web

DIRECTIONS If you were rewriting this paragraph to go on the Web, which sentences would be at the very beginning? Write the numbers of those sentences in the blank at the end of the paragraph in the order they would appear. Then circle the words or phrases that you would turn into hypertext, i.e., the highlighted words on a web page that are linked to additional websites, meant to deepen the reader's understanding of the material.

[1]It's long been said that laughter is the best medicine. [2]And certainly laughter, at the right moments, can do a lot to improve a tense emotional climate. [3]But, apparently, the notion of laughter as medicine needs to be taken more seriously. [4]Laughter, a new study shows, actually provides physical benefits for the heart. [5]In the 2012 annual meeting of the American College of Cardiology, Dr. Michael Miller reported on his study of twenty healthy subjects. [6]The study indicated that laughter improved artery function as effectively as aerobic exercise. [7]Laughter somehow affects the inner lining of blood vessels called the endothelium. [8]In response to laughter, the lining of the blood vessels relaxed and expanded. [9]That, in turn, increased the blood flow to the heart and to the brain.

_____

REVIEWING THROUGH WRITING

Read the following textbook passage and underline the information you consider most critical for web readers to know, giving a double underline to what you think is the most central idea in the text. Then paraphrase the original content that you've underlined and rewrite the excerpt—including the title—giving it the form of an inverted pyramid.

Cows, Memories, and Culture

If you were on a farm and saw 20 cows walk by, do you think you could remember the age, color, gender, and condition of all of them? Unless you are a dairy farmer, doing so would be quite a feat of memory. That's because we are most likely to remember information that is personally important or meaningful. Thus for a Maasai person from East Africa, it would be an easier task to sort out the cows and remember their individual details. Livestock are very important in Maasai culture. Thus the Maasai are prepared to encode and store information about cattle that would be difficult for most people in the United States to remember.

Culture affects our memories in other interesting ways. For example, American culture emphasizes individuals, whereas Chinese culture emphasizes membership in groups. In one study, European-American and Chinese adults were asked to recall 20 memories from any time in their lives. As expected, American memories tended to be self-centered. Most people remembered surprising events and what they did during the events. Chinese adults, in contrast, remembered important social or historical events and their own interactions with family members, friends, and others (Wang & Conway, 2004). In the United States, personal memories tend to be about "me"; in China, they tend to be about "us." (Adapted from Dennis Coon and John O. Mitterer, *Introduction to Psychology* 12e, © Cengage Learning.)

Use Hypertext Strategically

"The belief that readers can select for themselves which links in a network to follow rests on the assumption that readers know best what information they need and in what order they should read it."

—Davida Charney, "The Impact of Hypertext on Processes of Reading and Writing"

There was a time when many people believed that hypertext—highlighted words and terms on a computer screen that are linked to other reference works on the Web—was a godsend. Readers didn't need background knowledge anymore. They had hypertext. Any word, name, or term readers didn't immediately know they could discover with the click of the mouse.

That time has passed because, as journalist Nicholas Carr points out below, hypertext can distract as well as inform. People who use hypertext links heavily tend to comprehend less rather than more. The decrease in comprehension is the result of working memory—the part of your memory that takes information in and holds it temporarily while your long-term memory figures out what to do with it—becoming overwhelmed and unable to process all the ideas, facts, and figures attached to the various hypertext links. As Carr puts it,

> Links are wonderful conveniences, as we all know (from clicking on them compulsively day in and day out). But they're also distractions. Sometimes, they're big distractions—we click on a link, then another, then another, and pretty soon we've forgotten what we'd started out to do or to read.[2]

When you are searching out background knowledge on the Web, take Carr's warning to heart. Remember that relentless clicking of hypertext can prove a distraction. Instead of clicking every link you see, use hypertext strategically following the steps listed below.

How to Handle Hypertext
♦

1. Read through the material on the site that seems relevant, or related, to your search.

2. Note the names, words, and terms that appear in hypertext, usually in blue (see, for instance, the web page on Mendel, p. 31), but don't click on them until you finish reading the passage or page relevant to your assignment.

3. When you finish previewing the website material, see if you can sum up the information it provides by posing some basic *who, what, when, where,* and *why* questions.

---

[2]Nicholas Carr, "Experiments in Delinkification," www.roughtype.com/?p=1378.

4. If the answers aren't supplied by the text and they aren't part of your background knowledge, click on the hypertext link you think will fill in the gap.

5. Each time you read the information a link provides, see if you can better sum up the web page content, i.e., answer the question that stumped you before.

6. As soon as you can answer your questions, start your assignment and leave the remaining hypertext for another time. The mere presence of words in hypertext on a website does not mean you should click on all of them.

Putting the Strategy into Practice

Imagine that in an attempt to get background knowledge for a history text you had landed on a web page that offered you the following information:

The Federalist Papers

Published between 1787 and 1788, *The Federalist Papers* were a collection of essays all signed with the name "Publius" and published in New York newspapers. The papers were, however, the product of three men: Alexander Hamilton, John Jay, and James Madison. The purpose of the essays was to convince New Yorkers to ratify the recently created and highly controversial Constitution of the United States. At the time, a heated debate was underway about the type of government that would be best for the newly independent country. The question was, Should America go forward as a loosely united "confederacy," or union, of states in which each state made most of its own rules, while allowing the American Congress only the right to conduct international trade, declare war, and raise an army? Or should it have a federal government that could collect taxes, regulate interstate trade, and, above all, limit the independence of the individual states? While we all know now how that debate turned out, at the time it was not clear that the thirteen individual states—actually, only nine were needed for ratification, or formal approval—would agree to give up some of their independence.

There is a lot of hypertext in this passage. The question is, How much of it do you need to read?

The answer depends on how well you can answer three basic questions: (1) Who wrote *The Federalist Papers*? (2) What was their purpose? (3) Why were they called "Federalist" papers? As it turns out, the only question that can't be answered completely from the information on the site is the last one. That suggests you should click on the link "Federalist" to get an explanation like this: "A federalist believes in a union of individuals bound together by rules and a representative head." In other words, those who wrote *The Federalist Papers* were identifying themselves as men who wanted more than a loose union of the states. The essays they wrote supported and promoted a government with power broad enough to control many of the functions that had once been left to the states.

Despite all the hypertext on the web page, you only needed to open up one link to learn what you needed to know. As you read on the Web, you will have many experiences like this one.

TAKING **Short-Term Memory—Do You Know the Magic Number?**
STOCK

Looking The ability to remember is, for the most part, not a biological gift. The hu-
Ahead man memory can be trained. That doesn't mean, however, that you should
run out and buy software for memory improvement (most of which is
worthless). However, you should know how short-term memory works
to help new information make its way into long-term memory where it
might stay forever. The following reading will give you an idea of how
short-term memory functions.

Survey Steps

1. Pose a question or two based on the Looking Ahead preview
   and the reading title.

2. Read the first and last paragraphs.

3. Read the headings and italicized questions.

4. Read the first and last sentence of every paragraph.

5. Read through the *Sharpening Your Skills* questions on
   pages 52–55.

   Once you finish your survey, answer the questions or
   complete the statements in Part A below.

---

1 *Question: What are the features of short-term memory?* To make good use
of your memory, it is valuable to know something about the quirks and
characteristics of both Short-Term Memory (STM) and Long-Term Memory
(LTM). Let's start with a closer look at STM. How much information can be
held in short-term memory? For the answer, read the following numbers
once. Then close the book and write as many as you can in the correct
order.

   8 5 1 7 4 9 3

This is called a digit-span test. It is a measure of attention and short-term
memory. If you were able to correctly repeat 7 digits, you have an average
short-term memory. Now try to memorize the following list, again reading
it only once:

   7 1 8 3 5 4 2 9 1 6 3 4

This series was probably beyond your short-term memory capacity. Psychologist George Miller found that short-term memory is limited to the "magic number" 7 (plus or minus 1) information bits. A bit is a single meaningful "piece" of information, such as a digit. It is as if short-term memory has 7 slots or bins in which separate items can be placed. Actually a few people remember up to 9 bits, and for some types of information 5 bits is the limit. Thus an average of 7 information bits can be held in short-term memory.

2   When all the slots in STM are filled, there is no room for new information. Picture how this works at a party: Let's say your hostess begins introducing everyone who is there, "Chun, Daisia, Sandra, Roseanna, Cholik, Shawn, Kyrene . . ." Stop, you think to yourself. But she continues, "Nelia, Jay, Frank, Patty, Amir, Ricky." The hostess leaves, satisfied that you have met everyone. And you spend the evening talking to Chun, Daisia, and Ricky, the only people whose names you remember!

The Power of Chunking

3   Before we continue, try your short-term memory again, this time on letters. Read the following letters once, then look away and try to write them in the proper order.

TVIBMUSNYMCA

Notice that there are 12 letters or bits of information. If you studied the letters one at a time, this should be beyond the 7-item limit of STM. However, you may have noticed that some of the letters can be grouped, or *chunked*, together. For example, you may have noticed that NY is the abbreviation for New York. If so, the two bits N and Y became one chunk. Information chunks are made up of bits of information grouped into larger units.

4   *Question: Does Chunking Make a Difference?* Yes, chunking records (reorganizes) information into units that are already in LTM. In a classic experiment that used lists like this one, people remembered best when the letters were read as familiar meaningful chunks: TV, IBM, USN, YMCA. If you recoded the letters this way, you organized them into four chunks of information and probably remembered the entire list. If you didn't, go back and try it again; you'll notice a big difference.

5   Chunking suggests that STM holds about 5 to 7 of whatever units we are using. A single chunk could be made up of numbers, letters, words, phrases, or familiar sentences. Picture STM as a small desk again. Through chunking, we combine several items into one "stack" of information. This allows us to place 7 stacks on the desk, where before there was only room

for 7 separate items. While you are studying, try to find ways to link 2, 3, or more separate facts or ideas into larger chunks, and your short-term memory will improve. . . . The clear message is that creating information chunks is the key to making good use of your short-term memory.

Rehearsing Information

6   *Question: How long do short-term memories last?* They disappear very rapidly. However, you can prolong a memory by silently repeating it, a process called **maintenance rehearsal**. In a sense, rehearsing information allows you to hear it many times, not just once. You have probably used maintenance rehearsal to keep a phone number active in your mind while looking at your cell phone and dialing it.

7   Isn't saying stuff to yourself over and over also a way of studying? It is true that the more times a short-term memory is rehearsed, the greater its chance of being stored in LTM. This is rote learning (learning by simple repetition). But rote learning is not a very effective way to study.

8   **Elaborative encoding**, which makes information more meaningful, is a far better way to form lasting memories. Elaborative encoding links new information to memories that are already in LTM. When you are studying, you will remember more if you elaborate on the meaning of the information. As you read, try to reflect frequently. Ask yourself *why* questions such as "Why would that be true?" Also try to relate new ideas to your own experiences and knowledge. (Adapted from Dennis Coon and John O. Mitterer, *Introduction to Psychology* 12e, © Cengage Learning.)

Sharpening Your Skills

DIRECTIONS   Answer the following questions by filling in the blanks or circling the letter of the correct response.

Part A: Surveying

1. *True* or *False*. Overall the reading suggests we have some control over how poorly or well our memory performs.

2. On average, how many bits of information can be held in short-term memory?

    a. three

    b. six

    c. seven

    d. nine

3. *True* or *False*. Individual bits of information can be remembered more easily by grouping them into bigger units of information called *chunks*.

4. Based on your survey, how does chunking relate to the idea that short-term memory can absorb a limited number of information bits?

_____

_____

_____

5. **Maintenance rehearsal** refers to

   a. writing while reading.

   b. silent repetition.

   c. linking ideas to images.

Part B: Reading

1. In your own words, what did the psychologist George Miller claim about human memory?

_____

_____

2. Explain how the party example in paragraph 2 illustrates Miller's point about the "magic number" 7.

_____

_____

3. Which of these sentences does not chunk bits of information?

   a. The Civil War began in 1861.

   b. The Civil War began in 1861 following the attack on Fort Sumter.

   c. The Civil War, which Lincoln had tried so hard to avoid, began in 1861 after the attack on Fort Sumter.

Please explain your answer.

_____

4. Three paragraphs in the reading open with questions. Are they examples of rhetorical questions? _____ Please explain.

_____

_____

5. Explain what the authors mean by the heading "The Power of Chunking." What power are they referring to?

_____

_____

_____

6. Which one of the following would be the best marginal note for paragraph 5?

   a. Chunking gives you seven stacks, leaving more space on the desk.

   b. Chunking combines information bits, leaving more space in short-term memory.

   c. Think of short-term memory as a small desk in the corner of your mind.

7. Elena is preparing to take a test and wants to remember that Lyndon B. Johnson was the president who signed into legislation Medicare insurance for people over sixty-five. To remember that fact, she keeps on repeating to herself that Lyndon Johnson was responsible for Medicare insurance. What term from the reading describes how she tries to store information in long-term memory?

_____

8. Henry is taking the same test and wants to remember that the federal income tax officially became the law of the land in 1913 under President William Howard Taft. But Henry doesn't keep repeating the name, date, and event to himself. Instead, he links the information to something he already knows, the year World War I started. He tells himself that the constitutional amendment creating the federal income tax was ratified in 1913, one year before World War I started in 1914. To remember who the president was at that time, he also makes a mental note that Taft's tenure in office ended in the same year the income tax arrived. What term from the reading describes how he tries to store information in long-term memory?

_____

9. If you wanted to learn how to remember more of what you are reading, what search terms do you think would get you the information you need most quickly?

_____

10. If this reading were written for the Web, do you think it would open in the same way?

_____ Please explain.

_____

_____

▶ TEST 1   Recognizing an Accurate Paraphrase

DIRECTIONS Circle the letter of the most accurate paraphrase. *Note:* Because this is a test, the answers are more like the formal paraphrases you would use for writing.

1. A *dialect* is language—including vocabulary, grammar, and pronunciation—unique to a particular group or region. Audiences sometimes make negative judgments about a speaker based on his or her dialect. Such negative judgments are called *vocal stereotypes*. (Adapted from Bruce Gronbeck et al., *Principles of Speech Communication*, 13e. Longman Publishing Group, 1997, p. 100.)

Paraphrase

   a. A *dialect* is a particular way of speaking. Unfortunately, people sometimes judge others based on the way they speak. Southerners, for example, complain about being stereotyped because of their accent.

   b. The term *vocal stereotypes* refers to the negative judgments people make based on dialect. A *dialect* is speech unique to a group or region and includes vocabulary, grammar, and pronunciation.

   c. A *vocal stereotype* is a type of dialect. People who speak a particular dialect are critical of those who speak other dialects.

2. Professional nursing associations, like the National Federation of Licensed Practical Nurses, develop their own codes of ethics for nurses by means of consensus, or group agreement. These codes outline a nurse's obligation to clients and to society at large. The codes provide broad principles for determining and evaluating nursing care. (Adapted from Sue Roe, *Delmar's Clinical Nursing Skills and Concepts*, © Cengage Learning.)

Paraphrase

   a. The National Federation of Licensed Practical Nurses has created its own code of ethics to define the behavior of nurses. The code explains the relationship between doctors and nurses and defines the responsibility of each.

   b. The National Federation of Licensed Practical Nurses uses an ethical code to evaluate the nursing care of its membership. This is a practice that other nursing associations should imitate.

   c. Professional nursing associations create ethics codes based on standards agreed on by the group. The purpose of the codes is to define how nurses are supposed to act toward patients and toward society. Thus the codes can be used to judge nursing care.

3. During World War II, movies about Japan made little effort to develop a Japanese character or explain what Japan hoped to accomplish in the war. The Japanese remained nameless, faceless, and almost totally speechless. No attempt was made to show a Japanese soldier trapped by circumstances beyond his control or a family man longing for home or an officer who despised the slaughter even if he supported the military campaign. This was in sharp contrast to the portrayal of German soldiers, who were often shown as decent human beings altogether different from the Nazis. (Adapted from Clayton R. Koppes and Gregory D. Black, *Hollywood Goes to War*, p. 254, University of California Press, 1990.)

Paraphrase

a. During World War II, Hollywood filmmakers were applauded for engaging in racist propaganda. The 1942 film *Wake Island*, for example, with the story of 377 marines resisting a Japanese invasion, was a smash hit despite its racial stereotypes of Japanese soldiers. Today, such movies, even during wartime, would be sharply criticized.

b. Hollywood films made during World War II portrayed Japanese soldiers like robots, who followed government orders without question. Such films suggested that Japanese soldiers never experienced emotional conflict, unlike German soldiers who were shown disagreeing with their government's inhumane course of action. In the movies, Japanese soldiers always fulfilled their duty to Japan.

c. During World War II, Hollywood filmmakers made propaganda movies that failed to distinguish between the Japanese government's war machine and the Japanese soldier caught in that machine. This was very different from their treatment of German soldiers, who were occasionally shown to be decent people.

4. During the nineteenth and early twentieth centuries, the South American countries of Argentina, Uruguay, and Brazil had their own homegrown cowboys called *gauchos*. Derived from the Quechua[†] word *wáhcha*, the word *gaucho* usually referred to cowhands or horse handlers, but it could also refer to horse thieves and mercenaries, or soldiers for hire.

[†]Quechua: language spoken by people belonging to the Incan Empire.

Paraphrase

a. In Argentina, Uruguay, and Brazil, *gauchos* were considered romantic figures. Like America's cowboys, *gauchos* were the heroes of movies and novels. The most famous novel based on the life of the *gaucho* was *The Four Horsemen of the Apocalypse*, which also became a movie.

b. During the nineteenth and beginning of the twentieth centuries, American-like cowboys, called *gauchos*, worked the ranches of Uruguay, Argentina, and Brazil. The term *gaucho*, originating from the Quechua word *wáhcha*, means "cowhand" or "horse handler"; the word can also refer to horse thieves and soldiers of fortune.

c. *Gauchos*, the nineteenth- and early twentieth-century horsemen of Argentina, Uruguay, and Brazil, tended to be lawless robbers and guns-for-hire. When their American counterparts were wreaking havoc in the Old West, these South American cowboys were causing trouble in their homeland.

▶ **TEST 2** **Recognizing an Accurate Paraphrase**

DIRECTIONS Circle the letter of the most accurate paraphrase. *Note:* Because this is a test, these are the kinds of paraphrases you would use when writing term papers.

1. In 1960, researcher Jane Goodall went to Africa's Gombe Stream National Park to study chimpanzees. No one before her had attempted to observe the animals in their natural habitat and, initially, the chimps ran from her. However, when Goodall didn't give up, the animals gradually became used to her, letting her watch them for hours. In time, Goodall's pioneering fieldwork revolutionized primate[†] research: She was the first to observe that chimps eat meat, use tools, and engage in warfare.

Paraphrase

a. Jane Goodall, who studied chimpanzees in 1960 in Africa's Gombe Stream National Park, was a better researcher than anyone who had previously studied the shy animals. Unlike earlier researchers, she got the chimps to accept her. Their acceptance gave her the opportunity to observe them in the wild for long periods of time. As a result, she found out that chimps live exactly like humans do: They eat meat, use tools, and wage war.

b. In 1960, Jane Goodall became the first person to study chimpanzees in their natural habitat of Africa's Gombe Stream National Park. After patiently overcoming the chimps' initial resistance to her presence, Goodall significantly influenced primate research by witnessing and reporting on chimpanzee behaviors such as meat eating, tool use, and warfare, none of which had been documented before.

c. If Jane Goodall hadn't gone to Africa's Gombe Stream National Park in 1960, we never would have known that chimpanzees are meat eaters, use tools, and occasionally engage in cannibalism. Jane Goodall had a special talent for working with the animals and could communicate to them that they had nothing to fear. The chimps allowed her to get close enough to make some astonishing discoveries that heavily influenced primate research.

d. When Jane Goodall went to Africa's Gombe Stream National Park in 1960, she did not know how difficult it would be to study chimpanzees in their natural surroundings. Initially the animals would

---

[†]primate: refers to animals characterized by refined development of hands and feet; includes apes and humans among others.

not let her approach. Goodall didn't give up, though. She kept trying, and eventually the chimps permitted her to watch them for long periods of time.

2. People can successfully perform two different activities simultaneously. However, one of the two activities has to be performed automatically and require little or no attention. For example, we can drive a car and talk at the same time because we can steer, brake, accelerate, and so on, without close attention to each individual action. The actions necessary to driving are practically automatic and require little thought once they have been thoroughly learned. We can also do two things at the same time if the tasks or activities involved require different kinds of attention. It's possible to read music and play the piano simultaneously because each activity requires a separate mode of concentration. One forces us to pay attention to incoming stimuli; the other requires us to produce a response. What's nearly impossible is having a conversation and reading at the same time because both activities rely on similar types of attention.

Paraphrase

a. It is possible to do two different things at the same time. But one of those two things has to require little or no thought. It must be almost completely automatic. For instance, many people can drive while they talk because the motions of driving—steering, accelerating, braking, etc.—are automatic. They don't require close concentration. We can also do two things at the same time if the two tasks are quite different and thus require different types of concentration. We can, for example, read music at the same time that our fingers play the piano keys. Reading the notes forces us to attend to incoming external stimuli. When we play the piano, however, we are producing a response. But we can't talk and read at the same time because those tasks require similar kinds of attention.

b. To perform two activities at the same time, one of them has to be automatic. Driving, for example, is automatic, so we can usually drive while talking. When playing the piano, pressing the keys is an automatic response to reading the music. However, we cannot talk and read at the same time because we have to pay attention to both of these tasks. Neither one can be performed without thinking.

c. If two tasks require different kinds of attention, then they can be performed at the same time. For example, you don't really have to pay attention when you drive a car, which leaves you free to talk to your passengers. Plus, you don't have to think about how your fingers are moving over the keyboard, so you can read music while playing a piano. But reading and talking both force you to pay attention to what you're doing. Therefore, they cannot be performed simultaneously.

d. Because the human brain allows us to divide our attention, we can often do two things at the same time. For example, we can drive and talk at the same time because one of the tasks (driving) is automatic. Also, we can read music while playing the piano because each task requires the same kind of attention.

3. Local television news directors have long known that their primary goal is to attract audiences for their advertisers. However, thanks to a large increase in media choices, competition for viewers has become fiercer. Because it's difficult to write catchy stories about politics and government, many news directors have given up trying to cover that kind of news. Instead, they concentrate on TV news programs that mix action stories—short clips about murders, robberies, rapes, fires, and car accidents—with weather, sports, human interest stories, and friendly banter between the anchors.

Paraphrase

a. Television news programmers know they have to draw big audiences to please their advertisers. Because audiences have many programs to choose from, local TV news directors try to attract viewers with action-oriented shows featuring stories about crimes, accidents, and natural disasters with news about sports and weather and the chipper chatter of the newscasters. Because it's hard to write snappy stories about government and politics, most news programs feature very little information about these topics.

b. Local TV directors know that viewers won't watch dull news programs. They also know they must attract lots of viewers to please their advertisers. For those two reasons, today's local news programs rarely include much information about serious subjects like government and politics. Instead, they tend to focus mostly on violent action. Tune in to a local TV news broadcast, and you're likely to see attractive and smiling anchormen and anchorwomen introducing footage of mangled cars, raging fires, and storm damage, all accompanied by interviews with teary victims.

c. Local TV news directors know they have to create action-packed shows to draw in advertisers. Consequently, they have stopped covering politics and government. Most people would rather see video footage of crimes, accidents, weather forecasts, and sports events, particularly if it is interspersed with friendly conversation between the newscasters. News directors can't really be blamed for giving people what they want.

d. Local TV news directors know that advertisers prefer to place their ads in action-oriented shows with large audiences. They have given up trying to make subjects like government and politics interesting, and they put together shows filled with reports of murders, robberies, accidents, sports highlights, and weather information. They know people are interested in those subjects.

4. A *class-action suit* is a case brought into a court of law by a person who wishes to sue an organization not only for himself or herself but also on behalf of everyone who has been wronged in the same way by that organization. One of the most famous class-action suits was brought in 1954 by the National Association for the Advancement of Colored People (NAACP), which sued on behalf of Linda Brown, a black girl from Topeka, Kansas, who was denied admission to a white elementary school, as well as all other children who were forced to attend segregated schools. The resulting Supreme Court decision, *Brown v. Board of Education*, led to the desegregation of public schools.

Paraphrase

a. Class-action suits are brought by people who want to sue an institution not only on their own behalf but also on behalf of anyone who might have been unfairly treated by the same institution. Perhaps the most famous class-action suit was brought by the NAACP, which sued in the name of Linda Brown, an African-American girl denied entry to an all-white elementary school. The suit also included the names of all other children excluded by the practice of segregation in the schools. This class-action suit, which the NAACP won, was the first step in the desegregation of all public schools.

b. The term *class-action suit* is applied to those cases where a group of people are suing one institution. The lawsuit that led to the desegregation of schools, *Brown v. Board of Education*, was a class-action suit filed by the NAACP.

c. The first and most famous class-action suit ever brought into court was *Brown v. Board of Education*, which was the first step in the desegregation of all public schools. The NAACP, fearing it could not win its case in the name of a single child, decided to sue on behalf of all the children who had ever been denied access to a local school because of the practice of segregation.

d. A class-action suit is brought by someone who wants to sue an institution not only in the name of himself or herself but also in the names of any others who might have been wrongly treated by the same institution. The famous lawsuit *Brown v. Board of Education*, which paved the way for desegregation, is probably the best example of a class-action suit that had important consequences not just for a single person but also for a host of people. This is typical of class-action suits brought by the NAACP.

▶ TEST 3   Paraphrasing with Accuracy

DIRECTIONS   Paraphrase each of the following statements.

1. During the New Deal of the 1930s, Native Americans had two strong supporters in Secretary of the Interior Harold Ickes and Commissioner of Indian Affairs John Collier. Both opposed existing Indian policies that since 1887 had sought to destroy tribal culture. Together they helped pass the Indian Reorganization Act of 1934, which returned land and community control to tribal organizations. (Adapted from Carol Berkin et al., *Making America* 6e, © Cengage Learning.)

Paraphrase

_____

_____

_____

_____

_____

2. In the late 1950s, union leaders Walter Reuther and George Meany battled over how to define American labor's role in the world. The liberal Reuther wanted unions to think of themselves as part of an international labor movement. The more conservative Meany insisted that American union members should concentrate on their own interests and let workers in other countries take care of themselves.

Paraphrase

_____

_____

_____

3. It seems that Valentine's Day is hard on relationships. Researchers Katherine Morse and Steven Neuberg have shown that the overall odds of breaking up one week before or one week after Valentine's Day are higher than normal, 5.49 times higher than normal to be exact. Morse and Neuberg further determined that the negative effect of the holiday occurred mainly in couples whose relationship

was already deteriorating. The holiday had no effect on breakups among high-quality or improving relationships. (Adapted from Bryan Strong et al., *The Marriage and Family Experience* 10e, © Cengage Learning.)

Paraphrase

_____

_____

_____

_____

_____

4. Despite many enthusiastic claims about the benefits of e-government, five problems remain to be solved. Substantial investments are needed to pay for the necessary computer hardware and trained personnel. There is still an absence of staff expertise along with questions of liability, privacy, and security. There is also the possibility of cyberattacks and the difficulty of integrating software across multiple agencies and departments. (Adapted from Ann Bowman and Richard Kearney, *State and Local Government* 8e, © Cengage Learning.)

Paraphrase

_____

_____

_____

_____

_____

_____

Vocabulary Building
for College Reading

IN THIS CHAPTER, YOU WILL LEARN

- how to recognize words essential to your coursework.

- how context clues reveal word meaning.

- how knowing some common word parts can help you recall word meanings.

- how understanding a writer's allusions, or references, can improve your comprehension.

"Words are power, and pleasure. They are the individual cells that make up the body of language."
—Ben Macintyre, journalist

This chapter tells you more about how to develop the kind of academic vocabulary that will help you read your textbook assignments. The chapter also introduces the topic of **allusions**—references to specific people, places, and events that have, over time, taken on a more general meaning. Once you have finished Chapter 2, you will have noticeably enlarged your vocabulary and taken a giant leap forward on the road to academic achievement.

Master the Specialized Vocabulary in Your Courses

Some of your college courses will undoubtedly require you to master **specialized vocabulary**. A specialized vocabulary consists of words and phrases that rarely appear in ordinary conversation. They are, however, essential to mastering specific academic subjects.

For instance, you couldn't complete a biology text without seeing the word *respiration*, the process by which cells are supplied with oxygen. Similarly, reading a psychology text without running into the word *cognition*, the mental activity involved in thinking, is all but impossible.

Courses in business, biology, criminology, nursing, engineering, and astronomy, to name just a few, all employ specialized vocabulary words. To do well in these courses, you must master their specialized vocabulary. That means you need to recognize specialized vocabulary words when they first appear in your textbooks.

But recognizing specialized vocabulary is only the first step. You also have to note and record the definitions (in an online or paper notebook or on note cards).[†] Then you have to review both words and meanings until you know them as well as you know the meanings of words like *dog* and *house*.

Look for Words That Get Extra Attention

Textbook authors often rely heavily on a specialized vocabulary, words that seldom appear in everyday speech but are, nevertheless, essential to a particular subject. For that reason, authors are careful to highlight the words readers need to know and equally careful about supplying explicit definitions.

Look, for instance, at the following excerpt from a psychology text. The author knows that the words used to describe parts of the brain are unlikely to be familiar.

To make sure that readers learn the words that describe the brain, Nevid uses boldface to make specialized vocabulary stand out. He also supplies definitions within the passage and then repeats both words and definitions in the margins. Any words or phrases that get this much visual emphasis deserve your close attention.

medulla   A structure in the hindbrain involved in regulating basic life functions, such as heartbeat and respiration.
pons   A structure in the hindbrain involved in regulating states of wakefulness and sleep.
brainstem   The "stalk" in the lower part of the brain that connects the spinal cord to higher regions of the brain.

The Hindbrain

The lowest part of the brain, the hindbrain, is also the oldest part in evolutionary terms. The hindbrain includes the *medulla*, *pons*, and *cerebellum*. These structures control such basic life-support functions as breathing and heart rate.

The **medulla** and **pons** contain sensory neurons that transmit information from the spinal cord to the forebrain. The medulla is the section of the hindbrain that lies closest to the spinal cord. It forms the marrow, or core, of the **brainstem**, the "stem" or "stalk" that connects the spinal cord to the higher regions of the brain. (Jeffrey Nevid, *Psychology: Concepts and Applications* 3e, © Cengage Learning.)

[†]With the arrival of cloud technology, there are many online formats that allow you to make and store your notes. Evernote is one source, but there are certainly others you can explore. You can also use online flash cards.

Any time you see words that are not only highlighted in the text but also annotated in the margins, you can be sure that you are looking at specialized vocabulary crucial for understanding the subject matter. Readers who know the meanings of such specialized vocabulary *automatically*, without even thinking about them, have a huge advantage in reading their textbooks.

Look for Ordinary Words That Double as Specialized Vocabulary

Some words used in ordinary conversation take on a specialized meaning within the context of a particular subject. In biology, for instance, the word *producers* doesn't refer to the people who back Hollywood movies or Broadway plays. In the context of biology, the word *producers* refers to a category of organisms, or living things, that acquire energy and raw materials from environmental sources to make their own food. Similarly, the word *consumers* in the context of biology doesn't refer to shoppers. It refers to organisms that don't produce their own food and must feed off the tissue and waste of other organisms.

Ordinary words that take on a specialized meaning when appearing in textbooks are just as important as those specialized vocabulary words that almost never pop up in ordinary speech. If you see a word you think you know and are surprised at how it's used, note the specialized meaning and commit it to memory.

Use the Glossary for Troublesome Definitions

If you have any trouble understanding a specialized word or term an author has highlighted, check the glossary at the end of your textbook. This is where you can usually find brief definitions for all the specialized words in your text.

Use Specialized Online Dictionaries

If your textbook glossary provides a definition you still find hard to understand, check the Web for an online dictionary that deals solely with the subject you are studying. Then type the word into the online dictionary's search-engine box or check to see if the word appears in an alphabetical list. Much of the time, what you'll find in a specialized online dictionary is a definition simpler than the one that's in your textbook. Here, for example, is an online definition for *consumers* when it's used in the context of biology:

> An organism that generally obtains food by feeding on other organisms or organic matter due to lack of the ability to manufacture own food. (www.biology-online.org/dictionary/Consumer.)

Usually, reading the online definition followed by the textbook definition will clarify any confusion about the word's meaning. But because online definitions can occasionally be too simplified, you don't want to rely solely on them. Combining your textbook definition with that of an online source is a better option.

Here are a few of the discipline-specific dictionaries available to you:

1. http://allpsych.com/dictionary/index.html

2. http://sociology.socialsciencedictionary.com

3. www.biology-online.org/dictionary

4. www.historytoday.com/historical-dictionary

◆ EXERCISE 1   Identifying Specialized Vocabulary

DIRECTIONS   Make a list of the subjects you are currently taking. Underneath each subject heading, identify at least three specialized vocabulary words, along with their definitions. Keep adding to this list so that you learn the words essential to the subject. Included is an example to show you how to get started. *Note*: The definitions and the words are separated so that you can review by covering one or the other and then recalling either the definition or the word from memory.

EXAMPLE

Biology

1. DNA	the initials for deoxyribonucleic acid, the hereditary material for all living organisms and some viruses
2. receptor	a molecule or cellular structure that responds to a specific form of stimulation

3. mutations   slight changes in DNA

_____

_____

_____

_____

_____

 # Build Up Your General Academic Vocabulary

History, government, and sociology textbooks also highlight specialized vocabulary. In the following excerpt from a government textbook, for example, note how many different ways the author draws your attention to the word *filibuster*. It appears as a heading. Then it reappears in bold-face in the text, followed by a definition. That same definition appears in a marginal note, and the passage devoted to the word is followed by a cartoon illustration.

filibuster A prolonged speech or series of speeches used as a delaying tactic; a last ditch attempt to defeat a measure or bill.

Filibuster

A **filibuster** is a technique by which a small number of senators attempt to defeat a measure by talking it to death.[†] A filibuster consists of a prolonged speech, or series of speeches, made to delay action in a legislative assembly. It had become a common—and unpopular—feature of Senate life already by the end of the nineteenth century. Liberals and conservatives alike employed it for lofty-sounding and usually self-serving purposes. The first serious effort to restrict the filibuster came in 1917 after an important foreign-policy measure submitted by President Wilson had been talked to death by, as Wilson put it, "eleven wilful men." Efforts to end the filibuster continue to the present day. (Adapted from James Q. Wilson and John J. Dilulio, *American Government* 11e, © Cengage Learning.)

[†]The first sentence of the definition comes from *Safire's Political Dictionary* by political columnist William Safire.

The filibuster is considered by many people to be a time-wasting political tactic that should be abandoned by those on both sides of the congressional aisle.

Courtesy Ulrich Flemming

Here again, anytime you spot a word or phrase getting this much attention, both verbally and visually, you can be sure it's a word or phrase you need to know without hesitation.

However, you also need to realize that courses like history, sociology, and government don't necessarily rely as much on a specialized vocabulary as some other courses do. In these courses, there is more of an overlap, and many of the words will belong to a **general academic vocabulary**[†] appropriate to reading, speaking, and writing in classroom lectures, scholarly journals, and textbooks or reference works. But these words aren't restricted to a specific kind of knowledge or context. They are just typical of the kind of language used in an academic setting.

[†]Scholars from New Zealand have put together lists of words typically found in academic writing. A list of the words used most frequently is available here: www .victoria.ac.nz/lals/resources/academicwordlist/most-frequent

Pay Attention to Any Words Followed by Definitions

Subjects like government, history, and sociology don't have as many specialized vocabulary words as, say, biology, psychology, or oceanography do. Thus the textbooks for these subjects use fewer marginal notes to draw readers' attention to must-know words.

What they do more often is highlight words central to a particular discussion with italics or boldface and then weave a definition into the text itself. The definitions following highlighted words do not always announce that they are, in fact, definitions. Still, as soon as a word merits italics or boldface, you need to be on the lookout for a definition that fits the discussion. To illustrate, here's an example from a world history book. Note how the authors introduce and define the word *oligarchies*. Note, too, the use of the phrase "in other words," a common **transitional device**, or connective link, that tells the reader a restatement is coming up.

The city-states of the fourteenth and fifteenth centuries were princely *oligarchies. In other words*, a small group of wealthy people, headed by a prince with the powers of a king, ran the government (Philip J. Adler and Randall L. Pouwels, *World Civilizations* 6e, © Cengage Learning.)

As with boldface and definitions repeated in the margins, explicit definitions following or preceding a word, even if the word is *not* printed in bold or italic, are a signal of significance. Those definitions say to readers, the meaning of this word is important; make sure you learn it.

Notice Word Repetition

If you are going to build an academic vocabulary, you'll also need to be attentive to words or phrases that turn up repeatedly. Do the words *exempt* and *exemption* appear frequently in the discussion of taxes in your American government textbook? If they do, then make sure you know that both refer to being freed of some obligation that others must fulfill.

Building an Academic Vocabulary

Here, to get you started developing your academic vocabulary, is a list of words common to the study of psychology and sociology.

**Words
Common
to Psychology
and Sociology**
◆

1. **Dynamics**   The social, intellectual, or moral forces that produce an event, an effect, or a change.

    Sample sentence: The underlying social *dynamics* of online relationships have not received the attention they deserve.

2. **Norms**   Standards of behavior considered typical; unwritten but understood rules of society.

    Sample sentence: In addition to roles for its members, groups also establish *norms*, rules of conduct for members. (Sharon Brehm et al., *Social Psychology* 8e, © Cengage Learning.)

3. **Assertive**   Willing to put forth one's opinions and wishes.

    Sample sentence: In response to a demand for a change in behavior, people may conform or maintain their independence; they may comply with the demand or react by being *assertive*. (Adapted from Sharon Brehm et al., *Social Psychology* 8e, © Cengage Learning.)

4. **Stimulus**   Motive or cause of action.

    Sample sentence: The *stimulus* for the study was the appearance of an unusual virus that did not behave in typical fashion.

5. **Reciprocity**   A mutual exchange between what we give and what we receive—for instance, helping those who help us.

    Sample sentence: *Reciprocity* does mean that we will like everyone who likes us; studies show that we like to think that people who like us are selective in their affections. (Adapted from Sharon Brehm et al., *Social Psychology* 8e, © Cengage Learning.)

6. **Longitudinal**   Extending over a long period of time.

    Sample sentence: To prove or disprove Erik Erikson's theory about developmental stages spanning a lifetime, researchers need to do *longitudinal* studies of large sample populations.

7. **Genetic**   Due to heredity; inheritable; transmissible.

    Sample sentence: There may well be a *genetic* factor in the development of schizophrenia.

8. **Cognitive**   Related to thought rather than being a purely emotional response.

    Sample sentence: His *cognitive* skills were way ahead of his age, but on an emotional level, he was more child than teenager.

9. **Therapeutic** Having to do with the treatment of disease and producing a beneficial effect.

   Sample sentence: The *therapeutic* effects of psychoanalysis have never been scientifically tested.

10. **Correlation** Connection; relationship.

    Sample sentence: There seems to be a high *correlation* between active learning and long-term remembering.

♦ **EXERCISE 2** **Putting Words into Sentences**

DIRECTIONS Fill in the blanks with one of the words in the list below.

norms	reciprocated	genetic	cognitive	dynamics
assertive	stimulus	therapeutic	logitudinal	correlation

1. *The War Hotel* is the title of a book written by Arlene Audergon; it deals with the psychological _____ underlying human conflict.

2. In a(n) _____ setting, patients or clients should feel free to say things they are normally fearful of expressing.

3. Aware of the penalties they might pay, even the most independent and rebellious spirits have a difficult time ignoring society's _____.

4. A 35-year-long study showed a high _____ between consistent physical exercise and a healthy old age.

5. An environmental _____ like the smell of cookies baking in the oven can trigger powerful memories.

6. If members of a group are going to contribute time and energy to achieving the group's goals, they have to feel that their efforts are being _____.

7. _____ studies strongly suggest that personality may be as much a product of the genes as the environment.

8. It's a mistake to assume that the words _____ and *aggressive* are synonyms: The first describes a person who is not shy about expressing an opinion, the second a person who insists on making his or her opinion everyone else's as well.

9. _____ therapies generally rely less on medication and more on changing thought patterns.

10. It was once believed that an extra *y* chromosome caused a(n) _____ tendency toward criminal behavior.

Learn New Words by Creating Your Own Recall Cues

As you work on building your academic vocabulary, keep in mind the principle of *elaborative encoding* that you learned about in Chapter 1 (p. 52). The human brain struggles when it has to absorb isolated bits and pieces of unfamiliar or unrelated information. The more you can link new vocabulary to things you already know and embed that new vocabulary in a cluster of associations, the more likely you are to remember the meanings of new words. **Recall cues** are a concrete or visible illustration of this principle. They use information already stored in your long-term memory to help you call up or remember definitions of new words.

For instance, to learn the word *expenditures*, you might link it to the word *spend*, which you hear in the second syllable. You could also create a different recall cue by making up a sentence like this: "When we make expenditures, we are often spending money that we shouldn't."

After a few reviews, you'll learn the meaning of the word and be able to recall it automatically. But when you are first learning the meanings of unfamiliar words, recall cues are a huge help.

Linking Words to Images

You can also use images as recall cues. Say you are trying to remember that the word *elite* refers to those who are privileged or who have special privileges that others don't. You could go to Google images or browse online for pictures that you can copy into a vocabulary file or print out and paste onto the note card of the word you want to learn. Here, for instance, is the drawing of a snooty lion that you could use for the word *elite*.

Courtesy Ulrich Flemming

Use Antonyms as Recall Cues

You can also remember new word meanings by making use of **antonyms,** or words opposite in meaning. For instance, if you want to remember that a *partisan* is a person strongly in favor of someone or something, then, in addition to its definition, link the word to its antonym as shown here.

partisan   person strongly in favor of a theory or cause; a partisan or person who is partisan supports a particular idea or group; a partisan is the *opposite of a critic or detractor*

♦ **EXERCISE 3**   **Using Recall Cues**

DIRECTIONS Next to each word below, write down one or more recall cues that you can use to remember the word and meaning.

1. norms: _____

2. genetic: _____

3. stimulus: _____

4. embargo: _____

5. elite: _____

Use Context Clues

Textbook writers usually explicitly define the specialized vocabulary of their academic disciplines, or subjects. Still, they can't define every potentially unfamiliar word in a textbook. Readers sometimes have to use the **context**, or setting, of the word to **infer**, or figure out, an **approximate meaning**, one that doesn't match the dictionary definition but comes close enough to let readers continue without looking the word up. Based on the context, for example, what do you think *ideology* means in this excerpt?

> In English-speaking countries, the period from about 1850 to 1901 is known as the Victorian Age. The expression refers not only to the reign of England's Queen Victoria (1837–1901) but also to the *ideology* surrounding the family and governing the relations between men and women. According to the ideology that ruled the Victorian era, men were meant, by nature, to be strong and courageous, women to be nurturing and cautious. (Adapted from Richard W. Bulliet et al, *The Earth and Its Peoples.* © Cengage Learning.)

Because the passage illustrates how Victorian ideology functioned—it governed relations between men and women—you might correctly conclude that *ideology* is a "particular way of thinking about human behavior." To understand the point of the passage, this approximate definition for *ideology* would be fine even though dictionaries are likely to define *ideology* more generally as "the set of beliefs forming the basis for political, economic, or social systems."

Avoid Constant References to the Dictionary

Turning to the dictionary every time you encounter an unfamiliar word can disrupt your concentration. Before looking a word up, see if context can provide you with a meaning. Four of the most common context clues are **contrast, restatement, example**, and **general knowledge**.

Contrast Clues

Sentences containing contrast clues tell you what an unfamiliar word does *not* mean, often in the form of antonyms. For instance, suppose you were asked what *ostentatious* means. You might not be able to define it. After all, the word doesn't turn up that often in everyday conversation. Now suppose as well that word had a context, or setting, like the following:

> Contrary to what many of us assume, the really rich are seldom *ostentatious* in their dress. Secure in the status wealth provides, they can afford to look plain and unimpressive.

In this case, the context for the word *ostentatious* offers contrast clues to its meaning. The words *plain* and *unimpressive* are antonyms for *ostentatious*. Using the contrast clues, you could infer, or read between the lines and determine, that *ostentatious* means "being showy" or "trying to impress."

Restatement Clues

For clarity and emphasis, writers, particularly of textbooks, sometimes deliberately say the same thing two different ways. Look, for example, at this sentence:

> In addition to being a member of humanity, each of us also belongs to a particular social group, where we find our *peers*—like-minded people often close to us in age—with whom we can identify and relate.

Here the author tells us that in addition to being a member of the human race we all have other, more specific groups to which we belong. Among those groups are our *peers*, "like-minded people often close to us in age." Note how the author defines the word to make sure readers know what it means.

Example Clues

Be alert to passages in which the author supplies an example or illustration of an unfamiliar word. Examples of the behavior associated with a word can often give you enough information to determine an approximate definition.

Personification in writing is an effective device only if it is used sparingly. Unfortunately, if the tables are always groaning, the wind is always howling, and the lights are always winking, then the technique becomes tiresome.

You could correctly infer from the examples in this passage that *personification* means talking about things or events as if they were people.

General-Knowledge Clues

Although contrast, restatement, and example are common context clues, not all context clues are so obvious. Sometimes you have to base your inference solely on your familiarity with the experience or situation described in the text, as in the following example:

With only the most primitive equipment and maps to guide their journey, the explorers ended up taking a very *circuitous* route to India.

This passage does not contain any contrasts, restatements, or examples. But you can still figure out that *circuitous* means "indirect or roundabout," given that people are inclined to get lost or take a long time if they are guided by primitive equipment and bad maps.

CHECK YOUR UNDERSTANDING

For each sentence, define the italicized word and identify the type of context clue.

1. General George Patton demanded that his soldiers remain *stalwart*, no matter what threats they faced; Patton is famous for slapping two soldiers he considered cowardly, a gesture that ended his promising career.

   Context clue: _____

   Meaning: _____

2. Many voters believe that a candidate's marital status is *relevant*, or related to, his or her political performance.

   Context clue: _____

   Meaning: _____

3. The scientist's long, *abstruse* explanation left her audience speechless with incomprehension.

   Context clue: _____

   Meaning: _____

4. If you want to travel into the Grand Canyon, you have two choices of *conveyance*: your feet or a mule.

   Context clue: _____

   Meaning: _____

◆ **EXERCISE 4**   **Making Use of Context Clues**

DIRECTIONS   Use context to identify an approximate definition for each italicized word.

1. By the seventeenth century, nutmeg was a favorite spice of European cooks because of its flavor and *aroma*.

    a. taste

    b. appearance

    c. smell

    d. ingredient

2. *Proponents* of states' rights argued that letting the federal government interfere in state affairs was like asking for a return of the monarchy.

    a. critics

    b. supporters

    c. creators

    d. challengers

3. The music had a *cathartic* effect on the young man: Listening to the songs of his childhood, feelings long suppressed welled up to the surface and he started to weep.

    a. emotional

    b. angry

c. bland

d. comic

4. Angry at the *inequitable* distribution of wealth so obvious in the city's business district, roving bands of teenagers robbed the well-heeled tourists and distributed the money and valuables to friends and family.

a. luxurious

b. usual

c. unequal

d. changing

5. Most scholars consider the *Oxford English Dictionary* to be the most comprehensive dictionary available, and they turn to it for definitions of brand-new words as well as *obsolete* words or meanings no longer included in other dictionaries.

a. up-to-date

b. out-of-date

c. improperly used

d. grammatically correct

6. In the late nineteenth century, boxer John L. Sullivan *vanquished* all his opponents until "Gentleman Jim" Corbett demonstrated that speed and technique could subdue Sullivan's brute strength.

a. conquered

b. irritated

c. challenged

d. delayed

7. The story of the homeless woman's life did not make for a pleasing or happy *narrative*.

a. sound

b. joke

c. description

d. tale

8. Tabloid newspapers generally avoid serious news about government policy and international affairs; their focus is on more *titillating* stories about celebrity divorces, bloody crimes, and financial scandals.

   a. personally disinterested

   b. completely untrue

   c. exciting, stimulating

   d. casually described

9. The American writer Gertrude Stein claimed that when she took a final exam with the philosopher William James, she wrote a note saying, "I am so sorry, but I really do not feel a bit like an examination paper in philosophy today." According to Stein, James replied, "I understand perfectly how you feel; I often feel like that myself" and gave her the highest grade in the class. Stein, however, was known to *embellish* reality for the sake of a good story.

   a. enjoy

   b. exaggerate

   c. celebrate

   d. emphasize

10. The rule of the generals was meant to be *provisional*, but they ended up staying in power for more than a decade.

    a. rebellious

    b. strong

    c. failing

    d. temporary

◆ **EXERCISE 5   Using Context Clues**

DIRECTIONS Based on the context clues, write out definitions for the italicized words. *Note*: These words can turn up anywhere but are very likely to appear in textbooks devoted to U.S. government and history. And they are, for sure, going to turn up on the review test at the end of this chapter.

1. Worried about rumors of a terrorist background, the United States has questioned the *legitimacy* of Iranian president Ahmadinejad, since if the rumors are true the man should not be leading Iran's government

   Legitimacy: _____

2. While the *adherents*, who favored taxing corporations repeated their talking points, the opponents of such legislation barely paid attention.

   Adherents: _____

3. After the Revolutionary War (1776–1783), those in the *commercial* sector found their fortunes on the rise while those not involved in importing and exporting—farmers, for instance—could barely make ends meet.

   Commercial: _____

4. Initially, representatives of only nine states *ratified* the Constitution, but over time, all thirteen states agreed that the Constitution would be legally binding.

   Ratified: _____

5. The senator outraged most of his *constituents* when he publicly applauded a tax increase on alcohol and cigarettes.

   Constituents: _____

6. Military *expenditures* for the Iraq War dramatically increased the U.S. debt.

   Expenditures: _____

7. The U.S. commercial and financial *embargo* against Cuba has severely damaged the Cuban economy—some sources place the figure at over one trillion dollars—because, prior to 1960, the United States had been one of the biggest consumers of Cuban products.

   Embargo: _____

8. If you decide to run for president as a Democrat, do not trust too much the early polls identifying the front runner; among all the early front runners, like Edmund Muskie (1972), George Wallace (1976), Ted Kennedy (1980), Gary Hart (1988), Mario Cuomo (1992), and Joseph Lieberman (2004), only two *prevailed*, Walter Mondale (1984) and Al Gore (2000). (Adapted from James Q. Wilson and John J. DiIulio, *American Government* 11e, © Cengage Learning.)

   Prevailed: _____

9. The first meeting of the newly elected senator with the man she had defeated did not go well, and *subsequent* meetings were, if possible, even worse.

   Subsequent: _____

10. While Alexander Hamilton was determined to maintain the *supremacy* of the U.S. government, Thomas Jefferson was just as much inclined to undermine that *supremacy* in favor of giving the states more power.

   Supremacy: _____

Learn Common Word Parts

Knowing something about the parts of words can help you remember new word meanings. Trying, for instance, to learn the meaning of *primordial*, "existing first or very early in time," you could use the meaning of *prim* ("first") to remember the definition. Just tell yourself that something *primordial* has to be one of the *first* creatures or plants in history.

Then during reviews, you could use the word part *prim* as a recall clue to jog your memory and call up the word's meaning. That means, however, that you need to have a working knowledge of common word parts and their definitions. This section will help you develop that knowledge. However, it will be up to you to do regular reviews of the word parts and meanings shown below because there will be a test on word parts when you finish the chapter.

Prefixes[†]

Prefix	Meaning	Examples
a, ab, de	away, away from	asexual, absent, dethrone
a, an	not	anonymous, amoral
in, im, il, ir, non	not	incorrect, immoral, illegal, irregular, nonstop
ad, as	to, toward	adhere, associate
ante	before	anteroom
anti	against	antidote
circum	around	circumference
com, con, syn	with, together	complete, construct, synchronize
contra	against	contradict
de, dis	down from, away, not	decline, distance, disallowed
ex, e	out of	exclude, evade
in, im, il	into	incline, immerse, illuminate
inter	between	interstate
mono	one, alone	monarch
para	beside, beyond	paraphrase
phil	love	philanthropist
plut	wealth	plutocrat
poly	many	polygamy
post	after	postpone
pre, pro	before, forward, in place of	prepare, prophet, pronoun
re	back	refer, retreat
sub, suc, suf, sup, sus	under	submerge, succumb, suffer, support, suspend
super	above, over	supervise
trans	across, beyond	transmit

[†]prefix: a letter or letters at the beginning of a word that modify or change the core meaning, e.g., *in*spect and *re*spect.

Roots[†]	Root	Meaning	Examples
◆	*anthrop*	human	anthropology, philanthropy
	arch	chief	monarch, architect, archangel
	bibl	book	bibliography, Bible
	cap	head	capital, captain, decapitate
	ceed	move, yield	exceed, proceed, succeed
	chron	time	chronology, chronicle
	civ	city	civic, civilize
	cred	belief	credible
	dic	speak	dictate, diction, dictator
	equ	equal	equalize
	fid	faith	confide
	fin	end, finished	final
	flor	flower	florist
	flu, fluc, flux	flow	influence, fluctuate
	gam	marriage	bigamist
	gram, graph	write, written	grammar, graphic
	hetero	different	heterosexual
	homo	same	homosexual
	lingua, lingu	tongue, language	bilingual
	loc	place	location, local, allocate
	log, ology	speech, study	dialogue, geology, biology
	loqu	speech	loquacious
	memor	memory	memorial, memorize
	mit	send	admit, commit, permit
	mo	set in motion	move, remove, mobile
	ord	order	ordinary, ordain
	path	feeling, suffering	pathetic, sympathy
	phil, phile	love	philosopher
	physic, physio	nature	physical, physiology
	pon	place, put	postpone, opponent
	popul	people	popular, population
	port	carry	portable, porter, deportment
	reg, rect	straighten, rule	regular, regal, rectangle
	sequ, secu	follow	sequence, persecute
	spec	look	specimen, spectacle, spectator
	temp	time	temporary
	the	god	theology
	ven	come	prevent
	vid, vis	see	vision, visualize, video

[†]roots: the parts of words that contain the central or core meaning, e.g., in*spect* and re*spect*.

◆ **EXERCISE 6** **Adding Word Parts**

DIRECTIONS Fill in the blanks left in each word with one of the word parts[†] listed in the following box.

circum	around
merit	deserve, achieve, earn
pend	hang
homo	same
plut	wealth
phil	love
super	above
loqu, locu	speech

1. The awards, diplomas, and trophies in the lawyer's office had been placed there intentionally to show that she had many achievements _____ing public approval.

2. Some people claim that what we have in the United States is not a democracy but a _____ocracy, or rule by the wealthy.

3. A _____atelist is a person passionate about stamp collecting.

4. Some philosophers have argued that we would all be better off if we were led by a _____ocracy of the best and the brightest.

5. The heavy, _____ulous leaves of the plant were covered in a dark, slimy mold.

6. The members of the group were extremely _____geneous, which may be why everyone got along so well.

7. Because an important trial was _____ing, the district attorney couldn't concentrate on the renovation of her office.

8. The cafeteria col_____y between the student and her professor looked too intense to be interrupted.

——————————
[†]Not all the word parts in the exercises appear on the list on pages 85–86.

9. The crown prince had a _____cilious manner that made it clear he thought of himself as a very important man.

10. Once he had measured the garden's _____ference, he had a better idea of how many trees he needed to go around the border.

◆ **EXERCISE 7**   **Using Context Clues and Word Parts**

DIRECTIONS   Use context and the list of word parts on pages 85–86 to create approximate meanings for the italicized words in the following sentences.

1. She was a brilliant woman, but her *linguistic* skills did not match her cognitive abilities: She had a terrible time expressing herself.

   Linguistic means _____.

2. Although the runner's days as a great athlete were long gone, he liked looking at the *memorabilia* from his glory days.

   Memorabilia means _____.

3. The new city *ordinance* exacted huge fines from dog owners who let their dogs off the leash.

   Ordinance means _____.

4. Henry VIII used trumped-up charges of *infidelity* to win a divorce from his wife Anne Boleyn, whom he had beheaded when she could not give him a son.

   Infidelity means _____.

5. If the bird flu virus becomes capable of human-to-human transmission, it will spread like a wildfire among the *populace*.

   Populace means _____.

6. Fearful of criticism, the new *regime* took power and immediately clamped down on freedom of the press.

   Regime means _____.

7. The man's *diction* suggested that he was British rather than American.

   Diction means _____.

8. In India, the yearly *per capita* income is rising as more and more technology companies are outsourcing to India instead of hiring workers at home.

   Per capita means _____.

9. The two government officials tried to appear friendly, but their *antipathy* was obvious.

   Antipathy means _____.

10. Bear and bare, mite and might, there and their, are all *homonyms*.

    Homonyms means _____.

Make Allusions Part of Your Vocabulary Building

Allusions are references to specific people, places, and events that carry with them fixed associations. In speech or writing, allusions function as a kind of verbal shorthand. By alluding to a person, event or place, the writer or speaker calls up in the mind of listeners or readers a set of associations that help explain an idea. What, for instance, does the allusion to Martha Stewart in this passage suggest about the author's mother?

When I was growing up we were pretty poor, but I didn't realize it until I was practically an adult. On very little money, my mother set an example even Martha Stewart might have approved. True, we drank out of jelly glasses. But the glasses always matched and they had been washed and dried to a high shine. Wildflowers, fresh or dried, regularly sat on the kitchen table, and the brightly colored paper napkins were perfectly folded into neat triangles. The food, much of it provided by food stamps, was carefully arranged on the four unscratched dinner plates our family possessed because our mother always insisted that food should not just taste good. It should look good as well.

Because Martha Stewart's name is synonymous with gracious living, the author uses an allusion to her to convey her mother's refusal to let lack of money make her careless about how she and her family lived. The allusion to Stewart in the second sentence of the paragraph ties all the details together making them more meaningful than they would have been had she not been mentioned. That's the magic of allusions. They speak volumes if you pick the right one.

Allusions Vary with Your Audience

As a reader, you'll need to understand the role an allusion plays in a writer's message. But when you yourself are the writer, you'll need to choose your allusions with your audience in mind. If you are writing an article for a newsletter to be read by other college students your own age, then you're fine using allusions to *The Hunger Games* or rising star Amanda Seyfried. But if you are writing a letter to the editor to be printed in your local newspaper where people of all ages might be reading it, you might want to use other allusions not so specific to one age group, say *Pirates of the Caribbean* and Johnny Depp.

Allusions with Staying Power

Some allusions come and go as people and events grab the public's attention only to fade from memory after a few months.[†] Other allusions, in contrast, seem to last forever. After making their way into the English language, they have shown staying power and come to be considered **common knowledge**. Writers use such allusions without explaining them to readers. They assume their audience will know what the allusions suggest. Lady Macbeth from Shakespeare's play *Macbeth* is a good example of an allusion that writers expect readers to know:

> As the playwright envisions the character, she is a modern-day Lady Macbeth whose relentless determination to make her husband succeed produces tragic results.

[†]In the 1980s, people talked about a person or a career being "borked," meaning the person's reputation was destroyed by his or her enemies. The allusion referred to Judge Robert Bork's failure to become a Supreme Court justice after his critics got together and blocked his nomination. If you use the term *borked* today, many people will not know what you are talking about.

If the reader does not know that Shakespeare's Lady Macbeth drives her husband mercilessly to become king and ends up guilt-ridden about the bloodshed that task requires, then the meaning of the above sentence is considerably diminished. A reader who understands the allusion, in contrast, will have no problem getting the point: As the playwright portrays the character, she is a woman like Lady Macbeth. Her hunger for power drives her husband to do despicable deeds that have deadly consequences.

Learning Common Allusions

What follows are some explanations of five common allusions. They will help you increase the number of common cultural allusions you automatically know. As you complete the chapters in this textbook, note as well the boxes labeled **Allusion Alert**. They all introduce some frequently used allusions, which should be part of the background knowledge you bring to a text.

Allusions, like all new words and phrases, are easier to remember when placed in a larger context. Again, this is another illustration of elaborative encoding at work. Rather than trying to memorize just the allusion's meaning, learn the story of its origin. Once you know the story, you'll automatically remember the meaning.

Allusions Common to History, Politics, and Government ◆

1. **Waterloo**   In 1814, the French Emperor Napoleon Bonaparte was forced into exile on the island of Elba. However, in 1815 he escaped from Elba and returned to France, where he re-established his rule. To get the jump on his enemies, he then marched into Belgium and defeated the forces arrayed against him *until* he entered the battle of Waterloo. Facing British forces, Napoleon waited too long to attack. With that mistake, he gave the Germans time to reinforce the British troops, and, as a result, he was totally defeated. Once again he was exiled, this time to a more isolated island where he died in 1821. As a result of Napoleon's humiliating defeat, the allusion to Waterloo has come to mean a final and decisive failure as it does in the following sentence: "Elected by a landslide in 1964, Lyndon Baines Johnson met his Waterloo when he committed the country to waging war in Vietnam."

2. **Cold War** From roughly the late 1940s to the early 1990s, the Soviet Union and the United States did everything possible, short of all-out war, to undermine each other's power and influence. Although the term *cold war* mainly refers to this particular period and these two countries, it can also refer to other similarly "cool" conflicts that don't turn into "hot," open warfare, for instance: "When it came to the Chinese, the secretary of state had a cold war mentality that refused to acknowledge any evidence challenging her point of view."

3. **McCarthyism** This allusion originates with Wisconsin senator Joseph R. McCarthy. In the 1950s, in an attempt to increase his own political power, McCarthy aggressively accused, without any evidence, hundreds of people of being Communists or Communist sympathizers. While McCarthy's initial attacks successfully focused on members of the State Department, he eventually went too far and ended up being censured by the Senate. From then on, he was in disgrace, and he died a broken and forgotten man. When not used in reference to McCarthy's actual attacks, *McCarthyism* generally describes an atmosphere filled with unfounded accusations and suspicion; for example, "The new administration made it clear that McCarthyism, which had dominated the previous administration, was now a thing of the past."

4. **Laissez-faire** This French phrase, which, roughly translated, means "let alone," originated in the seventeenth century. The French minister of finance is said to have asked a wine merchant how he could be of assistance. Because Jean-Baptiste Colbert was famous for levying taxes, the wine merchant answered, "Let us alone." The story and the phrase were widely circulated, and the phrase *laissez-faire* became a common way to refer to an economy or approach that functioned without interference. The phrase has its widest use in the context of economics. However, it can also be used to describe theories and behaviors unrelated to economics, for instance, "When it came to education, the philosopher Jean-Jacques Rousseau took a *laissez-faire* approach. He believed that the children would instinctively learn what they needed to know."

5. **Main Street** Published in 1920 Sinclair Lewis's novel *Main Street* described the author's Minnesota hometown Sauk Centre, a place he thoroughly despised. Calling the fictional version of his hometown Gopher Prairie, Lewis painted its citizens as nosy and small-minded. For that reason, allusions to Main Street were once

used to describe people who were close-minded and couldn't stand anyone different from themselves. However, over time, the meaning of the allusion has changed. Most people who use it have never read the novel. They mainly remember that Lewis's *Main Street* describes ordinary people living in a small town. Thus allusions to Main Street suggest plain, hard-working Americans, for example, "Bruce Springsteen has not forgotten his New Jersey, working-class roots; he still writes songs that speak for the people of Main Street rather than Wall Street."

WEB QUEST   **The Stockholm Syndrome**

When someone makes an allusion to the Stockholm Syndrome, what specific event are they referring to?

_____

_____

_____

_____

When a writer or speaker alludes to the Stockholm Syndrome, what is the point of the allusion?

_____

_____

◆ **EXERCISE 8**   **Putting Allusions into Sentences**

DIRECTIONS Fill in the blanks with the correct allusion.

| laissez-faire | Waterloo | Cold War | McCarthyism | Main Street |

1. After the terrorist attacks of September 11, 2001, there were warnings against a return to _____ when the U.S. government arrested and questioned possible terrorists at home and

abroad. No one argued with the idea that rounding up the terrorists was a legitimate aim, but some wanted to make sure that there was sufficient evidence to take this step.

2. Titling his 2006 column "A(n) _____ Brewing Between the Press and White House Over Iran?" journalist Vaughn Ververs suggested that the press had become more ready to criticize presidential claims about nuclear threats than it had been prior to the Iraq War. If Ververs is correct, that may be why the White House, for its part, responded by harshly criticizing the media.

3. For years it looked as if Napoleon admirer and high-finance super-hero Conrad Black could always come back from seeming defeat. But as British journalist Jacquie McNish reported in *The Globe and Mail*, Black met his _____ in 2004 when a judge found him guilty and publicly criticized Black's business ethics.

4. Although the candidate was remarkably popular with members of the financial community, she didn't have the same appeal for those living on _____, who mistrusted her for everything from the way she dressed to how she held her knife and fork.

5. Even Adam Smith, the man most associated with the idea of a _____ economy, did not fully believe that the market could function effectively and fairly without some oversight.

REVIEWING THROUGH WRITING

Pick one of the descriptions listed below and use an allusion to communicate the experience or feeling described. You can pick your own allusion or use one from the list below. The first one is an example to help get you started. *Note*: Make sure to write a complete sentence.

Edward and/or Bella from the Twilight series	*The Scarlet Letter*	Shrek
	Harry Potter	*Romeo and Juliet*
Big Brother	Bambi's mother	*Alice in Wonderland*
Animal Farm		Dr. Seuss

1. Tell your reader about a book (or movie) that was extremely popular when you were a kid.

When I was growing up, for girls at least, Nancy Drew, girl detective, was my generation's Harry Potter.

2. Communicate your idea of the perfect mate.

_____

3. Tell your reader what grief or sadness feels like.

_____

4. Describe for your reader someone who looks menacing but is really harmless.

_____

5. Describe a new situation that left you feeling unable to figure out how to behave or respond because the experience was so unusual.

_____

6. Convey to your reader what it's like to fall in love for the first time.

_____

7. Describe for your readers someone who knows how to tell a great story.

_____

8. Explain how someone has been publicly shunned for bad behavior.

_____

If you want to learn more about allusions, here's a wonderful website that provides some great examples: poetryhandbookwinter.blogspot.com/p/winter-exercises.html.

TAKING STOCK The Science of Romantic Love

Looking Ahead The following reading talks about romantic love, past and present. It also talks about the effect of infatuation on the brain. You may be surprised at how powerfully "falling in love" can affect the human brain.

1 We like to think of this powerful force, this source of both danger and delight, as something that defies analysis. However, scientists have provided new perspectives on its true nature.

A Psychological View

2 According to psychologist Robert Sternberg, love can be viewed as a triangle with three faces: passion, intimacy, and commitment. Each person brings his or her own triangle to a relationship. If they match well, their relationship is likely to be satisfying.

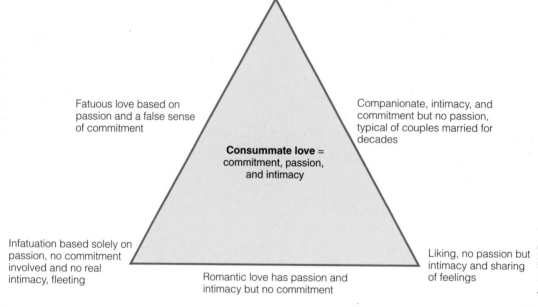

Fatuous love based on passion and a false sense of commitment

Companionate, intimacy, and commitment but no passion, typical of couples married for decades

Consummate love = commitment, passion, and intimacy

Infatuation based solely on passion, no commitment involved and no real intimacy, fleeting

Romantic love has passion and intimacy but no commitment

Liking, no passion but intimacy and sharing of feelings

Courtesy Ulrich Flemming

Sternberg identified six types of love:

- Liking, the intimacy that friends share.
- Infatuation, the passion that stems from physical and emotional attraction.
- Romantic love, a combination of intimacy and passion.
- Companionate love, a deep emotional bond in a relationship that may have had romantic components.
- Fatuous love, a combination of passion and superficial commitment in two people who lack a deep emotional intimacy.
- Consummate love, which combines passion, intimacy, and commitment over time.

An Anthropological View

3 When you first fall in love, you may be sure that no one else has ever known the same dizzying, wonderful feelings. Yet while every romance may be unique, romantic love is anything but. Anthropologists have found evidence of romantic love between individuals in most of the cultures they have studied—it seems to be a human universal, or, at the least, a near universal.

4 Anthropologist Helen Fisher, author of *Anatomy of Love: The Natural History of Monogamy, Adultery and Divorce*, describes romantic love "as a very primitive, basic human emotion, as basic as fear, anger, or joy." As she explains, it pulled men and women of prehistoric times into the sort of partnerships that were essential to child rearing.

5 But after about four years—just "long enough to rear one child through infancy," says Fisher—romantic love seemed to wane, and primitive couples tended to break up and find new partners. This "four-year itch" may well have endured through the centuries, contends Fisher, who notes that divorce statistics from most of the sixty-two cultures she has studied still show a pattern of restlessness four years into marriage.

A Biochemical View

6 The heart is the organ we associate with love, but the brain may be where the action really is. According to research on neurotransmitters (chemicals within the brain), love sets off a chemical chain reaction that causes our skin to flush, our palms to sweat, and our lungs to breathe more deeply and rapidly. The "love chemicals" within the brain—dopamine,

norepinephrine, and phenylethylamine (PEA)—have effects similar to those of amphetamines, stimulant drugs that intensify physiological reactions.

7   Infatuation may indeed be a natural high, but like other highs this rush doesn't last—possibly because the body develops tolerance for love-induced chemicals, just as it does with amphetamines. However, as the initial lovers' high fades, other brain chemicals may come into play: the endorphins, morphine-like chemicals that can help produce feelings of well-being, security, and tranquillity. These feel-good molecules may increase in partners who develop a deep attachment.

8   The hormone oxytocin, best known for its role in inducing labor during childbirth, seems particularly important in our ability to bond with others. By measuring blood levels of women as they recalled positive and negative relationships, researchers have found that women whose oxytocin levels rose when remembering a positive relationship reported having little dif-ficulty setting appropriate boundaries, being alone, or trying too hard to please others. Women whose oxytocin levels fell in response to remember-ing a negative emotional relationship reported greater anxiety in close re-lationships. (Adapted from Dianne Hales, *An Invitation to Health* 14e, © Cengage Learning.)

Sharpening Your Skills

DIRECTIONS   Answer the following questions by filling in the blanks or circling the letter of the correct response.

Surveying 1. A survey of the headings tells readers to expect how many perspectives on love? _____

2. Which of the following statements would be the more effective way to focus your reading?

   a. As you read, consider how the various views on love differ. Think about what you might say if you were trying to explain each one to someone who had not read the selection.

   b. As you read, consider how infatuation differs from love and how you might explain that difference to someone younger than you are.

Using Context Clues

3. What would be a good synonym for *contends* in the following sentence? "This 'four-year itch' may well have endured through the centuries, *contends* Fisher, who notes that divorce statistics from most of the sixty-two cultures she has studied still show a pattern of restlessness four years into marriage."

_____

4. What would be a good synonym for *wane* in the following sentence? "But after about four years—just 'long enough to rear one child through infancy,' says Fisher—romantic love seemed to *wane*, and primitive couples tended to break up and find new partners."

_____

5. What do you think *universal* means in this sentence? "Anthropologists have found evidence of romantic love between individuals in most of the cultures they have studied—it seems to be a human *universal*, or, at the least, a near *universal*."
   a. shared by certain portions of the population
   b. idea believed by many
   c. trait shared by all people

6. Based on the context, which definition would you choose for the word *tranquillity* in the following sentence? "However, as the initial lovers' high fades, other brain chemicals may come into play: the endorphins, morphine-like chemicals that can help produce feelings of well-being, security, and *tranquillity*."
   a. high anxiety
   b. dislike
   c. peace

Paraphrasing

7. Circle the letter of the best paraphrase for the following statement: "Infatuation may indeed be a natural high, but like other highs this rush doesn't last—possibly because the body develops tolerance for love-induced chemicals, just as it does with amphetamines."

a. Like other chemical rushes, becoming infatuated can leave you with a bad hangover once the chemicals are out of your system.

b. Falling madly in love can act like a drug and make you feel high, but once your body gets used to the effects of infatuation, the feeling wears off.

c. Many marriages fail because the two people involved got married under the influence of the chemical high that infatuation can cause.

8. Which of the following best paraphrases the anthropological view of love?

a. Prehistoric men and women fell in love just as readily as modern men and women do; only love never led to marriage because marriage did not exist.

b. The anthropological evidence suggests that love existed in prehistoric times, probably because it was useful to the human species and encouraged men and women to stay together long enough to get a child safely through infancy.

c. Love as we know it during prehistoric times did not exist. What existed, according to the anthropological evidence, was sexual attraction, and that rarely lasted long enough to raise a child, which is probably the reason behind the high rates of child mortality.

9. How would you paraphrase this sentence: "The heart is the organ we associate with love, but the brain may be where the action really is"?

_____

_____

Applying What You've Learned

10. Read the following description of a relationship in trouble. Then, based on your understanding of Robert Sternberg's theory (Paragraph 1), explain what went wrong: "When they met, Michelle and Tomas thought they were made for one another, and the two spent every waking minute together. But after about a year, tension entered the relationship. Tomas wanted Michelle to tell him everything about her past and present. Michelle, on the other hand, had come from a family that did not encourage the discussion of feelings, and she was uncomfortable with that degree of closeness. While Tomas wanted more intimacy, Michelle wanted less, and after six months of struggling to find a compromise, the couple broke up."

What would Sternberg say as to why this relationship did not work?

_____

▶ **TEST 1** **Reviewing New Vocabulary**

DIRECTIONS Fill in the blanks with one of the following words.

supremacy	commercial	expenditures
ratify	subsequent	partisan
prevail	embargo	
constituents	legitimacy	

1. Russia's lower house of parliament has finally voted to _____ the international treaty on climate change.

2. The senator was in favor of sex education in the schools but fearful of how his _____ might react.

3. No _____ trade should be allowed in protected wilderness areas.

4. Claiming the vote had been rigged, the rebels immediately challenged the _____ of the newly elected government.

5. As a(n) _____ of no political party, the judge seemed a good choice for the Supreme Court.

6. The _____ Act of 1807 forbade all international trade to and from American ports.

7. U.S. health care _____ neared $2.6 trillion dollars in 2010; that's more than 10 times what they were in 1980.

8. After World War I, President Woodrow Wilson did not _____ when he tried to convince the European powers to show mercy to the defeated.

9. In South Africa, the policy of apartheid, or strict separation of the races, was meant to guarantee white _____ in a country that was overwhelmingly black rather than white.

10. Initially, the two parties could not agree on a plan for reducing the budget, but in the _____ meetings that followed a huge public outcry, both sides seemed more ready to compromise.

▶ **TEST 2**   **Reviewing New Vocabulary**

DIRECTIONS Fill in the blanks with one of the following words.

> reciprocity   genetic   correlation   cognitive   stimulus
> therapeutic   norms   dynamics   longitudinal   assertiveness

1. For some people, society's _____ exist only to be ignored or challenged.

2. No one really understands the underlying _____ of physical attraction.

3. _____ therapy focuses on changing a person's thought patterns.

4. _____ studies of twins over the course of their lifetime suggest that, despite differences in environment, twins develop a similar behavior and temperament.

5. There is a positive _____ between smoking and lung cancer.

6. Trained to associate food with the sound of a bell, Pavlov's dogs responded to the _____ by salivating.

7. Oddly enough, when he took the anti-anxiety medication, his _____ increased, although normally he had difficulty expressing his opinions.

8. Research consistently shows a _____ component to both temperament and attitude.

9. Studies have undermined the belief that the herb St. John's Wort has a(n) _____ effect on depression.

10. Relationships in which there is no _____ of commitment usually do not survive.

▶ TEST 3   **Using Word Parts and Context Clues**

DIRECTIONS Use your knowledge of prefixes and roots, along with the context of each sentence, to fill in the blank or blanks with the correct word part.

re	cred	temp	in
viv, vit	corp	dis	

1. The teacher was openly _____ _____ulous about the student's claim that aliens had taken his term paper.

2. A devoted supporter of animal rights, the actress _____ avowed any connection to her former designer, who liked to create clothing decorated with fur.

3. The hope is that money from the stimulus plan will _____ _____alize the community, which has been hard hit by the loss of manufacturing.

4. No one who knows anything about fashion could consider bell-bottoms to be a con _____orary fashion; they are ridiculously dated.

5. The scientist was unlike the rest of her colleagues, who were quiet and withdrawn. She, in contrast, was very _____ acious.

6. At least once a day, everyone should remind themselves of the Latin expression _____us fugit, because time does indeed fly and life is over before we know it.

7. Both parents despised the idea of _____oreal punishment and were shocked to discover that their child's school principal believed in paddling kids for misbehavior.

8. A _____ible website will always provide a link to the person or group who hosts the site.

9. The ancient author's entire _____us of work was thought to have been destroyed by fire, but was rediscovered when the museum was renovated.

10. The detective stated that did not believe in ghosts, but the _____embodied form floating toward him certainly looked like one.

▶ TEST 4   **Using Context Clues and Word Parts**

DIRECTIONS   Use context and word parts to determine approximate definitions for the italicized words.

1. Currently, honeybees are disappearing and no one knows why. What scientists realize, however, is that the *ramifications* of the disappearance will be widespread. It won't just be harder to raise flowers, it will also be more difficult to produce a food supply rich in fruits and vegetables.

   Ramifications means _____.

2. When the author stood at the podium to speak, there were no signs of her previous *trepidation*. In contrast to her earlier mood, she was remarkably relaxed and calm. Her voice did not break, her hands did not shake, and she seemed totally in command of the situation.

   Trepidation means _____.

3. That kind of *vituperation* has no place in a political campaign; the candidate should be explaining positions, not spewing insults.

   Vituperation means _____.

4. When it comes to publicity, the *incumbent* president obviously has more access to the press than other candidates. As the person already holding the office, the president has automatic press coverage.

   Incumbent means _____.

5. He had come from an extremely *affluent* home where money was no object. But he gave it all up to live a life of poverty and serve those needier than he.

   Affluent means _____.

6. Although she wanted to, she could not *mitigate* the harshness of her criticism.

   Mitigate means _____.

7. The bulldog was remarkably *tenacious.* He wouldn't let go of the robber's leg even when the man rained blows down on his head. The dog only let go after his master yelled, "Stop!"

   Tenacious means _____.

8. Books on time management are popular mainly because *procrastination* is so common. After all, how many of us can honestly say we have never put off or postponed something we didn't want to do—washing the dog, writing a paper, cleaning the house—until the very last possible minute?

   Procrastination means _____.

9. After saving his mother from drowning, the twelve-year-old boy was *inundated* with letters praising him for his heroism.

   Inundated means _____.

10. Because of a *deterioration* in roads, bridges, canals, dams, and dikes, the government could no longer guarantee the reliability of its transportation systems, making foreign merchants anxious about engaging in trade agreements.

    Deterioration means _____.

▶ **TEST 5**   **Understanding Common Cultural Allusions**

DIRECTIONS In the blanks following every passage, explain what the italicized allusion is supposed to suggest.

1. In 2002, after American Civil Liberties Union president Nadine Strossen claimed that the word *terrorism* was "taking on the same kind of characteristics as the term *communism* in the 1950s," many civil rights and free-speech activists began publicly worrying about a possible return of *McCarthyism*.

   The allusion to *McCarthyism* implies that _____

   _____.

2. The Hundred Years' War between England and France began in 1337 and finally ended in 1453. Despite the conflict's name, however, fighting was not actually continuous for 116 years. Fighting was interspersed with extended periods of *cold war* and even periods of peace.

   The allusion to *cold war* implies that _____

   _____.

3. When it came to leadership, the administrator took a *laissez-faire* approach that left those working for him feeling confused about their duties.

   The allusion to *laissez-faire* implies that _____

   _____.

4. Even if he or she came from a wealthy family, a candidate hoping to win an election has to stay focused on *Main Street*.

   The allusion to *Main Street* implies that _____

   _____.

5. The World Champion met his *Waterloo* when he decided to fight an up-and-coming boxer ten years younger than himself.

   The allusion to *Waterloo* implies that _____

   _____.

3 Reviewing Paragraph Essentials

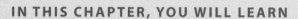

IN THIS CHAPTER, YOU WILL LEARN

- how to zero in on the essential elements of a paragraph: the topic, main idea, and supporting details.

- how transitions help direct readers to topic sentences and supporting details.

- how category words in topic sentences direct the reader's attention to major details.

- how major and minor supporting details further explain or prove the main ideas expressed in topic sentences.

"There is creative reading as well as creative writing."
—Ralph Waldo Emerson,
American philosopher and poet

There will certainly be times in your reading when the point of the paragraph seems to jump off the page. When this happens, your grasp of the author's message is immediate. You don't have to consciously think about it because you just get it without much effort. At other times, though, the topic might be so unfamiliar or the writer's style so complicated that, initially at least, you'll have to think your way through the paragraph sentence by sentence. The explanations that follow were written for precisely those times.

Recognizing the Topic

Whether you're reading a single paragraph or an entire chapter section, probably the first thing you need to think about is the **topic**, or subject matter, under discussion. Start your reading assignment with this question in mind: "Which person, event, practice, or idea is most frequently mentioned, referred to, or discussed throughout the paragraph?" To illustrate, let's use the following paragraph:

Sentence 1 introduces Personal Information Management software, which seems a likely topic.

The repetition in the remaining sentences confirms PIM as the topic.

Topic

[1]Personal Information Management, or PIM, software is the "Swiss Army knife" of personal software. [2]It provides a personal calendar to keep track of where you need to be and when. [3]You can set an alarm to remind you of an appointment. PIM also stores your personal to-do lists and address book. [4]Some PIM software comes with personal journal software so that you can record brilliant ideas or your life story. [5]PIM software is especially valuable when accessible from a smart phone anywhere, anytime. (Ken Baldauf and Ralph M. Stair, *Succeeding with Technology* 4e, © Cengage Learning.)

The topic of this paragraph is unmistakable. Every sentence refers to Personal Information Management (PIM) software. Also, many of the references to that software appear at the beginning of sentences. Sentence openings are typical locations for the words or phrases referring to the topic. Anytime you notice a word or phrase that's repeated or referred to at the beginning of several sentences, there's a very good chance that the word or phrase can help you identify the paragraph's topic.

Inferring the Topic

Don't be fooled, though, by the sample paragraph above. While it's true that writers often use repetition to identify the topic for readers, that's not always the case. When the subject under discussion is not something concrete that can be seen or touched, writers often rely on readers to **infer a topic**. They rely on their readers to spot words similar or related in meaning and come up with a word or phrase that includes or sums up all of those various references. Read the paragraph below for an illustration.

Sentence 1 says kids growing up in unloving homes are vulnerable to "crime-promoting forces."

Sentence 2 also suggests "unloving homes" might be the topic.

Nonetheless signals a shift in thought.

[1]Young people who grow up in households characterized by conflict and tension, and where there is a lack of familial love and support, are susceptible to the crime-promoting forces in the environment. [2]Even those children living in so-called high-crime areas will be better able to resist the temptations of the stress if they receive fair discipline, care, and support from parents who provide them with strong, positive, role models. [3]Nonetheless, living in a disadvantaged neighborhood places terrific strain on family functioning, especially in single-parent families that experience social isolation from relatives, friends, and neighbors. [4]Children who are raised within such distressed neighborhoods are at high risk for delinquency. (Larry J. Siegel, *Criminology: Theories, Patterns, and Typologies* 10e, © Cengage Learning.)

As you can see from the example, no one word or phrase stated in the paragraph is general or broad enough to sum up the different subjects mentioned. The paragraph isn't about "households" in general. It's also not about many different "crime-promoting forces."

However, if you read the paragraph closely, you'll see that every sentence refers to specific kinds of families, some inadequate, some not. Each sentence also mentions how those families contribute to the presence or absence of criminal behavior in young people. The question now is what word or phrase could sum up those different aspects of the paragraph. One answer might be "the effects of family on criminal behavior." Another could be "the influence of family life on delinquency," or even "when family leads to crime." There are any number of ways to express the topic of this paragraph. As long as the phrase sums up the two kinds of family life that can lead to criminal behavior, your topic would be correct.

Paragraphs in which the writer puts the topic into words for readers definitely make determining the topic easier. However, when ideas become more complex and more abstract—related to ideas rather than physical objects, things, or beings—you need to be prepared to infer or create the topic. You need to (1) pay close attention to the words and phrases that are similar or connected in some way and (2) come up with a word or phrase that covers them all.

◆ EXERCISE 1   Determining the Topic

DIRECTIONS   Read each paragraph. Then circle the letter of the word or phrase that sums up the topic.

1. Is it true that right-handed people live longer than left-handed people? It is true that there is a shortage of very old lefties. One possible explanation lies in the widespread finding that left-handers are more accident-prone. However, the supposed clumsiness of lefties may well be a result of living in a right-handed world. One study showed that left-handed locomotive engineers have higher accident rates and suggested that the cause was due to the design of locomotive controls. If it can be gripped, turned, or pulled, it's probably designed for the right hand. Even toilet handles are on the right-hand side. On the other hand, the shortage of very old lefties may just reflect the fact that, in the past, more left-handed children were forced to become right-handed. That makes it look like many lefties don't

survive to old age. In reality, they do, but many of them are masquerading as righties. (Dennis Coon and John O. Mitterer, *Introduction to Psychology* 12e, © Cengage Learning.)

Topic   a. life span of right-handed people

b. left-handed people

c. clumsy left-handers

d. left-handed locomotive engineers

2. Researchers are trying to develop new anti-malarial drugs and vaccines for Anopheles mosquitoes, which cause the deadly disease malaria. However, there are other ways to fight the disease. One is to provide poor people in malarial regions with long-lasting insecticide-treated bed nets and window screens for their dwellings. Another is to use zinc and vitamin A supplements to boost resistance to malaria in children. The number of malaria cases can also be greatly reduced by spraying the insides of homes with low concentrations of the pesticide DDT twice a year at a cost of about $10. Unfortunately, under an international treaty enacted in 2002, DDT and five similar pesticides are being phased out in developing countries. However, in 2006, the World Health Organization supported the use of DDT for malaria control. (Adapted from G. Tyler Miller Jr. and Scott E. Spoolman, *Sustaining the Earth* 9e, © Cengage Learning.)

Topic   a. fighting malaria

b. using DDT to fight malaria

c. malarial regions

d. pesticides

3. Conjoined twins are usually classified into three basic categories, depending on where their bodies connect. Twins of the first type are conjoined in a way that never involves the heart or the midline of the body. For example, about 2 percent of all conjoined twins are attached at the head only. About 19 percent are joined at the buttocks. Twins of the second type are always joined in a way that involves the midline of the body. Many twins joined at the midline share a heart. Around 35 percent are fused at the upper half of the trunk. Another 30 percent are joined at the lower half of their

bodies. The third major type of conjoined twins includes very rare forms of physical connection. In this category are those in which one twin is smaller, less formed, and dependent on the other, as well as cases in which one twin is born completely within the body of his or her sibling.

Topic

a. twins sharing a heart

b. twins

c. conjoined twins

d. categories of twins

4. *The Texas Chainsaw Massacre* and *Psycho* are two of the most popular horror films in American horror movie history. But popularity is not all the two films have in common. Both films are based on the life and crimes of one man, serial killer Ed Gein. Born in Wisconsin, Gein was the son of a deeply religious mother who preached relentlessly to her son about the evils of sexual desire. Like Norman Bates in *Psycho*, Gein was completely devoted to his mother and never recovered from her death. After she died, he seems to have lost all hold on his sanity. Although he started out robbing the graves of

Ed Gein, the inspiration for Leatherface in the horror movie *The Texas Chainsaw Massacre* was born in Wisconsin and never set foot in Texas

Everett Collection

recently deceased women, he graduated to murder of a particularly grisly kind, using the skin of his victims to make pieces of clothing and a mask reminiscent of the one worn by the killer in *The Texas Chainsaw Massacre.*

Topic
a. horror films

b. Ed Gein

c. *Psycho*

d. *The Texas Chainsaw Massacre*

5. When it comes to using formal or informal language, large cultural differences exist. The informal approach that characterizes conversations in countries like the United States, Canada, Australia, and the Scandinavian countries is quite different from the concern about using proper speech in many parts of Asia and Africa, where formality in language defines a person's social position. In Korea, for example, the language reveals a system of relational hierarchies.* Koreans have a special vocabulary for different sexes, levels of social status, degrees of intimacy, and types of social occasions. There are even different degrees of formality for speaking with old friends, acquaintances, and complete strangers. One sign of being a learned person in Korea is the ability to use language in a way that recognizes these relational distinctions. When you contrast these sorts of distinctions with the casual friendliness that Americans display even when talking to strangers, it's easy to see how a Korean might find an American boorish* in conversation while an American might consider a Korean stiff and unfriendly. (Ronald B. Adler and Russell F. Proctor, *Looking Out, Looking In* 12e, © Cengage Learning.)

Topic
a. Koreans in conversation with Americans

b. levels of formality in different cultures

c. informality in language

d. contrasting English and Asian rules for language

---

*hierarchies: levels or rankings of people based on authority or importance.
*boorish: crude, disrespectful of others, vulgar.

From Topics to Main Ideas and Topic Sentences

If your friends knew you went to the movies the night before and asked you what the movie you saw was about, you probably wouldn't say "the war in Afghanistan" and expect them to be satisfied with your answer. You'd know immediately that your friends wanted more than the film's topic. They posed their question to get a sense of the movie's **main idea** or general message. They wanted to know, that is, what the movie had to say *about* the topic. Thus, you'd probably respond to their question by saying something like "It was a documentary that showed the horrific physical and mental toll being taken on soldiers fighting the war in Afghanistan."

Whether you are watching a movie or reading a textbook, determining the topic is never an end in itself. It's only the start of discovering the main idea. Even while you are thinking about the topic, you need to be alert to clues that can help you figure out what the author wants to say *about* that topic.

Recognizing Main Ideas in Paragraphs

To discover the main idea of a paragraph, you have to determine what and how each sentence contributes to a larger, more general point. Sentence by sentence, you need to ask and answer questions like these:[†] (1) What does this sentence say? (2) What's the relationship of this new sentence to the one that came before it? (3) Does this new sentence contribute to, revise, or drop the idea that came before it? (4) What train of thought seems to be developing at this point?

Let's use the passage below as an example. The subject, or topic, is "diet." Notice how that word appears or is referred to in every sentence, a sign that it's the topic.

However, knowing just the topic only tells us the author's subject matter. What we have to think about now is what the author wants to say *about* diet. That means we have to consider each sentence's contribution to the topic of diet to discover what one general idea emerges when the sentences are all linked together.

[†]At a certain point, these questions become automatic, but, initially, especially with a difficult passage, it's not a bad idea to consciously think about them when you re-read a passage that has proved difficult on a first reading.

Sentence 1 links our diet to over eating.

Sentences 2–6 offer proof.

Sentence 7 restates, in more specific terms, the point of sentence 1, making it clear that sentence 1 states the main idea.

[1]It's highly likely that diet contributes to overeating. [2]Placing animals on a "supermarket" diet, for instance, can lead to gross obesity. [3]In one experiment, rats were given meals of chocolate chip cookies, salami, cheese, bananas, marshmallows, milk, chocolate, peanut butter, and fat. [4]Rats on this diet gained almost three times as much weight as animals that ate standard laboratory rat "chow." [5]It wasn't just that they consumed more calories. [6]Rats on the cookie and salami menu also consumed food in much greater quantities. [7]The study suggests that foods high in sweetness, fat, and variety encourage the desire to eat more. (Adapted from Dennis Coon, *Essentials of Psychology* 9e, © Cengage Learning.)

Recognizing Topic Sentences

Do you see from the model above how every sentence in the paragraph relates, in some way, to the opening sentence? That chain of connections is what tells you that sentence 1 is a topic sentence. **Topic sentences** are general sentences that sum up the paragraph's main idea and are further explained by almost all of the other sentences in the paragraph. While not all paragraphs include topic sentences, many do. This is particularly true of textbooks.

Look for a general sentence that seems to be developed in more specific detail by the sentences that follow. Once you spot that general sentence, you have probably discovered the topic sentence expressing the main idea. That's certainly the case in the above paragraph about diet.

Topic Sentence Locations

Although some discussions of reading comprehension suggest that the main idea always appears in the first sentence—this is particularly true of reading instruction on the Web—don't be fooled. While writers frequently make the first sentence the topic sentence, they often delay the introduction of the main idea to provide background or stimulate reader interest.[1] They start, that is, with an **introductory sentence** offering

---

[1]This statement does not apply to writing that is Web-specific. People who write to be published on the Web are inclined to make the first sentence the topic sentence, although not if they are writing book or movie reviews.

some background knowledge about the topic sentence. The introductory sentence, however, is not developed in the paragraph. It's strictly there to pave the way for the topic sentence expressing the real main idea. If this kind of paragraph were diagrammed, it would look something like this:

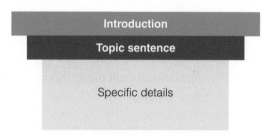

Introduction

Topic sentence

Specific details

Now here's a concrete illustration of a paragraph that opens with an introductory sentence:

> [1]When they hear the word *desert*, most people think of a vast expanse of sun-scorched earth. [2]Some deserts, however, *are actually mild in climate*, even cold. [3]There are, for instance, the deserts near cold ocean currents, like South America's Atacama Desert and Africa's Kalahari Desert. [4]Both are cooled by cold, dry ocean air. [5]Then, too, there are the dry, frozen, polar deserts found in places like northern Greenland, Arctic Canada, and Northern Alaska, where temperatures can dip well below zero. (Adapted from Stanley Chernicoff et al., *Earth: Geologic Principles and History.* © Cengage Learning.)

Sentence 1 talks about what "most people think," a sure sign this is not the topic sentence.

The paragraph is *not* discussing hot desert climates but mild or cold ones.

In this case, the introductory sentence identifies what "most people think" to be true about deserts. That phrasing "most people think" is a signal. Like the phrases "it's commonly assumed," "it's long been believed," and "for a long time now," it hints that the authors might challenge that traditional thinking. And indeed they do. In sentence 2, which is also the topic sentence, the authors point out that desert temperatures can be mild, even cold.

Such delayed introductions of the topic sentence are common. Delayed introductions like this one occur even in business texts, where writers generally make the first sentence the topic sentence. History texts, in particular, are heavy with introductory sentences. They need to be because many readers need some background to understand the main idea. Notice how the authors of the following reading offer some historical background to get readers ready for the main idea stated in sentence 4:

Sentences 1 and 2 start out discussing the reaction of African-Americans to the election of John F. Kennedy.

Sentence 3 moves the focus away from what Kennedy might do to focus on the civil rights movement.

[1]When John F. Kennedy was elected president in 1960, African-Americans showed a guarded enthusiasm. [2]They weren't convinced that the new administration would take a more active role in aiding the civil rights movement. [3]At the same time, most realized that the movement should not wait quietly for Kennedy to act. [4]Refusing to wait and see, civil rights activists continued to build on momentum created by the sit-in movement, which had begun in February 1960, when four black freshmen at North Carolina Agricultural and Technical College in Greensboro, North Carolina, decided to integrate the public lunch counter at the local F. W. Woolworth. [5]They entered the store, sat down at the lunch counter, and ordered a meal. [6]Refused service but not arrested, they sat until the store closed. [7]The next day twenty black A&T students sat at the lunch counter demanding service. (Adapted from Carol Berkin et al., *Making America* 6e, © Cengage Learning.)

The early civil rights activists were determined to end segregation no matter what the costs.

The Granger Collection, NYC

◆ EXERCISE 2   Identifying Topics and Topic Sentences

DIRECTIONS Read the following paragraphs. Circle the letter of the topic and write the number of the topic sentence in the blank.

Sentence 1 says that people want children for different reasons, suggesting that the author will tell readers what those reasons are.

By sentence 5, it's clear that the paragraph describes the different reasons for becoming a parent.

EXAMPLE [1]People have many different reasons for wanting children. [2]Some really like children and want an opportunity to be involved with their care. [3]Some women strongly desire the experience of pregnancy and childbirth, while some men are excited about becoming fathers. [4]Many young adults see parenthood as a way to demonstrate their adult status. [5]For people coming from happy families, having children is a means of reliving their earlier happiness. [6]For those from unhappy families, it can be a means of doing better than their parents did. [7]Some people have children simply because it's expected of them. [8]Because society places so much emphasis on the fulfillment motherhood is supposed to bring, some women who are unsure of what they want to do with their lives use having a child as a way to create an identity. (Kelvin Seifert et al., *Lifespan Development*. Houghton Mifflin, 2000, p. 484.)

Topic   a. childhood

(b.) the desire for children

c. parenting and past childhood experience

d. society's emphasis on child rearing

Topic Sentence ____1____

EXPLANATION The sample paragraph illustrates a very common explanatory pattern used in textbooks. The author opens by telling you there are many "reasons" why something occurs or many "ways" an event can be produced. As soon as you see that the second sentence introduces one of those reasons or ways, you know that the opening sentence is also the topic sentence.

1. [1]The zoo industry insists that elephants in zoos throughout the country are well taken care of. [2]The industry assures the public that there is no cause to be alarmed about the well-being of these magnificent creatures. [3]Animal rights activists, however, challenge the zoo

industry's claims, and there is an angry debate brewing about the health of elephants confined in zoos, with the federal government deciding to review the animals' situation in confinement. [4]According to Elliot Katz, a veterinarian and president of the California-based organization In Defense of Animals, "the state of elephant health in the U.S. is appallingly poor." [5]Katz claims that experts in the field believe elephants should not be walking back and forth on concrete floors. [6]Their feet are designed to walk miles on soil, but not back and forth on cold concrete. [7]Katz would seem to know whereof he speaks because in 2006 a number of zoo-held elephants died from complications brought on by sore feet. [8]Members of the zoo industry, however, consider the deaths exceptions. [9]Willie Theisseon, head elephant keeper at the Pittsburgh Zoo, argues that elephants dying of foot complications are probably older animals—elephants can live into their sixties—and probably came from facilities where their feet were injured. [10]He insists, though, that almost all such facilities have been upgraded so that the problem no longer exists. (Source of claims: www.idausa.org/.)

Topic
a. the treatment of animals by zoos

b. elephants in the wild versus elephants in zoos

c. debate over treatment of elephants in zoos

d. animal rights activists

Topic Sentence _3_

2. [1]Many people think that talking about *lifestyles*—tastes, preferences, and ways of living—is a trivial pursuit at best. [2]However, studying lifestyle differences reveals a lot about the differences in social classes. [3]Upper- and middle-class people think it important to be active outside their homes—in parent-teacher associations, charitable organizations, and any number of community activities. [4]They are also likely to make friends with colleagues and business associates, inviting them into their homes. [5]Usually, their spouses help cultivate these relationships. [6]In contrast, members of the working class are less likely to be involved in organizations not

directly related to their family. [7]They are also less inclined to entertain their co-workers at home, although outings after work for drinks or dinner are common. (Adapted from Alex Thio, *Society: Myths and Realities.* Allyn and Bacon, 2006, p. 211.)

Topic

    a. lifestyles of the middle class

    b. talking about lifestyles

    c. lifestyle class differences

    d. working class social behavior

Topic Sentence   _____

3. [1]When they are hungry, anxious, or scared, cats and dogs usually make noise. [2]For many pet owners, noisy pets present huge problems. [3]Landlords will evict owners of pets that bark or howl for hours. [4]Neighbors will lodge complaints with local police departments. [5]Sometimes, it's just a matter of the owner not getting enough sleep because a dog or cat is howling into the wee hours of the night. [6]Some pet owners who have been faced with these or similar problems have found a highly controversial solution: They have opted for having surgery performed on their pets' vocal cords so the animals can no longer bark or meow. [7]For them the surgery is a better solution than having to give up their pets. [8]But while the procedure may have solved the problem satisfactorily for pet owners, animal rights activists are outraged. [9]They consider the surgery to be painful mutilation and are trying to have it banned all across the country. [10]Currently, *vocal cordectomy*, as the procedure is called, is illegal in only three states: Massachusetts, New Jersey, and Rhode Island. [11]Even those who do not consider the surgery to be animal cruelty worry that surgery is not really a solution since it eliminates the symptom of the problem without answering a key question, Why was the animal making noise in the first place?

Topic

    a. vocal cordectomy on noisy pets

    b. cruelty to animals

    c. laws against vocal cordectomy

    d. evictions due to noisy pets

Topic Sentence   _____

4. [1]Society is struggling to define the extent to which employers should be able to monitor the work-related activities of employees. [2]On the one hand, employers want to be able to guarantee a work environment that is comfortable for all workers, ensure a high level of worker productivity, and limit the costs of defending against privacy-violations filed by unhappy employees. [3]On the other hand, privacy advocates want federal legislation that keeps employers from infringing on the rights of employees. [4]Such legislation would require notifying employees of the existence and location of all electronic monitoring devices. [5]Privacy advocates also want to restrict the type of information collected as well as the extent to which employers may use electronic monitoring. [6]As a result, many privacy bills are being introduced and debated at the state and federal levels. (Adapted from George W. Reynolds, *Ethics in Information Technology* 4e, © Cengage Learning.)

Topic
    a. privacy advocates

    b. electronic monitoring of employees

    ·c. society's struggles to regulate businesses

    d. employees' right to information

Topic Sentence _____

5. [1]The life of the leatherback turtle is a continuous series of transoceanic voyages to reproduce and find food. [2]From the very moment the leatherbacks hatch and emerge from their underground nest, they head straight for the open ocean. [3]During the early stages of their life, they live in waters that may be hundreds of thousands of miles from the beach where they hatched. [4]In these distant and watery locations, they feed mostly on jellyfish, squid, and other slippery prey. [5]Heavy feeders, leatherbacks are huge, and they grow faster than all other turtles. [6]Adults range in length from four to six feet and weigh from 650 to 1,200 pounds, making them the largest living turtle species on earth. [7]Leatherbacks reach sexual maturity when they are 13 to 14 years old and they live 30 years or more. [8]Male leatherbacks spend their entire lives in water. [9]Females, however, leave their breeding ground every two to four years and return to the same beaches from which they hatched to produce a new generation. (Adapted from Robert K. Noyd et al., *Biology: Organisms and Adaptations.* © Cengage Learning.)

Leatherback turtles can stay under water for up to 85 minutes.

Topic a. the early life of leatherbacks

b. leatherbacks

c. male leatherbacks

d. the sexual maturity of leatherbacks

Topic Sentence _____

REVIEWING THROUGH WRITING

Paragraph 3 in Exercise 2 introduced the topic of devocalizing cats and dogs and explained that the subject is controversial. Write a paragraph that opens with a brief explanation of what devocalizing is and why people do it to their pets. Then introduce a topic sentence that states your position in this controversy. Back up that topic sentence with reasons for your point of view.

Introductory Sentences Team Up with Reversal Transitions

Although they can appear on their own, introductory sentences in textbooks like the ones you worked with previously (p. 117) are often accompanied by **reversal transitions**. These are words and phrases like *however, yet, in contrast*, and *on the contrary*. Reversal transitions, however, aren't restricted to words or phrases. They can be entire sentences like "That's not how events unfolded" or "Things did not turn out as planned." Whether a word, phrase, or sentence, reversal transitions serve the same purpose: They signal to readers that the author is about to revise, challenge, modify, or flatly contradict what's just been said.

While reversal transitions can certainly appear in the middle or even at the end of a paragraph, they are especially important following introductory sentences at the beginnings of paragraphs. Miss the reversal transition and you might well miss the main idea. Notice, here, for example, how the reversal transition *yet* in the paragraph below says to the reader, "Get ready for a change in direction. This paragraph is *not* going to pursue the idea from the opening sentence." Then the underlined topic sentence announces the paragraph's real point.

Sentence 1 introduces what people are likely to think about losing sleep.

The transitional word *yet* signals a change of direction and paves the way for the main idea: sleep deprivation frequently causes motor vehicle accidents.

[1]If you miss a few hours of sleep, you may feel a little groggy for the next day but still believe that you can muddle through without difficulty. [2]Yet, perhaps not surprisingly, sleep deprivation is among the most common causes of motor vehicle accidents. [3]Such accidents are most likely to occur in the early morning hours when drivers are typically at their sleepiest. [4]This makes sense because sleep deprivation slows reaction times and impairs concentration, memory, and problem-solving ability. [5]Thus the effects of sleep deprivation make it more difficult to be a careful driver, making accidents more likely.

(Adapted from Jeffrey Nevid, *Essentials of Psychology* 3e, © Cengage Learning.)

Look at the topic sentence in the paragraph on lifestyles (p. 121) and then at the paragraph above, and you'll see that both topic sentences open with reversal transitions that tell readers, "There's a shift in thought coming up." In the paragraph on lifestyles, the reversal transition *however* suggests that thinking about lifestyles might actually be worth doing despite the paragraph's opening sentence. In the above paragraph, the word *yet* introduces the idea that whatever we may believe about losing sleep, the facts don't necessarily support that belief. If diagrammed, paragraphs that introduce the topic sentence in this way, would look something like this:

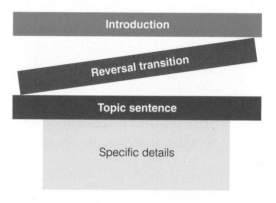

A reversal transition in the second (or third) sentence of a paragraph is a strong clue that the topic sentence is on its way to challenge the author's opening point. That means it's in your interest to learn the most common reversal transitions, which are listed below.

Reversal Transitions ♦	Actually	Nonetheless
	But	On the contrary
	Contrary to	On the other hand
	Conversely	Rather
	Despite the fact	Still
	Even so	Unfortunately
	However	While this might seem true [sensible, correct, right, etc.]
	In contradiction	
	In contrast	Yet
	In opposition	Yet in fact
	Ironically	Yet in reality
	Just the opposite	

REVIEWING THROUGH WRITING

Write a paragraph that challenges a piece of traditional wisdom, making your opening sentence signal your disagreement. For instance: "My parents always told me 'Don't lend money to friends.'" "Traditional wisdom claims that 'What goes around comes around'"; "Supposedly, it's a good idea to 'Keep your friends close, keep your enemies closer.'" Then use a reversal transition to pave the way for your topic sentence, which directly states your disagreement. "But I have always found it impossible not to lend money to friends in need since helping friends shouldn't stop at your wallet." Finally, explain why you think the traditional wisdom you are challenging is bad rather than good advice.

✔ CHECK YOUR UNDERSTANDING

1. Is it always possible to circle the topic of a paragraph? _____ Please explain.

_____

_____

2. What kinds of paragraphs are most likely to express the topic in a word or phrase?

_____

3. While you are trying to determine the topic, what else should you be looking for?

_____

4. What is the function of an introductory sentence?

_____

_____

5. What do reversal transitions following introductory sentences tell readers?

_____

6. Are introductory sentences always followed by reversal transitions? _____

◆ EXERCISE 3   Recognizing Topic Sentences and Reversal Transitions

DIRECTIONS   Read the following paragraphs. Write the number of the topic sentence in the blank. If the paragraph contains a reversal transition introducing the topic sentence, circle it. *Note*: Reversal transitions aren't restricted to introducing topic sentences, but in this exercise, circle only the ones that introduce the topic sentence.

1. ¹Most Americans see themselves as rugged individualists. ²They have a mind of their own and don't bow to group pressure. ³Several studies have shown, however, that many of us are profoundly influenced by group pressure. ⁴In a now classic study of group influence, for instance, social psychologist Solomon Asch (1952) told subjects that they were taking part in an experiment on visual judgment. ⁵The subjects then sat among members of a group and were asked to match up lines by length. ⁶Unknown to them everyone else in their group was a member of the experiment, and at some point in the experiment every one of those people intentionally mismatched the lines. ⁷By the end of the study, 37 percent of the subjects had agreed with the wrong answer given by other members of the group, even though it was obvious to the naked eye that the group answer was incorrect. ⁸The work of another sociologist, Philip Zimbardo (1975), also illustrated the influence of groups on individual behavior. ⁹Zimbardo recruited volunteers for an experiment in prison life, selecting 24 men, most of them college students. ¹⁰Some of the men were assigned to be prisoners and some to be guards. ¹¹The experiment was scheduled to run for 2 weeks. ¹²It ran for 6 days when Zimbardo called it off because the "guards" had become increasingly brutal and the "prisoners" were all becoming withdrawn and stressed out.

Topic Sentence   _____

2. ¹Most people think of beavers as cute, even appealing, animals, even though the animals belong to the rodent, or rat, family. ²Many people just don't realize that, like dogs and bats, beavers can become rabid and attack anyone who comes near them. ³In 2013, a fisherman from the eastern European country of Belarus spotted a beaver standing on the side of a country road. ⁴When he approached the animal to take a picture, the beaver bit him on the thigh. ⁵Tragically, his friends could not stem the flow of blood from the wound, and the man bled

to death. [6]Also in Belarus in 2003, a rabid beaver bit two farmers who tried to chase the animal out of a barn. [7]And rabid beavers can turn up closer to home as well. [8]In 2012, an 83-year-old woman was attacked by a rabid beaver while she swam in a Washington lake. [9]The beaver was two feet long and weighed 34 pounds. [10]Two young girls were also attacked while swimming in a lake in Virginia. [11]Anyone who doubts that beavers can be a threat just has to search YouTube for the video "Angry Beavers Are No Joke." [12]As a photographer tries to take a picture of a wet and crabby-looking beaver, the beaver races toward him and attacks. [13]Fortunately, the man lived to tell the tale and post the video, but that's not always the case.

Topic Sentence _____

3. [1]Extended solitary confinement has become a standard practice in many American prisons largely because, as prison punishments go, social isolation is not considered especially harsh or painful. [2]That is not the opinion, however, of a small group of psychiatrists, who believe that solitary confinement for extended periods of time—think years not days—is unbearable torture, bound to have devastating and long-lasting psychological effects. [3]At a hearing of the California State Assembly Public Safety Committee in 2011, Dr. Terry Kupers, a clinical psychiatrist, pointed out that one-half of all prison suicides are carried out by prisoners in maximum security prisons, who have been confined in isolation for long stretches of time. [4]The suicides, from his perspective, are the result of the "toxic conditions" created when prisoners must remain in cells the size of closets with no human contact for 23 hours a day. [5]Massachusetts psychiatrist Stuart Grassian, who has studied the psychiatric effects of long-term isolation for a decade, echoes Kupers's assessment of the practice. [6]Grassian insists that long-term isolation is a form of torture that should be eliminated from the list of prison punishments. [7]Arizona senator John McCain, who spent two years in solitary confinement as a prisoner of war in Vietnam would seem to agree. [8]Writing of his experience, McCain said, "It's an awful thing, solitary. [9]It crushes your spirit and weakens your resistance, more effectively than any other form of punishment."

Topic Sentence _____

4. [1]Genetic screening tests blood and tissue to detect evidence of genetic, or inherited, disorders. [2]Genetic screening provides information on the risks potential mothers run by giving birth. [3]It can also predict the potential occurrence of diseases like breast cancer and Huntington's disease.[†] [4]Hospitals also routinely do genetic screening on newborns. [5]Most newborns, for instance, are routinely tested for PKU, a genetic disorder that, if left untreated, can cause seizures and intellectual disability. [6]Because affected infants are now routinely discovered through screening, we see fewer individuals with symptoms of the disorder. [7]That's not to say, however, that there are no psychological risks associated with genetic screening. [8]How would you feel if you knew you had the potential to pass a disease on to your child or were at high risk for breast cancer? (Adapted from Cecie Starr et al., *Biology: The Unity and Diversity of Life* 12e, © Cengage Learning.)

Topic Sentence _____

5. [1]As many modern media watchers have complained, today's newspapers are all too often governed by "pack journalism." [2]These days, reporters aren't encouraged to search out unique stories or points of view. [3]Instead they are encouraged to make sure that they report on whatever story other newspapers are publishing. [4]In the nineteenth century, however, journalism was a highly competitive business with reporters hotly competing for stories, and no one was more competitive than famed reporter Nellie Bly. [5]In 1889 Elizabeth Cochran, who wrote under her pen name "Nellie Bly," came up with a circulation booster that may have been the first "manufactured news story." [6]Jules Verne's *Around the World in Eighty Days*, a story about a British gentleman who won a bet by circling the globe in eighty days, had been a bestseller. [7]Nellie thought she could beat the man's record. [8]She studied train and steamship timetables for connections and told the editors of Joseph Pulitzer's New York *World* that she could make the circuit in seventy-five days. [9]Bly insisted that the adventure would sell lots of papers. [10]The editors liked the idea but said they would send a man to do it. [11]They quickly changed their mind when Bly told them, "Send the man and I'll start the same day for some other newspaper and beat him." [12]She left on

---

[†]Huntington's disease: an inherited illness that destroys brain cells and grows progressively worse with time.

November 14, 1889, and returned to her point of departure on January 25, 1890. [13]Her trip took seventy-two days, and the *World*, thanks to Nellie Bly's exclusive story, increased its readership and its number of advertisers.

Topic Sentence _____

WEB QUEST   What Was the Pulitzer Formula?

Paragraph 5 in the previous exercise refers to Joseph Pulitzer, the man who turned the bankrupt *World* into the country's best-selling newspaper. Search the Web to discover what kinds of stories and writing style Pulitzer relied on—called the "Pulitzer formula"—to sell newspapers.

_____

_____

_____

_____

What Do You Think?

◆

In general do you think Americans are rugged individualists? Or are we prone to being influenced by the behavior of others?

◈ Addition Transitions Send a Different Message

If the author opens with one idea but follows it with a reversal transition, there's a good chance that the upcoming sentence is going to revise what's just been said and state the real main idea. **Addition** or **continuation transitions** are different. They do not contradict what came before. Just the opposite, they are the author's way of saying to readers, "I'm continuing the same train of thought that was introduced in the previous sentence."

Words and phrases like *first, second, for example, in several studies,* and *more precisely* (see the complete list below) are all considered addition or continuation transitions. If you see one of these words following the opening sentence, then there is a very good chance that the first sentence is also the topic sentence expressing the main idea.

The transition *in one study* says the writer is attempting to prove the train of thought from sentence 1.

The transition *further* signals continuation of the opening idea, making sentence 1 the topic sentence.

[1]Some police and police-citizen interactions seem to generate the most frequent use-of-force reports. [2]In one study, officers were shown to use force in an estimated 53 percent of vehicle pursuits. [3]Further, 47 percent of the surveyed suspects who fled from police reported that force was used. [4]Some police seem to get involved in use-of-force situations repeatedly, whereas others even in similar patrol neighborhoods rarely get involved in such altercations.* [5]According to the report by the Independent Commission on the Los Angeles Police Department, the top 5 percent of officers ranked by number of reports of use of force were responsible for more than 20 percent of all reports.

(Adapted from Joycelyn M. Pollock, *Ethical Dilemmas and Decisions in Criminal Justice*, 7e. © Cengage Learning.)

Addition or Continuation Transitions ◆		
Along the same lines	In more specific terms
Also	In one study; In several studies
An additional	In other words
Even better	In the same vein
Even more	More precisely
Even worse	Moreover
Finally	More to the point
First; second; third	One; two; three
For example; for instance	Then, too
In addition	Too

◆ EXERCISE 4   Using Transitions to Identify Topic Sentences

DIRECTIONS   Read each paragraph and write the number of the topic sentence in the blank at the end. If a reversal or addition transition helps you identify the topic sentence, circle that transition. Underline it if it's a sentence.

1. [1]During the nineteenth-century potato famine that decimated the population of Ireland, the country's English rulers claimed to be

---

*altercations: fights, disagreements.

doing everything they could to improve the situation. [2]But as historians have pointed out since, that claim was clearly untrue. [3]For the British, who generally held the Irish in contempt, "coffin-ships" were considered a sound solution to the starvation that plagued Ireland. [4]British landlords would tell their starving tenants that if they sailed overseas to British North America, i.e., Canada, they would find at the end of their journey clothing, jobs, food, and medical care, everything they needed to survive. [5]But, in fact, one in five Irish immigrants who made the journey died from starvation and disease, thus the nickname for the ships they sailed on. [6]Packed half-naked into overcrowded sailing boats, many of those fleeing the famine were already ill. [7]The long sea journey with poor food, cramped quarters, and no fresh air did not produce a cure. [8]Instead, deadly diseases like typhus spread like wildfire. [9]Those who arrived at their Canadian destination disease-free often became ill thanks to a fifteen-day quarantine that kept them on board with the ailing until they could be certified as "healthy." [10]The agents they had been told would help them get settled in their new home never materialized, and the Irish immigrants who survived were dumped onshore to fend for themselves as best they could.

Topic Sentence _____

2. [1]Whistleblowers, employees who disclose organizational wrongdoing to parties who can take action, are often isolated and humiliated by the companies they hope to improve. [2]For example, they may receive no further promotions or be given poor performance evaluations. [3]Many whistleblowers are fired or demoted, even for high-profile tips that proved true. [4]True, the Sarbanes-Oxley Act offers some protection for whistleblowers. [5]Employees who report fraud related to corporate accounting, internal accounting controls, and auditing have a way of gaining re-instatement, as well as back pay and legal expenses. [6]Nevertheless, more than half of the whistleblowers' pleas for help go ignored, and leaders at all levels have a responsibility to create a climate of safety for legitimate whistleblowing. (Adapted from Andrew J. DuBrin, *Leadership* 6e, © Cengage Learning.)

Topic Sentence _____

3. ¹There are two questions that need to be answered in understanding drug use. ²The first is at the individual level: Why does a given individual use alcohol or other drugs? ³One answer is that many individuals at high risk for drug use have been "failed by society." ⁴They are, that is, living in poverty, unemployed, victims of abuse, dependent on neglectful or addicted parents, etc. ⁵The second question asks why drug use varies so dramatically across societies, often independent of a country's drug policies. ⁶The United States has some of the most severe penalties for drug violations in the world, but has one of the highest rates of marijuana and cocaine use. ⁷In contrast, Portugal decriminalized personal possession of all drugs, and youth drug use is down. (Adapted from Linda A. Mooney et al., *Social Problems* 8e, © Cengage Learning.)

Topic Sentence   ____

4. ¹Butterflies are an agent in the fertilization of flowers. ²Like bees, they carry pollen from flower to flower and see to it that cross-fertilization takes place. ³In addition to their functional role in nature, though, butterflies play many different symbolic roles, and what they symbolize changes according to the culture. ⁴In Chinese culture, they are a symbol of long life. ⁵In Japan, butterflies, particularly in paintings and decoration, represent a happy marriage. ⁶The Greeks linked butterflies to the human soul, and the Greek word for butterfly and soul is the same, *psyche*. ⁷Among Mexico's ancient tribes, the butterfly was a symbol of fertility. ⁸To the early Mayan tribes of Mexico and Latin America, butterflies were the souls of fallen warriors returned to earth. ⁹The Irish once believed that butterflies were the souls of the dead waiting to descend into hell. ¹⁰Taking the connection between death and the butterfly one step further, legends from Eastern European countries claim that vampires can transform themselves into butterflies when in pursuit of their victims.

Courtesy Ulrich Flemming

Butterflies play different symbolic roles depending on the culture.

Topic Sentence   ____

Two Key Kinds of Topic Sentences

As you have already seen, topic sentences can and do appear anywhere in a paragraph, although some locations are more common than others. Particularly in textbooks, topic sentences are quite likely to be the first or second sentence in a paragraph. However, the following paragraphs illustrate two other methods of introducing the main idea that deserve some special attention.

Topic Sentences Arriving at the End

At the opening of chapter sections (more on the structure of chapter sections in Chapter 5), writers sometimes delay the topic sentence until the very end of a paragraph, making the shape of the paragraph look like this:

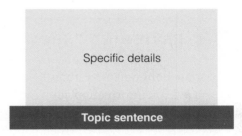

Specific details

Topic sentence

Now here's a concrete example. Note how the author describes a number of specific examples that build up to the general main idea at the very end of the paragraph.

Sentences 1 and 2 provide specific details about the fate of Chinese blogger Shi Tao.

Sentences 3–5 introduce examples of other bloggers severely punished for their posts,

[1]In China, blogger Shi Tao was sentenced to ten years in prison after his blog sent out details of how the government planned to handle the fifteenth anniversary of the Tiananmen Square massacre, during which protestors were killed or imprisoned because of their public demands for a more democratic government. [2]According to Reporters Without Borders, Yahoo!, the Internet service provider for Shi's email, helped the government link Shi's account to the offending messages. [3]In Iran, Kianoosh Sanjari was arrested for using his blog to provide details about the arrest of dissidents* by the Iranian government.

---

*dissidents: people who openly disagree with the policies of their government.

suggesting the author wants to point out that blogging can be dangerous.

Sentence 6 expresses the point of the examples: Some countries don't care about freedom of expression and punish dissident bloggers severely.

[4]Amnesty International claims that after Tunisian lawyer Mohammed Abbou posted two articles denouncing the government's torture of political prisoners, he was arrested and sentenced to four years in prison. [5]When Vietnamese blogger Nguyen Vu Binh wrote a series of articles demanding more political and economic freedom for his fellow citizens, he found himself sentenced to seven years in prison. [6]In the United States, bloggers are sometimes harshly criticized for their outspoken, even insulting expressions of opinion concerning political figures and government policies; however, countries that don't have the same respect for freedom of expression go much further in their determination to make bloggers toe the line.

In essays, paragraphs with a concluding topic sentence might turn up anywhere. In textbooks, however, they turn up most frequently at the beginning of chapter sections, where the concluding topic sentence unifies not just the individual paragraph but the paragraphs to follow as well.

REVIEWING THROUGH WRITING

Make the name of some nonhuman creatures like bees, cows, cats, crows, etc., part of a search term that will get you information about how this animal is portrayed in myth, legend, and superstition. Read through two or three sites that come up (remember to apply the savvy web searcher's checklist). Then paraphrase several examples of stories, superstitions, or beliefs associated with the animal.

Choose three paraphrases that describe the most colorful or the weirdest superstitions or legends and use them to write a paragraph that ends with a topic sentence. Your topic sentence should identify some characteristic or link that ties the examples together, for instance: "In all parts of the world, superstitions have associated black cats with witchcraft and evil."

Draft Outline

Paraphrase 1 _____

_____

_____

Paraphrase 2 _____

_____

_____

Paraphrase 3 _____

_____

_____

Topic sentence that states a common characteristic or thread: _____

_____

_____

Now revise to make each paraphrase move smoothly to the next and make sure your topic sentence identifies a common link.

The stories and legends surrounding most animals vary. The black cat, however, is uniformly associated with evil.

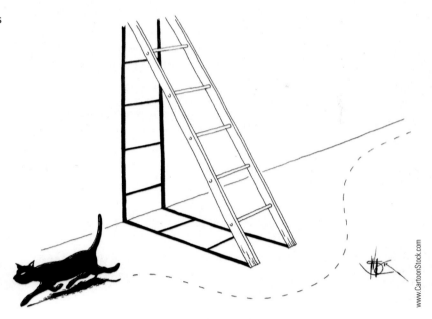

www.CartoonStock.com

Question-and-Answer Topic Sentences

Like paragraphs that present the main idea in the first or the second sentence, paragraphs that open with a question are extremely common in textbooks, particularly psychology textbooks. In paragraphs opening with a question, the answer is often stated in a nearby topic sentence, for instance:

Sentence 2 suggests the answer to that opening question is "no."

But the reversal transition *however* signals a change of direction.

Because the remaining sentences explain the link between CHD and hostility, sentence 3 is the real answer to the opening question. It's also the topic sentence.

¹Is there a connection between personality patterns and the risk of coronary heart disease? ²Although early research linked the Type A personality to an increased risk of coronary heart disease (CHD), later evidence casts doubt on this relationship. ³However, evidence points to a strong link between CHD and a component of the Type A personality, hostility. ⁴Hostile people tend to have "short fuses" and are prone to get angry easily and often. ⁵People who often experience strong, negative emotions, such as anger and hostility, stand an increased risk of developing coronary heart disease and other significant health problems. ⁶Their bodies also respond more strongly to stress, which, over time, can take a toll on their physical health in general and heart disease in particular. ⁷In contrast, a study of Mexican-American elders showed that those reporting more frequent positive emotions tended to have healthier blood pressures. (Adapted from Jeffrey S. Nevid, *Psychology*, 4e. © Cengage Learning.)

Using an opening question to draw the reader's attention to the topic sentence is a very popular strategy with writers in all fields. In textbooks, however, the author is just as likely to pose the question in the paragraph's heading. When that's the case, the answer doesn't necessarily follow on the heels of the question, although it can.

Look, for instance, at this next paragraph. Where's the answer to the question that appears in the heading?

Sentence 1 starts to answer the opening question by offering an expert opinion: Babies might understand quite a bit about the world around them.

Just How Much Do Newborns Understand About the World Around Them?

¹Child psychologist Jerome Bruner believed that babies are smarter than most people think. ²To prove his point, Bruner cited an experiment in which 3- to 8-week-old babies showed signs of understanding that a person's voice and body are connected. ³If babies heard their mother's voice coming from where she was standing, they remained calm. ⁴If her voice came from a loudspeaker several feet away,

The last sentence suggests Bruner is right: Babies understand a lot.

the babies became agitated* and began to cry. [5]Experiments like this one suggest that Bruner may be right:⌈The human mind is active from birth onward and babies are pretty smart and understand a lot about the world around them⌋ (Adapted from Dennis Coon, *Essentials of Psychology* 9e, © Cengage Learning.)

In this case, the answer to the question, or as much of an answer as anyone can supply, comes not at the beginning but at the end of the paragraph.

It doesn't matter if the question is posed in the heading or as the first sentence in the paragraph. You need to locate or infer an answer (more about inferring answers in Chapter 6), because the answer is very likely to be the topic sentence expressing the main idea.

◆ EXERCISE 5   Recognizing Topic Sentences

DIRECTIONS Read each paragraph and then write the number of the topic sentence in the blank. Circle any reversal transitions introducing the topic sentences.

1. [1]What does it take to achieve extraordinary success? [2]Psychologist Benjamin Bloom studied America's top concert pianists, Olympic swimmers, sculptors, tennis players, mathematicians, and researchers. [3]According to Bloom, drive and determination, not great natural talent, are what lead to exceptional success. [4]The first steps toward high achievement began when parents exposed their children to music, swimming, scientific ideas, and so on, "just for fun." [5]At first, many of the children had ordinary skills. [6]One Olympic swimmer, for instance, remembers repeatedly losing races as a 10-year-old. [7]At some point, however, the children began to actively cultivate their abilities. [8]Before long, parents noticed their children's progress and found an expert instructor or coach. [9]After experiencing successes, the youngsters began "living" for their talent and practiced many hours daily. [10]This continued for many years before they reached truly outstanding heights of achievement. (Adapted from Dennis Coon and John O. Mitterer, *Psychology: A Journey* 4e, © Cengage Learning.)

Topic Sentence   _____

---

*agitated: upset; disturbed, uneasy.

2. [1]Is there anything a couple can do to keep the honeymoon alive? [2]One key study suggests there is. [3]Arthur Aron and his colleagues think that after the exhilaration of a new relationship wears off, partners can combat boredom by engaging together in new activities. [4]By means of questionnaires and a door-to-door survey, these researchers found that the more new experiences these spouses said they had together, the more satisfied they were with their marriages. [5]To test their theory in a controlled experiment, the researchers brought randomly selected couples into the laboratory, spread gymnasium mats across the floor, tied the partners together at a wrist and ankle and had them crawl on their hands and knees, over a barrier from one end of the room to the other—all the while carrying a pillow between their bodies. [6]Other couples were given a simpler task of rolling a ball across the mat, one partner at a time. [7]A third group received no assignment. [8]As predicted, the couples that had struggled and laughed their way through the experiment reported more satisfaction with the quality of their relationships than did those in the simple and no task groups. (Adapted from Sharon S. Brehm et al., *Social Psychology* 6e, © Cengage Learning.)

Topic Sentence _____

3. [1]What causes plants to bloom? [2]Although you may think that plants flower based on the amount of sunlight they receive, they actually bloom according to the amount of uninterrupted darkness; this principle of plant bloom is called *photoperiodism*. [3]Plants that bloom in late summer and fall, like asters and sedum, are called short-day plants. [4]They require long periods of darkness and only short periods of light. [5]Plants that flower in late spring and early summer, such as daisies and poppies, are called long-day plants. [6]They need only short periods of darkness to blossom.

Topic Sentence _____

4. [1]On May 28, 1934, Elzire Dionne gave birth to five daughters who became famous as the Dionne Quintuplets. [2]Their birth made immediate headlines and was celebrated as a medical miracle. [3]Unfortunately, the little girls' fame was their downfall; almost from the moment of birth, they were exploited by everyone around them. [4]The parents of the quintuplets were poor and didn't know how to support their family, which already included six children. [5]Confused and desperate, they

agreed to put their five daughters on display at the Chicago World's Fair. [6]For a brief moment, it seemed as if the girls were saved from a miserable fate when the family physician, Dr. Allan Roy Dafoe, stepped in and insisted the girls were too frail to be on exhibit. [7]But after Dafoe took control of the girls' lives, he made himself rich by displaying the quintuplets to tourists and collecting fees for product endorsements.

Topic Sentence _____

5. [1]George W. Bush is only the second man, after John Quincy Adams, to follow in the footsteps of his father and serve as president of the United States. [2]John Quincy Adams, America's sixth president, was the son of second president John Adams. [3]The elder George Bush even calls his son "Quincy." [4]George W. Bush and John Quincy Adams share other similarities, too. [5]Both men are their fathers' oldest sons. [6]Both men held public office before being elected president. [7]Adams was a U.S. senator and served as secretary of state, while Bush was governor of Texas. [8]Both men were in their fifties when they successfully ran for president. [9]Both men also achieved the presidency in a contested election because neither of them had won the popular vote.

Topic Sentence _____

6. [1]On the surface, effective listening might seem to require little more than an acute sense of hearing. [2]But, in fact, there's a big difference between hearing and listening. [3]*Hearing* occurs when sound waves travel through the air, enter your ears, and are transmitted by the auditory nerve to your brain. [4]As long as neither your brain nor your ears are impaired, hearing is involuntary. [5]It occurs spontaneously with little conscious effort on your part. [6]*Listening*, in contrast, is a voluntary act that includes attending to, understanding, and evaluating the words or sounds you hear. [7]If you sit through a lecture without making an effort to listen, there's a good chance that the speaker's words will become just so much background noise. (Laraine Flemming and Judith Leet, *Becoming a Successful Student* 2e, Harper Collins, 1993, p. 93.)

Topic Sentence _____

7. [1]During periods of extreme emotion, when we become frightened or furious for example, our heartbeat speeds up, along with our

pulse and breathing rates. [2]The body's metabolism* accelerates. [3]It burns up sugar in the bloodstream and fats in our tissues at a faster rate. [4]The salivary glands also become less active. [5]That's why during periods of extreme emotion your mouth feels dry and it becomes hard to swallow. [6]Your sweat glands also respond, producing a dripping forehead, clammy hands, and "cold sweat." [7]Finally, the pupils of the eye get bigger, producing the wide-eyed look that is typical of both terror and rage. [8]Strong emotions are not without consequences for the human body.

Topic Sentence _____

8. [1]In pre-industrial societies, the primary unit of social attachment was not the family but the peer group. [2]The family provided for reproduction, child rearing, and economic support, but emotional attachments were primarily to persons of the same age and sex outside of the family. [3]Wives had close attachments to other wives, and husbands to other husbands. [4]Social life was highly segregated by sex and was based on childhood friendships and associations. [5]For example, a group of neighborhood boys would become close friends while still very young, and these friendships remained the primary ties of these people all their lives. [6]The same occurred among women. [7]While, no doubt, peer attachments provided people with a source of intimacy and self-esteem, they also probably hindered the formation of close emotional bonds within the family. (Adapted from Rodney Stark, *Sociology* 10e, © Cengage Learning.)

Topic Sentence _____

9. [1]In 1919, President Woodrow Wilson was serving his second term in office. [2]Suddenly, without warning, in September of that year, he suffered a near-fatal stroke that left him partially paralyzed and nearly blind. [3]When the president's doctors told Wilson's wife, Edith, that her husband was seriously ill and might need to resign, she made a momentous decision. [4]For more than six months, Edith Wilson concealed the seriousness of her husband's condition by running the country for him, thereby earning her nickname as "the secret president." [5]Edith read all of the documents sent to her husband for his

_____
*metabolism: a complex of physical and chemical processes in the body that maintain life.

signature and decided which ones would be brought to his attention and which not. ⁶When the president seemed too ill to concentrate, Edith took over and made decisions for him, communicating those decisions to his staff. ⁷Wilson never fully recovered and, in 1921, at the end of his presidential term, Woodrow and Edith retired. ⁸In 1924, after living three more years in virtual seclusion, President Woodrow Wilson died. ⁹Edith lived to be eighty-nine years old and died in 1961.

Topic Sentence _____

10. ¹Many people know that Joan of Arc was burned at the stake because she was suspected of being a witch. ²However, St. Joan was convicted of another crime as well—that of dressing as a man. ³This was a serious offense in 1481, based on the Biblical injunction*: "The woman shall not wear that which pertaineth unto a man, neither shall a man put on a woman's garment." ⁴What was Joan wearing that contributed to her death at the stake? ⁵On the battlefield she wore armor, but in camp, eyewitnesses claimed that she wore a long gray tunic, or blouse, over closely fitted hose or tights. ⁶Unlike today, women of the fifteenth century did not wear tights. ⁷They wore long dresses. ⁸During her trial, Joan, in a plea for mercy, did put on a dress. ⁹But she didn't wear it for long. ¹⁰It was less than a day before she once again donned tights, claiming that without them she feared rape at the hands of her guards. ¹¹Her captors considered her clothing change to be an act of defiance, and Joan of Arc lost all chance for mercy at their hands. (Adapted from Richard Zacks, *An Underground Education.* Anchor Books, 1999, p. 153.)

Topic Sentence _____

◆ **EXERCISE 6**   **Recognizing the Best Paraphrase**

DIRECTIONS   Read the paragraph and look closely at the underlined topic sentence. Then circle the letter of the best paraphrase.

1. ¹In 2009, a new treatment center called reSTART opened in Fall City, Washington. ²The center's goal is to treat what the owners believe is a growing population of "Web addicts," people who find it almost

_____
*injunction: law or rule forbidding certain actions or behavior.

impossible to stay off the Web for any length of time. [3]For around a thousand dollars a day, the five-acre center currently only handles about six patients at a time, but the managers of the center believe their space will enlarge to meet ever-growing numbers of people. [4]Although Internet addiction is not recognized as a disorder by the American Psychiatric Association and treatment is not covered by insurance, Cosette Dawna Rae, one of the center's owners, believes that centers like reSTART are going to multiply over time. [5]Such centers for video addicts are, in fact, already commonplace in China, South Korea, and Taiwan. [6]At reSTART, the treatment methods are much like the more traditional ones used for alcohol and drug addiction. [7]The patient goes cold turkey and is cut off from access to the Internet. [8]Instead, he or she spends the days in a variety of activities that include chores, exercise, and therapy sessions.

Paraphrase

a. Therapy centers designed to treat Web addiction are springing up around the country with reSTART in Fall City, Washington, being a good example of what such treatment centers have to offer.

b. Like other treatment centers for addiction, reSTART in Fall City, Washington, takes a cold-turkey approach to addiction, and patients are not allowed any access to the Web.

c. The therapy center reSTART in Fall City, Washington, was created to treat people who have become addicted to being on the Web.

d. Due to the growing number of people who seem addicted to playing video games, the owners of reSTART think that their new facility will be the first of many.

2. [1]If you have ever lived in the country, you are probably familiar with the croaking sound frogs make in the night. [2]For many country dwellers, it's a soothing, peaceful sound. [3]But unless strong action is taken immediately, the croaking of frogs might not be a sound anyone hears ten years from now. [4]All the evidence suggests that frogs and others in the class known as *amphibia*—for example, salamanders and toads—are threatened with extinction. [5]There are already reports that two-thirds of several amphibian species in Central and South America have vanished. [6]The twin causes of the amphibians' demise are pollution and humans invading their natural habitats. [7]Among the amphibians, though, frogs—the most populous group in the class—are under special attack. [8]For years

now, the chytrid fungus has been spreading around the world leaving dead frogs in its path. [9]The fungus coats the frogs' skin, closing off their pores. [10]As a result, the frogs have trouble breathing and absorbing water. [11]Ultimately, they die of dehydration, or fluid loss, and suffocation. [12]In an effort to save frogs and other amphibians, conservationists have founded Amphibian Ark, a project that contacts zoos around the globe and asks them to adopt and care for at least 500 members of the amphibian class. (Source of statistics: http://science .howstuffworks.com/bye-bye-kermie.htm.)

Paraphrase

a. The comforting sound of frogs croaking in the night is a familiar sound to anyone who has lived in the country.

b. The class of animals known as *amphibia* is under the threat of extinction.

c. The class of animals known as *amphibia* includes salamanders.

d. Many different species are currently under threat of extinction.

◆ EXERCISE 7   Practicing Paraphrasing

DIRECTIONS Read each paragraph and underline the topic sentence. Then paraphrase it in the blanks that follow. *Note*: For the purposes of this exercise, paraphrase in complete sentences as if you were paraphrasing for a term paper.

EXAMPLE [1]In an attempt to solve the problem, a number of elementary and middle schools around the country are making a strong effort to find a solution to bullying behavior in the schools. [2]At the administrative level, supervisors and principals are sending out questionnaires, asking students if they have ever been bullied. [3]The goal of the questionnaire is to determine how much bullying behavior occurs in a particular school. [4]Administrators are also increasing student supervision in places like the playground and the cafeteria, where trouble is likely to occur. [5]In addition, they are requesting that teachers actively patrol the halls and be alert to signs of bullying. [6]In classrooms, teachers are discussing the subject with students and asking them to write about what causes some students to bully others.

Paraphrase Nationwide, elementary and middle school administrators are introducing

strong measures to combat bullying among students.

EXPLANATION   Every sentence following the first one refers to bullying in the schools. Each sentence offers more specific information about the attempts that have been made to solve the problem. Thus sentence 1 is the topic sentence. Like the topic sentence, the paraphrase must indicate the two kinds of schools and the action they are taking against bullying.

1. ¹People in all societies communicate by manipulating the space that separates them from others. ²Sociologists commonly identify four zones of space that we use in our communication with others. ³In North America, an *intimate zone* extends about 18 inches from the body. ⁴It is restricted to people with whom we want sustained, intimate physical contact. ⁵A *personal zone* extends from about 18 inches to 4 feet away. It is reserved for friends and acquaintances, from whom we will accept a limited amount of physical contact. ⁶The *social zone* is situated in the area roughly 4 to 12 feet away from us. ⁷Except for a handshake, we do not allow for physical contact from people who enter this zone. ⁸The *public zone* starts around 12 feet from our bodies, and it's the space we employ when we are on stage or standing in back of a podium addressing an audience. (Adapted from Robert J. Brym and John Lie, *Sociology* 3e, © Cengage Learning.)

Paraphrase   _____

_____

2. ¹Between January and May 2007, beekeepers lost one-quarter of their colonies, which is a lot of bees. ²Anyone inclined to ho-hum at this information should think again because honeybees are not important just to gardeners, who need bees to pollinate† their flowers; on the contrary, the disappearance of honeybees could have much wider significance. ³The truth is the disappearance of honeybees, also known as "Colony Collapse Disorder," could cause a food crisis. ⁴Honeybees pollinate nuts, avocados, apples, celery, squash, cucumbers, cherries, and blueberries. ⁵And that's not even a complete list. ⁶Experts estimate that about a third of the human diet is insect-pollinated, and 80 percent of the time, the honeybee is the pollinator of choice. ⁷Honeybees are also part of the cycle that brings

†pollinate: to transfer pollen in order to encourage reproduction.

meat to the table. [8]Cattle feed on alfalfa, and alfalfa crops need bees as pollinators. [9]If scientists can't figure out why honeybees are disappearing, meat eaters might be forced to turn vegetarian precisely at the time when even vegetables are in short supply.

Paraphrase _____

_____

The Function of Supporting Details

"The idea emerges from the detail and the detail grounds the idea."

—Mike Rose, researcher and writer

As you know from the previous sample paragraphs, topic sentences always need additional and more specific explanation to communicate their message. That's where supporting details come into the picture. **Supporting details** are more specific sentences that further explain and clarify main ideas. Writers use them to anticipate and answer questions readers are likely to pose about the main idea. They are the writer's way of saying to readers, "I mean this, not that."

Take, for instance, the following paragraph:

Sentence 2 reverses the opening train of thought with the transition *however.*

Sentence 3 appears to be the topic sentence, but the sentences that follow it would need to continue the same train of thought. Do they?

[1]Think of birds and you think of delicate creatures that soar effortlessly into the air, revealing a speed and grace that even the most advanced airplane can never achieve. [2]Speed and grace, however, were not the defining characteristics of early birds. [3]Although the earliest known bird, the pigeon-sized Archaeopteryx, had feathers, its skeleton was essentially that of a small dinosaur. [4]It had digits and claws on its forelimbs, teeth on its jaws and many bones in its wings and vertebral column. [5]How could flight evolve in such an unbirdlike animal? [6]The theory is that Archaeopteryx didn't fly. [7]Like the dinosaur, it pursued its prey, using its feathered wings like fly swatters. [8]Larger wings would have given it extra lift when it jumped on prey. [9]Gradually over time, evolutionary modifications could have led to changes in the wing bones and muscles so that these clumsy creatures became capable of real flight. (Adapted from Peter J. Russell et al., *Biology: The Dynamic Science* 2e, © Cengage Learning.)

Let's say you knew right away that sentence 3 was the topic sentence expressing the main idea: Ancient birds had the skeletons of small dinosaurs. Great, you have grasped the main idea of the paragraph. But that's not all you need to take away from the paragraph. Suppose, for instance, that a test question on the above passage required you to do this: Describe how the skeleton of ancient birds was more like a dinosaur than a modern bird. If you hadn't taken note of and understood the supporting details, you wouldn't be able to answer the question.

It's also true that you often don't know for sure what the author's main idea is until you have read one or more of the supporting details. For example, in the paragraph below, sentence 3 looks to be the topic sentence expressing the main idea. But it's only by sentences 4 and 5, which are more specific supporting details, that we can confirm the author is focusing on what poor communication before marriage predicts about the success of a marriage. We can confirm that point as the main idea because the supporting details develop precisely this claim.

Sentence 1 has to be introductory: There is nothing more to say about this point.

Sentence 2 is too specific to be the main idea.

It isn't until sentences 4 and 5, both supporting details, that we know that the authors are focusing on poor communication and marriage.

> [1]"Drop dead, you creep!" is hardly the thing someone would want to say when trying to resolve a disagreement in a dating relationship. [2]But it may be an important clue as to whether such a couple should marry. [3]Many couples who communicate poorly before marriage are likely to communicate the same way after marriage, and the result can be disastrous for future marital happiness. [4]Researchers have found that how well a couple communicates before marriage can be an important predictor of later marital satisfaction (Cate and Lloyd, 1992). [5]In one study, researchers found that those premarital couples who responded more to each other's positive communications than to each other's negative communications were more satisfied four years after marriage than those who focused mainly on negative messages. [6]If communication is poor before marriage, it is not likely to significantly improve after marriage. (Adapted from Bryan Strong et al., *The Marriage and Family Experience* 11e, © Cengage Learning.)

If the topic sentence appears at the end of the paragraph, the supporting details will provide the clues that guide you to it. If it appears at the beginning, supporting details will develop that point to make sure you fully understand it. How they fulfill either function depends on the needs of the main idea, which dictates the form the supporting details will take.

REVIEWING THROUGH WRITING

Make one of these three statements the point of a paragraph for which you supply the supporting details. But before you start drafting the paragraph, identify at least two questions you think your supporting details would need to answer to make your point both clear and convincing. Once you have your questions, you also know the answers your supporting details need to provide.

1. Employers who block their employees from using social media sites are doing the right (or wrong) thing.

   _____

   _____

2. Many people believe that having children can save a failing marriage, but while children might save the marriage, they don't always improve the relationship between husband and wife.

   _____

   _____

3. MOOCs (Massive Open Online Courses) are going to change education forever.

   _____

   _____

Purpose Has an Influence on Supporting Details

Supporting details always have the same function—to make the main idea clear and convincing. But as you already know, they can vary in form. They can be reasons, examples, studies, steps, statistics, and stories. The form they take, however, depends a lot on the writer's purpose.

Much of what you read in school will have an **informative purpose**, where the writer's goal is to tell readers what's generally known or believed about the topic under discussion. Thus, little or no attempt is made to convey a personal point of view. In fact, writers with an informative purpose go out of their way to avoid expressing any personal opinions, carefully using **denotative language**, or language that packs little or no emotional punch.

When the writer's purpose is informative, you are more likely to get supporting details that provide illustrations, convey facts, or describe studies. If the supporting details take the form of reasons, they will be ascribed to other people, rather than to the author.

However, even academic writers sometimes write with a **persuasive purpose**. They convey an opinion that they want readers to share or at least seriously consider. When persuasion is the writer's intent, you are likely to see more supporting details that take the form of reasons explaining why readers should think the same way the author does. You may also find personal anecdotes, or stories, that are meant to touch readers' emotions and thereby persuade them to share the author's point of view.

CHECK YOUR UNDERSTANDING

1. From the writer's standpoint, what is the central purpose of supporting details?

_____

_____

2. From the reader's standpoint, what is the function of supporting details?

_____

_____

3. How does the author's purpose affect supporting details?

_____

_____

Knowing the Difference Between Major and Minor Details

Most paragraphs include two kinds of supporting details, major and minor. **Major supporting details** are the examples, reasons, studies, statistics, facts, and figures, etc., that directly explain, develop, or prove an author's main idea. **Minor supporting details** further explain or clarify major ones. For an illustration of supporting details at work, look at the following topic sentence: "Most people who have survived near-fatal automobile accidents have a lot in common when it comes to being either drivers or passengers." Given only this one sentence, could you be sure you understood the author's message? After all, that sentence could mean different things to different people. Perhaps survivors have nightmares or fears about their health. But then again maybe they just become really slow drivers.

Look now at the following paragraph. You'll see right away how the supporting details fill out the topic sentence. But, can you also tell which sentences are major details and which ones are minor? See if you can answer that question by filling in the blanks following the sentences with a capital *M* for major or a lowercase *m* for minor.

> ¹Most people who have survived near-fatal automobile accidents have a lot in common when it comes to being either drivers or passengers. ²They agonize about driving even a mile or two over the speed limit and flatly refuse to go any faster than the law allows. _____ ³If they themselves are not at the wheel, their terror increases. _____ ⁴They tend to compulsively hit the imaginary brake under their foot whenever the actual driver seems to be tailgating the car ahead. _____ ⁵They are probably among the most annoying passengers on earth, prone to offering advice about how to take a curve or where to stop for a light._____

In this instance, the two major supporting details—sentences 2 and 3—describe the two types of behavior that the author has in mind. Those illustrations are the author's way of answering questions such as, "What does 'have a lot in common' mean?" Sentences 4 and 5 are minor details that illustrate how people who have survived a deadly accident behave as passengers: (1) they are constantly hitting an imaginary brake, and (2) they constantly give advice.

Minor Details Can Be Essential

Don't be fooled by the labels *major* and *minor*. Sometimes minor details can be as meaningful as major ones. Therefore, you need to judge them in terms of what they contribute to the major details they modify. If a minor detail simply adds a personal note or provides emphasis, you don't need to think about it much. You certainly don't need to include it in your notes. But if a major detail doesn't make much sense without the minor one that follows, then both details are equally important and both should be paraphrased in your notes.

ALLUSION ALERT

Pygmalion

The sample paragraph for Exercise 8 alludes to the Pygmalion effect. According to myth, Pygmalion, the king of Cyprus, carved and then fell in love with the statue of a woman who was transformed into a human being. The phrase *Pygmalion effect* reflects the myth's suggestion that wishing or believing something can make it happen. However, the allusion is usually used without the word *effect* in statements like these: "Many of the popular stories and movies about vampires are a variation on the myth of Pygmalion, with the love of a good woman transforming an evil vampire into a loving caretaker, albeit* one with fangs."

✔ CHECK YOUR UNDERSTANDING

1. Describe the relationship between major and minor details.

_____

_____

2. Are minor details always nonessential? _____ Please explain.

_____

_____

---

*albeit: even though, notwithstanding.

◆ **EXERCISE 8**   **Connecting Topic Sentences and Supporting Details**

DIRECTIONS Read each paragraph and write the number of the topic sentence in the first blank. Then answer the questions that follow by circling the correct response or filling in the blanks.

EXAMPLE   [1]What makes an effective leader? [2]To be sure, no one characteristic or trait defines an effective leader. [3]It is true, however, that effective leaders get the most out of employees or group members by holding them to very high standards or expectations. [4]Setting high standards increases productivity because people tend to live up to the expectations set for them by superiors. [5]This is an example of the *Pygmalion effect*, which works in a subtle, often unconscious way. [6]When a managerial leader believes that a group member will succeed, the manager communicates this belief without realizing that he or she is doing so. [7]Conversely, when a leader expects a group member to fail, that person will not usually disappoint the manager. [8]The manager's expectation of success or failure becomes a self-fulfilling prophecy. [9]Thus it pays for a manager to expect the best from employees. (Adapted from Andrew J. DuBrin, *Leadership* 6e, © Cengage Learning.)

a. Topic sentence: __3__

b. The major details help answer what question or questions about the topic sentence? Why do effective leaders set such high standards?

c. *True* or (*False.*) Sentence 5 is a major supporting detail. Explain your answer. This supporting detail further explains the previous one, making it a minor but far from unimportant detail.

d. *True* or (*False.*) Sentence 6 is also a major supporting detail. Explain your answer. The point made in sentence 6 clarifies how the Pygmalion effect functions in a "subtle, almost unconscious way."

EXPLANATION   Sentence 3 answers the paragraph's opening question and most effectively sums up the paragraph. That makes it the topic sentence. Explanations for the *true* and *false* answers already appear in the blanks above.

1. [1]Despite its rapid spread, Islam is not a religion for those who are casual about regulations. [2]On the contrary, adhering to the rules of Islam takes effort and discipline. [3]One must rise before dawn to observe the first of five prayers required daily, none of which can take place without first cleansing oneself according to an established ritual or ceremony. [4]Sleep, work, and recreational activities take second place to prayer. [5]Fasting for the month of Ramadan,[†] undertaking the pilgrimage to Mecca at least once in a lifetime, paying tax for relief of the Muslim poor, and accepting Islam's creed require a serious and an energetic commitment. [6]On the whole, the vast majority of Muslims worldwide do observe those tenets.[*] (Adapted from Jan Goodwin, *Price of Honor,* Plume Books, 2002, p. 29.)

   a. Topic sentence: _____

   b. The major details help answer what question or questions about the topic sentence? _____

   _____

   c. *True* or *False.* Sentence 3 is a major supporting detail. Explain your answer. _____

   _____

   d. *True* or *False.* Sentence 4 is also a major supporting detail. Explain your answer. _____

   _____

2. [1]Those cuddly toys called teddy bears seem to have been around forever. [2]But actually the first teddy bears came into being when President Theodore "Teddy" Roosevelt showed himself too much of a sportsman to shoot a staked bear cub. [3]In 1902, Roosevelt visited Mississippi to settle a border dispute. In Roosevelt's honor, his hosts organized a hunting expedition. [4]To make sure that the president would bag a trophy, they staked a bear cub to the ground so that Roosevelt's shot couldn't miss. [5]To his credit, Roosevelt refused to

---

[†]Ramadan: Muslim holy month, the ninth month of the Islamic calendar.
[*]tenets: rules, principles, or beliefs held to be true by a person or an organization.

shoot the bear. [6]When the incident was publicized, largely through political cartoons, a Russian candy store owner named Morris Michtom made a toy bear out of soft, fuzzy cloth and placed it in his shop window with a sign reading "Teddy's Bear." [7]The bear was a hit with passersby, and teddy-bear mania spread rapidly throughout the country.

a. Topic sentence: _____

b. The major details help answer what question or questions about the topic sentence? _____

_____

c. *True* or *False*. Sentence 4 is a minor detail. Explain your answer. _____

_____

d. *True* or *False*. Sentence 6 is a major detail. Explain your answer. _____

_____

3. [1]Many people don't know the difference between a patent and a trademark. [2]However, the terms *trademark* and *patent* aren't synonyms; they refer to different things. [3]Granted for a specific number of years, a patent protects both the name of a product and its method of manufacture. [4]In 1928, for example, Jacob Schick invented and then patented the electric razor in an effort to maintain complete control of his creation. [5]Similarly, between 1895 and 1912, no one but the Shredded Wheat Company was allowed to make shredded wheat because the company had the patent. [6]A trademark is a name, symbol, or other device that identifies a product and makes it memorable in the minds of consumers. [7]Kleenex, JELL-O, and Xerox are all examples of trademarks. [8]Aware of the power that trademarks possess, companies fight to protect them. [9]They do not allow anyone else to use one without permission. [10]Occasionally, though, a company gets careless and loses control of a trademark. [11]Aspirin, for example, is no longer considered a trademark, and any company can call a pain-reducing tablet an aspirin.

a. Topic sentence: _____

b. The major details help answer what question or questions about the topic sentence? _____

_____

c. *True* or *False*. Sentence 4 is a minor detail. Explain your answer.

_____

_____

d. *True* or *False*. Sentence 6 is a major detail. Explain your answer.

_____

_____

WEB QUEST   **What Can Become a Trademark?**

In addition to names, what other kinds of things can be trademarked?

_____

_____

REVIEWING THROUGH WRITING

Using the Web for your research, write a paragraph in which the topic sentence identifies at least three different kinds of trademarks. Describe the trademarks with both major and minor details, marking the major detail with a capital *M* and the minor detail with a lowercase *m*.

Draft Outline

Topic Sentence Identifying Three or More Trademarks: _____

_____

_____

_____

1. Major Supporting Detail: _____

_____

Minor Supporting Detail: _____

_____

2. Major Supporting Detail: _____

_____

Minor Supporting Detail: _____

_____

3. Major Supporting Detail: _____

_____

Minor Supporting Detail: _____

_____

When you revise, consider giving your topic sentence an introduction and make sure that your supporting details clearly introduce each new type of trademark.

Using Category Words to Identify Major Details

Category words are general terms used to sum up a number of individual events, objects, elements, or people. Some examples of category words are *types*, *factors*, *events*, *parts*, *kinds*, and *components*. If you spot a category word in a topic sentence, you have also discovered an excellent clue to the major details because each new individual example of the category word is bound to be a major detail. What's the category word clue in the topic sentence of this paragraph? Write your answer in the blank at the end.

> [1]Around 1950, agriculture in the United States underwent a number of profound changes. [2]For one thing, agriculture became energy intensive.* [3]In 1950, an amount of energy equal to less than half a barrel of

---

*intensive: characterized by great power, strength, or force.

oil was used to produce a ton of grain. [4]By 1985, the amount of energy needed to produce a ton of grain had more than doubled. [5]Searching for ways to increase the yield of the lands already in use, farmers also began to rely heavily on inputs of water, chemical fertilizers and pesticides (many of which are petroleum-derived products), and high-yield strains of crops. [6]In some areas, especially the drier regions of the Southwest, irrigation projects allowed dry lands to be cultivated. [7]In contrast to past agricultural practices, farmers also began to concentrate on producing only one or two profitable crops as opposed to a variety of crops. (Adapted from Donald Kaufman and Cecilia Franz, *Biosphere 2000*. Kendall Hunt Publishers, 2000, p. 182.) _____

If you wrote, "changes" into the blank, you correctly identified the category word clue in sentence 1, which is the topic sentence. The next step is to use that category word to identify which sentences in the sample paragraph describe major details. Write the numbers of those sentences here: _____

With the help of the category word *changes*, you were probably able to identify sentences 2, 5, 6, and 7, leaving sentences 3 and 4 as minor details. Are those minor details unimportant? That depends on your background knowledge. For the reader who knows a lot about energy use, maybe not, but for most of us, the minor details provide insight into just how energy intensive agriculture became.

 REVIEWING THROUGH WRITING

Use a category word to start off a paragraph on any personal relationship you think you know something about. Write, for instance, about the different *qualities* that you consider essential to being a good friend or the *mistakes* people are likely to make in choosing a mate. Whatever relationship or category word you choose for this assignment, you need to provide at least three individual examples as major supporting details. You also need to flesh out at least two of those major details with minor ones.

◆ **EXERCISE 9** **Category Words and Major Details**

DIRECTIONS Underline the topic sentence. If there is a category word in the topic sentence, circle it. Then answer the questions that follow.

1. [1]Emotional intelligence is a difficult term to define precisely; however, the term can be generally described using four main characteristics. [2]The first key characteristic of emotional intelligence is self-awareness, or knowing one's own feelings. [3]This characteristic may, in fact, be the most important component of emotional intelligence. [4]Another key characteristic is the ability to manage one's emotions. [5]Emotionally intelligent people can soothe themselves in difficult times and bounce back quickly from disappointments. [6]People with high levels of emotional intelligence can also use their emotions in service of their goals. [7]Faced with a challenge, they can summon the enthusiasm and confidence necessary to pursue their desires. [8]In addition to these two characteristics, emotionally intelligent people are also likely to have empathy. [9]They are, that is, able to recognize and identify the feelings of others. [10]They possess what are commonly called "people skills." [11]The fourth and final characteristic of emotional intelligence is the ability to help others deal with their feelings. [12]This characteristic is an important factor in maintaining meaningful relationships. (Adapted from Douglas A. Bernstein and Peggy W. Nash, *Essentials of Psychology* 2e, © Cengage Learning.)

1. Use the numbers of the sentences to identify the major details in this paragraph: _____

2. Which sentences introduce minor details?

   _____

2. [1]Volcanic eruptions and their aftereffects are among the earth's most destructive natural events. [2]But whether a volcano poses an imminent threat to human life and property depends on its status as an *active*, a *dormant*, or an *extinct* volcano. [3]An active volcano is one that is currently erupting or has erupted recently. [4]Certain active volcanoes, such as Kilauea on Hawaii or Stromboli in the eastern Mediterranean, erupt almost continuously. [5]Active volcanoes can be found on all continents except Australia and on the floors of all major ocean basins. [6]Indonesia, Japan, and the United States are the world's most volcanically active nations. [7]A dormant volcano is one that has not erupted recently but is considered likely to do so in the future. [8]The presence of relatively fresh volcanic rocks in a volcano's vicinity is an indication that it is still capable of erupting. [9]The presence of hot water springs or small earthquakes occurring near a volcano may also indicate that the volcano is stirring to wakefulness. [10]A volcano is considered extinct if it has not erupted for a very long time (perhaps tens of thousands of years) and is considered unlikely to do so in the future. [11]A truly extinct volcano is no longer fueled by a magma[†] source and, thus, no longer capable of erupting. [12]Volcanoes, however, can surprise us. [13]Residents of the Icelandic island of Heimaey were convinced that their volcano Helgafell was extinct, until it erupted in 1973. [14]The eruption lasted 157 days. (Adapted from Stanley Chernicoff and Haydn A. Fox, *Essentials of Geology* 3e, © Cengage Learning.)

1. Use the numbers of the sentences to identify the major details in this paragraph. _____

2. Which sentences introduce minor details?

    _____

3. [1]In addition to using their senses, predators have a variety of methods that help them capture prey. [2]Herbivores[†] can simply walk, swim, or fly up to the plants they feed on. [3]Carnivores[†] feeding on mobile prey have two main options: pursuit and ambush. [4]Some, such as the cheetah, pursue and catch their prey by running fast; others, such as the American bald eagle, have keen eyesight and can fly; still others, such as wolves and African lions, cooperate to capture their prey by hunting in packs. [5]Other predators use camouflage to hide in plain sight and ambush their prey. [6]For example, praying mantises sit in flowers of a similar color and ambush visiting insects. [7]White ermines and snowy owls are the perfect color to hunt in snow-covered areas. [8]Some predators use chemical warfare to attack their prey. [9]For example, spiders and poisonous snakes use venom to paralyze their prey and to deter their predators. (Adapted from G. Tyler Miller, *Living in the Environment* 15e, © Cengage Learning.)

    1. Use the numbers of the sentences to identify the major details in this paragraph: _____

    2. Which sentences introduce the minor details?

        _____

[†]magma: heated rock material underneath the earth's crust.
[†]herbivores: plant-eating organisms, such as deer, sheep, and grasshoppers.
[†]carnivores: flesh-eating animals, such as lions and tigers.

◆ **EXERCISE 10   Identifying Major and Minor Details**

DIRECTIONS   Identify major and minor details by writing the appropriate sentence numbers in the boxes of the accompanying diagram.

EXAMPLE   [1]Twins can be either identical or fraternal. [2]Identical twins are formed from one fertilized egg that splits in two, resulting in two children of the same sex who look very much alike. [3]One-third of all twins born are identical. [4]Fraternal twins are formed from two different fertilized eggs; these twins can be of different sexes and look quite different from one another. [5]Two-thirds of all twins are fraternal.

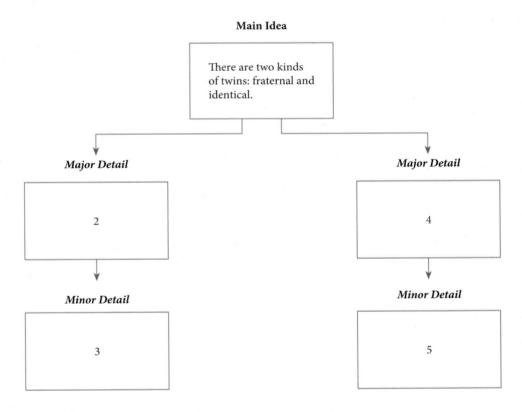

Main Idea

There are two kinds of twins: fraternal and identical.

Major Detail

2

Major Detail

4

Minor Detail

3

Minor Detail

5

EXPLANATION   In this example, each major detail fleshes out the two terms introduced in the topic sentence: *identical* and *fraternal*. Both details are followed by minor ones that give readers additional information about the different kinds of twins. *Note*: Although this paragraph neatly balances major and minor details, this is not the case in every paragraph and major details may or may not be followed by minor ones. It's also possible for one major detail to be followed by two minor ones.

1. [1]Nightclub acts that use lions and tigers may be entertaining, but they are, for a number of reasons, bad for both the animals and their trainers. [2]Making these animals learn tricks forces them to ignore their natural instincts. [3]Even worse, using lions and tigers for entertainment means that these proud creatures spend most of their lives in cages rather than roaming free in their natural habitat. [4]Club performances that feature lions and tigers are also bad because they are unsafe for both handlers and spectators. [5]These powerful beasts are fundamentally wild, and no amount of training can guarantee they will not, without warning, turn and attack. [6]The horrific attack that took place on trainer Roy Horn of the famed duo Siegfried and Roy is a tragic illustration of that fact. [7]Horn had thirty years of training performing tigers behind him, but all that experience did not prevent him from being attacked and severely injured by a tiger.

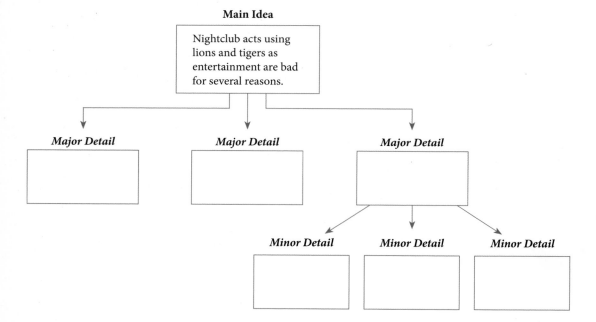

Main Idea

Nightclub acts using lions and tigers as entertainment are bad for several reasons.

Major Detail

Major Detail

Major Detail

Minor Detail

Minor Detail

Minor Detail

2. [1]Some psychologists believe there are five general aspects or components of human personality, which get mixed and matched in the process of biological inheritance. [2]The first of the five is *extraversion*. [3]This trait determines characteristics such as excitability, sociability, talkativeness, assertiveness, and intense emotional expressiveness. [4]*Agreeableness* is considered another core element of personality. [5]It covers characteristics such as trust, selflessness, kindness, and affection. [6]*Conscientiousness* is another central dimension of personality. [7]High levels of thoughtfulness, good impulse control, and goal-directed behaviors are characteristics of people whose personality includes a high degree of conscientiousness. [8]Those high in conscientiousness also tend to be organized and mindful of details. [9]Another, less positive component of personality is *neuroticism*. [10]Individuals high in this trait are likely to be nervous, moody, and irritable. [11]*Openness* is the fifth personality component. [12]This element of personality encourages characteristics such as imagination and insight. [13]People high in openness are also likely to have a broad range of interests. (Source of information: Kendra Cherry, http://psychology.about.com/od/personalitydevelopment/a/bigfive.htm.)

Main Idea

| Many current personality psychologists believe there are five core elements of personality. |

Major Detail   *Major Detail*   *Major Detail*   *Major Detail*   *Major Detail*

Minor Detail   Minor Detail   Minor Detail   Minor Detail   Minor Detail   Minor Detail   Minor Detail

WORD CHECK

The following words were introduced and defined in pages 115–157. See how well you can match the words with the meanings shown below, many of which have been slightly expanded. When you finish, make sure to check the meanings of any words you missed because the same words will turn up in tests at the end of the chapter.

1. hierarchies (p. 115) _____

2. boorish (p. 115) _____

3. altercations (p. 132) _____

4. dissidents (p. 135) _____

5. agitated (p. 139) _____

6. metabolism (p. 142) _____

7. injunction (p. 143) _____

8. albeit (p. 152) _____

9. tenets (p. 154) _____

10. intensive (p. 157) _____

a. fights, disagreements, battles

b. levels or rankings of people based on authority or importance; organizations or systems with a tight top-to-bottom structure

c. rules, principles, or beliefs held to be true by a person or an organization

d. upset, disturbed, uneasy; also, in its noun form, political unrest

e. law, rule, or decision forbidding something to occur

f. people who openly disagree with the policies of their government

g. characterized by great strength and force, concentrated, very focused

h. crude, disrespectful, loutish

i. chemical processes that occur in the body to maintain life

j. even though, notwithstanding

◆ **EXERCISE 11   More About Form and Meaning**

DIRECTIONS   Fill in the blanks with one of the words listed below.

altercation	hierarchy	metabolism	agitated	dissidents
boorish	intensive	injunction	albeit	tenets

1. Belief in the "gift of tongues" is one of the _____ of the Mormon faith. The gift of tongues occurs when someone translating the word of the Holy Spirit suddenly has the ability to speak in a strange and unknown language.

2. The young Winston Churchill, before he became England's prime minister, was said to be a delightful companion, _____ a bit overbearing.

3. The patient's movements were jerky and _____ until the drug finally took hold and he was able to calm down.

4. The actor Charlie Sheen was once known for his talent, but has become famous mainly for his _____ behavior.

5. Before the regime of Egyptian dictator Hosni Mubarak collapsed due to public protests in 2011, it was known for its especially brutal handling of _____, who went public with their distrust of the government.

6. There is no better example of a(n) _____ than the military; the top-to-bottom order is very strict with those on the lower rungs of the ladder obeying anyone higher up than they.

7. Why is it that people who overeat are always blaming their weight gain on their supposedly slow _____ ? The truth is they gain weight because they eat too much.

8. Anyone who wants to speak a foreign language within six months better be prepared to make a(n) _____ effort.

9. Once the judge issued a(n) _____ against an extension of the strike, the union had to find a new strategy.

10. The boxer didn't just fight in the ring. Even out of the ring, he was always getting into _____ with strangers who, in his mind, did not show the proper respect.

TAKING STOCK   What Causes Right- or Left-Handedness?

Looking Ahead   The paragraph on page 112 suggested that left-handed people might suffer some because there are so many more right-handed people than left. Look over the headings in the following reading. Do you think the author will continue or modify that point of view?

TEXTBOOK TIP   Psychology textbooks typically cite experts and studies to back up claims about human thought and behavior. If you see an expert or study cited, make sure you understand what general claim about human behavior or thinking the expert or studies support. Those claims should also probably make it into your marginal notes. Just remember to paraphrase rather than copy the author's words.

1   About 90 percent of all humans are right-handed; 10 percent are left-handed. Most people (about 75 percent) are strongly right- or left-handed. The rest show some inconsistency in hand preference. Which one are you? What causes handedness (a preference for the right or left hand)? Why are there more right-handed than left-handed people? How do left-handed and right-handed people differ? Does being left-handed create any problems—or benefits? The answers to questions about right- and left-handedness lead us back to the brain, where handedness begins.

2   *Is handedness inherited from parents?* Clear hand preferences are apparent even before birth and can be seen in fetal ultrasound images. According to British psychologist Peter Hepper, prenatal handedness persists for at least ten years after birth. This suggests that handedness cannot be dictated. Parents should never try to force a left-handed child to use the right hand. To do so may cause speech or reading problems.

3   Studies of twins show that hand preferences are not directly inherited like eye color or skin color. Yet, two left-handed parents are more likely than two right-handed parents to have a left-handed child. The best evidence to date shows that handedness is influenced by a single gene on the X (female) chromosome.

4   On the other hand, environmental factors such as learning, birth traumas, and social pressure can affect which hand you end up favoring. In the past, many left-handed children were forced to use their right hand for writing, eating, and other skills. This is especially true in collectivist cultures like India and Japan, where left-handedness is viewed as especially

negative. Not surprisingly, the proportion of left-handers in these societies is only about half that found in individualist cultures such as the United States and Canada.

Advantage Right

5 *Are there any drawbacks to being left-handed?* A small minority of lefties owe their hand preferences to birth traumas (such as prematurity, low birth weight, and breech birth). These individuals have higher rates of allergies, learning disorders, and other problems. Similarly, people with inconsistent handedness may be at risk for more immune-related diseases.

6 *Is it true that right-handed people live longer than left-handed people*? It is true that there is a shortage of very old lefties. One possible explanation lies in the widespread finding that left-handers are more accident-prone. However, the supposed clumsiness of lefties may well be a result of living in a right-handed world. One study showed that left-handed locomotive engineers have higher accident rates and suggested that the cause was due to the design of locomotive controls. If it can be gripped, turned, or pulled, it's probably designed for the right hand. On the other hand, the shortage of very old lefties may just reflect the fact that, in the past, more left-handed children were forced to become right-handed. That makes it look like many lefties don't survive to old age. In reality, they do, but many of them are masquerading as righties.

Advantage Left

7 Actually, there are some clear advantages to being left-handed. Throughout history a notable number of artists have been lefties from Leonardo da Vinci and Michelangelo to Pablo Picasso and M. C. Escher. Conceivably, because the right hemisphere is superior at imagery and visual abilities, there is some advantage to using the left hand for drawing or painting. At the least, lefties are definitely better at visualizing three-dimensional objects. This may be why there are more left-handed architects, artists, and chess players than would be expected.

8 **Lateralization** refers to specialization in the abilities of the brain hemispheres. One striking feature of lefties is that they are generally less lateralized than the right-handed. In fact, even the physical size and shape of their cerebral hemispheres are more alike. If you are a leftie, you can take pride that your brain is less lopsided than most! In general, left-handers are more symmetrical on almost everything, including eye dominance, fingerprints—even foot size.

9   In some situations, less lateralization may be a real advantage. For instance, individuals who are moderately left-handed or ambidextrous seem to have better than average pitch memory, which is a basic musical skill. Correspondingly, more musicians are ambidextrous than would normally be expected. The clearest advantage of being left-handed shows up where there is a brain injury. Because of their milder lateralization, left-handed individuals typically experience less language loss after damage to either brain hemisphere, and they recover more easily. (Adapted from Dennis Coon and John O. Mitterer, *Introduction to Psychology*, 12e. © Cengage Learning.)

Sharpening Your Skills

DIRECTIONS Answer the following questions by circling the letter of the correct response or filling in the blanks.

Making Predictions

1. The authors open this reading with a series of questions. Based on that opening, what should you expect the authors to do by the end of the reading?

   _____

2. Which headings are likely to introduce information about the benefits associated with being right- or left-handed?

   _____

Making Use of Explanatory Patterns

3. This reading illustrates what point made about topic sentences coming at the end of a paragraph?

   _____

   _____

4. In the first half of the reading, what explanatory pattern for paragraphs does the author seem to favor?

   _____

5. That pattern signals that the reader should be looking for

   _____.

Spotting Transitional Signals

6. What reversal transition appears in paragraph 3?

_____

7. Paragraph 4 opens with a reversal transition that signals a previous idea will be modified. What previous idea is that?

_____

Understanding Supporting Details

8. What do you think the psychologist Peter Hepper, mentioned in paragraph 2, would say to parents who were trying to train their five-year-old left-handed child to rely more heavily on her right hand so she would be more like her classmates?

_____

9. Imagine that a boxing match was taking place between two people who had never boxed together before. One person is right-handed, the other is left-handed. Who would have the advantage?

_____

_____

_____

Paraphrasing

10. Why is this *not* a good paraphrase for the definition of lateralization in paragraph 8? "Lateralization refers to specialization in the abilities of the brain hemispheres."

_____

11. Why is this paraphrase better? "The term *lateralization* describes how the sides of the brain specialize in certain activities."

_____

Using Word Parts

12. You know from Chapter 2 that *sym* means "alike" or "united." Based on your knowledge of that word part, what does the word *symmetrical* mean in this sentence from paragraph 8? "In general, left-handers are more *symmetrical* on almost everything, including eye dominance, fingerprints—even foot size."

Symmetrical means _____

13. You know from Chapter 2 that *ambi* means "both." Given your knowledge of the prefix, what does the word *ambidextrous* mean in this sentence from paragraph 9? "For instance, individuals who are moderately left-handed or *ambidextrous* seem to have better than average pitch memory, which is a basic musical skill."

   Ambidextrous means _____

Making Connections Between Major and Minor Details

14. Which of the statements below accurately describes the relationship between these two sentences from paragraph 8? "One striking feature of lefties is that they are generally less lateralized than the right-handed. In fact, even the physical size and shape of their cerebral hemispheres are more alike."

   a. Both sentences introduce major details.

   b. The first sentence is a major detail; the second sentence is a minor one.

   c. Both sentences are minor details.

Understanding Sentence Functions

15. Which of the statements below accurately describes the relationship between these three sentences from paragraph 9? "In some situations, less lateralization may be a real advantage. For instance, individuals who are moderately left-handed or ambidextrous seem to have better than average pitch memory, which is a basic musical skill. Correspondingly, more musicians are ambidextrous than would normally be expected."

   a. The first sentence is an introductory sentence; the second is a topic sentence; and the third is a major detail.

   b. The first sentence is a topic sentence; the second is a major detail; and the third is a minor detail.

   c. The first sentence is a topic sentence while the second and third sentences are both major details.

◗ **TEST 1**   **Recognizing Topics and Topic Sentences**

DIRECTIONS Read each paragraph and circle the letter of the correct topic. Then write the number of the topic sentence in the blank.

1. ¹A major cause of excessive water use and waste is the underpricing of this precious resource. ²Many water authorities charge a flat fee for water use and some charge even less for the largest users of water. ³For example, about one-fifth of all U.S. public water systems do not have water meters and charge a single low rate for almost unlimited use of high-quality water. ⁴Also, many apartment dwellers have little incentive to conserve water because water use is included in their rent. ⁵When Boulder, Colorado, introduced water meters, water use per person dropped by 40 percent. ⁶Researchers have found that each 10 percent increase in water prices cuts domestic water use by 3–7 percent. (Adapted from G. Tyler Miller, *Living in the Environment* 10e, © Cengage Learning.)

Topic   a. Boulder's use of water meters

b. use of water meters

c. cheap price of water

d. flat fees for water use

Topic Sentence   _____

2. ¹In a few high-profile cases, prosecutors have been censured after evidence of misconduct came to light. ²In Arizona, Kenneth Peasley, a prosecutor who was once named Prosecutor of the Year by the Arizona Bar Association, was disbarred for soliciting and using false testimony. ³Mike Nifong, in the Duke University lacrosse case, endured a highly publicized disbarment in 2007 because of his actions.† ⁴However, there are generally few controls on the behavior of prosecutors in the courtroom. ⁵Although voters have some control over who becomes a prosecutor, once in office most prosecutors stay in the good graces of the public unless there is a major scandal. ⁶Prosecutorial misconduct in the courtroom is

_____

†Nifong prosecuted a case against three students from Duke University, who were accused of rape. Despite evidence indicating their innocence, he continued with the prosecution.

all too often orally sanctioned by trial judges. [7]Even when convictions are overturned, prosecutors are rarely penalized in any way. [8]Many times, when there is clear misconduct with the prosecutor not turning over exculpatory evidence[†] or other forms of misconduct, the court rules it is a harmless error and does not even overturn the conviction. (Joycelyn M. Pollock, *Ethical Dilemmas & Decisions in Criminal Justice* 7e, © Cengage Learning.)

Topic

a. disgraced prosecutors

b. exculpatory evidence

c. prosecutorial misconduct

d. high-profile cases of prosecutorial misconduct

Topic Sentence   _____

3. [1]In 1987, Brazilian labor leader and environmentalist Francisco "Chico" Mendes was awarded the United Nations Global 500 Prize, along with a medal from the Better World Society. [2]Sadly, medals couldn't save Chico Mendes's life when he took on a group of cattle ranchers in Acre, Brazil. [3]Determined to drive out rubber workers like the ones Mendes represented, the ranchers used threats and violence to do it. [4]Mendes, who had both a reputation for courage and the respect of his fellow workers, was a special thorn in the ranchers' side, and they threatened his life. [5]To be sure, Mendes took their death threats seriously but refused to abandon his labor activities. [6]On December 15, 1988, he told a friend, "I don't think I'm going to live." [7]One week later, Mendes was shot in the chest as he stepped out of his house.

Topic

a. famous labor leaders

b. the murder of Chico Mendes

c. labor conditions in Brazil

d. honors given to Chico Mendes

Topic Sentence   _____

[†]exculpatory evidence: evidence that would clear the defendant on trial.

4. [1]The Underground Railroad was an informal network of routes traveled by American slaves escaping to freedom between 1840 and 1860. [2]These routes included paths through woods and fields; transportation such as boats, trains, and wagons; and homes where runaways hid from slave owners and law-enforcement officials. [3]In keeping with the idea of a railroad, slaves were referred to as "passengers," while homes that gave them shelter were "stations." [4]The people who assisted the slaves in flight were known as "conductors." [5]The conductors were abolitionists who defied fugitive slave laws to shelter and feed runaways and guide them along the safest routes out of the South to free states in the North. [6]Harriet Tubman, for example, liberated at least 300 slaves after she herself had used the Underground Railroad to escape the chains of slavery. [7]If it hadn't been for the Underground Railroad, hundreds of slaves, including Tubman, would never have escaped slavery's cruel bondage.

Topic

a. Harriet Tubman

b. the Underground Railroad

c. role of Quakers in the abolitionist movement

d. rules of the Underground Railroad

Topic Sentence   _____

▶ **TEST 2**   **Understanding the Function of Supporting Details**

DIRECTIONS Read each paragraph and write the number of the topic sentence in the blank. Then answer the questions about supporting details.

1. ¹In the past, young adults who went off to college would earn their degrees, get jobs, and move into their own homes or apartments. ²Today, however, twenty-something college graduates are more likely to return home for an extended period of time. ³In fact, one informal poll of college seniors revealed that 63 percent of them planned to move back home after graduation. ⁴This nationwide "back-to-the-nest" trend among young adults is the result of several factors. ⁵Because of the unstable economy, jobs are scarce, so recent graduates are often unemployed. ⁶Even those lucky enough to find jobs are concerned about keeping them. ⁷Plus, young people with entry-level salaries are finding it difficult to afford their own place to live. ⁸In high-cost-of-living cities, such as New York, Boston, and San Francisco in particular, recent college graduates often do not make enough money to pay the exorbitant rents. ⁹Even in lower-rent areas, young people in their twenties who have student loans to repay or who plan to attend graduate school cannot afford to pay their bills and live on their own.

Topic Sentence   _____

1. What word in the topic sentence is a clue to the major details?

    _____

2. Sentences 5 and 6 are
    a. both major details.
    b. a major detail followed by a minor one.
    c. both minor details.

3. Sentence 7 is a
    a. major detail.
    b. minor detail.
    c. transitional sentence.

4. Sentences 8 and 9 are

  a. both major details.

  b. a major detail followed by a minor one.

  c. both minor details.

2. [1]What is the difference between a computer virus and a computer worm? [2]After all, both can infect and damage computer systems. [3]Computer viruses and computer worms, however, differ in the way they damage the computer systems they invade. [4]A virus, which is short for "vital information resources under siege," is a program or code that secretly enters a computer by piggybacking on email messages, files, or programs shared between two different computer systems. [5]Then the virus infects its new host by attaching itself to the files within that computer and deleting or changing them or even overwriting entire programs. [6]Just like a biological virus in the human body, a computer virus replicates itself so that it will continue to be contagious when data is shared with another computer system. [7]In 2000, for example, the famous "Love Bug" virus, which traveled via email messages, destroyed files in computers all over the world. [8]Worms, too, are malicious programs that reproduce and spread. [9]But unlike viruses, they do not need to attach themselves to other files. [10]They are programs that run independently and spread on their own through computer networks. [11]Thus they do not require human intervention to make their way from one computer to another. [12]The famous Internet worm of 1988, for example, copied itself across the Internet, destroying many computer systems as it went. [13]Currently, computer analysts are worried about the Sasser worm, which has disabled computers in Britain, South Africa, and Taiwan.

Topic Sentence _____

1. Sentences 4 and 5 are

  a. both major details.

  b. a major detail followed by a minor one.

  c. both minor details.

2. Sentences 6 and 7 are

    a. both major details.

    b. a major detail followed by a minor one.

    c. both minor details.

3. Sentence 8 is a

    a. major detail.

    b. minor detail.

4. Sentences 9 and 10 are

    a. both major details.

    b. a major detail followed by a minor one.

    c. both minor details.

3. [1]Members of living history clubs are deeply passionate about history, so much so that they are not content to simply read about a particular era. [2]Instead, members of living history clubs seek to re-create life as it was lived in their favorite time period. [3]The 24,000 members of the Society for Creative Anachronism,[†] for example, study the European Middle Ages and Renaissance by re-creating the arts and skills of those eras. [4]Each participant makes and wears clothing from the period and creates a "persona," a person whom he or she would have liked to have been. [5]When the club's members gather at meetings, which may take the form of feasts or tournaments, they re-enact the behaviors of those who lived during that era. [6]They might, for instance, practice sword fighting or learn a craft like brewing, weaving, or candle making. [7]Similarly, hundreds of Civil War buffs frequently dress as soldiers and re-enact whole battles, often while a crowd of spectators looks on. [8]The re-enactors spend weekends camping in canvas tents, eating foods that were available to their historical counterparts, and trying to capture what it was like to have lived during the nineteenth century. [9]Other living history groups around the country focus on re-creating the Roman Empire, the pirate era, or the Wild West.

[†]anachronism: something that is out of its proper or appropriate order in time. For example, a play about ancient Rome would never have an actor looking at a watch because the watch is an anachronism.

Topic Sentence _____

1. Sentences 3 and 4 are
   a. both major details.
   b. a major detail followed by a minor one.
   c. both minor details.

2. Sentences 5 and 6 are
   a. both major details.
   b. a major detail followed by a minor one.
   c. both minor details.

3. Sentence 7 is a
   a. major detail.
   b. minor detail.

4. Sentences 8 and 9 are
   a. both major details.
   b. a major detail followed by a minor one.
   c. both minor details.

▶ TEST 3   Recognizing and Paraphrasing Topic Sentences

DIRECTIONS   Read each paragraph and write the number of the topic sentence in the blank. Then paraphrase the topic sentence on the lines that follow. *Note*: Please paraphrase using complete sentences.

1.   [1]In 1976 in an effort to combat the possible widespread outbreak of swine flu, President Gerald Ford directed the Centers for Disease Control (CDC) to launch a project called the National Influenza Immunization Program (NIIP). [2]In response, four manufacturers set out to make 200 million doses of swine flu vaccine because the CDC wanted every person in the United States to be vaccinated. [3]The CDC also developed a plan to take jet immunization guns into schools, factories, shopping centers, nursing homes, and health departments. [4]However, complications soon began to arise. [5]The vaccine, for instance, could not be produced as fast as initially planned. [6]This setback, along with legal issues, drastically disrupted the production timetable and delayed the beginning of the program by three months. [7]At the same time, the NIIP was suffering from public relations problems. [8]Although the program received widespread support at first, the media began to criticize it when no new cases of swine flu occurred. [9]Then when three elderly people died after being vaccinated, the press connected their deaths to the swine flu immunizations, despite a lack of evidence. [10]However, in time, a connection was established between the swine flu vaccination and a nervous system disease called Guillain-Barré syndrome (GBS). [11]The vaccine was thought to have caused 500 people to develop this complication, resulting in death for 25 of the victims and paralysis for many others. [12]When the NIIP was finally cancelled on December 16, 1976, only 24 percent of the population had been vaccinated, and the immunizations had killed more people than swine flu had. [13]When it was finally over, the 1976 National Influenza Immunization Program turned out to have been one of the greatest public health disasters of all time.

Topic Sentence   _____

Paraphrase   _____

                       _____

2. [1]Coral reefs perform many useful functions for the environment; above all, they provide a habitat for organisms that cannot survive elsewhere. [2]Yet coral reefs all over the world are being threatened by human activities. [3]Logging near the waters of Bacuit Bay in the Philippines has destroyed 5 percent of the coral reefs in the bay. [4]Dynamite fishing around the world has not only killed large numbers of fish, it has also blown apart a significant number of coral reefs in Kenya, Tanzania, and Mauritania. [5]Coral reefs have also fallen victim to the tourist industry. [6]Coral and shells are hot tourist commodities, and they have been collected in large quantities for sale to souvenir-hungry tourists. [7]Undoubtedly, the most violent assault on the reefs has come from nuclear testing. [8]France, for example, has exploded more than 100 nuclear devices in Polynesian waters once rich with coral reefs that are rapidly disappearing.

Topic Sentence _____

Paraphrase _____

_____

3. [1]In the nineteenth century, economic trends among women often began with one simple fact: Men were in short supply and women had to support themselves. [2]As their men headed West, for instance, many young women in New England supported themselves by spinning wool into yarn. [3]This practice became so widespread that the term "spinster" ceased to mean a female spinner and instead identified any unmarried woman of a certain age. [4]As the proportion of males in the region continued to decline and the number of women needing work increased, new inventions made it possible for huge textile mills to spring up in New England—built there because factory owners knew there was a large supply of unemployed females in the area. [5]New England textile factories thus relied on the labor of women, and the women relied on the factories for their income. [6]And it all started with men leaving home and heading West. (Adapted from Rodney Stark, *Sociology* 10e, © Cengage Learning.)

Topic Sentence _____

Paraphrase _____

_____

▶ **TEST 4**   **Reviewing New Vocabulary**

DIRECTIONS   Fill in the blanks with one of the words listed below.

metabolism	hierarchical	boorish	dissidents	injunction
agitation	tenets	albeit	intensive	altercations

1. The Chinese Communist Party, which has ruled China since 1949, has always been an intensely _____, top-down organization with all decisions and party _____ being under the control of the party's leaders and strict obedience demanded from the Chinese population. In 1989, however, the party's control appeared to be loosening and political _____ began to make their feelings known publicly. Aware of the political _____ that seemed to be growing daily, the government began to crack down. Initially there were small _____ between the government supporters and protesters. But when a huge student-led protest took place in Tiananmen Square in Beijing, China's capital, the government cracked down, first issuing an _____ against any further protest and finally sending in tanks and guns to subdue the demonstrators by any means necessary.

2. When cyclist Floyd Landis failed to pass a drug test and lost his crown as winner of bicycling's Tour de France, he blamed his body's fast _____ as a major source of his positive test results. When the body's physical processes speed up, water loss does occur more quickly, but exactly how that could affect the results of a drug test was anyone's guess. Landis's explanation was so far-fetched that it only encouraged the _____ investigations that had been going for years prior to Landis's being stripped of his medal. Eventually Landis gave up his original story and began pointing his finger at Lance Armstrong, the seven-time winner of the Tour de France. Armstrong had been accused before and was famous for his _____ and bullying response to anyone who suggested his performance had been enhanced by drugs. Landis's accusations were joined by the voices of others who had for years, _____ with some anxiety about how Armstrong would respond, accused Armstrong of taking drugs to win. At that point, there was just too much evidence for even Armstrong to deny, and he publicly apologized on television for betraying his fans and his family.

Identifying and Learning from Organizational Patterns

IN THIS CHAPTER, YOU WILL LEARN

- how to identify the most common patterns or methods of organization in paragraphs.

- how recognizing organizational patterns can focus your attention while you read.

- how knowing what's crucial to each pattern can help you with note-taking.

- how to respond to paragraphs that combine or mix organizational patterns.

"Making mental connections is our most crucial learning tool, the essence of human intelligence; to forge links; to go beyond the given; to see patterns. . . ."
—Marilyn Ferguson, writer

While no one rule exists for structuring information in writing, there are several organizational patterns or methods of development that make frequent appearances, especially in textbooks. This chapter introduces and describes seven of those patterns. Each one can be the **primary pattern** in a paragraph, that is, the one that organizes the majority of the details introduced. However, each of the seven can also team up with one or more of the others to communicate an author's ideas.

Pattern 1: Definition

Leaf through any textbook and, more often than not, you'll notice numerous definitions. In fact, as Chapter 2 showed with the word *filibuster*, textbook authors frequently devote whole paragraphs to defining the terms essential to their subject matter.

Usually, the definition pattern opens with the word or term being explained. That word is typically highlighted in some way, such as through boldface, color, or italics. The meaning then follows right on the heels of the highlighted word and is frequently introduced by phrases like *describes, refers to, is known* or *defined as, is called* or *termed.*

The remainder of the paragraph expands on the definition in one or more of the following ways: (1) gives an example of the word in context, (2) describes problems associated with the definition, (3) traces the history of the word, and (4) compares it to a word with a similar meaning.

To illustrate, here is a paragraph organized by the definition pattern. Note how the paragraph has been underlined and annotated to highlight both word and meaning.

Free association means you say anything that comes into your head.

Freud used free association as therapy.

Free Association. In **free association**, the client is instructed to say anything that crosses his or her mind, no matter how trivial or irrelevant it may seem. The father of psychoanalysis, Sigmund Freud, who first used free association as therapy, believed these free associations would eventually work their way toward uncovering deep-seated wishes and desires that reflect underlying conflicts. In classical psychoanalysis, the client lies on a couch with the analyst sitting off to the side, out of the client's direct view and saying little. By remaining detached, the analyst hopes to create an atmosphere that encourages the client to free associate. (Jeffrey Nevid, *Psychology: Concepts and Applications* 3e, © Cengage Learning.)

In this case, the paragraph is dedicated to defining the phrase "free association." In addition to an italicized title, the author uses boldface to highlight the term again, right before defining it. Thanks to these visual clues, the reader knows the phrase is important and is on the alert for its meaning.

Typically for the definition pattern, the author follows the word and meaning with a description of the context in which the word is used—a therapeutic setting. He also tells readers a little about the history: Sigmund Freud was the first to use free association as part of therapy.

Typical Topic Sentences

Sentences like these signal that conveying a definition is the goal of a paragraph:

1. **Sunshine laws** are regulations that try to ensure government meetings and reports are made available to the press.

2. The phrase "identification with the aggressor" describes victims who become dependent on those who hurt or oppress them.

3. One major category of waste is **solid waste**, which refers to any unwanted or discarded material we produce that is not liquid or gas. (G. Tyler Miller and Scott E. Spoolman, *Living in the Environment* 16e, © Cengage Learning.)

> ▶▶▶ **PATTERN POINTER**   To fully understand and remember a key definition, consider making a concept map like the one shown here.

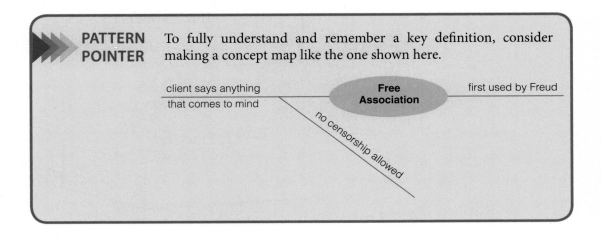

◆ **EXERCISE 1**   **Learning from the Definition Pattern**

DIRECTIONS   Read each passage and identify the term being defined. Paraphrase the definition. Then identify the method or methods the author uses to define the key term.

The paragraph focuses on the history of "white-collar crime," the term being defined.

Note that the definition is enclosed in quotation marks.

EXAMPLE

White-Collar Crime

[1]In the late 1930s, the distinguished criminologist Edwin Sutherland first used the phrase "white-collar crime" to describe the criminal activities of the rich and powerful. [2]He defined white-collar crime as "a crime committed by a person of respectability and high social status in the course of his occupation." [3]As Sutherland saw it, white-collar crime involved conspiracies by members of the wealthy classes to use their position in

Notice how the phrase "these actions" keeps the reader focused on the "conspiracies" that are another way of referring to white-collar crime.

commerce and industry for personal gain without regard to the law. [4]Often these actions were handled by civil courts because injured parties were more concerned with recovering their losses than with seeing the offenders punished criminally. [5]Consequently, Sutherland believed that the great majority of white-collar criminals did not become the subject of criminal study. [6]Yet the cost of white-collar crime is probably several times greater than all the crimes customarily regarded as the crime problem. (Larry Siegel, *Criminology* 10e, © Cengage Learning.)

WYNEM, DINEM & DINKEM INVESTMENTS

Brown.

"The accountants are here to cook the books, Mr. Blight."

The paragraph defines the following term or terms: white-collar crime

Restate the definition or definitions in your own words.

White-collar crime, as defined by Edwin Sutherland, refers to criminal behavior committed by people who, professionally, have powerful positions.

Which of the following methods does the author use to help define the key term or terms?

✓ The author gives an example of behavior or events that fit the definition.

✓ The author supplies a history of the word's development.

_____ The author describes a problem associated with applying the definition.

_____ The author compares the word defined to a word similar in meaning.

EXPLANATION The author tells readers who originally coined the term *white-collar crime* and provides the original definition along with a general example. *Note*: Paragraphs like this one that focus on the history of the term are commonly used to open a more general discussion of the term being defined.

1. [1]**Branding**, or the creation of a specific name to advertise a product, such as Quaker Oats for oatmeal or Coca-Cola for a soft drink, started to grow in importance in the late nineteenth century. [2]Prior to that time, manufacturers of flour and other basic products like candy, sugar, and beans sold merchandise in sacks without any names. [3]But over time manufacturers tried to distinguish their products from the products of others. [4]Henry Parsons Cromwell, for example, created the name *Quaker Oats* and launched an advertising campaign to extol the virtues of his product. [5]*Quaker Oats* was followed by a host of products with specific brand names, such as *Heinz ketchup, Borden's milk,* and *Pillsbury flour.*

(Adapted from Christopher Harper, *The New Mass Media*, Houghton Mifflin, 2002, p. 231.)

The paragraph defines the following term or terms: _____

Restate the definition or definitions in your own words.

_____

_____ .

Which of the following methods does the author use to help define the key term or terms?

_____ The author gives an example of behavior or events that fit the definition.

_____ The author supplies a history of the word's development.

_____ The author describes a problem associated with applying the definition.

_____ The author compares the word defined to a word similar in meaning.

2. [1]Created by the Constitution, the **Supreme Court** is the highest court in the land. [2]Although the original Supreme Court consisted of a chief justice and five associates, nine judges currently sit on the Supreme Court, and its decisions, once made, are irrevocable, or irreversible, making it the court of last resort. [3]Defendants displeased with a decision made by a lower court can appeal that ruling to the Supreme Court in the hopes of having it overturned. [4]In 2006, for instance, the Circuit Court of Appeals of New York found in favor of Evelyn Coke, a seventy-three-year-old employee in the home-care industry, who sued her employers for back payment of overtime compensation, which had been denied her based on a 1930s Department of Labor regulation created when home care for the elderly did not yet exist. [5]The court ruled that Coke deserved to be appropriately compensated for her overtime hours. [6]Coke's employers, Long Island Care at Home, appealed the decision to the Supreme Court in the hopes of having it reversed. [7]In 2007, the Supreme Court overruled the lower court's decision.

The paragraph defines the following term or terms: _____

Restate the definition or definitions in your own words.

_____

_____

Which of the following methods does the author use to help define the key term or terms?

_____ The author gives an example of behavior or events that fit the definition.

_____ The author supplies a history of the word's development.

_____ The author describes a problem associated with applying the definition.

_____ The author compares the word defined to a word similar in meaning.

REVIEWING THROUGH WRITING

When writers want to convey the formal definition or meaning of a word to readers, they often provide an example or examples of how the definition works or is applied in the real world. See if you can imitate that pattern by defining this term: *eureka moment* (also known as the *eureka effect*). Research it on the Web and collect several examples you think make good illustrations. Then write a paragraph that opens with a definition of the term followed by at least three examples.

Depending on how detailed you make the examples, the assignment may need to extend to two paragraphs.

◇ **Pattern 2: Process**

The process pattern orders events according to when they occurred and identifies the steps or stages necessary to explaining how something functions or works. To illustrate, here is a paragraph describing the digestion process. The passage is marked to highlight both the steps in the process and the kind of test question (TQ) such material might generate.

Digestive system prepares food to be turned into energy.

Four steps in process.

TQ: Explain the process of digestion.

In the human body, the digestive system breaks down food so that it can be used for energy. [1] As food enters the mouth, chewing, along with enzymes in the saliva, break it down into small pieces. [2] Next, the esophagus contracts and pushes the food into the stomach, where muscles, enzymes, and digestive acids turn the food into a thick liquid. That [3] liquid is emptied into the small intestine, where most of its nutrients are absorbed. [4] What remains travels to the large intestine, where water is removed from digested food and turned into waste.

Verbal Clues to the Pattern

Words such as *steps, stages, phases, procedures,* and *process* are all signs that you are dealing with a process pattern. So too are the transitions in the following list.

Transitions Identifying a Sequence of Steps ◆	Afterward	In the final stage
	At this point	In this stage
	By the time	Next
	Finally	Over time
	First; second; third	Then
	Gradually	Toward the end

Typical Topic Sentences

Sentences like the ones shown below are typical of the process pattern:

1. People who grieve for the loss of a loved one frequently pass through three basic stages of grief.

2. The bestowing of sainthood is a complex process.

3. Storing information in long-term memory requires several steps.

Flow Charts

Paragraphs organized according to the process pattern are often accompanied by flow charts. These are diagrams that use boxes or circles connected by arrows to map a sequence of steps, stages, or operations. For an example, read the following paragraph. Then look over the flow chart that accompanies it.

The word *process* in the opening sentence, along with the phrase "step by step" in the second, suggests the author will trace a sequence of steps.

The author traces the steps in the scientific process to prove his opening claim.

[1]There is nothing mysterious about the scientific process; we use it all the time to make decisions. [2]Here, for instance, is the scientific process applied, step by step, to an everyday situation. [3]*Observation*: You switch on your trusty flashlight and nothing happens. [4]*Question*: You ask yourself, Why in the world did the light not come on? [5]*Hypothesis*: Maybe the batteries are dead. [6]*Test the Hypothesis*: OK the new batteries are in, now all I have to do is turn it on. [7]*Result*: It still doesn't work. [8]*Revise the Hypothesis*: Maybe the bulb is burned out. [9]*Experiment*: Replace the bulb. [10]*Result*: Flashlight works when switched on. [11]*Conclusion*: The flashlight didn't turn on because the bulb was burned out. (Adapted from G. Tyler Miller, *Living in the Environment* 15e, © Cengage Learning.)

Repeated testing of hypotheses under controlled conditions produces scientific theories that explain events.

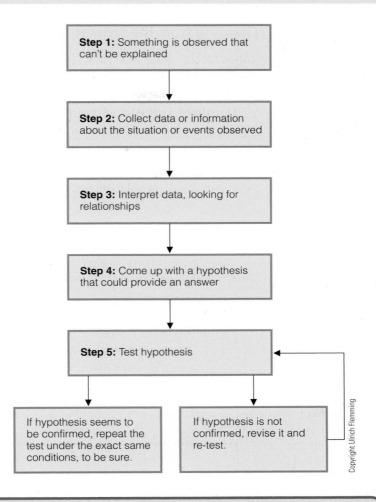

Step 1: Something is observed that can't be explained

Step 2: Collect data or information about the situation or events observed

Step 3: Interpret data, looking for relationships

Step 4: Come up with a hypothesis that could provide an answer

Step 5: Test hypothesis

If hypothesis seems to be confirmed, repeat the test under the exact same conditions, to be sure.

If hypothesis is not confirmed, revise it and re-test.

Copyright Ulrich Flemming

PATTERN POINTERS

1. Never get so caught up in the individual steps or stages that you lose sight of the larger process or sequence they describe. Keep thinking about what each step contributes to the whole.

2. If the process that the paragraph discusses seems hard to grasp, draw your own diagram or make a flow chart like the one shown with the sample paragraph.

3. During exam review, try to summarize, from memory, all the steps in a process, without missing a single one. Better still, see if you can draw your own flow chart.

◆ EXERCISE 2   Learning from the Process Pattern

DIRECTIONS   Read each paragraph. Then fill in the boxes in the accompanying flow chart. The first box of the first flow chart has been done for you.

1. Luminol and Bloodstains

[1]Tune in to television shows like the popular *CSI*, and you'll see plenty of crime-solving tools that are nothing but products of the writers' imaginations. [2]Luminol, however, isn't one of them. [3]Forensics specialists regularly use luminol to detect invisible bloodstains at crime scenes. [4]First, they close the curtains and turn off the lights. [5]Then they spray Luminol onto carpets, floors, walls, or furniture. [6]When the chemicals in Luminol combine with the iron in blood, the bloodstains glow greenish-blue. [7]Even miniscule amounts of blood will light up when the Luminol reacts to blood cells clinging to surfaces that have been washed with heavy-duty cleaning chemicals. [8]Investigators photograph or videotape the glowing patches, recording any sign of a pattern. [9]Finally, they collect samples and run additional tests to be completely sure that the substance causing the glow was indeed blood since Luminol can also produce a glow when the substance comes in contact with some plant matter and cleaning products.

Main Idea   Forensic specialists use Luminol to detect bloodstains at a crime scene.

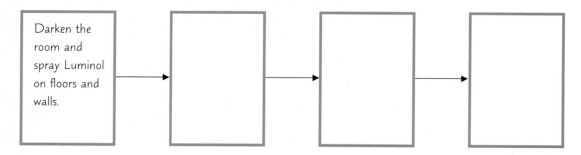

Darken the room and spray Luminol on floors and walls.

2. The Heimlich Maneuver

[1]You can save the life of a choking victim by performing the Heimlich maneuver. [2]If a person suddenly cannot breathe, cough, or speak, the person's airway is probably blocked by something that needs to be removed. [3]To perform the Heimlich maneuver, stand behind the victim and make a fist with one hand. [4]Then reach your arms around the person from behind. [5]Place your fist against the person's belly just above the belly button and below the rib cage. [6]Next, cover your fist with your

other hand and press into the belly with a quick, upward thrust. [7]If the object in the person's throat doesn't come flying out, perform another thrust. [8]Repeat thrusts over and over until you dislodge the object. [9]At the same time, yell for help and tell someone to call 911.

Main Idea The Heimlich maneuver can save the life of a person who is choking.

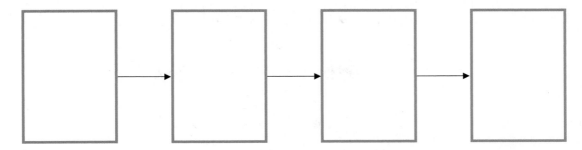

CHECK YOUR UNDERSTANDING

Fill in the blanks in the following sentences.

1. The definition pattern usually opens _____.

2. In the definition pattern, the word or term being defined is _____
   _____
   _____.

3. The process pattern orders events _____. The object of the
   process pattern is _____
   _____.

4. When you are reading a passage organized according to the process pattern, you
   should never _____
   _____.

5. While you are reading a paragraph organized according to the process pattern, keep
   thinking about _____.

REVIEWING THROUGH WRITING

Use the Web to learn about the steps that go into making or achieving the following:

1. water-processed decaffeinated coffee beans
2. glaciers
3. legal arbitration

Decide which process you want to describe. Then write a paragraph in which you (1) start off with an introductory sentence describing the final result of the process under discussion, e.g., "We handle paper money every day but seldom think about how it gets manufactured," and (2) use the process pattern to describe the steps that go into making or achieving that final result. "There are, however, six basic steps that go into making paper money."

Pattern 3: Sequence of Dates and Events

Authors who write about history and government frequently use a sequence of dates and events to explain or argue their overall point or message. The dates and events are presented according to the order in which they occurred. Here's an example.

TQ: What are the dates of the Mexican-American War?

TQ: What event helped to encourage a war with Mexico?

TQ: What treaty ended the Mexican-American War?

The Democrat James Polk became president of the United States in 1844. From the very beginning of his presidency, Polk made it clear that he intended to expand the boundaries of the United States. By 1846, he had ordered General Zachary Taylor to take troops into Mexican territory. On April 24 of the same year, the Mexican military fired on Taylor's troops, and war between the United States and Mexico began, even though Congress had not yet officially declared it. By 1847, U.S. troops had arrived in Mexico City and were claiming victory. (The opening phrase in the Marine Corps anthem—"From the halls of Montezuma"—is a reference to the arrival of those troops in Mexico's capital.) In 1848, Mexico and the United States signed the Treaty of Guadalupe Hidalgo,*** which ceded a portion of Mexican land that today includes Arizona, Utah, Nevada, and New Mexico to the United States. Polk had his wish: He had expanded and redefined

U.S. borders. But in an effort to assuage* the war's critics—and there were many who considered the war with Mexico unjust—the U.S. government paid the Mexican government $15 million.

Notice how many sentences in this paragraph open with dates. That's a sure sign that the author is using the sequence of dates and events pattern to organize information.

> **WEB QUEST   Polk and Manifest Destiny**
>
> **What does the term *manifest destiny* mean?**
>
> _____
>
> _____
>
> **What does the term have to do with Polk's decision to go to war?**
>
> _____
>
> _____

Transition Clues

Sequence of dates and events paragraphs are likely to use time-order transitions like those listed in the following box.

Time-Order Transitions ◆		
	After	
	During the period between	Between _____[†] and _____
	By the end of	On _____ of that year
	At the end of	_____ year(s) later
	In the years that followed	When _____ ended

Typical Topic Sentences

Along with numerous dates and events, the time-order transitions listed above are clues to the sequence of dates and events pattern. So, too, are topic sentences like those you see here.

---

*assuage: calm or soothe.
[†]Blanks indicate where dates, years, or numbers would go.

1. From 1753 to 1815, Native Americans cooperated and fought with or tried to avoid the Spanish, French, British, and Anglo-Americans who had intruded on their homelands. (Paul Boyer et al., *The Enduring Vision* 5e, © Cengage Learning.)

2. British children's writer Frances Hodgson Burnett started her career in 1853 at the age of four by telling stories to her siblings; by the time she died in 1924, she had written fifty-two books and thirteen plays.

3. Mexican singer Jenni Rivera died in a plane crash in 2012 at the age of forty-three, but in her brief time on earth, she accomplished a great deal both professionally and personally.

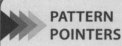

PATTERN POINTERS

1. Never lose sight of the main idea the dates and events are there to explain. Use the main idea to determine if all the dates and events are equally important.

2. If you think the paragraph is hard to understand and the sequence of dates and events difficult to follow, try making a time line like the one shown below.

3. When taking notes, make sure to line up the dates as shown in the sample notes. That will make the sequence of events easier to follow and remember.

Notes Based on a Time Line

Newly elected Polk has his heart set on expanding U.S. boundaries.

1844	Polk becomes president
	Wants to expand U.S. borders
1846	Orders Taylor into Mexican territory
April 24	Mexican troops fire on Taylor's troops
	War unofficially began
1847	U.S. troops in Mexico City claiming victory
1848	Mexico and U.S. sign Treaty of Guadalupe
	Hidalgo, ceding huge portion of Mexican land to U.S.

ALLUSION ALERT

The Garden of Eden

In the Bible, the Garden of Eden is the lush paradise where Adam and Eve are free to wander until they fall victim to Satan's trickery. Thus references to the Garden of Eden or Eden have come to suggest a place that is lush and beautiful—for instance, "With the passage of the Homestead Act, many Americans went west expecting an Eden, but what they found was dry, dusty desert."

◆ **EXERCISE 3**   **Learning from the Sequence of Dates and Events Pattern**

DIRECTIONS   Read each paragraph. Underline the topic sentence. Then paraphrase it and list the supporting details, making sure to use chronological order for the crucial dates and events. Abbreviate and paraphrase as much as possible without losing the original meaning. *Note*: Your paraphrasing here should be informal, as it would be for your reading notes.

The introductory sentence provides background about how break dancing got started with singer James Brown.

James Brown, however, disappears as the real main idea takes center stage.

The remaining sentences prove that "break dancing is far from dead."

Note how many of the opening transitional phrases provide a specific time frame.

EXAMPLE   [1]Break dancing first came to public attention in 1969 when the legendary James Brown performed the song "Get on the Good Foot," while performing wild, athletic dance moves that drew shouts and applause from his audience. [2]<u>Precisely because it's been around for so long, critics have been predicting the demise of break dancing for decades, yet break dancing is far from dead no matter what its detractors say.</u> [3]In the 1970s, the new style continued to develop as African-American and Latino young people incorporated movements from the martial arts, gymnastics, and acrobatics into their dancing. [4]By the 1980s, films like *Beat Street*, *Breakin'*, and *Flashdance* led to break dancing's entry into mainstream popular culture. [5]Because the media lost interest in the craze by the late 1980s, much of America assumed that the fad was over. [6]Yet in the late twentieth and early twenty-first centuries, break dancers were doing more daring moves than ever before while performing on television commercials as well as in music videos and competitions. [7]Now a new generation of young break dancers is spinning, kicking, and back-flipping to the beat. [8]The annual Battle of the Year international break-dancing competition is still held, and it attracts thousands of young fans, not to speak of hits on YouTube. [9]In 2012 Chris Brown starred in the movie *Battle of the Year*, which showed yet again that break dancing is alive and well and not to be performed by the faint of heart.

Break dancing is alive and well, and the moves are harder than ever to execute.

Stephen Stickler/Stone+/Getty Images

Main Idea	Break dancing is still popular no matter what its critics say.
Supporting Details	1. 1969: James Brown's song "Get on the Good Foot" gives break dancing its start.
	2. 1970s: African-Americans and Latinos incorporate moves from different sources, e.g., martial arts, gymnastics.
	3. 1980s: Movies like *Beat Street* popularize break dancing.
	4. Late 80s: Break dancing seems to fade but made a comeback.
	5. Now there's a new generation.
	—Chris Brown's movie in 2012, *Battle of the Year*, celebrates break dancing.

EXPLANATION As they should, the notes paraphrase the topic sentence and include the dates and events needed to prove that "break dancing is far from dead." *Note*: In this case, the introductory sentence also provides support for the main idea, so it appears as a supporting detail.

1. [1]In its earliest days, the United States might have started out as a melting pot of nationalities, but, by the 1960s, it had become a nation of the native-born, and that was no accident. [2]For decades, legislation had been systematically reducing immigration to a trickle.

[3]In 1882, the Chinese Exclusion Act, borne of economic anxiety and racism, halted Chinese immigration for the next sixty years. [4]A little over forty years later, the Immigration Act of 1924 dammed up the stream of new immigrants from Italy, Greece, Poland, and other Eastern European countries by establishing small quotas that severely limited the number of people from each of those countries that could be admitted yearly. [5]During the 1930s, the Immigration and Naturalization Service (NIS) recorded only 500,000 new arrivals. [6]Even during the 1940s, despite the repeal of the Chinese Exclusion Act and several congressional acts providing sanctuary for World War I refugees, just one million immigrants arrived in the United States. (Adapted from Joseph Conlin, *The American Past* 9e, vol. 2. © Cengage Learning.)

Main Idea

_____

_____

Supporting Details

_____

_____

_____

_____

_____

_____

_____

2. [1]In 1584, an English fort and settlement with more than 100 men was established on an island off the coast of present-day North Carolina. [2]The British settlers named the island Roanoke, describing it as an "American Eden." [3]However, they abandoned it within a year because of bad relations with the Native Americans already living there. [4]In 1587, another group of British colonists arrived on the island and, within a month, one of the women on the island gave birth to the first child born in the New World, naming her Virginia Dare. [5]Only a week after the birth, the baby's grandfather, Captain John White, returned to England for supplies. [6]Due to conflicts with

Spain, White did not return to Roanoke until 1590. [7]But upon his return, to his horror and shock, there was nothing left of the former colony. [8]The only signs of human presence were the letters "CRO" and "CROATAN" carved on two trees. [9]To this day, no one knows what happened to the colonists White left behind on Roanoke Island.

Main Idea

_____

_____

Supporting Details

_____

_____

_____

_____

_____

_____

_____

 REVIEWING THROUGH WRITING

Although you can certainly choose your own topics, the following are three possible chains of events to explore in writing: (1) how Joan of Arc went from being a poor farm maid to a condemned prisoner, (2) the events leading up to and including the Triangle Shirtwaist Factory fire, (3) the bombing of Pearl Harbor and America's entry into World War II. Make sure your topic sentence sets out the chain of events you are intent on exploring: "In 1972 Washington was rocked by a scandal that would end up being dubbed 'Watergate.'" And use sentence openings that help your reader understand how events unfolded over time: "Following the break-in at the Watergate Hotel, the Nixon administration tried to stonewall the press."

Pattern 4: Simple Listing

In passages using the process or sequence of dates and events patterns, the order of events and steps is extremely important. The writer who describes a process is not about to put the last step first or vice versa. The same is true for the sequence of dates and events pattern. No writer of a history text tracing the events in the Civil War is going to describe the battle of Antietam (1862) after the Battle of Gettysburg (1863).

In the simple listing pattern, however, all the major details are equally important and the order in which they occur doesn't matter. Thus they can be switched around to suit the writer. A writer who uses the simple listing pattern mainly wants to identify certain skills, factors, studies, reasons, and so on, related to a particular topic or issue—making the order in which they appear irrelevant. Look, for example, at the two paragraphs that follow. The content of each is the same. The order is not.

The topic sentence focuses the reader's attention on the "symptoms" of eating disorders.

The symptoms do not have to be presented in the order in which they occurred.

The word *victims* along with the pronouns *they* and *those* keep both the victims and their symptoms front and center in the reader's mind.

Paragraph 1

¹Victims of eating disorders display several distinct symptoms. ²They are preoccupied* with their weight or their physical appearance and often exhibit signs of low self-esteem. ³They are inclined to suffer from anxiety, moodiness, or depression and may also diet obsessively or avoid eating altogether. ⁴Or just the opposite, they may overeat, purge, and then start eating again. ⁵In either case, the victims exhibit rapid weight loss or pronounced weight changes. ⁶Those suffering from eating disorders may also exhibit compulsive* behaviors such as hoarding food or eating specific foods only on certain days. ⁷They are likely to wear baggy clothes to hide their bodies and withdraw from others, avoiding social situations that include food. ⁸Some victims even isolate themselves completely. ⁹Those in the grip of an eating disorder are likely to experience faintness, dizziness, and difficulty concentrating. ¹⁰Problems such as constipation or diarrhea are also common.

In Paragraph 1, the author announces that eating disorders have several symptoms. Expecting readers to ask, "What are those symptoms?" the author describes them in detail. Nothing in the paragraph, however, suggests that any one symptom is more important than the others

---

*preoccupied: overly concerned with something; also, absorbed in thought.
*compulsive: involuntary, uncontrollable.

or precedes the others in time. Thus, the author is free to list them in any way she thinks appropriate. Notice now how easily the order can be changed without changing the paragraph's meaning.

Paragraph 2

The writer lists the specific symptoms before introducing a topic sentence at the very end.

The order of the symptoms is quite different from the previous paragraph.

The topic sentence now comes at the end, another typical topic sentence location for the simple listing method.

¹Victims of eating disorders are likely to experience faintness, dizziness, concentration difficulties, and bowel problems like constipation or diarrhea. ²They are inclined to wear baggy clothes to hide their bodies and tend to withdraw from others, avoiding in particular any social situation involving food. ³Some completely isolate themselves and may exhibit obsessive behaviors such as hoarding food or eating specific foods only on certain days. ⁴They may diet obsessively and avoid eating, or just the opposite, they may overeat and purge; in either case, they exhibit rapid weight loss or pronounced weight changes. ⁵Often suffering from anxiety, moodiness, or depression, they are preoccupied with their weight and physical appearance and are likely to exhibit signs of low self-esteem. ⁶Although there are other less common symptoms, the ones listed here are the typical signs of an eating disorder.

Typical Topic Sentences

Topic sentences typical of the simple listing pattern almost always (note the qualifier *almost*) contain category words like those listed here.

advantages	drawbacks	inventions	symptoms
benefits	elements	parts	traits
cases	efforts	policies	virtues
changes	examples	principles	values
characteristics	factors	qualities	
components	ideas	roles	
decisions	illustrations	studies	

Topic sentences that suggest the simple listing pattern are also likely to include counting words and phrases like *several, numerous, many kinds of, just a few,* and *a number of.*

1. These are just a few of the numerous inventions that Dean Kamen has patented in the last two decades. (Note the wording, which is typical of simple listing topic sentences appearing at the very end of a paragraph.)

2. Before global warming threatened the very existence of polar bears, several inborn traits helped the bears survive and even thrive in the Arctic.

3. In places like China, Vietnam, Egypt, and Algeria, numerous efforts are being made to censor, even silence, bloggers who speak out against repressive governments.

PATTERN POINTERS

1. If the topic sentence contains a general category word that needs to be specifically itemized to be meaningful—for example, *statistics*, *studies*, *reasons*—use that word to guide your selection of major details. Any sentence that introduces a new case, characteristic, etc., is worth remembering and/or recording in your notes. Any sentence that doesn't is probably not especially significant.

2. The information in the simple listing pattern is often so loosely connected, the different details can be hard to remember. To help remember the details listed in this pattern, think about including a visual aid in your notes, perhaps making a concept map like the one shown below.

moodiness   **Signs that an eating disorder is present**   baggy clothes

overeating and purging   low self-esteem and anxiety

weight fluctuations

◆ **EXERCISE 4**   **Learning from the Simple Listing Pattern**

DIRECTIONS Read each paragraph. Then identify the topic sentence and the best paraphrase of that sentence by circling the appropriate letters. Write the crucial word or phrase from the topic sentence in the blanks and list the qualities, traits, etc., that clarify it.

The words "those shown here are the five most common" indicate that order is not critical to the paragraph.

The supporting details identifying personality disorders could be moved around without causing a major communication breakdown between reader and writer.

EXAMPLE [1]In total, the *Diagnostic and Statistical Manual of Mental Disorders*, a handbook for mental-health professionals, identifies ten different personality disorders; those shown here are the five most common. [2]People with a **narcissistic personality disorder** have an inflated or grandiose* sense of themselves, while those suffering from a **paranoid personality disorder** show a high degree of suspiciousness or mistrust. [3]Those with a **schizoid personality disorder** have little if any interest in social relationships, display a limited range of emotional expressions, and are perceived as distant and aloof. [4]Those with a **borderline personality disorder** tend to have stormy relationships with others, dramatic mood swings, and an unstable self-image. [5]**Antisocial personality disorder** (APD) is the most widely studied and is characterized by a complete disregard for all social conventions, or rules. [6]In the United States, personality disorders affect 10 to 15 percent of the population.

1. The topic sentence is

   (a.) sentence 1.

   b. sentence 2.

   c. sentence 3.

2. The crucial word or phrase in the topic sentence is <u>the five most common.</u>

3. The following supporting details help clarify and explain that word or phrase.

   1. Narcissistic personality disorder: believe that they are remarkably important to the rest of the world.

   2. Paranoid personality disorder: think everyone is trying to do them harm.

   3. Schizoid personality disorder: aren't interested in relationships and are limited in the emotions they can express.

---

*grandiose: having an exaggerated sense of one's importance or influence.

4. Borderline personality disorder: unstable self-image, wild mood swings and difficult relationships.

5. Antisocial personality disorder: couldn't care less about society's rules.

EXPLANATION   Because the topic sentence mentions five common personality disorders, notes on this paragraph would have to list five different types along with a brief description of each.

1. [1]New words and phrases are added to the English language all the time. [2]For instance, the phrase *muffin top*, used to refer to an unsightly roll around the waist of either sex, made it into the *2011 Oxford English Dictionary*. [3]It was followed in 2012 by the phrase *Tiger mother*, which refers to mothers who set extremely high standards for their children, and the word *illiterati*, which describes people who take pride in being ignorant. [4]The word *mondegreen* has also earned dictionary status. [5]It refers to the misunderstanding and continued misstatement of words or phrases that are repeatedly said or sung. [6]Kids, for example, often think that the sentence "I pledge allegiance to the flag" is "I led the pigeons to the flag." [7]In those dictionaries trying hard to be cutting edge, you'll also now find phrases like *Christmas bogus*, used to sarcastically identify the lack of a bonus from an employer along with *virtual Friday*, used to identify the last day of school or work thanks to an extended weekend.

   1. The topic sentence is

      a. sentence 1.

      b. sentence 2.

      c. sentence 3.

   2. The best paraphrase of that topic sentence is

      a. English is always adopting new words and dropping old ones.

      b. The *Oxford English Dictionary* tries hard to be cutting edge and adopts all of the latest slang expressions.

      c. New words are always being added to the English language.

      d. What makes the English language great is its ability to absorb new words.

3. The crucial word or phrase in the topic sentence is _____

_____.

4. Paraphrase the supporting details that help clarify and explain that word or phrase.

_____

_____

_____

_____

_____

_____

_____

What Do You Think?
◆

Do parents who demand the very best from their children have a positive or a negative influence on their children's performance?

2. [1]Is texting destroying the English language? [2]On the contrary, some observers believe that texting involves a range of conscious, stylistic choices. [3]As linguist Anne Curzan wrote in the March 2013 *Chronicle of Higher Education*, "Anyone who says that text language is chaotic isn't paying enough attention to the system of rules that users have developed to move real-time conversations into written form." [4]In a survey of her students, Curzan found that experienced users of what she calls Electronically Mediated Communication (EMC) use two double colons to indicate that the action described is currently going on (::getting anxious::). [5]If the person texting is in a particular hurry, then asterisks will also do (*Getting bored waiting*). [6]And if the person on the other cell phone is taking too long to text back, well, then an ellipsis plus a question mark is the way to respond (. . . ?). [7]While those not much given to texting might assume that LOL is still the way to indicate laughter, the more sophisticated know that LOL is now a way of saying that a message is *meant* to be funny. [8]Indicating laughter, however, requires at least three ha's (hahaha). [9]There are also subtle differences that can be conveyed with the two letters

o and *k*. ¹⁰Simple agreement about a plan is "ok." ¹¹But real excitement over the plan is "ok!" and the thought that the proposed plan might not turn out well is "ok…" ¹²You can also convey a wide range of emotions with just a few text symbols, for instance <> for amazed, :-o for appalled, and :-X for big sloppy kiss.

1. The topic sentence is _____.

2. The best paraphrase of that topic sentence is

    a. The English language can only be improved by the popularity of texting.

    b. Text messaging symbols are always changing.

    c. People who text use many different symbols to convey a wide range of ideas.

    d. Emotional subtlety is not possible in a text message.

3. The crucial word or phrase in that topic sentence is _____

    _____.

4. Paraphrase the supporting details that help clarify and explain that word or phrase.

    _____

    _____

    _____

    _____

    _____

    _____

    _____

    _____

    _____

    _____

    _____

REVIEWING THROUGH WRITING

All of the following topics lend themselves to the simple listing pattern. Pick one you think you can write about (again, feel free to choose your own topic): (1) things you should never do at an office party, (2) ways to build or break a friendship, (3) holiday traditions in your family, (4) the joys and/or drawbacks of pet ownership. Whichever topic you choose, remember that you need an opening or closing sentence that sums up the *mistakes*, *ways*, *drawbacks*, etc., that you list as supporting details.

Pattern 5: Classification

In the classification pattern, too, the order in which information is presented is unimportant. The significant difference between simple listing and classification is that paragraphs using the classification pattern always make the same point: They tell readers how some larger group can be broken down into smaller subgroups, or classes, each with its own set of specific characteristics. Here's an illustration.

Hippocrates classified people according to the four fluids in their body.

TQ: Explain Hippocrates' system of classifications.

Like other doctors of his time, the Greek physician Hippocrates believed that the human body consisted of four humors, or fluids: black bile, yellow bile, blood, and phlegm. Hippocrates' contribution was to classify human beings according to the predominant fluid in their bodies. Persons with an excess of black bile were labelled [1]melancholic and presumed to be depressed and pessimistic. The [2]choleric, had an excess of yellow bile and were considered quick-tempered and irritable, while the [3]sanguine had an excess of blood and were expected to be cheerful and optimistic. The [4]phlegmatic, possessing excess phlegm, were assumed to be cool and unemotional. Although the theory of the four humors is no longer taken seriously, the terms used to describe the four different personalities still exist.

Although most classification paragraphs have a topic sentence that names the number of categories, be aware that this is not always the case. Sometimes the author just describes the subgroups of a larger category and leaves it to readers to total up the number of categories mentioned.

Typical Topic Sentences

Topic sentences like those that follow are clues to the classification pattern. Note the presence of verb phrases such as "are classified" and "can be divided." Such phrases are typical of this pattern.

> 1. Burns are classified into three different types based on degree of severity.
> 2. The earth is divided into three layers, each with its own composition and temperature.
> 3. Web users fall into three distinct groups.

PATTERN POINTERS

1. Classification patterns can be quite lengthy. Don't, however, let the length intimidate you. Instead look for the larger group being divided along with the number and names of the categories, if names are present. Then search out the key characteristics of each group.

2. If the author explains how the categories are created—for example, "Burns are classified into three different types based on degree of severity"—make sure you remember and/or record the method of classification as well as the categories that are the end result.

3. Although most classification paragraphs have a topic sentence that names the number of categories, this is not always the case. Sometimes the author just describes the subgroups of a larger category and leaves it to readers to total up the number of categories. Make sure your notes record the number of subgroups.

4. The classification pattern differs from the simple listing pattern in two ways: (1) It always explains how some larger group can be broken down into smaller subgroups, and (2) the subgroups always account for the entire larger group described.

5. If you are having difficulty sorting out the categories in a paragraph using the classification pattern, try making a chart like the one that follows:

Three different kinds of burns based on severity		
First-degree burns	**Second-degree burns**	**Third-degree burns**
1. Burns are red and sensitive. 2. Burns affect the outer layer of skin and cause pain and swelling. 3. The skin may peel or appear whitish; it can also become clammy, as in sunburn.	1. Burns affect the epidermis and underlying dermis. 2. Burns cause redness, swelling, and blisters. 3. Burns often affect sweat glands and hair follicles.	1. Burns affect the epidermis, dermis, and hypodermis. 2. Visible burn areas may be numb, but the victim may still complain of pain. 3. Healing is slow and scarring present.

CHECK YOUR UNDERSTANDING

Explain how the simple listing and the classification pattern are both similar and different.

_____

_____

_____

_____

_____

◆ **EXERCISE 5**   **Learning from the Classification Pattern**

DIRECTIONS   Read each paragraph. Then fill in the blanks and list the subgroups along with brief descriptions of each one. *Note*: Paraphrase as much as possible.

1. ¹According to one theory of human behavior, nine different personality types exist. ²The *reformer* likes to create order and believes that he or she knows the right way of doing things in an imperfect world desperately in need of fixing. ³The *helper* feels a strong sense of personal responsibility for others and is fulfilled when lending a hand to those in need. ⁴The *motivator* places the highest value on the kind of success that can be recognized and acknowledged by others in the world. ⁵The *romantic* sees him- or herself as different from the rest of society and longs to be considered unique. ⁶The *thinker* doesn't want recognition. ⁷All he or she wants is a quiet place to think. ⁸The *skeptic* questions all authority even when it gets him or her into trouble, which it usually does. ⁹The *enthusiast* sees the world as a constant source of wonder and enjoys life's pleasures. ¹⁰Much like the reformer, the *leader* is convinced the world is heading toward ruin and is, therefore, eager to provide the necessary guidance. ¹¹The *vpeacemaker* believes passionately in harmony and is committed to resolving all conflict. (Source of information: www.9types.com.)

1. _____ is the larger group being subdivided into

   _____ smaller subgroups.

2. Does the author explain the basis for the classification? _____

   If so, what is the basis for the classification? _____

3. List and describe the subgroups in your own words.

   _____

   _____

   _____

   _____

   _____

   _____

   _____

   _____

   _____

   _____

2. [1]Fish are vertebrates[†] that live in water and breathe with gills. [2]Based on their skeletons, the 25,000 species of fish can be broken up into three main groups. [3]The *agnatha* class are the most "primitive." [4]They lack both a jaw and a bony skeleton. [5]Examples would be lamprey eels and hagfish. [6]Lacking true bones, fish in this group are extraordinarily flexible. [7]The hagfish, for instance, can tie itself into a knot. [8]Although their ancestors had real bones, the *chondrichthyes* have a skeleton made of cartilage. [9]These fish—sharks, skates, rays, and ratfish—have loosely attached lower jaws with big and very noticeable teeth. [10]The *osteichthyes* are called bony fish because their skeletons are made of calcium. [11]Catfish and trout belong to this group. [12]Like all bony fish, they are fast-moving and able to maneuver with ease. [13]Highly adaptable* creatures, they often have very specialized mouths, which help them to explore underwater resources with great efficiency.

1. _____ is the larger group being subdivided into

   _____ smaller subgroups.

2. Does the author explain the basis for the classification? _____

   If so, what is the basis for the classification? _____

3. List and describe the subgroups in your own words.

   _____

   _____

   _____

   _____

   _____

   _____

   _____

[†]vertebrates: creatures with a backbone.
*adaptable: able to adjust to new conditions, capable of being modified to fit the need or context.

REVIEWING THROUGH WRITING

Write a paragraph in which you use the classification method of development to describe one of the following: (1) kinds of ads on television, (2) main reasons why we overeat, (3) dancing styles, (4) types of movie monsters, (5) main causes of breakups, and (6) the key roles friends play in our lives. Make your topic sentence identify the number of categories and give each subgroup a name.

Pattern 6: Comparison and Contrast

In all kinds of textbooks, authors are likely to compare (discuss similarities) and/or contrast (cite differences). Sometimes, in fact, writers devote an entire chapter section to pointing out the similarities and differences between two topics, but more often the comparison and contrast pattern is confined to organizing a single paragraph, for example:

Assertive people stand up for their rights; aggressive people trample the rights of others.

Uncle Ralph assertive not aggressive.

TQ: Explain the difference between assertive and aggressive behavior and give examples for each.

Although assertive and aggressive behaviors sometimes share external characteristics, they are actually quite different in effect and intent. Assertive behavior involves standing up for your rights and expressing your thoughts and feelings in a direct, appropriate way that does not violate the rights of others. It is a matter of getting the other person to understand your viewpoint. People who exhibit assertive behavior skills are able to handle conflict situations with ease and assurance while maintaining good interpersonal relations. In contrast, aggressive behavior involves expressing your thoughts and feelings and defending your rights in a way that openly violates the rights of others. Those exhibiting aggressive behavior seem to believe that the rights of others must be subservient to theirs. Thus they have a difficult time maintaining good interpersonal relations. They are likely to interrupt, talk fast, ignore others, and use sarcasm or other forms of verbal abuse to maintain control. (Adapted from Barry Reece and Rhonda Brandt, *Effective Human Relations in Organizations* 7e. © Cengage Learning.)

The comparison and contrast paragraph divides into two parts. If you diagrammed it, it would look like this.

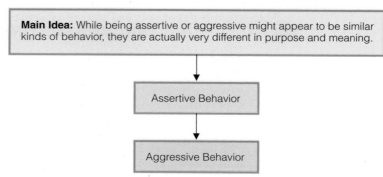

Main Idea: While being assertive or aggressive might appear to be similar kinds of behavior, they are actually very different in purpose and meaning.

Assertive Behavior

Aggressive Behavior

A paragraph like the one shown on page 211 with its two topics—assertive and aggressive behavior—and its emphasis on the difference between them has comparison and contrast written all over it. It all but cries out for you to predict a test question asking for a description of how the two topics are similar and/or different.

But paragraphs organized by the comparison and contrast pattern don't necessarily focus first on one topic and then the other as the paragraph shown above does. Sometimes the writer moves back and forth between the two topics, for example:

The opening sentence already suggests this idea will be challenged.

Sentence 2 intensifies the shift away from the opening point. Sentence 3 hones in on the real point of the reading.

Sentence 4 identifies the basic difference and the remaining sentences alternate illustrating the two types of rules.

[1]In casual conversation, we are likely to treat the words *morals* and *ethics* as synonyms. [2]But they aren't really synonymous. [3]Morals and ethics differ in subtle but important ways. [4]***Morals*** are personal rules about good or virtuous behavior, and they can contradict or undermine ***ethics***, which are rules defined by the larger group or society to which an individual belongs. [5]For instance, an attorney is ethically bound to defend a client to the best of his or her ability. [6]Yet that attorney, upon discovering that the client is actually guilty of a horrific crime, may feel immoral about providing the client with a good defense. [7]Similarly, the pharmacist who refuses to fill a prescription for a birth control pill is ignoring professional ethics in favor of obeying what are considered moral rules. [8]On an individual level, moral rules are also less subject to change than ethical rules are. [9]For instance, people who believe it's immoral to eat the flesh of animals don't usually change their mind about that belief, even if they resume eating meat. [10]Both morals and ethics, however, are strongly influenced by the cultural context. [11]While an American might consider it both moral and ethical to keep a secret revealed by a friend or relative, someone in Afghanistan might feel morally and ethically bound to reveal the secrets if they involved the betrayal of family honor.

Diagram this paragraph, and it would look something like this:

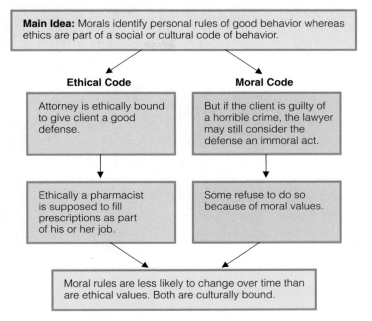

Typical Topic Sentences

Sentences like the ones that follow are also clues to the comparison and contrast pattern. Note the consistent presence of two topics (see underscores).

1. In the wild west of the nineteenth century, the life of a cowboy was not all that different from that of a cowgirl, and both lived a hard, hand-to-mouth existence.

2. The ancient Aztec civilization of Mexico and the early Incan civilization of Peru, both of which flourished in the sixteenth century, had very sophisticated cultures with similar beliefs and norms.

3. Falling in love and being infatuated may feel much the same, but there are crucial differences between love and infatuation that make confusing the two a mistake with huge consequences.

In Wyoming, Ellen Watson, whom the newspapers dubbed "Cattle Kate," was lynched for rustling cattle right alongside her husband.

Transitions

In addition to topic sentences like the three above, the following transitions are also clues to the comparison and contrast pattern.

Transitions That Introduce Similarity ◆	Along the same lines By the same token In like manner In much the same vein In the same manner	Just as Just like Likewise Similarly

Transitions That Signal a Difference ◆	And yet But Conversely Despite that fact However In contrast In opposition In reality	Nevertheless Nonetheless On the contrary On the one hand On the other hand Still Unfortunately Whereas

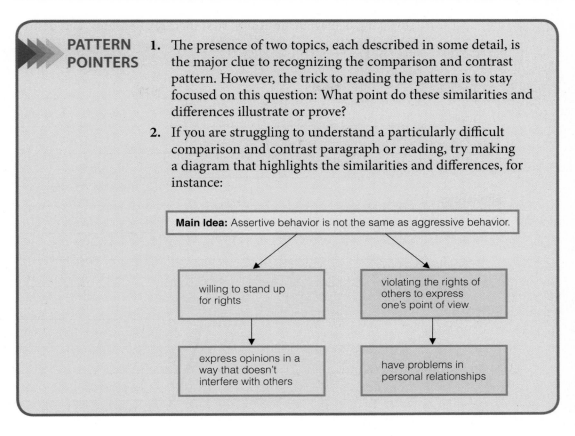

PATTERN POINTERS

1. The presence of two topics, each described in some detail, is the major clue to recognizing the comparison and contrast pattern. However, the trick to reading the pattern is to stay focused on this question: What point do these similarities and differences illustrate or prove?

2. If you are struggling to understand a particularly difficult comparison and contrast paragraph or reading, try making a diagram that highlights the similarities and differences, for instance:

> **Main Idea:** Assertive behavior is not the same as aggressive behavior.
>
> | willing to stand up for rights | violating the rights of others to express one's point of view |
> | express opinions in a way that doesn't interfere with others | have problems in personal relationships |

◆ **EXERCISE 6**   **Learning from the Comparison and Contrast Pattern**

DIRECTIONS   Read each paragraph. Identify the two topics. Then paraphrase the topic sentence along with the similarities and/or differences between the topics.

1. [1]Social drinking differs significantly from alcoholism. [2]Social drinkers control their drinking and consume alcohol in limited amounts. [3]Alcoholics, in contrast, can't control their drinking and consume alcohol in ever-increasing amounts. [4]They often drink until they pass out. [5]While social drinkers sip, alcoholics gulp. [6]Social drinkers drink to have more fun at social gatherings. [7]Alcoholics drink alone as a way of reducing stress or avoiding problems. [8]Social drinkers don't usually think or talk about drinking; alcoholics are preoccupied with how and when they will drink again. [9]Finally, social drinkers do not experience physical, psychological, or job-related problems caused by their drinking. [10]Alcoholics, however, often let

drinking damage their health, ruin their relationships, and destroy their careers. (Adapted from Douglas Bernstein *Essentials of Psychology* 5e, © Cengage Learning.)

Topic 1 _____

Topic 2 _____

Main Idea _____

_____

Similarities _____

_____

_____

_____

Differences _____

_____

_____

_____

2. [1]The use of chimpanzees in medical research has always been a controversial issue mainly because chimps are so remarkably similar to humans. [2]For example, the physical proportions for the body parts of both humans and chimpanzees are relatively close. [3]Both species also have similar hands, feet, legs, and facial features. [4]In fact, the DNA of humans and chimpanzees is 98.4 percent identical. [5]In addition to these physical similarities, chimpanzee societies are like human ones in a variety of ways. [6]Human beings establish political systems and fight wars. [7]Likewise, groups of chimpanzees form hierarchies with high-ranking and low-ranking chimps, and they too engage in warfare against other groups. [8]Moreover, observation of chimps in the wild has confirmed that chimpanzees display emotions similar to those humans experience. [9]Humans grieve for lost loved ones, and chimps do the same. [10]In one case, a healthy young chimp seemed to fall into a severe depression after his mother's death. [11]He eventually stopped eating and died. [12]Research on the brain suggests that emotions like grief arise from ancient parts of the brain found in both species.

Because of their similarities to humans, chimps are often used in research.

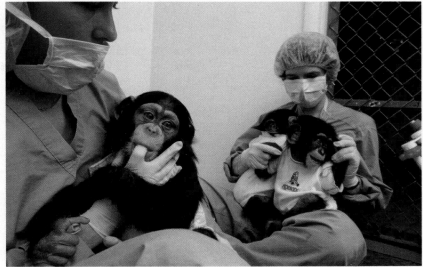

Robert Maass/Corbis

Topic 1 _____

Topic 2 _____

Main Idea _____

_____

Similarities _____

_____

_____

Differences _____

_____

_____

_____

WEB QUEST   A Better Future for the Government's Research Chimps

What plan for chimpanzees is underway at the National Institutes of Health?

_____

_____

 CHECK YOUR UNDERSTANDING

What key question do readers need to pose when they recognize the comparison and contrast pattern at work in a paragraph?

_____

 REVIEWING THROUGH WRITING

Outside of textbooks, where writers usually compare and contrast in order to show how people, places, or ideas are similar or different, writers generally compare and contrast in order to persuade. They cite similarities and differences to back up a topic sentence that offers a value judgment or points out an unexpected similarity, e.g., "On financial issues, the Democrats and Republicans are more similar than it might seem if one only listens to their speeches rather than comparing their voting records"; "When it comes to sheer talent as a singer and songwriter, Bruno Mars has no peer; one would have to go back some decades to the multi-talented singer and songwriter Little Richard to find Mars's equal."

Try your hand at comparing and contrasting to persuade. Pick two topics that share a relationship and explain how one is (1) obviously superior or inferior to the other or (2) really more similar to the other than one might think at first glance. You can pick two topics of your own or select from the list below.

1. the comedy of George Lopez and Paul Rodriguez
2. the singing and dancing talents of Beyoncé and Rihanna
3. the personalities of Bella Swan and Sookie Stackhouse
4. the plotlines in television's _Sons of Anarchy_ and Shakespeare's _Hamlet_
5. the pluses and/or minuses of e-books and print books as study tools

Pattern 7: Cause and Effect

Because connecting cause to effect is so basic to our thinking, you'll find cause and effect paragraphs in every type of textbook. No matter what the subject matter, at some point authors need to explain how one event (the cause) produces another event (the effect).

TQ: What are the effects of ultraviolet radiation?

[1]The <u>ultraviolet (UV) radiation</u> from the sun that reaches the earth's surface <u>is a health threat</u>. [2]At the very least, exposure to the sun's rays causes <u>aging</u> and <u>wrinkling</u> of the skin. [3]At the very worst, it is responsible for <u>cataracts</u>, <u>sunburn</u>, <u>snow blindness</u>, and <u>skin cancer</u>, which claims around 15,000 lives each year in the United States alone. [4]Exposure to UV radiation also <u>suppresses</u> the <u>immune system</u>, enabling cancers to become established and grow. [5]In addition, <u>radiation slows plant growth</u>, <u>delays seed germination</u>, and <u>interferes with photosynthesis</u>.[†] (Adapted from Donald G. Kaufman and Cecilia Franz, *Biosphere 2000* 3e, Kendall Hunt Publishing Company, 2000, p. 266.)

Cause and effect paragraphs are a likely source of test questions. When you encounter them in your reading, make sure you can (1) clearly identify both cause (or causes) and effect (or effects) and (2) explain how one led to or produced the other.

Typical Topic Sentences

Topic sentences like those listed here are typical of the cause and effect pattern.

1. The invention of air conditioning transformed the southern way of life.

2. Teacher and writer Paulo Freire (1921–1997) knew full well that poverty damages not just the body but the mind as well.

3. Whatever its benefit to individuals, the Homestead Act had a profound effect on the development of the American West.

[†]photosynthesis: process by which plants use sunlight to create food.

Common Transitions and Verbs

Along with topic sentences like those listed above, the transitions and verbs listed below are likely to make their way into paragraphs organized by cause and effect.

Transitions That Signal Cause and Effect ◆	As a result Consequently Hence In the aftermath	In reaction In response Therefore Thus

Verbs That Connect Cause and Effect ◆	brings about causes creates engenders evokes fosters generates induces	initiates leads to produces results in; results from sets off stems stimulates triggers

Common Connectives

Connectives are linking words that function as transitions, that is, they tie parts of sentences or whole sentences together by identifying their relationship. In paragraphs dealing with cause and effect, you are likely to see connectives such as *because, as,* and *since* used to introduce a cause (or causes). The conjunction *so* introduces an effect (or effects).

Be on the lookout for these words and phrases because they signal how you should respond to the information being offered: You need to identify the cause and effect relationship under discussion.

Additional Connectives That Signal Cause and Effect ◆	thanks to due to	as a result of following, stemming, resulting from	as a consequence of accordingly

Chains of Cause and Effect

Be alert to cause and effect paragraphs involving *chains of causes and effects* in which the effect of one event becomes the cause of another, for example:

Austin's disappointment over lack of hunting opportunities causes him to import rabbits.

The rabbit population explodes causing the next effect to unfold: The rabbits devastate the countryside.

The last sentence sums up the entire cycle.

[1]Thomas Austin was a dedicated British sportsman who had been an avid rabbit hunter while living in Britain. [2]After moving to Australia, Austin was dismayed to learn that there were no wild rabbits to hunt. [3]Determined to pursue his hobby, he ordered from England twenty-four rabbits to release into the wild and become prey for him and his hunter friends. [4]The rabbits, however, had no natural predators and an extraordinary ability to reproduce. [5]It wasn't long before the wild rabbit population exploded, leaving Austin with more rabbits than he had bargained for. [6]By 1867, Austin said he had killed almost 15,000 rabbits on his property alone. [7]Thanks to Austin's desire to pursue his hobby, vast tracts of land had also been devastated by rabbits, with Australia losing not just vegetation but entire species, thanks to millions of rabbits living off the land.

Diagrammed, the cause and effect relationship in this passage would look something like this:

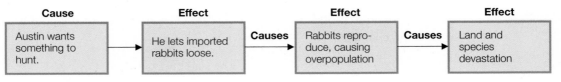

PATTERN POINTERS

1. If you feel that the cause and effect relationship under discussion is not completely clear, draw a diagram that highlights the relationship between cause and effect.

2. Once you recognize this pattern, see how well you can paraphrase the cause and effect relationship that is the basis for the pattern.

◆ **EXERCISE 7**   **Learning from the Cause and Effect Pattern**

DIRECTIONS   Read each paragraph. Then fill in the blanks and circle the letter of the statement that best describes the role of the supporting details.

The introduction describes how women are regarded in New Delhi in particular and India in general.

By sentence 2, the words "set to disappear" indicate a change taking place.

Sentence 3 explicitly states the cause and effect relationship.

The remaining sentences provide specifics about both the cause and the effect.

EXAMPLE   [1]In a country notorious* for its harsh treatment of women, New Delhi, India's capital, has earned the ugly nickname "rape capital." [2]But if hundreds of thousands of protesters have their way, that ghastly nickname, along with the attitudes that gave rise to it, may be set to disappear from the entire country, and not just its capital. [3]The death of a twenty-three-year-old medical student, who made the fatal mistake of getting on the wrong bus, has aroused the conscience of the country like no incident ever before. [4]The woman had gone to see a movie with a friend and boarded the bus home only to be savagely gang raped by five men. [5]While rape, even gang rape, is not that unusual in New Delhi, where a rape is reported every 18 hours, this one struck a chord in the men and women who took to the streets in protest.[†] [6]Early on, the protests consisted mainly of young women and girls. [7]But now they have been joined by men, many of whom say they don't want their young daughters to face a world that persistently threatens the lives of women. [8]As some of the female protestors said with a touch of bitterness, now that men have begun to protest the treatment of India's women, things are bound to change.

―――――――――
*notorious: famous for the wrong reasons, well-known for misdeeds.

1. In this paragraph, the author describes how <u>a young woman's tragic</u> <u>death</u> cause(s) or lead(s) to ___<u>a change in India's attitude toward women.</u>___

2. The supporting details

a. focus on the cause or causes.

b. focus on the effect or effects.

(c.) focus on both cause and effect.

EXPLANATION   Anytime the writer tells you that something is *set to disappear, about to vanish,* or *ready for change,* there is bound to be a cause and effect relationship providing the paragraph's structure.

1. [1]Instinctive behavior is caused by specific signals from the environment called *sign stimuli.* [2]Stalking behavior in cats, for example, may be "released" by the sight of prey. [3]Among male ring doves, the sight of an adult female triggers, or releases, the bowing associated with courtship. [4]Similarly, fighting behavior in territorial male European robins is released not only by the sight of another male invading their territories but also by the sight of red feathers located at a certain height. [5]This behavior is triggered because red feathers appear on the breasts of competitors. [6]Thus the sight of the feathers at a certain height sends a message that a rival is nearby and that triggers an aggressive response. [7]In other words, instinctive behavior may be released by only certain parts of the environment. (Adapted from Robert A. Wallace, *Biology* 4e, Harper Collins, p. 949.)

1. In this paragraph, the author describes how _____ cause(s) or lead(s) to _____

2. The supporting details

a. focus on the cause or causes.

b. focus on the effect or effects.

c. focus on both cause and effect.

[†] The statistic on rape comes from Sean O'Hare, "India's Rape Crisis Revealed." UKMailOnline.com, December 31, 2012.

2. [1]During the Civil War (1861–1865), the South had fewer men than the North to send to war. [2]Thus a larger proportion of southern families were left to the care of women. [3]Some women worked farms and herded livestock to support their families. [4]Others found themselves worse off: They and their families were left in poverty as the war turned the countryside black and dry. [5]Because of their dire straits, some women tried to persuade their husbands to desert. [6]One woman shouted to her husband, who was being drafted for the second time, "Desert again, Jake." [7]However, the vast majority of women on the domestic front fully supported the war despite the misery it caused them. (Adapted from Carol Berkin et al., *Making America* 5e, © Cengage Learning.)

   1. In this paragraph, the author describes how _____

   _____ cause(s) or lead(s) to _____

   _____

   2. The supporting details

      a. focus on the cause or causes.

      b. focus on the effect or effects.

      c. focus on both cause and effect.

 ## When Patterns Combine

Many of the paragraphs you encounter in textbooks will have one **primary pattern**, i.e., one single pattern that organizes the most important information in the text. However, when the main idea requires it, textbook writers, like writers of all kinds, combine or mix organizational patterns, sometimes in equal measure. Frequently, that's the only way they can fully communicate complex ideas, for instance: "The desire to attack from a distance during combat led to rocket-propelled grenades, which are easy to assemble and fire." In this case, the topic sentence outlines a cause and effect relationship that diagrammed would look like this:

| Combat need to attack from distance | → | Rocket propelled grenades |

But the reader still might ask, how can a weapon like that be easy to assemble and fire, which means the writer also needs to employ the sequence of steps pattern.

Unfortunately, it's not just the military that uses rocket-fired grenades. They are also a favored weapon of terrorists.

Stocktrek Images/Getty Images

By the same token, just imagine trying to develop the following idea without combining a sequence of dates and events with the cause and effect pattern: "As the Ugandan dictator Idi Amin steadily worked his way up the ladder of power, his growing paranoia led to ever more brutal acts." Some ideas simply require writers to combine methods of development without making one method more important than the other.

For a more detailed illustration, do a careful reading of the following paragraph:

The author begins with two critical dates.

The author defines "Hubbert's Peak" as background for the main idea: M. King Hubbert's prediction was correct.

In 1859, the United States was the first nation to produce oil. But oil is an exhaustible resource and by 1974 America had used up more than half of its once abundant* oil supply. The halfway production point of an oil field is called "Hubbert's Peak," named after M. King Hubbert, a geologist* with the U.S. Geological Survey. He predicted in 1956 that oil production in the United States would peak in 1970. At that time the United States was the world's largest oil producer. So nobody believed him, and oil company executives ridiculed

*abundant: existing in large quantities.

The author returns to the dates and events sequence to show just how correct Hubbert was.

him. Hubbert, however, was correct in his prediction. According to geologists, U.S. oil production peaked in 1974—just four years after Hubbert predicted—and has declined since then. Most geologists project that domestic oil production will reach the 80 percent depletion point by 2055. Already the United States produces most of its dwindling supply of oil at a high cost, about $7.50 to $10 per barrel compared to $1 to $2 per barrel in Saudi Arabia. As the oil supplies continue to decrease, we will become more dependent on foreign countries for oil, which is a far cry from our situation in the mid-nineteenth century. M. King Hubbert was right after all; oil is an exhaustible resource, and we may all soon discover the consequences of that simple fact. (Adapted from G. Tyler Miller, Living in *the Environment* 15e, © Cengage Learning.)

In this paragraph, the author relies most heavily on two organizational patterns—sequence of dates and events with cause and effect—to make his point. Both are equally important to the paragraph's main idea, which means your notes should take both patterns into account.

Good notes would record the dates and events indicating how oil supplies have diminished and describe how, over time, Hubbert's prediction about oil production came true. But they'd also need to describe the effects caused by the country's dwindling oil supplies. Depending on your experience with your instructor's tests and lectures, you might also include the definition provided for Hubbert's Peak.

Whenever you encounter paragraphs that mix patterns, you need to figure out which ones are the most important to the paragraph's main idea. Then you can look for the key elements of those patterns and decide which ones should go into your notes.

◆ **EXERCISE 8**   **Recognizing Primary and Mixed Patterns**

DIRECTIONS If the paragraph's information is organized by only one pattern of development, circle the letter of that pattern. If it is organized by more than one pattern, circle the letters of the patterns used in the paragraph.

---

*geologist: scientist who studies the past and present makeup of the earth.

1. [1]Individuals often respond differently in a group context than they might if they were alone. [2]Social psychologist Irving Janis examined group decision making among political experts and found that major blunders in U.S. history can be attributed to this pressure to conform, or fit in. [3]To describe the phenomenon, Janis coined the term "groupthink"—the process by which members of a group arrive at a decision that many individual members privately believe is unwise. [4]Why don't they speak up at the time? [5]Members usually want to be "team players." [6]They don't want to be the ones who undermine the group's sense of agreement or who challenge group leaders. [7]Consequently, members of a group often limit or withhold their opinions and focus on agreement rather than on exploring all possible options and determining the best course of action.

   (Adapted from Diana Kendall. *Sociology in Our Times* 9e, © Cengage Learning.)

   a. definition

   b. classification

   c. comparison and contrast

   d. cause and effect

2. [1]All of the gasoline now pumped into automobile and airplane tanks began as crude oil formed millions of years ago beneath ocean floors. [2]In ancient seas, when tiny aquatic plants and animals died, they sank to the bottom. [3]Sand and mud settled over them. [4]This process was repeated over and over, each time burying large quantities of organic* material and pushing it deeper and deeper into the earth as new layers accumulated on top. [5]The heavy weight of the layers created pressure and temperatures above 150° Fahrenheit so that the subterranean* organic matter began to "cook." [6]Over time, the heat transformed it into a liquid hydrogen and carbon substance. [7]This crude oil, lighter than both water and rock, drifted upward through tiny cracks in the rock until it was stopped by a layer of dense rock and forced to collect. [8]Today, oil companies drill down into these reservoirs to extract this energy-rich petroleum and send it to oil refineries to be converted into fuel for vehicles.

---

*organic: related to living matter.
*subterranean: beneath the earth.

a. definition

b. process

c. cause and effect

d. simple listing

3. [1]American house forms have changed over time as new building materials became available and living styles changed, but in the early days of America's history, there were essentially three types of houses. [2]Among the earliest and most common house types was the Cape Cod. [3]The typical Cape was two rooms deep with a huge central chimney and a roof that started just above the windows. [4]Because it had low ceilings and few rooms, a Cape was one of the easiest houses to heat, a big advantage when a fireplace was the main source of warmth. [5]Another early house type, the Classic Cottage, had a slightly higher front wall than the Cape and this allowed for a second tier of windows. [6]In the Classic Cottage, the chimney could be in the middle of the house or at the end. [7]The big advantage of the Cottage style was the increased amount of space it offered. [8]However, heating was more of a problem than it was for those who lived in a simple Cape. [9]The Colonial house was a one-and-one-half to two-story rectangle. [10]Its facade* emphasized the symmetry* of the building's design with the front door dividing up nine evenly placed windows, earning the design the nickname "five-over-four and a door." [11]Colonial houses were typically made of wood or brick and had columns or pediments[†] at the front-door entry. [12]The Colonial style house was associated with people of some wealth, who could afford to consider comfort as well as shelter.

a. sequence of dates and events

b. simple listing

c. classification

d. comparison and contrast

---

*facade: the face or front of a building; also a pretense or disguise.
*symmetry: being made up of similar parts that are evenly distributed and carefully matched on each side of a boundary or around a central point; also showing harmony and balance.
[†]pediments: triangular elements over a door or attached to a roof.

4. [1]Although everyone thinks it won't happen to them, house fires are one of the most common causes of deadly accidents, and no one is immune to the threat of a house fire. [2]Still, there are several precautions people can take to make sure they survive a house fire. [3]The most obvious is to install smoke detectors. [4]If you are renting, make sure the landlord installs smoke detectors, and be sure to check the batteries. [5]Get a fire extinguisher and have someone from the local fire station show you how to use it. [6]Keep an evacuation kit on hand. [7]The evacuation kit should include copies of identification; insurance cards or tags, including those for pets; and any essential medical supplies, such as insulin or blood-pressure medication. [8]Have an escape route and know where you plan to exit the house or apartment in case of a fire.[9]If you are living in a multi-story apartment building with a fire escape, make sure it is usable. [10]If it isn't, tell the landlord and make sure that he or she makes the proper repairs. [11]Know where the doors to the stairs are and take the stairs every once in a while to make sure you can negotiate them without difficulty.

a. simple listing

b. classification

c. comparison and contrast

d. cause and effect

5. [1]The legal term *due process* identifies an established course of action that must be followed during judicial* proceedings. [2]The basis for due process can be found in the Fifth Amendment of the Constitution, which says: "No person shall be deprived of life, liberty, or property without due process of law." [3]Due process reflects the Constitution's guarantee that criminal legal proceedings will be fair. [4]Because the courts must abide by due process, every individual tried by a court has to be notified that the proceedings are taking place. [5]Every person called to court for the prosecution of a crime must have an opportunity to defend himself or herself prior to any punishment that might involve the taking of life, liberty, or property. [6]In addition to the Fifth Amendment, the Fourteenth Amendment requires that the states, as opposed to the federal government, honor an individual's right to due process.

---

*judicial: related to the courts.

    a. definition

    b. process

    c. sequence of dates and events

    d. simple listing

6. [1]Dogs have been companions to humans for some 14,000 years, and the relationship probably began because dogs could be trained to help humans hunt for food. [2]Cats, in contrast, have been paired with humans for only one-third of that time. [3]Once cats teamed up with humans, though, they played a role very different from that of dogs. [4]In the past, and until fairly recently, dogs were usually considered the servants of humans. [5]They performed as guards, guides, and protectors in activities ranging from hunting to farming. [6]Cats, however, couldn't be trained to do anything they didn't want to do, which is perhaps why they were worshipped as gods in some societies. [7]The cat was held in such high esteem by the Egyptians, for instance, that there were laws protecting them from injury or death. [8]While many early cultures treated dogs with affection—the greyhound, for instance, appears in many Egyptian tomb carvings—there is little evidence that they ever achieved the status of a deity.*

    a. simple listing

    b. classification

    c. comparison and contrast

    d. cause and effect

7. [1]Thanks to his extraordinary talent for duplicity* and deception, the double-agent and traitor Harold Adrian Russell "Kim" Philby (1912–1988) avoided detection for more than thirty years. [2]From 1929 to 1933, while attending Cambridge University, Philby went to work for the former Soviet Union's feared intelligence agency, the KGB.[†] [3]Throughout the 1930s, under cover as a journalist, Philby continued to serve as a Soviet spy. [4]In 1940, Philby's activities as a

---

*deity: god.
*duplicity: double-dealing, deliberate dishonesty in behavior or speech.
[†]KGB: the Russian initials for what was, in fact, an agency of espionage and repression, the Committee for State Security.

journalist won the attention of the British Secret Intelligence Service (SIS), and he was offered a position as a British intelligence officer. [5]Philby seized this opportunity as a way of gaining access to information about British and American military strategy and, most important, atomic bomb production. [6]Yet even as he betrayed his native country by passing information on to his Soviet colleagues, Philby performed his duties so well that he rose rapidly to become head of the counter-espionage[†] division in 1944. [7]Then, in 1949, he was appointed to be the liaison* between the British Embassy and the U.S. Central Intelligence Agency (CIA). [8]However, in 1951, his double life came close to unravelling when he alerted two fellow KGB agents that they were under surveillance,* giving them time to avoid arrest and escape to Moscow. [9]Philby's British colleagues rightly suspected him of tipping off the two spies and asked him to resign. [10]But in 1955, after Philby had endured years of SIS interrogation* without cracking and admitting the truth, he was reemployed as an SIS officer. [11]In 1962, a captured Russian spy revealed Philby's double-agent status and Philby fled to the Soviet Union.

a. definition

b. cause and effect

c. sequence of dates and events

d. simple listing

8. [1]*Habeas corpus petitions* are frequently filed by individuals serving prison sentences. [2]Usually the petitions are written to show that the court ordering the imprisonment made an error of some sort, making the imprisonment illegal. [3]Habeas corpus petitions are also filed in family court by parents who have been denied custody of a child. [4]In *Brown v. Vasquez*, the Supreme Court ruled that "the writ of habeas corpus is the fundamental instrument for safeguarding individual freedom against arbitrary* and lawless state action." [5]In Latin, *habeas corpus* means "you have the body."

---

†counter-espionage: anti-spying.
*liaison: go-between.
*surveillance: observation.
*interrogation: formal questioning conducted by persons in authority.
*arbitrary: lacking any fixed rule or consistency, based on personal whim.

    a. definition

    b. process

    c. classification

    d. comparison and contrast

9. [1]Although the Indian caste, or class, system was officially outlawed in 1949 by the Indian Constitution, it persists to this day in one form or another and remains a source of political discontent. [2]India's caste system divides the population into four basic groups. [3]The *Brahmin* class includes priests and scholars. [4]Members of this class are not characterized by wealth or possessions, but its members are the object of regard and respect because of their spiritual and intellectual gifts. [5]Next come the *Kshatriyas*, whose members are rulers, warriors, and large property owners. [6]This class is likely to be characterized by the possession of great wealth. [7]Next in the hierarchy is the *Vaishyas* caste, which includes merchants and traders. [8]Those in this group may or may not have great wealth, but they are all engaged in some form of commercial transaction. [9]The *Shudra* caste includes those who wait on and serve members of the other three classes. [10]Those belonging to this group are servants and chauffeurs. [11]Outside the caste system entirely are the *harijans*, once known as the "untouchables." [12]Untouchables perform the jobs no one else wants to do, such as garbage collecting and leather dying. [13]Although the caste system has weakened with the passage of time, it still exists, although more in the country than in the city. [14]In some Indian regions, the caste system is mainly a state of mind, with some individuals believing themselves worthy of being treated as Brahmins while others feel as if the name "untouchable" still applies.

    a. simple listing

    b. classification

    c. comparison and contrast

    d. cause and effect

10. [1]David (Bruce) Reimer's life was a tragic and unintentional experiment that shed light on the complexity of gender identity. [2]After the boy's genitals were badly burned during circumcision, his parents

---

*renowned: famous, respected.

took him to the renowned* psychologist and sexual identity expert John Money. [3]Money advised Reimer's parents to raise him as a girl. [4]The boy was then named Brenda and started life as a female. [5]Although in 1972 Money reported that the boy had developed a female identity—which happened to fit Money's claim that sexual identity could be reshaped through surgery and training—independent follow-ups of the case have suggested a much different view. [6]By 1979, at the age of fourteen, Bruce, despite two years of estrogen therapy, was still fantasizing about being a boy rather than a girl. [7]Plagued by these dreams, he refused to continue his life as a female. [8]It was at this point that his parents informed the boy of his medical history. [9]Reimer responded by taking the name David and assuming the life of a man. [10]Although he married and adopted his wife's children, he was plagued by depression and rage. [11]In May 2004, David Reimer took his own life. (Adapted from Laura A. Freberg, *Discovering Biological Psychology,* © Cengage Learning.)

a. definition

b. process

c. sequence of dates and events

d. cause and effect

In the 1970s, John Money was a renowned expert on sexual identity, but in David Reimer's case Money made a colossal mistake.

PATTERN POINTERS

1. When an author uses two or more organizational patterns, it's up to the reader to decide the value of each one. If the main idea doesn't require any help from an organizational pattern present in the paragraph, then the pattern probably does little more than provide the introduction or organize a few minor details. In other words, it's not especially crucial to your notes.

2. Some standardized reading tests don't acknowledge the reality of mixed patterns. If you are taking one of those tests, let the transitional signals be your guide. They will usually help you identify the pattern or method of development you are dealing with.

3. If the exercise you completed on pages 226–233 suggested to you that cause and effect plays a role in many paragraphs that combine organizational patterns, you should congratulate yourself for being perceptive.

Common Combinations
◆

Process with Cause and Effect and/or Definition

Classification with Comparison and Contrast

Sequence of Dates and Events with Cause and Effect

Cause and Effect with Simple Listing

CHECK YOUR UNDERSTANDING

What should readers do when they realize that the writer has used more than one organizational pattern?

_____

_____

WORD CHECK

The following words were introduced and defined in pages 193–232. See how well you can match the words with the meanings shown below, some of which have been slightly expanded. When you finish, make sure to check the meanings of any words you missed because the same words will turn up in tests at the end of the chapter.

1. assuage (p. 193) _____
2. preoccupied (p. 199) _____
3. compulsive (p. 199) _____
4. grandiose (p. 202) _____
5. adaptable (p. 210) _____
6. notorious (p. 222) _____
7. abundant (p. 225) _____
8. geologist (p. 226) _____
9. organic (p. 227) _____
10. subterranean (p. 227) _____
11. facade (p. 228) _____
12. symmetry (p. 228) _____
13. judicial (p. 229) _____
14. deity (p. 230) _____
15. duplicity (p. 230) _____
16. liaison (p. 231) _____
17. surveillance (p. 231) _____
18. interrogation (p. 231) _____
19. arbitrary (p. 231) _____
20. renowned (p. 232) _____

a. a scientist who studies the past and present makeup of the earth
b. calm or soothe
c. related to the courts
d. god
e. double-dealing, deliberate dishonesty
f. having an exaggerated sense of one's importance or influence
g. the face or front of a building; a pretense or disguise
h. observation of a person or situation
i. lacking any fixed rule or consistency
j. go-between
k. formal questioning by persons in authority
l. being made up of similar parts that are evenly distributed, and carefully matched; having beautiful proportions.
m. able to adjust to new conditions; capable of being modified to fit the need of context
n. famous, respected
o. related to living matter
p. involuntary, uncontrollable
q. overly concerned with something; also, absorbed in thought
r. famous for the wrong reasons, well known for misdeeds
s. beneath the earth.
t. existing in large quantities

◆ EXERCISE 9   More About Form and Meaning

DIRECTIONS Fill in the blanks with one of the words listed below.

geologist	judicial	notorious	liaison	symmetry
interrogation	grandiose	renowned	facade	arbitrary
adaptable	compulsive	subterranean	organic	abundant
assuage	surveillance	duplicity	deities	preoccupied

1. For those who like _____ adventures, cave diving is a thrill.

2. The habit of speeding is likely to make you well-acquainted with our _____ system.

3. The last thing anyone would want to be is a(n) _____ between two feuding partners.

4. A child who likes to collect rocks might well grow up to be a(n) _____.

5. Vishnu, Aphrodite, and Jesus are all examples of _____.

6. The ancient Greeks made _____ the organizing principle of their architecture.

7. When crowds of people attend an event, there are usually numerous _____ cameras present.

8. Some individuals don't feel comfortable until they have closed doors or drawers a prescribed number of times; these people are exhibiting _____ behavior.

9. The man who is always smiling and cracking jokes while feeling devastated by the loss of his job is putting up a good _____.

10. At the beginning of the nineteenth century, passenger pigeons had been so _____ they darkened the sky when a group was in flight, but by the end of that century, they had all but disappeared.

11. Being famous can be the result of little more than publicity; being _____ takes a good deal more talent and work.

12. If you had a(n) _____ sense of your own importance, you would very likely be inclined to monopolize conversations and start every other sentence with the pronoun *I*.

13. The nanny wanted to please her employees by being _____ and changing her schedule to suit theirs, but when their schedule started to change daily, she insisted on a more fixed schedule.

14. For card sharks, who make their living by cheating at cards, _____ is nothing to be ashamed of.

15. Like bad luck, good luck is _____, and you can't plan ahead for it.

16. In the nineteenth century, Myra Maybelle Shirley Reed Starr (1848–1889) was a(n) _____ outlaw, better known as the Bandit Queen Belle Starr.

17. It's all but impossible to watch a crime drama like *Law & Order* and not see a(n) _____.

18. Because it's not _____, plastic won't disintegrate over time, which is one of the reasons that trash dumps are overrun with it.

19. Initially, grief over the loss of a loved one is impossible to _____.

20. It's not a good idea to be _____ with text messaging while driving.

TAKING STOCK **Why Should We Care About the American Alligator?**

Looking Ahead Alligators are not especially lovable creatures. It's not just their looks. It's also the fact that they've been known to put humans on the dinner menu. Given their appearance and their appetite, we have hunted them relentlessly and almost driven them to extinction. However, as the author of this reading points out, alligators are as tough as they look.

1   The American alligator is North America's largest reptile, has no natural predators except humans, and it plays a number important roles in the ecosystems, or biological communities, where it is found. The species outlived the dinosaurs and has been able to survive numerous dramatic changes in the earth's environmental conditions.

2   But starting in the 1930s, alligators faced a new challenge. Hunters began killing them in large numbers for their exotic meat and their supple belly skin, used to make shoes, belts, and pocketbooks. Other people hunted alligators for sport or out of hatred. By the 1960s, hunters and poachers had wiped out 90 percent of the alligators in the U.S. state of Louisiana, and the alligator population of Florida was almost extinct.

3   Those who did not care much for the American alligator were probably not aware of its important ecological role—its niche—in subtropical wetland communities. Alligators living in these regions dig deep depressions, or gator holes, which hold fresh water during dry spells, serve as refuges for aquatic life, and supply fresh water and food for fish, insects, snakes, turtles, birds, and other animals. Large alligator nesting mounds provide nesting and feeding sites for species of herons and egrets, and red-bellied turtles use old gator nests for incubating their eggs. Alligators eat large numbers of gar, a predatory fish. This helps maintain populations of game fish such as bass and bream.

Fearful looking creatures that they are, alligators still play a key role in maintaining the balance of nature.
FloridaStock/Shutterstock.com

4   As alligators move from gator holes to nesting mounds, they help keep areas of open water free of invading vegetation. Without these ecosystem services, freshwater ponds and coastal wetlands where these alligators live would be filled with shrubs and trees, and dozens of species would disappear from these ecosystems. Some ecologists classify the American alligator as a *keystone species* because of its important ecological roles in helping to maintain the structure, function, and sustainability of the ecosystems where it is found. And, in 2008, scientists began analyzing the blood of the American alligator to identify compounds that could kill a variety of harmful bacteria, including those that have become resistant to commonly used antibiotics.

5   In 1967, the U.S. government placed the American alligator on the endangered species list. Protected from hunters, the population made a

strong comeback in many areas by 1975—too strong according to those who find alligators in their backyards and swimming pools, and to duck hunters whose retriever dogs are sometimes eaten by alligators. In 1977, the U.S. Fish and Wildlife Service reclassified the American alligator as a threatened species in the U.S. states of Florida, Louisiana, and Texas, where 90 percent of the animals live. Today, there are one to two million alligators in Florida, and the state now allows property owners to kill alligators that stray onto their land.

6   To biologists, the comeback of the American alligator is an important success story in wildlife conservation. The tale of the alligator illustrates how each species in a community or ecosystem fills a unique role and it highlights how interactions between species can affect ecosystem structure. (Adapted from G. Tyler Miller and Scott E. Spoolman, *Living in the Environment* 16e, © Cengage Learning.)

Sharpening Your Skills

DIRECTIONS Answer the following questions by circling the letter of the correct response or filling in the blanks.

Using Context Clues

1. What would be a good synonym for the word *predators* in the following sentence? "The American alligator, North America's largest reptile, has no natural *predators* except humans . . ."

_____

Surveying

2. The question in the title assumes what about humans' attitude toward alligators?

_____

Paraphrasing

3. Which statement best paraphrases the topic sentence of paragraph 2?

   a. Humans have never minded killing animals if they could benefit from their death and the alligator is no exception to that general rule.

   b. Alligators came close to extinction because people just hated the look of them.

   c. In the 1930s, alligators came close to becoming extinct.

   d. Poachers almost wiped out the alligator population in the 1930s.

Recognizing Context Clues

4. According to the restatement clue in paragraph 3, what is a synonym for the phrase "ecological role"?

_____

Understanding Supporting Details

5. Paraphrase the three major details provided to prove the main idea in paragraph 3: People who don't care about what happens to the alligator don't know how important they are to the natural communities they inhabit.

   1. _____

   _____

   2. _____

   3. _____

   _____

6. It's correct to say that paragraph 4

   a. continues the main idea introduced in paragraph 3.

   b. introduces a new main idea about alligators.

   If your answer was *a*, explain how paragraph 4 continues the previous main idea. If your answer was *b*, paraphrase the new main idea paragraph 4 introduces.

   _____

   _____

Using Organizational Patterns

7. Paragraph 5 uses the cause and effect organizational pattern. Please explain in one sentence the cause and effect described.

   _____

   _____

8. What two organization patterns does the author use to structure the material in this reading?

   _____ and _____

Analyzing Language 9. Some scientists think of the alligator as a "keystone species". In architecture, a keystone is the stone at the top of an arch that locks the other pieces of the arch in place. What's the similarity between the alligator's role in the environment and the keystone of an arch?

_____

_____

Seeing the Big Picture 10. How does the author answer the question posed in the title?

_____

_____

▶ TEST 1   Recognizing Organizational Patterns

DIRECTIONS   Circle the letter or letters that identify the organizational pattern or patterns used in each paragraph.

1. [1]A **cartel** is an organization of independent firms whose purpose is to control and limit production and maintain or increase prices and profits. [2]A cartel can result from either formal or informal agreement among members. [3]Cartels are illegal in the United States but exist in other countries. [4]The cartel most people are familiar with is the Organization of the Petroleum Exporting Countries (OPEC), a group of nations rather than a group of independent firms. [5]During the 1970s, OPEC was able to coordinate oil production in such a way that it drove the market price of crude oil from $1.10 to $32.00 a barrel. [6]For nearly eight years, each member of OPEC agreed to produce a certain limited amount of crude oil as designated by the OPEC production committee. [7]Then in the early 1980s, the cartel began to fall apart as individual members began to cheat on the agreement. [8]Members began to produce more than their allocation in an attempt to increase profits. [9]As each member of the cartel did this, the price of oil fell, reaching $12 per barrel in 1988. [10]Oil prices rose again in 1990 when Iraq invaded Kuwait, causing widespread damage to Kuwait's oil fields. (Adapted from William Boyes and Michael Melvin, *Fundamentals of Economics* 3e, © Cengage Learning.)

a. definition

b. classification

c. sequence of dates and events

d. cause and effect

2. [1]Over the years, there have been many accounts of the Bermuda, or Devil's, Triangle, an area located off the southeastern Atlantic coast of the United States, where a number of ships and planes have supposedly disappeared. [2]The USS *Cyclops*, a Navy ship with 309 people aboard, disappeared there in 1918. [3]Also reported lost, supposedly without a trace, was an entire squadron of five Navy torpedo bombers that took off from Fort Lauderdale, Florida, in 1945. [4]Two years later, the same thing happened to the British airliner *Star Tiger.* [5]However, according to journalist

Larry Kusche, author of the book *The Bermuda Triangle Mystery— Solved*, there is no "mystery" to these disappearances and nothing especially significant about the Bermuda Triangle. [6]Kusche investigated all of the missing ships and planes cited to illustrate the Triangle's mystery only to discover that many of them never even disappeared. [7]Writers intent on making the Bermuda Triangle into a mystery—among them the author of a famous foreign language series, Charles Berlitz—just passed on rumors until they were treated as fact. [8]For the disappearances that really did happen, it turns out there are competing explanations that make technical malfunction or human error more likely than demonic influence. [9]*The Star Tiger*, for instance, was already off course before reaching the Bermuda Triangle and was known to have had problems with its heating system.

a. classification

b. simple listing

c. cause and effect

d. sequence of dates and events

3. [1]Eighteenth-century assemblies bore little resemblance to twentieth-century state legislatures. [2]Much of assembly business would today be termed administrative; only on rare occasions did assemblies formulate new policies or pass laws of real importance. [3]Members of the assemblies also saw their roles differently from those of modern legislators. [4]Instead of believing that they should act positively to improve the lives of their constituents, eighteenth-century assemblymen saw themselves as acting defensively to prevent encroachments on the people's rights. [5]In their minds, their primary function was, for example, to stop the governors or councils from enacting oppressive taxes, rather than to pass laws that would actively benefit their constituents. (Adapted from Mary Beth Norton et al., *A People and a Nation* 7e, © Cengage Learning.)

a. process

b. sequence of dates and events

c. comparison and contrast

d. cause and effect

4. [1]Numerous studies suggest that people who consider themselves happy have four key traits in common. [2]For instance, happy people generally have high self-esteem. [3]They have a good self-image and believe that they are intelligent, healthy, ethical, and personable. [4]A second trait common to happy people is a sense of personal control. [5]People who describe themselves as happy believe that they can make decisions which affect the course of their lives. [6]Another characteristic of happy people is an optimistic outlook. [7]Happy people are inclined to focus on positive experiences rather than negative ones. [8]The fourth trait associated with happiness is an outgoing personality. [9]Most happy people are extroverted and have a solid circle of friends and family that they can rely on for warmth and emotional support.

   a. definition

   b. simple listing

   c. process

   d. sequence of dates and events

5. [1]In the second century BCE, the Chinese developed a method of converting cast iron into steel by melting the iron and then blowing air on it, thereby reducing the carbon content. [2]But it wasn't until 1845 that American inventor William Kelly brought four Chinese steel experts to Kentucky, mastered the Chinese process, refined it, and then took out a patent. [3]Kelly, however, went bankrupt in the financial panic that gripped the country in 1857 and had to sign ownership over to Henry Bessemer, who had been working on a similar process of steel production. [4]By 1858, Bessemer had developed the first method of mass-producing steel. [5]He then set up the first steelworks in Sheffield, England. [6]Three years after Bessemer's triumph, the German-born inventors William and Frederick Siemens introduced the open-hearth furnace, capable of sustaining the high temperatures needed to make "Bessemer's process" work efficiently. [7]Once the Siemens's furnace was improved on by Pierre Émile Martin of France, the stage was set for a revolutionary change in industrial production of all kinds.

   a. classification

   b. simple listing

   c. sequence of dates and events

   d. cause and effect

▶ **TEST 2**   **Recognizing Organizational Patterns**

DIRECTIONS Circle the letter or letters that identify the organizational pattern or patterns used in each paragraph.

1. [1]In general, people use three different methods of learning, and most rely more heavily on one method than another. [2]**Visual learners** absorb new information best when they can see it represented in physical form. [3]Thus they are likely to take detailed notes with many diagrams and symbols. [4]If visual learners have a choice between learning by reading or listening, they are inclined to choose reading. [5]**Auditory learners** rely most on their sense of hearing to learn new material, preferring to learn from lectures, discussions, and tours. [6]At museums, they are the first to sign up for guided tours or make use of guides on tape by purchasing headphones. [7]**Kinesthetic learners** are at their best when they are physically active. [8]Thus they are likely to gesture while reviewing new information, and they like to use learning techniques that require movement. [9]For example, kinesthetic learners might jot notes on sticky pads and attach the notes to the pages of a textbook because this method allows for maximum physical involvement. [10]In the same vein, they are also likely to build models and take things apart to see how they work. (Source of information: "Three Different Learning Styles," University of South Dakota, http://sunburst.usd.edu/˜bwjames/tut/learning-style/styleres.html.)

   a. classification

   b. simple listing

   c. process

   d. sequence of dates and events

   e. cause and effect

2. [1]XML (Extensible Markup Language) and HTML (Hypertext Markup Language) are coding languages, or instructions to the computer, used for the design of web pages. [2]HTML was the brainchild of Tim Berners-Lee, a British physicist who wanted to find a way for researchers to share information over the Internet. [3]It was formally introduced in 1993. [4]XML is a cousin† to HTML and was introduced by the World Wide Web Consortium (W3C) in 1998.

---

†Some might liken them to brother and sister since both are offshoots of SGML (Standard Generalized Markup Language).

[5]HTML uses preexisting labels or "tags" to classify text and only text, whereas XML allows users to create their own tags, which can be applied to all kinds of data, including images. [6]For those who like their web pages with lots of bells and whistles, XML is the preferred markup language. [7]But HTML still has plenty of defenders who say that XML is not a replacement for HTML because the two have different goals and can complement one another. [8]In the words of Joe Burns, whose website offers tutorials in both languages, "HTML is not dead, nor is it breathing funny. . . . I believe I will be able to write HTML and post web pages as long as I live using HTML alone." [9]Burns is not alone in his sentiments, and the arrival of HTML5 has brought with it a host of new possibilities for the markup language that some once thought obsolete.

a. classification

b. simple listing

c. process

d. sequence of dates and events

e. comparison and contrast

3. [1]Bats and dolphins gather information about their surroundings by bouncing sound waves off objects in a three-step process. [2]First, both animals send sound waves into the atmosphere. [3]Bats make high-pitched sounds by moving air past their vocal chords, and dolphins transmit clicking sounds from nasal sacs in their foreheads. [4]Next, these sounds hit an object in the animal's vicinity, bounce off the object, and return in the form of echoes. [5]In the third step, the animal hears and interprets the echoes. [6]Its brain processes the information, assessing the object's size and shape to form a mental image of it. [7]It is even possible for bats and dolphins to determine how far away the object is based on how long it takes the echo to return.

a. simple listing

b. process

c. sequence of dates and events

d. comparison and contrast

e. cause and effect

4. [1]Dean Kamen is a self-taught physicist and highly successful inventor-entrepreneur with numerous inventions to his credit. [2]Kamen invented the first portable infusion pump capable of delivering drugs

like insulin to patients who otherwise would have spent their time in hospitals rather than at home. [3]Kamen also invented the first book-sized dialysis machine, allowing patients with kidney failure to receive treatment at home instead of in a hospital. [4]Then, after watching a man trying to negotiate a curb in his wheelchair, Kamen created the iBOT Transporter, a six-wheeled chair that can climb stairs and rocky terrain. [5]Moving away from the medical field, Kamen is currently at work on a machine that would generate power for industry and home use while simultaneously serving as a water purification system.

a. definition

b. classification

c. simple listing

d. process

e. sequence of dates and events

5. [1]Nathan Weaver, a student at Clemson University, is passionately committed to promoting the welfare of animals, and one of the animals Weaver would like to protect is the box turtle. [2]Aware that these slow-moving creatures are threatened with extinction, he tried to discover a way to save them from becoming road kill as they make their way across busy roads. [3]However, in his attempts at protecting the turtles, Weaver made an unpleasant discovery. [4]Many drivers actually swerve their cars to hit the turtles if they spot them on the road. [5]When the experiment was repeated, the results were the same with about 6 percent of 1,000 drivers swerving to intentionally squash the rubber turtle that had been placed roadside. [6]When Hal Herzog, a professor at Western Carolina University, was asked why anyone would do this, he suggested that some people feel the need to assert their status as the dominant species. [7]For them, squishing a helpless turtle seems to satisfy that desire. [8]As he put it, it's the "dark side of human nature." [9]Herzog also asked a group of over one hundred students whether any one of them had ever swerved intentionally to run over a turtle. [10]In response, thirty-four hands went up, most of them male.

a. definition

b. classification

c. simple listing

d. process

e. cause and effect

▶ **TEST 3** **Recognizing Organizational Patterns**

DIRECTIONS Circle the letter or letters that identify the organizational pattern or patterns used to explain that main idea.

1. [1]Given the limited tools at their disposal, it's amazing how many different kinds of webs spiders can spin, with the following being only a few of the most common. [2]*Sheet webs* consist of flat sheets of spider-spun silk strung between blades of grass or the branches of a tree. [3]They trap insects that fly into it head first, giving the spider, waiting on the edges, just enough time to attack. [4]*Gum-footed webs* are made of tightly woven silk threads and are attached at each end to tree branches. [5]The lower threads of the web are coated with a gummy substance that sticks to the feet of the spider's insect victims. [6]*Triangle webs* get their name from their shape. [7]The spider waits at one end of the triangle and shakes the web when an insect lands, catching it in the folds of the three-cornered web. [8]*Horizontal line webs* consist of one simple line dotted with sticky droplets and stretched low over vegetation or leaf litter. [9]Spiders keep the line taut until an insect lands, and then they let it loosen and tangle the struggling prey.

   a. definition

   b. process

   c. sequence of dates and events

   d. classification

   e. simple listing

   f. comparison and contrast

   g. cause and effect

2. [1]*Phishing* is the act of fraudulently using email to try to get the recipient to reveal personal data. [2]In a phishing scam, con artists send legitimate-looking emails urging the recipient to take action to avoid a negative consequence or to receive a reward. [3]This requested action may involve clicking on a link to a website or opening an email attachment. [4]*Smishing* is a variation on phishing that involves the use of Short Message Service (SMS) texting. [5]In a smishing scam, people receive a legitimate-looking text message on their phone telling them to call a specific phone number or to log on to a website. [6]This is often done under the guise of suggesting that there is

a problem with their bank account or credit card that requires immediate attention. [7]However, the phone number or website is phony and is used to trick unsuspecting victims into providing personal information such as a bank account number, personal identification number, or credit card number. [8]*Vishing* is similar to smishing except that the victims receive a voice mail telling them to call a phone number or access a website. (Adapted from George W. Reynolds, *Ethics in Information Technology* 4e, © Cengage Learning.)

a. definition

b. process

c. sequence of dates and events

d. classification

e. simple listing

f. comparison and contrast

g. cause and effect

3. [1]The United States (along with many Latin American nations) has a congress. [2]Great Britain (along with many Western European nations) has a parliament. [3]A hint to the difference between the two kinds of legislatures can be found in the original meanings of the words. [4]*Congress* derives from a Latin term that means "a coming together," a meeting, as of representatives from various places. [5]*Parliament* comes from a French word, *parler*, that means "to talk." [6]The differences implied by the names of the law-making groups are real ones, with profound significance for how laws are made and governments are run. [7]Ordinarily a person becomes a member of a parliament by persuading a political party to put his or her name on the ballot, with it being understood that the person chosen supports the national political party or program. [8]In elections, voters in a district then choose not between two or three personalities running for office but between two or three national parties. [9]By contrast, a person becomes a candidate for representative or senator in the U.S. Congress by running in a primary election. [10]Except in a very few places, political parties exercise little control over the choice of who is nominated for congressional office. [11]Voters then select candidates in the primaries based on the candidates' personalities and positions. [12]As a result of these differences, a parliament tends to be made up of people loyal to a national party or group. [13]A congress, on the other hand, tends to be made up of people who may or may not support the national party or group to which they belong. (Adapted from James Q. Wilson and John J. DiIulio, *American Government* 11e, © Cengage Learning.)

a. definition

b. process

c. sequence of dates and events

d. classification

e. simple listing

f. comparison and contrast

g. cause and effect

4. [1]The National Security Act of 1947, signed into law by President Harry S. Truman on July 26, 1947, called for a Secretary of Defense, whose job it would be to unify the military's training procedures and goals. [2]A secretary of the Navy for close to three years, James V. Forrestal seemed the perfect man for the job. [3]However, in less than two years, James Forrestal would leave his office in disgrace and despair. [4]A staunch cold warrior, Forrestal was inclined to see Communist threats everywhere. [5]He even coined the term *semi-war* to express his belief that the country needed to remain permanently on high alert. [6]In addition to feeling constantly under siege by Communists, Forrestal was deeply wounded on his home turf when, in 1948, tabloid columnists Drew Pearson and Walter Winchell accused him of everything from tax evasion to collaborating with the Nazis. [7]Things only got worse for Forrestal when he learned that Truman was ready to fire him because he was not fully supportive of the new plan to found the country of Israel on land already occupied by Arabs. [8]Rather than be publicly dismissed, Forrestal resigned on March 28, 1949. [9]Upon leaving his office, Forrestal seemed so distraught his government superiors sent him to Florida for a rest. [10]However, when Forrestal's behavior became increasingly erratic, he was rushed to a military hospital in Bethesda, Maryland. [11]On May 22, 1949, Forrestal jumped out a sixteenth-story window, the sash of his bathrobe wrapped tightly around his neck.

a. definition

b. process

c. sequence of dates and events

d. classification

e. simple listing

f. comparison and contrast

g. cause and effect

5. [1]Global positioning system (GPS) technology has been around since 1978 and put to a number of good uses, from tracing tanks on the battlefield to finding hikers lost in a snowstorm. [2]Now, however, parents of teenagers have discovered a brand-new use for GPS technology: helping them keep in touch with their kids so that they know, for instance, exactly where their children are and how fast they are driving. [3]Not surprisingly, this use of GPS technology has sparked an intense debate with the parents expressing the pros in the argument while teenagers just as intensely point to the cons. [4]Advocates of using the GPS devices in this way say they help reduce risky behavior and may even save lives. [5]More specifically, they argue that teenagers won't speed if they know their parents will be alerted—some GPS systems send an email to parents if kids go over the speed limit—and that teenagers driving at or below the speed limit might help reduce the number of kids who die in car crashes. [6]According to the National Highway Traffic Safety Administration, motor vehicle crashes are the leading cause of death among fifteen- to twenty-year-olds. [7]Jack Church, spokesman for Teen Arrive Alive, a Florida company that offers GPS-enabled cell phones, made exactly this point in a 2006 *San Francisco Chronicle* article: "This is about parents being given tools to better protect their kids. [8]That's not Big Brother. [9]That's parenting." (Source of quotations: www.pbs.org/newshour/extra/features/jan-june07/gps_2-19.html.)

a. definition

b. process

c. sequence of dates and events

d. classification

e. simple listing

f. comparison and contrast

g. cause and effect

▶ **TEST 4** **Reviewing New Vocabulary**

DIRECTIONS Fill in the blanks with one of the words listed below.

| judicial | abundant | notorious | facades | renowned |
| organic | duplicitous | subterranean | adaptable | grandiose |

1. On June 19, 1953, a middle-class, middle-aged couple, Ethel and Julius Rosenberg, were executed as spies. They had been convicted in 1951 for passing secrets to the Soviet Union and, at their sentencing, the judge in the case, Irving Kaufman, issued an angry statement, claiming that their activities had had _____ negative consequences. The judge even attributed the start of the Korean war to their unpatriotic and _____ activities. Following the conviction, there were public demonstrations of protest because many people believed the evidence against the Rosenbergs was insufficient to prove their guilt. The Rosenbergs' lawyers repeatedly applied for a(n) _____ review of the case, going as high as the Supreme Court. But they failed in their efforts and both Julius and Ethel were executed.[†] Since their execution, the case has become _____ for the fury and controversy it aroused. While evidence discovered later has indicated Julius was indeed guilty, there is no real evidence suggesting Ethel was a spy.

2. As their name implies, desert _____ termites live underground, and they can and do survive on _____ matter like decayed cactus. That does not mean, however, that their presence isn't a bad sign for homeowners. These termites do come above ground to search for food and, when they do, they can severely damage any wooden _____ within their reach. Because these termites normally live in moist, dark earth, the heat of the sun could kill them. The termites, though, are _____ creatures. They have learned to avoid this danger by building mud tubes that allow them to tunnel above ground while remaining protected from the heat and light.

[†]Later revelations have indicated that Julius was indeed a spy. Ethel, however, was not.

3. It appears that fame can provoke some _____ fantasies. Otherwise, it's impossible to explain how celebrities like Madonna, Tom Cruise, and Suzanne Somers[†] can publicly lay claim to knowledge about medical and scientific issues totally outside their expertise. Being _____ as entertainers does not mean they will be respected when they express their opinions on issues unrelated to their training or experience.

[†]Madonna has claimed to have a fluid that can clean up radioactive waste. Cruise has proclaimed his knowledge of psychiatry; and Somers promotes the use of specially formulated hormones that are, from her perspective, not dangerous to women's health.

> **TEST 5**   **Reviewing New Vocabulary**

DIRECTIONS   Fill in the blanks with one of the words listed below.

interrogate	arbitrary	preoccupied	surveillance	assuages
deity	liaison	geologist	symmetry	compulsively

1. Children suffering from autism, a mysterious and complex disorder that makes it hard for them to interact with others, are easily upset by changes in their ordinary routine. Oddly enough, arranging blocks, cards, or other objects in order to create an exact _____ frequently _____ their distress. Autistic children who have been kept under close _____ by doctors or parents also consistently display other typical and unusual behaviors. They are likely to become passionately attached to objects, show no fear of serious danger, and are given to rocking themselves or spinning objects for long periods of time.

2. If school officials are forced to summon police to school to deal with violence on the part of a student, administrators must carefully follow all the appropriate procedures. For instance, should police need to _____ a student on school grounds, the principal must notify the parents that such an interview is taking place. If at all possible, the parent or parents should be present during questioning. The interview should also be conducted by a(n) _____ officer who has experience working with both police and educators.

3. **Charles Darwin and Alfred Wallace**

   Opening the mail one day in June 1858, Charles Darwin, the famous naturalist and eventual author of *On the Origin of Species*, a book that changed scientific thinking forever, was, as usual, _____. For more than twenty years, he had been _____ pondering the discoveries he made on his voyage to the Galapagos Islands. Darwin believed he had discovered the _____ but powerful mechanism "natural selection," which could account for developmental change in all species, including humans. Cautious to a fault, though, Darwin was worried that his theory, if made public, would unleash a flood of criticism and controversy, largely because it suggested that the development of humanity was not under the control of a higher _____.

The package that came in the mail that day in June, however, shocked Darwin into focused attention. Alfred Wallace, a younger and much more daring colleague, had sent Darwin a paper in which he outlined, in different language, the very theory that Darwin had long been thinking about publishing. That paper was all Darwin needed to end his indecision. With the help of _____ Charles Lyell and biologist Joseph Hooker, Darwin went public with his theory and by 1859 his book was in print.

Understanding, Outlining, and Summarizing Longer Readings

IN THIS CHAPTER, YOU WILL LEARN

- how to adapt what you know about reading paragraphs to multi-paragraph selections.
- how to create informal outlines.
- how to summarize longer readings.

"Observation is the key to good reading."
—James W. Sire, *How to Read Slowly*

In Chapter 5 you'll use some of the same skills introduced in previous chapters. However, you'll apply those skills, with a few modifications, to readings longer than a paragraph. In addition, you'll learn how to take notes with informal outlines and how to revise those outlines as you get closer to exams. Chapter 5 also offers some pointers for summarizing, or condensing, multi-paragraph readings.

 ## Understanding Longer Readings

To thoroughly understand a paragraph, you need to answer three questions: (1) What's the topic? (2) What's the main idea? and (3) Which supporting details are central to understanding that main idea? Fortunately, the same questions apply to readings longer than a single paragraph. Still, that's not to say there are no differences between reading a single paragraph and reading longer selections. There are several crucial differences you need to take into account.

The Main Idea Controls More Than a Paragraph

In longer readings, one main idea unifies not just a single paragraph but all or most of the paragraphs in the selection. Because it controls the content of the other paragraphs, you can think of this main idea as the "controlling main idea." It controls the content of the paragraphs that precede and follow it. These paragraphs exist to introduce, explain, clarify, or argue the controlling or overall main idea. (For a diagram illustrating this point, see page 260.)

Several Sentences May Be Needed to Express the Main Idea

The main idea of an entire reading can often be summed up in a single sentence. But expression of the controlling main idea often requires several sentences, maybe even a paragraph. For that reason, composition textbooks frequently use the term **thesis statement** to refer to the stated main idea of a research paper or an essay. Following that tradition, we'll use that term throughout the remaining chapters to emphasize that the main idea of a multi-paragraph reading cannot always be summed up in a single sentence.

Ideas Can Get Bigger

With more space available for explanation, longer readings frequently explore broader, more general ideas than the more specific ones paragraphs address. While a paragraph might discuss how pet owners are using the free web service "If This, Then That" to monitor the air-conditioning in their homes so that elderly animals don't overheat while their owners are away, a longer reading selection would be likely to make a broader point like this one: "A growing number of home owners are using the Web to oversee the household while they are away."

From your standpoint as a reader, this means you have more supporting details to evaluate in terms of their importance to your understanding of the main idea. But the mental process you engage in remains the same as it was for paragraphs. Once you determine the controlling main idea, figure out how much of the remaining information is essential to your understanding of the author's central point.

Purpose Becomes Easier to Identify

When you are dealing with a single paragraph, it's often hard to identify the author's purpose in writing, unless, of course, the language is especially emotional in tone. Individual paragraphs don't usually provide you with enough evidence to judge the author's purpose. However, when you have an entire reading available, you can usually determine the author's primary, or main, purpose in writing based on the context, content, and style of the writing.

Introductions Can Get Longer

In paragraphs, introductions are usually limited to only a few sentences. However, in longer readings, providing background for the main idea may require an entire paragraph, maybe even two. While it's true that textbook authors are very likely to present readers with the main idea in the first or second paragraph of a multi-paragraph reading, you can't always assume that to be true. With multi-paragraph readings, if you don't find a statement of the main idea in the first two paragraphs, it might well turn up in the third.

The Author May More Frequently Conclude Rather Than Begin with the Main Idea

If you are reading a multi-paragraph text and there is no hint of the thesis statement by the middle of the reading, it's very possible that the author has decided to conclude with it. So read the last paragraph with extra attention. Be on the lookout for a general thesis statement that sums up what came before.

However, if there is no general statement in the last paragraph, it's quite possible that the controlling main idea is not expressed in a thesis statement. Instead, you might have to infer it, drawing your own conclusion based on what the author actually says in the reading. (More on this subject in Chapter 6.)

One Supporting Detail Can Take Up Several Paragraphs

In longer readings, explaining one major supporting detail can take up a paragraph or more. The author may, for instance, introduce a main idea and then provide two paragraphs of illustration or explanation.

A Minor Detail Can Occupy an Entire Paragraph

As they do in paragraphs, minor details in longer readings further explain major ones. But like major details in longer readings, one minor detail can take up an entire paragraph. This means it's especially important for readers to determine which minor details add truly relevant information and which ones do not.

Main Ideas Aren't All Equal

In longer selections, readers have to mentally move back and forth between the controlling main idea and the main ideas in the rest of the selection. With each new paragraph, the reader has to connect or relate a new main idea to the overall or controlling main idea of the entire selection.

For an illustration of why determining the relationship among main ideas is important, read the following selection and look at the accompanying diagram. The diagram provides a picture of the reading's underlying structure.

Research on Leadership

Thesis Statement

1   In business, managers have to be leaders. Thus it comes as no surprise that researchers have been studying the nature of leadership in business. At the <u>University of Michigan</u>, <u>researchers</u> have <u>found</u> that <u>leadership behavior among managers</u> can be divided into two categories—<u>job-centered and employee-centered</u>.

Topic Sentence   2   <u>Job-centered leaders</u> closely <u>supervise their employees</u> in an effort to <u>monitor</u> and <u>control</u> their <u>performance</u>. They are primarily concerned with getting a job done. They are far <u>less concerned</u> with the <u>feelings</u> or attitudes <u>of their employees</u>—<u>unless</u> those attitudes and <u>feelings affect</u>

the task at hand. In general, they don't encourage employees to express opinions on how best to accomplish a task.

Topic Sentence 3   In contrast, employee-centered leaders focus on reaching goals by building a sense of team spirit. An employee-centered leader is concerned with subordinates' job satisfaction and group unity. Employee-centered leaders are also more willing to let employees have a voice in how they do their jobs.

Topic Sentence 4   The Michigan researchers also investigated which kind of leadership is more effective. They concluded that managers whose leadership was employee-centered were generally more effective than managers who were primarily job-centered. That is, their employees performed at higher levels and were more satisfied. (Adapted from David Van Fleet and Tim Peterson, *Contemporary Management* 3e, Houghton Mifflin, 1994, p. 332.)

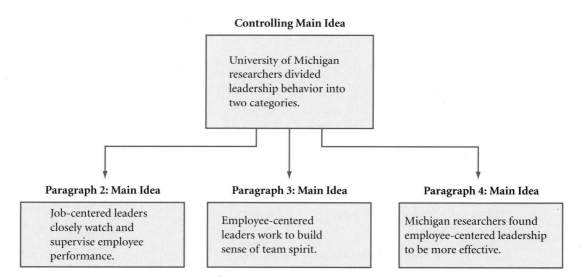

The diagram illustrates how thesis statements and topic sentences work together. The thesis statement introduces the reading's overall main idea. Then the topic sentences of supporting detail paragraphs each introduce a main idea that helps clarify the overall point.

CHECK YOUR UNDERSTANDING

Without looking back at the text, describe how longer readings differ from single paragraphs. When you finish, compare your list to the original explanation.

1. _____

_____

2. _____

_____

3. _____

_____

4. _____

_____

5. _____

_____

6. _____

_____

7. _____

_____

8. _____

_____

◆ EXERCISE 1   Identifying Thesis Statements

DIRECTIONS Read each of the following selections and underline the thesis statement. *Note*: Remember the thesis statement does not always open the reading, and it can consist of more than one sentence.

EXAMPLE

The Death Penalty Through the Ages

The title suggests a sequence of dates and events organizational pattern.

The opening paragraph suggests the author will focus on the death penalty in the U.S.

The time-order transition "In times past" connects to the time-order phrase in the title, making sentences 1 and 2 the thesis statement.

The supporting details provide numerous illustrations for the meaning of the word *trivial* introduced in the thesis statement.

Note how a time-order transition guides the reader through the passage of time.

1   In the United States today, the federal government and 35 states have statutes allowing the death penalty for certain crimes. Still, the death penalty, or capital punishment, is reserved almost exclusively for those who commit murder. Nationwide fewer than 100 criminals are executed every year, and between 1976, the year the death penalty was reintroduced as punishment, and 2010, there were 1,202 executions, all of them for the crime of homicide.

2   In times past, though, the death penalty was much more widely imposed. Often the death penalty was used to punish offenses that were rather trivial by modern standards. In ancient Babylon, for example, the Code of King Hammurabi allowed the death penalty for 25 different crimes. None of them involved the taking of a life. The Egyptians imposed the death penalty for killing a cat, an animal considered sacred. In the seventh century BCE, the Draconian[†] Code of Athens prescribed death as the punishment for every crime committed. In the fifth century BCE, the Romans punished with death anyone who sang insulting songs, burned a stack of corn too close to a house, committed perjury, or disturbed the peace in the city at night. In 438, the Code of Theodosius designated more than 80 different crimes as worthy of the death penalty.

3   During the Middle Ages, the death penalty was used for a number of major as well as minor crimes. In Britain, people were put to death for everything from stealing a loaf of bread to sacrilege* or treason. From 1509 to 1547, during the reign of Henry VIII, as many as 72,000 people were executed for various offenses. By the 1700s, the list of crimes punishable by death increased to 220 offenses. These offenses included stealing, cutting down trees, sending threatening letters, and producing counterfeit money.

[†]Draconian: The word exists today and means harsh or severe. It derives from Draco, a Greek politician who codified the country's laws, and in the process made them as severe as possible.
*sacrilege: treating religious objects with disrespect; showing a disrespect for accepted ideas and traditions.

The writer uses the sequence of dates and events pattern throughout to describe how executions were meted out in what was then called the New World.

By the end, the writer has moved away from trivial crimes to emphasize that the death penalty covered a wider range of crimes than it does now.

4 ⟶ English settlers in America initially brought with them to the New World the idea of severe punishments for crimes both large and small. In addition to executing murderers, the Capital Laws of New England, in effect from 1636 to 1647, punished with death anyone convicted of witchcraft, adultery, assault, blasphemy, and perjury. In 1665, the New York colony imposed capital punishment on anyone found guilty of challenging the king's rights or striking a parent. Although these laws were relaxed for fear of discouraging new colonists, by 1780 the Commonwealth of Massachusetts was still executing those convicted of crimes such as burglary, homosexuality, and arson. As late as 1837, North Carolina required death for the crimes of assisting with arson, engaging in bigamy, encouraging slaves to riot, and hiding slaves with the intention of freeing them

EXPLANATION Because the point made in the opening sentences of paragraph 2 is picked up and developed outside the paragraph, those two sentences make up the thesis statement of the entire selection.

1. Is Your Home Clean?

1 Surveys show that, overall, Americans scrub and wipe down their homes fairly often. A Bounty Home Care Council survey, for example, revealed that bathrooms are cleaned an average of five times a month, and that 42 percent of people clean their bathrooms twice a week or more. However, environmental biologist Dr. Charles Gerba of the University of Arizona has shown that many clean homes just look clean. In reality, they are often breeding grounds for bacteria. Indeed, the homes that seem the cleanest are often the ones teeming with the most disease-causing germs. This happens because tools used to clean the house are not always properly handled and as a result they spread germs during cleaning.

2 Dr. Gerba's research has shown that a clean bathroom is often smeared with millions of harmful microorganisms. This is because about half the population uses sponges and rags to clean. Yet only 24 percent of those Americans disinfect the rags and sponges after each use. About 40 percent rinse them only with water, and 16 percent just put the sponges and rags away after using them. Consequently, bathroom sponges and rags are filled with germs. The more the sponges and rags are used, the more germs are spread.

3 Clean kitchens, too, often harbor more dangerous bacteria than messy kitchens. As a matter of fact, research has shown that even in the most spotless of homes, bacteria associated with fecal matter,[†] such as E. coli,

---

[†]fecal matter: waste eliminated from the bowels.

are regularly found in the sink and on countertops. These germs are spread by unwashed hands; raw meat; and the sponges, dishrags, and dish towels used to clean up. For example, a kitchen sponge that has been used for only two or three days is filled with millions of bacteria. The more it's used to wipe surfaces, the more it spreads germs around.

4   Dr. Gerba's research has also shown that freshly laundered clothes are not truly clean either. In one study, he swabbed the inside of 100 household washing machines in Florida and Arizona and found that more than 60 percent tested positive for coliform bacteria, which comes from fecal matter. Another 20 percent tested positive for staphylococcus, a major cause of food-borne illness. Swabs of dryers showed that even high-heat settings don't kill salmonella and another bacteria (mycobacterium fortuitum) that causes skin infections. Thus every time a new load of clothes or towels goes into either the washer or the dryer, these harmful germs get into the fabrics.

5   However, Dr. Gerba and other experts say that changing to different tools and techniques will help kill and stop the spread of germs. They recommend cleaning with sturdy paper towels and then throwing them away. They also suggest using bleach on surfaces and in the laundry, as well as putting rags, towels, and sponges in the microwave for at least one minute after each use. (Sources of statistics: Amanda Hesser, "Squeaky Clean? Not Even Close," *New York Times*, January 28, 2004, p. F1; "Paper Towels Help Wipe Out Harmful Bathroom Germs," PR Newswire, November 22, 2000.)

2. If Bats Become Extinct

No matter how much they look like something out of a horror movie, bats do much more good than harm.
Kirsanov Valeriy Vladimirovich/ Shutterstock.com

1   Worldwide there are 950 known species of bats—the only known mammals that can fly. But bats have two traits that make them vulnerable, or exposed, to extinction. First, they reproduce slowly. Second, many bat species live in huge colonies in caves and abandoned mines, which people sometimes close up. This prevents them from leaving to get food, or it can interrupt the hibernation if they have to leave their shelter to escape being trapped.

2   Bats play important ecological roles. About 70 percent of all bats feed on crop-damaging nocturnal insects and other insect pests such as mosquitoes. This makes them the major nighttime SWAT teams for insects.

3   In some tropical forests and on many tropical islands, pollen-eating bats pollinate flowers, and fruit-eating bats distribute plants throughout the forests by excreting undigested seeds. As keystone species, such bats are vital for maintaining plant biodiversity and for regenerating large areas of tropical forest that has been cleared by humans. If you enjoy bananas, cashews, dates, figs, avocados, or mangos, you can thank bats.

4   Many people mistakenly view bats as fearsome, filthy, aggressive, rabies-carrying bloodsuckers. But most bat species are harmless to people, livestock, and crops. In the United States, only ten people have died of bat-transmitted disease in more than four decades of record keeping. More Americans die each year from being hit by falling coconuts.

5   Because of unwanted fears of bats and lack of knowledge about their vital ecological roles, several bat species have been driven to extinction. Currently, about one-fourth of the world's bat species are listed as endangered or threatened. And thousands of bats are dying from an unknown illness in the northeastern United States. Because of the important ecological roles bats play, conservation biologists urge us to view bats as valuable allies who need to be saved from threatened extinction. (Adapted from G. Tyler Miller and Scott E. Spoolman, *Living in the Environment* 16e, © Cengage Learning.)

WEB QUEST   Why Are Bats Dying?

What is the name of the mysterious disease in the Northeast that is destroying the bat population? _____

What is the first symptom of the disease? _____

_____

Thinking More About Purpose

You already know that a writer's purpose can vary. Writers intent on informing will explain an idea, event, or issue without taking a stand on it or asking you to take one. In informative writing, the point of view expressed is attributed to other people, for example, "The highly successful movie *Zero Dark Thirty* was roundly criticized for suggesting that the film was based on fact even though it falsified the role torture played in the capture of Osama Bin Laden."

Writers whose intention is to persuade, in contrast, are more likely to personally evaluate a particular idea, issue, or event without attributing their point of view to anyone else, for instance: "When it comes to suspenseful, edge-of-your seat movie-making, Kathryn Bigelow, the director of *Zero Dark Thirty*, gets an A for effort. However, when it comes to recounting history with any degree of accuracy, she gets a D−."

But illustrations of the difference in purpose aside, the more basic question to answer is this: Why should readers care what the author's purpose is? The answer is simple: Purpose shapes content. The more intent writers are on persuasion, the more likely they are to supply supporting details that encourage their point of view while leaving out details that don't. While writers with an informative purpose are inclined to give you both sides of an issue, writers with a persuasive intent are likely to leave out or underplay information that discredits their position. That's why you as a reader need to get a clear sense of the author's purpose.

Recognizing the writer's purpose will help you decide how critically you have to read what the author has to say. It will also help you decide how much time you need to spend double-checking the writer's content and sources for accuracy.

Writers Whose Primary Intent Is to Inform ♦	1. choose titles that report information without offering a value judgment, e.g., "Instagram's Popularity Rises While Facebook's Declines."
	2. state or suggest a controlling idea that reveals no personal perspective on the topic under discussion, e.g., "The federal government has announced that all chimpanzees currently under the control of the National Institutes of Health will be retired from public service and live out the remainder of their lives in a laboratory setting with the facilities to care for them or be sent to a chimpanzee sanctuary, where they will be cared for."
	3. employ a tone that is neutral rather than expressive, e.g., "Critics claim torture is still used in Egypt."
	4. avoid revealing their personal point of view by attributing opinions to another person or group, e.g., "Many hackers[†] in the online community believe that making information free to the public should not be treated as a crime because, in their mind, 'information wants to be free.'"
	5. rely mainly on facts, studies, and statistics and include personal points of view only to indicate what people other than the writer think about the topic or issue, e.g., "As observers said at the time, the students in the study responded favorably when the teacher began the class by explaining the meaning of photosynthesis but showed frustration when they had to figure it out for themselves."

[†]hackers: people who use their computers to gain unauthorized access to information.

Writers Whose Primary Intent Is to Persuade ◆	**1.** often use titles that express a personal judgment, e.g., "Hallelujah! Teens Are Tiring of Facebook!"
	2. state or suggest a controlling main idea that identifies a value judgment, an unusual state of affairs, or an action that must be taken, for instance, "The federal government's decision to finally ban the use of chimpanzees in medical research conducted by the National Institutes of Health is a step in the right direction. Now we need to ban the use of chimps in all medical research."
	3. use emotionally charged language, e.g., "Kathryn Bigelow's harrowing film *Hurt Locker*, about the daily horrors soldiers endured on duty in Iraq, allegedly takes no position on the war itself, but in its devastating scenes of violent destruction it is a profoundly antiwar movie."
	4. include the writer's personal opinion, e.g., "As an employer, let me say that I don't find arguments about social networks improving productivity to be especially convincing."
	5. use rhetorical questions that require no answers because the answer is considered obvious, e.g., "Would you let a known criminal teach in your child's school?"
	6. suggest a knowledge of the audience's state of mind, e.g., "The Boston Marathon will remain a tradition, but we will never view it in quite the same way again."[†]

◆ **EXERCISE 2**   **Identifying Purpose**

DIRECTIONS   Read the following selections and underline the thesis statement. Then put *I* or *P* in the blank at the end to indicate if you think the author's purpose is primarily informative or persuasive.

1. Our Oldest Enemy: The Locust

1   In 2009, Australian farmlands were invaded by vast armies bent on nothing less than total destruction. The enemy had entered the country on foot, creeping along at just a mile an hour at first. But in time it took to the air, swooping in from the skies to plunder the land. Covering hundreds of miles a day, it obliterated everything in its path.

[†]In 2013, bombs exploded at the finish line of the Boston Marathon, killing three people and injuring more than 260.

2   In response to the long-awaited attack, emergency teams went into action. Aircraft roared into the skies, flying only sixty-five feet above the ground to battle the enemy at close quarters with deadly chemicals. Allies took flight to help increase Australia's airborne forces. The initial battle went on for close to a week. Then there were a series of brief encounters to finish off the last of the invaders. At war's end, the enemy dead numbered in the billions.

3   It had been no human invasion but a far more fearsome and rapacious* threat that attacked Australia's fields: The attack was launched by a plague of locusts. Using chemicals sprayed from aircraft and employing thousands of locust-eating birds, humans eventually wreaked havoc* on these hugely destructive pests. Nevertheless, throughout most of history, the reverse has been true. When a plague of locusts arrives, it has usually been people who suffered more than the insects.

4   The earliest written record of a locust plague is probably in the Bible's Book of Exodus, which describes an attack that took place in ancient Egypt: "They covered the face of the whole land, so that the land was darkened . . . ; not a green thing remained, neither tree nor plant of the field, through all the land of Egypt" (Exodus 10:12–15). Another biblical account, in the book of Job, describes trees "made white" as locusts stripped even the bark from the branches.

5   Locusts have always spelled disaster for humans. In a single day, a typical large swarm (about 40 million insects) can eat 80,000 tons of corn, devouring a city's food supply for an entire year in just hours. In 125 BCE locusts destroyed the grain crop in northern Africa. More than 80,000 people died of starvation. In 591 AD, a plague of locusts in Italy caused the death of more than a million people and animals. In 1613, disaster struck the French region of La Camargue when locusts ate enough grass in a single day to feed 4,000 cattle for a year, leaving the animals in the region to starve and the people to die.

6   Between 1873 and 1877, locusts blackened the skies of the American West from California to Missouri, causing $200 million in crop damage. At the time, the U.S. government pronounced the locust to be "the most serious impediment to the settlement of the West." In 1889, the Nile valley of Egypt suffered a similar disaster when locusts so thoroughly destroyed crops over an estimated 2,000-square-mile area that even the mice starved in their wake. But, make no mistake, swarms of locusts and the damage they can do are not restricted to the pages of history books. Between 1949

---

*rapacious: greedy and destructive.
*havoc: widespread destruction; often used with the verb *wreak* meaning "inflict" and rhyming with *week*.

and 2004, locust swarms in Africa have been a major cause of starvation, resulting from the insects sweeping in and devouring fields of crops. In November 2008, Australia was again hit hard by a plague of locusts that measured 3.7 miles long and ate all the vegetation in its path.

_____

2. A Three-Part Theory of Love

1   What is love? No one knows for sure. However, researcher R. J. Sternberg has a theory. According to Sternberg, love consists of three separate ingredients. Each one is crucial to falling in love or staying in love.

2   Passion is one of the three key ingredients, and it plays a primary role at the start of a loving relationship. Passion involves not just a feeling of heightened sexual arousal but also a strong, romantic attraction. In the throes* of passion, each lover feels that life is barely worth living unless the other is present. Unfortunately, passionate feelings almost always diminish over time, although they remain essential to the beginning of a loving relationship. Luckily, if there's a strong sense of intimacy between the partners, the loss or decrease of passion can be accepted and the love maintained.

3   Within the framework of Sternberg's theory, intimacy—feelings of closeness, sharing, and affection—is essential to staying in love. Both partners need to feel that they view the world in similar ways so that they can turn to one another in times of great sadness or joy. If the one you love is not the one you feel particularly intimate with, or close to, over time, love may not last. Typically in a relationship, intimacy grows steadily at first and then levels off.

4   Commitment is the third ingredient of Sternberg's three-part framework. As he sees it, this ingredient is the hardest to develop and maintain. More conscious and logical than the other two, commitment requires a decision to stay with a relationship even when things are not going smoothly. While passion requires no effort, it comes spontaneously, and intimacy tends to develop naturally through shared experience and activities, commitment depends on the individual's conscious decision to stick with the relationship. It depends on the willingness of a person to say, "This relationship matters to me. I'm going to hold on to it no matter what."

_____

_____

*throes: caught up in excitement.

3. The Moon Landing and the Conspiracy Theorists

1 Despite all evidence to the contrary, there are people who insist on claiming that NASA's Apollo space program never really landed men on the moon. These people claim that the moon landings were nothing more than a huge conspiracy, perpetuated* by a government desperately in competition with the Russians and fearful about losing face.

2 These conspiracy theorists claim that the United States knew it couldn't compete with the Russians in the space race and was therefore forced to fake a series of successful moon landings. As evidence, the advocates of a conspiracy cite several pieces of what they consider evidence. Crucial to their case is the claim that astronauts never could have safely passed through the Van Allen belt, a region of radiation trapped in earth's magnetic field. If the astronauts had truly gone through the belt, say conspiracy theorists, they would have died.

3 Yet those scientists who don't doubt the reality of Apollo's successful mission have a twofold answer for this alleged* evidence. They point to the fact that the metal hulls of the spaceship were designed to block radiation. Then, too, the spacecraft passed so quickly through the Van Allen belt, there wasn't time for the astronauts to be affected. As might be expected, conspiracy theorists remain unconvinced by this straightforward and, at least for rational people, convincing explanation.

4 Proponents of the "moon landing was faked" school also want to know why the U.S. flag planted on the moon is rippling when it should be still because there is no air on the moon. Here again, they simply refuse to listen to any reasonable explanation, which, it turns out, reputable* scientists can provide. The flag shown rippling in photographs only did so because an astronaut was adjusting the flag's rod at the time the picture was taken. But that, of course, is too simple an explanation for those who insist on believing, despite all evidence to the contrary, that the moon landing was faked. Zealously* committed to their beliefs, they treat factual explanations that explain away their "evidence" as little more than irritating distractions. In other words, no amount of logical counterargument or evidence can convince them to change their mind.

_____

----

*perpetuated: something negative that is carried out and maintained, preserved.
*alleged: claimed but not yet proven beyond a doubt.
*reputable: having a good reputation.
*zealously: enthusiastically, often excessively so.

Outlining Longer Readings

With longer readings that cover fairly familiar or uncomplicated material, you can probably prepare for class discussions and exams just by reviewing your underlining and your marginal notes. However, if the material is at all complicated, you should probably take notes using an informal outline.

Like a formal outline, an informal outline identifies relationships by aligning or indenting sentences, words, or phrases. With informal outlines, though, you needn't worry about using all sentences or all phrases, and you don't have to fuss over consistency of capital or lowercase letters. You can use whatever symbols seem appropriate to the material and combine letters, numbers, abbreviations, dashes, and so on, as you need them. Informal outlines are not governed by a rigid set of rules.

The main thing to keep in mind is the goal of your informal outline: Your goal is to create a clear blueprint of the author's ideas and their relationship to one another. The following pointers should help you achieve that goal.

Start with the Title

The title of an essay, an article, or a chapter section usually identifies the topic being discussed. Sometimes it even identifies the main idea of the entire reading. Start your outline with the title next to the left margin.

Follow with the Thesis Statement

Follow the title with a paraphrase of the thesis statement or a statement of the main idea you think is suggested but not explicitly stated. Because indenting to show relationships is crucial to outlining, your paraphrase should be aligned with the left-most margin.

Use Key Words in the Thesis Statement to Select Details

The thesis statement often provides a clue to what should be included in your outline. For instance if the thesis statement is something like

"Three major studies indicate that working memory can be improved through training," then you know immediately that your outline should paraphrase the results of three studies. By the same token, a main idea along the lines of this one—"In the last decade, hurricanes have gotten bigger and more destructive"—tells you that your outline has to identify precisely how much bigger and more destructive hurricanes have become.

Streamline the Major Details

In longer readings you may find that an entire paragraph is devoted to explaining one major detail. When this is the case, you have to decide how much of the paragraph is essential to your understanding of that one detail. Only what's essential goes into your outline.

Include Any Essential Minor Details

Minor details in a paragraph should be included in your outline only if they are essential to an understanding of the major ones. If you can't explain a major detail without the help of a minor one, then the minor detail should be in your outline. Outlining, like underlining, requires conscious and consistent selectivity. When you outline, the key question to answer is always, "How important is this information to my understanding of the controlling main idea?"

Indent to Reveal Relationships

Remember, outlines are blueprints. Even a quick look at yours should tell you which ideas are the most important. While the symbols used to separate different ideas help show relationships, the indention of sentences and phrases says even more. Ideas that are aligned are equal in importance, or **coordinate**, for example:

Coordinate Statements

a. Judges confining themselves strictly to the language of the Constitution are said to be practicing the *judicial restraint approach.*

b. Judges applying the underlying principles of the Constitution to respond to moral principles and the passage of time are called *judicial activists.*

However, if one sentence or phrase is indented beneath another, then the top one is independent, or more important, while the indented item is not equal to the statement above it. It's **subordinate** or dependent. That means it's only in the outline to clarify a previous point.

Independent and Subordinate Statements

a. Techniques used in therapy to recover memories of sexual abuse in childhood can encourage false memories.

—Events recalled during hypnosis often subject to distortion.*

Be Consistent

Letters, numbers, dashes (—), or asterisks (**) can help you separate major and minor details. Whichever symbols you use, be sure to use them consistently within the outline. Don't switch back and forth, sometimes using numbers for major details and then switching to letters. In the long run, this kind of inconsistency will only confuse you when you get ready for exam reviews.

◆ EXERCISE 3　Outlining Longer Readings

DIRECTIONS　Read each selection. Then fill in the part or parts of the outline that have been left unfinished.

EXAMPLE

Inducing Compliance: Turning No into Yes

The word *strategies* suggests the reading will use the simple listing pattern.

1　Although it would be nice if they did, other people don't always do what we wish them to, at least not at first. Over the years, however, social scientists interested in determining how people can be made to comply without the use of force have identified a number of strategies that are effective in inducing compliance, or agreement.

The beginning of paragraph 2 confirms the prediction that the reading will enumerate the various strategies available.

2　One way of encouraging compliance is to use the *foot-in-the-door* strategy. The name comes from a technique used in the days when salespeople went door to door selling their products. As the saying went at the time, "If you can get your foot in the door, the sale is almost a sure thing." In psychological terms, the foot-in-the-door strategy means that if a person is willing to comply with some small request, he or she may also be willing to comply with a much larger demand.

Paragraph 2 supplies a major detail by defining the first strategy.

*distortion: being changed for the worse, made incorrect.

As the transition indicates, paragraph 3 provides a minor detail that illustrates the strategy just introduced.

Another minor detail paragraph explains *why* the strategy works. A pattern is emerging: The strategy is defined in one paragraph and further explained in another.

Paragraph 5 supplies the next major detail, a definition of the second compliance strategy.

The example comes in the same paragraph as the definition.

Again, a minor detail paragraph follows up to explain why the strategy works.

In paragraph 7, the author doesn't use the word *strategy*. But the italics announce that the "low-ball technique" is the next one to be discussed.

A "for example" transition identifies the function of this minor detail paragraph.

3   For example, if the committee to re-elect your local mayor wants you to put a huge sign in your front window promoting her candidacy, members of the committee might first ask you to display a bumper sticker. Once you agree to display the bumper sticker, they might ask you to wear a button. Once you've agreed to those two smaller requests, you would more than likely be ready to put that sign in your window.

4   Psychologists suspect that the foot-in-the-door strategy works because we are inclined to observe our own behavior. Recognizing that we have agreed to a small request, we convince ourselves that the next, larger demand isn't all that different. At that point, we are ready to comply.

5   The *door-in-the-face* strategy—the name was coined by psychologist Robert Cialdini—is a variation on foot-in-the-door, and it works like this: If you have flatly said no to a large and inconvenient request ("slammed the door in someone's face"), you're more likely to agree to a smaller bid for help. Say, for example, your neighbor comes by and asks you to pick up his daughter at school for the next week while he is working overtime. Chances are you will say no because fulfilling the request takes up too much time. But if your neighbor comes back the next day and says he got a friend to handle Monday, Wednesday, and Friday, you are likely to agree to take over on Tuesday and Thursday.

6   This strategy works because it seems as if the person making the request is being reasonable and making a concession.* For that reason, the person doing the favor feels that it is only fair to comply with the smaller request.

7   If you or someone you know has ever purchased a car, you will recognize the *low-ball technique* of encouraging compliance. In the context of car-buying, the salesperson offers a "low-ball" price that is significantly less than that of the competition. Once the customer seems interested, the salesperson begins to bump up the price. In other words, the low-ball technique gets you to comply with a request that seems to cost little or nothing. Once you say yes, the person starts tacking on additional items.

8   For example, your roommate asks for a ride to the local ticket office, where she hopes to get tickets for an Alicia Keys concert. Because the ticket office is only five minutes away by car, you say, "Sure, no problem." It's at that point that your roommate tells you she has to be there by 5:00 in the morning because that's when the line starts forming. If you agree, you've just succumbed to the low-ball technique. (Source of labels: Dennis Coon, *Essentials of Psychology* 9e, © Cengage Learning.)

---

*concession: admission of agreement or defeat.

Title Inducing Compliance

Main Idea There are three major ways to induce compliance in people who are reluctant to agree to a request.

Supporting Details 1. "Foot in the door " approach comes from days when salespeople went house to house and literally put their foot in the door to make a sale.

 a. get person to agree to a little request and they will agree to a bigger one.

 Ex: if they put a bumper sticker on the car, they might put up a lawn sign too.

2. "Door in the face" strategy works after you have flatly said no to a bigger task, you might well say yes to a smaller request.

 a. Friend asks you to pick up his daughter at school for the entire week and you say no but if he comes back and asks for only two days, you say yes.

3. "Low-ball" strategy makes an offer that can't be refused but once it's accepted the demands keep increasing.

 a. Typical ploy of car salespeople.

 b. Having said yes to the larger request, you don't know how to say no to the smaller ones.

EXPLANATION In this outline, what needed to be added were the descriptions of the strategies for compliance and the details that illustrate and explain them.

1. The Five Languages of Love

1 According to relationship expert Dr. Gary Chapman, author of *The 5 Love Languages*, people not only have very different personalities, they also express love in different ways. Chapman believes that every individual best expresses love—and prefers to receive love—through one of five different communication styles. He calls these styles "love languages."

2   Some people feel that love is best expressed through quality time spent as a couple. Quality time, according to Dr. Chapman, does not mean simply being in the same room together; instead, it involves doing things as a couple and devoting attention to one another. People who prefer quality time as their love language feel loved when their partners set aside time for them, even if it's just to chat for a few moments.

3   Other people, however, prefer words of affirmation as a way of giving or receiving love. These individuals like to be told that they are loved. They expect to hear "I love you" or "I appreciate you" often. They like compliments, encouragement, and praise. They like to hear statements such as "That dress looks great on you" or "You have a wonderful smile."

4   Gifts are yet another love language. People who use this language see presents as much more than material objects. For them gifts are symbols of love and signs of affection. In their mind, no presents equals no love.

5   People who express love through acts of service, however, aren't impressed by gifts. They believe that helping others is the best expression of love. Voluntary acts of service are what makes them happy. Cooking, doing chores, changing the baby's diaper, and walking the dog are ways to make members of this group feel cared for and supported.

6   According to Chapman, physical touch is the fifth kind of love expression. People using this form of communication prefer to communicate their feelings for their partners by holding hands, kissing, hugging, or having sex. They feel secure and loved when they can touch and be touched in return.

7   Chapman believes that problems arise when two people involved in a romantic relationship have different styles of expression. If each person expresses him- or herself in a language the partner doesn't really understand or recognize, then expressions of affection may go unnoticed and undermine the relationship. For example, people who prefer expressing love through sharing quality time may doubt their partner's affection if the partner doesn't want to do lots of things as a couple. Similarly, people who need to hear words of affection will feel rejected if their partners don't tell them how much they care. But while it's true that speaking different love languages can lead to misunderstanding, there is hope. If couples become aware of the different love languages and learn to give and receive affection in a partner's preferred style, they can enhance, even revitalize, a romantic relationship. (Sources of language description: www.fivelovelanguages.com/thefivelovelanguages/index.html.)

Title   The Five Languages of Love
_____

Main Idea   According to author Gary Chapman, there are at least five different
_____

languages, or ways, to express love.
_____

Supporting Details   _____

_____

_____

_____

_____

_____

_____

_____

_____

_____

_____

_____

_____

_____

2. The Roman Circus

1   Although nowadays we think of the circus as an amusing entertainment for kids, originally it was not such a harmless event. To be sure, the
first circus, like its modern counterpart, included death-defying events.
But there was one big difference. In the early Roman circus, death was
a frequent visitor, and circus spectators were accustomed to—and
expected—bloodshed.

2   The Roman "Circus Maximus" began under the rule of emperor Julius
Caesar, and it specialized in two big events—brutal fights between

gladiators (or between gladiators and animals) and equally bloody chariot races. In most cases, both events ended in the death of either a person or an animal. If nobody died, the audience was likely to be disappointed. Even worse, the emperor would be displeased.

3 Not surprisingly, the circus event that was in fashion usually reflected the taste of the man in power. Julius Caesar, for example, favored aggressive chariot races. Because the charioteers were usually slaves, racing frantically to earn their freedom, the horses pulling the chariots were driven unmercifully, making tragic accidents an exciting possibility that kept members of the audience on the edge of their seats. In the hope of surviving the event, the charioteers wore helmets and wrapped the chariot reins around their bodies. They also carried knives to cut themselves free if they became entangled. Spills occurred more often than not. When they did, the charioteers would be thrown from the chariot and dragged around the ring by runaway horses. Knives and helmets notwithstanding, most did not survive this kind of horrible mishap, not that the screaming crowd cared. For the audience death was part of the thrill.

4 During the reign of Augustus, from 27 BC to 14 AD, a fight to the death between man and beast was the most popular circus event, and more than 3,500 lions and tigers perished in the circus arena, taking hundreds of gladiators with them. Under the half-mad Emperor Nero, who ruled during the first century AD, the most popular circus spectacle was lion versus Christian, with the Christians the guaranteed losers. Fortunately for both Christians and the slaves who followed in their wake, this savage circus practice was outlawed in 326 AD by the Emperor Constantine.

5 Although the pitting of Christians against lions was staged in a special arena, most of the circus events that took place in Rome were staged in the largest arena of them all—the Coliseum. The capacity of this great stadium, completed in 79 AD, was enormous. It seated close to 50,000 people. In one Coliseum season alone, 2,000 gladiators went to their deaths, all in the name of circus fun. (Sources of dates and figures: Charles Panati, *Browser's Book of Beginnings*, Houghton Mifflin, pp. 262–264.)

Title The Roman Circus

Main Idea The circus began in ancient Rome, but it was much bloodier than the circus we know today.

Supporting Details   1. The first circus, Circus Maximus, originated under Julius Caesar.

_____

_____

_____

_____

_____

_____

_____

_____

_____

_____

_____

_____

_____

_____

_____

_____

_____

ALLUSION ALERT

Bread and Circuses

With the discussion of circuses still in mind, it's a good time to introduce the allusion "bread and circuses." This allusion originated with the Roman writer Juvenal, who claimed that if the ordinary people of Rome were discontented about something, they could be easily distracted by the promise of food and entertainment. Juvenal's comment has survived in an allusion implying that when problems seem large, difficult, or unpleasant, we—or those in power—opt for distractions rather than a solution.

Based on that explanation of the allusion, how would you interpret the following sentence: "Evita Perón knew how to distract the people of Argentina from her extravagant spending habits: If complaints about her free-spending ways began to surface, the people could always count on Evita for a rich diet of bread and circuses."

_____

_____

_____

WEB QUEST   How Does Compliance Relate to Social Impact Theory?

Look up "social impact theory." How does knowing about this theory add to your knowledge of compliance strategies? Does it confirm what you learned in the reading or suggest you should revise what you learned?

_____

_____

_____

_____

WORD CHECK I

The following words were introduced and defined in pages 262–274. See how well you can match the words with the meanings. When you finish, make sure to check the meanings of any words you missed because the same words will turn up in review tests at the end of the chapter.

1. sacrilege (p. 262)	_____	a. maintain, continue, or preserve something that is bad or negative
2. rapacious (p. 268)	_____	
3. havoc (p. 268)	_____	b. admission of agreement or defeat
4. throes (p. 269)	_____	c. trustworthy, respected
5. perpetuate (p. 270)	_____	d. being changed for the worse, made incorrect
6. alleged (p. 270)	_____	e. claimed but not yet proven true
7. reputable (p. 270)	_____	f. midst or state of great excitement
8. zealously (p. 270)	_____	g. wide-ranging destruction
9. distortion (p. 273)	_____	h. full of enthusiasm that is often excessive
10. concession (p. 274)	_____	i. treating religious objects with disrespect; expressing contempt or disrespect for objects or ideas sacred to others
		j. greedy, destructive

◆ EXERCISE 4   More About Form and Meaning

DIRECTIONS Fill in the blanks with one of the words listed below.

sacrilege	distortion	allegedly	zealous	throes
havoc	perpetuate	reputable	rapacious	concessions

1. Someone who enters a religious shrine and smashes all the objects inside is guilty of committing _____.

2. Unfortunately, lawyers who advertise on television are not always _____.

3. People who have just recently taken up an exercise program are often extremely _____ for about a month before losing interest.

4. Cuddly and cute as they are, it seems wrong to use the word _____ to describe koala bears, but the adjective fits: The bears eat 2.5 pounds of eucalyptus leaves per day. Between the koala bears' appetite and global warming, supplies of the leaves are dwindling.

5. Our memories are subject to _____, which is one of the reasons eyewitness testimony is not as reliable as we might like to think.

6. The loss of electricity for almost twenty-four hours wreaked _____ with the schedule.

7. A willingness to make _____ is a key part of negotiating.

8. If a journalist reports that a person has just been arrested for a robbery but not yet been proven guilty, then the person arrested is only _____ guilty.

9. It's altogether appropriate to describe a person newly in love as being in the _____ of passion.

10. Constant tax reductions have helped _____ economic inequality.

 ## Summarizing Longer Readings

> *"Thinking back . . . I couldn't imagine a more crucial skill than summarizing; we can't manage information, make crisp connections, or rebut arguments without it."*
>
> —Mike Rose, *Lives on the Boundary*

Your summaries should condense or abbreviate longer readings by eliminating all but the controlling main idea and most important supporting details. Like paraphrasing, summarizing can tell you if you have really mastered the difficult chapter section you just read. If you cannot tell the important information from the unimportant, you probably haven't fully understood the author's message.

While you clearly can't jot summaries in the margins of your texts— well, maybe very brief ones—you can jot them into the pages of a notebook. Summarizing a chapter section will tell you how well you have understood both the author's general point and the specific details used to explain it.

But the ability to write a summary has other benefits. Sooner or later almost every instructor assigns a summary of some sort, whether it's a request to summarize an outside reading or a part of a question on an essay exam. The same is true for professional writing, where summaries are a key part of applications and reports. As the quote from researcher, teacher, and scholar Mike Rose suggests, summarizing is a core writing skill, and you need to know how to do it if you are going to be successful in both school and work.

Goal of Summarizing

"When you take down almost everything, it becomes a disease."

—Professor Peter Burke, from a conference on note-taking

Good summaries reduce the original text to an abbreviated version that (1) paraphrases the overall message or main idea and (2) includes one or two essential details explaining or proving the author's point. Background information, colorful but nonessential details, repetition for emphasis, etc., are all eliminated from a summary.

Pointers for Summary Writing

To get you off to a good start, here are some tips on how to write a summary. The first six apply to all kinds of summaries, whether they are written for your own personal use or for an instructor's assignment. The last two apply mainly to summaries written for other people to read. Keep that in mind as you get to the end of the list.

Use the Margins to Paraphrase the Key Point of Each Paragraph

Generally, how you annotate pages should vary with the material. For instance, if you are annotating a text in a familiar field, and think the material is not too difficult, a few key phrases to jog your memory during review may be all you need. But if you are annotating in preparation for writing a summary, then you really should identify the key point of every paragraph, noting it in the margins (or on a separate sheet of paper). When you are finished, you can go through your marginal list and put an asterisk or checkmark next to the ideas essential to your summary. Cross out any ideas you think are not central to explaining the overall main idea.

Use the Author's Main Idea to Guide Your Selection of Details

If the thesis statement or controlling main idea of the text you are summarizing identifies a set number of theories, stages, studies, and so on—for example, "Erik Erikson described four stages of psychosocial development"—then your summary needs to include one of each theory, stage, or study. Skip one and you haven't fully explained the overall main idea. You can, however, abbreviate each stage. Although the author might have given each stage three or four sentences of description apiece, you could still describe each one in a sentence.

However, if the central point is something like "Adolescence is an especially turbulent time of life" and the rest of the chapter section describes four or five ways in which adolescence is a time of conflict and change, then it's probably safe to include only two or three of the illustrations given. After all, what makes adolescence so turbulent is largely general knowledge, even common sense. You don't need lots of examples to prove that point.

Maintain the Same Organizational Patterns

As you read, try to determine how the author connects ideas as he or she moves from sentence to sentence. Is the author identifying the specific causes of one event or comparing and contrasting opposing points of view on the same subject? Does he trace a series of dates and events that preceded some major social change? Or is she listing the various solutions experts have proposed for a pressing problem? When you summarize, maintain the same organizational patterns. *The relationships exemplified by those patterns are as much a part of the summary as the content.*

Mark and Annotate the Text Before You Summarize It

As Chapter 1 explained, underlining and annotating your text, especially if it's difficult or unfamiliar, can help solidify your understanding of the material. Thoroughly marking up the text you plan on summarizing is also a good way of deciding which sentences or passages are essential and which ones are not. In fact, some people prepare for summary writing by penciling a line through any sentences they consider nonessential.

Get Right to the Point

Although textbook writers are more inclined than most to open with the controlling main idea of a chapter section, they, too, frequently start with an introductory sentence or two. Here's an example:

Original

President Theodore Roosevelt was not alone in thinking that many American companies were becoming monopolies. Activists in favor of social change had been saying for years that big industries were controlling the economic market, rather than letting it regulate itself through supply and demand. Roosevelt, however, was the first president who decided to do something about the growing power of big business. It was Roosevelt's attack on big business that earned him his reputation as a "trust buster."

In this paragraph, the author leads up to the main idea of the passage by telling readers how others before Roosevelt were concerned about monopolies' growing influence. But that information is purely introductory. The real point of the passage is what Roosevelt did about the problem. Thus, a summary of the above passage would eliminate the introductory material and start off with Roosevelt's taking action to bust up monopolies.

Sample Summary

Theodore Roosevelt was the first president to attack the growing power of monopolies. That's what earned him the nickname "trust buster."

Don't Insert Opinions

Whether you are summarizing for research or for an assignment, your goal is to create an accurate version of the original material. That means you shouldn't distort the original by adding a value judgment that wasn't there in the first place. A summary should be a miniature version of the author's ideas and express only the author's thoughts. If the author's goal is to persuade rather than inform, that should be clear in your summary. But your summary should never make the author's purpose seem persuasive when it's not.

Connect Sentences with Transitions That Clarify Relationships

Summaries require you to **synthesize** information—to pull ideas from different sentences or paragraphs and link them together into a new and original whole (more on this subject in Chapter 7). But this restructuring of information sometimes produces a summary with an awkward, choppy style. While summaries used as chapter notes don't necessarily have to flow smoothly, even at a glance, you should be able to determine *why* one sentence follows another. The quickest way to achieve such clarity is to use transitions like the ones listed on the chart below.

Common Transitional Signals and the Author's Message ◆	Transition	Message
	For instance, As illustration, For example, To be more precise	"An example or illustration is on the way."
	Consequently, Thus, Therefore, As a result, In response, As a reaction	"Having identified causes, I'm now listing effects."
	Afterward, In the next step, At the next stage, In the following year, At this point	"I'm trying to show readers how steps or events occur or occurred in real time."
	Similarly, Likewise, In the same vein, Along the same lines	"I want readers to notice how these two people or ideas resemble one another."
	In contrast, However, In opposition, Whereas	"I want readers to focus on how two people, ideas, or events don't resemble one another."

Identify the Author, Article, and Source

Summaries you write for note-taking don't require you to put the author's name and textbook into the opening. But if you are writing a summary that's been assigned, your instructor probably hasn't read the article. That means you need to identify the author, title, and source of your summary. If your instructor does not give you a set format, then your opening sentence should read something like this: "In the December 2012 issue of *Wired* magazine, Clive Thompson argues that it won't be long before most household objects are in constant communication with their owners."

From Text to Summary

Read through the original excerpt from a history text. As you do, pay close attention to the underlined thesis statement and the marginal notes that describe how a skilled reader would evaluate the content.

Even a quick glance at the title and first paragraph says the Pony Express is the topic.

The opening lines suggest a sequence of dates and events pattern.

The author introduces two general points about the topic: Pony Express riding was a romantic adventure, but it was also hard and dangerous.

The remainder of the paragraph focuses on the hard and dangerous aspect of Pony Express riding.

The last sentence tells you how effective the Pony Express was at achieving its goal.

The Pony Express

1   The Pony Express lasted only eighteen months, from April 1860 to the fall of 1861. But longevity* was never the point of the Pony Express. It was never meant to be more than a temporary means of communication while telegraph lines were strung from Missouri to California. The Pony Express cut twelve days off the time it had taken for Washington to communicate with Sacramento via steamships.

2   Pony Express riding was a genuinely romantic adventure: lone riders walking, trotting, now and then sprinting their ponies across half a continent to carry a few pounds of government dispatches and some very expensive private letters. <u>But being a Pony Express rider was both hard and dangerous.</u> According to the company's Help Wanted advertisement, what was wanted were "young, skinny, wiry fellows, not over eighteen." However, they also had to be "expert riders willing to risk death daily . . . orphans preferred."

3   Pony Express riders maintained a demanding schedule. They were based at large stations 75 to 100 miles apart. At each relay station, which was little more than a shack and a stable, they changed their sweating ponies for fresh mounts that were saddled and ready to go. The intrepid* riders made 308 cross-continent runs for a total of 606,000 miles. Riders carried almost 35,000 pieces of mail. In the eighteen months the Pony Express was in existence, only one mail pouch was lost. (Adapted from Joseph Conlin, *The American Past* 9e, vol. 1, © Cengage Learning.)

Here's a summary of that excerpt. Pay attention to what's been left in and what's been eliminated:

---

*longevity: lasting over an extended period of time; long life or duration.
*intrepid: brave, fearless, bold.

Summary

Often risking their lives, the riders of the Pony Express, which operated between 1860 and 1861, reduced the amount of time needed for transcontinental mail delivery by twelve days. Working in relays, the horsemen would bring mail to stations set at regular intervals along the Pony Express route, changing mounts and exchanging mail pouches at each station. The Pony Express ended when telegraph service began. By that time, it had carried almost 35,000 pieces of mail, losing only one pouch in the process.

This summary gets at all the essentials of the original by answering three key questions: Who or what was involved? When did these events occur? What was attempted or accomplished? Would you say that the following summary is as effective?

Summary

At each new station, Pony Express riders would switch to a fresh horse. Using this system, one rider was able to cover 75 to 100 miles of the 1,966-mile route before another rider took his mail pouch and continued on. As they moved across deserted parts of Missouri, Kansas, Nebraska, Wyoming, Utah, Nevada, and California, Pony Express riders faced hazards like robbers and blizzards.

If your answer was no, you are absolutely correct. This summary doesn't supply a time frame. It also adds details that weren't in the original and doesn't identify what the Pony Express system set out to do or how effectively it accomplished its goal, i.e., reduce the time it took to get mail from one part of the country to another.

Effective summaries answer the same kinds of questions good paraphrases do. Some of those questions were mentioned in Chapter 1 (see p. 23). But for your convenience, here is a list of questions that summaries should answer. The number and kind of questions will vary with the text. But every well-written summary will answer at least two or more of these questions.

Who or what was involved?

When did these events happen?

Who or what caused them?

What was attempted or accomplished?

What was the outcome?

Where did events take place?

What was the time frame?

How were the people or events involved related?

What's the underlying organizational pattern?

WEB QUEST   **From the Pony Express to International Fame**

What Pony Express rider went on to become a world famous traveling showman? What was his nickname and the name of his traveling show?

_____

_____

◆ EXERCISE 5   Recognizing an Effective Summary

DIRECTIONS   Read each selection. Then circle the letter of the better summary.

1. Kennedy and Vietnam

1   South Vietnam represented one of the most challenging issues President John F. Kennedy faced at the start of his presidency in 1960. Like Eisenhower, Kennedy saw South Vietnam as a place where the United States' flexible response could stem communism and develop a strong democratic nation. But by 1961, the president of Vietnam, Ngo Dinh Diem, was losing control of his nation.

2   South Vietnamese Communist rebels, known as the Viet Cong, controlled a large portion of the countryside, having battled Diem's troops, the Army of the Republic of Vietnam (ARVN), to a standstill. In response, U.S.

military advisers argued that the use of American troops was necessary to turn the tide.

3   Kennedy was more cautious. "The troops will march in, the bands will play," he said privately, "the crowds will cheer; and in four days everyone will have forgotten. Then we will be told we have to send in more troops. It's like taking a drink. The effect wears off and you have to take another."

4   But Kennedy gave in. The South Vietnamese forces would have to continue to do the fighting, but the president agreed to send more "advisers." By November 1963, the United States had sent $185 million in military aid and had committed sixteen thousand advisers to Vietnam—compared with only a few hundred in 1961. (Carol Berkin et al., *Making America* 5e, © Cengage Learning.)

Summary

a. **Kennedy and Vietnam**

When President John F. Kennedy came into office in 1960, he was faced with the challenge of Vietnam. Believing that Vietnam should become a democracy, he wanted to stop the Communists from taking over. Yet the man Kennedy supported, Ngo Dinh Diem, was fast losing control of his country. More in control were the Viet Cong, the South Vietnamese Communist rebels. Correctly evaluating the situation, military advisers argued that the president had to send more troops. While Kennedy was cautious, he basically agreed with that evaluation. He gave in and sent more troops, all the while insisting that the South Vietnamese forces had to do the bulk of the fighting. By 1963, the United States had committed sixteen thousand troops to Vietnam, compared to just a few hundred in 1961.

b. **Kennedy and Vietnam**

Arriving in office in 1960, President John F. Kennedy was faced with a deteriorating situation in Vietnam. The man the United States supported, Ngo Dinh Diem, was losing control of the country and the Communists were gaining ground. In response to the situation, U.S. military advisers were saying the president should send in more troops. Kennedy, however, wasn't sure that was the right idea. Still, he gave in and by 1963 the United States had committed 16,000 troops to the region, a huge increase over the few hundred sent there in 1961.

2. Hispanic and Latino Power

1 By the late 1960s, many Hispanic and Latino Americans felt that their interests and needs were not being served by either their state or local governments. Thus they grew both visible and vocal in their protests.

2 In November 1968, for instance, Mexican-American students walked out of their high school in the small south Texas school district of Edcouch-Elsa. The activists demanded dignity, respect, and an end to "blatant discrimina-tion," including corporal punishment—paddling—for speaking Spanish outside Spanish class.

3 The school board claimed outside agitators were to blame and sus-pended more than 150 students. But as in other school districts, the protests brought results. The Edcouch-Elsa school district implemented Mexican-American studies and bilingual programs, hired more Mexican-American teachers and counselors, and created programs to meet the unique needs of migrant farm children.

4 And it was not only in the West that Latino and Hispanic Americans were becoming more visible. In the urban Northeast, for instance, the Puerto Rican population had increased while job opportunities had de-creased. In response, the National Puerto Rican Forum lobbied the federal government for more jobs and job training. The more militant Young Lords in Chicago and New York began organizing younger members of the Puerto Rican population while emphasizing their island culture and Hispanic heritage.

Summary

a. Hispanic and Latino Power

By the late sixties, many Latino and Hispanic Americans felt their interests were being ignored by both state and local governments. In response, members of both communities began organizing. Students who had been forbidden to speak Spanish staged a walk-out from their schools and won the right to use their own lan-guage. In the Northeast, the National Puerto Rican Forum began organizing to get more jobs and funds from the government.

b. Hispanic and Latino Power

By the late sixties, many Latino and Hispanic-Americans felt that state and local governments were not addressing their interests. Angry over the situation, both groups began organizing to change it.

At a school in south Texas students staged a walkout to protest what they considered an injustice: being punished for speaking their own language. Like similar protests in other districts, this one brought results with more attention being paid to the needs of Mexican-American students. In the urban Northeast, Puerto Rican groups like the National Puerto Rican Forum and the Young Lords began organizing to win jobs and promote ethnic pride.

◆ EXERCISE 6 Writing Summaries

DIRECTIONS Read each selection. Underline the thesis statement and then summarize the reading in the blanks that follow.

1. The Gains and Losses of Beauty

1   No doubt about it, extremely good-looking people have a social advantage. They are less lonely; less socially anxious (especially about interactions with the opposite sex); more popular; more sexually experienced; and . . . more socially skilled (Feingold, 1992b). The social rewards for physical attractiveness appear to get off to an early start. Mothers of highly attractive newborns engage in more affectionate interactions with their babies than do mothers of less attractive infants (Langlois et al., 1995). Given such benefits, one would expect that the beautiful would also have a significant psychological advantage. But they don't. Physical attractiveness (as rated by objective judges) has little if any association with self-esteem, mental health, personality traits, or intelligence (Feingold, 1992b).

2   One possible reason why beauty doesn't affect psychological well-being is that actual physical attractiveness, as evaluated by others, may have less impact than self-perceived physical attractiveness. People who view themselves as physically attractive do report higher self-esteem and better mental health than those who believe they are unattractive (Feingold, 1992b). But other people's ratings of physical attractiveness are only modestly related to self-perceived attractiveness. When real beauties do not see themselves as beautiful, their appearance may not be psychologically valuable.

3   Physically attractive individuals may also fail to benefit from the social bias for beauty because of pressures they experience to maintain their appearance. In contemporary* American society, such pressures are particularly strong in regard to the body. Although both facial and bodily

---

*contemporary: modern, current; person living in the same time or era.

appearance contribute to perceived attractiveness, an unattractive body appears to be a greater liability* than an unattractive face. Such a "body bias" can produce a healthy emphasis on nutrition and exercise. But it can sometimes lead to distinctly unhealthy consequences. For example, men may pop steroids in order to build up impressive muscles. Among women, the desire for a beautiful body often takes a different form.

4   Women are more likely than men to suffer from what researcher Janet Polivy and her colleagues call the "modern mania for slenderness." This desire for thinness is promoted by the mass media. Popular female characters in TV shows are more likely than popular male characters to be exceedingly thin; women's magazines stress the need to maintain a slender body more than do men's magazines (Silverstein et al., 1986b). Thus some good-looking women suffer, despite their good looks, because they don't feel their body is thin enough. (Adapted from Sharon Brehm et al., *Social Psychology* 6e, © Cengage Learning.)

Summary   _____

_____

_____

_____

_____

_____

_____

_____

2. But If It's Natural, It Must Be Good for You

1   Depending on who's doing the estimating, Americans spend between $5 and $10 billion per year on herbal supplements with funny-sounding names like echinacea, ginseng, and golden seal. The production, marketing, and selling of herbal supplements is a lucrative* business with countless people consuming a variety of herbal medicines in an effort to cure both minor and major health problems. Yet herbal medicines are not

_____

*liability: drawback.
*lucrative: profitable.

regulated by the Food and Drug Administration. As a matter of fact, few scientific studies are available to prove their medicinal powers. There are even fewer to detect the possibility that some herbal medications might cause harm.

2   Amazingly, American consumers don't seem to care that there is so little empirical* evidence backing up claims for herbal medicines. Generally, consumers don't even seem worried about the ill effects of ingesting herbs. The reigning* assumption* is that herbs are natural and anything natural can't hurt you. However, that assumption is misguided, even dangerous—just try ingesting* a leaf of "natural" poison ivy. If they really want to take care of their health, consumers should demand more proof that herbal supplements can do what their makers claim. More to the point, consumers should wonder about the side effects of taking supplements that have not undergone much, if any, rigorous testing.

3   The herb widely known as comfrey, for example, is sold as a gel or an ointment for treating minor cuts and burns. To be sure, comfrey does contain allantoin, a chemical that aids in skin repair. However comfrey is also sold as a treatment for ulcers and stomach upsets, even though there is no compelling evidence that it can help either condition. On the contrary, some evidence shows that it can destroy liver cells, so ingesting* it might be extremely dangerous. Still, you are unlikely to find any warning label on a bottle of comfrey tablets, and the herb is a popular item in natural food stores.

4   It's been widely claimed that another herbal supplement, ginseng, can improve memory and mood while also boosting energy. In Germany, where there is a formal body that regulates the sale of herbal medicine, ginseng has undergone repeated testing, and the herb seems to live up to claims about its benefits. The problem with ginseng is less that the claims are exaggerated and more that authentic ginseng is hard to find and extremely expensive. Thus a bottle of tablets or powder labeled as ginseng may have very little of the herb but quite a few additives, or fillers, and some of those additives might be harmful.

5   Anyone who thinks of herbs as "all natural" and therefore beneficial should also recall what happened around a decade ago to some of those

---

*empirical: based on experiment, observation, and fact.
*reigning: showing dominant or widespread influence; holding royal office.
*assumption: widely held belief that is left unstated and rarely questioned.
*ingesting: taking into the body by swallowing or absorbing.

who took an alleged weight-loss herb known as ephedra or ma huang. Ephedra contains ephedrine, a substance that acts as a stimulant to the body and seems to encourage weight loss. But the amount of ephedrine in each plant varies according to the conditions under which the herb was grown. If a particular batch of the herb contains extremely high levels of ephedrine, then ingesting the herb can cause both blood pressure and heart rate to soar.

6   No wonder then that ephedra caused problems such as fluctuating* blood pressure, dizziness, and heart rhythm irregularities. When ephedra was being marketed as one of the components of "herbal phen-fen," an allegedly miraculous, "all natural" diet drug, scores of people who used it suffered permanent heart valve damage. At least a dozen people died as a result of taking the dietary supplement, which is more proof that the label "all natural" does not equal safe for human consumption.

Summary   _____

_____

_____

_____

_____

_____

_____

_____

_____

_____

_____

_____

_____

_____
*fluctuating: changing, going up and down.

CHECK YOUR UNDERSTANDING

1. What's the difference between a list of the main ideas in a reading and an outline of them?

   _____

2. When statements are aligned with one another, that means they are _____

   _____.

3. When one statement is indented underneath another, that means that it _____

   _____.

4. A summary is an _____ version of a longer reading. A summary should include only _____.

5. What should be the first item in your summary? _____

6. If your summary gets choppy, smooth it out with _____.

WORD CHECK II

The following words were introduced and defined in pages 287–295. See how well you can match the words with the meanings. When you finish, make sure to check the meanings of any words you missed because the same words will turn up in tests at the end of the chapter.

1. longevity (p. 287)   _____   a. changing, going up and down
2. intrepid (p. 287)   _____   b. widely held belief that is rarely questioned
3. contemporary (p. 292) _____   c. based on observation and experiment
4. liability (p. 293)   _____   d. profitable
5. lucrative (p. 293)   _____   e. modern, current; person living in the same era
6. empirical (p. 294)   _____   f. having wide influence; holding royal office
7. reigning (p. 294)   _____   g. long life, duration of life
8. assumption (p. 294)   _____   h. handicap, drawback
9. ingesting (p. 294)   _____   i. brave, fearless
10. fluctuating (p. 295)   _____   j. taking into the body by swallowing or absorbing

◆ **EXERCISE 7**   **More About Form and Meaning**

DIRECTIONS Fill in the blanks with one of the words listed below.

longevity	empiricist	fluctuations	intrepid	lucrative
ingested	contemporary	liability	assumptions	reigning

1. Who among the following could not be called a(n) _____ president: Bill Clinton, George W. Bush, Jimmy Carter, or Thomas Jefferson?

2. The word _____ is used to describe gains and losses in stocks, weight, and price.

3. For a young girl determined to play professional basketball, being average height would be considered a(n) _____.

4. Action heroes in movies are expected to be _____; if they aren't, audiences want their money back.

5. In analyzing other people's arguments we are quick to challenge their underlying _____; what's harder to do is recognize and examine our own.

6. Most people dream of making _____ investments; except to save on taxes, not too many people search out those that have low earnings.

7. In Shakespeare's play *Othello*, the villain Iago tells Othello that his wife has been unfaithful and Othello responds by saying that he wants "ocular proof," or evidence that can be seen with the eye.

   That makes Othello a(n) _____.

8. Belief in "The Great Chain of Being" was one of the _____ concepts, or ideas, of the seventeenth century, when every individual, creature, and idea was believed to have its specific place in a divinely ordered hierarchy.

9. In January 2010, the world's oldest living dog, according to the Guinness book of records at least, was put to sleep. The dog, Otto, was twenty years and eleven months, which is remarkable

   _____ for a dog.

10. Nancy Hazle was one of the most notorious women of the twentieth century. Dubbed the "Giggling Grandma" by the press, she baked prune tarts sprinkled with arsenic for at least ten people,

    and no one who _____ the tarts lived long enough to complain about her baking.

ALLUSION ALERT

Impressionism

The reading that follows will compare remembering to an impressionist painting. To make sense of that allusion you need to know that the impressionist painters belonged to a nineteenth-century movement that turned away from realism in favor of putting their personal impressions of the world on canvas. Impressionists didn't record the world as it was; they painted pictures of the world as it appeared to them.

TAKING STOCK Can We Trust Our Memories?

Looking Ahead
Chapter 1 described how paraphrasing and note-taking could act as memory aids. The following reading will tell you more about the workings of memory. The more you know about memory, the better equipped you are to make use of techniques that enhance your ability to remember what you read.

1   Although we'd like to think that our memories accurately reflect events we've witnessed or experienced, our recollections may not be as reliable as we believe them to be. Contemporary memory researchers reject the view that long-term memory works like a video camera that records exact copies of experience. Their view, generally called **constructionist theory**, holds that memory is a reconstructive process. What we recall from memory is not a replica of the past, but a re-creation, or *reconstruction*, of the past. We stitch together bits and pieces of information stored in long-term memory to form a coherent, or unified, account of past experiences and events. Reconstruction, however, can lead to distorted memories of events and experiences.

2   According to constructionist theory, memories are not carbon copies of reality. From this vantage point, it is not surprising that people who witness the same event or read the same material may have very different memories of the event or of the passage they read. Nor would it be surprising if recollections of your childhood are not verbatim records of what actually occurred but rather reconstructions based on pieces of information from many sources—from old photographs, from what your mother told you about the time you fell from the tree when you were ten, and so on.

3   Constructionist theory leads us to expect that memories may be distorted. These distortions can range from simplifications, to omissions of details, to outright fabrications or lies. Even so, we shouldn't presume that all memories are distorted. Some may be more or less accurate reflections of events. Others, perhaps most, can be likened more to impressionist paintings than to mental snapshots of experiences.

4   **Recovery of Repressed Memories** Controversy has swirled around the issue of whether long-repressed memories of childhood experiences that suddenly surface in adulthood are credible. In most cases, such memories come to light during hypnosis or psychotherapy. On the basis of recovered memories of sexual trauma in childhood, authorities have brought charges of sexual abuse against hundreds of people. A number of these cases have resulted in convictions and long jail sentences, even in the absence of

corroborating, or supporting, evidence. But should recovered memories be taken at face value?

5   A total lack of memory of traumatic childhood events is rare, although it is possible that such memories may be lost in some cases (Bradley & Follingstad, 2001). We also know that false memories can be induced in many subjects in experimental studies (Zoellner, Foa, Brigidi, & Przeworski, 2000). Entire events that never happened can enter a subject's memory and seem just as real and accurate as memories of events that really did occur. However, evidence of false memory creation in experimental studies does not prove that recovered memories in actual cases are, in fact, false.

6   In sum, many investigators believe that some recovered memories may be genuine and that others are undoubtedly false. The problem is that in the absence of corroborating evidence, we simply lack the tools to differentiate between true memories and false ones.

7   From a constructionist standpoint, we should not be surprised that memories may be distorted, even when the person believes them to be true. The use of suggestive interviewing or therapeutic techniques or hypnosis can heighten suggestibility to false memories. Psychologists and other mental health professionals need to be cautious about assuming the veracity of recovered memories and vigilant about monitoring their own roles so that they don't contribute to the construction of false memories.

(Adapted from Jeffrey Nevid, *Psychology* 4e, © Cengage Learning.)

Sharpening Your Skills

DIRECTIONS Answer the following questions by circling the letter of the correct response or filling in the blanks.

Using Context Clues

1. Based on the context, how would you define the word *replica* in the following sentence? "What we recall from memory is not a *replica* of the past, but a re-creation, or reconstruction, of the past."

    a. copy

    b. remainder

    c. memory

    d. thought

2. In paragraph 2, which two phrases restate the word *replica* in paragraph 1?

    _____

3. Based on the context, how would you define the word *corroborating* in the following sentence? "The problem is that in the absence of *corroborating* evidence, we simply lack the tools to differentiate between true memories and false ones."

   a. irrelevant

   b. challenging

   c. supporting

   d. distracting

Understanding the Controlling Main Idea

4. What is the topic of the reading?

   _____

5. Which of the following best expresses the main idea of the entire reading?

   a. Memory researchers now believe that with enough effort we can completely avoid distorting our memories of past events. However, to avoid distortion we have to give conscious attention to what happens in the present.

   b. Recovered memories, despite the controversy surrounding them, are authentic, and the fact that they exist fits perfectly with the constructionist notion of how we remember past events.

   c. Memory researchers now believe that when we remember we combine bits of information stored in long-term memory to re-create some version of past experience that makes sense. Unfortunately, in constructing the past we remember we can be mistaken about what happened and what didn't.

   d. In contrast to the constructionist theory of memory, new research suggests that we store exact copies of our experiences in long-term memory, which is one reason why recovered stories of abuse need to be considered hard evidence of a crime committed in the past.

6. Which paragraph introduces the thesis statement?

a. paragraph 1

b. paragraph 2

c. paragraph 3

7. What is the author's answer to the question posed in the title? _____ Please explain.

_____

_____

_____

_____

Spotting Transitional Signals

8. What two reversal or contrast transitions appear in paragraph 1?

_____

Recognizing Organizational Patterns

9. Which is the primary pattern of organization in paragraph 1?

a. simple listing

b. definition

c. comparison and contrast

d. classification

10. Based on that pattern what piece of information from paragraph 1 must appear in your notes?

_____

11. Which two patterns unify the entire reading?

a. cause and effect; comparison and contrast

b. sequence of dates and events; cause and effect

c. cause and effect; definition

d. classification; cause and effect

Paraphrasing 12. Which of the following best paraphrases the topic sentence from paragraph 3?

a. Constructionist theory proves that memories of past childhood abuse are completely false.

b. Using constructionist theory to explain remembering encourages the idea that some memories can be false.

c. Research on constructionist theory suggests that all memories involve some distortion.

Understanding Supporting Details 13. Which of the following best describes the relationship between the three sentences that make up paragraph 7?

a. topic sentence, major detail, minor detail

b. introductory sentence, topic sentence, major detail

c. topic sentence, major detail, major detail

Summarizing 14. Which of the following best summarizes the section of the reading following the heading "Recovery of Repressed Memories"?

a. Although complete amnesia about traumatic experiences in childhood is rare, there is research evidence showing that people can be encouraged by others to remember what never happened. That doesn't mean that all recovered memories are false, but it does mean that it's impossible to know which ones are true and which ones not. Thus mental health professionals working with those who believe they have remembered a buried experience of child abuse need to be very careful about not influencing what their patients or clients remember and they can't assume all recovered memories are accurate accounts of what really happened.

b. Controversy always erupts when people say that they have recovered a repressed memory of childhood abuse, usually because these memories are likely to come to light during hypnosis. In the past when someone has recounted a long-suppressed memory, the response has been swift, and authorities have brought charges against hundreds of people based on recovered memories of abuse. In several instances, these charges have led to convictions and lengthy jail sentences despite the fact that there was no other evidence except for the recovered memory.

Recognizing Purpose

15. What is the primary purpose of the section about repressed memories?

   a. to inform readers about the existence of repressed memories

   b. to tell readers that accounts of repressed memories have always been proved true when subjected to investigation

   c. to persuade readers that repressed memories are always true and need to be taken seriously

   d. to convince readers that accounts of repressed memories need to be carefully evaluated because they may not always be accurate

REVIEWING THROUGH WRITING

Summarize the previous reading, making sure that your summary opens with the main idea. In this case, you don't need to include the author or the source. Start with a paraphrase of the overall main idea and then sum up, in your own words, the most essential supporting details needed to explain it.

▶ **TEST 1**   **Identifying the Controlling Main Idea and Purpose**

DIRECTIONS   Circle the appropriate letter to identify the controlling main idea of each selection. Then identify the reading's primary purpose by writing *I* or *P* in the blank at the end.

1. Social Media's Role in Criminal Investigations

1   As anyone who hasn't been living in a cave for the last decade must have noticed, social networking has become quite popular. That popularity has not gone unnoticed by police departments, and the police have successfully jumped on the social media bandwagon to combat a number of different law-breaking activities.

2   In addition to maintaining department websites, many police agencies have Facebook pages. Others report calls for service on Twitter, in real time, so concerned citizens can track crime trends and read details about what is happening in their communities—and where. In one case, a storeowner helped detectives investigate the theft of a valuable collector's jersey from his store. Detectives zeroed in on the store's Facebook friends list and quickly identified the four thieves because they were on the list. With successes like these, some departments have gone so far as to assign detectives to full-time monitoring of sites like Facebook for leads on criminal activity.

3   Police have even made drug busts after people arranged drug sales via Facebook! The people arranging the deals were actually dumb enough to boast about them on the social media site. Police have also used Facebook to combat underage drinking by zooming in on incriminating photos posted by underage drinkers. While it is true that Facebook requires people to be confirmed as friends to view the details of a person's page, some people are less than careful with their security settings and end up posting their information for the world to see. Also, it's not particularly difficult to become a person's Facebook friend. In one case, police worked with teenage volunteers to investigate cyber bullying. The volunteers would become friends with the suspects and then share information with the police. As one detective put it, "We'd be foolish not to use social networking as an investigative tool." (Adapted from Larry J. Siegel and John L. Worrall, *Essentials of Criminal Justice* 8e, © Cengage Learning.)

——————

**Recognizing
the Controlling
Main Idea**

a. Police departments all across the country have had enormous success controlling gang violence through the use of social media.

b. Police departments are using social media to monitor underage drinking.

c. Police are successfully using social media to fight crime.

2. Marital Satisfaction in New Families

1   Almost all studies that measure marital satisfaction before and after the birth of the first child have found that the birth of a child is a mixed marital blessing. Researchers have found that couples who were least satisfied with their marriages before the birth were most likely to report a decline in satisfaction after. Problems that existed before were likely to have been magnified by the additional stresses brought on by the birth.

2   Babies, however, do not appear to create severe marital distress where none existed before; nor do they bring couples with distressed marriages closer together. Rather, the early postpartum[†] months bring on a period of disorganization and change. The leading conflict in these first months of parenthood is division of labor in the family. Couples may regain their sense of equilibrium in marriage by successfully negotiating how they will divide the new responsibilities. The husbands' participation in child and home care, for instance, seems to be positively related to marital satisfaction after the birth. One study found that the more the men shared in doing family tasks, the more satisfied the wives were at six and eighteen months postpartum and the husbands at eighteen months postpartum.

3   While many couples experience a difficult transition to parenthood, they also find it rewarding. Children affect parents in ways that lead to personal growth; enable reworking of childhood conflicts; build flexibility and empathy; and provide intimate, loving human connections. They also give a lot of pleasure. In follow-up interviews of new parents when their children were eighteen months old, Philip Cowan and Carolyn Cowan found that almost every man and woman spoke of the delight they felt from knowing their child and watching the child develop. They reported feeling pride for and closeness to their spouses, more adult with their own

---

[†]postpartum: after birth.

parents, and a renewed sense of purpose at work. (Adapted from Kelvin Seifert et al., *Lifespan Development* 2e, Houghton Mifflin, 2000.)

_____

Recognizing the Controlling Main Idea

a. Studies of marital happiness suggest that children are the key to a happy marriage.

b. While the birth of a first child is a plus for a marriage, more than one child can be a strain.

c. Studies of marital happiness suggest that a baby can unite an unhappy couple.

d. Studies of marital satisfaction suggest that the birth of a first child has both positive and negative effects.

▶ **TEST 2** **Recognizing Thesis Statements and Supporting Details**

DIRECTIONS Underline the thesis statement. Then answer the questions by filling in the blanks or circling the letter of the correct response. *Note*: To decide if a detail is major or minor, you will probably need to look at the sentences in the context of the paragraphs where they appear. The numbers in parentheses identify the paragraph where the detail appears.

1. Feminist Objections to Pornography

1   Beginning around 1978, some—though not all—feminists became very critical of pornography and many remain so to the current day. Although many younger feminists do not share the early generation's strong objections to pornographic literature and films, those who are opposed are vehement in their sense that pornography is a direct threat to the lives of women. In support of their claim, they offer four basic objections to the idea that pornography does no harm.

2   First, they argue that pornography debases women. Even milder, soft-core pornography portrays women as sex objects, whose breasts, legs, and buttocks can be purchased for the viewing entertainment of men. Those who object to the sale of pornographic films argue that watching naked women for entertainment encourages disrespect for women in general.

3   The second objection revolves around the way pornography associates sex with violence toward women. As such, some feminists argue, it contributes to rape and other forms of violence against women and girls. Long-time feminist Robin Morgan famously said that "pornography is the theory and rape is the practice."

4   According to the third objection, pornography glamorizes unequal power relationships between women and men. A common theme in pornography is that of men forcing women to have sex. Thus the power of men and subordination of women are emphasized. Consistent with this point, feminists do not object to sexual materials that portray women and men in equal, humanized relationships—what we would term *erotica*.

5   Feminists also argue that pornography may serve to perpetuate traditional gender roles. By seeing or reading about dominant males and obedient dehumanized females, men are encouraged to devalue women. Even worse for future generations, adolescent boys are being encouraged to think of themselves as the controlling figure in sexual relationships. (Adapted from Janet Shibley Hyde et al., *Understanding Human Sexuality* 2e, McGraw-Hill, 2004, p. 524.)

1. Based on the title, what question should you use to guide your reading?

   _____

2. In your own words, what is the main idea of the reading?

   _____

   _____

3. What clue in the thesis statement should you use to identify the major details?

   _____

   _____

4. Which of the following is *not* a major detail?
   a. Pornography associates sex with violence toward women. (3)
   b. Robin Morgan put it bluntly: "Pornography is the theory and rape is the practice." (3)

5. Which of the following is a minor detail?
   a. Feminists argue that pornography debases women. (2)
   b. Pornography glamorizes unequal power relationships. (4)
   c. A common theme in pornography is that of men forcing women to have sex. (4)

2. The Meaning of Touch

1   Touching and being touched is an essential part of being human. However, the amount and meaning of touch change with age, purpose, and location. Infants and their parents, for example, engage in extensive touching behavior, but this decreases during adolescence. The amount of touching behavior increases after adolescence as young people begin to establish romantic relationships. No matter how much we are touched, however, most of us want to be touched more than we are (Mosby, 1978).

2   In general, the meaning of touch varies with the situation, and there are five basic categories of meaning. *Positive affective touches* transmit messages of support, appreciation, affection, or sexual intent. *Playful touches* lighten our interactions with others. *Control touches* are used to get other

people's attention and to gain their compliance. *Ritualistic touches* are those we use during communication rituals such as greeting others and saying goodbye. *Task-related touches* are those that are necessary for us to complete tasks on which we are working. Touches also can fit into more than one category at a time. We can, for example, touch others as part of a ritual to express affection.

3   Age, sex, and region of the country also influence the amount people touch. To illustrate, people between eighteen and twenty-five and between thirty and forty report the most touching, while old people report the least (Mosby, 1978). Women find touching more pleasant than men do, as long as the other person is not a stranger (Heslin, 1978). Finally, people who live in the South touch more than people who live in the North (Howard, 1985).

4   The United States is generally a noncontact culture. People do not engage in a great deal of touching. There are, however, situations in which people are likely to touch (Henley, 1977). People are more likely to touch, for example, when giving information or advice than when receiving information or advice. People are more likely to touch others when giving orders than when receiving orders, when asking for a favor than when granting a favor, or when trying to persuade others than when being persuaded. (Adapted from William B. Gudykunst et al., *Building Bridges*, Pearson, 1994, pp. 319–320.)

1. Based on the title, what question would you use to guide your reading?

   _____

2. In your own words, what is the main idea of the reading?

   _____

   _____

3. Which of the following is a major detail?

   a. People who live in the South touch more than do people who live in the North. (3)

   b. Age, sex, and region influence the amount people touch. (3)

   c. People are more likely to touch, for example, when giving information or advice. (4)

4. Which of the following is a major detail?

    a. In general, the meaning of touch varies with the situation, and there are five basic categories of meaning. (2)

    b. We can, for example, touch others as part of a ritual to express positive affection. (2)

    c. People between eighteen and twenty-five and between thirty and forty report the most touching. (3)

5. Which of the following is a minor detail?

    a. Women find touching more pleasant than men do, as long as the other person is not a stranger. (3)

    b. The amount and meaning of touch change with age, purpose, and location. (1)

    c. Age, sex, and region of the country also influence the amount people touch. (3)

▶ **TEST 3** **Outlining Longer Readings**

DIRECTIONS Read each selection and underline the thesis statement. In the blanks that follow, create an informal outline of the reading.

1. Defense Mechanisms Protect the Ego

1   Threatening situations tend to produce anxiety. When you are anxious, you feel tense, uneasy, apprehensive, worried, and vulnerable. This unpleasant state of mind can lead to emotion-focused coping that is defensive in nature. Psychologists have identified several defense mechanisms that allow us to reduce anxiety caused by stressful situations. What follows are three of the most common.

2   A **defense mechanism** is any mental process used to protect our self-image. Almost all the defense mechanisms that psychologists recognize today were identified by the Austrian psychoanalyst[†] Sigmund Freud, who believed they operated unconsciously. And it does seem to be true that the use of defense mechanisms creates blind spots in awareness.

3   **Denial** One of the most basic defenses is denial (protecting oneself from an unpleasant reality by refusing to accept it or believe it). For instance, if you were told that you had only three months to live, how would you react? Your first thoughts might be "Aw, come on, someone must have mixed up the X-rays" or "The doctor must be mistaken." Denial and disbelief are common reactions to the unexpected death of a friend or relative.

4   **Repression** Freud also noticed that his patients had tremendous trouble recalling shocking or frightening events from childhood. It seemed that powerful forces were holding these painful memories from awareness. Freud termed this response **repression**, and said that we use it to protect ourselves by blocking out threatening thoughts or impulses. Feelings of hostility toward a family member, the names of people we dislike, and past failures are common targets of repression. When these feelings emerge, we block them as quickly as possible.

5   **Reaction Formation** In reaction formation, impulses are not just repressed; they are held in check by exaggerating the opposite behavior. For example, a mother who resents the responsibility of children may, through reaction formation, become absurdly over-protective and over-indulgent. Her real thoughts of "I resent them and wish I had some time away from them" are replaced by thoughts like "I adore them and never want them out of my sight."

(Adapted from Dennis Coon and John O. Mitterer, *Psychology: A Journey* 4e, © Cengage Learning.)

[†]psychoanalyst: a therapist who looks to childhood for the source of one's psychological problems.

Main Idea

_____

_____

Supporting Details

_____

_____

_____

_____

_____

_____

_____

_____

2. Phobias Can Be Crippling

1   *Phobias* are intense and irrational fears of everything from spiders to open spaces. Some of the more common phobias are fear of heights, blood, flying, dogs, and enclosed spaces. The key element distinguishing a phobia from a normal fear is irrationality. Phobias are not based on reason. For instance, someone who is phobic about spiders would be just as terrified by a harmless Daddy Long Legs as by a deadly tarantula. In the United States, phobias are the most prevalent of the anxiety disorders. They affect 7 to 10 percent of adults and children.

2   Perhaps the most disabling phobia is *agoraphobia*. Agoraphobia is an intense fear of being away from a safe place like one's home; of being away from a familiar person, such as a spouse or close friend; or of being in a place from which departure might be difficult or help unavailable. For those who suffer from agoraphobia, attempts to leave home cause extreme anxiety. Thus agoraphobics are often severely housebound. For them, theaters, shopping malls, public transportation, and other potentially crowded places are particularly threatening. Most individuals who suffer from agoraphobia also have a history of panic attacks. In fact, their intense fear of public places starts partly because they don't want to go where they feel panicking would be dangerous or embarrassing.

3   Social phobias revolve around the fear of being negatively evaluated by others or acting in a way that is embarrassing or humiliating. This anxiety

is so intense and persistent that it impairs the person's normal functioning. *Common social phobias* are fear of public speaking or performance ("stage fright"), fear of eating in front of others, and fear of using public restrooms (Kleinknecht, 2000). A *generalized social phobia* is a more severe form in that victims experience fear in virtually all social situations (Mannuzzi et al., 1995). Sociocultural factors can alter the form of social phobias. For example, in Japan, where cultural training emphasizes group-oriented values and goals, a common social phobia is *taijin kyofusho*—fear of embarrassing those around you (Kleinknecht, 1994). (Adapted from Douglas Bernstein et al., *Psychology* 6e, © Cengage Learning.)

Main Idea

_____

_____

Supporting Details

_____

_____

_____

_____

_____

_____

_____

_____

_____

_____

_____

_____

_____

▶ **TEST 4**   **Recognizing the Best Summary**

DIRECTIONS   Read the selection. Then circle the letter of the summary that best fits the pointers on summary writing introduced in the chapter.

1. The Controversy Over the Death Penalty

1   Obviously, a great deal of controversy continues to surround the issue of executing criminals. Researchers generally agree that if punishment is to discourage future criminal behavior, it must be swift and certain. Neither of these conditions is met by the death penalty in the United States, and few reasonable and informed people today argue that capital punishment acts as a deterrent, except in the specific case of the individual who is executed. Studies comparing homicide rates between states with and without death penalties either find no significant difference or disclose that states with capital punishment actually have higher rates of homicide.

2   Also disturbing is the fact that personal characteristics of judges influence their decisions. Republicans are much more likely to vote for the death penalty, as are older judges and those with previous experience as a prosecutor. In this sense, the death penalty resembles a lottery. Application of the death penalty can also be shocking, in more ways than one. Florida's "Old Sparky" overheated in 1997, causing flames and smoke to erupt from a leather mask worn by the unfortunate murderer, Pedro Medina. (This gruesome scene helped to convince Florida officials to replace the chair with lethal injection in January 2000.) Perhaps most distressful of all aspects of the death penalty is the possibility that an innocent party may be executed. (Excerpted from Ann O'M. Bowman and Richard C. Kearney, *State and Local Government 5e,* © Cengage Learning.)

   a. In the United States, the death penalty is extremely controversial, and many people oppose its use because it is said to be ineffective, unfair, and cruel. However, death-penalty opponents tend to exaggerate these so-called flaws. They also ignore the fact that execution has been a just form of punishment for hundreds of evildoers who deserved to pay the ultimate price for taking a life and, in some cases, lives.

   b. The death penalty is a flawed form of punishment that studies show does not affect the homicide rate. The threat of the death penalty fails to deter people from committing murder. It is also applied inconsistently, and judges differ in their readiness to exact the death penalty. In addition, as the 1997 Florida execution of Pedro Medina illustrates, the application of the death penalty can cause inhumane suffering to those being executed.

c. The case of Pedro Medina is a perfect illustration of why Americans should follow the Europeans and abolish the death penalty. Medina was executed in an electric chair so old it was nicknamed "Old Sparky." After officials pulled the switch on Medina, the machine overheated and flames erupted from the executed murderer's head. Is it any wonder Florida officials replaced the electric chair with lethal injection?

2. Toxic Agents

1   There are three major types of potentially toxic agents. *Mutagens* are chemicals or forms of radiation that cause or increase the frequency of mutations, or changes, in the DNA molecules found in cells. Most mutations cause no harm but some can lead to cancers and other disorders. For example, nitrous acid, formed by the digestion of nitrate preservatives in foods, can cause mutations linked to increases in stomach cancer in people who consume large amounts of processed foods.

2   *Teratogens* are chemicals that cause harm or birth defects to a fetus or an embryo. Ethyl alcohol is a teratogen. Drinking during pregnancy can lead to offspring with low birth weight and a number of physical, developmental, behavioral, and mental problems. Other teratogens are arsenic, benzene, chlorine, chloroform, chromium, DDT, lead, mercury, PCBs, thalidomide, and vinyl chloride.

3   *Carcinogens* are chemicals or types of radiation that can cause or promote cancer—a disease in which malignant cells multiply uncontrollably and create tumors that can damage the body and often lead to death. Examples of carcinogens are arsenic, benzene, vinyl chloride, chromium, PCBs, and various chemicals in tobacco smoke. (Adapted from G. Tyler Miller, *Living in the Environment* 15e, © Cengage Learning.)

a. Toxic agents are generally classified into three basic categories. "Mutagens" encourage genetic changes that can sometimes lead to cancer, for instance, nitrates in processed foods are linked to stomach cancer. "Teratogens" are chemicals that can harm the growth of a fetus or an embryo. Alcohol is an example of a teratogen. "Carcinogens" come in the form of chemicals or radiation, and they can cause or promote cancer. In addition to being classified as a teratogen, arsenic is also considered a carcinogen.

b. Toxic agents are deadly chemicals that can cause cancer. Nitrates in processed food, for example, are linked to cancer of the stomach. Alcohol is another deadly chemical that can cause birth defects. Carcinogens also promote cancer. Arsenic is a good example of a carcinogen that can also cause serious birth defects.

c. *Mutagens* are chemicals or forms of radiation that cause or increase the frequency of mutations, or changes, in the DNA. *Teratogens* are chemicals that cause harm or birth defects to a fetus or an embryo. *Carcinogens* are chemicals or types of radiation that can cause or promote cancer.

▶ TEST 5   Summarizing Longer Readings

DIRECTIONS Read each excerpt and summarize it on the blank lines that follow.

1. Going West

1   In nineteenth-century America, many people were convinced that moving West would give them a better life. Railroad expansion had made remote farming regions accessible, and the construction of grain elevators eased problems of shipping and storage. As a result of population growth, the demand for farm products had grown rapidly, and the prospects for commercial agriculture—growing crops for profit—seemed more favorable than ever.

2   Life on the farm, however, was much harder than the advertisements and railroad agents suggested. The newly arrived easterners often encountered shortages of essentials they had once taken for granted. The open prairies contained little lumber for housing and fuel. Pioneer families were forced to build houses of sod and to burn manure for heat. Water was sometimes as scarce as timber. Few families were lucky or wealthy enough to buy land near a stream that did not dry up in summer and freeze in winter. Machinery for drilling wells was scarce until the 1880s, and even then it was very expensive.

3   The weather was seldom predictable. In summer, weeks of intense heat and parching winds often gave way to violent storms that washed away crops and property. In winter, the wind and cold from blizzards piled up mountainous snowdrifts that halted all outdoor movement. (Adapted from Mary Beth Norton et al., *A People and a Nation* 5e, © Cengage Learning.)

Summary _____

_____

_____

_____

_____

_____

_____

2. Taking a Conversational Turn

1　Have you ever conversed with another person who wouldn't stop talking? If so, you may have wondered whether that person was clueless, obnoxious, or just playing by a different set of cultural rules. Whatever the reason for such behavior, lopsided conversations usually remind us that turn-taking is a fundamental part of the give and take we expect from others in our everyday interactions. Because most people don't verbalize intentions to speak or listen, learning to navigate conversational twists and turns can be a real challenge. The signals we use to regulate the flow of speech consist largely of verbal cues and gestures.

2　When we are speaking and want to continue speaking, we use signals that communicate our intention to listeners. These signals prevent unwanted interruptions. They include raising the volume of our voice, uttering *um*'s and *ah*'s, continuing to gesture, gazing away from the listener, and so on.

3　However, if we don't want to continue speaking, we can relinquish our turn by dropping the volume and pitch of our voice, slowing the tempo of our speech, pausing, not gesturing, making eye contact with a listener, or raising our eyebrows. These are turn-yielding signals. Some research shows that conversants are more inclined to take turns when speakers use these signals (Duncan, 1972).

4　As listeners, we also employ turn-taking signals. To express a desire to speak, we employ various turn-requesting signals. These signals include an open mouth, audible inhalations, a raised index finger or hand, forward body lean, eye contact, quickened or exaggerated head nods, and simultaneous speech (i.e., listener's speech overlaps the speaker's). (Adapted from Martin S. Remland, *Nonverbal Communication in Everyday Life* 3e, Pearson, 2008, pp. 255–256.)

Summary　_____

_____

_____

_____

_____

_____

_____

▶ **TEST 6**   **Reviewing New Vocabulary**

DIRECTIONS   Fill in the blanks with one of the words below.

assumption	fluctuations	zealous	rapacious	longevity
lucrative	distorted	reigning	perpetuate	contemporary
alleged	liability	havoc	throes	ingested
empirical	intrepid	sacrilegious	concede	reputable

1. Boom and Bust in the 1920s Stock Market

1   Throughout the 1920s, the stock market experienced an unprecedented boom. While historically the American economy had experienced intense, boom-and-bust _____, most of those investing in the stock market during the twenties seemed to be undergoing a bout of amnesia. Among investors, the _____ _____ was that the boom would go on forever. Pouring money into the market, the most _____ investors assured one another that stock market crashes were a thing of the past. Financial depressions and crashes belonged to the country's history but would play no part in _____ affairs, they insisted. To disagree with that optimistic prediction was considered _____, so convinced were investors that they could keep on making the _____ investments that had amassed huge fortunes over the last decade.

2   But then came 1929 and Black Tuesday. Suddenly the country plunged into the _____ of a financial depression, the likes of which had not been seen since the 1870s. Even the most _____ and _____ of investors backed away from the market. However, it was too late. Not just the stock market but the entire country seemed to be plunging into a bottomless pit of misery. Even the richest Americans felt the financial pinch, and suicides among failed investors and brokers occured across the country. Some jumped out the window while others used a gun. A few _____ poison. All the while, the poor wondered how they were going to find food and shelter to survive another day. By 1933, stocks had hit rock bottom, and the most devoted fan of stock market investment had to _____ that the risks had been much greater than anticipated. Stocks were now worth only 20 percent of their original value.

3   By the time Franklin D. Roosevelt was inaugurated in 1933, the entire banking system had ceased to function. Checks, even those written on accounts of the most _____ banks, were worthless as payment because no one knew for sure the banks had the funds to make the checks good. In response to this liquidity crisis,[†] the government set up the Federal Deposit Insurance Corporation (FDIC), to eliminate the bank "runs" in which so many investors lined up to get their money the banks ran out of cash. The federal government also banned commercial banks from investing depositors' money in stocks so that banks could no longer lose that money in the market.[†] It took time and a good deal of federal money, but the country eventually emerged from its devastating financial collapse.

2. General Motors and the Fate of the Corvair

1   In the early 1950s, U.S. automakers seemed to believe that Americans would buy only big cars. However, automakers realized their mistake when compact imports like the Volkswagen Beetle began winning a substantial share of the U.S. market. In response to the European threat, General Motors introduced the Corvair, a car meant to compete with Germany's Volkswagen Beetle. With an engine made almost entirely of aluminum, the car was both lightweight and durable.

2   Initially the Corvair was a hit. *Motor Trend* magazine named it Car of the Year in 1960, and GM's new compact car looked like it might have serious _____ as a market favorite. However, it wasn't long before rumors began to surface. It was _____ that the car had handling problems and was inclined to skid on curves. Aware that such rumors could prove a serious _____ to success in the marketplace, General Motors completely redesigned the car, focusing particularly on the rear suspension in order to make the Corvair more stable. In 1964, GM debuted the 1965 second generation Corvair. Once again the car appeared to have a bright future.

3   But then disaster struck. An aggressive young lawyer named Ralph Nader published *Unsafe at Any Speed*, an attack on the auto industry's safety record. To GM's dismay the entire first chapter was devoted to the Corvair's handling problems. And Nader wasn't just repeating

---

[†]A liquidity crisis means there is no cash available.
[†]Most of the safeguards instituted by the Roosevelt administration were eventually eliminated, and there are those who think that's one of the reasons for the financial crash of 2008.

rumors. He had _____ proof in the form of a GM whistle blower named George Caramagna, an engineer at the company, who had documented the Corvair's handling problems and fought with management about changing the design. In the end, it didn't matter that GM had changed the design and that the Corvair suspension Nader described was on the old models, not the newer ones. The book wreaked

_____ with the Corvair's sales. They dropped by half. By 1969 the car was no longer on the market.

4   The Corvair may be gone, but it's never quite been forgotten. It still has passionate advocates who love the car and sing its praises. Some have gone to extreme lengths to prove their devotion. Rose Martin so loved her Corvair, she was buried in it in 1998. Needless to say, Ralph Nader did not endear himself to the car's fans when he wrote a book that forever tarnished the Corvair's reputation. To this day, the Corvair's biggest defenders insisted he seriously _____ the car's safety record and helped _____ a negative image of the car long after its problems had been solved. (Source of decline in sales: www.conceptcarz .com/vehicle/z7043/chevrolet-corvair.aspx.)

Reviewing with Longer Readings

Courtesy and © Ulrich Flemming from *Found Art Around the World*

The following reading selections will give you a chance to apply what you have learned to longer, multi-paragraph readings. The questions accompanying the readings will ask you to think more about everything from making predictions based on the title to what goes into a good outline and a useful summary. However, you'll also be asked to form your own opinions about the topics and issues discussed in these readings. Understanding how other people think is extremely important to your success in and out of school. But you can't stop there. Comprehending the ideas of others should be the first step toward developing and refining your own views on the world.

◆ **READING 1**

Heredity or Environment: What Can Identical Twins Tell Us?

Jim Henslin

Looking Ahead This reading from a sociology textbook focuses on identical twins and uses them to explore a question that has been discussed for decades: Which plays a bigger role in who we are and what we become, our experience or our genes?

Getting Focused Anytime a writer poses a question in the title, read for the answer. By the time you finish, you should be able to sum up how this author responds to the question suggested by the title: What can identical twins tell us about the role of heredity and environment in our lives?

> **TEXTBOOK TIP** Authors of sociology texts use studies to prove a point about human behavior. Whenever you see a study cited, be sure you can determine what the study is meant to prove. Then make a marginal note indicating what idea about human behavior the study or studies support.

If an author starts off by saying what should be, what do you expect will follow?

1 Identical twins share exactly the same genetic heredity. One fertilized egg divides to produce two embryos. If heredity determines personality—or attitudes, temperament, skills, and intelligence—then identical twins should be identical not only in their looks but also in these characteristics.

2   The fascinating case of Jack and Oskar helps us unravel the mystery of which affects us more, our heredity or our environment. From their experience, we can see the far-reaching effects of the environment—how social experience takes precedence over biology.

3   Jack Yufe and Oskar Stohr are identical twins born in 1932 to a Jewish father and a Catholic mother. They were separated as babies after their parents divorced. Oskar was reared in Czechoslovakia by his mother's mother, who was a strict Catholic. When Oskar was a toddler, Hitler annexed this area of Czechoslovakia, and Oskar learned to love Hitler and to hate Jews. He joined the Hitler Youth, a sort of Boy Scout organization, except that this one was designed to instill the "virtues" of patriotism, loyalty, obedience—and hatred.

Paragraph 2 suggests the author is on which side of the nature/nurture debate?

4   Jack's upbringing was a mirror image of Oskar's. Reared in Trinidad by his father, he learned loyalty to Jews and hatred of Hitler and the Nazis.

The author suddenly becomes more specific in paragraph 3. What does that suggest about paragraph 2?

After the war, Jack and his father moved to Israel. When he was 17, Jack joined a kibbutz,[†] and later, served in the Israeli army.

5   In 1954, the two brothers met. It was a short meeting and Jack had been warned not to tell Oskar that they were Jews. Twenty-five years later, in 1979, when they were 47 years old, social scientists brought them together again. These researchers figured that because Jack and Oskar had the same genes, any differences they showed would have to be the result of their environment—their different social experiences.

6   Not only did Oskar and Jack hold different attitudes toward the war, Hitler, and Jews, but also their basic orientations to life were different. In their politics, Oskar was conservative while Jack was more liberal. Oskar enjoyed leisure, while Jack was a workaholic. And as you can predict, Jack was very proud of being a Jew. Oskar, who by this time knew he was a Jew, wouldn't even mention it.

7   That would seem to settle the matter. But there was another side. The researchers also found that Oskar and Jack had both excelled at sports as children, but had difficulty with math. They also had the same rate of speech and both liked sweet liqueur and spicy foods. Strangely, both flushed the toilet both before and after using it and enjoyed startling people by sneezing in crowded elevators. (James Henslin, *Sociology: A Down-to-Earth Approach* 9e, © Jim Henslin, p. 66.)

Reviewing Concepts and Skills

DIRECTIONS Answer the following questions by filling in the blanks or circling the letter of the correct response.

Making Predictions 1. What does the title suggest about identical twins?

_____

_____

Recognizing the Controlling Main Idea 2. What's the topic of the reading?

a. heredity

b. identical twins

c. the identical twins Jack and Oskar

_____

[†]kibbutz: an Israeli group living arrangement, typically a farm.

3. Which is the thesis statement?

a. Identical twins share exactly the same genetic heredity. One fertilized egg divides to produce two embryos.

b. If heredity determines personality—or attitudes, temperament, skills, and intelligence—then identical twins should be identical not only in their looks but in these characteristics.

c. The fascinating case of Jack and Oskar helps us unravel the mystery of which affects us more, our heredity or our environment. From their experience, we can see the far-reaching effects of the environment—how social experience takes precedence over biology.

d. Jack Yufe and Oskar Stohr are identical twins born in 1932 to a Jewish father and a Catholic mother. They were separated as babies after their parents divorced.

Recognizing the Author's Purpose

4. What would you say is the author's purpose?

a. to inform

b. to persuade

What about the reading made you select that choice?

_____

_____

_____

Using Context Clues

5. Based on the context, what does "mirror image" mean in the following sentence from paragraph 4: "Jack's upbringing was a mirror image of Oskar's"?

_____

Making Connections Between Paragraphs

6. Paragraph 7 opens with this statement, "That would seem to settle the matter." What in the previous paragraph (6), do "that" and "the matter" refer to?

_____

_____

_____

Understanding Sentence Functions

7. In paragraph 7, what function does the following sentence fulfill: "But there was another side"?

    a. topic sentence

    b. major detail

    c. reversal transition

Understanding the Function of Supporting Details

8. Many of the supporting details describe how the twins grew up. What word or phrase in the thesis statement do these details make more specific?

    _____

Identifying Organizational Patterns

9. What three organizational patterns are at work in the reading?

    a. definition

    b. classification

    c. comparison and contrast

    d. cause and effect

    e. sequence of dates and events

    Are they all equally important? _____

Drawing an Inference

10. What point does the author want to make when he tells readers the following about the two men: "They also had the same rate of speech and both liked sweet liqueur and spicy foods. Strangely, both flushed the toilet both before and after using it and enjoyed startling people by sneezing in crowded elevators" (paragraph 7)?

    _____

    _____

    _____

WEB QUEST **Twins Apart and Together**

Use the Web to find out more about Paula Bernstein and Elyse Schein. How do they fit into a discussion of what's called nature versus nurture or experience versus genetic inheritance?

_____

_____

_____

_____

_____

_____

_____

_____

What Do You Think? Do you think that experience or genes play a more significant role in deciding who we are? Or do you think it's a combination of both? Whichever you believe, state your position and explain what made you develop that point of view.

Thinking Through Writing Write a paragraph in which you describe an early experience or a relationship that you believe influenced who you are as a person. For instance, do you tend to stick with things even when they become difficult because your mom always told you, "When the going gets tough, the tough get going"? Open the paragraph with a statement about the characteristic you are going to trace back to childhood, e.g., "It's hard for me to give up on a task, even when I want to. I tend to stick with a job until it's finished." Then describe the origin of that characteristic.

◆ **READING 2**   ## Legalizing of Marijuana Raises Health Concerns

Roni Caryn Rabin

Looking Ahead   Some states are doing what advocates for decriminalizing marijuana use have long asked for: They are making the recreational use of marijuana legal. Other states have followed California's example and begun to allow the drug's use for medical purposes. The author of this reading wonders aloud if such changes are truly a sign of progress.

Getting Focused   The title uses the category word *concerns*. Just as with paragraphs, that category word should guide your attention. By the time you finish the reading, you should be able to summarize the concerns identified by the author.

Based on the title, do you think the rest of the reading will focus on the 1960s?

1   In the '60s, marijuana was a hallmark of the counterculture, along with free love, bellbottoms, long hair and bandannas. But marijuana has had the most staying power. This month [January 2012], in a remarkable first, the recreational use of marijuana became legal (depending on your definition) in Colorado and Washington. Over a dozen other states have decriminalized possession of small amounts, and Massachusetts recently became the 18th state to allow its use for medicinal purposes. Though federal law still bans both the sale and possession of marijuana, President Obama has said the federal government has "bigger fish to fry" and won't aggressively prosecute tokers in states where its use is legal.

Which sentence in paragraph 1 looks like it might be the thesis statement for the entire reading?

2   The rise of marijuana as an adult pastime is a victory for those who've always felt that its hazards were overblown. Proponents of legalization argue that marijuana is much safer to use than alcohol, pointing out that it is virtually impossible to overdose on marijuana. While marijuana can be addictive, scientists generally agree that fewer than 10 percent of marijuana smokers become dependent on the drug, compared with 15 percent for alcohol, 23 percent for heroin and 32 percent for tobacco. Marijuana does contain carcinogens, including tar and other toxins similar to those found in tobacco, but people generally do not smoke marijuana in the same amounts as cigarettes.

Did paragraph 2 confirm your prediction about the thesis statement?

3   Still, legalization takes health consumers into murky territory. Even though marijuana is the most commonly used illegal drug in the United States, questions about its health effects remain. For starters, this is not your parents' pot. Today's marijuana is much more potent: The mean concentration of THC, the psychoactive ingredient, in confiscated cannabis more than doubled between 1993 and 2008. Increased potency may be having unforeseen consequences. The human brain's cannabinoid receptors are typically activated by naturally occurring chemicals in the body

At this point, what direction is the reading taking, for or against the legalization of marijuana?

called endocannabinoids, which are similar to THC. There is a high density of cannabinoid receptors in parts of the brain that affect pleasure, memory and concentration. Some research suggests that these areas continue to be affected by marijuana use even after the "high" dissipates. "It's much more potent marijuana, which may explain why we've seen a pretty dramatic increase in admission to emergency rooms and treatment programs for marijuana," said Dr. Nora D. Volkow, director of the National Institute on Drug Abuse. "When we hear, 'Well, I smoked and nothing happened to me,' we need to think about the context of when these people started to take it, how frequently they used and how active the marijuana was."

When the author tells you that the increase in marijuana's potency may have unforeseen consequences, what should you start looking for?

4   Those in favor of legalizing marijuana say the increase in potency has been exaggerated, and that when users have more powerful pot, they adjust their consumption and actually smoke less. Teenagers may be more vulnerable to addiction, however, and those who start smoking pot at a younger age are at higher risk. Approximately one in six will become addicted, Dr. Volkow said. Young adults who start smoking marijuana at earlier ages also tend to smoke much more, and more often, than those who start in their later teens, researchers say. In users who develop a dependence or addiction, quitting can cause intense withdrawal symptoms, like anxiety, trouble sleeping, lack of appetite, mood swings, irritability and depression, experts say.

The author opens paragraph 4 by describing those who favor the legalizing of marijuana and why. What word signals the author will not pursue this line of thought?

5   Both Colorado and Washington restricted marijuana use to adults age 21 and over when they legalized recreational use in November. But experts worry that the perception of marijuana is changing because its stigma as an outlawed drug has eroded. "When people can go to a 'clinic' or 'cafe' and buy pot, that creates the perception that it's safe," said Dr. A. Eden Evins, director of the Center for Addiction Medicine at Massachusetts General Hospital in Boston. "Before we unleash the powers of the marketplace to woo people to use this addictive substance, we need to better understand who is at risk. . . . Once moneyed interests are involved, this trend will be difficult to reverse," she added.

How does paragraph 6 follow up on the warning from Dr. Evins?

6   The most disturbing new studies about early teenage use of marijuana showed that young adults who started smoking pot regularly before they were 16 performed significantly worse on cognitive tests of brain function than those who had started smoking later in adolescence. They performed particularly poorly on tests assessing executive function, which is responsible for planning and abstract thinking, as well as understanding rules and inhibiting inappropriate responses.

Does paragraph 7 continue the same train of thought begun in paragraph 5 or introduce a new point?

7   Imaging scans also found detectable differences in how their brains worked, said Staci Gruber, the lead author of these studies and director of the Cognitive and Clinical Neuroimaging Core at the Brain Imaging Center at McLean Hospital in Boston. Imaging scans found alterations in the frontal cortex white matter tracts of the brain in the early-starters, she said, that are associated with impulsiveness. "The frontal cortex is the last part of the brain to come online, and the most important," Dr. Gruber said. "Early exposure perhaps changes the trajectory of brain development, such that ability to perform complex executive function tasks is compromised."

What does the phrase "especially troubling" suggest about the content of the previous paragraph?

8   A recent study showing a drop in IQ scores among teenagers who are regular pot smokers is especially troubling, Dr. Evins said. A more recent study found that people who started smoking marijuana as teenagers and used it heavily for decades lost IQ points over time, while those who started smoking as adults did not, though some critics have said these differences may not be meaningful. Older survey studies had indicated that regular pot smokers were less likely to graduate from high school or pursue higher education, but it was never clear which came first, difficulty in school or the drug use.

What connection is the writer implying between prep courses and the cognitive effects of marijuana?

9   "If parents who are spending thousands of dollars on SAT prep courses knew about the cognitive effects marijuana has on their kids' brains, they would be up in arms," Dr. Evins said. Other health concerns about marijuana are less well documented but may turn out to be significant. States that legalized marijuana prohibit driving under its influence, and studies have found marijuana smoking increases weaving between lanes and slows reaction times. And although marijuana is not as damaging to the lungs as tobacco, in part because people do not smoke a pack of joints a day, a regular habit can eventually take a toll on the lungs.

10   At the very least, the new studies suggest parents who recall their own pot parties may want to suggest greater moderation to their children. And teenagers who insist on trying marijuana are better off waiting until they're older. "It's the same message as with alcohol," Dr. Gruber said. "Just hold on, it's worth it to wait." ("Legalizing of Marijuana Raises Health Concerns" by Roni Caryn Rabin from *The New York Times*, January 7, 2013. Copyright © 2013 The New York Times. All rights reserved. Used by permission and protected by the Copyright Laws of the United States. The printing, copying, redistribution, or retransmission of this Content without express written permission is prohibited.)

Reviewing Concepts and Skills

DIRECTIONS Answer the following questions by filling in the blanks or circling the letter of the correct response.

Recognizing the Controlling Main Idea

1. Which paragraph introduces the thesis statement?

   a. paragraph 1

   b. paragraph 2

   c. paragraph 3

   How would you paraphrase the thesis statement?

   _____

   _____

2. What phrase in the thesis statement should guide your attention while reading?

   _____

Using Transitions

3. In paragraph 3, the third sentence opens with the transition, "For starters." Based on that opening phrase, what should the reader expect?

   a. This sentence sums up the problems associated with marijuana legalization.

   b. This sentence introduces the first problem associated with marijuana legalization.

   c. This sentence sums up all of the reasons why decriminalizing marijuana use is a good thing.

   d. This sentence introduces the first reason why legalizing marijuana is a positive move.

Making Connections Between Supporting Details

4. Which statement below best describes the relationship between these two supporting details from paragraph 3? "[1]For starters, this is not your parents' pot. [2]Today's marijuana is much more potent: The mean concentration of THC, the psychoactive ingredient, in confiscated cannabis more than doubled between 1993 and 2008."

a. The first sentence is a major detail. The second sentence is a minor detail that modifies the previous sentence.

b. The first sentence is a major detail. The second sentence is also a major detail that further explains the controlling main idea.

c. Both sentences are minor details that modify a previous major detail.

Analyzing Paragraphs   5. In paragraph 4, which sentence is the topic sentence?

a. sentence 1

b. sentence 2

c. sentence 3

Seeing Relationships   6. A cause and effect relationship ties together the sentences in paragraph 6. The cause is _____ and the effect is _____.

Summarizing   7. Which of the following summaries does a better job paraphrasing and summing up the information in paragraphs 6 and 7?

a. Researchers are worried about new studies suggesting that kids who start smoking marijuana before the age of 16 do poorly on tests of brain function. Researchers are also concerned about brain scans that show changes in the brains of those who started smoking marijuana at an early age.

b. Researchers have found that marijuana smoking at an early age severely and permanently damages the brain. More specifically they are concerned about the damage to the frontal cortex, which has consistently shown up in imaging scans.

Identifying Organizational Patterns   8. What is the primary pattern organizing the information in this reading?

a. comparison and contrast

b. definition

c. cause and effect

d. classification

Recognizing the Author's Purpose

9. What's the purpose of this reading?

   a. The author wants to tell readers about the new laws concerning marijuana.

   b. The author wants to convince readers that decriminalizing marijuana is a huge mistake.

   c. The author wants to encourage readers to be skeptical about the benefits of decriminalizing marijuana use.

   Please explain why you chose that answer.

   _____

   _____

   _____

Using Context Clues

10. Based on the context, how would you define the word *detectable* in this sentence: "Imaging scans also found *detectable* differences in how their brains worked. . ."? (Paragraph 7)

   _____

What Do You Think?

Do you think pre-teens and teenagers who read this article would be too scared to smoke marijuana? Why or why not?

WEB QUEST **The Pros and Cons of Decriminalizing Marijuana**

Come up with a search term that will get you a list of both the pro and con arguments for decriminalizing marijuana. Read at least two articles that are in favor and two that are against.

Thinking Through Writing

Write a few paragraphs that express your approval or disapproval of the current trend toward decriminalizing marijuana. For the introduction, refer to the states that have decriminalized marijuana for recreational and/or medicinal use. Then introduce a thesis statement that acknowledges the opposing point of view before stating your own, for instance, "Although some state legislatures seem comfortable about making marijuana accessible to the public, the movement toward decriminalization of marijuana use is a bad, bad idea" or "Many people are outraged that some states are decriminalizing marijuana. But their outrage is out of proportion to the minimal risks involved. Decriminalization is actually a sensible move on the part of the states." Follow the thesis statement with reasons or evidence that backs up your point of view.

♦ **READING 3**   # Dealing with Conflict

Roy M. Berko, Andrew D. Wolvin, and Darlyn R. Wolvin

Looking Ahead   In Chapter 4, you learned about the difference between aggressive and assertive behavior. In response to a conflict or disagreement, some people are aggressive, i.e., they get angry and counterattack. Others are assertive; they state their position and hold their ground but don't escalate the emotional tension. These two responses, however, do not cover all the possible ways people react to conflict. As this reading explains, there are a number of others.

Getting Focused   Even a very quick survey should tell you that this reading identifies and defines some basic ways of responding to conflict. That means you should focus on reading to identify the different types of conflict described and to determine the characteristics of each one. Also be on the lookout to see if the authors compare and contrast the different types of conflict. If they do, make sure you understand how they are similar or different.

In the opening paragraph, what organizational pattern are you dealing with and what should you be looking for?

1   Most of us use a primary style for confronting conflict. Knowing your style and its ramifications can be helpful in determining whether you are satisfied with your conflict style. If you are not, you may need to acquire the skills to make a change in your habitual pattern. The basic styles of conflict management are (1) avoidance, (2) accommodation/smoothing-over, (3) compromise, (4) competition/aggression, and (5) integration.

Avoidance

Given the headings, what should the reader be looking for?

2   Some people choose to confront conflict by engaging in conflict avoidance: They sidestep, postpone, or ignore the issue. They simply put up with the status quo no matter *how unpleasant*. While seemingly unproductive, avoidance may actually be a good style if the situation is a short-term one or of minor importance. If, however, the problem is really bothering you or is persistent, then it should be dealt with. Avoiding the issue often uses up a great deal of energy without resolving the aggravating situation. Very seldom do avoiders feel that they have been in a win-win situation. Avoiders usually lose a chunk of their self-respect since they so clearly downplay their own concerns in favor of the other person's. Avoiders frequently were brought up in environments in which they were told to be nice and not to argue, and eventually bad things would go away. Or they were brought up in homes where verbal or physical abuse was present, and to avoid these types of reactions, they hid from conflict.

Once the authors describe a particular method of dealing with conflict, what do they do next?

Accommodation/Smoothing-Over

3 Accommodators meet the needs of others and don't assert their own. In this situation, the accommodator often feels like the "good person" for having given the other person his own way. This is perfectly acceptable if the other person's needs really are more important. But unfortunately, accommodators tend to follow the pattern no matter what the situation. Thus, they often are taken advantage of, and they seldom get their needs met. Accommodators commonly come from backgrounds where they were exposed to a martyr who gave and gave and got little but put on a happy face. They also tend to be people who have little self-respect and try to earn praise by being nice to everyone.

4 A form of accommodation known as *conflict smoothing-over* seeks above all else to preserve the image that everything is okay. Through smoothing-over, people sometimes get what they want, but just as often they do not. Usually they feel they have more to say and have not totally satisfied themselves.

5 As with avoidance and accommodation, smoothing-over occasionally can be useful. If, for example, the relationship between two people is more important than the subject they happen to be disagreeing about, then smoothing-over may be the best approach. Keep in mind, however, that smoothing-over does not solve the conflict; it just pushes it aside. It may very well recur in the future.

Does paragraph 6 carry on the point introduced in paragraph 5 or switch directions?

6 Those who use this technique as their normal means of confronting conflict often come from backgrounds in which the idea was stressed that being nice was the best way to be liked and popular. And being liked and popular was more important than satisfying their needs.

Compromise

7 Conflict compromise brings concerns into the open in an attempt to satisfy the needs of both parties. It usually means "trading some of what you want for some of what I want. It's meeting each other halfway." The definition of the word "compromise," however, indicates the potential weakness of this approach, for it means that both individuals give in at least to some degree to reach a solution. As a result, neither usually completely achieves what she or he wants. This is not to say that compromise is automatically a poor method of conflict management. It is not, but it can lead to frustration unless both participants are willing to continue to work until both of their needs are being met. Those who are effective compromisers normally have had experience with negotiations and know that you have to give to get, but you don't have to give until it hurts. Those who tend to be weak

The transition "as a result" tells you to expect what concerning the compromise method of conflict resolution?

in working toward a fair and equitable compromise believe that getting something is better than getting nothing at all. Therefore, they are willing to settle for anything, no matter how little.

Competition/Aggression

8 The main element in conflict competition is power. Its purpose is to "get another person to comply with or accept your point of view, or to do something that person may not want to do." Someone has to win, and someone has to lose. This forcing mode, unfortunately, has been the European-American way of operation in many situations—in athletic events, business deals, and interpersonal relations. Indeed, many people do not seem to be happy unless they are clear winners. Realize that if someone wins, someone else must lose. The overaggressive driver must force the other car off the road.

9　The value of winning at all costs is debatable. Sometimes, even though we win, we lose in the long run. The hatred of a child for a parent as a result of continuous losing, or the negative work environment resulting from a supervisor who must always be on top, may be much worse than the occasional loss of a battle. In dealing with persons from other cultures, European Americans sometimes are perceived as being pushy and aggressive. Many sales, friendships, and relationships have been lost based on the win-at-all costs philosophy. Many of the aggressive behaviors in the personal lives of professional athletes are directly credited to their not being able to leave their win-at-all-costs attitude on the athletic field.

Integration

How is the description of integration different from the other descriptions?

10 Communicators who handle their conflicts through conflict integration are concerned about their own needs as well as those of the other person. But unlike compromisers, they will not settle for only a partially satisfying solution. Integrators keep in mind that both parties can participate in a win-win resolution and are willing to collaborate. Thus, the most important aspect of integration is the realization that the relationship, the value of self-worth, and the issue are important. For this reason, integrative solutions often take a good deal of time and energy.

What does that difference suggest?

11　People who are competitive, who are communication-apprehensive, or who are nonassertive find it nearly impossible to use an integrative style of negotiation. They feel that they must win, or that they cannot stand up for their rights, or that they have no right to negotiate. In contrast, people who tend to have assertiveness skills and value the nature of relationships usually attempt to work toward integration.

12   Avoidance, accommodation, and smoothing-over are all nonassertive acts; the person's needs are not met. Competition is an aggressive act in that the person gets his needs met at the expense of another person. Integration is assertive since the objective is to get one's needs met without taking away the rights of someone else. Compromise, depending on how it is acted out, can be either nonassertive or assertive. (Roy M. Berko, Andrew D. Wolvin, and Darlyn R. Wolvin, *Communicating* 9e, pp. 185–192,' © Pearson Education Inc. Reproduced by permission of Pearson Education, Inc. Boston, MA.)

Reviewing Concepts and Skills

DIRECTIONS   Answer the following questions by filling in the blanks or circling the letter of the correct response.

Making Predictions   1. The title of the reading should immediately raise what question?

_____

Recognizing the Controlling Main Idea   2. Where does the thesis statement appear?

a. paragraph 1

b. paragraph 2

c. paragraph 3

d. paragraph 4

Recognizing Explanatory Patterns   3. This reading illustrates what about topic sentences coming at the end of the paragraph?

_____

_____

Using Context Clues   4. Based on the context, how would you define the word *equitable* in this sentence: "Those who tend to be weak in working toward a fair and *equitable* compromise believe that getting something is better than getting nothing at all" (paragraph 7)?

_____

Paraphrasing   5. Paraphrase the authors' explanation of conflict avoidance.

_____

_____

6. In your own words, what's the drawback commonly associated with compromise as a response to conflict?

_____

Understanding the Function of Supporting Details

7. Would you call the detail about professional athletes (paragraph 9) a major or minor detail? _____ Explain your answer.

_____

_____

Understanding Sentence Functions

8. Which of the following best describes the relationships among these sentences? "The value of winning at all costs is debatable. Sometimes, even though we win, we lose in the long run. The hatred of a child for a parent as a result of continuous losing, or the negative work environment resulting from a supervisor who must always be on top, may be much worse than the occasional loss of a battle" (paragraph 9).

a. Topic Sentence → Major Detail → Minor Detail

b. Introductory Sentence → Topic Sentence → Major Detail

c. Topic Sentence → Major Detail → Major Detail

Applying What You Have Learned

9. Marc and Brittany are arguing over Marc's failure to complete his part of their shared research paper. Marc is insisting that his share of the paper was much greater than Brittany's and therefore he shouldn't be blamed for not getting it done on time. Brittany listens to his explanation and says, "I understand. You did have more research to do than I did. I'm just tense about getting the paper in on time and getting a good grade." Marc responds by saying, "You shouldn't have yelled at me. I am overworked as it is and I'm doing more than my fair share." Marc is engaging in _____ while Brittany is engaging in _____.

Recognizing the Author's Purpose

10. What is the authors' purpose?

a. to inform

b. to persuade

WEB QUEST **Who Were Thomas and Kilmann?**

Why do people who study conflict resolution know the names Kenneth Thomas and Ralph Kilmann?

_____

_____

_____

What Do You Think? How would you describe your own style of dealing with conflict? How does your style match the authors' descriptions? Does it fit one of the types described or do you need a new category?

Thinking Through Writing Write a paragraph that opens by paraphrasing the authors' explanation of one type of conflict resolution. Follow the definition with a specific example that illustrates the meaning of the term in a concrete way. In moving from the definition to the example, try to come up with a transitional word, phrase, or sentence that gets the reader from one point to the other.

◆ **READING 4**   # White-Collar Criminals: Swindlers and Chiselers

Larry Siegel

Looking Ahead   The following reading returns to the subject of white-collar crime (p. 183), which can take a number of different forms. In this reading, you'll get a detailed description of two, swindling and chiseling.

Getting Focused   Because the author clearly makes a distinction between the two kinds of crimes, read to get a sense of the difference between them. When you finish the chapter section, you should be able to generally define the two kinds of white-collar crime and recall, or remember, at least two examples of each.

1   White-collar crime represents a range of behaviors involving individuals acting alone and within the context of a business structure. Although criminologist Mark Moore has identified seven different categories of white-collar crime, the two types that are most likely to affect ordinary citizens are swindling and chiseling.

Swindling

Given the title and first heading, what information do you expect to get at this point?

2   For more than a decade, the Gold Club in Atlanta was the hottest spot in town, the destination of conventioneers and businessmen looking for a rowdy night filled with good cigars, strong drinks, and nude dancers. It became the home away from home for well-known professional athletes who stopped by to receive sexual favors from the girls who worked at the club. The Federal government filed charges claiming that the Gold Club manager, Steven Kaplan, was in cahoots with the Gambino organized crime family of New York to overcharge or double bill credit cards of unsuspecting customers. The club owners were also charged with ordering women in their employ to provide sexual services to professional athletes and celebrities to encourage their presence at the club. The scheme depended in part on the victims' reluctance to come forward and press charges, fearing negative publicity. The government won its case when Kaplan pleaded guilty and received a three-to-five-year prison sentence and a $5 million fine. Ironically, as part of the deal, the federal government took over the Gold Club, making it the manager of one of the largest strip clubs in the nation!

Were your expectations met by the paragraph?

What does paragraph 3 add to your understanding of paragraph 2?

3   Kaplan and his co-conspirators were found guilty of engaging in a *sting* or *swindle*, a white-collar crime in which people use their institutional or business position to trick others out of their money. Offenses in

Why has the author included Truly Unique Collectibles in the reading?

this category range from fraud involving the door-to-door sale of faulty merchandise to selling bogus or counterfeit products. Truly Unique Collectibles, for instance, made a fortune selling forged and fraudulent posters, photos and other items. Their celebrity-signed pictures and posters were obtained by "runners," people who happen to catch a celebrity at an event and obtain a signed picture there. Though runners may have obtained one or two signatures from famous athletes, they simply forged many more, claiming all genuine. An investigation found that the overwhelming number of celebrity-signed photographs and posters being sold throughout the world are sold under this pretense; they are almost all forged.

What's the connection between BCCI and Truly Unique Collectibles?

4   The collapse of the Bank of Credit and Commerce International (BCCI) in 1991 is probably the most costly swindle in history, costing depositors an estimated $10 billion. BCCI was the world's largest private bank, with assets of about $23 billion. Investigators believe bank officials made billions of dollars in loans to confederates who had no intention of repaying them. Its officers helped clients, among them dictators Saddam Hussein and Ferdinand Marcos, launder money, finance terrorist organizations, and smuggle illegal arms. BCCI officers helped Colombian drug cartel leaders launder drug money so it could be shifted to legitimate banks. After the bank was closed, in addition to the billions in lost deposits, hundreds of millions were spent to pay auditors to liquidate the bank's holdings.

What shift in the author's focus does the heading for paragraph 5 suggest?

5   **Swindling the Desperate** When oil prices skyrocketed in 2003 and 2004, one enterprising swindler of the Albany, Kentucky-based Vision Oil Company, lured investors into risky schemes by claiming that God (and not geologists) guided her company's oil exploration: "God gave me a vision of three oil wells," she said in a letter sent to potential investors. State regulators found that Linda Stetler and her company engaged in illegal practices, including inadequate disclosures of risks and selling to unsuitable investors. Vision Oil and its agents were fined by the state and ordered to pay restitution to investors.

6   Swindlers love to target the poor and the desperate, taking advantage of their hope. Religious people are a common target. It is estimated that fake religious organizations bilk thousands of people out of $100 million per year. Swindlers take in worshippers of all persuasions: Jews, Baptists, Lutherans, Catholics, Mormons, and Greek Orthodox have all fallen prey to religious swindles. How do religious swindlers operate? Some create fraudulent charitable organizations and convince devout people to contribute to their seemingly worthwhile cause. Some use religious television and radio shows to sell their products. Others place verses from the scriptures on their promotional literature to comfort hesitant investors.

7   Another particularly cruel swindle is to prey upon couples desperate to adopt children and use religious organizations or local ministries to conduct their scams. In one Indiana case, Victoria Farahan approached the director of a new local adoption ministry and said she could provide healthy newborns from Hospital 31 in Moscow. Couples were provided with pictures of the babies (which turned out to be Farahan's own children).

Chiseling

8   Chiseling is another category of white-collar crime. It involves regularly cheating within the context of an institution. Chiselers may be individuals looking to make quick profits in their own businesses or employees of large organizations who decide to cheat on obligations to their company or its clients. Chiseling can involve charging for bogus or inept auto or home repairs. It can also involve short-weighting (intentionally tampering with the scales used to weigh products being sold). In one scheme, some New York City cab drivers routinely taped the dashboards of their cabs with pens loaded with powerful magnets to zap their meters and jack up the fares.

9   Chiseling may even involve illegal use of information about company policies that have not been disclosed to the public. The secret information can be used to make money in the stock market. (This is called "insider trading.") Use of the information violates the obligation to keep company policy secret.

10   **When Chiseling Is a Matter of Life or Death** It is not uncommon for professionals to use their positions to chisel clients. This is true even of health care professionals. Pharmacists have been known, for example, to alter prescriptions or substitute low-cost generic drugs for more expensive name brands. In one of the most notorious cases in the nation's history, Kansas City pharmacist, Robert R. Courtney was charged with fraud when it was discovered that he had been selling diluted mixtures of the cancer medications Taxol, Gemzar, Paraplatin, and Platinol, which are used to treat a variety of illnesses including pancreatic and lung cancers, advanced ovarian and breast cancers, and AIDS-related Kaposi's sarcoma. In one instance, Courtney provided a doctor with only 450 milligrams of Gemzar for a prescription that called for 1,900 milligrams, a transaction that netted him a profit of $779.00.

11   After he pleaded guilty, Courtney told authorities that his drug dilution activities were not limited to the conduct he admitted to at the time of his guilty plea. His criminal activities had actually begun in 1992, or even

---

Margin notes:

Does the opening of paragraph 7 suggest the author is going to continue to discuss religious swindles or introduce a different kind?

What would you expect the writer to do following this heading?

What does the heading of paragraph 10 suggest about the content of the upcoming section?

earlier, affected the patients of 400 doctors, involved 980,000 prescriptions, and harmed approximately 4,200 patients.

12 **Investment Chiseling** Richard Banville and Harold Howell, two men from Orange County, California were indicted in 2005 on fraud charges stemming from their operation of a scheme that defrauded elderly and retired victims out of nearly $1.7 million. Promising huge returns on investments, they told potential investors that they were really in luck because a world-renowned trader—David Zachary of La Jolla, California—would be doing the trades. Though they promised returns of 10 percent to 40 percent per month, they failed to mention that David Zachary did not really exist. When victims asked to withdraw their monies, Banville and Howell explained that an "early withdrawal penalty" of up to 75 percent would be assessed in order to disguise the fact that the scheme diverted victims' money for the personal benefit of Banville and Howell. (Adapted from Larry Siegel, *Criminology* 10e, © Cengage Learning.)

Reviewing Concepts and Skills

DIRECTIONS Answer the following questions by filling in the blanks or circling the letter of the correct response.

Recognizing and Paraphrasing the Controlling Main Idea

1. Which of the following statements fits the organization of this reading?

   a. The thesis statement opens the reading and the supporting details introduce two types of white-collar crime.

   b. There is a thesis statement unifying the paragraphs following each heading but no overall thesis statement that covers the entire reading.

2. How would you express the controlling main idea of this entire reading in your own words?

   _____

   _____

Recognizing the Author's Purpose

3. What is the author's purpose?

   a. He wants to suggest that not enough is being done to catch the swindlers and chiselers who cheat the public.

   b. He wants readers to agree that white-collar crime is as bad as a street crime.

   c. He wants to tell readers about two kinds of white-collar crime.

Summarizing 4. Which one of the following passages does a better job summarizing the description of the scam run by Truly Unique Collectibles?

a. Truly Unique Collectibles made a good deal of money selling forged and fraudulent posters. They got their signed photos from "runners," people who happened to run into a celebrity at an event and got the celebrity's autograph. Some of the photos and posters were legitimate. Many of the photos, however, were not actually signed by the celebrities themselves. Instead their signatures were forged. Then Truly Unique Collectibles marketed the photos and posters as genuine.

b. Truly Unique Collectibles used "runners," people who ran into celebrities and got their autographs, to get some of their photos and posters signed. But for the most part, they forged the signatures and made a fortune selling them on their website until the government put an end to their swindle. According to the government, most celebrity-signed photos and posters on the market are fakes.

Analyzing Paragraphs 5. In paragraph 6, which sentence is the topic sentence?

a. sentence 1

b. sentence 2

c. sentence 3

d. sentence 4

Please explain why you chose that answer.

_____

_____

6. Which method of introducing topic sentences does this author seem to favor?

a. He likes opening paragraphs with the topic sentence.

b. He favors paving the way for the main idea with an introductory sentence or two.

c. He likes to use examples that lead up to the main idea.

d. He doesn't favor any one particular method.

7. In paragraph 8, the description of the cab drivers is a

   a. major detail.

   b. minor detail.

   Please explain why you chose that answer.

   _____

   _____

Summarizing 8. Which of the following does a better job summarizing paragraph 10's description of the crimes committed by pharmacist Robert Courtney?

   a. In one of the most serious cases of professional chiseling on record, Kansas City pharmacist Robert R. Courtney was charged with fraud after it was discovered that he had been substituting diluted cancer medications for far stronger prescriptions. Courtney began substituting prescriptions in 1992 and before he was caught, Courtney harmed over four thousand patients.

   b. In one of the most despicable cases of professional chiseling, pharmacist Robert R. Courtney substituted weaker medications for stronger ones and caused deadly harm to thousands of patients.

Recognizing Organizational Patterns 9. Which pattern or patterns do you see at work in this reading?

   a. definition with sequence of dates and events

   b. process with simple listing

   c. definition

   d. comparison and contrast with sequence of dates and events

Outlining 10. If you were making an outline of this reading, which of these statement pairs are correctly aligned to indicate the relationship between them?

a.

> **1.** In swindles or stings, people use their professional position to take other people's money without giving them anything in return.
>
> —Chiseling involves the consistent cheating of an organization or clients.

b.

> **1.** In swindles or stings, people use their professional position to take other people's money without giving them anything in return.
>
> **2.** Chiseling involves the consistent cheating of an organization or clients.

What Do You Think? There are some, like philosopher Jeffrey Reiman, who argue that our society doesn't treat white-collar crime harshly enough. People in this camp say that we are harsh on street crime but soft on white-collar crime. What do you think? Should we view the two kinds of crime in the same light or not? Should the man or woman who robs the elderly of their life savings by selling them phony stocks get the same treatment as the person who breaks into their house and steals their possessions?

Thinking Through Writing Victoria Farahan, the woman who bilked six couples out of close to $100,000 by claiming she could get them Russian children to adopt, did not go to jail. She was sentenced to two years of home detention because she was seriously ill with lupus. Some of her victims thought the sentence did not do justice to her crime. Was justice served in her case? Write a few paragraphs that start out with a description of her swindle followed by a description of the verdict. (Use the Web to get the specific details.) Then, in a sentence or two, explain what you think about her sentence and offer at least two reasons for your opinion.

The Role of Inferences in Comprehension and Critical Reading

6

> **IN THIS CHAPTER, YOU WILL LEARN**
>
> ● how inferences are essential to helping readers identify which words are central to the author's discussion.
>
> ● how to infer main ideas that are implied but not stated in paragraphs.
>
> ● how to infer the connections between supporting details.
>
> ● how to draw personal conclusions that might *not* have been intended by the author but are still implied by the text.

"Language does not carry meaning in sentences, but rather triggers or releases meaning . . . in the mind of the reader."

—Walter B. Weimer and David S. Palermo,
Cognition and the Symbolic Process

This chapter shows you how to draw inferences, or put into words what the author suggests but doesn't say outright. Essential to understanding an author's meaning, drawing logical inferences also lies at the heart of critical reading. You need to draw inferences to understand the author's message. However, you also need to draw inferences to come to your own conclusions about both the author and the content. Ultimately it's your own conclusions that are the key component of critical reading.

 ## Inferences and the Author's Train of Thought

You already know from Chapter 3 that writers sometimes expect readers to infer a topic that is implied rather than explicitly stated. This chapter elaborates on that point and will talk about paragraphs in which the reader infers not just the topic but also the main idea of a paragraph.

Drawing inferences, however, is already crucial at the level of individual sentences. As the following examples demonstrate, writers create **chains of repetition and reference** to make sure that words central to their meaning stay in the forefront of the reader's mind. They rely, that is, on *pronouns, category word substitutes,* and *synonyms,* as well as *associated words and phrases* to help the reader follow the thematic progression of their thought.

Nouns and Pronouns

One way writers create a chain of repetition and reference is to introduce a key noun[†] and then refer to it with pronouns. It's the reader's job to infer the connections between pronouns and antecedents, or the nouns to which pronouns refer. Here's a fairly straightforward illustration:

Edward Thorndike (1874–1949) is a famous figure in educational theory. He conducted several experiments with animals to gain further understanding of the learning process. He also formulated many important laws of learning. (Adapted from Barbara Engler, *Personality Theories* 7e, © Cengage Learning.)

The pronoun *he* in the second sentence is the author's way of saying, "I am still talking about Edward Thorndike. Because I can't always call him by name—it would be repetitive and tedious—I'm using the pronoun *he*." Notice, though, that the author expects readers to keep track of the original topic, in this case Edward Thorndike, by inferring the relationship between pronoun and antecedent.

Tricky Pronouns and Antecedents

The example about Edward Thorndike might make it seem as if inferring relationships between pronouns and antecedents is so easy the subject is not worth mentioning. But connecting the two can get tricky, particularly

---

[†]noun: The grammatical term *noun* refers to people, places, ideas, and objects—e.g., *president, country, socialism,* and *house* are all nouns.

if there is more than one pronoun and antecedent relationship or if the noun is followed by a pronoun clause[†] rather than a single word.

Staying on the trail of pronouns and their antecedents can also become more difficult when the nouns to which the pronouns refer are far away. In the following passage, the pronouns are italicized. When you finish reading the excerpt, fill in the blanks in parentheses with the nouns each pronoun represents, or stands in for.

[1]One problem with court-assigned counsel for the poor concerns degree of effort. [2]Although most attorneys assigned by the court to defend *those* who cannot afford counsel (_____) probably take *their* (_____) job seriously, some feel only a loose commitment to *their* (_____) clients. [3]Paying clients, in *their* (_____) eyes, deserve better service and are apt to get *it* (_____). (Frank Schmalleger, *Criminal Justice Today* 9e, Prentice Hall, p. 41.)

In this case, the first pronoun represents, or acts as a substitute for, the clients who cannot afford to pay. The next string of pronouns represents the attorneys, with the last pronoun *it* referring not to a person but to better service, or a good defense. In every instance, it's up to readers to infer the relationship between pronoun and antecedent based on clues in the text and the reader's knowledge of English.

Looking at *This* and *That*

Writers sometimes use *this* or *that* to refer to an entire idea rather than a single noun. Look, for example, at the following pair of sentences:

[1]No public figure wants to be crucified for having concealed warnings of terrorist attacks if the attacks actually occur because the warnings would almost certainly be revealed. [2]On the simplest level, *this* is why we've had two warnings from the administration against unspecified terrorist threats. (Adapted from Allan J. Cigler, ed., *Perspectives on Terrorism*, Houghton Mifflin, 2002, p. 19.)

In this example, *this* doesn't refer to a single word. It refers to an entire thought: Public officials fear that if they get a warning of a terrorist attack

---

[†]Pronoun clauses include a verb, e.g., "The philosopher Ayn Rand was a woman *who knew what she wanted* and therefore thought she knew what everyone else wanted as well."

but don't reveal it and the warning then becomes a reality, they will be harshly criticized by the public and the media. That entire thought is packed into the pronoun *this*. As you can see, it is the reader's job to unpack the pronoun by drawing the right inference.

In the next example, you need to connect two *that* pronouns to their antecedents. Read the passage and explain what the two italicized pronouns represent.

> [1]Researchers who study the history of animal migrations are performing a crucial task. [2]Their intention is to discover geographical and biological changes *that* propelled mass movement of animal populations over the decades, as well as the feeding patterns *that* have altered as a result of changes in location.

The first *that* in sentence 2 refers to "geographical and biological changes." This phrase has to be the antecedent for the first *that*. "Researchers" couldn't be the antecedent because they study the mass movement of animals. They don't stimulate or propel the migration.

The second *that*, however, has a different antecedent. This time, it refers to "feeding patterns." Here again, the reader has to draw an inference to connect the pronoun to its rightful antecedent.

From the standpoint of grace and style, writing with lots of *this* and *that* pronouns is not very engaging to read. Nevertheless, academic writing makes heavy use of these pronouns, sometimes positioning the pronoun far from the antecedent it represents. *Whenever you are struggling with a hard-to-read passage, it pays to slow down and consciously connect pronouns to antecedents.* Connecting the two will unlock the author's meaning.

Keep an Eye on *Which*

Like *this* and *that*, the pronoun *which* can also refer to a thought larger than a single word or phrase. Consider this example:

> [1]Power is an ingredient in almost every relationship. [2]Yet the role of power, or who has more of *it*, is seldom discussed, *which* may be the reason why personal relationships can be so stressful.

In this excerpt, the pronoun *it* refers to, or stands in for, one single word, *power*. But the pronoun *which* represents a whole string of words: "the role of power, or who has more of it, is seldom discussed." You have probably been advised in writing classes to not use, or to use sparingly, pronouns such as *this*, *that*, or *which* when referring to lengthy antecedents that encompass an entire sentence. That's good advice. But sometimes it's necessary to make pronouns represent complex ideas. That's the reason pronouns like *this*, *that*, and *which* need your close attention. Pass them over too quickly and you might connect them to a single word instead of the broader idea they really represent.

General Category Substitutes

Instead of a pronoun, writers can also use a more general term that can include and, therefore, refer to the person, event, or idea they want to focus on throughout the passage. Here again, it's the reader who has to infer the right connection. For instance, in the excerpt that follows, the word *document* is a more general stand-in for "the Constitution."

[1]Once the states received copies of the Constitution, Americans began an intense discussion about whether to ratify the changes it proposed. [2]They expressed a great spectrum of opinions about different provisions within the *document*, and they used the press, the pulpit, and public podiums to spread their views on *it* to every layer of society.

(Adapted from Steven M. Gillon and Cathy D. Matson, *The American Experiment* 2e, © Cengage Learning.)

In this example, the author uses *document*, a general word stand-in, along with the pronoun *it*, to keep readers' attention focused on the Constitution, which is the topic of the discussion. Because writers don't want to bore their readers, they need to find substitutes for the key words used to express their ideas. In response, it's important for readers to be on the lookout for how references to key words change.

Substitute by Association

Writers sometimes build a chain of repetition and reference by using words associated with the key word already introduced. In the following passage, for instance, the author starts out using pronouns to refer to the dogs in the bomb squad, "*their* behavior." But by the end of the second sentence, she uses a phrase associated with dogs to tell readers, "I'm still talking about dogs."

[1]The dogs in the bomb squad had been carefully trained to stay at attention until the whistle blew. [2]But once it did, their behavior changed dramatically, and there was much wild *yipping and tail wagging.*

Here, the author uses the phrase "yipping and tail wagging" to signal to readers that dogs are still her focus. It's not unusual for writers to use associated words to represent the topic, for example, a passage discussing King George III might use "the crown" for a repeat reference to the king while a passage talking about cats might use "meowing and hissing" to indicate that cats were still the subject.

Spotting the Links in the Chain

The four methods discussed above are among the most common ways writers help readers keep track of the people, places, events, and experiences that are central to the overall meaning of a reading. But there are other ways writers keep reminding readers of how new information links up to old. You will be quicker at spotting them if you mentally ask yourself about each new sentence, "How is the author linking this new sentence to what I already read?" The link might be a pronoun. It might also be an example, a common association, or a different form of a word used in the previous sentences. What's important is that you notice how references to key words are threaded through a passage. Following those threads will help you re-create the author's intended meaning.

◆ **EXERCISE 1**   **Filling in the Gaps with Inferences**

DIRECTIONS   Read each passage. Then answer the questions by filling in the blanks.

EXAMPLE   [1]According to World Bank estimates, 90 percent of the more than half billion women living around the world do not have access to credit. [2]Small loans of $100 would go a long way in helping women to start their own businesses, which could substantially improve their economic conditions. (Adapted from Gary Ferraro and Susan Andreatta, *Cultural Anthropology* 9e, © Cengage Learning.)

In sentence 2, the pronoun *which* refers to <u>women starting their own business</u> while the phrase *their economic conditions* refers to the <u>half billion women living around the world</u>.

1. [1]It is possible to speak of social character types or orientations* that are frequently shared by the people of a particular culture. [2]The psychologist Erich Fromm identified five personalities that are common in Western societies. (Adapted from Barbara Engler, *Personality Theories* 7e, © Cengage Learning.)

   In sentence 2, the word _____ refers to the "social character types or orientations" introduced in sentence 1.

2. [1]Psychologist Alison Gopnik has argued that Stanislas Dehaene, the author of *Reading in the Brain*, may not really mean it when he claims that the brain cannot overcome the limitations of working memory. [2]Gopnik may be right, but in fact, there is not a single sentence in the book that suggests she is correct in her assumption.

   In sentence 2, the word *book* refers to _____ while

   the word *assumption* refers to the _____

   _____.

3. [1]Sir Isaac Newton's book *Mathematical Principles of Natural Philosophy* was published in Latin in 1687, when he was forty-five. [2]It is considered by many to be the most important publication in the history of physics.

   In sentence 2, the pronoun *it* and the word *publication* refer to

   _____.

4. [1]Family science researchers use the **scientific method**—well-established procedures used to collect and analyze information about family experiences. [2]This approach allows other people to know the source of the information and to be confident of the accuracy of the findings. (Adapted from Bryan Strong et al., *The Marriage and Family Experience* 11e, © Cengage Learning.)

   The second half of sentence 1 defines the phrase _____ introduced in the first half. In sentence 2, the words *this approach*

   refer to _____ introduced in sentence 1.

---

*orientations: leanings, tendencies, inclinations.

5. [1]Already in childhood, it was clear that Lewis Carroll, the author of *Alice's Adventures in Wonderland*, was a math prodigy,* whose gift for numbers astonished his elders. [2]Equally obvious, though, was the writer's fascination with language, evidenced by his love of rhymes and puns.*

In sentence 2, the words *writer's*, and *his* refer to

_____ introduced in sentence 1.

6. [1]The colonists who chose to protest taxation by the British government in 1765 and 1767 did not think of themselves as rebels or revolutionaries. [2]Indeed, most of them would have been shocked at the suggestion that they were no longer British patriots.

In sentence 2, the pronouns *them* and *they* refer to the word

_____ introduced in sentence 1.

7. [1]In the late 1960s, many celebrities, including the Beatles and the Beach Boys, followed the Indian guru* Maharishi Mahesh Yogi. [2]But when the Beatles went to India to spend three months studying under the Maharishi, Ringo Starr returned home with his wife, Maureen. [3]The couple was apparently unhappy with the great sage's accommodations. (Adapted from Mark Kurlansky, *1968: The Year that Rocked the World*, Random House, 2005, p. 30.)

In sentence 3, the word _____ refers to Ringo Starr

and his wife from sentence 2 and _____ refers to the Maharishi Mahesh Yogi introduced in sentence 1 and mentioned in sentence 2.

8. [1]Studies of how brain injuries affect memory provide evidence about which parts of the brain are involved in various kinds of memory. [2]For example, damage to the hippocampus often results in anterograde amnesia, a loss of memory for any event occurring after the injury. (Adapted from Douglas A. Bernstein, *Essentials of Psychology* 5e, © Cengage Learning.)

In sentence 2, the words _____ are a reference to brain injuries mentioned in sentence 1.

---

*prodigy: someone who shows great talent at an early age.
*puns: plays on words that exploit their similarity in sound or their multiple meaning. For example: "The sign at the rehab center said, 'Keep Off the Grass.'"
*guru: wise person.

9. [1]To the tech-savvy activists who engineered the uprising across the Arab world, headlines like "FACEBOOK REVOLUTION" and "TWITTER REBELLION" were ridiculous. [2]Social networks don't overthrow governments—people do, courageous people who, despite the risk of retribution or even death, take to the streets because they have had enough. [3]Yet dismissing technology's role in the Arab spring[†] is mistaken. (Adapted from David Wolman, "Arab Spring" in *Wired*, May 2013, p. 28.)

In sentence 2, the words *social networks* refer to _____ from sentence 1. In sentence 3, the word *technology* is a reference

to _____ in sentence 2 and _____

and _____ in sentence 1.

10. [1]Emotional responses may hurt negotiations between members of different cultures if they are deemed inappropriate in one of the cultures. [2]Expressions of pride are more likely to be received positively in individualistic cultures, whereas expressions of shame are more likely to be received positively in collectivistic cultures. (Saul Kassin et al., *Social Psychology* 8e, © Cengage Learning.)

In sentence 2, the phrases *expressions of pride* and *expressions*

of shame are references to _____ introduced in sentence 1, while *individualistic cultures* and *collectivistic cultures*

are a reference to _____ in sentence 1.

Inferring Main Ideas

Now that we've looked at the way readers infer connections between sentences, we need to look at the way readers infer main ideas when the topic sentence is missing. Sometimes that's just a matter of piecing together parts of sentences to come up with the implied main idea.

[†]Arab spring: refers to the pro-democracy uprisings that swept the Middle East starting in the spring of 2011 and were powered in part by the use of social media as an organizational tool.

The supporting details describe the Fox sisters' "clever, but cruel act."

None of the sentences in the paragraph sums up the main idea: The sisters were frauds.

[1]In the nineteenth century, the Fox sisters, Margaret and Kate Fox, were famous for their ability to communicate with the dead. [2]When the sisters arrived in town, men, women, and children flocked to see them speak with the spirits and, if an audience member was lucky, bring back a message from a lost loved one. [3]Unfortunately, for those eager and hopeful fans, the sisters were not what they seemed to be. [4]Their communication with the spirits was a clever but cruel act. [5]Margaret and Kate would ask questions of the spirits, and the spirits would seem to reply. [6]They would rap once for "no" and three times for "yes." [7]But those raps didn't come from the spirit world. [8]Both women could crack the joints of their toes and ankles at will, and they cracked them every time they needed the spirit world to answer.

Although the paragraph makes it clear by the end that the Fox sisters were con artists, none of the sentences in the paragraph makes that point, although sentences 3 and 4 come close. Thus, it's up to the reader to piece together a main idea statement that goes something like this: "Although the Fox sisters were famous for their ability to communicate with the dead, their communication with the spirits was a clever but cruel act."

Sometimes, though, particularly in subjects like history and sociology, the writer won't give you either a topic sentence or the sentence parts to create your own main idea statement. Instead, the writer will give you several clues to the implied main idea, and it will be up to you to draw an inference that sticks close to what the author says but still goes beyond it to sum up the implied point of the paragraph, for example:

The philosopher Arthur Schopenhauer lived most of his life completely alone and tended to keep to himself. Separated from his family and distrustful of women, he had neither wife nor children. Irrationally* afraid of thieves, he kept his belongings carefully locked away and was said to keep loaded pistols near him while he slept. His main companion was a poodle named Atma (a word that means "world soul"). However, even Atma occasionally disturbed his peace of mind. Whenever she chewed his shoes or barked too much, her master would grow irritated and call her *mensch*, the German word for "human being."

In this paragraph, the author supplies a number of specific details about Schopenhauer's character and behavior: (1) he lived most of his life alone, (2) he distrusted women, (3) he always expected to be robbed, (4) his only companion was a dog, and (5) he called his dog a "human

---

*irrationally: without reason or logic, not based on reason.

being" when she irritated him. However, none of those statements sums up the point of the paragraph.

This is a case where the author leaves it to the reader to infer a main idea that can sum up all the specific details in the same way a topic sentence might. In this instance, a main idea like the following would fit the bill: "Schopenhauer had little faith in his fellow human beings." That idea follows logically from the details presented in the paragraph, and it's expressed in a general sentence that could sum up the paragraph's supporting details. In other words, that same sentence could easily function as the paragraph's topic sentence.

The Difference Between Logical and Illogical Inferences

When readers can't find a general sentence to sum up a paragraph, they infer one that fits or follows from the details the author included. However, they are careful to make their inference logical. They base it solidly on the author's statements because they know illogical inferences can lead them away from, rather than toward, the author's intended meaning.

Seeing the Difference

For an illustration of the difference between a **logical** and an **illogical inference**, imagine that we had come up with this implied main idea for the paragraph about Schopenhauer: "Schopenhauer's miserable childhood made it impossible for him to have healthy relationships with other people." Although the paragraph makes it quite clear that Schopenhauer must have been difficult, it doesn't completely rule out *all* relationships with other people. Based on the paragraph, we can't say if he did or didn't have any relationship with other human beings (In fact, he did).

The paragraph also doesn't refer to his childhood. Based on what the author actually says, we can't claim that his early years soured him on life. In other words, both parts of that implied main idea about Schopenhauer's childhood stem from illogical inferences, i.e., inferences that are not backed up by what the author says.

The confusion an illogical inference can sow becomes clear when we take a look at the second paragraph in the reading.

Yet, however negatively Schopenhauer was inclined to view his fellow human beings, his philosophy suggests his famously introspective[*] personality had another side. Whatever his personal life, in his work

---

[*]introspective: given to examining one's own thoughts; withdrawn.

Schopenhauer encouraged his readers to stop focusing on themselves and see compassion for others as the basis for morality. This emphasis on the need for empathy is so strong in his writing, that other philosophers have dubbed Schopenhauer, the "compassionate curmudgeon."[†]

Making the mental move from our original implied main idea, "Schopenhauer mistrusted his fellow human beings," to the point of the above paragraph—his philosophy showed another side—is easy enough to do. But the ease with which we can connect one paragraph to another decreases if we start out with the second implied main idea: "Schopenhauer's miserable childhood made it impossible for him to have healthy relationships with other people."

The second statement suggests that the writer is going to further explain the cause and effect relationship between Schopenhauer's childhood and his lack of a healthy relationship with others. But the second paragraph doesn't touch on either. That's the problem with an illogical inference. It doesn't keep you connected to the writer's train of thought. On the contrary, it leads you away from it.

The Author's Words Count Double

While your personal experience and background knowledge always contribute to the author's meaning, it's important that you never let what you think about a topic overwhelm the author's actual statements. When it comes to interpreting the author's meaning, the actual words on the page should carry more weight than your thoughts on the subject.

Logical Inferences ◆	1. are solidly grounded in, or based on, the author's words.
	2. are not contradicted by any statements in the passage.
	3. rely more heavily on the author's words than on the reader's background knowledge, experience, or common sense.

Illogical Inferences ◆	1. do not fit the author's actual statements.
	2. are contradicted by what the author says.
	3. rely too heavily on the reader's personal experience or general knowledge rather than on the author's words.

[†]curmudgeon: a cranky, ill-tempered person.

ALLUSION ALERT

The Fountain of Youth

The fountain of youth turns up in ancient legends, which claim that bathing in a mysterious fountain can make the old young again. In 1512 the Spanish explorer Juan Ponce de León set off to find the legendary fountain that could stop the passage of time. He landed in Florida, where he settled, even though his search had failed. Nowadays, an allusion to the fountain of youth, with or without any reference to Ponce de León, suggests that some behavior, lotion, or activity restores or tries to restore youth—for example: "Exercise does seem to be a fountain of youth for some; in his seventies exercise guru Joseph Pilates had the body of a much younger man."

WEB QUEST **The Fox Sisters Start a Trend**

The Fox sisters are often credited with starting a trend in late nineteenth-century culture. What trend would that be?

_____

How did the public discover that the Fox sisters were fakes?

_____

◆ EXERCISE 2 Implied Main Ideas

DIRECTIONS Read each passage. Then circle the letter of the implied main idea.

The writer opens with a reference to a youth-restoration therapy.

Sentence 3 suggests what about cell therapy?

EXAMPLE ¹Over the years, countless numbers of men and women have paid large sums of money for a treatment commonly known as cell therapy. ²Their reason was simple: They believed lamb-cell injections could help them maintain their youth. ³Such people apparently don't know that animal cells, when injected into the human body, are destroyed by the immune system. ⁴Others in a similar pursuit of youth have tried *chelation therapy*, which is supposed to pull heavy metals like lead and mercury from the body. ⁵Proponents claim that the treatments improve

Sentences 4 through 10 introduce a therapy only to suggest it is fraudulent.

cell function, inhibit the aging process, and prevent heart disease, all by eliminating poisons from the body, yet research shows no such effect. [6]In fact, critics question the idea of there being poisons in the body to begin with, suggesting that the therapy has nothing to treat. [7]Other seekers of the fountain of youth use human growth hormone (HGH) tablets or sprays. [8]These sprays and tablets can allegedly accomplish everything from eliminating wrinkles to improving memory and concentration. [9]Yet such treatments have no research backing up these claims. [10]There is, however, evidence that HGH in any form may produce side effects like an increased risk of cancer and cardiovascular disease.

Implied Main Idea

a. Therapies designed to keep people young are generally worthless.

b. Therapies for staying younger should be available for everyone, not just for those rich enough to afford them.

c. Treatments designed to help people maintain youth invariably do more harm than good.

EXPLANATION The author's pattern of describing a therapy to restore youth and then saying it's useless makes inference *a* the best choice for an implied main idea.

1. The founding fathers based the Constitution of the United States on republican rather than democratic principles. In other words, laws were to be made by the representatives of citizens, not by the citizens directly. Yet whatever the intentions of the founding fathers may have been, eighteen U.S. states provide for legislation by popular initiative. For instance, voters can place legislative measures (and sometimes constitutional amendments) directly on the ballot as long as they get the required number of signatures on a petition. In addition, forty-nine states allow for *referendums*, a procedure that lets voters reject a measure adopted by the state legislature. Fifteen states permit *recalls*. If enough signatures can be collected, an elected official has to go before the voters, who may well vote him or her out of office. This is precisely what happened to Governor Gray Davis of California in 2003—a recall election propelled him out of office. The election took place because many of the same citizens who had elected Davis were unhappy with his performance and wanted him gone. Governor Scott Walker of Wisconsin, however, did not meet the same fate in 2012 when he was the subject of a recall. Walker kept his chair in the governor's office.

Implied Main Idea

   a. Whatever the founding fathers had in mind, there are still several ways in which Americans practice direct democracy.

   b. The founding fathers were fearful of a democracy in which the majority ruled.

   c. In the last ten years, U.S. citizens have consistently challenged the legality of the Constitution through initiatives like recalls and referendums.

2. Like Jackie Robinson, who broke the color barrier in baseball in 1947, Asian-American basketball player Jeremy Lin, who challenged stereotypes about Asian athletic prowess, has been the target of racial stereotyping. But while those who shouted racist insults at Robinson as he tore around the bases weren't ashamed of themselves, the same is not true today. ESPN's praise of Lin's performance as a "chink in the armor" of the opposing team, for instance, caused public outrage and calls for an apology from the sports network, which promptly issued one. In Robinson's time, racism was a part of the culture and was just beginning to be publicly challenged by civil rights activists. Lin, in contrast, is playing basketball in an era when anyone with a conscience would be embarrassed to be caught voicing racial or ethnic slurs. Yet that doesn't mean stereotyping has disappeared from sports. As journalist Sean Gregory of *Time* magazine correctly said, Lin has been a victim of "racial profiling." The coaches who early on in his career ignored Lin's obvious ability and failed to draft him were inclined to think of Asian-Americans as intellectual achievers who couldn't possibly possess athletic prowess as well. Lin himself has said that he thinks, initially at least, his athletic abilities went unrecognized because he was Asian-American.

Implied Main Idea

   a. Jackie Robinson and Jeremy Lin were both victims of racism, and their extraordinary athletic skills were not readily acknowledged by those prejudiced against people of color.

   b. Asian-American Jeremy Lin may not have faced the overt racism that Jackie Robinson did, but he has still been a victim of racial stereotyping; it's just more subtle than it used to be.

   c. Asian-Americans are often stereotyped as intellectual overachievers who can't possibly be good at sports too.

3. On July 28, 1945, the Allies[†] delivered an ultimatum to Japan. Promising that the Japanese people would not be "enslaved," the Potsdam Declaration[†] called for unconditional surrender or suffer "prompt and utter destruction." In response, Tokyo radio announced that the government would respond with *mokusatsu* (literally "kill with silence"). On August 6, 1945, a B-29 bomber, the Enola Gay, dropped an atomic bomb above Hiroshima, igniting a firestorm and killing 130,000 people. Tens of thousands more would suffer from radiation poisoning. On August 8, the Soviet Union declared war on Japan. On August 9, the United States used a second atomic bomb on Nagasaki, killing sixty thousand people. Five days later, Japan surrendered. Recent histories argue that the Soviet declaration of war played a more significant role in Japan's surrender than America's use of atomic weapons. (Mary Beth Norton et al., *A People and a Nation*, Brief Edition, 9e, © Cengage Learning.)

Implied Main Idea

a. Recent histories suggesting that the Soviet Union's declaration of war did more to make Japan surrender than the United States' decision to drop the atomic bomb are accurate in their interpretation of events.

b. The bombing of Hiroshima and Nagasaki brought World War II to an end.

c. No one can say for sure which action compelled Japanese surrender during World War II, the Soviet Union's declaration of war or the dropping of the atomic bomb.

4. At Yale University's School of Law, president-to-be William Clinton met and set up housekeeping with fellow student Hillary Rodham, who also had big ambitions. Her background was rather different from Clinton's, although not one in which he was uncomfortable. She was a midwesterner from a family several social notches above the smoking, drinking, card-playing Clintons of Little Rock, Arkansas. She was a Republican—an active one—when she went to Wellesley College. There she was surrounded by girls talking about civil rights, protesting the Vietnam war, and groping their way toward feminism. She was soon conflicted, telling an adviser she "was a mind

---

[†]During World War II, the Allies were Britain, France, the United States, and, by the end of the war, Russia.
[†]Potsdam Declaration: statement defining the terms of Japan's surrender.

conservative and a heart liberal." By the time she got to Yale Law, she was a certified Democrat of the "political correctness" persuasion. (Adapted from Joseph Conlin, *The American Past 9e*, vol. II, © Cengage Learning.)

a. Hillary Rodham Clinton may have changed parties in her youth, but she remains a Republican at heart.

b. Hillary Rodham Clinton's peers in college influenced her thinking enough for her to switch from Republican to Democrat.

c. It wasn't until she went to college that Hillary Rodham Clinton began to think about a political career.

5. In 2009, Samuel Bragg confessed to his pastor John Vaprezsan that he had assaulted a nine-year-old girl. Vaprezsan later testified about the assault at Bragg's trial, unleashing a flood of objections by the defendant's lawyer, who claimed a jury would be more inclined to believe the pastor than the defendant. As a result of an appeal, the pastor's testimony was thrown out of court by a judge who said it violated state law, which did not require a priest or pastor to report crimes acknowledged in a religious context. Vaprezsan himself seemed uninterested in the position of the state, saying that he thought his job was to help people, and, in this case, he chose to help a nine-year-old girl rather than the man who had confessed. However, had the same case been tried in New Hampshire or West Virginia, the state would have sided with the pastor and the defendant would have had no basis for challenging the testimony. These states deny any right to what's known as "clergy-penitent privilege" in cases of child abuse or neglect. Legal challenges might have also been useless in Connecticut and Mississippi, where the privilege is not addressed specifically. Application of the clergy-penitent privilege becomes even more complicated in states that grant it only to the person making the confession, not to the minister.

a. States like New Hampshire and West Virginia have the right idea when it comes to clergy-penitent privilege.

b. Where child abuse is concerned, states vary markedly in their willingness to grant clergy-penitent privilege.

c. Pastor John Vaprezsan has the right attitude toward doing his duty as a pastor; he should do what's right, not what's legal.

REVIEWING THROUGH WRITING

Study the sample paragraph about the creams, lotions, and treatments people resort to in a generally hopeless attempt to find the fountain of youth. Notice how the listing of specific examples is used to imply a main idea. Then research on the Web any one of the following: (1) the behavior of crows, (2) legends about bluebirds, (3) the calorie count of cheeseburgers, (4) fad diets, (5) the number three in fairy tales, or (6) flashbulb memories. As you read, look for specific illustrations that you think suggest a pattern and a point. Then select at least three illustrations that make the same point and write a paragraph that implies the main idea without stating it.

What Do You Think?
♦

If you could apply a uniform policy statewide to clergy-penitent privilege in cases of child abuse, what would it be?

♦ EXERCISE 3   Inferring Main Ideas

DIRECTIONS   Read each passage. Then circle the letter of the implied main idea.

1. The widely acclaimed singer and guitarist Buddy Holly died in a 1959 plane crash at age 22. Famed singer Otis Redding was only 26 when he was killed in a plane crash in 1967. At age 27, legendary rock guitarist Jimi Hendrix died from suffocation in 1970 after swallowing a mix of liquor and pills. Jim Morrison, lead singer of the popular rock band The Doors, was also only 27 when he died of mysterious causes in 1971. Just two weeks after Hendrix's death, rock-and-roll idol Janis Joplin died of a heroin overdose, also at the age of 27. In 1979, Sid Vicious, the 21-year-old bass player of the influential Sex Pistols punk-rock band, took his own life. In 1994, Kurt Cobain, world-renowned lead singer for the band Nirvana, committed suicide; he was also only 27 years old. In 1996, Rapper Tupac Shakur was only 25 years old when he was shot four times after watching Mike Tyson fight in Las Vegas. The rapper died of his wounds six days later. Christopher George Wallace, popularly known as Biggie Smalls, or The Notorious BIG, was only 24 when he was killed in a drive-by shooting in Los Angeles on March 9, 1997. The rap musician and music producer Disco D was only 27 when he committed suicide in 2008, after a long bout with depression.

Implied Main Idea
 a. Plane crashes have taken the lives of many of rock's biggest stars.

 b. Many celebrities have died when they were at the peak of their fame.

 c. Many of rock and hip-hop's biggest stars died young.

 d. Like hip-hop, the world of rock music was plagued by violence.

2. The island of Ikaria, which lies around 30 miles off the western coast of Turkey, is small, only 99 square miles. Tiny as it is, though, Ikaria gets a good deal of attention. Researchers are interested in the island because its inhabitants reach the age of 90 at double the rate people in the United States do. Ikarian men, in fact, are four times more likely to reach 90 than American men are. In general, elderly Ikarians also suffer less from depression and Alzheimer's disease than Americans of a similar age do. The question posed by researchers is, Why? The residents think their longevity comes from the mountain tea they brew, which is made from herbs grown on the island. They also think that the honey they eat, produced on the island, has medicinal qualities that keep diseases at bay. It appears that their claims might not be old wives' tales. When researchers analyzed the herbal tea and honey, they found them filled with antioxidants known to fight disease. The Ikarian diet is also naturally designed to combat disease and prolong life. It's short on red meat and long on olive oil and red wine, which reduce bad cholesterol while raising levels of the good. Their diet is also low on refined sugar, which may account for the population's low levels of diabetes. In trying to explain the good health the elderly residents enjoy, researchers also point to their active lifestyle, a necessity given how much of their diet is based on garden produce they grow themselves. Researchers also believe that the island's communal lifestyle, forced on the Ikarians by their relatively isolated location, has contributed mightily to the inhabitants' ability to lead a life that is not just long but healthy.

Implied Main Idea
 a. Ikarians live a long time because they know how to relax.

 b. A number of different factors contribute to the Ikarians' longevity.

 c. If Americans would adopt the Ikarian lifestyle, they could easily add twenty years to the average life span.

 d. Most people overestimate their chances of developing cancer.

3. Cleveland child psychologist Sylvia Rimm interviewed 5,400 children in eighteen states about their worries, fears, relationships, and self-confidence. She also talked with another 300 children in focus groups. She discovered that overweight children feel less intelligent and less confident than their normal-weight peers. Overweight children also worry more than their slimmer peers and experience more anxiety. Rimm discovered as well that heavier children are lonelier and sadder than other kids. They also describe family relationships more negatively than average-weight children describe theirs. Sadly, Rimm also found that overweight kids are forced to endure their peers' hurtful taunts and ridicule much more frequently than normal-weight kids do.

Implied Main Idea

   a. According to Sylvia Rimm, average-weight children are very cruel to overweight children.

   b. Sylvia Rimm's research indicates that negative emotions and problems lead children to overeat and become overweight.

   c. Sylvia Rimm's survey indicates that overweight children have a more difficult childhood than their average-weight peers do.

   d. Childhood obesity is a growing problem in the United States.

4. In June 1840, Lucretia Mott and Elizabeth Cady Stanton attended the World Anti-Slavery Convention in London. Although both were activists in the cause of abolition, Mott was an actual delegate to the convention as were several other American women. Mott, though, never took her convention seat. It was denied her after several male delegates, among them Stanton's husband, vehemently expressed their disapproval of women abolitionists participating in the convention on an equal footing with men. Although there were strong protests to the exclusion of women from the proceedings, those opposed to the female delegates carried the day, and all the women attending were restricted to sitting in the balcony of the meeting hall and assuming the role of onlookers rather than participants. Still, it was in the balcony that Mott struck up a friendship with Elizabeth Cady Stanton. The two women bonded because of their mutual anger at being excluded. As a result of their exclusion, the two vowed to found their own movement and hold their own convention. Mott and Stanton were true to their word. Eight years later, in 1848, the first women's rights convention took place in Seneca Falls, New York. The Seneca Falls Convention is now considered the official starting point of a feminist movement that would forever change the social role of women in the United States and eventually give them the right to vote in 1920.

Implied Main Idea

a. The 1848 Seneca Falls Convention forever changed the role of women in the United States.

b. Thanks to Lucretia Mott, Elizabeth Cady Stanton was inspired to become a feminist who spoke for an entire generation of women.

c. Had Mott and Stanton not been excluded from the World Anti-Slavery Convention, the very influential Seneca Falls Convention might never have taken place.

d. Lucretia Mott profoundly influenced the life of Elizabeth Cady Stanton, who went on to become a leader of the nineteenth-century feminist revolution.

WEB QUEST   **Elizabeth Cady Stanton's Speech of a Lifetime**

What is the title of the speech Elizabeth Cady Stanton gave when she retired from the National American Woman Suffrage Association in 1892?

_____

In the speech's opening lines, Stanton gives a very explicit reason why women needed equality with men. What is that reason?

_____

_____

_____

◆ **EXERCISE 4**   **Recognizing Implied Main Ideas**

DIRECTIONS   Read each passage. Then circle the letter of the implied main idea.

1. Why do only humans have language? No one is quite sure. For centuries, people assumed that only humans were sufficiently intelligent to develop speech. But in recent decades, many careful observers of the higher apes, such as chimpanzees, have been uneasy with this assumption. Through long observation of ape behavior, they became convinced that apes display considerable intelligence. Their ability to solve problems, for example, is sufficient to suggest that they are smart enough to learn a language, which has led to a series of efforts

to teach chimpanzees to speak. (Adapted from Rodney Stark, *Sociology* 10e, © Cengage Learning.)

Implied Main Idea

a. Some people believe that chimpanzees' problem-solving abilities are proof that they are smart enough to learn a language, and efforts have been made to teach chimps to speak.

b. For centuries, we have assumed that only humans can use language, but as it turns out, chimpanzees are language users as well.

c. Apes display the same degree of intelligence that humans do, especially when it comes to problem solving.

d. Efforts made to teach chimps speech have been highly successful and prove that chimps can use language in the same way humans can, which should have been obvious from the animals' problem-solving skills.

2. In 1822, James Forten responded to the American Colonization Society's proposal that free blacks like him "return" to Africa: "My great-grandfather was brought to this country a slave from Africa. My grandfather obtained his own freedom. My father never wore the yoke. He rendered valuable service to his country in the war of our Revolution; and I, though then a boy, was a drummer in that war. I have since lived and labored in useful employment, have acquired property, and have paid taxes. . . . Yet some ingenious* gentlemen have recently discovered that I am still an African; that a continent three thousand miles away—and more—from the place where I was born is my native country." (Adapted from Joseph Conlin, *The American Past* 9e, vol. I, © Cengage Learning.)

Implied Main Idea

a. Many freed slaves followed the suggestion of the American Colonization Society and returned to Africa, but James Forten was not among them.

b. Many African-Americans distinguished themselves during the Revolutionary War but none more so than James Forten.

c. James Forten was contemptuous of the American Colonization Society's idea that free African-Americans like himself should "return" to Africa.

d. Like many other do-gooder groups throughout history, the members of the American Colonization Society had little real experience with the people they wanted to help.

*ingenious: clever, forward-thinking.

3. At this point, a convincing body of evidence suggests that the Wild West was never as wild as it is imagined by most Americans. Books like Richard Slotkin's immensely readable *Gunfighter Nation* have convincingly argued that while violence and lawlessness were present in the early days of the western states, there were actually many more attempts to cooperate and build primitive codes of law than there were gunfights. In fact, as Terry L. Anderson and Peter J. Hill, the authors of *The Not So Wild, Wild West: Property Rights on the Frontier*, point out, probably no more than a dozen bank robberies occurred in the heyday of the so-called Wild West, the years between 1869 and 1900. Yet Americans don't seem to care. Tourists still line up in droves to re-enact the gunfight at the O.K. Corral between Wyatt Earp and the Clanton boys. And those same tourists keep dude ranches and fake ghost towns booming. Tourists in pursuit of the Wild West are probably also the main reason why groups like the "Cheyenne Gunslingers Association," "Gunfighters for Hire," and "Cowboys of the Old West" continue to multiply.

Implied Main Idea

a. Writers of history textbooks are completely out of touch with the interests of the American people.

b. Americans' fascination with the Wild West continues despite convincing evidence that the West was not nearly as wild as people imagine.

c. The people who travel west to re-enact the adventures that supposedly took place in the heyday of the Wild West (1869–1900) are just wasting their money.

d. If historians didn't write dry, dusty prose, perhaps more people would pay attention to books claiming to dispel the myth of the Wild West.

4. In 2010, the International Center for Media and the Public Agenda decided to explore the idea that many of today's students are addicted to social media. Titled "24 Hours: Unplugged" and performed by researchers at the University of Maryland, the study asked 200 students what they would do if they had to spend a day without being hooked up to social media. Subjects in the study had to give up cell phones, Facebook, Twitter, etc., and then answer questions about their experience by blogging on a private website. Although the researchers had expected subjects to dislike not having access to social media, even they were surprised by their subjects' responses.

One student wrote that without access to texting or instant messaging, she felt "quite alone and secluded from my life." Those feelings were echoed by many of the other students in the study, who reported symptoms similar to addicts withdrawing from a drug: They were jittery, anxious, and miserable. As one student expressed it, "Although I started the day feeling good, I noticed my mood started to change around noon. I started to feel isolated and lonely." Susan D. Moeller, the project director, said that for many students in the study, "going without media meant, in their world, going without their friends and family." It was that feeling of being cut off from loved ones that made not using any social media, even for twenty-four hours, seem unbearable. (Source of quotations: Jill Laster, "Students Denied Social Media Go Through Withdrawal," *The Chronicle of Higher Education*, April 28, 2010.)

Implied Main Idea

a. The suggestion that young people today are addicted to social media seems to be more than idle chatter; studies show that students denied access to social media are incapable of functioning.

b. Students today no longer have a personal connection to friends and family; they have replaced their family and friends with a variety of social media that act as substitutes for relationships the students don't have.

c. All the students in a study conducted by the International Center for Media and the Public Agenda behaved like addicts withdrawing from a drug after they were denied access to social media.

d. One 2010 study conducted by the International Center for Media and the Public Agenda suggests that some students, initially at least, may suffer addiction-like symptoms of withdrawal if they have no access to social media.

◆ EXERCISE 5   Inferring Main Ideas from Paragraphs

DIRECTIONS Read the paragraph. Then write a sentence that expresses the implied main idea.

Sentences 1–3 identify kudzu's original purpose—feeding livestock.

EXAMPLE ¹The plant known as kudzu was introduced to the South in the 1920s. ²At the time, it promised to be a boon* to farmers who needed a cheap and an abundant food crop for pigs, goats, and cattle. ³Because it grows like a weed, it was assumed that kudzu could provide

_____

*boon: gift, benefit.

There's nothing kudzu can't eventually overrun.

smartstock/iStockphoto.com

Sentence 4 moves away from the opening point. It suggests a main idea that contrasts the original hope with the current reality.

an inexpensive and a plentiful supply of food for agricultural animals. [4]However, within half a century, kudzu had overrun seven million acres of land, and huge patches of the plant had developed root systems weighing up to three hundred pounds. [5]Currently, no one really knows how to keep kudzu under control. [6]It's creating problems for everyone from boaters to farmers.

Implied Main Idea Intended to help farmers feed their livestock, kudzu has proven to be more harmful than beneficial.

EXPLANATION While readers would vary in the words they used, the implied main idea has to unite the two different perspectives described in the paragraph.

1. Following the tragic shooting at an elementary school in Newtown, Connecticut, the *Journal News*, a newspaper in Westchester County, New York, decided to perform what they called a public service. They published an interactive map showing the names and addresses of handgun permit holders in the area. The map was made up of dots, each one linked to an address. Readers who clicked on a dot could see the name and address of a permit holder. The map received more views than any other posting in the paper's history, but the public's response may not have been what the paper's managers expected. One common complaint was that, thanks to the *Journal News*, criminals would know

where they could go to get guns. Others complained about the paper's shameless invasion of privacy. But perhaps the most telling indicator of the public's reaction to the map is that, after publishing its public service announcement, the newspaper had to hire armed guards.

Implied Main Idea _____

_____

2. If dieting works, why are hundreds of "new" diets published each year? The answer is that although dieters do lose weight, most regain it soon after they stop dieting. In fact, many people end up weighing even more than before. Why should this be so? Dieting slows the body's rate of metabolism (the rate at which energy is used up). In effect, a dieter's body becomes highly efficient at conserving calories and storing them as fat. (Dennis Coon and John Mitterer, *Introduction to Psychology* 12e, © Cengage Learning.)

Implied Main Idea _____

_____

3. On the evening of January 24, 1848, a carpenter from New Jersey, James Marshall, took a walk along the American River where it tumbles through the foothills of the Sierra Nevada. Marshall was working for John Augustus Sutter, a colorful Swiss adventurer, who had turned a Mexican land grant into a feudal domain.[†] Marshall was building a sawmill for Sutter on the river. He was inspecting a ditch that returned water to the river when he noticed a curious metallic stone. "Boys," he told his crew, "I think I have found a gold mine." He had, and that was it for the sawmill. Sutter's employees dropped their hammers and set to shoveling gravel from the river, separating the sand and silt from what proved to plenty of gold dust and nuggets. Marshall's discovery briefly ended the existence of San Francisco. A town of 500 on a huge harbor, it was depopulated when "everyone," including a recently arrived military unit, headed for the hills. (Joseph Conlin, *The American Past* 9e, © Cengage Learning.)

Implied Main Idea _____

_____

[†]feudal domain: land that is completely under the control of the owner as it was during the Middle Ages.

4. In 1923 Wiley College, an all-black college in the Northeast corner of Texas, hired poet and educator Melvin B. Tolson as a professor of speech and English. As part of his job, Tolson proceeded to build up the school's debating team to the point where it challenged and beat the mighty University of Southern California for the 1935 national debating championship. Wiley's victory shocked and outraged much of the country's white population even as it instilled pride in African-Americans, providing them with a shining model of academic achievement and motivating black youth to reach for new heights. There was a lesson to be learned from Wiley's victory. No self-fulfilling prophecy condemning black students to mediocrity because of their history operated at Wiley. To the contrary, with the backing of the administration, Tolson worked his students hard, demanded excellence, and expected the best. Supported by their friends, their family, and their school, the students rose to the challenge. (Adapted from Robert J. Brym and John Lie, *Sociology* 3e, © Cengage Learning.)

Implied Main Idea

_____

_____

_____

5. Vegetarianism is on the rise in the United States, with more people, especially among young people in college, deciding to ban meat from their diet. There was a time when vegetarians were considered oddballs for refusing to eat meat, and college students in particular considered hamburgers a diet staple. But that attitude is changing and for good reason. Hamburgers on a bun may be as American as apple pie, but, unfortunately, they often supply consumers with more than protein. A 2010 report by the U.S. Department of Agriculture found that beef can contain a number of veterinary drugs, some of which are harmful to humans. In addition to big doses of antibiotics, the report cited worming medications and anti-inflammatories. Under analysis, pork hasn't fared much better. A 2012 study from Iowa State University found MRSA, the superbug strain of bacteria, in 7 percent of the pork samples tested. Turkey met a similar fate. A 2011 study published in the journal *Clinical Infectious Diseases* found staph bacteria in 80 percent of the samples analyzed.

Implied Main Idea _____

_____

REVIEWING THROUGH WRITING

Melvin Tolson had a powerful effect on the students he taught. Use the Web to read about both the man and his influence. Then write a description of his personality and its effect on his students. Try to make that effect clear to readers without using a topic sentence or thesis statement.

CHECK YOUR UNDERSTANDING

1. Explain the difference between logical and illogical inferences.

_____

_____

2. What's the drawback associated with making an illogical inference when you read?

_____

Drawing Inferences About Supporting Details

Even when the topic sentence is present in a paragraph, readers still need to draw other kinds of inferences. Above all, the most important are **bridging inferences**. These are the inferences readers draw to understand how supporting details relate to one another and contribute to the main idea. Bridging inferences answer questions like these: What does this sentence add to what I already learned from the paragraph? What is this sentence's relationship to the one that came before?

Although bridging inferences are not essential to every supporting detail in a paragraph, they are necessary for a good many. Without them, it would be difficult for readers to follow the writer's train of thought. Here's an example:

Sentence 2 picks up on the "fear of spoiling the land," confirming that sentence 1 is the topic sentence.

To connect sentences 4 and 5, readers have to infer that Harrison's actions and the opening phrase "such policies" are one and the same.

[1]In the nineteenth century, questions about natural resources caught Americans between the desire for progress and the fear of spoiling the land. [2]After the Civil War, people eager to protect the natural landscape began to coalesce* into a conservation movement. [3]Among them was Western naturalist John Muir, who helped establish Yosemite National Park in 1890. [4]The next year, under pressure from Muir and others, Congress authorized President Benjamin Harrison to create forest reserves—public land protected from cutting by private interests. [5]Such policies met with strong objection. [6]Lumber companies, lumber dealers, railroads, and householders were accustomed to cutting timber freely for fuel and building materials. [7]Public opinion on conservation also split along sectional lines. [8]Most supporters of regulation came from the eastern states. [9]In the East, resources had already become less plentiful. [10]Opposition was loudest in the West, where people were still eager to take advantage of nature's resources.

(Adapted from Mary Beth Norton et al., *A People and a Nation* 8e, © Cengage Learning.)

In the previous paragraph, the writers describe how the early conservation movement got its start in the United States. The paragraph describes the first conservationists along with those who opposed them. But as you can see from the marginal notes, it's the reader's job to infer the connections that bind the sentences together and move the meaning of the paragraph forward.

For an illustration of how important the reader's bridging inferences are, look at sentence 3, which reads, "Among them was Western naturalist John Muir, who helped establish Yosemite National Park in 1890." To understand why sentence 3 follows sentence 2, readers need to supply the following information:

1. The antecedent for *them* is "people eager to protect the natural landscape." They are the ones coalescing "into a conservation movement."

2. John Muir agrees with the conservationists that the land's natural resources cannot be sacrificed to progress.

3. Establishing a park is one method conservationists use to protect the land.

The need for reader-supplied inferences persists throughout the passage. Look closely, for instance, at sentences 8 and 9: "Most supporters of regulation came from the eastern states. In the East, resources

---

*coalesce: combine, form around, connect.

had already become less plentiful." The connection between these two sentences is implicit rather than explicit, leaving the reader to infer the cause and effect relationship that connects the two: *Because* the eastern states were beginning to notice that resources were less plentiful, they were more inclined to be supporters of regulation.

✔ CHECK YOUR UNDERSTANDING

What are *bridging inferences*?

_____

_____

✎ REVIEWING THROUGH WRITING

Write two sentences that require a bridging inference to communicate their meaning.

_____

_____

_____

◇ Writers and Readers Collaborate

You may be accustomed to thinking that writers supply every bit of text you need to understand their message. But, in fact, writers do only part of the job. They try to put enough information on the page to explain or prove their point. However, if they include every word necessary to creating their meaning, the result would be so repetitive and long, no one would read it. Thus writers always rely on readers to supply some of the information necessary to their intended meaning.

No matter what you may have thought in the past, you need to think of reading as an act of collaboration in which you help create the text you read. If you don't collaborate with the author, the text's meaning may well elude you.

◆ EXERCISE 6   Making Connections Between Sentences

DIRECTIONS   Read each passage. Then circle the letter of the correct answer or fill in the blanks.

Sentence 1 provides a time frame.

Sentence 2 is general enough to be a topic sentence.

But sentences 3 and 4 make it clear that the focus is on the size of the public meetings.

EXAMPLE   [1]In the 1820s American politics was not just a matter of voting in periodic elections. [2]On the contrary, vast numbers of Americans participated directly in politics. [3]One gauge of this was the huge number of public meetings involving large audiences that attended for the purpose of discussing current political issues. [4]On occasion, audiences were so large that members of the elite even grew fearful that the meetings would get out of hand and democracy would take the form of "mobocracy." [5]The organizers, however, were overjoyed that the meetings included not only a cross section of the electorate but many others who lent valuable collective support, even though they could not vote.

(Adapted from Steven M. Gillon and Cathy D. Matson, *The American Experiment* 2e, © Cengage Learning.)

1. What is the stated or implied main idea of this passage?

   a. In the early days of American independence, the wealthy were worried about democracy turning into mob rule.

   b. In the 1820s, organizers of large public meetings worked hard to make large numbers of people attend.

   (c.) In the 1820s, the size of public meetings made it clear Americans wanted to participate in political decisions.

2. In sentence 3, the pronoun *this* refers to <u>Americans' participation in</u> <u>politics; Americans' direct political participation.</u>

3. What inference do readers need to make to understand the function of sentence 3 in the paragraph?

   a. Sentence 3 reverses the train of thought introduced in sentence 2.

   (b.) Sentence 3 offers proof of the claim made in sentence 2.

   c. Sentence 3 repeats for emphasis the point of sentence 2.

4. What inference do readers need to make to understand the function of sentence 4 in the paragraph?

   a. Sentence 4 reverses the claim made in sentence 3.

   (b.) Sentence 4 describes a consequence of the events mentioned in sentence 3.

   c. Sentence 4 repeats for emphasis the point made in sentence 3.

5. What inference do readers need to make to understand the function of sentence 5 in the paragraph?

   a. Sentence 5 describes a criticism of events mentioned in sentence 4.

   (b.) Sentence 5 describes a response that contrasts with the one described in sentence 4.

   c. Sentence 5 offers proof of the claim made in sentence 4.

EXPLANATION In this passage, the main idea has to be pieced together from sentences 1, 2, and 3. The supporting details then describe the huge public meetings and the response to them in more detail.

1. ¹There is no denying the importance of the future. ²In the words of the scientist Charles F. Kettering, "We should be concerned about the future because we will have to spend the rest of our lives there." ³However, concern about the future doesn't make it easy to predict. ⁴In 1877, when Thomas Edison invented the phonograph, he thought of it as an office machine for taking dictation and lost interest in it. ⁵Recorded music did not become popular until twenty-one years later. ⁶When the Wright brothers offered their newly invented flying machine to the U.S. government and the British Royal Navy, the brothers were told airplanes had no future in the military. ⁷In 1900, a study commissioned by Mercedes-Benz estimated that worldwide demand for cars would not exceed 1 million, primarily because of the limited number of available chauffeurs. ⁸In 1899, Charles H. Duell, the Commissioner of the U.S. Patent and Trademark Office, said, "Everything that can be invented has been invented." (Adapted from George Beekman and Michael J. Quinn, *Computer Confluence* 7e, © Cengage Learning.)

1. What is the stated or implied main idea of this passage?

   a. People who predict the future are frequently mistaken.

   b. Although it's not easy, correctly predicting the future of technology can be done.

   c. "Expert" opinion about the future of new technology has often been wrong.

2. What inference must readers make to understand the function of sentence 3 in the paragraph?

   a. Sentence 3 modifies and revises the point made in sentence 1.

   b. Sentence 3 repeats the point made in sentence 1.

   c. Sentence 3 illustrates the point made in sentence 1.

3. What inference do readers need to make to understand the function of sentence 4 in the paragraph?

   a. Sentence 4 offers a criticism of the point made in sentence 3.

   b. Sentence 4 further illustrates the point made in sentence 1.

   c. Sentence 4 illustrates the point made in sentence 3.

4. What inference must readers make to understand the function of sentence 6 in the paragraph?

   a. Sentence 6 offers a contrasting opinion to the point made in sentence 4.

   b. Sentence 6 illustrates the point made in sentence 4.

   c. Sentence 6 offers another illustration of the point made in sentence 3.

5. What inference do readers need to make to understand the function of sentence 8 in the paragraph?

   a. Sentence 8 continues a sequence of dates and events begun in sentence 4.

   b. Sentence 8 illustrates the point made in sentence 6.

   c. Sentence 8 further illustrates the point made in sentence 3.

2. [1]In thirty-nine states, voters select judges to sit on the bench, making judges face elections like any other political candidate. [2]In theory at least, elections maximize the value of judicial accountability.* [3]It's worth observing, however, that electing judges is almost unknown in the rest of the world, where judges are appointed based on merit. [4]In the United States, voter turnout is very low in most judicial elections. [5]This fact is a major criticism leveled against choosing judges by election. [6]If the voter turnout is small, the winners can't be truly accountable to the people, which is the principal advantage associated with elections. [7]Yet low rates of voter interest and participation frequently combine with low-key, unexciting, and issueless campaigns to keep many judges on the bench as long as they run for re-election. [8]One study indicates that less than 10 percent of the judges who run are defeated. (Adapted from Ann O' M. Bowman and Richard C. Kearney, *State and Local Government* 5e, © Cengage Learning.)

1. What is the stated or implied main idea of this passage?

a. It's typical of American democracy that many state judges have to face regular elections if they are to rule in state courts.

b. Electing judges seems like a sound democratic idea, but it has some serious drawbacks.

c. Electing judges may sound like a good idea, but it doesn't work because campaigning for a judgeship requires money, and that means people with money can have more say in the election of a judge than ordinary people do.

2. What word or phrase signals that the authors are going to shift gears and modify the second sentence of the paragraph?

_____

3. What inference do readers need to make to understand the function of sentence 3 in the paragraph?

a. Sentence 3 brings the reader back to the point made in sentence 1.

b. In different words, sentence 3 repeats the point made in sentence 2.

c. Sentence 3 begins to challenge the point of sentence 2.

_____

*accountability: being held responsible.

4. Which phrase in sentence 5 refers to or stands in for the information presented in sentence 4? _____

5. Sentence 6 clarifies what word in sentence 5?

_____

3. [1]What's likely to happen if a person's defenses failed or if the person appraised a threatening situation as hopeless? [2]Martin Seligman[†] studied the case of a young marine who seemed to have adapted to the stresses of being held prisoner during the Vietnam War. [3]The marine's health was related to a promise made by his captors: If he cooperated, they said, he would be released on a certain date. [4]As the date approached, his spirits soared. [5]Then came a devastating blow. [6]He had been deceived. [7]His captors had no intention of ever releasing him. [8]He immediately lapsed into a deep depression. [9]He refused to eat or drink and died shortly thereafter. (Adapted from Dennis Coon and John O. Mitterer, *Psychology* 4e, © Cengage Learning.)

1. What's the stated or implied main idea of this passage?

   a. The case studied by Martin Seligman suggests that hopelessness breeds the kind of deep depression that destroys the will to live.

   b. Most people who feel hopeless about their lives just give up and welcome death.

   c. Martin Seligman started his career by studying people in situations that seemed hopeless; among them was a young marine being held as a prisoner of war.

2. What inference do readers need to make to understand the relationship between sentences 1 and 2?

   a. Sentence 2 turns the focus of the paragraph away from the question posed in sentence 1.

   b. Sentence 2 introduces a study that will help answer the question posed in sentence 1.

   c. Sentence 2 answers the question posed in sentence 1.

[†]Martin Seligman is a psychologist famous for his research on "learned helplessness," and he is often referred to as the "father of positive psychology," which suggests that happiness is a state of mind that can be acquired through positive thinking.

3. What inference do readers need to make to understand the relationship between sentences 3 and 4?

   a. Sentence 4 describes the promise made in sentence 3.

   b. Sentence 4 revises the point made in sentence 3.

   c. Sentence 4 describes a consequence of the promise mentioned in sentence 3.

4. Sentences 6 and 7 clarify what key phrase mentioned in sentence 5?

   _____

5. What inference do readers need to connect the opening question, the reference to Martin Seligman, and the marine betrayed by his captors?

   _____

   _____

WORD CHECK I

The following words were introduced and defined in pages 354–381. See how well you can match the words with the meanings. When you finish, make sure to check the meanings of any words you missed because the same words will turn up in tests at the end of the chapter.

1. orientations (p. 354) _____

2. prodigy (p. 355) _____

3. puns (p. 355) _____

4. guru (p. 355) _____

5. irrationally (p. 357) _____

6. introspective (p. 358) _____

7. ingenious (p. 369) _____

8. boon (p. 371) _____

9. coalesce (p. 376) _____

10. accountability (p. 381) _____

a. teacher, wise person

b. plays on words that emphasize similarity in sound

c. taking responsibility, the obligation to answer for one's actions

d. original, forward-thinking, imaginative

e. favor, benefit, blessing

f. combine, unite, gather around

g. someone who shows special talents at a very young age

h. serious, inward-looking

i. lacking in reason or logic

j. leanings, tendencies

◆ EXERCISE 7　　More About Form and Meaning

DIRECTIONS　Use one of the words listed below to fill in the blanks.

irrational	puns	ingenious	coalesce	orientations
introspective	guru	prodigy	boon	accountability

1. Someone who tells you that he or she is interested in global warming because it is a very heated topic probably has a weakness for

   _____.

2. Although Lady Gaga might be so in real life, no one who has ever seen her perform or heard her interviewed would imagine that she

   is _____.

3. Only a cynic would call steroids a(n) _____ to baseball.

4. Although it's common to ask someone to be reasonable, it would be unusual to make the opposite request—that they be

   _____.

5. Someone who studies yoga, meditates, and has the cash to spare might well consider traveling to India in search of a(n)

   _____.

6. The how-to book for household jobs had some _____ ideas for how to use WD-40 in the kitchen.

7. People readily _____ around an issue or get behind a cause that directly relates to their lives.

8. Tennis player Andre Agassi was a tennis _____, who was swinging a racquet and hitting the ball soundly already at the age of three.

9. Sometimes political _____ can become so strong they can turn into prejudices against those who don't share them.

10. Citizens have a right to expect _____ from their government.

Implied Main Ideas in Longer Readings

Longer readings, particularly those in textbooks, generally include thesis statements expressing the main idea of the entire reading. However, even writers of textbooks occasionally imply a main idea instead of explicitly stating it. When this happens, you need to respond much as you did to paragraphs lacking topic sentences. Look at what the author explicitly says and ask what inference can be drawn from those statements. That inference is your implied main idea.

To illustrate, here's a reading that lacks a thesis statement, yet still suggests a main idea.

J. Edgar Hoover and the FBI

The opening date with the phrase "rise to real power" hints at a sequence of dates and events pattern.

1 Established in 1908, the Federal Bureau of Investigation (FBI) was initially quite restricted in its ability to fight crime. It could investigate only a few offenses, such as bankruptcy fraud and antitrust violations, and it could not cross state lines in pursuit of felons. The passage of the Mann Act in 1910 began the FBI's rise to real power. According to the Act, the FBI could now cross state lines in pursuit of women being used for "immoral purposes," such as prostitution. Prior to the Mann Act, the FBI had been powerless once a felon crossed a state line; now at least the FBI could pursue those engaged in immoral acts.

Paragraph 2 suggests Hoover is the focus more than the FBI. Notice how references to him begin to take over the reading.

2 It was, however, the appointment of J. Edgar Hoover in 1924 that truly transformed the FBI. Hoover insisted that all FBI agents had to have college degrees and undergo intensive training at a special school for FBI agents. He also lobbied* long and hard for legislation that would allow the FBI to cross state lines in pursuit of all criminals. He got his wish in 1934 with the Fugitive Felon Act, which made it illegal for a felon to escape by crossing state lines. Thanks to Hoover's intensive efforts, the way was now open for the FBI to become a crack crime-fighting force with real power.

---

*lobbied: worked to influence government officials.

The opening of paragraph 3 suggests a positive view of Hoover and the bureau.

A key date and event identifies an increase in Hoover's power.

The reversal transition "unfortunately" signals what about the attitude toward Hoover?

In paragraph 5 the phrase "tendency toward paranoia" emphasizes the shift in attitude toward Hoover.

3   And fight crime the agency did. Its agents played key roles in the investigation and capture of notorious criminals in the 1930s, among them John Dillinger, Clyde Barrow, Bonnie Parker, Baby Face Nelson, Pretty Boy Floyd, and the boss of all bosses—Al Capone.

4   In 1939, impressed by the FBI's performance under Hoover, President Franklin D. Roosevelt assigned the FBI full responsibility for investigating matters related to the possibility of espionage* by the German government. In effect, Roosevelt gave Hoover a mandate* to investigate any groups he considered suspicious. This new responsibility led to the investigation and arrest of several spies. Unfortunately, J. Edgar Hoover did not limit himself to wartime spying activities. Instead, he continued his investigations long after World War II had ended and Germany had been defeated.

5   Suspicious by nature, Hoover was prone to seeing enemies of the United States everywhere. His tendency toward paranoia increased with the onset of the sixties and the eruption of protests over civil rights, the Vietnam war, and women's role in society. His investigations began to cast a wider and wider net. In secret, the agency went after the leaders of student and civil rights groups. Even esteemed* civil rights leader Martin Luther King Jr. was under constant surveillance by the FBI. Investigation techniques during this period included forging documents, burglarizing offices, opening private mail, conducting illegal wiretaps, and spreading false rumors about sexual or political misconduct. It wasn't until Hoover's death in 1972 that the FBI's secret files on America's supposed "enemies" were made public and these investigations shut down.

If you look for a sentence or group of sentences that sums up the two parts of this reading—the positive and the negative portraits of Hoover's tenure at the FBI—you're not going to find it. It's up to the reader to infer a main idea like the following: "J. Edgar Hoover was a powerful influence on the FBI. Although he did some good, he also tarnished the agency's reputation and image."

This implied thesis statement neatly fits the contents of the reading without relying on any information *not* supplied by the author. It is also *not* contradicted by anything said in the reading itself. In short, it meets the criteria, or standards, of a logical inference.

_____

*espionage: spying.
*mandate: legal right, authority; also used as a verb meaning to authorize or enact a law.
*esteemed: respected.

Some critics thought director Clint Eastwood was too kind to Hoover in his movie *J. Edgar*, but they generally praised Leonardo DiCaprio's portrayal of the FBI chief.

Keith Bernstein/Warner Bros. Pictures/Everett Collection

◆ EXERCISE 8   Recognizing Implied Main Ideas in Longer Readings

DIRECTIONS Read each selection. Write an *I* or a *P* in the blank to indicate the author's purpose. Then circle the letter of the statement that most effectively sums up the implied main idea of the entire reading.

1. The Hermits of Harlem

1 On March 21, 1947, a man called the 122nd Street police station in New York City and claimed that there was a dead body at 2078 Fifth Avenue. The police were familiar with the house, a decaying three-story brownstone in a rundown part of Harlem. It was the home of Langley and Homer Collyer, two lonely recluses* famous in the neighborhood for their eccentric—the unkind called it crazy—ways.

2   Homer was blind and crippled by rheumatism. Distrustful of doctors, he wouldn't let anybody but Langley come near him. Using his dead father's medical books, Langley devised a number of odd cures for his brother's ailments, including massive doses of orange juice and peanut butter. When he wasn't dabbling in medicine, Langley liked to invent things, like machines to clean the inside of pianos or intricately wired burglar alarms.

3   When the police responded to the call by breaking into the Collyers' home, they were astonished and horrified. The room was filled from floor to ceiling with objects of every shape, size, and kind. It took them several hours to cross the few feet to where the dead body of Homer lay, shrouded

---

*recluses: people who want to be alone and shun the presence of others.

in an ancient checkered bathrobe. There was no sign of Langley, so authorities began to search for him.

4   When they found him, he was wearing a strange collection of clothes that included an old jacket, a red flannel bathrobe, several pairs of trousers, and blue overalls. An onion sack was tied around his neck; another was draped over his shoulders. Langley had died some time before his brother. He had suffocated under a huge pile of garbage that had cascaded down upon him.

5   On several occasions, thieves had tried to break in to steal the fortune that was rumored to be kept in the house. Langley had responded by building booby traps, intricate systems of trip wires and ropes that would bring tons of rubbish crashing down on any unwary intruder. But in the dim light of his junk-filled home, he had sprung one of his own traps and died some days before his brother. Homer, blind, paralyzed, and totally dependent on Langley, had starved to death.

Purpose _____

Implied Main Idea   a. In the end, the Collyer brothers' eccentric and reclusive ways led to their deaths.

       b. The Collyer brothers' deaths were probably suicides.

       c. The Collyer brothers have become more famous in death than they ever were in life.

The Collyer household.

2. Obsessions and Compulsions

1 Obsessions are images or thoughts that intrude into consciousness against a person's will. You have probably experienced a mild obsessional thought in the form of some song or stupid commercial jingle that is repeated over and over in your mind. This may be irritating, but it is usually not terribly disturbing.

2 True obsessions are so disturbing that they cause anxiety or extreme discomfort. The most common obsessions are about doing harm to other people, being dirty or unclean, whether one has performed some action such as turning off the stove, or the possibility of committing immoral acts.

3 Obsessions usually give rise to compulsions. These are irrational acts a person feels driven to complete. Often the compulsive act helps control or block out anxiety caused by the obsession. For example, a minister who finds profanities popping into his mind might take up compulsively counting his heartbeat to prevent himself from thinking "dirty words."

4 Many people with compulsions can be classified as *checkers* or *cleaners*. Thus a person who feels guilty or unclean about behavior perceived as immoral might feel driven to wash his or her hands hundreds of times a day. And a young man or woman who has fantasies of stabbing someone might check repeatedly to see that all the knives are locked away. (Adapted from Dennis Coon, *Essentials of Psychology* 7e, © Cengage Learning.)

Purpose _____

Implied Main Idea a. Most people have experienced some degree of obsessional behavior without needing to seek treatment for it.

b. Obsessive disorders are frequently accompanied by compulsive behaviors.

c. People troubled by compulsive behavior repeat the same actions over and over, sometimes more than one hundred times per day.

3. Would You Want Your Essay Graded by a Machine?

1 Every day it seems some new start-up company emerges to claim that grading essays can be done more quickly and efficiently by machines than by people. The National Council of Teachers of English (NCTE), however, begs to disagree. In April 2013, the group issued a statement saying students "are ill-served when their writing experience has been dictated by tests that ignore the evermore complex and varied types and uses of writing found in higher education." Chris M. Anson, who chaired the committee that drafted the statement, says that the goal of

the statement was to encourage policy-makers and designers of standardized tests to re-consider the value of evaluating writing through an
algorithm.[†]

2   Predictably, those involved in developing programs designed to correct
writing by machines were outspoken in their mistrust of the NCTE statement. Also critical was Mark D. Shermis, a professor of educational founda-
tions at the University of Akron, who conducted a study comparing short
essays that were corrected by machines with short essays corrected by
teachers. Since the study showed little difference between the two kinds of
scoring, Mr. Shermis called the NCTE's statement "political posturing" and a
"knee-jerk reaction."

3   However, those on the side of the NCTE position, including
Professor Les C. Perelman of the Massachusetts Institute of Technology,
criticized the study's methodology and showed how computers respond
favorably to big words where real readers might respond by calling
the very same writing style pompous and overblown. Perelman's point
is simple: Machines aren't readers with taste or experience. They are
impressed by big words and fancy syntax. They are likely to give higher
scores to the writer who says, "In a fury, the thief engaged in an act of
violent defenestration" and lower grades to the one who says, more simply,
"In a fury, the thief hurled the chest out the window."[†]

4   Those critical of the NCTE's position on machine-grading of writing
and in favor of using machines to grade exams admit that computers
guided by algorithms will probably never be able to tell if a student has,
for instance, improved his ability to use original and illuminating metaphors or made progress in her ability to create an engaging tone. But for
them, those issues—issues that are essential to people who care about
both writing and reading—are beside the point. As Mr. Shermis puts it,
the technology to grade writing is here and "There's nothing we can do
to stop it. It's whether we can shape it or not." (Source of quotations: Dan Brett,
"English Teachers Reject Use of Robots to Grade Student Writing," *The Chronicle of Higher
Education*, May 3, 2013, p. 11.)

Purpose _____

[†]algorithm: a formula for, in this case, evaluating word order, vocabulary use, and co-
herence, or unity of thought.
[†]The quotation on defenestration is not part of the *Chronicle*'s article.

Implied Main Idea a. By challenging the role machines can play in evaluating writing, the NCTE is simply sticking its head in the sand and refusing to acknowledge the role machines can play in teaching writing.

b. Computers will never be able to evaluate the progress students have made in their writing.

c. The NCTE is correct to suggest that machine-grading of writing is inadequate to meet the needs of college students.

◆ EXERCISE 9 Inferring Main Ideas in Longer Readings

> **DIRECTIONS** Read each selection. Write the implied main idea in the blanks that follow, along with an *I* or a *P* to indicate the author's purpose.

1. Women and the Grange

1 The story of American agriculture after the Civil War is gloriously exciting mainly when looked at in the aggregate.* But for the individuals who opened up the Great Plains, life was often laborious, dirty, and lonely. Winters were marked by long stretches of subzero weather and ferocious blizzards so intense men and women had to find their way from house to barn via a rope strung between the buildings. Summers were equally intense. Blistering hot, the only shade was under a wagon.

2   Much of the era's writing about farm life dwells on its loneliness. This is especially true for women, who never forgot their early isolation. Even in middle age, many farm matrons told their granddaughters about arriving at the new home their husbands had built on the wide, empty plains. If the men celebrated the women's arrival, the women had a different response: They sat down and wept.

3   And, in general, life for women on the plains did not improve. The nearest neighbors lived half a mile away. With work demanding attention dawn to dusk, women saw only their husbands and children, and other people only briefly while marketing in town on Saturday and after church on Sunday.

4   But some of the women's loneliness was diminished in 1867, when a federal employee at the Department of Agriculture, Oliver Hudson Kelley, grew distressed over the lack of sound agricultural practices in the southwestern and western regions of the country. In an effort to educate inexperienced farmers about proper agricultural methods, Kelley formed the *National Grange of the Patrons of Husbandry*,† which was organized into

---

*aggregate: as a whole, in combination with other elements, in the big picture.
†husbandry: a rather old-fashioned way of talking about agricultural practices.

local Granges, or farm associations. The official goal of the group was to encourage sound farming practices. However, in the early years, Grange lodges often served an unofficial function as social and cultural centers for isolated rural areas. For that reason, Grange meetings often included dances and dinners, an addition not everyone approved of but many were grateful for, particularly women.

5   By 1900, the Grange had a million members. Surprisingly for the time, women enjoyed equality with men in decision-making and other Grange activities. Visitors consistently observed the same phenomenon:* Farm wives, rather than husbands, held the associations together during the Grange's early days. The women planned and administered the activities and, of course, cleaned up after them. In many ways, it was the women who kept the Granges going. (Adapted from Joseph Conlin, *The American Past* 9e, vol. 2, © Cengage Learning.)

Purpose _____

Implied Main Idea _____

_____

2. Will African Penguins Go the Way of the Passenger Pigeon?

1   One hundred years ago, a million and a half African penguins waddled and swam along the coasts of South Africa and Namibia. Today, only about 120,000 African penguins remain, and they are confined to a few small islands off the coast of South Africa. Fortunately for the penguins' future, they are adorable. Only two feet tall with big eyes and a black stripe around their bellies, the birds attract human visitors in droves. If they are lucky, their popularity with humans will keep them alive.

2   African penguins feed on anchovies and sardines, which until recently could readily be found in nearby waters. But around 1997, the sardines began to disappear from waters near the penguins' habitat. Some of the fish were relocating because global warming had increased water temperature and sent the fish in pursuit of cooler temperatures. However, tons of sardines and anchovies were also swept up in the nets of commercial fishermen, who have been depleting the fish population along the coast of Africa. The disappearance of their usual food supply has left the penguins stranded and starving.

3   The islands where the penguins live are also home to feral, or wild, cats who have made a meal out of penguin chicks whenever they could find

_____
*phenomenon: happening, event.

them. In addition to the cats, penguin parents have had to protect their chicks from the aggressive kelp gull, a tough predator that searches out unprotected nests in order to swoop down and devour vulnerable chicks. The penguins used to be able to dig their nests so deep they could escape the threat of gulls, but settlers have dug out so much penguin guano to use as fertilizer, the ground is not as soft as it used to be, and it is harder for the birds to dig deep nests. As if threats by land and air weren't enough, in 2000 an oil spill made the waters even more dangerous than the beach. A huge bird-rescue operation saved almost forty thousand penguins, but thousands more did not survive.

4   Environmentalists are currently mounting a campaign to save the African penguin. While relocating the birds would be difficult, supporters of the campaign are raising money to build igloos, where the birds can be protected from the sun's heat and gulls' attacks. Environmentalists are also overseeing the removal of feral cats from the island in the hopes of increasing the penguins' slim chances for survival. (Source of figures: Michael Wines, "Dinner Disappears, and African Penguins Pay the Price," *New York Times*, June 4, 2007, www.nytimes.com/2007/06/04/world/africa/04robben.html.)

Purpose _____

Implied Main Idea _____

_____

Being adorable may be the African penguins' key to survival.

WEB QUEST **The Grange Movement and Victory in the Supreme Court**

By the mid-1870s, the Grange had become a powerful force in a number of agricultural states. Grangers even got state laws passed that limited railroad rates. The railroads retaliated by challenging the laws in court. In 1877, the Grange won what was viewed as a huge Supreme Court victory over the railroads. What was the name of the case, and why was it a victory for the Grange?

_____

_____

_____

_____

ALLUSION ALERT

A Man for All Seasons

A Man for All Seasons, the 1954 play by Robert Bolt, focused on Sir Thomas More, an adviser to King Henry VIII. The play's title comes from what a contemporary, Robert Whittington, said about More. Citing More's ability to be witty and serious, learned and plain-speaking, Whittington called More "a man for all seasons." It was the play, however, and the movie of the same name that followed, which made the phrase famous. It's now used to describe anyone who has numerous and varied talents, for instance, "A highly acclaimed actress and a much-admired member of the British parliament, Glenda Jackson can rightly be called a woman for all seasons."

Making Connections Between Paragraphs

Like inferring the connections between sentences, inferring connections between paragraphs is essential to understanding multi-paragraph readings. Look, for example, at these two paragraphs from a reading discussing the reality and the myth of frontiersman Davy Crockett.

Davy Crockett: A Man for All Seasons

<div class="margin-notes">
Initially, the reading seems to focus on the television version of Davy Crockett.

Notice how the TV show disappears from the text as the writer focuses on John Wayne and how he used the image of Davy Crockett to support his presidential candidate.

Why Wayne would have "spun in his grave" to hear how someone else used the allusion to Crockett is the question readers need to answer.
</div>

1   The Walt Disney version of Davy Crockett's life, *Davy Crockett: Indian Fighter*, became a runaway hit in 1954 when an unknown actor named Fess Parker donned Crockett's trademark coonskin cap and played him on television. The show spawned several movies—and millions of coonskin caps— among them the 1960 smash hit *The Alamo*, starring John Wayne. In an attempt to use the film's popularity to support his favored presidential candidate, Richard Nixon, Wayne even helped finance a movie ad that showed Crockett at the Alamo.[†] The caption for the ad—"There were no ghostwriters at the Alamo, only Men"—slyly alluded to rumors that John F. Kennedy, Richard Nixon's opponent in the presidential race, had used a ghostwriter for his Pulitzer Prize–winning book, *Profiles in Courage*. A long-time Republican, Wayne was no fan of Kennedy, a Democrat, and he was deeply disappointed when Nixon was defeated, despite Wayne's attempt to link him to the heroic Davy Crockett.

2   Wayne, who died of stomach cancer in 1979, must have spun in his grave when Paul Andrew Hutton's 1989 essay, "Davy Crockett: An Exposition on Hero Worship," was published. Hutton argued that young men volunteering for the Vietnam War had been inspired by their twin heroes, John F. Kennedy and Davy Crockett. According to Hutton, when Kennedy "issued a clarion call to fight for freedom in a distant land," young men answered the call because "they knew full well what he was talking about, for they had been brought up on those same liberal values by Disney's Davy Crockett." (Source of quotation: Allen Barra, "American Idols," *Salon.com*, April 10, 2004.)

To move smoothly between these two paragraphs, readers need to infer a cause and effect relationship: John Wayne, a staunch supporter of Republican Richard Nixon, would have spun in his grave *because* he would have hated the idea of Crockett being linked to Kennedy, the man who challenged and beat his political favorite. Notice, though, that the author doesn't include that information in the supporting details. It's up to readers to infer the right connection.

◆ **EXERCISE 10   Making Connections Between Paragraphs**

> **DIRECTIONS**   Read the following selection. Then circle the appropriate letters to identify the implied main idea and the connections between paragraphs that readers need to infer.

[†]Alamo: In the war to make Texas part of the United States, the battle of the Alamo was a decisive one; it was also the battle in which Crockett died.

A Boy Soldier's Story

1   When Ishmael Beah was interviewed on Jon Stewart's *The Daily Show*, the normally wise-cracking Stewart showed a serious side. Even he, whose gift for on-the-spot quips* seems genetically inspired, couldn't find anything amusing to say about Beah's book, *A Long Way Gone: Memoirs of a Boy Soldier*. Beah, who now lives in Brooklyn, New York, grew up in Sierra Leone, Africa, and writes about being a twelve-year-old soldier in the civil war that tore his country apart throughout the 1990s until an uneasy peace was achieved in 2002. The book does not make for good bedtime reading, unless, of course, the reader is looking for nightmares.

2   Beah's journey into hell began when members of the rebel army, the Revolutionary United Front (RUF) led by Foday Sankoh, entered his village, intent on slaughtering everyone in it. Along with several other young boys, Beah ran away, only to end up moving from village to village, desperately trying to find shelter and food. When he did finally find what appeared to be a safe haven, it was on a government military base.

3   But Beah's new-found safety came at a price. He was given a choice: Become a soldier or leave the base and face the rebel army, notorious for amputating the arms of its victims. Since this was no choice at all, Beah accepted the AK-47 handed to him and became one of the government's child soldiers. Fueled by the mix of cocaine and gunpowder all the boys were given to keep them as mindless and conscience-free as possible, Beah and his cohorts were willing to do anything asked of them no matter how bloody or horrible. As Beah writes of one incident, "We walked around the village and killed everyone who came out of the houses and huts."

4   Jon Stewart was right to skip the jokes during his interview with Beah. There are few bright moments in his largely tragic story, unless one counts the time where Beah escaped the anger of rebel supporters by having some rap cassettes with him when he was captured. Miming the lyrics and dancing to the sounds of LL Cool J and Naughty by Nature among others, Beah entertained the villagers intent on maiming or killing him. In exchange, they gave him his freedom.

5   Yet what is probably most astonishing about *A Long Way Gone* is that its author seems to have survived "childhood" with his humanity intact. When his commander volunteers Beah and a few other very young boys for rehabilitation, it seems to prove the truth of his father's motto, "If you are alive, there is hope for a better day." Although he and the other boys initially fought all attempts to make them give up being child soldiers,

---

*quips: clever, brief remarks, one-liners.

their resistance finally gave way, and they began to act like what they were, children.

6   After leaving the rehabilitation center, Beah lived for awhile with his uncle because the rebels who had driven him from his village had kept their word: They had destroyed the village and slaughtered Beah's parents, along with the rest of the inhabitants. At fifteen, Beah had no home to go to, so his relatives took him in. While living with his uncle, Beah was selected to speak at the United Nations because the international delegates wanted to better understand the fate of child soldiers. The UN appearance led to Beah's coming to the United States, where he graduated from high school and Oberlin College with a degree in political science.

7   Beah has grown up, but he hasn't forgotten his nightmare past. Instead, through his memoir, he uses it to make a point: "I believe children have the resilience to outlive their sufferings if given a chance." Ishmael Beah's life is a testament to those words. (An interview with Ishmael Beah is available here: www.npr.org/templates/story/story.php?storyId=7519542.)

1. What is the implied main idea of the reading?

   a. The civil war in Sierra Leone destroyed the lives of countless children.

   b. Ishmael Beah's life story illustrates how tragic war is, especially for children, who seldom recover from war's psychological wounds even if they survive the physical ones.

   c. Tragic as Ishmael Beah's early years were, his story still suggests that his father was right: "If you are alive, there is hope for a better day."

   d. Although Ishmael Beah's horrifying time as a child soldier is over, he is still haunted by the experience.

2. To understand why paragraph 2 follows paragraph 1, the reader has to infer which connection?

   a. Paragraph 2 illustrates why the peace mentioned in paragraph 1 is considered "uneasy."

   b. Paragraph 2 explains why Beah decided to write his memoirs.

   c. Paragraph 2 illustrates why the book can cause the "nightmares" mentioned in paragraph 1.

3. To understand why paragraph 3 follows paragraph 2, the reader must infer which connection?

   a. Paragraph 3 further explains why the book can cause nightmares.

   b. Paragraph 3 offers an exception to the book's description of a tragic time in Ishmael Beah's life.

   c. Paragraph 3 reverses the suggestion of a "safe haven" introduced in paragraph 2.

4. To infer the relationship between paragraphs 4 and 5, the reader cannot afford to miss what word? _____

5. What word or phrase does the author use to help readers follow the order of events and connect paragraph 5 to 6?

   _____

REVIEWING THROUGH WRITING

Look closely at the opening sentences in paragraphs 2–6 of the previous reading. Revise each opening sentence to make the paragraphs connect without using the exact same language.

Drawing Personal Conclusions

Readers truly intent on mastering an author's message don't limit themselves to drawing just the inferences intended by the author. To deepen their understanding, readers frequently draw **personal conclusions**. These are inferences that follow from the reading but were not necessarily intended by the author. This next passage and the two conclusions that follow provide an illustration.

Exit exams are tests that high school students in some states must take to successfully pass a course or earn a diploma. Although exit exams have numerous supporters, they have come under persistent fire where diplomas are concerned. In Massachusetts, for instance, state officials had to quell a rebellion of school superintendents who wanted to award diplomas to 4,800 students who had failed the exam. In Florida, protesters demanded that the governor give diplomas to 14,000 seniors who had failed the exit exam. Given all this controversy, the question that has to be answered is, What's wrong with exit exams? After all, high school exit exams ensure that a diploma accurately indicates how much information students have actually absorbed from their courses. This is important because it's widely assumed that grade inflation is rampant in some schools. Thus the passing grades that allow students to get a diploma are not necessarily proof that they have mastered the course material. However, when that diploma is backed up by an exit exam, we can be sure students have mastered the courses identified on their transcripts. By the same token, exit exams should help reassure prospective employers who have begun to lose faith in the diploma as proof of achievement. In short, the presence of an exit exam grade on a student's transcript will add value to the diploma.

The implied main idea in the above passage is something like this: "Exit exams are a good idea and school administrators should not cave in to the pressure to abandon them." The author does not say this explicitly. Instead, she implies her main idea by offering reasons why exit exams are valuable for documenting achievement.

However, based on what the author says, you can also draw two personal conclusions that she does not address in the paragraph: (1) the author would probably agree with legislation that made high school exit exams mandatory throughout the nation and (2) the author would probably be unwilling to sign a petition demanding that students who failed their exit exams be allowed to receive diplomas anyway. Given what the author actually says, these are legitimate or logical conclusions. Both follow from what the author says about exit exams even though nothing in the paragraph explicitly addresses either conclusion.

Far less logical would be the following personal conclusion: "The author believes that the school superintendents should have been allowed to give diplomas to the 14,000 students who failed in Florida." Under some specific conditions, the author might possibly agree. But given what she says about trust in the meaning of diplomas dwindling and using exit exams to make them more respected, there's no evidence in the paragraph that could support this conclusion.

✔ CHECK YOUR UNDERSTANDING

1. How do personal conclusions differ from the inferences described in the preceding section of the chapter?

_____

_____

2. What do inferences necessary to understanding a reading and personal conclusions have in common?

_____

_____

◆ EXERCISE 11   Drawing Personal Conclusions

DIRECTIONS   Read each passage. Circle the letter of the personal conclusion that might logically be drawn from the passage.

1. In his book *After Virtue*, philosopher Alasdair MacIntyre argues that virtue is the product of social training. From MacIntyre's point of view, virtue can be acquired only in a community where the young are consciously initiated into the reigning social values, including what it means to be a good person. MacIntyre interprets the word *community* in its broadest sense, making it refer to families, schools, religious institutions, political groups, and even sources of entertainment. From his perspective, it's important that these aspects of the community be respected because a sense of their authority is what persuades the child to accept their teachings and pursue the path of virtue. Far from simplistic in his thinking, MacIntyre recognizes that communities are historical entities that can change over time. It follows, then, that the virtuous life can also be redefined as the character of the community undergoes historical change.

Which personal conclusion could be logically drawn from the reading?

a. MacIntyre is probably a modern-day disciple of Plato, who believed that virtue was inborn in special people who had a natural knowledge of perfection.

b. MacIntyre is following in the footsteps of St. Augustine, who believed that virtue is a gift of God.

c. MacIntyre would probably take the side of Aristotle, who believed that virtuous behavior is not inborn but must be learned.

2. Periodically, the price of gasoline soars and infuriated Americans blame Congress, the White House, and the Organization of the Petroleum Exporting Countries (OPEC). According to an editorial in the *Miami Herald*, however, if Americans want to know who is really responsible for high gas prices, they should look in the mirror. "The real cause of gas-pump sticker shock," says the *Herald*, "is American consumers' addiction to the automobile and the lifestyle it allows." The editorialist goes on to point out that far too many Americans act as if they are entitled to own big, gas-guzzling cars and oversized pickup trucks, which together account for a sizable portion of the vehicles sold in this country. The result? America has an insatiable* appetite for oil, and OPEC simply takes advantage of our dependence on its product. Rather than demanding lower gas prices, says the *Herald*, Americans should be driving as little as possible and insisting that their leaders do more to make mass transportation available, reliable, and affordable. (Source of quotation: "Gas-Guzzling Americans Drive Oil Prices Higher," *Charlotte Observer*, April 4, 2004, p. 5E.)

Which personal conclusion could be logically drawn from the reading?

a. The *Miami Herald* editorialist quoted in the passage would heartily agree with those who advocate drilling in the Arctic National Wildlife Refuge as a way of solving the oil shortage.

b. The *Miami Herald* editorialist is likely to endorse policies designed to force OPEC to lower its prices so that gas and oil will be available at cheaper prices.

c. The *Miami Herald* editorialist is likely to be in favor of legislation that improves the quality of mass transportation across the country.

---

*insatiable: never satisfied.

3. All segments of society have a great deal to gain by changing the health care system. The emphasis through the years has shifted from the "caring" to the "system," and the medical care industry has become the biggest business in the United States. In 1950, the cost of health care was $12 billion, but it was more than a trillion dollars by the end of the century, having risen faster than any other item in the cost of living. Despite the exorbitant bills, however, the system has failed for many citizens. About 43 million people at the Census Bureau's last count are denied access to health care because they lack insurance. But even if people do have health insurance, their coverage may be limited because companies profit not by providing insurance but by trying to avoid paying for its use. The costs of the enormously complicated health care industry—the doctors, the health care workers, the hospitals, the clinics, the nursing homes, the prescription drug industry—continue to increase. Although patients are referred to as health care consumers, they are not the ones to decide, as they may with other services and products, what and how much medical care to buy. Generally, they take what they can get. (Ethel Sloane, *Biology of Women* 4e, © Cengage Learning.)

Which personal conclusion could be logically drawn from the reading?

a. The author of this reading would agree that the United States should become more like other industrialized countries and make affordable health care the right of every citizen.

b. The author of this reading would not agree with the underlying assumption that guides health care throughout Europe: Health care is a citizen's right rather than a product with a price tag.

c. The author would be against any attempts to change the existing health care system by instituting a public option, which would allow the government to offer health insurance to people too young to qualify for Medicare.

4. In the May 2013 issue of *Wired*, political blogger and *Slate* magazine's business and economics correspondent Matthew Yglesias turned to a more personal topic—how he met his wife, Kate. Turns out he met her via Match.com and initially at least was embarrassed by the source of their first connection. Both parties, in fact, felt the

need to exercise discretion* and told others that they met through mutual friends rather than admit to meeting online. But as Yglesias points out, his attitude, as well as his wife's, has changed. One reason for that is the simple fact that a few months after meeting up via the Internet, both Iglesias and Kate were invited, separately, to the same party, leading him to rethink his original position on the role the Internet can play in romance: "The Internet didn't introduce me to a person I never could have met otherwise; it did something more valuable—offering an easier, more appealing way of interacting with someone already in my circle." And Yglesias is not the only one to suggest that finding a partner via the Internet should no longer be an embarrassment on the assumption that relationships flourishing in cyberspace are completely trivial, purely sexual, or maybe even dangerous. According to a study done by Andriana Bellou of the University of Montreal, there seems to be a causal link between re-gional broadband adoption and an increase in marriage rates. She cites a 13–30 percent increase in the marriage rate among young peo-ple of marriageable age once broadband Internet access became avail-able where they live. (Source of quotation: Matthew Yglesias, "Online Dating," *Wired*, May 2013, p. 128; Source of study: Matthew Yglesias, "Internet Access Promotes Marriage," *Slate*, May 2, 2013.)

Which personal conclusion could be logically drawn from the reading?

a. The author of the reading on Matthew Yglesias and his wife found her husband by searching on the Internet.

b. If a friend of Matthew Yglesias were bemoaning his inability to meet women he really liked, Yglesias might well recommend that the friend try an Internet dating service.

c. Andriana Bellou probably believes that within a decade people will no longer bother trying to meet dates or mates face to face anymore but will instead turn first to the Internet.

---

*discretion: behaving in a way that avoids revealing information; showing sound judg-ment, thought.

WORD CHECK II

The following words were introduced and defined in pages 385–403. See how well you can match the words with the meanings. When you finish, make sure to check the meanings of any words you missed because the same words will turn up in tests at the end of the chapter.

1. lobbied (p. 385)	____	a.	admired, respected, trusted
2. espionage (p. 386)	____	b.	people who purposely live apart from society
3. mandate (p. 386)	____	c.	event or happening; remarkable person or occurrence
4. esteemed (p. 386)	____	d.	clever, brief remarks or jokes, one-liners
5. recluses (p. 387)	____	e.	attempted to influence actions of legislators or other public officials
6. aggregate (p. 391)	____		
7. phenomenon (p. 392)	____	f.	in combined form, as a group
8. quips (p. 396)	____	g.	authorize; legal right, law
9. insatiable (p. 401)	____	h.	never satisfied
10. discretion (p. 403)	____	i.	spying
		j.	behaving in a way that avoids revealing information; showing sound judgment, thought

---

◆ **EXERCISE 12   More About Form and Meaning**

DIRECTIONS Use one of the words listed below to fill in the blanks.

> lobbyists   mandate   reclusive   phenomenon   insatiable
> espionage   esteemed   aggregate   quips   discretion

1. You are unlikely to find _____ people attending a neighborhood block party.

2. Having a lot of money can make you envied, but it may not make you _____.

3. When people speak about the hive mind at work, they are talking about people in the _____ coming up with ideas.

4. After a number of _____ about the media's constant references to her changing hair styles, the candidate suddenly turned serious and wondered aloud if women could ever be in positions of power without having their looks evaluated along with their performance.

5. Presidents who win a lot of votes in an election often talk about having a(n) _____ from the people to make decisions of national importance.

6. Even if they are completely full, people at a pie-eating contest have to pretend to be _____ and just keep eating.

7. Although the word normally applies to events, an individual who is really good at something is likely to be called a(n) _____.

8. Kids with concerned parents who monitor their comings and goings would probably like to accuse their parents of _____, but parents are supposed to keep an eye on their children; that's not an illegal activity.

9. People who put photos of themselves on their Facebook wall showing them suffering the ill effects of too many beers could hardly be accused of having too much _____.

10. It's not especially reassuring to see elected officials lunching day after day with _____.

TAKING STOCK

J. Robert Oppenheimer and the Manhattan Project

Looking Ahead

J. Robert Oppenheimer, one of the men responsible for the explosion of the atomic bomb that, depending whom you talk to, may or may not have forced the Japanese to surrender, was one of the most controversial men of the twentieth century. He was a hero to some and a villain to others. The following reading explains why historians, to this day, consider him a fascinating and mysterious figure.

1 [1]Initially at least, J. Robert Oppenheimer (1904–1967) seemed destined to lead a charmed life. [2]Handsome, brilliant, and charming, Oppenheimer had been born into a well-to-do family that readily indulged his varied interests in everything from writing poetry to collecting and analyzing minerals. [3]As a young man, he had whizzed through Harvard and earned his doctorate in physics by the age of twenty-three.

Robert Oppenheimer was thrilled about his role in building the atomic bomb until he saw it explode in the air and recognized its destructive power.
Roger Ressmeyer/Historical/Corbis

2 [1]Oppenheimer was just thirty-eight when what seemed to be the biggest plum of all fell into his lap. [2]In 1942, the Army engineer General Leslie Groves was looking for someone to head "The Manhattan Project."[†] [3]The project's top-secret goal was to develop an atomic bomb that would turn the United States into a military superpower. [4]Its success would require the work of many gifted scientists, ranging from chemists to mathematicians.

3 [1]While Groves was no scientist, he was also no fool. [2]He knew that geniuses often have egos to match their intellect. [3]Thus someone had to be found who could understand the complicated work of those participating in the project and simultaneously play peacemaker during those unavoidable moments when egos might collide and the project be endangered. [4]Groves found the man he wanted in J. Robert Oppenheimer.

4 [1]Oppenheimer gathered together the cream of the scientific world and persuaded the group to live in almost total isolation, for some twenty-plus months, hidden away in New Mexico, having little or no contact with the outside world. [2]On December 2, 1942, the Italian physicist Enrico Fermi, one of the men working at Los Alamos, created the first self-sustaining, nuclear chain reaction on Stagg Field in the University of Chicago football stadium. [3]At that point, the energy was available for the explosion of an atomic bomb, and on July 16, 1945, in Alamogordo, New Mexico, Groves and Oppenheimer watched as an enormous ball of fire followed by a mushroom cloud rose in the skies over the flat, dry desert.

[†]The project got its name from the fact that much of the money raised to get it underway came from Columbia University in Manhattan.

5   [1]At the sight, Oppenheimer, who had been hell-bent on building an atomic bomb, is said to have quoted a sentence from Hindu scripture: "I am become death, the shatterer of worlds." [2]The physicist's sense of doubt was apparently not momentary. [3]Shortly after, Oppenheimer wrote to his former high school teacher expressing his "misgivings" about the alleged accomplishment of The Manhattan Project: "You will believe that this undertaking has not been without its misgivings; they are heavy on us today, when the future which has so many elements of high promise, is yet only a stone's throw away from despair." [4]The bombing of Nagasaki and Hiroshima in August 1945 only intensified Oppenheimer's change in feeling from enthusiasm to shame.

6   [1]Hiroshima's streets were teeming with people when the first atomic bomb, nicknamed "Little Boy," struck, killing 100,000 people (by 1950, radiation deaths would swell the number to 200,000). [2]Nagasaki was hit three days later with an atomic bomb called "Fat Man." [3]The bomb obliterated 44 percent of the city and 54 percent of the people.

7   [1]Oppenheimer was devastated by his role in the destruction and never really accepted the government's explanation—that dropping the atomic bomb forced the Japanese to surrender and avoided even greater bloodshed. [2]He informed government officials that he and most other scientists involved in creating the atomic bomb would not continue working on the project, particularly if the government wished to pursue the even bigger and potentially deadlier hydrogen bomb. [3]Oppenheimer also expressed his guilt to Harry Truman, the president who had made the decision to drop the bombs on Hiroshima and Nagasaki. [4]Oppenheimer told Truman at a meeting, "I feel we have blood on our hands." [5]Truman was not especially sympathetic, telling Oppenheimer the blood on his hands would "come out in the wash."

8   [1]If Truman was unsympathetic, Oppenheimer's fellow scientist Edward Teller was outraged by his colleague's comments. [2]Teller had expected Oppenheimer's help convincing government officials that they needed to build a hydrogen bomb, and he was convinced that Oppenheimer's public handwringing was seriously undermining support for what many called the super bomb, or simply "The Super." [3]By the time the Soviets had detonated an atomic bomb of their own in 1949, Teller was even more obsessed with the need to build The Super, but Oppenheimer was still, as were many other scientists, dead set against it.

9   [1]When the time came and he had his chance, Teller made sure that Oppenheimer suffered for what, in Teller's mind, was a personal and, even worse, a national betrayal. [2]In 1954, the country was at the height of its

hysteria over Communists in the U.S. government, and Oppenheimer was called to Washington for a security clearance review. [3]Most of those called to testify gave Oppenheimer unqualified praise and approval. [4]Teller, however, said that he had serious doubts about Oppenheimer being given a security clearance that would allow him access to government secrets: "I would feel personally more secure if public matters would rest in other hands." [5]Because Lewis Strauss, the head of the Atomic Energy Commission, already detested Oppenheimer for what he considered the man's arrogance, Oppenheimer was denied security clearance. [6]From then on, he would never again play a role in how the government used the destructive weapons he, perhaps more than anyone else, had made possible.

10   [1]Oppenheimer continued to work as the director for the Institute for Advanced Study in Princeton, New Jersey, but he was never the same. [2]The review of his security clearance and its subsequent withdrawal had been a public humiliation for his proud spirit. [3]Oppenheimer's security clearance was reinstated in 1963 by Lyndon Baines Johnson, but it made little difference. [4]Four years later, J. Robert Oppenheimer was dead of throat cancer.

(Sources of quotations and statistics: Harold Evans, *The American Century*, Knopf, 2000, pp. 323–327, 376, 448–449; David Halberstam, *The Fifties*, Ballantine Books, 1994, pp. 24–40.)

Sharpening Your Skills

DIRECTIONS   Answer the following questions by circling the letter of the correct response or filling in the blanks.

Inferring the Implied Main Idea

1. Which of the following best expresses the implied main idea of the reading?

   a. The personal animosity Edward Teller felt for J. Robert Oppenheimer destroyed Oppenheimer's career, and Oppenheimer never forgave Teller for his betrayal.

   b. The Manhattan Project, which was initially considered a feather in Oppenheimer's cap, was the cause of his personal and professional downfall.

   c. J. Robert Oppenheimer's guilt over the success of The Manhattan Project is understandable and appropriate given what he let loose on the world.

   d. Harry Truman and J. Robert Oppenheimer were of very different minds when it came to evaluating the success of The Manhattan Project.

Making Predictions 2. In the first sentence of paragraph 1, what does the phrase "initially at least" signal about how Oppenheimer's life will unfold?

_____

Using Repetition and Reference 3. The pronoun _its_ opening sentence 4 in paragraph 2 refers to

_____.

4. In sentence 2 of paragraph 3, the pronoun _their_ refers to

_____.

5. In paragraph 3, sentence 3, the word _egos_ is a stand-in, or substitute,

for _____.

Inferring Connections Between Sentences 6. To understand sentences 1 and 2 in paragraph 7, readers need to infer what connection?

a. Oppenheimer refused to do any more work on the atomic bomb because he didn't want to work alone.

b. Oppenheimer refused to do any more work on the atomic bomb because the Japanese had surrendered and there was no longer any reason for the bomb to be used.

c. Oppenheimer refused to do any more work on the atomic bomb because he was horrified by the bombing of Hiroshima and Nagasaki and his role in the destruction.

d. Oppenheimer refused to continue working on the atomic bomb because he hated Edward Teller.

Inferring Connections Between Paragraphs 7. To connect paragraphs 4 and 5, which inference does the reader need to draw?

a. The reality of the explosion made Oppenheimer think about how destructive the bomb could be.

b. Oppenheimer was the kind of man inclined to quote poetry at every opportunity.

c. Oppenheimer felt proud because he had helped create such a destructive weapon.

d. Oppenheimer was a Buddhist, and building the atomic bomb contradicted his beliefs.

8. To connect paragraphs 5 and 6, which inference do readers need to draw?

   a. The U.S. government had purposely picked a time when many civilians would be on the street.

   b. The numbers of deaths estimated from the bombings of Hiroshima and Nagasaki rose with time.

   c. The number of civilians killed in the bombings was a major reason for the change in Oppenheimer's feelings.

Paraphrasing　9. Which of the following best paraphrases the topic sentence of paragraph 4?

   a. Oppenheimer brought together brilliant people whose egos matched their talent and still managed to make them get along with one another.

   b. Oppenheimer brought together the finest minds in the scientific world and convinced them to live separated from the rest of the world in an isolated area of New Mexico for over twenty months.

   c. Oppenheimer gathered together the cream of the scientific world and convinced them to live in almost total isolation for some twenty-plus months in a remote area of New Mexico.

Recognizing Organizational Patterns　10. What organizational pattern do the first two paragraphs of the reading rely on?

   _____

11. What organizational pattern does paragraph 8 rely on?

   _____

12. What combination of patterns is used to organize the entire reading?

   _____

   Which of those patterns are the most important?

   _____

Identifying the Author's Purpose

13. Which of the following statements do you think best describes the author's purpose?

   a. The author wants to describe the events that led up to the dropping of the atomic bomb on Hiroshima and Nagasaki.

   b. The author wants to persuade readers that Harry Truman did the right thing when he ordered the dropping of the atomic bomb on Hiroshima and Nagasaki while Oppenheimer was misguided in his opposition.

   c. The author wants to explain to readers why Oppenheimer was such a controversial figure in American history.

Drawing Inferences

14. Why does the author include the quotation from Hindu scripture in paragraph 5? What does the author want you to infer about Oppenheimer's state of mind?

   _____

   _____.

Drawing Personal Conclusions

15. Based on the reading, what conclusion seems more likely?

   a. Harry Truman abandoned all work on the hydrogen bomb.

   b. Harry Truman eventually went along with Teller and gave the go-ahead for a project devoted to The Super.

   Please explain your answer.

   _____

   _____

   _____

▶ **TEST 1**   **Drawing Inferences About Pronouns and Other Noun Substitutes**

DIRECTIONS   Answer the following questions by circling the letter of the correct response or filling in the blanks.

1. ¹In the early 1800s, leading Republicans had hoped to end the nation's political divisions. ²*They* sought compromise among sectional interests and welcomed the remaining Federalists into their fold. ³*They* praised the one-party system. (Adapted from Steven M. Gillon and Cathy D. Matson, *The American Experiment* 2e, © Cengage Learning.)

In sentences 2 and 3, the pronoun *they* refers to _____.

Sentences 2 and 3 continue the point of sentence 1 by _____

_____ .

2. ¹When researcher Frans de Waal observed a group of chimps and recorded their grooming and food-sharing behaviors, he noted striking evidence of reciprocal altruism among the chimps. ²If Chimp A groomed Chimp B, B became much more likely to then share his or her food with A. ³It was as if they were operating under a norm of "You scratch my back, I'll scratch yours, and maybe I'll give you some of my apples." (Adapted from Saul Kassin et al., *Social Psychology* 8e, © Cengage Learning.)

In sentence 2, the description of grooming and food-sharing is an

illustration of _____ mentioned in sentence 1.

In sentence 3, the quotation is used to further illustrate _____

_____ introduced in sentence 1.

3. ¹In the policymaking process, *earmarking* involves attaching a tag to some special project included in a bill so that it stands out from the other provisions—the herd, if you will—to allow for special treatment. ²Such special treatment might mean that the project is automatically funded or that it moves to the top of the list of priorities. (Adapted from Alan R. Gitelson et al., *American Government* 10e, © Cengage Learning.)

In sentence 1, the pronoun *it* refers to _____

____ and the *herd* is a reference to _____.

In sentence 2, the references to automatic funding and moving to the top of the priority list are specific examples of the general term

_____, which is another way of talking about _____.

4. [1]After his father retired as the head of IBM, Thomas Watson Jr. took over and led IBM into the computer field with a vengeance, dwarfing all competitors in the decades to come. [2]After establishing its first microcomputer as the business computing standard in 1981, the conservative giant was slow to adjust to the rapid-fire changes of the 1980s and 1990s, *which* made it possible for more nimble companies to seize emerging markets. (Adapted from George Beekman and Michael J. Quinn, *Computer Confluence* 7e, © Prentice Hall, 2005, p. 72.)

What word or phrase in sentence 2 is used as a stand-in, or substitute, for *IBM* introduced in sentence 1?_____

In sentence 2, to what does the pronoun *which* refer?

a. IBM's establishing of the first microcomputer

b. IBM's becoming the de facto business standard

c. IBM's slowness to adjust to rapid-fire changes

d. Thomas Watson's taking over for his father as head of the company

5. [1]The problem with power imbalances and the misuse of power within the family is the negative effects they have on intimacy. [2]If partners are not equal, self-disclosure may be inhibited. [3]It is not easy to change unequal power relationships after they become embedded in a relationship. [4]Yet they can be changed. (Adapted from Bryan Strong et al., *The Marriage and Family Experience* 11e, © Cengage Learning.)

The second half of sentence 1 defines which word from the first half?

a. problem

b. power

c. family

d. misuse

Sentence 3 refers to the power imbalances from sentence 1 with

what phrase? _____

▶ **TEST 2**   **Recognizing the Implied Main Idea**

DIRECTIONS   Read each paragraph. Then circle the letter of the implied main idea.

1. Every year desperate cancer victims travel to the Philippines hoping to be cured by people who call themselves "psychic surgeons." These so-called surgeons claim to heal the sick without the use of a knife or anesthesia, and many victims of serious illness look to them for a cure. But curing the sick is not what these surgeons do. When they operate, they conceal bits of chicken and goat hearts in their hands; then they pretend to pull a piece of disease-ridden tissue out of the patient's body. If a crowd is present, and it usually is, the surgeons briefly display the lump of animal tissue and pronounce the poor patient cured. Not surprisingly, psychic surgeons cannot point to many real cures.

Implied Main Idea   a. More people than ever before are flocking to psychic surgeons.

b. Psychic surgeons are frauds.

c. When people are desperate, they are inclined to abandon their skepticism.

d. Psychic surgeons should be imprisoned for the harm they do to their poor victims.

2. Up until recently, the Japanese word *Nisei* referred solely to the children of Japanese immigrants who had never lived in their parents' birth country. But in its twenty-year anniversary issue, *Wired* magazine writer Jerry Adler put a new spin on the term, calling those who grew up with the Internet the "digital Nisei." The digital Nisei have never had to adjust to the new world of technology because they were born into it. As Adler describes them, this new generation has no patience with traditional wisdom and is quick to use information found on the Web to challenge what others tell them. But if they are bold about challenging received opinion, they are far less comfortable when such confrontations take place face to face. Like Sherry Turkle, the author of *Alone Together*, who worries that technology is destroying our ability to communicate in person, Adler describes a group of young people who seem easily intimidated by something previous generations took for granted, phone conversations. Their preference for e-mailing and texting instead of using the phone is

linked to the need to present one's self in the very best light. According to Adler, the digital Nisei like the idea of being able to craft a personality that suits the occasion or the person. However, one of the young people Adler interviewed for the article poses an interesting question about the ease with which the digital Nisei construct and convey a tailored-to-order personality online. Citing her friends who spend an "inordinate amount of time composing e-mails to impress," a nineteen-year-old from Washington D.C., asks, "What will they do when they meet in person and have to talk?" (Source of quotation: Jerry Adler, "1993," *Wired*, May 2013, p. 190.)

Implied Main Idea
a. While being born into a world where the digital revolution has already happened has some definite benefits for the generation writer Jerry Adler calls the "digital Nisei," there may also be some serious drawbacks.

b. Having been born into a world where the digital revolution has already happened, the digital Nisei don't have the fear of technology and what it can do the way a previous generation does.

c. The digital Nisei are perfectly comfortable having as little to do with the real world as they possibly can; for them virtual reality is where real life is lived.

d. Typically for *Wired* magazine, Jerry Adler's article "1993" celebrates all things digital, and the generation born after the digital revolution seems perfectly comfortable in a world the older generation looks upon with a mixture of admiration and fear.

3. Social scientists have been studying the phenomena of speed dating for a while now, with some interesting results. At the University of Pennsylvania, Robert Kurzban and Jason Weeden studied more than 10,000 clients of HurryDate—a company that gathers men and women together for a round robin of speed dates lasting about three minutes each. At the end of the "dates," those attending find out who was interested in dating whom. Kurzban and Weeden found that the women attending the group dating sessions were much pickier than the men. Women usually got a "yes, I'd like to see her again" from about half the men they chatted with. Men who participated got that response from only about one-third of the women they talked to. A similar German study found that the female subjects—attractive women in particular—were very choosy about whom they would see again. The men, in contrast, indicated that they wanted to get

acquainted with most of the women they had encountered during the speed-dating sessions. In another study of more than 20,000 online daters, the results indicated that women were interested in more than looks. They wanted to know about the men's level of education and their profession. Although education didn't rate high with men, a woman's having blond hair appeared to be a distinct advantage.

Implied Main Idea

a. Studies of speed dating indicate that men are much pickier than women about whom they will date.

b. Studies of speed dating indicate that women care more about a man's education and profession than they do about his looks.

c. Studies of speed dating suggest that women tend to be more selective than men.

d. Men engaged in speed dating do not tend to marry the women they meet, so they spend little time thinking about anything but appearance.

4. *Troll* is a term for an anonymous person who is abusive in an online environment. It would be nice to believe that there is only a minute troll population living among us. But in fact, a great many people have experienced being drawn into nasty exchanges online. Everyone who has experienced that has been introduced to his or her inner troll. I have tried to be aware of the troll within myself. I notice that I can suddenly become relieved when someone else in an online exchange is getting pounded or humiliated, because that means I'm safe for the moment. If someone else's video is being ridiculed on YouTube, mine is temporarily protected. But that also means I'm complicit in the mob dynamic. (Jaron Lanier, *You Are Not a Gadget*, 2010, Vintage Books, p. 60.)

Implied Main Idea

a. Trolls can be particularly abusive about videos posted on YouTube.

b. Everyone is a troll under the right circumstances.

c. The troll population is a good deal larger than many of us like to think.

d. Participating in online anonymous discussions tends to bring out the worst in people.

▶ **TEST 3**　　　　　**Drawing an Effective Inference**

DIRECTIONS　Write a sentence that expresses the implied main idea of the passage.

1. When the Barbie doll first appeared in pre-feminist 1959, she had large breasts, a tiny waist, rounded hips, shapely legs, and little feet shod in high-heeled shoes. Barbie wore heavy makeup, and her gaze was shy and downcast. She was available in only two career options: airline stewardess or nurse. In the 1960s era of feminism, though, Barbie had her own car and house. A "Barbie Goes to College" playset was also available. In 1967, Barbie's face was updated to sport a more youthful, model-like appearance with a direct and fearless gaze. By the 1970s, Barbie's career options had expanded to include doctor and Olympic medalist. She also got another facelift that left her with a softer, friendlier look. She now had a wide smile and bright eyes. During the 1980s and 1990s, when girls were encouraged to grow up to be independent wage earners, Barbie's options increased even more to include professions such as business executive, aerobics instructor, and firefighter. Today Barbie has a thicker waist, slimmer hips, and smaller breasts, and she comes in black, Asian, and Latina versions.

Implied Main Idea　　＿＿＿＿＿＿＿＿＿＿＿＿＿＿＿＿＿＿＿＿＿＿＿

＿＿＿＿＿＿＿＿＿＿＿＿＿＿＿＿＿＿＿＿＿＿＿

2. In 1984, Congress passed a law prohibiting anyone from selling one of his or her organs to a person needing a transplant. Since then, however, the number of people on waiting lists to receive an organ has risen steadily, and now about 6,000 individuals die every year because the need for organs greatly exceeds the number donated. As a possible solution, the American Medical Association has begun encouraging transplant centers and organ procurement organizations to study whether more people would donate organs if they or their loved ones received a small financial reward for doing so. In response to such policy changes, critics of offering financial incentives have repeatedly quoted a landmark article by Dr. Gregory W. Rutecki from the Center for Bioethics and Human Dignity. In a 2002 article titled "Is It Ethical to Buy Organs? One Physician's Perspective," Dr. Rutecki insisted that any financial incentives offered for organs were likely to lead to ethical and moral abuses. Dr. Rutecki claimed that even modest financial incentives would quickly deteriorate into an organ black market, where human body parts are sold to the highest bidder.

Even worse was the possibility that human organs, once payment was involved, would be taken without individual consent.

Implied Main Idea _____

_____

3. Over billions of years, the human body has evolved to function and to thrive in a gravity-controlled environment. Thus when astronauts spend extended periods of time in outer space, where there is no gravity, they lose muscle mass. That's because weightlessness in space lets many muscles in the body go unused. Lacking the constant pull of gravity to work against, the muscles become weak, and astronauts who spend months aboard a space station can barely stand when they first return to Earth. Their heart muscles also deteriorate. Living in an atmosphere lacking the weight of gravity also decreases bone mass, which makes the skeletal system weaker. Moreover, the redistribution of fluids in a zero-gravity environment also causes fluid loss, making dehydration a potential problem. The human immune system also does not function as effectively in a gravity-free environment, so astronauts are more readily prey to viruses they might otherwise have fought off.

Implied Main Idea _____

_____

4. Based on simple observation, it's clear that animals experience fear. Many mammals, for example, exhibit an anxious "fight or flight" response when confronted by a threatening predator. In addition to the emotion of fear, animals seem to feel grief as well. Observers say that elephants, for instance, mourn for days over dead or dying family members. Chimpanzees who lose a relative also exhibit signs of depression and some even refuse to eat. Along with grief, many animals display obvious affection for their partners. Mating whales, for example, stroke each other with their flippers and swim slowly side by side during courtship. It's also clear that many creatures, besides humans, exhibit happiness when at play. Mammals such as dolphins frolic and chase each other, especially when they're young. Scientists claim that young dolphins are not just developing adult skills. They are displaying the joy they take in play.

Implied Main Idea _____

_____

▶ TEST 4   Inferring Main Ideas and Supporting Details

DIRECTIONS Read each paragraph. Then answer the questions about supporting details by filling in the blanks.

1. [1]Next time you hear complaints about how long it takes the U.S. Food and Drug Administration to approve a new drug, you might want to remind the person complaining about the 1950s thalidomide scandal. [2]Thalidomide was produced by a small German pharmaceutical firm called Chemie Grünenthal and appeared on the market around 1957. [3]Sold as a tranquilizer and treatment for morning sickness, thalidomide was inadequately tested. [4]Yet, assured by the drug's makers that it was safe, doctors prescribed it, and thousands of patients, most of them pregnant women, dutifully ingested it. [5]Then in the early 1960s, hospitals in Germany, the United States, Canada, Great Britain, and the Scandinavian countries began to report the births of babies with horrifying deformities. [6]The infants had hands but no arms, feet but no legs. [7]However, it wasn't until Dr. William McBride, a physician in Australia, made the connection between thalidomide and the babies' deformities that the drug was finally removed from the market. [8]But that was in 1961. [9]By that time, 12,000 deformed infants had already been born. [10]Astonishing as it might seem in the light of its tragic past, thalidomide actually made a comeback in the 1990s when it was discovered that the drug might be useful in the treatment of leprosy and AIDS.

Implied Main Idea _____

_____

Implied Supporting Detail In sentence 9, the author does not say what caused 12,000 infants to be born with deformities. Instead, she expects readers to infer what detail?

_____

_____

2. [1]In the process of what sociologists call *groupthink*, the initial tendencies or leanings of a group often become more exaggerated and harder to change or revise once a discussion of those plans takes place. [2]Consider, for instance, one of the greatest disasters in U.S. history: the decision to invade Cuba in 1961. [3]President John F. Kennedy had

assembled in his administration what many considered "the best and the brightest" political minds in the country. [4]But Kennedy had also inherited a plan from the previous administration to invade Cuba and spark a revolt against communist-leaning Fidel Castro's government. [5]After some deliberation, Kennedy and his advisers approved the plan to invade. [6]Yet had Kennedy and his advisers consulted a map, they might have noticed that a huge swamp separated the U.S. invaders from the location of anti-Castro forces they needed for back-up. [7]Ultimately the invasion failed miserably. [8]The invaders were quickly killed or captured; the world was outraged at the United States, and the United States was humiliated. [9]After the fiasco, Kennedy himself wondered, "How could we have been so stupid?" (Adapted from Saul Kassin et al., *Social Psychology* 8e, © Cengage Learning.)

Implied Main Idea _____

_____

Implied Supporting Detail   In sentence 7, the authors do not say why the invasion failed miserably. They expect readers to infer that it failed because the invaders

_____

_____

3. [1]In 2012, technology writer Paul Miller took a big step. [2]He disconnected himself from the Internet for one solid year, thinking that unplugging would make his life richer and fuller. [3]In 2013, he went back and wrote about the experience for *The Verge*, an online magazine. [4]As Miller tells it, some things in his life certainly changed for the better. [5]Without the Internet, he couldn't get caught up in reading blog posts or article summaries, so he bought and read whole books and newspapers. [6]The difference between reading print or digital texts, an issue fraught with controversy for many, didn't make much of a difference to Miller except for the fact that he read more and at greater length. [7]His experience seemed to fulfill what many technology critics have maintained: The Internet supplies us with endless snippets of information but distracts us from exploring ideas in any depth. [8]However, Miller had also expected to have more intense and more face-to-face, real-time interactions once he was unplugged. [9]When his mailbox filled up with letters and cards from people wanting to hear about his experiment, the sight of all that human interest was a thrill. [10]But lacking the ability to text, tweet, email, or post, answering so much mail seemed an insurmountable chore, one he never got around to. [11]When his best long-distance friend moved to China, Miller couldn't keep up with him on Facebook, and the two lost touch. [12]Miller even lost touch with a close friend who lived nearby. [13]In the end, much of Miller's year away from the Internet was spent at home alone, reading or playing video games. [14]As Miller describes it, it took plugging back into the Internet, a year later, to get him back in touch with real people.

Implied Main Idea

_____

_____

Implied Supporting Detail

In sentences 11 and 12, the author does not say why Miller lost touch with his two friends, but she expects readers to infer that _____

_____ .

4. [1]Charter schools are publicly and privately funded elementary or secondary schools that have been freed from some of the rules and regulations governing public schools because their charter, or statement of goals, makes the schools accountable for only the specific objectives defined in the charter. [2]Exactly how or what a school's charter has to achieve varies from state to state. [3]The National Education Association (NEA), like many other individuals and groups, has been vocal about its enthusiasm for charter schools. [4]As the NEA website expresses it, "NEA believes that charter schools and other non-traditional public school options have the potential to facilitate education reforms and develop new and creative teaching methods that can be replicated in traditional public schools for the benefit of all children." [5]Yet, so far at least, the key word in that statement is "potential." [6]In 2004, the National Assessment Governing Board (NAGB) released a report widely referred to as "The Nation's Report Card." [7]The report found that, on average, charter school students were performing less well than students in public schools. [8]A 2009 report showed similar results, while a 2012 report from the National Association of Charter School Authorizers (NACSA) acknowledged that many charter schools were not performing as hoped. [9]Greg Richmond, the president and CEO of NACSA said at

the time the report was published that at least 900 charter schools across the country were performing "in the lowest 15 percent of all public schools within their state."

Implied Main Idea

_____

_____

Implied Supporting Detail

Although the author does not explicitly say it, the quotation from the NEA in sentence 4 is meant to illustrate _____

_____, while the reports from the NAGB and NACSA in sentences 6–8 are included in order to _____

_____ .

▶ **TEST 5**   **Drawing Personal Conclusions**

DIRECTIONS   Answer the following questions by circling the letter of the correct response.

1. Research has shown that people are more likely to help others when they're in a good mood. Psychologists call this tendency the *good mood effect*. In one experiment conducted over the course of a year, pedestrians in Minneapolis were stopped and asked to participate in a survey. When researchers examined the responses in the light of the weather conditions, they found that people answered more questions on sunny days than on cloudy ones. In another experiment, researchers found that the more the sun was shining, the larger the tips left by restaurant customers. Yet another experiment focused on pedestrians at a shopping mall, who were asked to change a dollar. Researchers discovered that when the request occurred outside a bakery or coffee shop, where strong, pleasant odors like freshly baked chocolate chip cookies or freshly brewed French roast coffee were in the air, people were more likely to help than they were if the request was made in a place with no pleasant smells emerging from it. (Source of information: Sharon Brehm et al., *Social Psychology* 6e, © Cengage Learning.)

   Which personal conclusion follows from the passage?

   a. If you're trying to raise money for your favorite charity, you would be better off stationing yourself outside a doughnut shop than in front of your neighborhood cleaners.

   b. Someone who tries to raise money for charity by standing in front of the local police station in hopes of donations will never collect a dime.

   c. If you want to raise money for your local basketball team, you should probably go door to door accompanied by two of the team members.

2. Throughout the United States, one or more lanes on some of the nation's busiest highways have been converted into Express Lanes. These pay-as-you-go express routes allow individual drivers[†] to buy their way out of traffic jams and sail past nonpaying motorists stuck in a line of cars. Many states are allowing private companies

---

[†]Those who carpool have free access to Express Lanes.

to build new toll lanes in exchange for the revenue generated from them. Others are designating existing lanes as Express Lanes. Not surprisingly, some people object to this growing trend. Several driver-advocacy groups claim that tolls amount to yet another tax on people who have no choice but to drive. Others have dubbed the new routes "Lexus Lanes." These people see the pay-as-you-go lanes as a luxury for those who can afford to pay. Advocates of the whiz-through toll lanes, however, disagree. They say that Express Lanes are just like any other convenience that some people choose to pay for and some people don't. This position, however, ignores the fact that some of those individuals "willing to pay" may not also be in the "can afford to pay" category.

Which personal conclusion follows from the passage?

a. Supporters of Express Lanes were probably happy to hear that the number of freeways with Express Lanes, currently at fourteen, is expected to double, perhaps triple during the next decade.

b. Critics of Express Lanes are likely to agree with those who think toll lanes will be good sources of revenue for cash-strapped state governments.

c. The author of this passage is firmly opposed to adding more Express Lanes to our nation's busy highways.

3. Is it ethical to keep animals in zoos? Some animal rights groups say no. They believe that animals have a right to be free and conclude, therefore, that *all* zoos are wrong because they deprive wild creatures of their freedom. Those in favor of zoos, however, argue that the need for species conservation outweighs the cost to individual animals. They justify the existence of zoos because of the role they play in the preservation of animal populations, particularly through captive breeding programs. Furthermore, they maintain that the alternative to zoos—letting species simply dwindle or perish altogether in the wild—is the less ethical choice. However, Dr. Michael Hutchins of the Department of Conservation and Science for the American Zoo and Aquarium Association believes that even zoos that focus on conservation may not be doing enough to justify keeping animals in captivity. According to Dr. Hutchins, "A strong commitment to individual animal welfare is equally important." Many agree with Dr. Hutchins that zoos behave ethically *only* if they work toward the dual goals of conserving species while providing

high-quality care in as natural an environment as possible. (Source of information: Bridget Kuehn, "Is It Ethical to Keep Animals in Zoos?" *Journal of the American Veterinary Medical Association*, December 1, 2002.)

Which personal conclusion follows from the passage?

a. Dr. Michael Hutchins probably agrees that it is perfectly acceptable for traveling circuses to include animals in their acts.

b. Dr. Michael Hutchins would be likely to defend researchers who keep animals in laboratories to conduct experiments on them.

c. In all likelihood, Dr. Michael Hutchins would be willing to donate or raise funds for zoo renovation projects devoted to re-creating an animal's natural habitat in the wild.

4. Controversial Dutch author and filmmaker Ayaan Hirsi Ali may have been named one of *Time* magazine's most influential people, but reactions to the story of how she came to reject Islam and advocate an end to what she calls its persecution of women have been mixed. Born in Somalia in 1969, she and her family eventually moved to Kenya, where she was raised in the religion of Islam. In 1992, according to her biography, Hirsi Ali balked at the idea of an arranged marriage to a distant cousin in Canada. To avoid the marriage, Hirsi Ali fled to the home of a female relative in the Netherlands. While living there, she earned a degree in political science and worked as a Somali-Dutch translator, often translating for battered Muslim women who sought refuge from abusive male relatives. Although she did not renounce her religion until 2002, it was at this point that Hirsi Ali's quarrels with Islam truly began. According to Hirsi Ali, the September 11, 2001, terrorist attacks on the United States led her to conclude that she could no longer believe in the God worshipped by the nineteen Muslim terrorists. Thus, in 2002, Hirsi Ali not only became an atheist, she also began to argue against what she called a "politically correct" approach to religious communities whose cultural values violated fundamental human rights along with the law. She was particularly outspoken about the role of women in the Muslim world, insisting that "the position of women is, in my view, nowhere as bad as it is in the Muslim world." While Hirsi Ali has won the admiration of many, she has her share of critics. Her challengers insist that she stereotypes all Muslim women as victims and fails to make distinctions between distortions of Islamic thought and authentic Islamic beliefs. Critics also say she persistently

misrepresents her former faith, particularly in her reading of the Koran, which, they insist, does not justify the mistreatment of women as Hirsi Ali claims.

Which personal conclusion follows from the passage?

a. Critics are correct to claim that Hirsi Ali's view of Islam stems from her own unhappy experience, not from her knowledge of Islamic thought and practice.

b. Despite her ideas about Islam, Hirsi Ali would probably agree that *madrasahs*, schools that include education in the religion of Islam, deserve public support.

c. Hirsi Ali would probably not send a child of hers to a school that included Islamic religious training in the curriculum.

▶ TEST 6   Inferring Implied Main Ideas in Longer Readings

DIRECTIONS Read each selection and write the implied main idea in the blanks.

1. Obedience—Would You Electrocute a Stranger?

1   The question is this: If ordered to do so, would you shock a man with a heart condition who is screaming and begging you for help? Certainly, few people would obey. Or would they? In Nazi Germany, obedient soldiers (once average citizens) helped slaughter more than 6 million people in concentration camps. Do such inhumane acts reflect deep character flaws? Are they the acts of heartless psychopaths or crazed killers? Or are they simply the result of obedience to authority? These are questions that puzzled social psychologist Stanley Milgram, when he began a provocative series of studies on obedience.

2   **Milgram's Obedience Studies** Imagine answering a newspaper ad to take part in a "learning experiment at Yale University." When you arrive, a coin is flipped and a second subject, a pleasant looking man in his fifties is designated the "learner." By chance you have become the "teacher."

3   Your task is to read a list of word pairs. The learner's task is to memorize them. You are to punish him with an electric shock each time he makes a mistake. The learner is taken to an adjacent room and you watch as he is seated in an "electric chair" apparatus. You are then escorted to your position in front of a "shock generator." There are 30 switches on this device, marked from 15 to 450 volts. Corresponding labels range from "Slight Shock" to "Extreme Intensity Shock" and finally "Danger: Severe Shock." Your instructions are to shock the learner each time he makes a mistake. You are to begin with 15 volts and then move one switch (15 volts) higher for each additional mistake.

4   The experiment begins and the learner soon makes his first error. You flip a switch. More mistakes. Rapidly, you reach the 75-volt word level. The learner moans after each shock. At 100 volts he complains he has a heart condition. By 300 volts, he screams he wants to be released, then goes silent.

5   At some point, you protest to the person in charge of testing. "That man has a heart condition" you say; "I'm going to kill him if I keep increasing the voltage." The leader of the experiment says calmly, "The experiment requires you to continue." Would you continue? You are probably shaking your head no, but what Milgram discovered is that most of his subjects would. And they didn't even know the truth. The screams were faked as

were the shocks. The subjects of Milgram's now infamous experiment just did what they were told because the person in charge told them they should. (Adapted from Dennis Coon and John O. Mitterer, *Introduction to Psychology* 12e, © Cengage Learning.)

Implied Main Idea _____

_____

_____

2. The Link Between Attitude and Behavior

1   People take for granted the notion that attitudes influence behavior. We assume that voter's opinions of opposing candidates predict the way they vote on Election Day. We tend to think that consumers' attitudes toward competing products influence their purchases and that feelings of prejudice trigger negative acts of discrimination. Yet as sensible as these assumptions seem to be, they fail to fully describe reality.

2   Sociologist Richard LaPiere was the first to notice that attitudes and behavior don't always go hand in hand. In the 1930s, LaPiere took a young Chinese-American couple on a three-month, 10,000-mile automobile trip, visiting 250 restaurants, campgrounds, and hotels across the United States. Although prejudice against Asians was widespread at the time, the couple was refused service only once. However, when LaPiere wrote back to the places they had visited and asked if they would accept Chinese patrons, more than 90 percent of those who returned an answer said they would not. According to LaPiere, self-reported attitudes did not match actual behavior.

3   As critics pointed out, however, this study was revealing but seriously flawed. LaPiere measured attitudes several months after his trip, and during that time the attitudes may have changed. He also did not know whether those who responded to his letter were the same people who had greeted the couple in person. It was even possible that the Chinese couple were served wherever they went only because they were accompanied by LaPiere.

4   Despite these issues, LaPiere's study was the first of many to reveal a lack of correspondence between attitudes and behavior. In 1969, Allan Wicker reviewed the research and concluded that attitudes and behavior are correlated only weakly, if at all. Sobered by this conclusion, researchers were puzzled. Could it be that the votes we cast do *not* follow from our political opinions, that consumers' purchases are *not* based on their

attitudes toward a product, or that discrimination is *not* related to an underlying prejudice? Is the study of attitudes useless to those interested in human social behavior? Not at all.

5   During subsequent years, researchers went on to identify the conditions under which attitudes and behavior are correlated. For instance, the strength of the attitude plays an important role. If the attitude is not particularly strong, then the chances of its affecting behavior vary from experience to experience. Also the degree to which an attitude is reinforced by others is significant. Our attitudes are more likely to affect our behavior when we know that our beliefs are shared by those around us. (Adapted from Saul Kassin et al., *Social Psychology* 8e, © Cengage Learning.)

Implied Main Idea   _____

_____

_____

▶ **TEST 7** **Reviewing New Vocabulary**

DIRECTIONS Use one of the following words to fill in the blanks.

esteemed	recluse	accountable	introspective	prodigy
boon	ingenious	aggregate	phenomenally	guru

Loving Loneliness

1 In the age of Facebook—and the general zeal for sharing—the notion of

being a(n) _____ is probably unthinkable to many. Yet

some highly _____ people have chosen to live alone

rather than be part of a social _____. For such people,

being alone is a(n) _____, not a deficiency.

2 Disappearing from public view was, for instance, the choice of cartoon-

ist Bill Watterson, _____ creator of the famous *Calvin and

Hobbes* comic strip. _____ by temperament, Watterson

just dropped from sight when the _____ popular car-

toon strip ended. The same is true of J. D. Salinger, creator of that smart-

mouthed _____ Holden Caulfield, who, until recently[†] was
embraced by generations of teenagers aspiring to be like him.

3 Seeming to share Holden's sense of alienation, Salinger refused all interviews and avoided the press and people in general. Those who expected

Salinger to play the role of cultural _____ dispensing
wisdom about how to lead the authentic life his character Holden admired
were disappointed to discover that Salinger wanted nothing more than

to be left alone and wasn't about to be made _____ for
anyone other than himself.

[†]In 2009, the *New York Times* ran an article saying that teenagers today thought Holden
was a whiner in need of antidepressants.

▶ TEST 8   **Reviewing New Vocabulary**

DIRECTIONS   Fill in the blanks with the words listed below. *Note*: In the second excerpt, you will have to use the same word twice, changing the ending to fit one of the blanks.

insatiable	lobbied	discretion	coalesced	espionage
quipped	mandated	irrationality	orientation	puns

1. Truman and the Loyalty Oath

In 1947, President Harry Truman was _____ by members of his own party to do something that would prove the Democrats were *not* soft on communism. In response to political

pressure, Truman _____ that everyone holding a federal appointment would have to sign a loyalty oath. In any realistic sense, the oath was worthless. Having government employees swear that they were loyal was not going to keep Russian spies intent on

_____ out of government. A spy with even a minimal

sense of _____ would just swear his or her loyalty and then go back to the business of snooping for the Soviet Union.

   However, the _____ of the oath did not disturb

those groups with a strong anti-Communist _____. For these people, the loyalty oath was only a step in the right direction and a small step at that. Intent on ridding the country of any groups they perceived to be leaning toward the left, from civil rights activists to conservationists, they rejected Truman as too liberal and

_____ around the political figure of Senator Joseph McCarthy, who built his entire career on his reputation for hunting down Communists and destroying thousands of innocent lives in the process.

2. No Laughing Matter

_____ treat homonyms, or words that sound alike, as synonyms. For fans, therein lies their humor. Writer Richard Lederer celebrates them in his essay "Get Thee to a _____nery," claiming they reveal the richness of language.

Asked for a slogan appropriate to a legal firm, Lederer showed he was among the quickest of wits when it came to double meanings. Without

hesitation, he _____ "Remember the Alimony," which associated the specialty of divorce lawyers—winning their clients alimony—with the battle cry of the doomed Texas fort, the Alamo.

While some, like the playwright Oscar Wilde,[†] have an almost

_____ desire to use such wordplay, there are those who have exactly the opposite reaction. They consider it the lowest form of humor and aren't especially shy about openly sneering when someone engages in wordplay wit. For these wet blankets, a line like Groucho Marx's[†] famous "Time wounds all heels" is more likely to produce a bored groan than a smile or a chuckle.

[†]Oscar Wilde: the nineteenth-century playwright's humor is heavy with plays on words.
[†]Groucho Marx: A member of the famed Marx brothers, whose movie comedies delighted audiences in the thirties, Groucho went on to television fame. His joke is based on the line "Time heals all wounds."

7 Synthesizing Sources

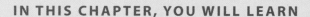

IN THIS CHAPTER, YOU WILL LEARN

- how to read different writers on the same topic and infer a relationship that links them together.

- how to use that link to create a synthesis statement that sums up the relationships or suggests your own point of view.

"Get into the habit of analysis—analysis will in time enable synthesis to become your habit of mind."
—Frank Lloyd Wright,
American architect

Chapter 7 builds on everything you have learned so far while taking you deeper into critical thinking territory, where readers apply, evaluate, and elaborate on what they've read. In this chapter, you'll learn how to **synthesize**, or link together, different readings on the same topic. Through the process of synthesizing, you will not only better understand each reading individually, you'll also come up with your own original perspective, or position, based on how you combine the main ideas of each reading into a whole new thought.

As you can probably guess, synthesizing similar or competing ideas on the same topic is a critical academic skill. Being able to synthesize various viewpoints can give you the ideas you'll need to answer essay questions and write good term papers.

 ## Synthesizing Sources

Imagine you are assigned to read an account of President John Adams's[†] tenure in the White House, and the reading celebrates Adams's efforts to

---

[†]John Adams (1735–1826): the second president of the United States (1797–1801).

stop the country's undeclared war with the French. Now imagine as well that you are assigned an additional reading on the same topic. This reading, however, harshly criticizes Adams's role in bringing about passage of the Alien and Sedition Acts.[†] Having read about two different sides of the same subject, John Adams's tenure in the White House, how do you think you should proceed? Should you take notes on each reading separately? Or should you try to synthesize, or combine, the two different positions into one unified or connected whole?

If you opted for the second choice, it may be because you already know the basic rule of remembering: The human mind is better at storing related pieces of information than isolated ideas, theories, or facts. Keep that principle in mind whenever you read different authors who discuss the same subject. See if you can synthesize the point each author makes into a broader statement that refers to or acknowledges the different points of view. If you can synthesize several ideas on the same topic, you have understood them thoroughly enough to write about them, whether it's for an exam or a term paper.

Consider the two readings about Adams just mentioned. Each one focuses on a different aspect, or side, of Adams's career. One reading notes a positive accomplishment; the other focuses on a more negative achievement. A statement like the following synthesizes the two readings and acknowledges both perspectives, or points of view, on Adams's career: "Fans of John Adams like to point to his role as a peacemaker during the conflict with the French, but his critics can't forget that the Alien and Sedition Acts came into being during his presidency." Using that sentence as your thesis statement, you can write a term paper. You can also prepare for a test by trying to recall the supporting details from both readings as a method of review.

Taking the time to synthesize two, three, or even four different sources of information into a statement that links them together does more than encourage remembering. It also deepens your understanding of individual viewpoints.

To synthesize different sources on the same subject, you have to determine the main idea for each one. Then you have to infer how those main ideas, along with the supporting details used to develop them, relate to one another. This prolonged processing of information

---

[†]Alien and Sedition Acts: acts that discriminated against the foreign born and blurred the distinction between political dissension and attempts to overthrow the government.

improves both comprehension and remembering. It will also take the terror out of writing term papers because you will know how to make sense of your research.

Synthesizing to Inform or to Persuade

Synthesizing is particularly important when you write research papers. Keep in mind, however, that synthesis statements, like longer readings in general, can vary in their purpose. Sometimes they merely inform readers, while at other times they are clearly designed to persuade.

For example, imagine that you were assigned a paper on the USA Patriot Act, which came into being in response to the terrorist attacks on September 11, 2001. From your research, you might discover that there is much disagreement, some of it quite heated, on the effectiveness of the Patriot Act. Some people say it is essential to protecting the country. Others, however, argue that it is ineffective.

If the goal of your synthesis is mainly to inform—and that may be a requirement of the assignment—then the synthesis statement[†] you use to draft your paper would connect what you've read on the topic without expressing your personal opinion—for example, "Since the moment it was formulated, the Patriot Act has been a source of controversy, with many people supporting it and probably an equal number challenging its effectiveness."

However, if your paper is expected to persuade, then your final paper might synthesize your point of view with the ideas of others into a statement like the following: "While portions of the Patriot Act were certainly necessary given the threat that faced the country following September 11, 2001, in current and calmer times, some elements of the Act need to be modified because they do more to undermine civil rights than they do to eliminate terrorism."

Then again you might argue the opposite: "While it is easy to understand the widespread criticism of the Patriot Act because it does, in fact, intrude on civil rights, it's also clear that in times like the current ones, even the portions of the Act that intrude on our civil liberties are necessary."

[†]If the term *synthesis statement* is starting to seem synonymous with *thesis statement*, that's because thesis statements for term papers are the result of synthesizing sources.

Step-by-Step Synthesizing ◆	Synthesizing two or more sources into one statement requires these steps:

Synthesizing two or more sources into one statement requires these steps:

1. Identify and paraphrase the main idea of each reading.

2. Determine what makes the readings similar or different (For questions to guide your analysis, see the list on pages 437–438.)

3. Write a sentence or two that identifies, in fairly specific terms, the relationship among different authors focused on the same topic. Look, for example, at the following synthesis statement, which connects the theories of three different psychologists:

   > For Sigmund Freud, unacknowledged sexual desires were the main source of neurotic behavior in adults, but Freud's pupils Carl Jung and Alfred Adler publicly refused to follow in his footsteps. While Jung emphasized the power of historical patterns to alter behavior, Adler focused on the way in which a sense of inferiority could motivate both positive and negative reactions to the world.

4. Include the names of the people taking each position if those names are (1) central to the opinion being expressed (e.g., almost no one else holds the opinion) or (2) the instructor wants the names included in the assignment.

Keep Your Purpose in Mind

If you are synthesizing for a paper, you might also need a fifth step, depending on your purpose. The synthesis statement shown above is fine as is *if* the purpose of the paper is strictly informative. However, if part of your assignment is to argue for a particular point of view, then you need to indicate whether you (1) agree with the sources you've read, (2) disagree wholly or in part, or (3) hold a completely different point of view.

Here, for instance, is how the informative synthesis statement above could be rewritten with a persuasive purpose:

> His disciples Carl Jung and Alfred Adler both rejected Sigmund Freud's theory that repressed sexual desires caused neurosis. Instead, they went on to formulate their own theories about the causes of psychic disturbance. However, of the two, it is Adler's theory of low self-esteem which has proven the most useful for therapeutic purposes. Jung's ideas about ancient mythic figures dominating our unconscious make interesting reading but don't allow for much practical application.

Writing and Synthesizing

Keep in mind that you are never locked into your first synthesis statement. What your first synthesis statement can do, though, is help you uncover what really interests you. For example, if you began writing to develop the previous synthesis statement, you might find as you went along that you were actually drawn more to Jung than to Adler and preferred to make this point rather than the previous one:

> Although Carl Jung is often treated as psychology's stepchild, the man whose emphasis on myth rather than sex alienated his mentor Sigmund Freud. Jung's theories, when closely studied, are far from ridiculous, and Jung uses myths to construct paradigms* of human behavior.

As you can see, Adler has dropped out of the picture and Freud is just a backdrop for Jung. Changes like these are bound to happen when you write. That's what real writers do. They use their writing to discover what they think.

Ten Questions for Synthesizing Sources

Sometimes the connections among sources are obvious. This is particularly true when the writers all agree or disagree. But when the connections between different texts on the same topic are not so obvious, the following questions will prove useful.

1. Do the authors generally agree but for different reasons?
2. Does one author interpret events in a way that is challenged by the others?
3. Do the authors express a similar point of view only in different forms, say poem and essay, fiction and nonfiction?
4. Do the authors completely disagree or only partially disagree?
5. Do the authors address the same topic or issue from different time frames, for instance, past and present—or from different perspectives—the digital native versus

*paradigms: instructive patterns, models.

the technological novice,* or the struggling farmer versus the CEO of an agribusiness?

6. Does one author focus on the cause or causes of a problem while the other looks more closely at solutions?

7. Does an author zero in on the causes of a historic event while the others concentrate on the aftermath or effect of the same event?

8. Do the authors employ the terminology and tools of different disciplines? Does one author focus on the psychological roots of an event while the other views it from an economic perspective?

9. Did the ideas of one author influence the work of another?

10. Does one author offer a personal account of events that the others only know secondhand?

◆ EXERCISE 1   Synthesizing Brief Passages

DIRECTIONS Read each group of passages. Then circle the number of the statement that most effectively synthesizes all three. *Note*: Remember the synthesis statement should not contradict anything said in the original sources.

EXAMPLE

Sources

The focus here is on the misery faced by migrant workers who struggled to find work, food, and shelter.

a. John Steinbeck's *The Grapes of Wrath* movingly conveys the misery facing the migrant workers who, throughout the Depression, traveled Route 66 across the country searching for work. Steinbeck writes, "Route 66 is the path of a people in flight, refugees from dust and shrinking land, from the thunder of tractors and shrinking ownership, from the twisting winds that howl up out of Texas, from the floods that bring no richness to the land and steal what little richness is there."

Here the emphasis is on members of the financial world,

b. Statistics suggest the magnitude of the Great Depression's effect on the business world. The stock market crash in October 1929 shocked investors and caused a financial panic. Between 1929 and

---

*novice: beginner, inexperienced, newcomer.

who suffered devastating losses during the Depression.

1933, 100,000 businesses failed; corporate profits fell from $10 billion to $1 billion; and the gross national product was cut in half. Banks failed by the thousands. (Adapted from Mary Beth Norton et al., *A People and a Nation* 5e © Cengage Learning.)

In the third selection, the population affected by the Depression has changed again. But the desperation remains the same.

c. Unemployment soared during the Great Depression, leaving the working people in the cities without the money to pay their rent or mortgage. In 1932, a squad of New York City police officers arrested 29 men in "Hoover Valley," a village of tents and crates constructed in Central Park. All over the country, people were so poor they were forced to live in miserable little camps called "Hoovervilles," named in sarcastic honor of President Herbert Hoover, whose policy on the Depression was to pretend it wasn't happening.

Synthesis Statement

1. During the Great Depression, statistics show that no one suffered more than the men and women who earned their living as migrant workers.

2. Whether we look at fictional or historical accounts of the Great Depression, it's clear that this massive economic downturn took a terrible toll on people from all walks of life, from bankers to migrant workers.

3. John Steinbeck's description of the hardships people faced during the Great Depression is enormously moving to this day, and Steinbeck's novel is more real than any statistic.

EXPLANATION   Statement 1 is not a good synthesis statement because it makes a claim about statistics not mentioned anywhere in the original source material. The second synthesis statement is effective because it identifies the common thread in all three passages without inventing any facts that weren't there initially. Statement 3 is incorrect because it focuses solely on Steinbeck's novel and ignores the other sources. *Note*: All three are informative synthesis statements. But that is not necessarily the case with those that follow.

Sources 1. a. When World War II broke out in Europe on September 1, 1939, the United States was the only world power without a propaganda agency. Since World War I, Americans had been suspicious of the claim that propaganda could be used to good effect. Many believed that British propaganda against the Germans had helped maneuver the United States into World War I. They also had not forgotten the bloody anti-German riots touched off by movies like the silent, B-movie *Kaiser: Beast of Berlin* (1918). To most Americans, *propaganda* was simply a dirty word, no matter what its purpose.

b. In 1939, the president of the United States, Franklin Delano Roosevelt, applied pressure on Hollywood to make feature films that were little more than propaganda vehicles. Hollywood producers, however, were reluctant to give Roosevelt what he wanted. Committed to the doctrine* of pure entertainment, pure profit, and, above all, a desire to stay out of the war, lest ticket sales decline, most balked at making films that reflected the horror engulfing Europe.

c. The Japanese bombed Pearl Harbor on December 7, 1941. Astonished and outraged, the United States entered World War II. On December 17 of the same year, President Roosevelt appointed Lowell Mellett as head of the Hollywood propaganda office. Mellett's job was to make sure that Hollywood films aided the war effort. In the aftermath of Pearl Harbor, Hollywood producers were happy to cooperate by making films that celebrated the war effort and castigated* America's enemies by exploiting crude stereotypes.

Synthesis Statement

1. Until the bombing of Pearl Harbor, the United States did not have an official propaganda office, a terrible mistake that had horrifying consequences.

2. Before the Japanese bombed Pearl Harbor (December 7, 1941), Hollywood movie makers, like most Americans, mistrusted propaganda. But after Pearl Harbor, propaganda became an acceptable part of the war effort, and Hollywood embraced it with a vengeance using the worst stereotypes to describe America's enemies, particularly the Japanese, which may be one reason why the internment of Japanese-Americans aroused hardly a ripple of protest.

3. During wartime, it is very likely that propaganda is a necessity; unfortunately, the effects of propaganda sometimes live on after the war ends, when those vilified* as our enemies have once again become allies, and we need to somehow forget the hatred and disgust wartime propaganda consciously promotes.

---

*doctrine: principle, theory.
*castigated: harshly criticized or punished.
*vilified: insulted or attacked character.

Propaganda during World War II demonized both the Japanese and the Germans in an effort to maintain the public's support for the war.

Sources 2. a. The Egyptians revered Ma'at, the goddess of justice. She was depicted weighing the hearts of the dead on a scale, with an ostrich feather on one side and a heart on the other. A balance between the two guaranteed a happy afterlife because an almost weightless heart showed an absence of evil deeds. An imbalance of the scale, however, promised torment for the deceased.

b. The ancient Greeks worshipped Dike as the goddess of mortal, rather than divine, justice. When the Romans inherited her, they renamed her Justitia and represented her with a blindfold around her eyes to symbolize her lack of bias, or prejudice, in favor of one side or the other.

c. After the advent of Christianity and the rejection of gods and goddesses, justice in the western world was represented by "Lady Justice," who, like her predecessors, held scales and a sword. But unlike earlier images of Lady Justice, more modern depictions have frequently suggested suspicion of the lady's ability to be fair. Lady Justice has even been depicted holding an unevenly balanced pair of scales to pointedly suggest that justice is not always applied impartially.

Synthesis Statement

1. The ancient portrayals of justice created by the Egyptians, Greeks, and Romans suggest a worldview where justice is fairly dispensed. However, some more modern representations of Lady Justice imply skepticism about the justice system's ability to be fair.

2. The Greeks appear to have had no goddess of divine justice, which makes sense. The gods of ancient Greece were answerable to no one except Zeus, the supreme God of ancient Greece, and Zeus was accountable to no one.

3. When one country conquers another, the conquerors usually try to wipe out the religion of the occupied population. It follows, then, that the Christians wanted little or nothing to do with the gods and goddesses associated with earlier civilizations.

Sources 3. a. Roger M. Witten knows a good deal about the effect of money on politics. He was a Watergate special prosecutor who investigated attempts by President Richard M. Nixon and his staff to raise and keep secret funds that were being collected before the arrival of new campaign financing legislation. A strong supporter of campaign finance laws that limit the ability of groups to make financial contributions, which, in turn, buy them influence, Mr. Witten is anxious about the effect of money on the political process. Eying the huge sums raised by the most recent political candidates, he has said, "I think we are in the middle of a scandal that hasn't quite gelled yet. A tremendous amount of ground has been lost. We'll have to relearn the lessons of Watergate—that money corrupts the system." (Source of quotation: http://articles.washingtonpost .com/2012-06-16/politics/35462700_1_watergate-corporations-and-unions-limits-on-individual-campaign.)

b. The effect of the campaign finance reform law in 1973 was to encourage the growth of political action committees (PACs) that raise money for the candidates of their choice. Some people worry that the existence of all this political money has resulted in our having "the finest Congress that money can buy," as Senator Edward Kennedy put it. More likely the increase in the number of PACs has had just the opposite effect. The reason is simple: With PACs so numerous and so easy to form, it is now probable that there will be money available on every side of almost every conceivable issue. As a result, members of Congress can take money and still decide for themselves how to vote. (Adapted from James Q. Wilson and John J. DiIulio, *American Government* 11e, © Cengage Learning.)

c. In 2010, the Supreme Court of the United States reversed a long-standing limitation on the right of corporations and unions to promote their favorite political candidates through financial contributions. It's now legal for corporations and unions to use monies from their treasuries to underwrite ads for the candidate of their choice. Long-time watchdogs of campaign financing are dismayed, believing that candidates in need of funding will be inclined to favor those individuals or groups giving them the most money. Those backing the Supreme Court decision insist that giving money to candidates is just another form of free speech, which cannot be denied to corporations or unions. From their perspective, the decision was a fair one.

Synthesis Statement

1. As the quotations from Roger Witten and Edward Kennedy suggest, money has corrupted our political process, which is probably the main reason why so many people don't vote. They think it's money, not votes, that really count.

2. Political action committees (PACs) and their contributions to political campaigns have been much discussed over the past decade. However, no one has ever proven that PAC contributions affect the political decisions of those on the receiving end of PAC generosity, and it's unlikely that anyone ever will.

3. The long-standing controversy about the role money plays in both political campaigns and the running of our government has heated up since a 2010 Supreme Court decision lent legal support to those claiming campaign contributions by corporations are a form of free speech guaranteed by the Constitution.

Sources 4. a. Perhaps you've seen the videos online. They are uncomfortable, to say the least. Patricia Walsh-Smith, 52, who was being divorced by her husband, 76-year-old theater executive Philip Smith, turned her marital crisis into a public spectacle by airing a series of self-made videos on YouTube. In one, she reports that though she and Philip were not physically intimate, he had a supply of condoms, pornography, and Viagra. Attempting to garner attention, sympathy, and support from the public, and to generate revenue by selling music videos online, Walsh-Smith lost her case and had to vacate the New York penthouse she lived in and settle for the $750,000 prescribed by her prenuptial agreement. (Bryan Strong et al., *The Marriage and Family Experience* 11e, © Cengage Learning.)

b. James Rachels is an American philosopher who, in 1975, wrote an essay titled "Why Privacy Is Important." He started the essay with the question, "Why, exactly, is privacy important to us?" Rachels then described a number of different responses. Among them was the need to protect secret information in competitive situations or the need to avoid the consequences total exposure of one's secrets might produce. Rachels also included the need to keep some parts of one's life secret from friends or loved ones, who might not be comfortable knowing every detail of our lives. In 1975, both the question and the answers seemed to make perfect sense.

c. Alessandro Acquisti, a researcher from Carnegie Mellon University, has been investigating privacy issues for years and has discovered that despite widespread claims about its importance, we are remarkably careless about protecting our privacy. In one study, mall patrons were told they were participating in a survey. As a reward for their participation, they were told they would receive a gift card. They could choose either a $10 gift card that could not be traced to the recipients or a $12 dollar gift card that would reveal to marketers the recipients' names, addresses, and purchases. At least half of those participating in the study chose the $12 gift card. With their decision they confirmed what other similar studies have shown. People are willing to put aside privacy concerns for small, in this case, very small, financial rewards. Acquisti's studies also suggest that the less privacy people have, the less they care about it.

Synthesis Statement

1. Although people claim to be concerned about privacy, they do nothing to protect it. Time and time again, they will endanger their personal privacy because they don't want to take the time to understand what actions are necessary to maintain privacy. According to a recent survey by the Ponemon Institute, which specializes in privacy and security issues, only 7 percent of Americans are willing to change their behavior to protect their privacy.

2. With the popularity of reality television shows, social media, and Internet tracking software, privacy seems to be an outdated concept, which may well be why most of us make so little effort to protect it.

3. When James Rachels wrote his essay "Why Privacy Is Important" in 1975, there was no question in people's minds that it was. But that was before our culture underwent profound technological changes that have undermined the notion that privacy is something to be valued and protected.

Sources 5. a. With its brilliant and innovative techniques, D. W. Griffith's *The Birth of a Nation* dramatically changed the face of American movies forever. Before Griffith, movies contained neither close-ups nor fade-outs. It was Griffith who brought those two techniques to the screen. With the exception of Orson Welles and the film *Citizen Kane*, no other director and no other film have been as influential as Griffith and *The Birth of a Nation*.

b. By 1910, motion pictures had become an art form, thanks to creative directors like D. W. Griffith. Griffith's most famous work, *The Birth of a Nation* (1915), an epic* film about the Civil War and Reconstruction, used innovative techniques—close-ups, fade-outs, and battle scenes—that gave viewers heightened drama and excitement. Unfortunately, the film fanned racial prejudice by depicting African-Americans as a threat to white moral values. An organized black protest against it was led by the infant National Association for the Advancement of Colored People (NAACP). (Mary Beth Norton et al., *A People and a Nation* 5e, © Cengage Learning.)

c. Despite the film's famed innovations, it's nearly impossible for moviegoers to take pleasure in D. W. Griffith's *The Birth of a Nation*. Powered by racism, the film enrages more than it entertains, and it's no wonder that African-American groups picketed the film when it first appeared, fearing, correctly as it turned out, that Griffith's film would revitalize the Ku Klux Klan.

Synthesis Statement 1. Famed film director D. W. Griffith changed the face of the American film with his masterpiece *The Birth of a Nation*.

---

*epic: dealing with big topics; important.

2. Despite the technical contributions that D. W. Griffith's *The Birth of a Nation* made to filmmaking, many people were and are rightfully appalled by the film's racism.

3. No one before or after has influenced movie making as profoundly as D. W. Griffith. His film *The Birth of a Nation* became the model for the modern American film.

WEB QUEST   *The Birth of a Nation* **and the Ku Klux Klan**

What was the original title of D. W. Griffith's movie *The Birth of a Nation*?

_____

What effect did the movie have on membership in the Ku Klux Klan?

_____

_____

_____

What Do You Think?
◆

If we are at war with a country, is it morally acceptable to use propaganda that makes our enemy seem less than human, as was done with the Japanese and the Germans during World War II?

◆ EXERCISE 2   Writing Synthesis Statements

Excerpt *a* focuses on the plight of the Jews in World War II, with no names of specific individuals or groups.

DIRECTIONS   Read each set of statements. Then write a synthesis statement that links them together.

EXAMPLE

a. Even before the war, Nazi officials had targeted Jews throughout Europe for extermination. By war's end, about six million Jews had been forced into concentration camps and had been systematically killed by firing squads, unspeakable tortures, and gas chambers.

(Mary Beth Norton et al., *A People and a Nation* 5e, © Cengage Learning.)

Excerpt *b* refers to the plight of the Jews but focuses on what one woman did to protest what was happening.

Excerpt *c* also describes an individual response to the situation.

b. To protest Hitler's treatment of the Jews during World War II, the French philosopher Simone Weil went on a prolonged hunger strike. In the end, Weil starved to death rather than take food because she knew that concentration camp prisoners were being turned into walking skeletons. If they were starving, so would she.

c. Born to a wealthy Swedish family, Raoul Wallenberg could easily have ignored the horror Adolf Hitler unleashed on the world. But he chose not to. Using his considerable daring, charm, and brains, Wallenberg saved the lives of thousands of Jewish refugees who would have died a horrible death without his help.

Synthesis Statement

During World War II, the tragic plight of the Jews stirred people like Simone Weil and Raoul Wallenberg to extraordinary acts of heroism.

EXPLANATION The synthesis statement links together the first text's description of the tragic situation and the two individual responses to it described in passages *b* and *c*.

 Sources 1. a. Every society is concerned with the socialization of its children— that is, with making sure that children learn early on what is considered socially correct and morally ethical behavior. Gender socialization is the aspect of socialization that teaches specific messages and practices concerning the nature of being female or male in a specific group or society. (Adapted from Diana Kendall, *Sociology in Our Times* 9e, © Cengage Learning.)

b. In Asian societies, the family is considered the most important agent of socialization. And children are taught that misbehavior is a great source of shame to the family. It follows, then, that worry about the family's reputation is one reason why Japanese children raised in the traditional fashion are likely to be very well-behaved. They do not want to dishonor their families.

c. In the last decade, a number of studies have suggested that in the United States a child's peer group may be overtaking the family as the most powerful agent of socialization. Values and attitudes that the family has patiently tried to teach children are often profoundly challenged by their interaction with their peers. Children who want to fit in are inclined to behave and think like their peers, even when that behavior and those thoughts go against what's been learned at home.

Synthesis Statement _____

_____

_____

Sources 2. **a.** Don Tapscott, the author of books such as *Growing Up Digital* and *Grown Up Digital* believes that the Internet and the search engine Google are ushering in a new age of learning when students no longer need to be taught anything. In Tapscott's view, they will be their own teachers, turning to the Internet to find out everything they want or need to know about the world. In his enthusiastic vision of the future, this is "an extraordinary period in human history . . . for the first time the next generation can teach us how to ready our world for the future." Tapscott wants parents, in particular, to recognize that "digital immersion is a good thing for their kids." (Source of quotation: Don Tapscott, *Grown Up Digital*, McGraw-Hill, 2008, p. 8.)

b. In his book *The Dumbest Generation: How the Digital Age Stupefies Young Americans and Jeopardizes Our Future*, English professor Mark Bauerlein voices his concerns about the effects of technology on the brains of the next generation. The word *concerns* is an understatement since Bauerlein is a prophet of doom, who believes that young people today are losing the ability to focus on and analyze the information they are bombarded with when they log on to the Web. Although Bauerlein cites a number of reasons for a decline in analytical reasoning ability, his major target is the huge amount of time kids spend on computerized gadgetry. For him, video games, social networking, web surfing, text messaging, and email are distractions from the focused work of learning. The more kids let themselves be distracted, the less they learn. Bauerlein has little or no patience with those proclaiming that technology has given kids a host of new and different ways to learn. From his perspective, it's given them a host of new ways to waste their time, and they are learning less than ever before. In Bauerlein's dark view, the society of the future will pay a high price for what technological progress has brought in its wake.

c. Writing in this best-selling book, *The Shallows*, Nicholas Carr makes it clear that he relies on the Internet for research. But Carr, who also penned the controversial article "Is Google Making Us

Stupid?" has some concerns about what our newfound access to multiple sources of information that can be viewed simultaneously is doing to our brains. Carr believes that the brain, which is highly plastic, i.e., capable of changing in response to experience, is getting into a mental rut and becoming incapable of giving new information anything more than a superficial response. As he puts it, "Because there is so much information at our fingertips, we can get stuck just constantly uncovering new relevant information and never stopping and actually reading and thinking deeply about any one piece of information." Carr's point needs serious consideration because groundbreaking research, the kind that gave birth, for instance, to the Internet, requires that individuals be capable of focusing on and analyzing information gathered from various sources. Leapfrogging from site to site to collect bits of information is fine. However, if that's all our brains can do, we have lost more than we have gained.

Synthesis Statement

_____

_____

_____

Sources 3. a. The custom among the Pirahã Indians of Brazil is that women give birth alone. The linguist Steve Sheldon once saw a Pirahã woman giving birth on a beach, while members of her tribe waited nearby. It was a breech birth, however, and the woman started crying in agony. "Help me, please! The baby will not come." Sheldon went to help her, but the other Pirahã stopped him, saying that she didn't want his help. The woman kept up her screams. The next morning both mother and baby were found dead. (David Brooks, "Tribal Lessons," Book Review, *New York Times*, January 13, 2013, p. 20.)

b. Most Koreans, especially older people, are very conservative and frown upon any show of public affection between boys and girls. This includes kissing, touching each other on the face, and even holding hands. Quite surprisingly though, public shows of affection between friends of the same gender are very common, and it is not odd in the least to see two men or two women sitting side-by-side, walking arm-in-arm, or even holding hands. (www .planetesl.com/information/behaviour.html.)

Among members of the Dani tribe in Indonesia, amputating the top part of the finger was a way of showing the proper respect for the dead.

Eric Baccega/AGE Fotostock

c. Although the practice of cutting off finger joints to symbolize the suffering endured during the period of mourning is now banned, visitors to the Dani tribe from Papua, Indonesia, will still notice that some older members of the tribe, particularly females, are missing the tops of their fingers. That's because finger amputations were once considered the proper way to mourn the dead. The physical pain of the amputation was meant to mirror the emotional suffering that the death had produced. The ashes of the amputated fingers were buried in a sacred place because they were believed to ward off evil spirits.

Synthesis Statement _____

_____

_____

 ## Synthesizing Longer Readings

The following readings are a good deal longer than any you have synthesized so far. However, they all deal with a subject you already know something about from Chapter 6—President Harry Truman's decision to drop the atomic bomb on the Japanese cities of Hiroshima and Nagasaki.

Steps in Creating a Synthesis

As you read each excerpt, try to determine what the author or authors have to say about the topic. Write the overall main idea into the blank lines that follow. Then, as soon as you get to the second reading, start thinking about the ways in which the authors agree or disagree. Does one reading challenge the other? Or are the authors similar in what they think? Are the authors writing in the same time period? Or are the readings widely separate in time?

Here's the first reading:

What's the Japanese position?

How does Truman respond to the Japanese?

What's another option Truman and his advisers are pondering?

Reading 1: Truman's Decision

1 Early in the summer of 1945, Japan began to send out peace feelers. Japan was not, however, willing to accept the "unconditional surrender" terms on which the Allied leaders had agreed at the Potsdam Conference, which was called to decide the fate of Japan. Thus Truman and his advisers chose not to pursue a negotiated peace. By this time, U.S. troops were mobilizing for an invasion of the Japanese home islands. However, the experience of Iwo Jima and Okinawa weighed heavily in the planning. Japanese troops had fought on well past any hope of victory, and death tolls for Japanese and Americans had been enormous. News of the success of the Manhattan Project offered another option, and President Truman took it. Using atomic bombs on Japan, Truman believed, would end the war quickly and save American lives.

2 Historians still debate Truman's decision to use the atomic bomb. Why would he not negotiate surrender terms? Was Japan on the verge of an unconditional surrender, as some argue? Or was the anti-surrender faction of Japanese military leaders strong enough to prevail? Truman knew the bomb could give the United States both real and psychological power in negotiating the peace. How much did his desire to demonstrate the bomb's power to the Soviets influence his decision? Did racism or a desire for retaliation play a role? How large were the projected casualty figures for invasion and were they accurate? No matter the answers on these ongoing debates, bombing fit the established U.S. strategy of using machines rather than men whenever possible. (Adapted from Mary Beth Norton et al., *A People and a Nation* 8e, © Cengage Learning.)

Main Idea _____

_____

_____

The next excerpt is taken from a textbook published in 1965. As you read it, consider how this author's perspective compares with the one expressed in the previous reading.

Reading 2: Truman's Choice

The reading opens with the author taking what stand?

Although many Americans have expressed contrition over exploding the first atomic bombs, it is difficult to see how the Pacific war could otherwise have been concluded, except by a long and bitter invasion of Japan. . . . The explosion over Hiroshima caused fewer civilian casualties than the repeated B-29 bombings of Tokyo, and those big bombers would have had to wipe out one city after another if the war had not ended in August. Japan had enough military capability—more than 5,000 planes with kamikaze-trained[†] pilots and at least two million ground troops—to have made our planned invasion of the Japanese home islands in the fall of 1945 an exceedingly bloody affair for both sides. And that would have been followed by a series of bitterly protracted battles on Japanese soil, the effects of which even time could hardly have healed. Moreover, as Russia would have been a full partner in these campaigns, the end result would have been partition of Japan, as happened in Germany. (Samuel Eliot Morison, *The Oxford History of the American People*, Oxford University Press, 1965, pp. 1044–1045.)

How do you see the author of this reading differing from the previous authors?

Main Idea _____

_____

_____

To get a sense of how much people differ on the subject of Truman's decision to drop the atomic bomb, look now at reading 3 from Harold Evans, author of *The American Century*.

Reading 3: The Myth of the Atomic Bomb

The author cites research to prove what claim?

1   Research over five decades has confirmed that Truman and his civilian advisers knew enough early on to appreciate that a siege strategy of sea blockade and non-atomic bombing had a prospect, though not a certainty, of ending the war before the November date set for Operation Olympic, the invasion of Kyushu.[†]

[†]kamikaze: pilots trained to fly what were suicidal crash-attacks.
[†]"Operation Olympic" and "invasion of Kyushu" both refer to an invasion of Japan.

<table>
<tr><td>

Why does the author quote the journal *Diplomatic History*?

</td><td>

2   The state of knowledge was summarized in a review in *Diplomatic History* (Spring 1995) by J. Samuel Walker: "The consensus among scholars is that the bomb was not needed to avoid an invasion of Japan and to end the war within a relatively short time. It is clear that alternatives to the bomb existed and that Truman and his advisers knew it." It is clear, too, that this last fact is the one there has been the most effort to fudge. The myth of Hiroshima the unavoidable seems to have embedded itself in the American psyche in a remarkable manner. It has survived for five decades in high school and college textbooks and in popular journalism. In the publications and television programs on the fiftieth anniversary of Hiroshima and Nagasaki, there was an emotional aversion to acknowledging the summation of research. Critical historians were denounced as "diabolical* revisionists" as if history were not a continual process of discovery and revision.

</td></tr>
</table>

In this context, what does the word *fudge* mean?

How does the author's word choice differ from that of the first excerpt?

What attitude is the author referring to here?

3   The most dramatic manifestation of the attitude was the response to an exhibition planned for the Smithsonian National Air and Space Museum in Washington, [D.C.,] in 1995. The exhibit, focused on the Enola Gay B-29, intended to highlight all aspects of the bombing, including pictures of the victims. It was canceled because of a hue and cry, led by the American Legion† and then taken up by sections of Congress, that to discuss the bombing was unpatriotic, pro-Japanese and a dishonor to American servicemen. This is curious. It is not as if the servicemen had anything to do with the decision to drop the bombs. The Smithsonian's mistake may have been to confuse a simple commemoration of the sacrifices made by American servicemen with an attempt at dramatizing a complex history, to offer a seminar instead of a salute. But what was striking about the responses was the eruption of hostility to presenting any fact—anywhere at any time—that does not conform with the official version of the events of 1945. (Harold Evans, *The American Century*, Knopf Publishing, 2000, p. 324.)

Main Idea

_____

_____

_____

Samuel Eliot Morison may have thought that Truman had no alternatives, but Harold Evans is equally convinced of the opposite: He says bluntly that Truman had an alternative to dropping the atomic bomb, and there is "research" to prove that claim.

---

*diabolical: tricky enough to be the devil.
†American Legion: an association of war veterans.

Step 1: Creating a Synthesis

Here's a list of the main ideas from each of the readings. Look them over to see how they might be synthesized into a statement that accurately reflects all three viewpoints.

1. Textbook author Mary Beth Norton and her colleagues: Truman really believed that he had no choice but to drop the atomic bomb.

2. History author Samuel Eliot Morison: Truman had no choice but to drop the bomb on Hiroshima; he had to do it because it was the only way to save many lives.

3. History author Harold Evans: Americans may not want to admit it, but Truman had an alternative to bombing Hiroshima and Nagasaki.

Step 2: Look for Connections

The first and most general connection to be made is that the authors of readings 2 and 3 are equally convinced about their point of view. There is no middle ground for them. The authors of reading 1 differ from the other two in their neutrality about the rightness of Truman's decisions. They think Truman believed he was making the right decision but don't take a stand on whether or not dropping the atom bomb on civilians really was the correct thing to do.

Also, readings 1 and 3 are both relatively current whereas reading 2 belongs to a much earlier era. Thus one possible synthesis statement might read something like this:

In the decades immediately following Truman's detonation of the atomic bomb, it was possible to argue, as Samuel Eliot Morison does in *The Oxford History of the American People*, that Harry Truman had no choice but to bomb Hiroshima and Nagasaki. But as new evidence emerged, it became harder to make that argument, and more current historians are less inclined to defend Truman's decision. Some, like Harold Evans, are openly critical, while others, like the authors of *A People and a Nation*, acknowledge the controversy without passing judgment.

What Synthesizing Accomplishes

Getting into the habit of synthesizing different sources on the same topic is one of the best things you can do for your academic career. Synthesizing fosters **analysis**. It encourages you to see and understand how the different ideas in a text relate not just to one another but also to the ideas of other writers. In addition, synthesizing encourages a deeper understanding of hard-to-understand material, ensuring that new information finds a place in your long-term memory.

But, as you can see from the previous paragraph, synthesizing can also help you create what your instructors ask for in writing assignments: original ideas, ideas that don't just repeat what you have read in your textbook or heard in a lecture. Thinking about how different sources focused on the same topic relate to one another will do more than enhance your understanding. It will also provide you with original ideas that can be turned into papers.

Synthesis Statements Aren't Created with a Cookie Cutter

Here are three more synthesis statements, all of which illustrate additional ways to combine these three points of view into one synthesis statement that takes them all into account. As you read them, keep in mind that there is no one way to write a synthesis statement. The end result depends on two things: (1) the purpose of your synthesis, whether to inform or to persuade, and (2) the relationship you choose to emphasize.

All of the following are possible synthesis statements. There could be more, particularly if the author has a persuasive purpose in mind. While an informative purpose leads to a synthesis statement that generally lays out the different points of view equally, a persuasive purpose tends to produce a synthesis statement that encourages readers to take sides. Note, too, that when the thesis becomes persuasive, the writer chooses to push one point of view into the foreground while the others become an introduction.

1. In the 1960s, many historians argued that the bombing of Hiroshima was necessary to end the war, which is what the Truman administration had claimed. By the 1990s, however, more doubt had crept into the discussion. In fact, some, like Harold Evans,

the author of *The American Century*, bluntly call Truman's explanation a "myth."

2. In the 1960 textbook *The Oxford History of the American People*, Samuel Eliot Morison, like so many other historians of the time, insisted that Harry Truman had no other choice but to bomb Hiroshima. However, four decades later, the authors of the textbook *A People and a Nation* are not completely sure that Truman's decision was the right one. But, unlike Harold Evans, the author of *The American Century*, they do not doubt Truman's integrity in making it.

3. Some modern historians are inclined to doubt Truman's claim that dropping the atomic bomb on Hiroshima and Nagasaki was unavoidable. But earlier ones who were closer to the actual events show no such doubts. Interestingly, it is the earlier historians who seem more in touch with the public's perception of Truman's decision.

Note the differences in emphasis among these three statements. Fueled by a persuasive purpose, statement 1 sides with the more current interpretation. Statement 2 also notes how time has affected the evaluation of Truman's actions. But the focus of this statement is on Truman's personal feelings about his decision. Statement 3 highlights an element of the readings unmentioned by any of the others: the public's tendency to side with Truman no matter what historians may say.

ALLUSION ALERT

Hedonism

Among the ancient Greeks, Hedonism referred to a school of philosophy that claimed pleasure was the highest good. But nowadays, the philosophical associations have pretty much disappeared. To call someone a hedonist or speak of hedonism is to suggest that some person or group is interested solely in personal pleasure or gain, often of a sexual nature—for example, "Unlike the male stars of rock or rap, male country-and-western singers don't portray themselves as hedonists."

✔ CHECK YOUR UNDERSTANDING

1. When you synthesize, you combine _____ to come up with
   _____.

2. As a reader, knowing how to synthesize different sources on the same topic can
   _____ and _____.

3. As a writer, the ability to synthesize sources will provide you with _____.

4. If three different people synthesize the same three sources, do the resulting synthesis
   statements need to be fairly similar?

   _____

5. A synthesis statement can reflect an _____ or a _____ purpose.

◆ **EXERCISE 3**   **Recognizing Effective Synthesis Statements**

DIRECTIONS Read the selections and identify the purpose and main idea for each one. Then choose a synthesis statement that best expresses the relationship among the three.

1. **Reading 1: Television Still Wins Out in Prime Time**

1   With all the attention the media gives to the digital revolution, you might well be thinking no one except the very elderly watches television anymore. That perception is understandable, but not especially accurate. Family members aren't all going their separate ways to download a new phone application, check their text messages, or look at the latest photo trend on Instagram. Instead, the 2012 Nielsen[†] report of television viewing habits shows that the average American child between the ages of 2 and 11 watches about 24 hours of TV per week, with teenagers watching the least amount of television, about 22 hours. Adults over the age of 25 watch

   _____
   [†]Nielsen is a company that does marketing and media research.

about 34 hours per week, with those over 65 spending nearly 7 hours per day or 48 hours per week in front of a television screen.

2   If anything, in the harsh economic times that began in 2008 and still haven't ended, television viewing may have increased as many Americans have been forced to cut back on spending for entertainment. As one entertainment analyst expressed it, "consumers are choosing to invest in the enhancement of their TV experience." In other words, with the times being tight, consumers are buying flat-screen TVs because they don't know when they will be able to afford the movies again. (Source of quotation: www.homemediamagazine.com/research/npd-america-a-nation-couch-potatoes-17868.)

1. What's the main idea of this reading?

_____

_____

2. What's the author's purpose?

    a. The author wants to report on a study of television viewing.

    b. The author wants to convince readers that television viewing hasn't been considerably reduced by the arrival of the technology revolution.

Reading 2: Less Television, More Computer Games Not Such a Bad Idea

1 In 2008, researchers in the United States and Spain studied 111 children ages 3–8. Throughout the study, the children were monitored so that researchers could tell how much time the children spent in inactive pursuits. Overall the children spent about five hours each day in inactive, or minimal movement, pursuits such as playing computer games or watching television.

2   When researchers further analyzed those periods of inactivity, they made a surprising discovery: When it comes to children's health, watching television is definitely the bigger threat. Children who watched more television than played computer games tended to be overweight and had higher blood pressure. In part that's due to television's being such a completely passive activity as opposed to computer games, where movement is involved.

3   But it's also caused by, or at least the study's authors suggest, children's snacking habits as they watch television. While watching TV, children tend

to eat fast food, and they eat a lot of it. Bags of chips or plates of fries are likely to be consumed without children realizing how much they are eating. They are too involved in their television program to notice.

4   Parents worried about their kids being too involved with social media or too addicted to computer games might want to re-think their concern. Computers seem to be better for children than their other, steady companion, the TV. As David Ludwig, director of the Optimal Weight for Life Program at Children's Hospital, Boston, expresses it, "TV-viewing really is the worst of all sedentary activities." (Source of quotation: Alice Park, "Watching TV: Even Worse for Kids Than You Think," *Time*, August 4, 2009.)

1. What's the main idea of this reading?

_____

_____

2. What's the author's purpose?

a. The author wants to describe for readers a study that monitored how much young children engage in inactive pursuits.

b. The author wants to persuade readers that computer games might be a better choice for kids than watching television.

Reading 3: Teenagers Are Looking More at Monitors Than at Television Screens

1   The results of a survey released by the Centers for Disease Control and Prevention (CDC) in 2012 will not be music to the ears of television executives. According to the study, children are spending more time in front of computer monitors and less time in front of television screens. The 2011 Youth Risk Behavior Surveillance Survey says that 31.1 percent of high school students spend three hours or more on the computer every day. In 2007 that figure was 24.9 percent, and in 2005 it was 21.1 percent. Where computer monitors are concerned, the trend is upward with a marked increase in students who spend more time on the computer than they do watching television.

2   With television screens, however, the trend is downward. The survey found that currently 32.4 percent of high school students are watching at least three hours of television per day. That's a decrease from 35.4 percent in 2007 and 37.2 percent in 2005. The Youth Risk Behavior Surveillance Survey is based on over 15,500 questionnaires completed by a representative sample of students from grades 9 through 12, and it suggests that as

computers get faster and applications and websites become more enticing, students will turn more and more to their computers for both entertainment and information.

3   Television executives, however, can take comfort from one aspect of the survey. Not all the states participated. Minnesota, Oregon, and Washington chose not to take part. California, Missouri, Nevada, New Hampshire, Pennsylvania, and Vermont didn't get enough completed responses to determine differences in viewing preferences for either television or computers. Perhaps in those states, television is still a big draw, but somehow that conclusion seems doubtful.

1. What's the main idea of this reading?

_____

_____

2. What's the author's purpose?
    a. The author wants to pass on information about a study of children's television viewing habits versus the time they spend working and playing on the computer.
    b. The author wants to convince readers that television is losing ground in the battle for viewers as kids turn more and more to computers for both work and play.

3. Which synthesis statement does the best job of combining all three readings into a new main idea?
    a. Although the media likes to portray television and computers in a battle to the death, there is almost no hard evidence that the computer monitor has replaced the television screen when it comes to providing entertainment and news.
    b. Television revenues from advertising might plummet dramatically as kids spend more time playing games on their laptops or buying television shows that no longer have commercials attached.
    c. While families may still be watching television, kids on their own are spending more time in front of the computer than the television, a practice that may provide a health benefit since one study suggests television viewing encourages the consumption of junk food.

2. Reading 1: Photographs of a Tragedy: Compassion or Exploitation

1 When an earthquake crumbled Haiti in 2010, photographs of the destruction and death were front-page news. The *New York Times*, in particular, displayed heartrending photos. One showed a woman walking along a street, her eyes glazed over in shock. In the background, corpses of people lying where they fell were clearly visible. Other pictures were even more distressing, so much so that the *Times* received numerous letters protesting the photos as a gross exploitation* of human suffering.

2 Some readers were so offended that Clark Hoyt, the *Times* public editor, acting as the intermediary* between the paper and the public, ran a column titled "Face to Face with Tragedy." In it, he quoted some of the people who had been appalled by the pictures. Said one writer, "I feel that the people who have suffered the most are being spectacularized by your blood-and-gore photographs." Hoyt responded to the letters by publishing the comments of others who supported the photos' publication. In a letter to the *Times* defending the photos, one woman asked, "How else can you motivate or inspire someone like me to donate money?" Hoyt also quoted several photographers who insisted that quake victims had implored them to come into their homes to photograph what was left of their lives and let people know what had happened to them.

1. What's the main idea of this reading?

   _____

   _____

   _____

2. What's the author's purpose?

   a. The author wants to convey to readers the different reactions readers have to photographs taken of people experiencing deadly tragedy.

   b. The author wants to convince readers that taking pictures of people who are suffering already is a horrible invasion of privacy.

---

*exploitation: using others to benefit one's self.
*intermediary: liaison, person acting as a link between people or groups.

Reading 2: A Picture Tells the Story

1   One of the most famous photos ever taken shows a young girl, burned by napalm, running toward the camera, her face contorted from the pain of her burning skin. It won the photographer who took it, Nick Ut,[†] a Pulitzer Prize and probably did more than any editorial ever could to turn the American public against the Vietnam war. Another Pulitzer Prize–winning photograph, by photographer Eddie Adams, was also taken during the Vietnam War. It shows the execution of a Viet Cong officer by a South Vietnamese officer at the moment of the bullet's impact. Then there are the tragic photos showing President Kennedy's motorcade speeding away from Dealey Plaza, while the life of the mortally wounded president ebbs away.

2   Robert H. Jackson of the *Dallas Times-Herald* won a Pulitzer for his photo capturing the murder of Lee Oswald by Jack Ruby in the basement of the Dallas police station. In 2000, photographer George Kochaniec earned a Pulitzer for his photograph of children anguished and traumatized by the murders they had just witnessed at their school, after two classmates opened fire and killed thirteen people. These photographs all bear witness to human tragedies. They all tell important stories.

3   If they are going to keep the public informed, newspaper editors have to run photographs like these. These are the photos that make readers pay attention to what's happening in parts of the world they will never see. They put a human face on tragedies that might otherwise leave readers emotionally unscathed.* Speaking about photographs of the twin towers that came crashing down in flames on September 11, 2001, Jim Fisher, a former photojournalist and war photographer, now a professor at the University of Utah, identified the purpose of photos that capture horrific tragedy: "Being aware of the truth of the day's events sometimes takes extra effort—not to search for it but to face it."

1. What's the main idea of this reading?

_____

_____

_____

[†]Ut was the one who got the girl to a hospital. She survived and the two remain in contact to the present day.
*unscathed: untouched, unmoved.

2. What's the author's purpose?

    a. The author wants readers to know about several famous photos that went on to win Pulitzer Prizes.

    b. The author wants to suggest to readers that it's the photojournalist's job to make viewers experience tragedy both emotionally and intellectually.

Reading 3: Catastrophes Are News

1 Violence and tragedy are staples of American journalism because readers are attracted to gruesome stories and photographs. "If it bleeds, it leads" is an undesirable rule of thumb. Judges of contests also have a fatal attraction. Pulitzer Prizes are most often awarded to photographers who make pictures of gruesome, dramatic moments. *Milwaukee Journal* editor Sig Gissler summed up the newspaper profession's sometimes hedonistic philosophy when he admitted, "We have a commercial interest in catastrophe."

2   Ethical problems arise for photographers and editors because readers are also repulsed by such events. It is as if readers want to know that tragic circumstances take place but do not want to face the uncomfortable details. After the publication of a controversial picture that shows, for example, either dead or grieving victims of violence, readers in telephone calls and in letters to the editor often attack the photographer as being tasteless and adding to the anguish of those involved. As one writer noted, "The American public has a morbid fascination with violence and tragedy, yet this same public accuses journalists of being insensitive and cynical and of exploiting victims of tragedy" (Brown, 1987, p. 80). (Excerpted from Paul Martin Lester, *Photojournalism: An Ethical Approach*, 1991, Lawrence Erlbaum Associates.)

1. What is the main idea of this reading?

_____

_____

2. What's the author's purpose?

    a. The author wants to describe some of the conflicted attitudes the media faces in its attempt to report tragic news.

    b. The author wants to persuade readers that if photojournalists take invasive photographs, it's because the public demands them.

3. Which synthesis statement does the best job of combining all three readings into a new main idea?

   a. When tragedy strikes, photographers are always among the first to arrive on the scene, given that catastrophes draw viewers and sell papers. Photojournalists, however, insist that the pictures they take serve the public good and make people more deeply aware of what's happening in the world because pictures can touch the emotions in a way words cannot.

   b. Those who make and publish photos of human misery in times of catastrophe offer a convincing argument for what they do: Photographs give viewers and readers a deeper insight into a human tragedy than words could ever convey.

   c. Readers and viewers may complain that photographs of people suffering the effects of a tragedy increase the victims' pain, but these are the photographs that people remember. They are also the photographs that win Pulitzer Prizes, suggesting that photographs of people in the throes of suffering serve an important purpose by recording a history we might otherwise turn away from.

WORD CHECK

The following words were introduced and defined in pages 437–462. See how well you can match the words with the meanings. When you finish, make sure to check the meanings of any words you missed because the same words will turn up in tests at the end of the chapter.

1. paradigms (p. 437)   _____

2. novice (p. 438)   _____

3. doctrine (p. 440)   _____

4. castigated (p. 440)   _____

5. vilified (p. 440)   _____

6. epic (p. 445)   _____

7. diabolical (p. 453)   _____

8. intermediary (p. 461)   _____

9. exploitation (p. 461)   _____

10. unscathed (p. 462)   _____

a. beginner, inexperienced newcomer; just beginning, new

b. unmoved, untouched, or unharmed

c. typical examples or models of behavior; worldviews that underlie theories

d. tricky like the devil, evil

e. dealing with important topics; heroic, in the tradition of famous epics like *The Iliad* and *The Odyssey*

f. person who acts as a link between two people or groups

g. using people or a tragic situation to benefit one's own interests

h. policy, set of guiding principles

i. insulted or attacked character

j. harshly criticized or punished

◆ **EXERCISE 4   More About Form and Meaning**

DIRECTIONS Fill in the blanks with one of the words listed below.

| intermediaries | castigated | exploitation | novices | diabolical |
| doctrine | unscathed | vilify | paradigm | epic |

1. At the most basic level, puzzle making is a _____ for reading.

2. Miraculously, the driver of the race car emerged from the practically demolished car _____.

3. A courtroom is a likely place for people to be _____.

4. Except for horror movies like *The Exorcist* and *The Omen*, it's unusual for children to be described as _____.

5. People who are rude and tactless don't generally make good _____.

6. Those who are _____ at tennis will never get a chance to play at the U.S. Open.

7. "Sticks and stones will break my bones, but names will never hurt me" is one way to respond to someone who tries to _____ your reputation.

8. The rules for playing poker would not be called a(n)

   _____, but the principles that guide governments would.

9. While admirers of *The Iliad*, *The Odyssey*, and *The Aeneid* might not agree, in the minds of younger readers and movie viewers, Katniss Everdeen of *The Hunger Games* series is a hero of

   _____ proportions.

10. No matter what their children think, parents who expect their children to do some chores around the house cannot be accused of

    _____. That word is appropriate for people who employ illegal aliens to work for them so that they can pay very low wages and threaten them with deportation if they complain.

TAKING STOCK The Kikuyu's Painful Passage into Adulthood

Looking Ahead The readings on pages 449–450 described some customs from other cultures. This reading is longer, but it too focuses on cultural difference. It describes the initiation ritual of the Kikuyu tribe from East Africa. The focus of the reading is on a ritual that initiates, or introduces, girls and boys to adulthood.

For the women of Kenya's Kikuyu tribe, weddings are not necessarily a cause of celebration, despite the colorful clothing and body paint.

Niels Busch/The Image Bank/Getty Images

1 The Kikuyu, like other traditional East African societies, practice initiation ceremonies as a way of ensuring that children will become morally and socially responsible adults. Despite some regional variations, the Kikuyu initiation rite includes certain rituals that conform to a threefold scheme.

2 Kikuyu initiation into adulthood involves a physical operation—circumcision for males and clitoridectomy for females. Days before the physical operation, the initiates go through rituals designed to separate them from society and their old status and place them in close relationship to god. First, the initiates are adopted by an elder man and his wife; this event symbolically separates them from their own parents. Second, the initiates spend the night before the circumcision singing and dancing in an effort to solicit the guidance and protection of the ancestor gods. Third, the initiates have their heads shaved and anointed, symbolizing loss of the old status. And finally, they are sprayed with a mixture of honey, milk, and medicine by their adoptive parents in another separation ritual, which anthropologists John Middleton and Greet Kershaw call the *ceremony of parting*.

3 In the second phase of the Kikuyu initiation ceremony, the initiates undergo the dramatic and traumatic circumcision or clitoridectomy as a vivid symbolization of their soon-to-be-assumed responsibility as adults. Both male and female initiates are physically and emotionally supported during the operation by their sponsors, who cover them with cloaks as soon as the operation is completed. Afterward, the initiates spend four to nine days in seclusion in temporary huts (*kiganda*), where they are expected to recover from the operation and reflect upon their impending status as adults.

4 The third and final phase of Kikuyu initiation rituals involves the incorporation of the initiate (with his or her new status) back into the society as a whole. At the end of the seclusion period, the new male adults have ceremonial plants put into the large loops in their earlobes (a form of body mutilation practiced during childhood), symbolizing their newly acquired status as adult men. This phase of incorporation (or reintegration) involves other rituals as well. The men symbolically put an end to their transition stage by burning their *kiganda*; their heads are again shaved; they return

home to be anointed by their parents. The men then ritually discard their initiation clothing, and are given the clothing and weapons of warriors. Once the incorporation rituals are completed, the young people become full adults with all of the rights and responsibilities that go along with their new status. (Adapted from Gary Ferraro and Susan Andreatta, *Cultural Anthropology* 9e, © Cengage Learning.)

Sharpening Your Skills

DIRECTIONS Answer the following questions by circling the letter of the correct answer or filling in the blanks.

Identifying the Controlling Main Idea

1. Which statement best expresses the overall main idea of this reading?

a. The Kikuyu practice a particularly cruel form of initiation into adulthood.

b. The Kikuyu of East Africa make their children separate from their parents at an early age.

c. The Kikuyu use a three-step initiation ceremony to mark the transition from childhood to adulthood.

d. The Kikuyu are known as warriors, and their initiation ceremony marks the moment at which women turn to the home and the men prepare for war.

Using Repetition and Reference

2. In paragraph 1, the word _____ in sentence 2 is a reference to the word *ceremony* introduced in sentence 1.

Recognizing Clues to Patterns

3. What word or phrase in the opening paragraph suggests that the process pattern will play a primary role? _____

Inferring Connections Between Paragraphs

4. In the opening sentence of paragraph 2, the author expects readers to infer what connection to paragraph 1?

_____

Spotting Transitional Signals

5. What four transitions organize the supporting details in paragraph 2?

_____

Using Context Clues 6. Based on the context of this sentence from paragraph 2, which definition for the word *anointed* makes the most sense? "Third, the initiates have their heads shaved and *anointed*, symbolizing loss of the old status."

    a. pointed

    b. oiled

    c. dried

    d. patted

Recognizing the Author's Purpose 7. Which statement best expresses the purpose of the reading?

    a. The authors want to describe the customs of the East African Kikuyu.

    b. The authors want to describe the initiation ritual of the Kikuyu.

    c. The authors want to persuade readers that the initiation ritual of the Kikuyu is a barbaric form of mutilation for both sexes.

Drawing Personal Conclusions 8. Which statement seems to follow logically from the reading?

    a. The authors consider circumcision and clitoridectomy as equally traumatic.

    b. The authors consider circumcision a much more traumatic and devastating experience than clitoridectomy.

    c. The authors view clitoridectomy as a much more traumatic and devastating experience than circumcision.

Please explain why you chose this answer.

_____

_____

Synthesizing Sources 9. Which of the following does the best job synthesizing this reading with the three excerpts on pages 449–450?

    a. Korean culture is very similar to American culture, but that claim could not be made for African tribal cultures, which are completely different from ours.

b. While American and Korean cultural customs concerning affection differ, they are grounded in similar notions about public and private couple behavior. A similarity of worldview, however, is hard to detect in the rituals of some African and Indonesian cultures, which inflict particularly intense pain on women.

c. Americans are quick to be appalled by the customs of other cultures. What they don't seem to realize is that some people from other parts of the world find many of our customs equally appalling. This is especially true for customs concerning the independent behavior of women, which would not be tolerated in many other parts of the world.

Detecting Bias **10.** The subject of removing the clitoris of females is a highly controversial topic with critics saying it is a barbaric practice that should be eliminated and others claiming that cultures different from our own have a right to their customs and outsiders should not pass judgment or interfere. Which side do you think the authors are on?

a. They are appalled by the practice.

b. They understand that cultures differ in what they consider appropriate.

c. They give no indication of their personal thoughts.

WEB QUEST **The Kikuyu Fight for Independence**

The Kikuyu played an important role in Africa's early attempts to throw off the rule of the European nations. What country ruled Kenya in the early part of the twentieth century? _____When the Kikuyu rose up against the Europeans who controlled their country, what name were they given by the people they were fighting? _____

REVIEWING THROUGH WRITING

Describe a cultural ritual that you either know from personal experience or have researched on the Web. Use the process, or sequence of steps, organizational pattern to describe that ritual for readers, making sure to describe not just the individual steps but the meaning or purpose of the ritual. Some possibilities are religious baptisms, the *quinceañera*, couvade rituals, Indian suttee, and the South American ritual of the bullet ant gloves.

▶ **TEST 1**   **Recognizing Correct Synthesis Statements**

DIRECTIONS Once you finish the reading that follows, turn to the pages indicated and re-read the related passages. Then select the synthesis statement that you think most effectively combines the information of all the readings.

The White Rose Remembered

1   In 1941, a group of students in Munich decided to do what many others— allegedly older and wiser than they—were not doing: They decided to resist the terrifying power of Adolf Hitler and the Nazi Party. Because the brutality of the Nazi regime was well known, many other Germans just put their heads down and hoped the government's iron hand would leave them untouched.

2   That self-serving approach to survival, however, was not acceptable to the group of young people who called themselves "The White Rose."[†] Hans, Sophie, and Inge Scholl, along with Christoph Probst, Alexander Schmorell, Willi Graf, and Jürgen Wittenstein, the founding members of the group, chose to fight back, engaging in acts of passive resistance that eventually got all but one of them executed for sedition, or crimes against state authority.

3   Inspired by a sermon given by a pastor openly critical of Hitler's government, the young members of The White Rose started out painting anti-Nazi slogans like "Down with Hitler" on building walls. But with the help of their philosophy instructor, Kurt Huber, they were able to print thousands of leaflets, which they distributed throughout the city. The leaflets made their position on the government and their resistance to it dangerously clear.

> We want to try to show them that everyone is in a position to contribute to the overthrow of the system. It can be done only by the cooperation of many convinced, energetic people—people who are agreed as to the means they must use. . . . The meaning and goal of passive resistance is to topple National Socialism, and in this struggle, we must not recoil from our course, any action, whatever its nature.

4   Not surprisingly, the Nazis were outraged at the open resistance, and the hunt was on for the authors of the pamphlets. On February 18, the group's two leaders, Hans and Sophie Scholl, were distributing leaflets

---

[†]The origin of the name is unclear. One theory is that the name was picked because a white rose symbolized purity, another that the group members named themselves after a poem titled "The White Rose" written by the German romantic poet Clemens Brentano.

at the university when Jakob Schmidt, a member of the Nazi Party spotted them. Schmidt immediately reported their names to the police. Within hours, the brother and sister were arrested. When their house was searched, the police discovered a handwritten note from Christoph Probst. He too was taken into custody.

5   Two days later, the three young people appeared in court, where the judge delivered a furious lecture on their vile and unpatriotic behavior. However, even he was shocked by Sophie Scholl's cool response as she explained, "Somebody, after all, had to make a start. What we wrote and said is also believed by many others. They just don't dare express themselves as we did." Not surprisingly, nothing the accused said made a difference to the verdict. The three were found guilty of sedition. Only a few hours later, they were executed by guillotine. Their comrades Schmorell, Graf, and Huber met a similar fate in the same year.

6   Although reviled by the government in their lifetime, members of The White Rose are now considered heroes in Germany. They are celebrated as examples of "good Germans," who did not turn away when they saw others brutalized, imprisoned, and murdered. Instead, they stood up to be counted and paid with their lives. A square next to the university in Munich is named for the Scholls, while streets, squares, and schools all over Germany bear the names of the other founding members of the group called The White Rose.

Left to right: Hans and Sophie Scholl and Christoph Probst shortly before they were captured.

George (Jürgen) Wittenstein/akg

Related Readings Re-read the passages on page 447 and decide which of the following synthesis statements does the best job of combining the main ideas of all four readings.

a. When the German people came under the diabolical rule of Adolf Hitler, the population, in general, refused to acknowledge what was happening around them as Jews, Communists, gypsies, homosexuals, and anyone who did not meet the Nazi idea of perfection lost their lives. Sadly, the few voices that spoke out in protest at Nazi brutality were foreigners like Simone Weil and Raoul Wallenberg, whose lives could have remained untouched by the dark shadow of Nazism had they been willing to just look the other way. But they couldn't, which raises the question: What motivates the kind of altruism that made Wallenberg and Weil take action? The answer has several parts.

b. The phrase "good Germans" is often used in its negative sense, to refer to Germans who took orders under Hitler's rule without asking the questions that needed to be asked. But in the case of The White Rose, the term is a form of praise rather than criticism.

c. History has rightly praised people like French philosopher Simone Weil and the Swedish diplomat Raoul Wallenberg for refusing to look the other way when those less fortunate than they were suffering a harrowing and deadly fate. However, it shouldn't be assumed that only foreigners were courageous. The Germans also had homegrown heroes. They had, for instance, the extraordinary group of young students known as The White Rose, who gave their lives fighting to free their country from Hitler's deadly grip.

▶ **TEST 2**   **Recognizing Effective Synthesis Statements**

DIRECTIONS   Read each set of passages. Then identify the synthesis statement that effectively combines them.

1. **a. Eleanor Roosevelt Did Not Stand on Ceremony**

1   Eleanor Roosevelt (1884–1962) shattered the traditional, ceremonial role of the first lady and used her position and talents to make her own positive contributions to American society. She assisted her husband, Franklin D. Roosevelt, by traveling all over the country to gather information about the American people and their needs.

2   However, she also took up her own causes. Eleanor worked hard to promote civil rights for African-Americans, and it was she who convinced her husband to sign a series of executive orders that prevented discrimination in the administration of his New Deal projects. She also devoted her considerable energies to many different organizations dedicated to social reforms. In particular, she argued for equal rights and equal opportunities for women. She advocated women's right to work outside their homes and secured government funds to build child-care centers.

3   Eleanor Roosevelt also used her gifts for public speaking, writing, and organizing to work toward the elimination of child labor. She managed to overcome society's stereotypical views of presidential wives to effect, in her own right, many significant improvements in social justice and equality.

b. Hillary Clinton, an Activist First Lady

1   As first lady, Hillary Rodham Clinton (1947–) used her intelligence and talents to improve the lives of people across the United States and all over the world. Before becoming first lady, she worked on issues affecting children and families. While in the White House, she published a book, *It Takes a Village*, in which she argued that all areas of society must work together to improve the lives of American children. Also during the two-term presidency of her husband, Bill Clinton, she headed a task force devoted to improving the health care system. In this position, she traveled all over the country, talking to health care professionals and American citizens about how the government could provide access to high-quality, affordable medical care.

2   In addition, she visited many countries, serving as a goodwill ambassador for the United States and supporting human rights, women's rights, and health care reform. At the end of her term as first lady, she managed to do what none of her predecessors had done before: She established

an independent political organization and successfully ran for the U.S. Senate in New York State. By 2007, to no one's surprise, she was running for president, and in 2009 President Barack Obama named her Secretary of State. Having formally resigned as Secretary of State in 2013, Clinton might run for president again.

c. Busy Bess Was No Activist

1   On April 12, 1945, after serving a mere eighty-two days as vice president, Harry Truman became the president of the United States and his wife, Bess, became the first lady. It wasn't long before Bess Truman became known as one of the busiest and most hard-working hostesses in Washington. What she wasn't known for, though, was holding press conferences. She abolished the custom—established by her predecessor Eleanor Roosevelt—of holding regular meetings with reporters. Unused to being in the spotlight, Bess Truman was more interested in public service. She served as honorary president of the Girl Scouts and the Washington Animal Rescue League.

2   She also held honorary memberships in the Daughters of Colonial Wars and the Woman's National Farm and Garden Association. Known for her ability to remember the names of everyone she met at state affairs, Bess also made it a habit to personally answer the letters she received as the president's wife. Like her husband, Bess Truman was considered extremely down-to-earth, and she was proud of her frugal ways, which did not change with her improved status as a president's wife. During her time in the White House, she never spent more than three dollars on a manicure and, instead of having an in-house hairdresser, she made it a point to have her hair styled off the premises.

Synthesis Statement

a. As first ladies go, Bess Truman was probably the nicest and most frugal woman to ever live in the White House.

b. In their political ambitions, Eleanor Roosevelt and Hillary Clinton were very similar first ladies.

c. As first ladies, Eleanor Roosevelt and Hillary Clinton were very active politically; Bess Truman, however, kept her distance from politics.

d. Bess Truman carefully dismantled the political organization Eleanor Roosevelt had established while her husband was in office, and it wasn't until Hillary Clinton's term as first lady that a president's wife, once again, displayed a desire for political power.

2. a. The Warren Report

1   When President John F. Kennedy was assassinated in Dallas, Texas, on November 22, 1963, a traumatized American public wanted to know who was responsible. Police promptly captured ex-marine Lee Harvey Oswald and charged him with the murder, but when he too was gunned down one day later by local nightclub owner Jack Ruby in the police department's basement, new questions immediately arose. Had Oswald acted alone, or had he and Ruby been involved in a conspiracy to murder America's leader? Had Ruby been sent to silence Oswald and prevent him from exposing his co-conspirators?

2   In an attempt to answer these and other questions, Kennedy's successor, President Lyndon Johnson, quickly appointed a group that included two senators, two members of Congress, and two attorneys. It was headed by Supreme Court Justice Earl Warren. Known as the Warren Commission, this group was instructed to "evaluate all the facts and circumstances surrounding [the] assassination, including the subsequent violent death of the man charged with the assassination." Over the next ten months, the commission attempted to reconstruct the sequence of events surrounding Kennedy's and Oswald's murders by reviewing the investigative reports of the Dallas police department, the Federal Bureau of Investigation, the Secret Service, the Central Intelligence Agency, and other federal agencies. Members of the commission heard the testimony of 552 witnesses and visited Dallas to see the crime scene.

3   The culmination of this investigation was an 888-page final report presented to President Johnson on September 24, 1964. In this document, the Warren Commission concluded that Oswald was a psychologically disturbed person. The commission also concluded that he acted alone to kill President Kennedy and wound Texas governor John Connally. In addition, the commission endorsed the theory that one bullet had missed while the other two bullets had caused all of the injuries. The first of those two bullets had struck President Kennedy in the upper back, passed through him, and then hit Governor Connally, who had been sitting directly in front of the president in an open limousine. The second of those two bullets had hit Kennedy in the head, fatally wounding him.

4   Although the Warren Commission did not completely rule out the possibility of a domestic or foreign plot to kill the president, it stated that it had been unable to find any evidence of one. Unable to uncover any connection between Oswald and Ruby, the commission found Ruby innocent of conspiracy, concluding that he was motivated by rage. Ruby had simply decided to appoint himself Oswald's judge and executioner.

5   To most Americans, these conclusions seem perfectly sound. The Warren Commission, they believe, fulfilled its mission by thoroughly investigating the matter, finding the truth, and providing much-needed reassurance during a time of national crisis.

b. Doubts About the Warren Commission

1   In the wake of President John F. Kennedy's murder in Dallas, Texas, on November 22, 1963, a seven-member panel headed by Supreme Court Chief Justice Earl Warren undertook the task of investigating the assassination and determining whether the alleged assassin Lee Harvey Oswald had acted alone. After examining all of the evidence related to the events, the Warren Commission published a report concluding that neither Lee Harvey Oswald nor Jack Ruby, the man who shot and killed Oswald the day after he was arrested, had been involved in any type of conspiracy to murder Kennedy. Instead, the commission stated, both men had been mentally unstable, lone gunmen.

2   But almost before the ink on the Warren Commission's report was dry, people began to criticize its findings. Books such as the influential *Inquest* by Edward Jay Epstein and *Rush to Judgment* by Mark Lane, both published in 1966, argued that the commission's investigation had not been thorough enough to be conclusive. Others attacked the commission's conclusions as a "whitewash" and criticized its methods while pointing out errors and the omission of important information.

3   Although two more U.S. government investigations—in 1968 and 1975—agreed with the Warren Commission's conclusions, President Johnson himself and even four of the seven members of the commission were said to have privately expressed doubts about the findings. In 1967, New Orleans district attorney Jim Garrison fueled suspicions about the existence of a conspiracy by trying businessman Clay Shaw for participating in a plot to kill the president, but Shaw was acquitted because of lack of evidence.

4   In 1978–1979, a special committee of the House of Representatives re-examined all the evidence and declared that Oswald had indeed fired the fatal shots but had probably been part of a conspiracy. This conclusion was based on evidence that a fourth bullet, which missed, had been fired by a second assassin on the ground. Yet, so far at least, no one has been able to disprove the Warren Commission's conclusions. Still, the doubts remain. In 2013, John F. Kennedy's nephew, Robert F. Kennedy Jr., said publicly that he didn't believe the story about his uncle being killed by a lone gunman. Kennedy called the Warren report a "shoddy piece of craftsmanship."

c. Bullets Don't Lie

1   By conducting a new type of bullet analysis, a research team has undermined the theory that a lone gunman assassinated President John F. Kennedy in 1963. The team, which included a top former FBI laboratory expert and two Texas A&M University scientists, obtained boxes from two of the four total lots of Mannlicher-Carcano bullets manufactured in 1954. The ammunition used by assassin Lee Harvey Oswald to kill the president came from one of these lots.

2   Selecting 30 bullets, ten from each of three different boxes, and using techniques not available in the 1960s, the researchers then analyzed the bullets' chemical composition. They found that many bullets within the same box have a similar composition. This means that bullet fragments having the same chemical makeup don't necessarily come from the same bullet. Researchers also discovered that one of their test bullets, which was not even in the same box of ammunition used by Oswald, matched one of the five bullet fragments found at the assassination scene.

3   These findings are significant because they call into question the number of bullets that were fired when Kennedy was shot. Scientists who first analyzed the lead in the bullet fragments found at the scene of the crime claimed that each of the bullets in a box of ammunition had a unique chemical composition. This suggested that the recovered fragments, which were similar in chemical composition, had to have come from just the two bullets traced to the batch in Oswald's possession.

4   This conclusion supported the theory that Oswald was the lone assassin. As it turns out, though, this conclusion was based on the technology of the time. Newer methods of analysis suggest that more than two bullets may well have been fired.

5   Only two of Oswald's bullets struck President Kennedy. Therefore, if the fragments found actually came from *three or more* bullets, then at least one other bullet might have been fired by a second shooter. Although the researchers did not go so far as to say that their study supports theories that Oswald was involved in a conspiracy, they did point out that their analysis of the ammunition does not conclusively rule out the possibility of a second assassin. They also urged authorities to reexamine the five bullet fragments recovered after the assassination. (Sources of findings: John Solomon, "Scientists Cast Doubt on Kennedy Bullet Analysis," *Washington Post*, May 17, 2007, p. A03; "Bullet Evidence Challenges Findings in JFK Assassination," *Science Daily*, May 17, 2007.)

**Synthesis
Statement**

a. While some have always accepted the Warren Commission report as accurate, the controversy about its findings continues to this day.

b. New research has now conclusively proven what was once considered a ridiculous and unfounded rumor—that Lee Harvey Oswald did not assassinate John F. Kennedy.

c. Current research supports the findings of the 1964 Warren Report.

d. Despite all evidence to the contrary, conspiracy theorists refuse to believe that the assassination of John F. Kennedy was the act of one lone gunman.

▶ **TEST 3**   **Creating Synthesis Statements**

DIRECTIONS   Read each of the following selections and answer the questions by circling the letter of the correct response or filling in the blanks. When you finish, write a synthesis statement that connects all three.

1. **Dogs at War**

1   Bounding along a dusty road in Afghanistan, the young Labrador could be any dog out for a run. It's only when the Lab called Crush stops short and turns motionless that it becomes clear, Crush is not just any dog, and he's not at play. Crush is on the job and out with four other marines looking for bombs. When he finds one, he freezes, sticks out his tail, and lies down with his head on his paws, mission accomplished. He's found one.

2   Dogs like Crush are trained by the U.S. government under a program run by the Defense Department. After the training, which begins when they are puppies, the dogs are shipped to locations like Iraq and Afghanistan, where bomb detection is essential for military missions. Labs, rather than guard dogs like German shepherds, are the preferred animals for bomb-squad training. Labs are fast learners and less aggressive than other breeds bred to be guard dogs. Possessed of a more tranquil temperament, Labs are easier to train. Bred as hunting dogs, they can pick up a scent from as much as 500 yards away.

3   Schooling bomb-sniffing dogs is extremely expensive, but the results seem worth the time, money, and effort. According to dog handler Corporal Andrew Guzman, the dogs "are 98 percent accurate" when it comes to detecting a bomb. In Guzman's opinion, they are better than "metal detectors and mine sweepers." The dogs also help psychologically as well. Wherever they go, there are plenty of soldiers who miss their pets at home. Playing with the Labs during off-duty hours helps the soldiers, many away from home for the first time, fight homesickness.

4   By 2010, there were at least seventy dogs in Afghanistan alone and, given their success rate at detecting bombs, plans were afoot to send more. (Source of quotations: Jason Gutierrez, "Dogs of War Saving Lives in Afghanistan," *Yahoo News*, January 28, 2010.)

1.   What's the overall main idea of the reading?

_____

_____

2. The purpose of the reading is to

    a. describe the training of bomb-sniffing dogs that aid soldiers at war.

    b. praise the bomb-sniffing dogs that go into the battlefields with the soldiers.

2. Dogs in Armor

1   K9 Storm of Winnipeg, Canada, earns a tidy profit making armor for dogs used by the U.S. Army, Navy, Marines, Special Forces, police departments, and security firms. A small firm, it has done well for itself. However, the big test may still be ahead. In 2010, the company launched K9 Storm Intruder, a specially designed bulletproof dog vest with a built-in wireless camera, speaker, and microphone, which will allow the handler to see and hear what the dog does. According to the company's owner, Glori Slater, the new vest will dramatically "change the way dogs are managed in emergencies" and "extend the range of the handler to 300 yards."

2   The inspiration for the company came when Slater's husband, a former handler for the Winnipeg police department, had to subdue a prison riot with the help of his German shepherd guard dog Olaf. The prisoners were armed with screwdrivers and other makeshift weapons, and Slater was worried about his dog being attacked. After the riot was over, Slater created a makeshift flak jacket to offer the dog some padded protection. Other canine officers were soon asking him where he got the jacket, and K9 Storm was born.

3   For the Slaters, the K9 Storm Intruder is another step forward in canine protection. Extremely lightweight, it allows the dog to have mobility without leaving the watchful eye of the handler. Although the newly designed vests aren't cheap—starting at $20,000 per vest—the Slaters say they have dozens of orders, especially from the military, which spends as much as $50,000 purchasing and training dogs for military duty. However, even nonmilitary sources have been able to order the vests, thanks to the generosity of donors like football player Ben Roethlisberger. Roethlisberger donated $250,000 to the Pittsburgh police and fire departments, earmarking the money for canine armor. (Source of quotations: Jonathan Blum, "Armor to Guard $50,000 Dogs," CNNMoney.com, November 30, 2009.)

1. What's the overall main idea of the reading?

    _____

    _____

2. The purpose of the reading is to

a. inform readers that the K9 Storm Intruder exists.

b. persuade readers that the K9 Storm Intruder is a terrific new product.

3. Dogs and Humans: How It All Got Started

1 We will probably never have conclusive evidence to tell us how dogs and humans first formed their personal and working relationship with each other, but it is most likely the case that man did not initially choose dogs; rather dogs chose man. Dogs were likely attracted to human campsites because humans, like dogs, were hunters, and animal remains, such as bones, bits of skin, and other scraps of offal[†] from recent victims were likely to be scattered around human campsites. The ancestors of today's dogs (being ever food conscious) learned that by hanging around man's habitations, they could grab a quick bite to eat now and then, without all the exertion involved in actual hunting.

2 Although primitive man may not have been very concerned with cleanliness, health issues, or sanitation, it is still true that rotting food stuff does smell, and attracts insects that will make humans uncomfortable. Thus it is likely that dogs were initially tolerated around the perimeter of camps simply because they would dispose of the garbage. This waste disposal function continued for countless centuries and is still being fulfilled by the pariah dogs[†] in many less developed regions of the world.

3 Anthropologists studying primitive tribes in the South Pacific have noticed that on those islands where people keep dogs, the villages and settlements are much more permanent. Villages without dogs have to move every year or so simply to escape the environmental contamination caused by rotting refuse. This has even led to the suggestion that dogs may have been a vital element in the establishment of permanent cities in that bygone era before we learned the importance of public sanitation.

4 Once the wild canines that would eventually become dogs were attracted to human settlements, our ancestors noticed an added benefit. Remember early humans lived in dangerous times. There were large animals around which looked on humans as potential sources of fresh meat. There were also other bands of humans with hostile intentions. Since the canines around the village began to look upon the area as their territory,

---

[†]offal: guts of dead animals.
[†]pariah dogs: wild dogs that live near human communities and survive by eating garbage.

whenever a strange human or wild beast approached, the dogs would sound the alarm. This would alert the residents in time to rally some sort of defense. As long as dogs were present, the human guards did not need to be as vigilant, thus allowing for more rest and a better lifestyle. It takes only a short journey to get from dogs guarding the village to a personal house dog. ("Dogs and Humans: How It All Got Started." Reprinted with permission of The Free Press, a Division of Simon and Schuster, Inc. from *The Intelligence of Dogs: Canine Consciousness and Capabilities* by Stanley Coren, Copyright © 1994 by Stanley Coren. All rights reserved.)

1. What's the main idea of the reading?

   _____

   _____

2. The purpose of this reading is
   a. to describe how the relationship between dogs and humans got started and developed over time.
   b. to suggest that humans have benefitted so much from the presence of dogs, they should take better care of them.

3. Write a synthesis statement that connects the three previous readings.

   _____

   _____

   _____

   _____

   _____

▶ **TEST 4**   **Reviewing New Vocabulary**

DIRECTIONS Use one of the following words to fill in the blanks.

castigated	intermediary	paradigm	novice	epic
doctrine	vilified	unscathed	diabolical	exploit

1. Seeing Red

1   In the aftermath of World War II, the Russian and Chinese Communists were

seen as dangerous and _____ forces that had to be con-

trolled. The Communist state was considered a _____ for
the control and repression of every natural human impulse and instinct.

2   The fear of communism's spread is certainly one of the reasons why
President Harry Truman, in 1947, gave a speech on what came to be known

as the Truman _____ . Worried that the Communists were

going to _____ postwar chaos in an effort to undermine
democratic governments, Truman made it clear that any person or group in-
terfering with the United States' attempts to encourage democracy around

the world would not emerge from a confrontation _____ .
He also said that countries rejecting communism would receive economic

aid from the United States. _____ by some and celebrated
by others, Truman's new foreign policy made it clear that postwar America was
now a superpower ready to flex its muscle if its interests were threatened.

2. Nancy Wake: The Spy Who Lived to Tell the Story

1   New Zealand–born Nancy Wake was an independent and imaginative child, but it was precisely those qualities that got her repeatedly

_____ by her strict and very religious mother. Fed up
with the harsh scoldings of her home life, young Nancy left home at
sixteen. She traveled to Europe after an aunt gave her the money for the
trip. While in Europe, Wake watched in horror as Hitler's forces grew in
power and brutality. It wasn't long before she decided to become a spy
for the Allied forces.

2   Although a _____ at espionage, Nancy Wake had a
gift for sabotaging the enemy's efforts. She was so good at it, she ended
up on the Germans' "Most-Wanted" list, thanks to her successful work as

a(n) _____, who helped link the Allied military forces to the various citizen groups fighting the German occupation. Adept at handling guns, explosives, and radio communications, Wake always managed to be just a step ahead of the Germans, making one harrowing escape after another. Because of the way she repeatedly slipped through their fingers, the Germans nicknamed her "The White Mouse." When the

_____ struggle that was World War II finally concluded, Wake had become the Allies' most decorated servicewoman.

Understanding the Difference Between *Fact* and *Opinion*

8

IN THIS CHAPTER, YOU WILL LEARN

● how to tell the difference between *fact* and *opinion*.

● how to recognize statements that mix opinion with fact.

● how to distinguish between *informed* and *uninformed* opinions.

● how to recognize *irrelevant facts* and *reasons*.

● how textbooks often include opinions as well as facts.

"In all matters of opinion, our adversaries are insane."
—Oscar Wilde[†]

The goal of this chapter is to provide you with a clear set of criteria, or standards, for deciding if a statement is a fact or an opinion. Once you can quickly tell the difference between a fact and an opinion, you'll be in a better position to evaluate how effectively writers use facts to support their opinions. You'll also be well-prepared for Chapter 9, "Analyzing Arguments," where you'll learn how facts and opinions team up to persuade readers that the author's point of view is worth sharing or, at least, considering.

 ## Facts Versus Opinions

"Facts are stubborn things; and whatever may be our wishes, our inclinations or the dictates of our passion, they cannot alter the state of facts."
—John Adams, second president of the United States

Statements of **fact** provide information about people, places, events, and ideas that can be **verified**, or checked, for accuracy. Facts do not reveal the author's personal perspective, or point of view. The following are all statements of fact:

[†]This quote has also been attributed to Mark Twain. Since I first encountered it as attributed to Wilde, I include him as the source.

487

- Twitter was the creation of software engineer Jack Dorsey.

- In 2011, two-thirds of graduating college seniors had close to $26,000 in loan debt.

- Pluto is no longer considered a planet.

- Sony's robot "Curio" comes with foot sensors that allow it to play soccer.

- In February 1903, more than 1,200 Mexican and Japanese farm workers organized the Japanese-Mexican Labor Association.

These facts can be verified, or checked, in any number of print or Web reference works and they will always be the same. Facts do not vary with place or person. Whether you live in Dayton, Ohio, or Fairbanks, Alaska, if you look up Barack Obama's date of birth, it will be the same: August 4, 1961.

Obscure Facts

Because facts can be checked, they are generally not subject to question or argument. However, statements of fact may be questioned if they are obscure, or not widely known. For example, it's a fact that Muhammad, the Arab prophet who founded Islam, preached several sermons devoted to the rights of women. But since that fact is not widely known, it's likely to be questioned.

Changing Facts

Then, too, facts can and do change over time as new discoveries come to light or methods of research improve. This is especially true in fields like science, history, and medicine, where information is considered factual only insofar as it is based on existing knowledge. As scientists and historians gain more precise knowledge of the world, the facts on which they base their theories sometimes undergo dramatic change.

For example, it was once considered a fact that the sun revolved around the earth. But in the sixteenth century, a Polish astronomer named Nicolaus Copernicus used the laws of planetary motion to challenge that "fact." Copernicus proved that, *in fact*, the earth revolves around the sun.

Generally, though, facts are fixed pieces of information. They often consist of dates, names, and numbers that are not affected by the writer's background or training. Facts can be verified, or *proved* accurate or inaccurate, to the satisfaction of most people. Thus, unless they are newly discovered, facts are not often the subject of disagreement.

Statements of Fact ◆	• can be verified for accuracy by outside sources.
	• can be proven true or false.
	• are not influenced by the writer's background or training.
	• rely heavily on names and events, along with dates, numbers, and other units of measurement.
	• are not usually the subject of disagreement unless they are not widely known.
	• rely mainly on **denotative** language, or words that evoke no emotion in the reader.

Calling It a Fact Doesn't Necessarily Make It One

Because people tend to accept facts without giving them too much thought, some writers and speakers preface opinions with phrases like "the fact is," as in the following sentence: "*The fact is* that Sarah Palin was totally unprepared to be John McCain's running mate in 2008." Despite the opening phrase, this statement is an opinion. Many people would not agree with it. What the author tries to do with that beginning phrase is bully readers into agreeing that the statement is an indisputable, or unquestioned, fact.

Generally speaking, beware of expressions like "it's a well-known fact that," "in point of fact," "without a doubt," "obviously," and "without question." Writers sometimes use this kind of confident language to discourage readers from actually thinking about and evaluating opinions disguised as facts.

Finding Facts on the Web

If you are using a search engine like Google to locate facts via the Web, always double-check the results of your search. This advice is especially important if the website addresses you explore don't end in the letters *edu*, *gov*, or *org*, endings that indicate large (and generally reliable) institutions.

One of the wonderful things about the Internet is that it allows ordinary people to share their knowledge or expertise with others. However, many of these amateur experts, while knowledgeable, don't necessarily have a team of editors to verify their information. Thus they unwittingly can, and occasionally do, misinform.

One Web search, performed by the author of this text, revealed—to the author's amazement—that Frances Hodgson Burnett, the creator of a famous children's book, *The Secret Garden*, had an amazingly long life. According to one website, Burnett was born in 1849 and died in 1974, making her 125 years old at the time of death. Now this "fact" is impressive. Unfortunately, it's also incorrect. Burnett was born in 1849, but she actually died in 1924, a fact confirmed by a quick search of *several sites* related to Burnett's life and work. Someone managing the website had missed the error.

Where the Web is concerned, this kind of error is not all that unusual. Books, particularly reference and textbooks, have usually been double-checked by teams of people. Websites, however, are often the product of a few overworked souls, who sometimes make mistakes. They don't always have a copy editor and proofreader waiting in the wings to spot their errors. Thus the errors remain until some sharp-eyed reader spots it and notifies the appropriate website manager.[†]

As you know from Chapter 1, the Web is a wonderful source of factual information. But you should always confirm the accuracy of your facts by checking to see if two or more websites agree.

CHECK YOUR UNDERSTANDING

1. Facts are _____

_____.

2. Give three examples of factual statements.

_____

_____

_____

[†]Where errors are concerned, this is less true of websites based on print products such as the website maintained by the *New York Times* or *Time* magazine.

Opinions

Statements of **opinion** cannot be verified with outside sources because they reflect the writer's perspective on the subject being discussed. Shaped by an author's personal experience, training, and background, opinions about the same subject can vary from person to person, group to group, and place to place. For an illustration, ask a group of teenagers how they feel about high school dress codes. Then ask their parents. Don't be shocked if you uncover a marked difference of opinion.

You Can't Verify Opinions

Opinions are too **subjective**—too personal—to be checked in reference books or historical records. The following are all statements of opinion:

- If Facebook administrators continue to infringe on users' right to privacy, they will continue to see a decline in their consumer base.

- Thanks to acclaimed cellist Yo-Yo Ma, the glorious music of Argentinean Astor Piazzolla is now more widely known.

- Pet owners deserve to be held legally accountable if their animals do someone harm.

- Amazon's purchase of the book recommendation website goodreads .com has given Amazon too much control over the book-buying market.

- Young women under the age of thirty are unlikely to consider themselves feminists.

Because opinions are so heavily influenced by individual training, knowledge, and experience, it's impossible to talk about them as *accurate* or *inaccurate*, *right* or *wrong*. For example, if you own a dog and firmly believe that dogs make more desirable pets than cats, no cat lover can *prove* you wrong because you're expressing an opinion, not stating a fact.

Statements of Opinion
◆

- can be evaluated but cannot be verified for accuracy.
- cannot be proven true or false, right or wrong (although they can be termed *ethical* or *unethical*, *informed* or *uninformed*).
- are shaped by the writer's knowledge, background, or training.
- often communicate value judgments, indicating that the author thinks something is right or wrong, good or bad.
- use language that expresses or arouses personal feelings—for example, *effective*, *ineffective*, *slender*, *skinny*, *delightful*, *disgusting*.

In addition to the characteristics listed in the preceding box, the author's language is another important clue to the presence of opinions.

The Language of Opinions
◆

- often includes verbs or adverbs such as *suggests*, *appears*, *seems*, *might*, *could* or *should be*, *possibly*, *probably*, *likely*, *apparently*, *presumably*, *arguably*, *allegedly*, *supposedly*.
- frequently makes comparisons using words such as *more*, *most*, *better*, *best*, *greatest*, *finest*.
- is likely to include words that make value judgments such as *beautiful*, *perfect*, *significant*, *interesting*, *critical*, *key*, *crucial*.
- is frequently prefaced, or introduced, with phrases such as *one interpretation of*, *another possibility is*, *this study suggests*, *in all likelihood*, *it would seem*, *arguably*, *supposedly*.
- is likely to challenge preexisting beliefs or traditions such as *Although it's often said that*, *While in the past we have*, *Even though for years now*.

REVIEWING THROUGH WRITING

Give three examples of opinion statements.

_____

_____

Now take the subject of those opinions and write a factual statement about each one. Feel free to do some Web searching to find the right fact.

_____

_____

CHECK YOUR UNDERSTANDING

What's the essential difference between facts and opinions?

_____

◆ **EXERCISE 1**   **Identifying Facts and Opinions**

DIRECTIONS   Label each statement *F* for fact or *O* for opinion.

_____ 1. All this uproar about animal rights is nonsense. Animals don't have rights.

_____ 2. In 1909, Ernest Rutherford showed that atoms were mostly space.

_____ 3. Historians differ over the original name of Los Angeles, but Bill Bryson, author of *Made in America*, favors *El Pueblo de Nuestra Señora la Reina de los Angeles del Río de Porciúncula*, which means "The Town of Our Lady the Queen of the Angels by the Little Portion River."

_____ 4. Using Craigslist to find romance is a dumb and potentially dangerous idea.

_____ 5. Martin Luther King Jr.'s "Letter from Birmingham Jail" was published in 1963 by the American Friends Service Committee, a Quaker organization.

_____ 6. Michael Jackson's death at such an early age was a tragedy.

_____ 7. Jaron Lanier, the author of *You Are Not a Gadget* and *Who Owns the Future?*, is correct to argue that digital networks "should make our economy grow, not shrink."

_____ 8. Although the singer Selena has been given most of the credit, it was the band La Mafia that made *tejano* music popular in the United States.

_____ 9. Dionysus was the Greek god of wine and fertile crops.

_____ 10. The fastest a raindrop can fall is 18 MPH.

ALLUSION ALERT

Dionysus, the Greek God of Wine

Dionysus (also known as Bacchus) was the Greek god of wine. For precisely that reason, he was associated with wild, drunken rituals, called the Dionysian rites. Allusions to Dionysus, which usually take the form of a modifier, now suggest events associated with or fueled by alcohol and marked by a lack of all restraint or inhibition—for instance, "Few parents can acknowledge to themselves the kind of Dionysian revels their children are exposed to at school parties."

An image of Bacchus is bound to include grapes.

◇ Be Alert to Opinions Mixed in with Facts

Evaluating how well an author backed up opinions with facts would probably be a good deal easier if authors kept statements of fact and opinion neatly divided. But they don't. Whether consciously or unconsciously, writers—and textbook authors are no exception—don't always avoid coloring their facts with opinions.

As a critical reader, your job is to make sure you recognize when and where a writer's language blends some opinion in with the facts. That way you won't mistakenly accept as fact an opinion you haven't consciously thought through or considered. Take, for example, the following sentence:

> At least thirty-eight states have sensibly decided to give terminally ill patients the right to refuse medical treatment.

At a quick glance, this sentence might appear to be a statement of fact. It's easy enough to verify how many states have given terminally ill patients the right to reject medical treatment.

But think again about the author's use of the word *sensibly*. This word has positive **connotations**, or associations. If you call a decision "sensible," then you give it your approval. A decision labeled "not sensible" would be lacking in logic or common sense and suggest disapproval. What the author has done in the above sentence is to include her opinion of the action taken by those thirty-eight states. That makes the statement a blend of both fact and opinion.

Connotative Language Is the Language of Personal Evaluation

Writers dealing in pure fact tend to rely heavily on denotative language that suggests little more than dictionary definitions—for example, "The flying fox is a bat with a wingspan that can extend to five feet."

However, writers who express opinions are more likely to use connotative language that implies a value judgment. Think here of words like *effective, intelligent, hard-working*, and *determined*. These words all have positive associations, and all of them reveal the writer's point of view. For an illustration, compare these two descriptions of the same events:

Hard-working, *determined*, and *meticulous** in his attention to detail, the new liaison between the Indians' tribal organizations and the federal government was *committed to finding out* if all the royalties on mineral rights had been paid into the appropriate account.

The new liaison between the Indians' tribal organizations and the federal government checked to see if all the royalties on mineral rights had been paid into the appropriate account.

In the first sentence, the language suggests the writer is impressed by the efforts of the liaison to get the job done, especially since the phrase "committed to finding out" implies the job isn't easy. The second sentence is more descriptive, with the writer telling readers what the liaison between the two groups is responsible for. In this sentence, it's not clear if the writer approves or disapproves of how well the liaison has performed.

As you know from the box on page 492, words that make value judgments are a strong sign that an opinion is present. But many of the words that make those value judgments are more subtle than you might realize. Words like *good*, *bad*, *moral*, and *immoral* obviously express a value judgment. In contrast, words like *effective*, *convincing*, *pointedly*, *clearly*, and *surprising* don't scream out value judgment. Yet they do nudge readers to respond in a specific way.

 REVIEWING THROUGH WRITING

Here is a largely denotative description of two people having dinner. Rewrite it to make the language more connotative than denotative. Revise it in a way that makes the language reveal what is going on between the two people.

The man and woman sat across from one another. The man's head was tilted to the side while the woman spoke, and he was drumming his fingers. He shook his head twice while she gestured with her hands. He appeared to be in his mid-thirties, while his dinner companion looked to be in her late fifties. She had short red hair and was wearing a suit. She also wore modest heels and carried a large black bag. He was dressed in slacks and a T-shirt with a brand name on the front. He had leather sandals on his feet. After the appetizers arrived, they ate without speaking. When they had finished eating, she paid the check and left. He immediately pulled out his phone and started texting.

---

*meticulous: very careful, precise, focused.

◆ EXERCISE 2   Recognizing When Fact and Opinion Combine

DIRECTIONS Read each sentence and look carefully at the italicized word or words. Then label each statement *F* for fact, *O* for opinion, or *B* for a blend of both.

___F___ **EXAMPLE** *Twentieth-century author* Gertrude Stein spent most of her life in France.

EXPLANATION The phrase "twentieth-century author" does not carry with it any positive or negative associations. It simply identifies the time in which Stein lived. The amount of time Stein actually spent in France can also be verified.

_____ 1. E. L. James's book *Fifty Shades of Grey* has sold millions of copies, and given the writing, *it's hard to understand* why so many people wanted to read this book, not to speak of all of its sequels.

_____ 2. "Zulu" is a *general name* for some 2.5 million Bantu-speaking peoples who live in South Africa.

_____ 3. The Amazon River is the *second-longest river* after the Nile.

_____ 4. Nuclear weapons are a *major plague of this century*.

_____ 5. In the nineteenth century, Marshal James "Wild Bill" Hickok was *fearless* in his pursuit of outlaws.

_____ 6. *Famed revolutionary hero* Emiliano Zapata was *worshipped* by the poor of Mexico.

_____ 7. Gospel music is *intense, joyful music* that *makes the spirit sing*.

_____ 8. Francisco de Goya was a Spanish painter of the *late eighteenth and early nineteenth centuries*.

_____ 9. The nineteenth-century naturalist John James Audubon was a painter *of extraordinary skill*.

_____ 10. *Astonishing as it may seem*, John D. Rockefeller, founder of the Standard Oil Company and *one of the most ruthless businessmen in a remarkably ruthless era*, became known for his charity work.

◆ **EXERCISE 3**   **Recognizing When Fact and Opinion Combine**

DIRECTIONS Some of the following statements are purely factual. Others blend fact and opinion. Label the purely factual statements with an *F*. Label the statements blending fact and opinion with a *B*. For those sentences you mark with a *B*, underline the word or words that led you to your conclusion.

___B___ **EXAMPLE** Singer Ednita Nazario's <u>splendid</u> album *Corazón* was produced by Dolores del Infante, an alias for Latin singer Robi Rosa.

EXPLANATION In this statement, the author provides factual information about the album, but the word *splendid* announces the author's opinion of the music.

_____ **1.** According to the Television Bureau of Advertising, an extraordinary 98.2 percent of all American households have a television set.

_____ **2.** Psychiatrist Bruno Bettelheim spent decades meticulously studying fairy tales and their effect on children.

_____ **3.** An astounding number of people have tattoos covering 98 percent of their body.

_____ **4.** Amazingly, Diane Nash was only twenty-two years old when she led the campaign to desegregate the lunch counters in Nashville, Tennessee.

_____ **5.** In 2010, cognitive scientists from the University of Rochester performed a study that indicated people who play video games make faster real-life decisions than those who don't.

_____ **6.** Juan Rodríguez Cabrillo explored the coast of California in 1542.

_____ **7.** At the end of World War I, victorious Britain and France greedily divided up the Turkish Empire.

_____ **8.** Highly acclaimed for her book about textbook censorship, *The Language Police*, Diane Ravitch returned to the subject of education in her 2010 book *The Death and Life of the Great American School System*, proving once again her commitment to educating our young people.

_____ **9.** After World War II, Great Britain turned Palestine over to the United Nations, which in November 1947 voted to create the State of Israel.

_____ **10.** In 1908, the phenomenal Jack Johnson became the first African-American to win the world heavyweight championship.

Jack Johnson was one of the greatest boxers of all time.

WEB QUEST **Jack Johnson and *The Great White Hope***

Use the Web to find out why the play and movie based on Jackson's life was called *The Great White Hope*.

_____

_____

_____

_____

_____

REVIEWING THROUGH WRITING

Use each word in two different contexts. One sentence should use the word in its denotative sense. The other should make it assume connotations. If necessary, you can change the word ending to make it more connotative or denotative. For instance, "They decided on tile for the *floor* because it would be easier to clean" and "The instructor was *floored* when the student defied the rule and used his cell phone in class."

1. home

_____

_____

_____

2. crack

_____

_____

_____

◇ Informed Versus Uninformed Opinions

You probably know the expression, "Everybody has a right to an opinion." That's certainly true. It doesn't follow, though, that every opinion deserves the same degree of attention or respect.

Imagine, for example, that a friend saw you taking an aspirin for a headache and told you that chewing a clove of garlic was a far better remedy. When you asked why, he shrugged and said: "I don't know. I heard it someplace." Given this lack of explanation or support, it's unlikely that you would start chewing garlic cloves to cure your headache. **Uninformed opinions**—opinions lacking sufficient or appropriate supporting details—usually do (and should) fail to persuade.

Informed Opinions Have Backup

More likely to convince are **informed opinions** backed by facts and reasons. For an example, look at this paragraph, which opens by expressing an opinion about the Internet's darker side.

Sentence 1 states the author's opinion.

Sentence 2 offers the first reason for saying the Internet has a darker side. Then sentences 3 and 4 offer more specific examples that can be verified.

Sentences 5 and 6 offer additional reasons for saying the Internet has a dark side.

[1]Although the Internet provides us with a convenient way to conduct research and to shop, it also has a darker side. [2]Every day, hundreds of people report that they are victims of online stalking. [3]In 2000, police arrested John Edward Robinson, the first Internet serial killer, who murdered at least five women he met and corresponded with online. [4]In 1999, the FBI investigated 1,500 online child solicitation* cases, a number more than double that of the previous year. [5]Criminals are also using the Internet to steal credit card numbers, thereby costing cardholders and issuers hundreds of millions of dollars per year. [6]Still other criminals are using the Internet for adoption fraud. [7]For example, Internet adoption broker Tina Johnson caused much heartache and created an international dispute in 2001 when she took money from two couples in two different countries for the adoption of the same infant twin girls. [8]Internet crimes have also involved the distribution of illegal drugs such as anabolic steroids. [9]In September 2007, the FBI made a number of arrests involving men distributing steroids through MySpace.com profiles. [10]In 2010, four men were indicted for illegally earning over $25 million by hacking into sites like Ticketmaster.com and reselling tickets to the hottest concerts and shows. (Source of dates and events: www.cybercrime.gov/porterindict.htm.)

This passage starts with the author's opinion—the Internet, whatever its advantages, also has a "darker side." Aware, however, that not everyone will agree, the author follows that opinion with a number of facts and reasons. These supporting details are designed to convince readers that the opening opinion is informed and worth sharing.

Notice that all of the supporting details are **relevant**, or related, to the opinion expressed. They all describe and illustrate dangers associated with the Internet. Thus they help prove the author's claim that the Internet has a dark side. What about this paragraph, though? Are we again dealing with an informed opinion?

---

*solicitation: the act of approaching someone for sexual or monetary purposes; to persuasively ask for something other than money or sex—for instance, votes or information.

[1]Given that at least thirty thousand patients per year die from bloodstream infections, health care workers need to spend more time washing their hands before handling patients. [2]When patients enter a hospital for treatment, they expect to be cured of their illness or injury; they don't expect to acquire another problem, especially not a deadly one. [3]Yet that's precisely what happened to Carol Bradley when she entered a hospital to be treated for stomach cancer. [4]As a result of the bloodstream infection, Bradley spent three weeks in intensive care and more than a year on antibiotics. [5]Some hospitals that have taken precautions to prevent infections have virtually eliminated them altogether. [6]*Consumer Reports* lists 105 hospitals reporting zero incidents of bloodstream infection. (Source of Carol Bradley's story: http://abclocal.go.com/wabc/story?section=news/consumer&id=7253884.)

The opinion expressed in the paragraph is clear. But does that make it an informed opinion? Not quite. What's not at all clear is how the case of Carol Bradley is relevant or connected to the author's insistence that health care workers need to do more hand washing.

Nor do readers know why the list from *Consumer Reports* is in the passage since it isn't directly tied to the central opinion. Put another way, the author hasn't yet shown readers why and how the supporting details are relevant to the main idea.

To make readers take this opinion seriously, the author needs to provide more **statements of connection**. These are like the bridging inferences described on pages 375–377 of Chapter 6. The only difference is that they are explicit rather than implicit. Explicit statements of connection are the writer's way of being considerate to readers by giving them the information that either tells them how two ideas are related or provides them with enough information to make a bridging inference possible.

Note how this revised version of the previous paragraph carefully explains the connection between Carol Bradley's experience and the need for medical personnel to wash their hands.

The paragraph opens with the same opinion as the previous paragraph.

[1]Given that at least thirty thousand patients per year die from bloodstream infections, health care workers need to spend more time washing their hands before handling patients. [2]In intensive-care units, long flexible catheters,[†] called "central lines," can quickly deliver desperately needed fluids, nutrition, and medication. [3]However, if

---

[†]catheter: a hollow flexible tube that can be inserted into the body to allow the passage of fluids.

The writer connects the use of catheters to the importance of hand washing.

The phrase "That's what happened to Carol Bradley" is a connection statement.

those central lines are inserted by caretakers who have not properly washed their hands, the lines can also deliver deadly bacteria. [4]That's what happened to Carol Bradley when she was treated in a hospital for stomach cancer. [5]It wasn't the cancer that almost killed her; it was the bloodstream infection that kept her in intensive care for three weeks and taking antibiotics for over a year. [6]Bradley now says that if she "went into the hospital again, I would try to make sure I had my family available around the clock to make sure everyone did . . . good hand washing." [7]Her sentiments are echoed in statements put out by the Centers for Disease Control and Prevention (CDC). [8]In 2013, the CDC even partnered with the Association for Professionals in Infection Control and Epidemiology[†] and Safe Care Campaign to distribute a video on the importance of hand hygiene for both patients and health care providers.

Opinions in Casual Conversation Versus Written

If you're in conversation with a group of friends, it's easy enough to discover that your friends, or maybe even you yourself, haven't really thought through the basis for your opinions. Someone says, for instance, "People who spend time on Facebook are just interested in gossip; Twitter is for people who are really interested in political issues and current events."

Annoyed by the claim, someone else responds that Facebook helped connect lost animals with their families in the aftermath of Hurricane Sandy in 2012 and that the people with the biggest number of followers on Twitter are celebrities and entertainers, so why would anyone claim Twitter was for news junkies while Facebook was for gossip? If that response leaves the person who favored Twitter over Facebook speechless, you know for sure that he hasn't thought his opinion through with much care.

While being caught expressing an uninformed opinion in conversations is embarrassing, it's also common. With our friends, we don't always think before speaking, and we say things that, if challenged, we can't always back up. But that's hardly a major error. While expressing uninformed opinions in a conversation shouldn't be encouraged, it doesn't mean you can't trust the person who makes the mistake once or even twice.

[†]epidemiology: branch of medicine dealing with the spread and control of disease.

Uninformed opinions expressed on the page, whether on the Web or in print, however, are different. These opinions have been put into words by people with a specific and conscious purpose in mind. They want to convince other people to think as they do. At the very least, they want others to consider sharing their point of view. If these people can't be bothered supporting their opinions with relevant facts and reasons, you might think twice, not just about sharing the opinions they express, but also about whether you want to read more of what they write.

✔ CHECK YOUR UNDERSTANDING

1. What's the difference between informed and uninformed opinions?

_____

_____

_____

2. Explain the difference between relevant and irrelevant supporting details.

_____

_____

3. Why are statements of connection important to relevant supporting details?

_____

4. Should you judge uninformed opinions expressed in conversation in the same way you judge them in writing? _____ Please explain.

_____

_____

_____

_____

◆ **EXERCISE 4**   **Recognizing Informed and Uninformed Opinions**

DIRECTIONS In each of the following passages, the opinion the writer wants to express has been underlined. In the blank that follows, write an *I* if you think the writer expresses an informed opinion supported by relevant details. Write a *U* if you think the author has not adequately supported his or her opinion.

1. Diversity on the Supreme Court?

1   When Barack Obama tapped Solicitor General Elena Kagan to replace the retiring Supreme Court Justice John Paul Stevens, several pundits* were concerned that Kagan was, like Sonia Sotomayor, a woman with no children. Others wondered if the Court didn't need a Protestant judge since, with Stevens's retirement, the Supreme Court would be without a single Protestant. But for some reason, far fewer news analysts highlighted what is a much more worrisome omission on the Supreme Court: diversity of academic background.

2   Look over the résumés of U.S. Supreme Court justices and you'll think that the Ivy League is apparently the only place to find qualified judges, despite the fact that law schools at Notre Dame University, George Washington University, and the University of Texas are ranked among the nation's top twenty-five schools of law. Yet diversity in academic training is important because the Supreme Court justices are somewhat detached from the concerns of ordinary life to begin with. That tendency is then compounded by presidents who repeatedly choose justices with the same or very similar academic backgrounds. As legal scholar and law professor Jonathan Turley succinctly expresses it, "The high court is a cloistered[†] enough institution as it is—so why risk making it even more detached from the rest of us by turning it into a Harvard–Yale Law Review[†] reunion." (Source of quotation: Tim Padgett, "Is the Supreme Court Too Packed with Ivy Leaguers?" Time.com.)

———

————

*pundits: public sources of opinion, people who give an opinion through the mass media and who, allegedly, are knowledgeable about the topic discussed.
[†]cloistered: a cloister is a monastery or convent, but in this case the word is used figuratively, rather than realistically, to mean isolated or set apart from the public.
[†]Law Review: a scholarly journal published by law school students. To be selected to be on the Law Review is a huge honor.

2. Global Warming False Alarms

1   Every year it seems that the public is treated to another alarmist report about the desperate state the planet is in. We are warned that New York City may sink beneath floodwaters, while Austin, Texas, may be set aflame by out-of-control forest fires that spread across the state. Many people are frightened by these warnings. As a result, they willingly accept the new legislation, new taxes, and new studies paid for with the taxpayer dollars that these doom and gloom prophecies invariably generate. For a long time, those of us who challenged the reality of global warming were treated with contempt. But now we have proof that we were not wrong. It was the true believers who were mistaken. Global warming is, indeed, a hoax.

2   A slew of anonymous email messages have been posted on the Web by an anonymous hacker. What those largely anonymous emails show is that those scientists claiming global warming is upon us and bringing with it chaos and death are worried about how best to frame their message so the public will accept it. They are worried, that is, about using the right PR to get their message out. As journalist James Delingpole says, "If you're going to bomb the global economy back to the dark ages with environmental tax and regulation . . . then at the very least you owe it to the world to base your policies on sound, transparent, evidence-based science rather than on politicized . . . junk." (Quotation from James Delingpole, "Uh Oh, Global Warming Looms: Here Comes Climategate II" http://blogs.telegraph.co.uk/news/jamesdelingpole/100119087/uh-oh-global-warming-loons-here-comes-climategate-ii/.)

------

3. Questioning the Value of Grief Counseling

1   Whenever there is a tragedy, grief counselors rush to the scene to offer their services. Generally, this act is applauded as a public service. Most people take on faith the idea that grief counseling is helpful, particularly when death is sudden and unexpected. We also assume that grief counseling helps people who have experienced the loss of a loved one in ordinary circumstances. But is grief counseling in either context really necessary? Probably not. The truth is, grief counseling does more harm than good.

2   Think about it. When people experienced the death of family, friends, or colleagues fifty years ago, grief counseling did not exist. Yet its absence did not mean that everyone affected by the loss of a friend, loved one, or co-worker was unable to stop grieving. Grief does abate* with time after all, so

------
*abate: cease, stop.

what's the matter with letting nature take its course? Grieving is a normal process. It's about adjusting to the loss of a loved one. Although it's a cliché to say it, time does heal all wounds. Time can heal the misery of grief without the help of grief counselors.

_____

4. Mozart Has No Effect

1   Although the so-called Mozart effect has been widely accepted by many educators, parents, legislators, and music marketers, it doesn't stand up very well under close examination. In fact, if anything, new evidence suggests that the Mozart effect does not exist.

2   In 1993, researchers at the University of Wisconsin claimed that college students who listened to ten minutes of a Mozart sonata prior to taking a spatial*-reasoning test significantly improved their ability to perform tasks such as cutting and folding paper. This study gave birth to the belief that listening to Mozart's music helps increase intelligence. However, researchers have not been able to duplicate the results of this first experiment. As a matter of fact, a Harvard University graduate student analyzed the conclusions of sixteen similar studies and found no scientific proof that music increased IQ or improved academic performance. Researchers at Appalachian State University and two Canadian universities have come to the same conclusion.

_____

5. Celia Cruz, the Queen of Latin Music

1   The legendary queen of salsa Celia Cruz (1925–2003) had a long and influential career that had an impact on both American music and culture. During her half-century career, the Cuban-born Cruz recorded more than seventy albums and traveled all over the world, entertaining four generations of fans with her extraordinary voice and flamboyant performances. Cruz's music helped define salsa, an Afro-Cuban musical style characterized by Latin rhythms. The singer also received numerous awards and honors— including the prestigious National Medal of Arts, a Grammy Award, and an honorary doctorate degree from Yale University—all in recognition of her contributions to encouraging the acceptance of cultural diversity.

2   Just as important, Cruz is widely credited with helping to break down racial and cultural barriers in the United States. Through her voice and

_____

*spatial: related to location in space.

Celia Cruz was an influential musical figure—in her native country of Cuba, in her adopted country, the United States, and all around the world.

AP Photo/Kevork Djansezian

magnetic personality, she won a mainstream audience over to Latin music. Thus it seems only appropriate that one of Cruz's gowns, a wig, and a pair of her shoes are part of the permanent collection of the National Museum of American History. She was an entertainer who brought cultures together and through her music gave them a common ground. Proud of her accomplishments, Cruz always credited them to her father, saying, "In a sense, I have fulfilled my father's wish to be a teacher as through my music, I teach generations of people about my culture."

————

What Do You Think?

◆

Do you think shared music can break down cultural barriers and bring people together?

Checking for Relevance in Longer Readings

As readings get longer, readers have to become even more vigilant. Sometimes writers start with relevant facts and reasons that support their position. But they end up drifting off and piling up details that add little more than length to the reading. Is that what happens in this example?

Walter Hickel's Transformation

What does the title suggest readers should look for?

1 In the early days of his political career in Washington, Walter Hickel, the former Alaskan governor and Secretary of the Interior, who died in 2010, was considered a foe of environmentalists. Environmental activists were furious when Richard Nixon selected Hickel in 1968. They fought hard to defeat his confirmation. Prior to becoming Nixon's choice for Secretary of the Interior, Hickel had aroused conservationists' ire by suggesting that they were mindlessly protecting every plant and creature in nature while at the same time ignoring human concerns. He was, as he put it, opposed to those who believed in "conservation for conservation's sake."

How did Hickel start out?

2 But when a Chevron Oil platform caught fire in the Gulf of Mexico in 1970, pouring more than 40,000 barrels of oil into the gulf, Hickel was outraged by the company's failure to have a response plan ready for such an event and determined to make sure the company cleaned up the mess. He was equally determined to make sure that similar environmental disasters would be avoided in the future. His response to the platform fire and oil spill in the Gulf of Mexico made Hickel a hero to environmentalists.

Notice the reversal transition opening paragraph 2. This signals the change in Hickel might be coming up.

What changed and why?

3 They cheered when Hickel demanded an investigation and were delighted when he also insisted that the Justice Department charged Chevron with 900 violations of the Outer Continental Shelf Lands Act of 1953. Truly disgusted by the scope of the environmental disaster Chevron had created, Hickel wrote regulations designed to control offshore drilling and make the oil industry financially responsible for any blowouts or spills that occurred.

4 During his twenty-two-month tenure as the Secretary of the Interior, Hickel also led a successful campaign to stop the construction of a jetport in the Everglades, wrote legislation protecting endangered alligators and whales, and published the names of companies that were polluting the country's rivers and lakes with mercury. In addition, he proposed banning billboards on federal lands and enthusiastically supported making Earth Day a national holiday.

Paragraph 4 provides Hickel with more environmentalist credentials.

But what's
going wrong in
paragraph 5?

5   Hickel was also admired because he bluntly told his boss, President
Richard M. Nixon, that he was badly mismanaging youthful opposition to
the Vietnam War. Nixon did not appreciate the advice. Shortly after voicing
his criticism of presidential policy, Hickel was dismissed as Secretary of the
Interior.

6   Those opposed to the war loved Hickel for his stand-up attitude. The
president of the United States, however, did not share the public's affection
for his outspoken Secretary of the Interior. Nixon sent Hickel back home,
where he ran for governor four times before finally winning in 1990.

Until paragraph 5, the reasons and facts used to support the claim that
Walter Hickel's reputation among environmentalists was transformed
are tightly connected to the controlling main idea. By paragraph 5,
however, the author starts losing sight of that overall main idea. Instead
of Hickel's growing reputation as an environmentalist hero, the author
talks about the secretary's disapproval of how Richard Nixon handled
the peace movement. That information doesn't support the reading's
opening opinion. Both paragraphs 5 and 6 include details not really relevant to the author's opinion.

If it turns out that a writer does include some irrelevant details in a
reading, that doesn't mean you should completely dismiss the author's
opinion as uninformed. It does mean, however, that you should double-
check how opinion and support match up throughout the selection. If
the author included one irrelevant detail, there might be more.

◆ **EXERCISE 5**   **Checking for Relevance in Longer Readings**

DIRECTIONS   Read each selection and underline the opinion being put
forth. Then write *R* or *I* in the blank at the end. *R* indicates that all the facts
and reasons are relevant. *I* indicates that you spotted one or more irrelevant
facts or reasons. If you write *I* in the first blank, indicate on the blank below
what reason or fact you consider irrelevant along with the paragraph number in which it appears. Leave that blank empty if all the details are related
to the opinion that forms the controlling idea of the reading.

1. **Emphasis on Sound Nutrition Trumps Common Sense**

1   In his quest to improve the health of New York City's residents, Mayor
Michael R. Bloomberg has come up with some excellent ideas. Except for
diehard smokers, most people in New York City rejoiced at the ordinance*

———————
*ordinance: rule or regulation.

banning cigarette smoking in bars and restaurants. In addition, follow-up studies of the air in restaurants and bars showed an 85 percent drop in nicotine by-products. No one worried about the deadly effects of second-hand smoke can quarrel with that result.

2   However, in 2012, the health-conscious mayor went overboard in his efforts to legislate good health and showed again what many have complained of in the past: The mayor is out of touch with the needs of the poor. As a multi-millionaire, the mayor just doesn't understand what life is like for poor people. This time around, Bloomberg's good intentions combined with lack of empathy for those less fortunate than himself have led the mayor seriously astray.

3   The mayor, you see, has placed a ban on food donations to homeless shelters. What's the reason for the ban? Well, it's not worries about the donations being contaminated by dangerous bacteria like E. coli or salmonella. What worries the mayor is that people forced to rely on homeless shelters to stay warm and get food supplies might end up consuming food that doesn't properly limit salt and trans fats while including healthy doses of fiber. Yes, you read that correctly. The mayor is worried that people who might well be starving could get fed with food that doesn't have the proper nutritional content. While this concern makes perfect sense for those people with enough money to overindulge in food that will, in the years to come, probably injure their health, it seems downright loony in relation to people whose stomach pains stem from lack of any food, never mind food that's bad for them.

4   In addition to having his ban on food donations lambasted by homeless advocates from all over the city, the Bloomberg administration received an additional blow to its efforts to help the poor when the new numbers on homelessness in New York were published. A 2012 survey registered 41,000 people using homeless shelters for a place to sleep. Prior to 2012, the people sleeping in homeless shelters had never gone over 40,000.

———

——————————————————————————————————

——————————————————————————————————

2. **Getting Smart**

1 For decades now, there have been numerous much-publicized claims that intelligence was inherited, with books like Arthur Jensen's *The g Factor* (1998) and Charles Murray and Richard Herrnstein's *The Bell Curve* (1994) fueling debate over which contributes more to intelligence, genetic inheritance or environmental training and experience. Both books suggest, and in some chapters insist, that nature, or genetic inheritance, plays an overwhelming role in the development of human intelligence, at least as it's measured by IQ tests.

2 In his 2009 book *Intelligence and How to Get It: Why Schools and Cultures Count*, the esteemed cognitive psychologist Richard E. Nisbett begs to differ. Nisbett has looked closely at the research supporting heritability claims, and doesn't find it or the claims convincing. Nisbett is, however, enthusiastic about studies suggesting that a child's environment and personal character are crucial influences on the development of intelligence. These studies suggest that genes are less important than the context or environment in which a child is raised, and they provide the basis for the carefully argued and altogether convincing thesis of his book.

3 From Nisbett's point of view, studies showing that identical twins, after being separated and raised miles apart, often have similar IQ levels are not especially compelling evidence, even though, in the past, such studies were cited to prove the role of genetic inheritance in intelligence. Nisbett insists that twins participating in such studies are usually raised by parents belonging to the same social class. Thus each twin was almost always given similar intellectual and cultural advantages or, for that matter, disadvantages, a fact that could just as easily account for the similarity in IQ scores.

4 Unfortunately, people are all too readily beguiled* by the subject of twins, largely because there is so much popular folklore* surrounding their existence. There are stories of twins who felt one another's physical pain when one of them fell ill or was injured and even more tales of twins who lived in different cities yet somehow managed to buy the exact same dress or suit. This common lore about the mystical* connection between twins may be one reason why identical-twin studies have made such an impression on the public's mind.

5 In making his point about the way environment shapes intelligence as much as or more than genes, Nisbett eventually moves away from twin

---

*beguiled: fascinated.
*folklore: accumulated facts, traditions, knowledge, often with the implication of being informally learned or acquired.
*mystical: spiritual, mysterious.

studies to talk about the relationship between personal traits and intellectual achievement. As he sees it, parents who raise their children to have the right mindset about learning—that is, to be self-disciplined and exert impulse control—are doing their kids a huge favor. In support of this belief, Nisbett cites the work of psychologists Martin Seligman and Angela Duckworth.

6   Duckworth and Seligman studied student achievement in an effort to determine which factor was a bigger predictor of success, a child's IQ score or an ability to be focused and self-disciplined about completing tasks. What they found was that IQ was not nearly as good a predictor of academic success as the presence of what Nisbett calls "strong self-discipline."

7   As he puts it, "If you had to choose for your child a high IQ or strong self-discipline, you might be wise to pick the latter." Self-discipline, of course, is not a characteristic that's inherited; it's something we learn by example and experience. Thus studies like the ones performed by Duckworth and Seligman go a long way toward proving Nisbett's claim that our environment—that is, how we are raised and what we experience—is the main ticket to getting smart. (Source of quotation: Richard Nisbett, *Intelligence and How to Get It: Why Schools and Cultures Count*. W.W. Norton, 2010, p. 17.)

_____

_____

_____

What Do You Think?
◆

Why did Richard Nisbett subtitle his book "Why Schools and Cultures Count"?

ALLUSION ALERT

- -

Tweedledee and Tweedledum

Numerous allusions revolve around twins. But perhaps the most famous of them is the allusion to the twins Tweedledee and Tweedledum. Although the twins made an appearance in early English nursery rhymes, their true claim to fame comes from their appearance in Lewis Carroll's book *Through the Looking Glass and What Alice Found There*, which tells the story of Alice in Wonderland. They also appeared in the Walt Disney and Tim Burton movies about Alice's trip to Wonderland.

The two brothers are almost always portrayed as identical, even mimicking one another's speech. Thus allusions to them suggest that the two topics under discussion, despite any outward signs of difference, are exactly the same—for instance, "Ralph Nader was widely quoted when he referred to the Democratic and Republican Parties as Tweedledee and Tweedledum."

The twins Tweedledee and Tweedledum are often used to suggest that two seemingly different people, ideas, or groups are really exactly the same.

AF archive/Alamy

 WEB QUEST   Another Twin Allusion

Use the Internet to find answers to these questions: According to Roman mythology, the founders of Rome were twins. What were their names? Who was nursing them when they were discovered? Who was alleged to be their father?

Separate Fact and Opinion in Textbooks

Many students assume that textbook writers restrict themselves to facts and avoid expressing any opinions. Although that may be true for some science texts, it's not true for textbooks in general, particularly in the areas of psychology, history, and government.

Look, for example, at the following passage, where the author describes Americans in 1952:

> In 1952, Americans wanted a change of pace, not radical change. They had learned to live with the Cold War; they had no choice. They wanted out of Korea, where soldiers were dying daily for reasons the Democrats could not persuasively explain. . . . Ordinary people were weary of reformers' moral demands—and the sacrifices the war had required. They wanted to kick back and taste the fruits of living in the world's richest nation. (Joseph Conlin, *The American Past* 9e, vol. II, © Cengage Learning.)

This description of the country in the early fifties may be absolutely accurate. But we will never know for sure since there is no way to determine what all Americans were thinking or feeling in 1952. Statements about Americans as a whole are pretty much impossible to verify. In other words, this is not a factual description of the country at that time. It's an opinion or personal interpretation of many different events and millions of people.

That's not to say, though, that the author is trying to trick you. He's just offering you his version of what the public's mood was in the early fifties. Another history author might focus more on the political tensions in the fifties[†] and describe this period as a time of anxiety. Neither author would be engaging in deception. Rather, each one would be offering you his or her opinion on the most significant social trends of the times. That's the thing about opinions; they are shaped by personal perspective, which is why they can vary so much.

Opinions in textbooks are almost always present when the writer is talking about human behavior. The presence of opinions in textbooks is not a problem. It only becomes a problem if readers unknowingly absorb the opinions, right along with the facts.

[†]The fifties were a period when the United States and the Soviet Union seemed to be locked in a cold war, and Senator Joseph McCarthy was accusing innocent people of Communist sympathies.

Check That Opinions Are Backed by Supporting Details

To illustrate how widespread opinions are in textbooks, here's an excerpt from a sociology text. Read the passage. As you do, keep asking yourself which statements are factual and which express an opinion. In the blank after each sentence, put an *F* for fact, an *O* for opinion, or a *B* for a blend of both.

What does the phrase *may be as good* suggest about sentence 1?

[1]Examining the experience of those who divorce may be as good a way as any to see how much our married self becomes part of our deepest self. _____ [2]When people separate or divorce, many feel as if

Can the information in sentence 2 be verified?

they have "lost an arm or a leg." _____ [3]This comparison, as well as the traditional marriage rite in which a man and a woman are pronounced "one," reveals an important truth about marriage: the constant association of both partners makes each almost a physical part of the other.

Can statement 3 be proved "true"?

_____ [4]This is true even if two people are locked in conflict; they too are attached to each other (Masheter 1991). _____ (Adapted from Bryan Strong et al., *The Marriage and Family Experience* 11e, © Cengage Learning.)

If you filled in the blanks with the letters *O* and *B*, you are good at telling fact from opinion. You have also learned something important about textbooks, especially textbooks devoted to history, sociology, and psychology. They do not deal in pure fact. Often there's plenty of opinion threaded through the explanations they provide.

However, the more you think about the difference between facts and opinions, and the more experienced you become at spotting the difference, the more you will see that textbooks differ in the degree that they balance fact and opinion. And the balance is what really counts. When authors present you with opinions, they should also provide reasons or factual evidence.

The previous excerpt offered only one study as support for the authors' claims about marriage and divorce. Compare that paragraph to the one below, which also starts off with an opinion: The effects of diversity on groups are very mixed. That's an opinion because those who champion diversity might disagree, saying that the weight of research falls on the side of its importance. In contrast, those who don't think diversity in groups is so critical might argue that the results of the research are decidedly negative rather than mixed. Look how these authors handle the fact that they are presenting readers with an opinion:

[1]The evidence from group empirical research concerning the effects of diversity on group performance is decidedly mixed (Hackman, 2010; Mannix & Neale, 2005; van Knippenberg & Schippers, 2007). [2]On the one hand, diversity is often associated with negative group dynamics (Levine & Moreland, 1998; Maznevski, 1994). [3]Miscommunication and misunderstandings are more likely to arise among heterogeneous group members, causing frustration and resentment and damaging group performance by weakening coordination, morale, and commitment to the group. [4]Cliques often form in diverse groups, causing some group members to feel alienated. [5]On the other hand, research has also demonstrated positive effects of diversity, like increased socialization and complexity of group discussions (Antonia et al., 2004; Juvonen et al., 2006). [6]Samuel Sommers (2006) found that racially diverse juries exchanged a wider range of information, cited more facts about the case being decided, and made fewer errors in their deliberations* than racially homogeneous juries. (Adapted from Saul Kassin et al., *Social Psychology* 8e, © Cengage Learning.)

In this example, the authors identify the studies on which their opinion is based and define some of the plusses and minuses of diversity that make them consider the research results "mixed." In general, this is what you should expect textbook authors to do when they offer opinions or interpretations of events that might well vary from person to person.

◆ **EXERCISE 6**   **Detecting Textbook Opinions**

DIRECTIONS   Read each textbook passage. Fill in the blank at the end with an *F* to indicate that the passage is purely factual or a *B* to indicate that opinions are blended in with the facts. Underline as well any words that you think give away the presence of opinions.

1. Voting is only one way of participating in politics. It is important (we could hardly be considered a democracy if nobody voted), but it is not all-important. Joining civic associations, writing to legislators, fighting city hall—all these and other activities are ways of participating in politics. It is possible that, by these measures, Americans

---

*deliberations: forming of careful judgments; efforts to think carefully before coming to conclusions.

participate in politics more than most Europeans—or anybody else, for that matter. Moreover, it is possible that low rates of registration indicate that people are reasonably well satisfied with how the country is governed. If 100 percent of all adult Americans registered and voted, it could mean that people were deeply upset about how things were run. In short, it is not at all clear whether low voter turnout is a symptom of political disease or a sign of political good health. (Adapted from James Q. Wilson and John J. DiIulio, *American Government* 11e, © Cengage Learning.)

———

2. Methaqualone was first synthesized in 1951 in India, where it was introduced as an antimalarial drug but found to be ineffective. At the same time, its sedating effects resulted in its introduction in Great Britain as a safe . . . sleeping pill. The substance subsequently found its way into street abuse; a similar sequence of events occurred in Germany and Japan. In 1965, methaqualone was introduced into the United States as the prescription drugs Sopors and Quaalude. It was not listed as a scheduled (controlled) drug. By the early 1970s, "ludes" and "sopors" were part of the drug culture. Physicians prescribed the drug for anxiety and insomnia, believing that it was safer than barbiturates. Thus the supplies for street sales came primarily from legitimate sources. (Adapted from Howard Abadinsky, *Organized Crime* 8e, © Cengage Learning.)

———

3. People who filter daily experiences through a negative attitude tend to focus on what is going wrong and find it difficult to achieve contentment or satisfaction in any aspect of their lives. It makes no difference how attractive, intelligent, or skilled they are; their attitude holds them back. (Barry L Reece and Rhonda Brandt., *Effective Human Relations in Organizations* 8e, © Cengage Learning.)

———

4. Filipinos began settling in the Yakima River Valley around 1918–1920. The majority of those who settled there became agricultural laborers. By the late 1920s, there were many who worked on truck farms, in orchards, and in packinghouses. Some leased plots for independent farming. . . . If Filipinos were going to settle in the Yakima River Valley, they had to secure work within agriculture; Yakima was a single-economy region. By 1927, Filipinos had engendered the resentment of many whites who viewed them as competitive sources of labor. So deep was the anti-Filipino animosity that mob attacks took place the same year. Filipinos were attacked wherever vigilante groups encountered them. Some Filipinos were even assaulted in their homes, while others were forcibly rounded up and placed on outbound trains. (Sucheng Chan et al., *Peoples of Color in the American West,* © Cengage Learning.)

———

5. Most authorities agree that there is room for improvement in business ethics. A more problematic question is: Can business be made more ethical in the real world? The majority opinion on this issue suggests that government, trade associations, and individual firms indeed can establish acceptable levels of ethical behavior. The government can encourage ethical behavior by legislating more stringent regulations. For example, the landmark Sarbanes-Oxley Act of 2002 provides sweeping new legal protection for those who report corporate misconduct.... Among other things, the law deals with corporate responsibility, conflict of interest, and corporate accountability. However, rules require enforcement, and the unethical businessperson frequently seems to "slip something by" without getting caught. Increased regulation may help, but it surely cannot solve the entire ethics problem. (William M. Pride et al., *Business* 10e,© Cengage Learning.)

———

WORD CHECK

The following words were introduced and defined in pages 496–517. See how well you can match the words with the meanings. When you finish, make sure to check the meanings of any words you missed because the same words will turn up in a test at the end of the chapter.

1. meticulous (p. 496) _____
2. solicitation (p. 501) _____
3. pundits (p. 505) _____
4. abate (p. 506) _____
5. spatial (p. 507) _____
6. ordinance (p. 510) _____
7. beguiled (p. 512) _____
8. folklore (p. 512) _____
9. mystical (p. 512) _____
10. deliberations (p. 517) _____

a. related to location in space
b. rule or regulation
c. fascinated, enchanted
d. accumulated facts, traditions, knowledge, often with the implication of being informally learned or acquired
e. spiritual, mysterious
f. forming careful judgments; efforts to think carefully before coming to conclusions
g. very careful, precise, focused
h. the act of approaching someone for sexual or monetary purposes; to persuasively ask for something other than money or sex, e.g., votes or information
i. public sources of opinion, people who give an opinion through the mass media and who, allegedly, are knowledgeable about the topic discussed
j. cease, stop

◆ **EXERCISE 7**   **More About Form and Meaning**

DIRECTIONS Fill in the blanks with one of the words listed below.

pundits	mystical	meticulous	beguiled	folklore
soliciting	abate	ordinances	deliberating	spatial

1. People newly in love find it easy to be _____ by one another; the trick is to have the same ability after twenty years together.

2. Judges, scholars, and scientists are all capable of _____ long and hard before arriving at their conclusions.

3. Those who are incapable of being _____ in their attention to detail should give up any dreams of being programmers, because where software code is concerned, details really count.

4. Architects have to be good at imagining different _____ relations among forms.

5. It seems that the more a town needs to raise money, the more _____ there are with financial penalties attached.

6. How is it that many political _____ can consistently get everything wrong yet still be seen on television giving their opinion?

7. According to herbal _____, echinacea can reduce the length of the common cold.

8. Anyone with a toothache prays for it to _____.

9. The owners of the house received a letter _____ information about the former tenants.

10. People expect to have _____ feelings in places of worship, but similar feelings can also occur out of doors.

TAKING STOCK   What Exactly Is a Frivolous Lawsuit?

Looking Ahead   Close to twenty years ago, Stella Liebeck spilled a cup of McDonald's coffee on her skin and as a result of her injuries, she sued the company and won over $2 million in damages.[†] That lawsuit, however, became grist for a nationwide movement pushing for "tort reform." The claim was that frivolous lawsuits were hurting the country economically and socially, and damage awards resulting from lawsuits should be dramatically reduced.

1   The lawsuit seventy-nine-year-old Stella Liebeck launched against McDonald's in 1994 after spilling hot coffee on herself as she went through the drive-through lane immediately became the stuff of comedy. A *Seinfeld*[†] episode had a character sue for damages after he spilled coffee on himself. But the general attitude toward the suit, on television and off, was summed up in the response of another *Seinfeld* character, Elaine, who expressed puzzlement at the very idea of a lawsuit involving hot coffee being spilled and McDonald's being somehow liable: "Who ever heard of this anyway? Suing a company because their coffee is too hot? Coffee is supposed to be hot."

2   What got left out of all the jokes, though, were the actual details of the case. Liebeck suffered third-degree burns, which are the most serious kind, especially for a woman her age. Plus, there had been at least 700 previous cases of people being scalded by McDonald's coffee before Liebeck went to court. McDonald's had settled other claims but did not want to give Liebeck the $20,000 compensation she had requested. The case went to court.

3   What Liebeck's lawyers proved was that McDonald's was making its coffee 30 to 50 degrees hotter than other restaurants. In fact, the Shriner's Burns Institute had already warned McDonald's not to serve coffee above 130 degrees. Yet the liquid that burned Liebeck was the usual temperature for McDonald's brew—about 190 degrees. As a result of Liebeck's suit, McDonald's coffee is now sold at the same temperature as most other restaurants.

4   Yes, trivial lawsuits are probably filed on a regular basis. But Liebeck's wasn't one of them. It's actually ironic that the "hot coffee" lawsuit, as it's come to be called, is often cited as an illustration of why the country desperately needs tort reform. Yet a closer examination of this issue suggests that citizens might want to think twice before joining in the chorus of calls to enact tort reform.

[†]The judge reduced the amount to $.5 million.
[†]*Seinfeld* was a popular sitcom that aired between 1989 and 1998.

5   Tort reform legislation, in place or pending, differs from state to state. Thus one of the questions involved in the debate is how tort reform should go forward. Should it be on a state or federal level?

6   In general, though, the tort reform movement focuses on three goals: (1) the need to limit the circumstances under which injured people may file a lawsuit after being injured by a product or procedure, (2) the goal of making it more difficult for people injured by a product or procedure to obtain a trial by jury, and (3) the desire to place limits on the amount of money injured parties may be awarded.

7   In the eyes of some, like political activist and organizer Jon Greenbaum, the need for tort reform is a myth. From his perspective, the right to sue corporations or companies if their products were defective or their procedures badly managed or fraudulent was a consumer victory won in the 1950s, and now is no time to abandon that right. In his eyes, tort reform would be a step backward for consumers, not a step forward: "It will limit our ability to hold corporations accountable for their misdeeds. Corporate America has succeeded to a great extent in buying up our legislators and capturing regulatory bodies. We must not let them wrest control of the judicial system as well."

8   That, however, would not be the position of Court Koenning, the president of Citizens Against Lawsuit Abuse of Houston. For him, lawsuits demanding compensation for injury due to defective products or procedures reveal a growing canker on American society—the abdication of personal responsibility. As he writes, "The 'somebody's gotta pay' attitude is pervasive and that does not bode well for future generations. We need to reacquaint ourselves with personal responsibility and stop playing the blame game. We need to realize that every dilemma or personal disappointment is not fodder for a lawsuit and does not warrant a treasure trove of cash."

9   These are all stirring sentiments. But they need to be viewed in the light of what consumers "playing the blame game" in court have actually tried to accomplish. In Los Angeles, California, consumers have gone to court to stop health insurers from cancelling polices of people newly diagnosed with a serious illness. The insurance cancellations, usually based on technicalities, seem to target people who will require long-term and expensive care, for which the insurance companies would have to pay if the policies weren't cancelled.

10   In Harrisburg, Pennsylvania, consumers went to court to take action against "mortgage rescue" companies who, for a fee, claimed they could help those falling behind on their payments. After the fee was paid, the help was not forthcoming. In Hartford, Connecticut, consumers also went to

court against a pharmaceutical company that was blocking generic alternatives to the high-priced drugs on which the company's profits were based.

11   This is not to say that all personal injury complaints taken to court are worthy of respect. Did anyone really want to see the woman who sued a cosmetics company for changing the shade of her hair become a millionaire? But many of the personal injury lawsuits brought by consumers do real good, helping not just the litigant but the public in general. We might want to consider that fact next time we hear or read another argument advocating tort reform because what we might be reforming is our own right to seek justice by legal means. (Source of quotations: www.setexasrecord.com/ arguments/226869-starbucks-hot-tea-lawsuit-highlights-a-void-in-personal-responsibility; Jon Greenbaum, "McDonald's Hot Coffee Lawsuit and Beyond: The Tort Reform Myth Machine," CommonDreams.org.)

Sharpening Your Skills

DIRECTIONS   Answer the following questions by circling the letter of the correct response or filling in the blanks.

Paraphrasing the Controlling Main Idea

1. Which of the following statements accurately paraphrases the main idea of the reading?

    a. The movement for tort reform is spreading throughout the country, thanks to the frivolous lawsuits that have been waged over the last few decades; they are clogging the system and something needs to be done to put an end to them.

    b. Consumers who take their concerns to court should be praised rather than criticized for their efforts; personal injury lawsuits have never done anything but good.

    c. While some personal injury claims may be worthless, many are necessary to hold corporations and companies accountable for their actions, and we should think twice about supporting tort reform.

    d. The tort reform movement is in control of the country's big corporations, and it is yet another way to deny citizens their right to social justice.

**Recognizing the
Author's Purpose**

2. The author's purpose is

  a. to inform readers about the tort reform movement's history and goals.

  b. to tell readers about Stella Liebeck's suit against McDonald's.

  c. to persuade readers that the tort reform movement has some serious drawbacks.

  d. to persuade readers that there is no such thing as a frivolous lawsuit.

**Spotting Transitional
Signals**

3. In paragraph 2, what transitional signal does the author use to reverse the previous paragraph's train of thought? _____

**Analyzing Sentence
Functions**

4. In paragraph 4, the first sentence is

  a. an introductory sentence.

  b. a transitional sentence.

  c. a topic sentence.

Paraphrasing

5. Paraphrase the three goals of the tort reform movement.

  1. _____

  2. _____

  3. _____

**Using Repetition
and Reference**

6. What idea does "That" refer to at the beginning of paragraph 8?

  _____

  _____

**Inferring Main
Ideas**

7. What is the implied main idea of paragraph 9?

  _____

  _____

Using Repetition and Reference

8. What word in paragraph 11 provides a link to paragraph 10?

_____ That word represents what from the previous paragraph?

_____

Understanding the Difference Between Fact and Opinion

9. At the end of paragraph 11, the author says, "We might want to consider that fact." In your own words, what does the word *fact* refer to?

_____

Does the word *fact* actually refer to a fact? _____ Please explain your answer.

_____

_____

Summarizing

10. Which summary of paragraphs 9 and 10 better fits the criteria outlined on pp. 523–524.

a. Consumers who want to play the blame game have gone to court repeatedly over trivial issues. This is particularly true in California, where consumers brought lawsuits against mortgage rescue companies that asked a fee for helping those who had gotten behind in their mortgage payments. When the fee got paid, no help was forthcoming.

b. Critics who argue that consumer lawsuits illustrate a failure of responsibility are ignoring the important goals of some consumer lawsuits. In California, for example, consumers used the courts to stop insurance companies from cancelling the policies of those who got a serious illness. In Pennsylvania, they took legal action against mortgage rescue companies that provided no rescue.

WEB QUEST   **Defining Product Liability**

What does the term *product liability* mean?

_____

_____

REVIEWING THROUGH WRITING

Use the Web to find at least three websites that describe product liability lawsuits in detail. Then make two lists, one describing the pros, the other the cons of such suits. Decide which view you consider most convincing and write an editorial-like paper that you think might convince other people to be for or against the tort reform that would place strict limits on such lawsuits. Start your paper with your opinion on tort reform, but make sure to provide factual evidence about cases that illustrate *why* you think consumers should or should not turn to the courts for compensation if they are injured through the use of a product. Here's one website that does a great job summing up the pros and cons: www.scu.edu/ethics/publications/iie/v4n1/pay.html. Now you need only find two others.

▶ **TEST 1**   **Distinguishing Between Fact and Opinion**

DIRECTIONS   Label each of the following statements *F* for fact, *O* for opinion, or *B* for a blend of both.

_____   1. As George Orwell so correctly said, "The great enemy of clear language is insincerity."

_____   2. Among people suffering from depression, one portion of the brain is significantly smaller than the other.

_____   3. The planet Neptune was discovered in 1846 by the German astronomer Johann G. Galle.

_____   4. The devastating flooding that overwhelmed parts of Tennessee in May 2010 did not get nearly the media attention such a disaster deserved.

_____   5. The Mexican revolutionary Emiliano Zapata (1879–1919) had a profound influence on modern Mexico.

_____   6. Louise Brown, the world's first test-tube baby, was born on July 25, 1978.

_____   7. We should return to the days when films were made in black and white rather than color.

_____   8. Iraq has the world's second-largest reserves of crude oil.

_____   9. People who walk along the street with cell phones pressed to their ears are just trying to prove they have friends who want to talk to them.

_____ 10. The Centers for Disease Control and Prevention in Atlanta, Georgia, estimates that every year 48 million people are sickened by food-borne diseases.

▶ TEST 2   Checking for Relevance

DIRECTIONS Read each passage and underline the opinion being expressed. Write *R* or *I* in the blank at the end. *R* indicates that all the facts and reasons are relevant. *I* indicates that you spotted one or more irrelevant facts or reasons. If you write *I* in the blank, follow it with the number of the sentence or sentences introducing irrelevant facts or reasons.

1. [1]Even though Elvis Presley died on August 16, 1977, he is certainly not forgotten. [2]On the contrary, the legend of Elvis lives on. [3]To honor the twentieth anniversary of his death, RCA released a four-volume CD set, *Elvis Presley Platinum: A Life in Music.* [4]It was so popular that record stores couldn't keep it on the shelves. [5]In honor of that same anniversary, more than fifty thousand fans descended on Graceland, Elvis's Tennessee home. [6]*Elvis Lives, The Ultimate Tribute Artists Tour* still sells out coast to coast while sightings of Elvis, real and bogus, continue to be reported to this day. [7]Anyone who needs further proof that for many "The King" lives on in memory need only type his name into a search engine and sit back to watch the results pile up to well over 50 million.

_____

2. [1]Are you one of those people assuming that any produce or product bearing the word *organic* on the label has got to be better for you than produce lacking such a label? [2]If you are, you might want to think twice about automatically picking up higher-priced organic produce, meat, and dairy products because you want to avoid eating fruit sprayed with pesticides or meat containing antibiotics. [3]Unfortunately, the word *organic* on the label doesn't necessarily guarantee that fruits and vegetables have been grown or raised without pesticides and human-made fertilizers. [4]On the contrary, the meaning of the label *organic* varies from state to state. [5]Some states' certification programs allow organic produce to be grown with certain fertilizers and insecticides that other states specifically prohibit. [6]Remember, too, that there are three levels of claims behind organic food labels. [7]"100-percent organic" on a label means that the United States Department of Agriculture (USDA) has certified that the product has used no pesticides, antibiotics, or non-organic additives. [8]The plain label "organic," however, certifies that 95 percent of the ingredients used to create the product were organic. [9]The other 5 percent need not be. [10]The "made with organic ingredients" label does not get the USDA seal and this label appears when 70 percent of the ingredients used were organic. [11]That means at least one-third of the ingredients involved in growing the product could be antibiotics, pesticides, or growth hormones.

———

3. [1]In the wake of several recent cases of gun violence in schools, states would be wise to enact laws requiring public school teachers to be armed while in the classroom. [2]Many U.S. cities and towns are struggling with shrinking budgets, which often result in cutbacks in police and fire personnel. [3]These cutbacks translate into a longer response time if police are called to a potential crime scene in the schools, and this gives a gun-wielding attacker more time to slaughter innocent children and their instructors. [4]In the event of such a threat, gun-carrying teachers who have been properly trained would be able to prevent the fatalities that have occurred in too many school shootings. [5]Arming our educators would also serve to prevent these crimes from occurring in the first place, as criminals would be deterred by the possibility of encountering teachers armed with guns and ready to defend themselves and their students. [6]Furthermore, Americans need to stand up and demand that our Second Amendment right to bear arms be protected. [7]Sadly, today's society requires us to go beyond supplying our teachers with books, computers, pencils, and paper. [8]Give our teachers the tools they need not only to educate our children, but also to keep them safe: firearms.

———

4. [1]Autism is a brain disorder that is generally diagnosed when a child is between the ages of one and three. [2]As the disease takes its toll, the children have difficulties with speech, imaginative play, and interaction with others. [3]Despite claims to the contrary, the disease has become an epidemic. [4]In a landmark 2007 case, some 4,800 petitioners sued the federal government, claiming that ordinary vaccinations against childhood diseases had caused their children to develop autism. [5]As Roy Richard Grinker points out in his book *Unstrange Minds: Remapping the World of Autism*, psychiatrists have broadened the definition of autism making the term apply to more

people. [6]Because more people have been included in the definition of the disease, it is also more widely known, making more child psychiatrists prepared to diagnose it. [7]A 2004 study by the Institute of Medicine found no compelling evidence linking autism to childhood vaccines, but there are undoubtedly other environmental factors contributing to the epidemic that is claiming more and more victims. (Source of information: Richard Monastersky, "Is There an Autism Epidemic?" *Chronicle of Higher Education*, May 11, 2007, pp. A-24–27.)

———

5. [1]Given the number of people that suffer and even die from food poisoning every year, the safety of our food supply should be a concern for everyone. [2]To that end, the Food and Drug Administration (FDA) has been working for several years to implement tighter regulations designed to protect the U.S. food supply. [3]The current system of waiting until people have already fallen ill from eating contaminated food *before* opening an investigation is illogical. [4]The emphasis in food safety should be placed on prevention, so that bad food no longer sickens one out of six people every year. [5]Improved FDA food policies could also prevent close to 130,000 people from being hospitalized and 3,000 people from dying each year as the result of consuming tainted food. [6]Anti-government advocates who argue against any federal government "intrusion" on their lives may not realize it, but by ignoring these sobering statistics they are indirectly increasing the possibility that contaminated food will make its way to the market. [7]Let's hope the FDA's new guidelines will be strict enough to keep contaminated foods out of our stores and off our kitchen tables. [8]Too many people are suffering from diabetes because they are eating foods heavy with corn syrup and sugar, so we have to pay more attention to what we eat.

———

▶ **TEST 3**   **Checking for Relevance**

DIRECTIONS   Read each passage and underline the opinion being expressed. Write *R* or *I* in the blank at the end. *R* indicates that all the facts and reasons are relevant. *I* indicates that you spotted one or more irrelevant facts or reasons. If you write *I* in the blank, follow it with the number of the sentence or sentences introducing irrelevant facts or reasons.

1.   [1]The penny still plays several necessary roles, so Americans should not eliminate this coin as some pundits have been suggesting. [2]First, rendering the penny obsolete would hurt the poor. [3]Because merchants usually round up to the nearest nickel on cash purchases, lower-income Americans, who conduct most of their business using cash, would wind up paying more. [4]The non-profit organization Americans for Common Cents claims that rounding will cost consumers an additional $600 million a year. [5]Those who advocate keeping the penny also say that eliminating it would hurt charities because they collect millions of dollars in donated pennies. [6]Finally, the penny should remain in circulation because Americans are fond of it. [7]According to Americans for Common Cents, polls consistently show that up to 65 percent of Americans oppose getting rid of this coin.

_____

2.   [1]In the United States, the ability to speak Spanish can be an advantage personally and professionally. [2]The Hispanic population is growing rapidly. [3]As of 2011, the Hispanic population in the United States had surpassed 50 million. [4]In many communities, their numbers have doubled in the last decade, and in many cities and counties, even in states like Kansas, Hispanics now account for almost half the population. [5]Thirty-eight percent of all California residents are now Hispanic. [6]With this many Spanish-speaking neighbors, English-speaking citizens will see the Spanish language entering more and more into pop culture like television commercials and music. [7]Speaking Spanish will also be a tremendous asset in the workplace as increasing numbers of businesses seek to hire bilingual employees who can communicate with Hispanic customers. [8]In particular, professionals who interact with the public on a daily basis—such as law-enforcement officers and nurses—will benefit from knowing Spanish.

_____

3. [1]Titan Books has done a fabulous job of putting the artwork from two popular video games into digital books that cost only $9.99, *The Art of Dead Space* and *Awakening: The Art of Halo 4*. [2]Included in the books are not only gorgeous, high-resolution photos but information-rich videos that offer the artists' take on their creations. [3]If the world needed any more proof that those big, clumsy and expensive art books are a thing of the past, here it is in the form of these exquisite collections. [4]After all, it's a lot easier to carry around a digital reader than it is to tote around a heavy print art book. [5]Now that collections of artwork can be looked at in digital form, art books will no longer be relegated to the book shelf or coffee table and taken out only when one has the time to sit down and look at them. [6]In addition, art lovers will be overjoyed at being able to indulge their passion without having to pay the hefty prices charged for print books. [7]And for those who say the art images will be smaller in digital formats, just remind them that a little pinching or zooming can enlarge whatever features the reader might have trouble viewing. [8]*Dead Space* had many famous movie ancestors like *Alien* and *The Thing*, and it's no surprise that its graphics have made it an instant classic.

---

4. [1]The laws that prohibit convicted felons who have served out their sentences from voting are both inconsistent and unfair. [2]For starters, the laws vary significantly from state to state. [3]In some states, for instance, felons on parole can't vote, but those on probation can. [4]In other states, felons can apply to have their voting rights restored. [5]However, local governments can, without giving a reason, deny the application. [6]Unfortunately, the states that do restore felons' voting rights once their sentence has been served are not always efficient when it comes to notifying the men and women leaving prison that their voting rights have been restored. [7]Supporters of Al Gore insist that the removal of suspected felons from the voter rolls in Florida tipped the 2000 election scales in the direction of George W. Bush. [8]It's not surprising that several different appeal courts have ruled that taking away voting rights from those who have served time for a felony may well violate the Voting Rights Act of 1965.[†]

[†]On August 6, 1965, President Lyndon Johnson signed into law legislation designed to protect voters from discrimination by state governments that placed restrictions, conditions, or limitations on voting rights.

5. [1]Video bloggers, or vloggers, regularly record video diaries of their most intimate thoughts and feelings and put them on the Internet so that they can share them with the world. [2]This is just one more example of what Professor Jean Twenge of San Diego State University has correctly suggested in her study of today's college students: They belong to the most narcissistic generation in all of academic history. [3]While college students of a decade ago were obsessing about whether all the good jobs were disappearing, these kids are obsessing about how many hits their video got on YouTube or how many followers they have on Twitter. [4]Michael L. Wesch, an assistant professor of cultural anthropology at Kansas State University, has written a paper about social networking on the Web and, to test some of his ideas, he made a video and put it on YouTube. [5]Within a few weeks, Wesch's video had had more than two million hits and was a testament to the way the Internet is changing how we communicate. [6]Unfortunately, the Internet seems to be changing our notion of privacy as well, and more and more people are using it to discuss their childhood traumas along with their sexual triumphs and inadequacies. [7]Privacy is the last thing they are interested in. [8]Quite the contrary, their focus is on getting as much public attention as possible.

_____

▶ **TEST 4**   **Reviewing New Vocabulary**

DIRECTIONS Fill in the blanks with one of the words listed below.

meticulously	solicit	ordinances	beguiled	deliberated
mystical	abate	pundits	folklore	spatial

1. In 2009 when a resident of Wishek, North Dakota, erected a 39-foot wind turbine[†] in his backyard, he was fined for violating city

   _____ about structures erected in residential zones.

   The zoning laws said _____ restrictions needed to be carefully observed and the owner of the turbine had not done so.

   When the story broke, _____ on the right and left had a field day interpreting the events in Wishek. Those on the left praised the man for "going green" and preserving the environment. Those on the right insisted he should be allowed to do whatever he wanted with his own property.

2. The American psychologist Abraham Maslow coined the term *peak experiences* to describe _____ moments in life when a person, for no apparent reason, feels an intense sense of happiness. Although peak experiences are quick to _____, Maslow thought that some individuals could learn to induce and control the sensation to make it longer lasting. These longer-lasting sensations of being deeply happy and in tune with the world he called "plateau experiences." Certainly a good deal of religious

   _____ suggests that Maslow was correct in assuming that such spiritual moments do not have to be fleeting.

3. **In Darwin's Shadow**

   Already as a boy, the future naturalist Alfred Wallace was

   _____ by the world of plants and animals. As a young man, he decided to travel to faraway places to gather plants, animals, and insects for wealthy collectors. Wallace did not come

   _____
   [†]turbine: a machine powered by wind and capable of generating electricity.

from a well-to-do family. Collecting specimens for those with the money to pay his way was his only chance to do what he loved and still avoid ending up in one of England's notorious poorhouses.

While he was on his travels, Wallace _____ about the variety in the related plants and creatures he _____ collected and labeled for his clients. It wasn't long before he came up with virtually the same theory Charles Darwin[†] had developed to explain how plants and animals evolved, or changed over time. Darwin, however, was in constant contact with the most famous scholars of his time and could use their expertise to enhance and promote his ideas. Wallace was working alone. The one man he did _____ for help was the man he most admired, Charles Darwin. Unfortunately, that request only made Darwin go forward with publishing his own theory and, in effect, laying claim to the discovery of natural selection, the mechanism which induced evolutionary change. That left Wallace to become the man who *almost* discovered the principle of evolution.

[†]Charles Darwin (1809–1882): the man credited with discovering the mechanism that propels evolutionary change in everything from plants to humans.

Analyzing Arguments

IN THIS CHAPTER, YOU WILL LEARN

- how arguments and persuasion go hand in hand.

- how to recognize the typical opinion statements that are the focus of arguments.

- how becoming familiar with common introductions to an argument helps you spot the author's main idea.

- how to identify the essential elements of an argument and reduce it to its bare bones, making it easier to evaluate.

- how writers use tone to be persuasive.

> *"Keep cool. Anger is not an argument."*
> —Daniel Webster, American senator famous
> for his powers of persuasion

Now that you have thought about the difference between facts and opinions, you are ready to look more closely at the role both play in arguments used to persuade. That's not to say, however, that writers intent on persuasion try to pick a fight. The word *argument* in this context means stating an opinion along with relevant supporting details, which function as evidence for a specific point of view.

But when an author is writing to persuade, there are other elements of an argument to consider as well. For instance, does the author acknowledge opposing points of view? How does the author handle them? Does she have an answer for the opposition?

You'll need to consider as well the author's tone, or voice, in explaining his position. Does he assume a tone that suggests complete confidence in his perspective, implying that no questions need to be answered? Or does she admit doubts, all the while suggesting that her position still seems to be the best one to support? Tone is a tool of argument, which means that critical readers shouldn't let themselves be unconsciously influenced by the way an author "speaks" in print.

Opinion Statements Form the Foundations of Arguments

You can't really have an argument without an opinion. People don't argue much over statements of fact, such as William Jefferson Clinton served as president of the United States for two terms. With statements like this one, there is nothing to dispute, or disagree about. Any reference work will confirm its factual accuracy, so what would be the point of mounting an argument to defend it?

But if you tell someone that Bill Clinton was a great president, be prepared to argue that statement of opinion. You'll need to offer relevant evidence that might convince someone who disagrees with you. After all, Clinton is a controversial figure. Some people love him. Some people despise him. Others have mixed emotions about both the man and his presidency. While you could probably not convince those who despise him no matter what you said, a good argument might win over those in the middle. It might even raise a doubt or two in the minds of those who think Clinton was a disaster as president.

What this discussion of Bill Clinton illustrates is that all arguments begin with an opinion, point of view, or belief that the writer wants known and shared. Thus the first thing skilled readers do is scan the opening paragraphs of an article or essay, looking for the thesis statement expressing the writer's opinion.

In pursuit of that thesis statement, experienced readers are especially alert to three categories of opinion statements that are likely to become the main idea of numerous arguments: statements of value, statements of policy, and statements of condition.

Statements of Value

Statement of value opinions express approval or disapproval in any number of ways. They might tell readers that an idea, activity, or object is worthless or priceless, logical or illogical, savvy or silly. Authors who express a statement of value opinion strive to make their readers evaluate or assess the topic of their argument in the same way that they do. The following are all statements of value:

1. Among popular sports, boxing is the most dangerous and dehumanizing.

2. Publishers of digital textbooks insist that e-books are, in every way, superior to print. Yet the empirical evidence for such claims is lacking. On the contrary, when it comes to reading for study purposes, print books seem to have some definite advantages.[†]

3. The Executive Order, "Assignment of National Security and Emergency Preparedness," signed by President Obama in July of 2012 has not received the critical attention it deserves. Some sections of the order give the Department of Homeland Security too much decision-making power over the Internet during "emergencies" that aren't clearly defined.

4. Standardized tests are limited in their ability to evaluate how much students have learned from a course. This is especially true for courses that involve interpretation.

5. Educational programs claiming to train your right brain to be more creative are not based on anything more than the desire to make money.

Statements of Policy

Statement of policy opinions insist that a particular action should or should not be taken in response to an existing condition or situation. They tell readers that something must be changed, improved, revised, or abandoned. With this kind of opinion statement, facts are likely to play a big supporting role but so too are reasons that tell readers what great things can be accomplished or what bad things will happen if this action is, or is not, taken. As you might expect, helping verbs like *must*, *need*,

---

[†]For a review of what some people see as the disadvantages of digital textbooks, see the April 11, 2013, issue of *Scientific American*, which contains an article by Ferris Jabr titled "The Reading Brain in the Science of the Digital Age."

and *should* appear frequently in statements of policy. The following are all statements of policy:

1. The Internet needs to be covered by strict censorship laws that protect children from access to pornographic material.

2. College athletes who do not maintain a B average should be prohibited from playing any team sports.

3. Rate hikes by insurance companies should undergo a strict review by state boards empowered to approve or deny any increase in insurance premiums.

4. Parents need to let their children experience failures as well as successes.

5. The federal government must provide funding for jobs programs in urban areas where gang violence is prevalent.

Statements of Condition

Statement of condition opinions assert that a specific situation or state of affairs exists or existed. Unlike statements of value and policy, statements of condition appear to be purely factual, but they are actually more opinion than fact because they involve personal interpretations of events. (See the discussion of how writers might disagree on what the fifties were like on p. 515.) They also describe situations or attitudes that are unlikely to be known to general readers and therefore require supporting details meant to convince. The following are all statements of condition:

1. The nuclear family seems an ancient institution but, in fact, it hasn't been around for very long.

2. If today's parents are accused of coddling their children, the same could not be said of parents in the sixteenth century, when children, even children of the wealthy, were expected to act like little adults. The children of

the poor were expected to not just behave like adults but to do as much work as their age and size would allow.

3. Currently, the notion of privacy is under attack and many people are worried we are losing the concept of a private life not shared with the general public. But in the ancient world, one's private life was considered too unimportant to be kept secret, and the idea of personal embarrassment was all but unknown.

4. Although Henry David Thoreau celebrated solitude in his now classic book *Walden*, he actually spent relatively little time alone.

5. In 2013, women were formally granted the right to take part in military combat. But, in truth, this new rule is playing catch up with reality. Many women in the military engaged in combat long before they received formal permission.

Long before it became law, women were finding ways to go into combat.

U.S. Army photo by Spc. Jacob Kohrs

Although reasons play a role in almost every argument, arguments grounded in a statement of condition are particularly reliant on factual evidence.

Combination Statements

If you are wondering whether these three types of statements can be combined, the answer is yes. Here's an example: "Despite the cloud of shame surrounding his name, baseball player Shoeless Joe Jackson was never convicted of any crime. As one of the most talented players in the history of baseball, he should be admitted to the Baseball Hall of Fame." In this example, we have a statement of value: "Jackson was one of the most talented players in baseball history." We also have a statement of condition, "Despite the shame that surrounds his name, Jackson was never convicted of a crime," along with a statement of policy: "Jackson should be admitted to the Baseball Hall of Fame."

However, statements of policy, value, and condition don't have to team up to be at the heart of an argument. Plenty of writers base their arguments on a statement of value, policy, or condition without combining them.

✔ CHECK YOUR UNDERSTANDING

1. Give an example of a statement of value:

   _____

   _____

2. Provide an illustration for a statement of policy:

   _____

   _____

3. Offer an example of a statement of condition:

   _____

   _____

◆ EXERCISE 1   Identifying Opinion Statements

DIRECTIONS   Read each opinion statement. Then in the blank line that follows write *V* for statement of value, *P* for statement of policy, or *C* for statement of condition. If a statement combines more than one kind of opinion, indicate that by writing the letters for each one.

1. Finding just the right brand name is essential to a product's success, and a lot of thought went into naming some of our most famous products such as Pentium, Lexus, and Apple. It's no wonder that companies like Catchword Branding earn huge sums of money for coming up with just the right name for new products. Their track record is impressive.

   _____

2. Great surgeons need to have more than expert skills with a scalpel; they also need personal communication skills, something far too few possess, suggesting that medical schools might consider including a course for surgeons in how to interact with human beings who are not under anesthesia.

   _____

3. It's easy to ridicule the idea of wealthy people hiring personal coaches to help them manage their lives, but the idea of having an expert coach you into a better performance, whether it be at your job, in relationships, or on the basketball court, is not silly at all. Now all we have to do is make acquiring a personal coach affordable for everyone, not just for the wealthy.

   _____

4. The American version of *The Girl with the Dragon Tattoo* was a pleasant enough action film, but it lacked the complexity and energy of the Swedish original, which had a good deal more than action to offer.

   _____

5. Although some names of men and women active in the early civil rights movement have become household words, others, like Fred L. Shuttlesworth and Robert Zellner, have remained largely unknown.

   _____

6. For at least a decade, literature classes have been taken over by the reader-response approach to literature, which emphasizes the reader's interpretation of the text. But if students are to master the art of reading difficult prose, our classrooms need to return to close readings of complex texts, where the emphasis is more on the writer's intentions than the reader's personal impressions.

———

7. Dolphins aren't just cute and friendly creatures; they also have an amazingly tight-knit social structure. The dolphins' complex social network suggests the animals are highly intelligent and extremely compassionate.

———

8. A growing body of evidence indicates that the concussions endured during high school football games can cause serious brain damage that only makes itself known later on in life. Given that fact, parents need to decide if they truly want their children to play football under the existing conditions of play.

———

9. If incidents of bullying in the schools continue to increase, there should be penalities put into place that make the price of bullying behavior too high to pay.

———

10. Some cognitive scientists are claiming that the virtues of hypertext reading have been, pardon the pun, over-hyped, because of limitations on the processing abilities of the human brain. However, the very fact that our brains have become so exquisitely adapted for reading letters instead of shapes suggests that our brains can evolve to meet this new challenge." (Adapted from Alison Gopnik, "Mind Reading," *New York Times*, January 3, 2010, p. 15.)

———

Five Common Introductory Statements

Becoming familiar with the three most common forms of opinion statements that can focus an argument will help you analyze and ultimately evaluate persuasive writing. The same is true for five common types of introductions writers are likely to use when persuasion is their goal. Become familiar with them and you will be amazed at how quickly you get to the heart of an argument. With that goal in mind, here are five ways writers are likely to introduce opinions they want readers to share.

Statements of opinion are likely to follow close on the heels of opening statements that . . .

1. **contrast the opinion central to the argument with a different point of view:** "What's clear to most of us in teaching is that the Internet is a powerful educational tool. However, it is *not* a magic bullet."

2. **describe a long-held tradition or belief before challenging it with a new point of view:** "For years, we've been told that vigorous exercise was a boon to the body. Yet now it appears that vigorous exercise involving long periods of cardio can actually harm the body."

3. **cite new research as evidence for a new perspective:** "The assumption has long been that humans must be taught how to dance. However, a recent study from Stanford University suggests we may have to revise that hypothesis because researchers have discovered that their infant subjects were bouncing to the beat at less than five months old. The desire to dance may just be part of our genetic inheritance."

4. **make a prediction:** "I want to dust off my crystal ball and make a prediction: In the future, the biggest land animals will be smaller than they are now. Here's why I think so . . . ." (Olivia Judson, "Divide and Diminish," *New York Times*, March 16, 2010.)

5. **relate a personal anecdote showing the source of the opinion:** "I never paid much attention to the issue of banning assault rifles until my neighbor lost her child to a lunatic who was able to kill twenty-two helpless children without having to reload. Now I'm an advocate of banning them and wondering how anyone could think an assault rifle owned by an individual is a Constitutional right."

Are there additional ways to introduce the opinions that anchor an argument? Absolutely. But the five methods listed above are among the most common.

REVIEWING THROUGH WRITING

Flip through the pages of this chapter to find a topic you think you could make the subject of a written argument, such as privacy settings on Facebook, becoming an organ donor, or the role of women in combat. Once you have a topic (you can also invent your own topic), write an opinion statement that does one or all of the following: (1) makes a value judgment, (2) suggests a policy, or (3) identifies an existing condition.

◆ EXERCISE 2   Identifying the Point of the Argument

DIRECTIONS Read each passage and in the blanks below paraphrase the opinion the writer wants readers to share. Then at the end of your paraphrase write a *V* for statement of value, *P* for statement of policy, or *C* for statement of condition. If the opinion expressed is a mix of statement types, write the letter of each type used.

1. Some feminists think high heels are a symbol of male dominance. For them, high heels, because they place restrictions on movement, are akin to the ancient Chinese practice of foot binding. What those who despise high heels don't seem to recognize is that heels can also symbolize female confidence and authority. Viewed from a more open-minded perspective, wearing high heels is actually a way of flaunting female power. However, high heels are only a weapon in the female arsenal if the person wearing them knows how to walk without stumbling. For that reason, let me address the *dos* and *don't*s of how to wear high heels with pride rather than embarrassment.

   _____

   _____

   _____

2. So you think that your brain is sleeping soundly when you are? Well, think again. Brain-scanning technology suggests that the brain is more active during sleep than it is during its waking hours. And it's active for a reason. What the research shows is that the brain uses the hours of sleep to process and reorganize new information received during the day. That's one reason why brain scans made during the hours of REM sleep are often strikingly similar to the patterns of activity revealed during the day. During sleep, the brain seems to be rehearsing new skills acquired during its waking hours. In effect, it's re-enacting what it did earlier in the day.

_____

_____

_____

3. For close to a decade now, those of us capable of managing just one task at a time have been hanging our heads in shame when confronted by the seemingly supernatural powers of our multi-tasking friends. Thankfully, though, we no longer need feel ashamed. A growing body of research compiled since 2000 suggests that multi-tasking and superior performance do *not* go hand in hand. In fact, research shows that multi-taskers are downright mediocre when it comes to focusing their attention and storing or organizing information in long-term memory.

_____

_____

_____

4. Most people know about the sinking of the *Titanic*, the British luxury liner that hit an iceberg on April 14, 1912, and sank into the ocean taking with it the lives of over 1,500 passengers. Almost equally well-known is the tragedy of the British liner *Lusitania*, which was torpedoed by a German submarine in an attack that cost the lives of

around 1,200 people. Far less well-known, although equally tragic, is the sinking of the ship *Empress of Ireland*, which disappeared beneath the sea on May 29, 1914.

_____

_____

_____

5. Evgeny Morozov, author of *The Net Delusion*, offers a sobering and convincing rebuttal to those who unthinkingly celebrate the Internet as a democratic weapon against dictatorship. While not denying that the Internet can encourage democracy, Morozov is all too aware of the way governments, particularly dictatorships, have caught on to how much political power can be commanded by taking over cyberspace. Among the many examples he cites is China's Fifty Cent Party, a network of bloggers paid by the government. The goal of the group is to "safeguard the interest of the Communist Party by infiltrating and policing a rapidly growing Chinese Internet." These government-paid bloggers push pro-Communist Party positions through blogs and web comments. They also participate in chat rooms, book groups, and web forums, pretending to be ordinary citizens rather than what they are—government stooges.

_____

_____

_____

6. For years, I have rescued dogs from the pound and watched them turn into devoted and loving pets, and until a year ago my advice to anyone thinking of adopting a dog was always, "Get a rescue dog." But now I am the loving, if not always proud, owner of Caesar, a two-year-old rottweiler that was so badly abused he lost all trust in human nature. He seems, under my care, to have regained some of that faith, but woe betide those friends or strangers who knock at my door unannounced without my having prepared Caesar for

their arrival and shown him that they are welcome. Having paid the medical bills of a postal carrier, the UPS man, and a census taker, I have now modified my advice to anyone thinking of adopting a dog. These days I say, "Get a rescue dog, but make sure you know the dog might well come with problems because of its past. Make yourself as informed as possible about those problems. Even more important, think about your ability to deal with them because you are not doing yourself or the dog any favors if you adopt the dog and then have to give it back because you weren't prepared for the problems you encountered."

_____

_____

_____

Five Common Types of Support

"No man's opinion on any subject is worth a damn unless backed up with enough genuine information to make him really know what he's talking about."

—H. P. Lovecraft

Writers who want their arguments to be taken seriously know they have to do more than state their opinion. To be persuasive, they also have to provide their readers with supporting details that make the opinion being argued clear and convincing.

Critical readers, for their part, need to recognize and evaluate that support, deciding if it is both relevant and up to date (more about evaluating support in Chapter 10). Although there are many different ways people argue their position—compare, for instance, Ann Coulter with Paul Krugman[†]—five common types of support are particularly likely to be used in an argument: personal experience, reasons, examples and illustrations, the opinions of experts, and research results.

[†]If you are not familiar with the work of either, check online to see the *enormous* difference in political viewpoints.

The female albatross flies far distances to forage for food for her chicks but often mistakenly brings home pieces of plastic that kill the chicks instead of nourishing them.

following author uses examples to persuade readers that plastic litter floating in the ocean is more than unsightly. It's also deadly.

Plastic accounts for anywhere from 60 to 80 percent of ocean litter, and that litter isn't just unsightly, it's lethal to many, if not most, of the creatures that inhabit ocean waters. Whales and sea turtles, for instance, mistake plastic debris for squid, which is normally part of their diet. Plastic, however, can't be digested. If the whales and turtles don't choke to death on the plastic immediately, it will clog their intestines making them unable to excrete the waste that will slowly kill them. Seals and sea lions have a different problem. They get their heads stuck in the plastic rings that bind soft drinks and beer bottles together. When that happens, the animals can't open their jaws, and they starve to death. Plastic string and binding can also get entangled in a marine animal's flippers so that the animal is unable to swim and forage* for food. Seabirds are also not exempt from plastic's threat. One study found that 95 percent of all dead albatross chicks had plastic in their stomachs and at least 40 percent of those chicks died due to eating plastic debris.[†]

In this example, the author piles example on example in an effort to convince readers that plastic litter can be lethal to creatures living in the ocean.

Statistics as Examples

Note, too, how the author of the previous paragraph uses statistics to cite large numbers in examples. Where persuasion is concerned, relevant examples plus statistics are a knock-out combination. With this double-whammy approach, the writer avoids the two obstacles examples and statistics can pose: (1) the reader notes the specific examples but thinks they aren't all that common or typical or (2) the reader sees the statistics, but the numbers carry so little emotional impact the reader doesn't care. By citing both examples and statistics together, the writer has a better chance of persuading his audience to share his concerns.

Expert Opinions

To persuade, writers often call on one or more experts who support their position. In the following passage, for instance, the author suggests that

---

*forage: search widely for food.
[†]albatrosses: large, white sea birds.

cloning geniuses may not be a good idea. To make her point, she gives a reason and cites an expert.

Cloning Is No Guarantee

1   After the birth of Dolly, the first successfully cloned sheep, in 1996, it was often suggested that we could now consider the human gene pool a natural resource. We could, if we wished, clone a Pulitzer Prize–winning writer like Junot Díaz or a star athlete like Serena Williams and thereby create a population of gifted and talented people. What could be wrong with that? Well, in the long run, probably a lot.

2   There's simply no guarantee that the clones would be everything the originals were. After all, genes don't tell the whole story, and the clone of a prize-winning scientist, if neglected as a child, might well end up a disturbed genius, no matter what the original gene source. As John Paris, professor of bioethics at Boston College, so correctly said on the subject of cloning, "Choosing personal characteristics as if they were the options on a car is an invitation to misadventure." (Source of quotation: Jeffrey Kluger, "Will We Follow the Sheep?" *Time*, March 10, 1997, p. 71.)

In this case, the author doesn't just let her argument rest solely on her own reasoning. She also makes it clear that at least one knowledgeable expert is very much on her side.

Question the Experts

When an author uses experts to back up an opinion, see if he or she also tells you something about the expert's background and affiliation, or official attachment to an organization. If the author quotes a scientist who claims that global warming is not a real threat, you need to know if the scientist's background is in climate studies rather than cancer research. Similarly, if an author argues that animal rights activists are exaggerating the suffering of factory-raised chickens and quotes a veterinarian who agrees with that position, it's important to know whether the veterinarian has any ties to chicken farmers. (For more on questioning the experts, see Chapter 10.)

Research Results

In the same way they use experts, writers who want to persuade are likely to use the results of research—studies, polls, questionnaires, and surveys—to argue a point. In the following passage, for example, the author uses an expert *and* a study to support a statement of condition: There's a quiet revolution taking place among Amish[†] women.

> Katie Stoltzfus's shop *Country Lane Quilts* is attached to the side of a farmhouse in Pennsylvania's Lancaster County. The shop is a little bit off the beaten path. Yet people still seem to find their way there, motivated by Mrs. Stoltzfus's reputation as a doll and quiltmaker. A mother of nine, Mrs. Stoltzfus is a highly successful businesswoman, whose business has been consistently earning a profit for more than a decade. She is one of the many women in the Amish community who have been quietly building their own businesses and in the process revolutionizing the role of women in the Amish community. Notwithstanding their image as shy wives and stay-at-home moms, many Amish women are savvy businesswomen. According to a study by Donald B. Kraybill, a professor of sociology and religious studies at Elizabethtown College, women run over 20 percent of the one thousand businesses in Lancaster County. They are, he says, blazing a new trail for women of their faith: "These women are interacting more with outsiders, assuming managerial functions they never had before, and gaining more power within their community because of their access to money." (Source of quotation: "More Amish Women Are Tending to Business," *Toledo Blade*, March 11, 1996.)

To make sure that readers seriously consider his position, the author cites a study and identifies the person who conducted the study, making it clear that his opinion is grounded in solid research.

Some Amish women have turned out to have a real head for business.

Matthew Cavanaugh/EPA/Newscom

[†]The Amish: a religious group that generally avoids contact with the modern world.

Question the Research

When writers use research to back up the opinion they are arguing, experienced critical readers don't assume any research will do. As with expert opinion, they want to know something about the person or group performing the research. Here again, background and affiliation are important. Some corporations hire researchers to perform studies proving the effectiveness of their products. If you are reading an argument claiming that new arthritis medications are making this painful disease a thing of the past, then, for obvious reasons, you need to know if the research cited was funded by the company whose medications are being evaluated.

You should also know the timing of the study. A thirty-year-old study saying that radon gas is not a problem potential home buyers seriously need to think about should not convince you, or anyone else, that radon gas is no cause for worry. Even the study cited in the example on Amish businesswomen is questionable. Who knows if that figure about the number of businesses owned by Amish women is still accurate. In general, studies need to be accompanied by dates since study findings can become obsolete with the passage of time.

✔ CHECK YOUR UNDERSTANDING

1. Name the five ways writers support their opinions when using arguments intended to persuade:

   _____

   _____

2. What should readers check when an author provides expert opinion as support?

   _____

3. What should readers look for when an author provides research results as proof that an opinion is correct?

   _____

WEB QUEST   The Albatross as a Poetic Figure

In what poem does the albatross play a key role?

_____

Who wrote the poem? _____ Because of that poem, allusions to an albatross hanging around a person's neck have come to mean that the

person is _____.

◆ **EXERCISE 3   Identifying Support for Opinions**

DIRECTIONS   Each group of statements opens with an opinion or a claim that needs to be argued. Circle the letters of the two sentences that help argue that point.

EXAMPLE   Eyewitness testimony is far less reliable than most people think.

(a.) The testimony of eyewitnesses can often be influenced by the desire to please those in authority.

(b.) Studies of eyewitness testimony conducted by the researcher and psychologist Elizabeth Loftus reveal an astonishingly high number of errors.

c. Eyewitness testimony carries a great deal of weight with most juries.

EXPLANATION   Statements *a* and *b* both undermine the reliability of eyewitnesses and thereby provide reasons why eyewitness testimony cannot always be considered trustworthy. Statement *c*, however, is not relevant, or related, to the claim made about eyewitness testimony.

1. Uniforms should be compulsory* for all high school students.

   a. Most students hate the idea of wearing a uniform.

   b. Parents on a strict budget would no longer have to worry about being able to provide expensive back-to-school wardrobes.

   c. If uniforms were mandatory in high school, students would not waste precious time worrying about something as unessential as fashion.

_____

*compulsory: mandatory, binding by either rule or law.

2. All zoos should be abolished due to the cruelty they inflict on their imprisoned inhabitants.

   a. Zoos encourage the notion that animals are on earth for the amusement of human beings and discourage the idea that they are creatures with needs separate from our own.

   b. If all zoos were closed, no one has any idea what would happen to the animals now living in them.

   c. Although many zoos have improved the living conditions for the animals they possess, those animals still lack the freedom to roam that they have in the wild.

3. When teenagers commit violent crimes, members of the public often insist that they be tried as adults. But that's a mistake. Teenagers are not capable of evaluating the consequence of their actions in the way adults are.

   a. Research by Beatriz Luna of the University of Pittsburgh suggests that the brain's ability to control impulsive behavior is not fully established until the mid-to late twenties.

   b. Sending a teenager to a prison with hardened criminals destroys any chance they have to avoid becoming hardened criminals themselves; teenagers convicted of crimes should go to juvenile facilities, where rehabilitation is still possible.

   c. Teenagers want to be treated as adults. It follows then that they should be tried as adults.

4. Migraine headaches are much more painful and debilitating* than people who do not suffer from them realize. Migraines often leave their victims unable to function, and the government needs to fund more research for a cure.

   a. Hemiplegic migraine, although rare, is devastating: it can cause a paralysis that lasts for several days.

   b. Thomas Jefferson, Virginia Woolf, and Winston Churchill are just a few of the famous people who suffered from migraines.

   c. The onset of a migraine can cause reduced vision, making it impossible for the sufferer to carry on with ordinary, daily activities.

---

*debilitating: weakening, causing a lack of energy.

◆ EXERCISE 4   Identifying Opinion and Support

DIRECTIONS Read each passage. Then answer the questions that follow.

The passage opens with a statement of condition.

To provide proof for that claim, sentence 2 introduces the first example of a rebellion.

Sentences 6 and 7 describe more rebellions. Notice how the rebellions are marked by dates.

EXAMPLE [1]Unfortunately, some people still believe that African-Americans endured slavery without protest, but nothing could be further from the truth. [2]In 1800, for example, Gabriel Prosser organized an army of a thousand slaves to march on Richmond. [3]However, a state militia had been alerted by a spy. [4]The rebellion was put down and Prosser was taken prisoner. [5]He was executed for refusing to give evidence against his co-conspirators. [6]In 1822, Denmark Vesey plotted to march on Charleston, but he, too, was betrayed by an informer. [7]The most deadly revolt occurred in 1831 under an African-American known as Nat Turner. [8]For two days, Turner and his fellow rebels moved from plantation to plantation killing the inhabitants. [9]Turner had hoped to set off a chain of rebellions, but he and his followers, around seventy-five in total, were overwhelmed by a two-thousand-men-strong state militia. [10]Turner escaped but was eventually discovered hiding in a swamp. [11]After a period of imprisonment, he was executed along with more than a hundred black men and women, many of whom had nothing to do with the rebellion.

1. What is the point of the author's argument?

It's not true that African-Americans endured slavery without fighting back.

2. Paraphrase the examples used to support that point.

1. In 1800, Gabriel Prosser organized an army of slaves to march on
   Richmond.

2. In 1822, Denmark Vesey plotted to take over Charleston.

3. In 1831, Nat Turner and more than 75 rebels revolted, hoping to set off
   a chain of rebellions, but they failed and were executed.

1. A 2012 Gallup poll indicates that women are buying guns in increasing numbers. In fact, a whopping 23 percent of the women polled reported owning a gun. That's a ten-point increase over an early 2005 poll. It's also yet another sign that women are taking charge of their lives. Although anti-gun activists are wringing their hands over the rise in female gun ownership, they shouldn't be. Like men, women have a right to defend themselves. Ever since Betty Friedan wrote *The Feminine Mystique*,[†] feminists have been urging women to be independent and self-sufficient. What better evidence of female independence than women no longer having to rely exclusively on the police (still mostly male) for protection? We should applaud every woman who is skilled in handgun use for freeing herself from fear while walking on a dark street or driving on a country road late at night. For years, feminists have been hosting *Take Back the Night* demonstrations, which were an effort to get better protection for women who go out alone at night. If women keep arming themselves in ever-greater numbers, such demonstrations will be a thing of the past. (The point of this argument was made originally by talk show host Laura Ingraham, in an article titled "Armed and Empowered" and published in the *Pittsburgh Post Gazette*.)

1. What is the point of the author's argument?

_____

_____

2. Paraphrase the reasons used to support that point.

_____

_____

_____

_____

[†]Betty Friedan's *The Feminine Mystique* was published in 1963, and it was one of the first books to suggest that being a wife and mother might not be all a woman needed to be happy.

2. All states should consider limiting tractor-trailer traffic on crowded highways. Over the past few decades, the number of tractor-trailers on our nation's roads and interstates has doubled and that number is still increasing. By 2020, the number of trucks will probably have doubled again. During this period, though, the capacity of our roads and highways has either remained the same or slightly expanded. Put these two factors together and it's clear that the growing number of trucks on the road is increasing the danger of accidents. Already, around 4,500 drivers and passengers die every year in truck-car accidents because smaller, lighter cars are easily crushed by the much bigger rigs. That fatality rate will only continue to rise as the number of trucks increases. Obviously, the solution to this problem is to limit trucks to traveling in truck-only lanes and to prohibit them from traveling during rush hours. By restricting truckers in these ways, state officials can make the roads safer for everyone.

1. What is the point of the author's argument?

_____

_____

2. Paraphrase the reasons used to support that point.

_____

_____

_____

3. It's never too late to get physically fit. For over at least two decades now, studies published in the *New England Journal of Medicine* have consistently shown that taking up weight training can reverse some of the effects of aging. In one experiment, nursing home residents ranging in age from eighty-six to ninety-five participated in a supervised, eight-week weight-training program. All of these elderly people increased their strength and improved their balance. Another, more recent, study conducted by the University

of Pennsylvania Medical School has shown that elderly people who take up weight training can improve their bone density and reduce arthritic pain.

1. What is the point of the author's argument?

_____

_____

2. Paraphrase the results of the studies used to support that point.

_____

_____

_____

_____

4. Almost every college student has experienced pre-finals terror—the horrible anxiety that puts your stomach on a roller coaster and your brain in a blender. Few escape those final-exam jitters because everyone knows just how much is riding on that one exam, often more than half of the course grade. Yet therein lies the crux* of the problem. Infrequent high-stakes exams don't encourage students to do their best work. More frequent tests—given, say, every two or three weeks—would be a much more effective method of discovering how well students are or are not mastering course concepts. With more frequent testing, students would be less anxious when they take exams; thus anxiety would no longer interfere with exam performance. More frequent testing also encourages students to review on a regular basis something that a one-shot final exam does not do. Lots of tests also mean lots of feedback, and students would know early in the course what terms or concepts required additional explanation and review. They wouldn't have to wait until the end of the semester to find out that they had misunderstood, or missed altogether, a critical fact or idea.

_____

*crux: core, heart, key point.

1. What is the point of the author's argument?

   _____

   _____

2. Paraphrase the reasons used to support that point.

   _____

   _____

   _____

 REVIEWING THROUGH WRITING

Jot down the opinion statement you came up with for the Reviewing Through Writing assignment on page 546. Then write down underneath it any examples or reasons you think support your position. Look them over and put a check next to the ones you think are the most convincing. Let the list sit for anywhere from an hour to a day. Then go back and look it over again. See if any other kinds of evidence come to mind. Ask yourself if you need to do research to prove your point to your readers. If you do, complete the research, then go back and write the first draft of your argument. Don't think about the introduction until you have finished drafting. It's great if an introduction just comes to you while drafting, but if it doesn't, don't worry about it. Introductions are usually easier to write once the body of the paper is complete.

 ## Identifying the Opposing Point of View

Any argument worthy of the name has to include an opinion along with relevant and up-to-date support. Arguments, however, also frequently include the author's response to opposing points of view. Shown below is an article on homeschooling. In which paragraph does the author start responding to the opposition?

The first sentence introduces the author's main point: What's wrong with education can be fixed by homeschooling.

Already in the first paragraph, readers get a reason why homeschooling is the answer; no chance for distractions.

The opening phrase "at home" keeps the topic of homeschooling front and center and introduces another reason for its superiority over public education.

Notice the use of comparison and contrast to prove the point of the paragraph.

Paragraph 3 announces the next advantage: The home is a familiar and non-threatening environment.

Paragraph 4 introduces the opposing point of view: Schooled at home, kids don't get the same teaching quality.

The Benefits of Homeschooling

1 Although it has been harshly criticized by many—often by those who have a vested interest* in supporting the status quo*—homeschooling just may be the answer to our current educational crisis. In public schools kids are distracted by the presence of other children who don't always have an interest in learning. Teachers also can't monitor the increasingly huge classes they face. Thus children who aren't motivated to learn can easily spend most of the class time checking their Facebook page or texting one another. As a result, many of our children are not facing the future with the skills they need to get ahead professionally. But if these children were homeschooled, there would be nothing to distract them from the important task of learning the skills and concepts that will arm them for the future.

2 At home, children can learn one-on-one or in small groups. If they need some additional explanation or instruction, the home tutor can readily supply it. In public schools, in contrast, children often sit in classrooms with twenty or thirty other students. Such class numbers make it almost impossible for teachers to give students the individual attention they often need. There are so many competing voices and questions, a teacher can't possibly respond to all of them. Someone has to go consciously unattended or unconsciously ignored.

3 Another advantage of homeschooling is that it allows children to learn in a comforting, familiar environment. Any parent who has ever delivered a weeping child to the door of his or her classroom knows full well how terrifying some children find the classroom atmosphere with its noisy hubbub. Children who learn at home are familiar with their surroundings. They aren't frightened by them. Nor are they inhibited or made anxious by the presence of other children who might unthinkingly laugh at their mistakes or set a poor example by chatting or texting.

4 Critics who claim that homeschooling can't provide children with the breadth of knowledge they need always assume that the parents doing the teaching don't have the necessary qualifications. Yet of the parents I know personally who teach their children at home, two have a master's degree in physics, another has a doctorate in psychology, and still another is a former elementary teacher with ten years of teaching experience. Parents who take on the responsibility of homeschooling do not do so lightly. They

---

*vested interest: a special reason to promote or protect that which gives one a personal advantage.

*status quo: existing state of affairs.

Here's the author's response.

know that they must provide their children with an education that prepares them for the world they will eventually enter. Thus they make sure that they themselves or the people who come into their homes to tutor are well-prepared to teach their children what they need to know.

As you can see, the author introduces the opinion she wants readers to share in the very first paragraph: Homeschooling may be the answer to what she considers an "educational crisis." The next two paragraphs then offer reasons that support this claim:

1. Kids will get the attention they need when they need it; they won't be ignored.
2. They will be in a familiar environment that won't cause them anxiety.

By paragraph 4, though, the author feels she has to answer criticism of homeschooling. She does it by claiming that parents who homeschool are informed about the subjects they teach and, even if they are not, the tutors they employ are.

Analyzing the Writer's Response to Objections

In writing meant to persuade, writers frequently do address objections to their position. When they do, critical readers need to go beyond evaluating the clarity of an author's opinion and the soundness of the support supplied. For instance, in the reading on homeschooling the writer responds by telling readers, "We know our teachers have to be well-trained and we make sure that they are." But she offers no proof for that claim. Her response would be more convincing if she were able to say something like "In a 2013 survey of parents who homeschool conducted by the Pew Research Foundation, 75 percent of the parents involved in homeschooling had advanced degrees with 85 percent of outside tutors showing advanced training in their subject matter."

Often, it's in describing and responding to the opposition that writers are most likely to reveal the limitations of their argument. In the homeschooling argument, the author's response to the opposition is rather vague and the reader is left with little to go on except the author's personal claim that homeschooling teachers are qualified. The other tip-off that an author is on shaky ground is the use of an overtly annoyed or disrespectful tone in response to an opposing point of view.

WEB QUEST **Schooling Inside and Outside the Home**

Which state was the first to make public school mandatory for children, and when did that happen?

_____

Is the number of parents who homeschool increasing or decreasing?

_____

What is the main reason why parents homeschool?

_____

◆ EXERCISE 5   Analyzing Arguments

DIRECTIONS   Read each of the following selections and answer the questions that follow. Check to see how the writer responds to opposition. _Note_: If there is no response to an opposing point of view, then leave the lines for that question blank.

EXAMPLE

Homeschooling Isn't Really School

The opening paragraph ends with the statement of value that needs to be argued.

Paragraph 2 provides the first reason: Children who are homeschooled have gaps in their education.

Paragraph 3 offers the second reason: Homeschooled kids have

1   As a public school teacher, I have to admit I cringe every time I hear the word _homeschooling_. I know that many parents believe they are helping their children by teaching them at home. But in my experience, homeschooling is not in the best interest of the children involved.

2   Children who enter my class after a long period of homeschooling usually have huge gaps in their education. True, they often read and write better than the average fifth grader, and their spelling is good. But they know very little about the social sciences, and science itself seems to be a foreign word.

3   In addition, children who have been schooled at home frequently have difficulty working with other children. Unused to the give-and-take of group interactions, they quickly show their discomfort or displeasure. Their response is understandable since they have spent years at home in a class of one or two at most.

difficulty when they work with other children.

The author responds to the opposition.

4   I know that many parents believe homeschooling protects their children from dangerous or corrupting ideas and experiences. To some degree, they are probably correct in that assumption. Unfortunately, the protection homeschooling provides may cost too heavy an intellectual price. In general, parents do not have the necessary training or background to give their children the wide-ranging and up-to-date education they need. And certainly parents cannot provide the kind of peer socialization found in schools outside the home.

1. What is the point of the author's argument?

Homeschooling may do more harm than good.

2. What two reasons does the author give in support of that point?

Children can end up with big gaps in their education.

Children schooled at home usually have difficulty working in groups.

3. Identify the opposing point of view mentioned in the reading.

Parents believe that they are protecting their children from bad experiences

and inappropriate ideas.

4. Paraphrase the author's response.

The protection costs too much socially and intellectually.

EXPLANATION   Although the author responds to an opposing point of view at the end of the reading, this is not necessarily standard. Answers to objections can just as easily be sprinkled throughout. And while the way the author responds to objections cannot be faulted as it was in the reading written in support of homeschooling, notice that the reasons backing up the main opinion expressed in this reading have no outside evidence supporting the author's claims, something that should give readers pause. (More about evaluating responses in Chapter 10.)

1. Teacher Performance Linked to Pay

1   In both Britain and the United States, there is a growing movement to determine teacher's pay by student performance. Teachers whose students score well on standardized tests would see pay increases while teachers

whose students did not score well would get no salary increase. If the scores did not improve after two years, teachers would be terminated. Although opposed by many teachers and teachers' organizations, this plan of action should be implemented in all of our nation's public schools.

2   The recommendation makes sense for a number of reasons. For one, compensating teachers based on classroom results would replace an archaic,* decades-old system that pays a good teacher the same as a poor one. Currently, teachers' salaries are based only on years of experience, so an ineffective teacher who has taught for twenty years earns far more than a newer but far more effective one. According to supporters of the plan, the current system does nothing to reward excellence. In other words, it would be fairer to the hardest-working teachers to reward them with bigger pay checks.

3   Opponents of performance-based pay argue that such a plan ignores the many factors affecting student performance, such as poverty or family back-ground, which are outside teacher control. Their position is that the teacher can't be blamed if a student comes to school hungry and therefore has a hard time concentrating. Opponents also argue that standardized tests are not an accurate measure of what students learn in the classroom. Poorly constructed questions may elicit incorrect answers and teachers end up being the ones who get the blame. Standardized tests also don't measure intangible im-provements such as increased self-confidence or better language skills.

4   These arguments are just a smoke screen for the real issue, which is teachers don't want to be judged by any standards except their own. After all, teacher evaluations are designed to take factors like poverty and a poor home life into account. What's more, other professions use performance-based pay plans. As former IBM chairman Louis V. Gerstner Jr. has pointed out, other professions base pay on performance. "Lawyers do it, engineers do it, businesspeople do it. All professional people ultimately come up with methodology* to judge the difference between great performance and mediocre performance. Just because it's hard doesn't mean we can't do it." (Source of quotation: The Teaching Commission, "Teaching at Risk: Blue-Ribbon Panel Calls for Overhaul of Teacher Education and Compensation to Recruit and Retain Talent in America's Public Schools," Press Release, January 14, 2004.)

1. What is the point of the author's argument?

_____

_____

-----

*archaic: ancient, out of date.
*methodology: a system for getting something accomplished.

Identify the three reasons used to support that point.

a. _____

_____

b. _____

c. _____

2. Identify the opposing points of view mentioned in the reading.

_____

_____

_____

_____

3. Paraphrase the author's response.

_____

_____

_____

2. **The Baby Business**

1   The American Bar Association (ABA) believes that the various state laws governing the practice of surrogacy—the process in which a woman carries a child for an individual or a couple who cannot give birth—need to be standardized while the procedure in general needs more and better regulation. Given the current chaotic state of affairs, with some surrogacy agreements causing a good deal more misery than joy, it's hard to imagine how anyone could argue with this position. Probably the only people who might disagree with the ABA are those who are making huge sums of money from what is, in effect, the buying and selling of babies.

2   Although many surrogacy arrangements work out well with minimal trauma, others become a source of misery for everyone involved. That applies with special intensity to the babies involved in a surrogate arrangement. When the parties to what is officially titled "third-party reproduction" start quarreling, the infant or infants over whom they are fighting can end up spending time in foster homes, while the courts decide who has the

legal right to custody, the surrogate mother or the individuals who paid the mother to have what they consider "their" child.

3   Part of the problem haunting surrogacy arrangements is the amount of money involved. To put it bluntly, surrogacy is big business. Once all the medical expenses and fees are paid, the cost of a successful surrogacy is somewhere between $80,000 and $120,000. One agency advertising on the Web claims it can arrange for a surrogate mother to give birth for under $50,000. In other words, they offer bargain babies.

4   Not surprisingly, given sums of money that can soar into six figures, the surrogacy business has attracted some unscrupulous characters, who willingly engage in criminal activities to cash in on the desperation of would-be parents. The Central American country of Guatemala has been particularly hard hit by illegal baby rings, which either coerce women into having children that can be sold or kidnap children outright. Guatemala is an impoverished country, and the women who are targeted for this treatment have little recourse when their children are taken from them. Uniform state laws that make it impossible to adopt children born to anonymous mothers living in foreign countries would go a long way toward curbing these horrific practices.

5   Yet heartbreaking problems can arise even when the surrogacy agreements are arranged and carried out completely within the United States. As the *New York Times* reported in a 2009 article titled "Building a Baby, with Few Ground Rules," Amy and Scott Kehoe thought they did everything right. Using the Web, Amy Kehoe found a pre-med student at the University of Michigan to donate her eggs. She found an anonymous sperm donor the same way. Using the website surromomsonline.com, the couple also found Laschell Baker of Ypsilanti, Michigan. Mrs. Baker had four children of her own and had previous experience acting as a surrogate. Once Mrs. Kehoe had hired a fertility clinic, also located online, everything seemed to be in order.

6   Initially things did go smoothly, with Mrs. Baker giving birth to twins, Bridget and Ethan, and the Kehoes taking home what they believed were their babies. One month later, though, police arrived at the Kehoes' home to take the twins away. Mrs. Baker had discovered that Mrs. Kehoe was under the treatment of a psychiatrist and had to take medication to keep her illness under control. Even the testimony of the psychiatrist, who said Mrs. Kehoe would be a good mother, could not calm her anxiety: "I couldn't see living the rest of my life worrying and wondering what had happened, or what if she hadn't taken her medicine or what if she relapsed."

7   Laschell Baker demanded and got the babies back. Had the surrogacy arrangement been carried out in California, it's likely the Kehoes would have kept the children. California has legislation friendly to surrogacy

agreements. Michigan does not. The state holds that such agreements are unenforceable. Mrs. Baker was, therefore, within her rights to change her mind and assume care of the children.

8   It is precisely this kind of crazy quilt of legislation that the American Bar Association thinks should be addressed. While making the legislation uniform would not completely eliminate the heartbreak that can accompany surrogacy arrangements, it would at least ensure that both parties knew exectly what they might be getting into when they set out to engage in third-party reproduction.

1. What is the point of the author's argument?

_____

_____

Identify the three reasons used to support that point.

a. _____

_____

b. _____

_____

c. _____

_____

_____

2. Identify the opposing point of view mentioned in the reading.

_____

_____

3. Paraphrase the author's response.

_____

_____

_____

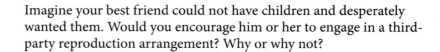

REVIEWING THROUGH WRITING

Add to your original draft (see Reviewing Through Writing on page 562) by (1) referring to an opposing point of view and (2) responding to the opposition.

What Do You Think?
◆

Imagine your best friend could not have children and desperately wanted them. Would you encourage him or her to engage in a third-party reproduction arrangement? Why or why not?

CHECK YOUR UNDERSTANDING

1. When you analyze an argument, what are the two essential elements you absolutely must pin down?

   _____

2. What's the third element you should watch for?

   _____

Using and Responding to Tone

Tone in writing was introduced in Chapter 1, where you were cautioned not to get basic background knowledge from websites that described people and events in a tone conveying strong positive or negative emotions. The topic of tone came up again in Chapter 5, where you learned about the connection between the neutral tone associated with informative writing versus the more emotion-charged tones likely to be present when the author wants to persuade.

Tone appears in this chapter because it's an important tool of writers using arguments to persuade. Writers passionately committed to their subject, for instance, may purposely use a strong, confident tone to make their readers feel that anyone who speaks with such confidence has to be correct. Writers who are skeptical of a new government policy or medical procedure may consciously create a tone laced with doubt as a way of encouraging skepticism in their audience.

Readers, for their part, need to recognize the effect tone has on their response to what they read. They have to recognize, for example, when they might be ready to accept a writer's ideas mainly because they like the down-to-earth, no-nonsense tone of the writing. By the same token, readers shouldn't let their dislike of a formal and professorial tone interfere with their ability to appreciate ideas that are both original and informed.

A Writer's Tone Consists of Many Different Elements

Tone is the result of many different choices made by the writer. Decisions about sentence length, word choice, references to the audience, expressions of personal preferences, type of grammar (formal or informal), selection of detail, use of figurative language,[†] and choice of imagery, among other things, all contribute to a writer's tone. Notice here, for instance, how the writer uses personal pronoun references to help create a folksy, down-to-earth tone.

Note the use of *we* to emphasize the shared point of view.

The direct address to the audience—"All you have to do"— emphasizes shared agreement.

> We all know what it's like to feel that we have been left in the lurch by those we thought we could trust. All you have to do, then, to understand the feelings of people standing knee- to neck-deep in water during Hurricane Katrina is to multiply that feeling by a hundred, because that's how the inhabitants of New Orleans felt when local and federal officials were slow to pitch in and save not just their city but the lives and property of the people in it. In the eyes of those stranded in New Orleans, the betrayal by the officials who were supposed to help them in a crisis was equal in magnitude* to the storm that savaged their city.

A different writer, though, might avoid such a personal approach in favor of an admiring tone that makes no reference to anyone's personal feelings, neither the writer's nor the audience's. The following writer, for instance, uses glowing language that encourages the reader to share the writer's admiration for his subject.

[†]figurative language: language that makes sense in imaginative terms rather than realistic ones. Here's an example from Lauren Groff's novel *Arcadia*, where stories are described as if they had the physical power to hurt: "They can wound, stories, they can blister." See pages 582–584 for more on figurative language.
*magnitude: size, importance, greatness.

Injuries and Creativity

The opening statement of value argues that what Dr. Sacks has to say is important.

An example illustrates the connection between injury and creativity.

The word choice in paragraph 2 is a major contributor to the admiring tone.

1   In his book *An Anthropologist on Mars*, the <u>renowned</u> neurologist[†] Dr. Oliver Sacks gives readers <u>an important and insightful perspective</u> on injuries and disorders of the brain. According to Sacks, some injuries and disorders result in greater creativity and achievement. He describes, for example, a painter who becomes color-blind through a car accident. Initially in despair, the painter eventually starts painting stunning black-and-white canvases that win him more critical acclaim than he had received before his mishap.

2   As in his previous works, Dr. Sacks offers readers an <u>unexpected and unusual perspective</u> on disease and injury. In *An Anthropologist on Mars*, <u>he once again makes us rethink and reconsider our most cherished beliefs about health and illness. His book should be required reading</u> for anyone interested in the power of human beings to adapt to and ultimately overcome loss.

As these two examples illustrate, the ingredients that go into tone can be mixed to create a variety of voices in print, some of which are listed in the chart below, but first a note on what it means when a writer's tone is ironic.

Tone and Irony

No discussion of tone would be complete without some mention of **irony**—the practice of saying one thing while implying exactly the opposite. This might sound confusing at first, but, like most of us, you've probably used irony more than once in your life. Haven't you ever had a really horrible day and said to someone, "Boy, what a great day this was!" Or, seeing a friend wearing a sad expression, maybe you said, "Gee, you look happy."

If either of these examples sounds familiar, then you know more about irony than you think. Thus you're well prepared for writers who assume an ironic tone like the one used in the following passage.

> The school board has decided to reduce the school budget once again. But why take half measures? Why not eliminate the budget altogether and close our schools? After all, a little learning is a dangerous thing. Better to keep our children totally ignorant and out of harm's way.

[†]neurologist: a doctor who specializes in the workings and diseases of the nervous system.

The author of this paragraph doesn't want his readers to take what he says *literally*, or at face value. After all, who would seriously suggest that keeping children ignorant is a good idea? The author's point is just the opposite of what he actually says. He doesn't want the school budget further reduced. But instead of saying that directly, he makes an outrageous suggestion that draws attention to where the cuts could lead.

When writers present what seems to be an outrageous or impossible opinion as if it were obvious common sense, critical readers assume the writer is being ironic, and they respond by inferring a message directly opposed to the author's actual words. As you might expect, an ironic tone is a good indicator of a persuasive purpose. That makes it wise to start looking for the author's argument as soon as you sense that an ironic tone is in play.

A Range of Tones Writers Can Use ♦		
	admiring	enthusiastic
	amused	generous
	angry	horrified
	annoyed	humorous
	anxious	insulted
	appalled	insulting
	astonished	ironic (saying the opposite of what is intended)
	awed (filled with wonder)	
	bullying	joyful
	cautious	mistrustful
	confident	neutral
	contemptuous	nostalgic (looking fondly toward the past)
	critical	
	cynical	outraged
	disgusted	passionate
	disrespectful	playful
	dumbfounded (very surprised)	puzzled
	embarrassed	regretful
	engaged (deeply involved)	sad
		sarcastic

shocked	sorrowful
solemn	surprised
soothing	trusting

 REVIEWING THROUGH WRITING

Look over the draft you have been working on and consider what tone would help you convince your readers. Pay particular attention to the language you use in addressing the opposition. Are you consistent in the way you describe your point of view as well as opposing ones? Do you need to change or add any language that would heighten or decrease the intensity, or strength, of your tone?

◆ **EXERCISE 6** **Recognizing Tone**

DIRECTIONS After reading each selection, circle the letter of the word or phrase that best fits the author's tone.

The writer opens by referring to the opposition.

The transition *but* signals a shift in the writer's opinion: Freedom of speech should only go so far.

Notice how the author repeats the opening pattern of "yes the opposition has a point but I still think . . ."

EXAMPLE I take seriously the worries expressed by those who believe that censoring individual speech harms free speech in general. But, still, I am uncomfortable guaranteeing the right to spew hate and bigotry. True, such language might not provoke any immediate threat, but it probably paves the way for future ones, and that concerns me. For that reason, I support academic codes that punish students who publicly use hate speech to humiliate and hurt others. I understand the position of the American Civil Liberties Union (ACLU), which insists that speech should not be censored. They may well be right in arguing that censoring hate speech leads to more censorship while failing to address the feelings that elicited the language. But I'm more convinced that not censoring racist language encourages other people to think it is acceptable, and for me that's a more fearful prospect.

    a. angry

    b. casual

    c. disgusted

    d. concerned

EXPLANATION The author's repeated recognition of opposing points of view at the same time that she restates her own position makes her sound concerned but still willing to listen to opposing points of view.

1. Jazz singer Ella Fitzgerald was a quiet and humble woman who experienced little of the love she sang about so exquisitely for more than fifty years. Her voice, even in later years when she suffered from crippling arthritis, was always filled with a clear, light energy that could make even the stodgiest* listeners start tapping their toes. Although Fitzgerald, an African-American, came of age in an era when racism was rampant, whatever bitterness she felt never spilled over into her music. She sang the lyrics of a white Cole Porter or a black Duke Ellington with the same impossible-to-imitate ease and grace, earning every one of the awards heaped on her in her later years. When she performed with Duke Ellington at Carnegie Hall in 1958, critics called Fitzgerald "The First Lady of Song." Although she died in 1996, no one has come along to challenge her title, and Ella Fitzgerald is still jazz's first lady.

Tone

    a. coolly objective

    b. enthusiastic

    c. neutral

    d. skeptical

2. There is something happening here. The Net Generation has come of age. Growing up digital has had a profound impact on the way this generation thinks, even changing the way their brains are wired. And although this digital immersion* presents significant challenges for young people—such as dealing with a vast amount of incoming information or ensuring balance between the digital and physical worlds—their immersion has not hurt them overall. It has been positive. The generation is more tolerant of racial diversity and is smarter and quicker than their predecessors. These young people are remaking every institution of modern life, from the workplace to the marketplace, from politics to education, and down to the basic structure of the family. (Don Tapscott, *Grown Up Digital*, 2008, McGraw-Hill, p.10.)

---

*stodgiest: dull, uninspired, lacking energy or imagination.

*immersion: deep involvement, concentration; the physical act of sinking into water.

Tone   a. neutral

b. heated

c. enthusiastic

d. ironic

3. No one who knows anything about horses could call horse racing a barbaric sport. By nature, horses love to run. Dr. Larry Bramlage of the American Association of Equine[†] Practitioners says it best, "You don't force a racehorse to race. They love running. If you came to where I am right now, with all the yearlings in the field, you'd see them out there trying to prove who runs the best." Those who say that horse racing is animal cruelty are speaking theoretically and have no experience with the animals themselves. What they know about horses probably comes from watching old-fashioned westerns on television. It certainly doesn't come from experience with real animals.

Tone   a. annoyed

b. concerned

c. neutral

d. ironic

4. As a mail carrier for more than twenty years, I can tell you firsthand that we are much maligned* members of the population. Customers see only the flaws in mail delivery. They never appreciate the huge effort that makes service both speedy and efficient. For an absurdly small price, you can send mail anywhere in the country, from Hawaii to Alaska. You'd think this would impress most people, but no. Instead of thanking us for services rendered, they whine and complain about the few times mail gets lost or a two-cent price increase. And just because a few members of the postal service have engaged in violent behavior, people now use the insulting expression *going postal* to refer to unexpected outbreaks of violence brought on by stress. This phrase unfairly insults the rest of us hardworking employees who do our jobs without complaint day in and day out.

[†]equine: related to horses.

*maligned: criticized in a spiteful manner.

Tone
    a. comical

    b. insulted

    c. neutral

    d. worried

5. According to one of your readers, insufficient attention has been paid to the possibility that men are also victims of domestic violence. It is his opinion that men are, in fact, just as likely to be victimized by women as women are by men. The difference is that men, for fear of looking unmasculine and weak, fail to report it. Well, I'm just all broken up at the thought of this new social problem. I can imagine how horrible it is for a 220-pound male to be terrorized by a 120-pound female. The poor thing must live in terror at the thought of her menacing approach. A man like that is certainly as much in need of our sympathy as are the women who end up hospitalized or worse in the wake of a domestic dispute.

Tone
    a. ironic

    b. friendly

    c. neutral

    d. sympathetic

6. In 1999, the world champion of chess, Garry Kasparov, agreed to play against the entire world. The game was played on the Internet, with the World Team's decision coming as a result of majority or plurality vote. Four young chess experts were asked to suggest possible moves, but the world was entitled to do as it wished. To promote extended thinking, moves were slowed down to permit one move every two days. Before the game began, it was widely expected that Kasparov would win easily. How could the majority or plurality view of the world's players, almost none of them anywhere near Kasparov's level, hope to compete with the world's champion? But the game turned out to be exceptionally close. After four grueling months, Kasparov ultimately prevailed. But he acknowledged that he had never expended as much effort on any game in his life. (Cass Sunstein, *Infotopia*, 2008, Oxford University Press, p. 22.)

Tone   a. cautious

b. sad

c. neutral

d. ironic

7. It is refreshing to note that many right-thinking citizens are calling for a ban on the celebration of Halloween because the holiday encourages devil worship. Hallelujah? It doesn't take the intellect of a TV evangelist to see that the wearing of "Casper the Friendly Ghost" costumes leads children to the wanton embrace of Beelzebub.[†] And it is a fact that candy corn is the first step toward addiction. Only the devil (or an underemployed dentist) would knowingly offer popcorn balls to innocent children. But why stop at Halloween? Many other holidays conceal wickedness behind a vicious veil of greeting cards and Bob Hope TV specials. (Steve Ruebal, "Toss Out Halloween? Let's Not Stop There," *USA Today*, October 29, 1991, p. 11A.)

Tone   a. confident

b. sarcastic

c. neutral

d. friendly

8. A financial instrument called credit default swaps (CDSs) played a large role in the financial problems that emerged in the United States during 2008. A credit default swap is a form of insurance in which the seller of the swap insures the bond or loan of the buyer. Should the bond or loan default or lose money, the seller will pay the buyer the value of the insurance. CDSs have existed since the 1990s, but their popularity increased greatly starting in 2003. Because credit default swaps were, until 2010, largely unregulated, there was no way to ensure that the seller of the swap could repay a buyer who lost money on a loan or bond. When many mortgage loans failed in 2008, buyers who owned CDSs on mortgage-based funds turned to the seller for the money owed them, based on their original agreement. But in some cases the sellers of the CDSs did not have the funds on hand to make the payment. This had a huge, negative effect on the economy.

[†]Beelzebub: another name for the devil.

Tone
    a. neutral

    b. disgusted

    c. disbelieving

    d. ironic

9. Before readers start mounting protests outside my home, let me say this: I have been a cat lover for years. My wife and I currently possess one three-month-old gray-and-white kitten and an ailing, twelve-year-old tabby, whose sky-high vet bills we pay without a murmur. That being said, we are thinking twice about letting the new kitten go out of doors when she is big enough, as we have with all the cats that came before her, and we'd like to suggest that other responsible pet owners keep their cats indoors as well. A new report by the Smithsonian Conservation Biology Institute and the U.S. Fish and Wildlife Service makes it clear that cats, no matter how cuddly indoors, are a danger to other wildlife and should not be allowed to roam freely. Perhaps you are thinking it's just rats and mice that cats kill. Not so, it's chipmunks, squirrels, and rabbits as well. According to the report, between 1.4 and 3.7 billion birds and close to 15 billion mammals are killed every year by cats. Those are eye-popping figures and reason enough for all of us to keep our cats indoors. They might not like it at first. Many cats do like to roam. But they will get used to it, and we cat lovers won't have so much blood on our hands.

Tone
    a. neutral

    b. concerned

    c. comic

    d. questioning

10. The brilliant Mexican painter Diego Rivera (1886–1957) considered himself a political artist on a mission: He wanted his art to express the dreams, longings, and needs of ordinary people. There is probably no better example of how well he succeeded at his goal than the twenty-seven frescoes[†] titled *Detroit Industry* and painted between 1932 and 1933. Financed by the head of the Ford Motor Company, Edsel Ford, and commissioned by the director of the Detroit Institute of Arts, Rivera's paintings celebrate not the power and influence

---

[†]frescoes: paintings done on wet plaster.

of the automobile or the company that produced it, but rather the hard physical labor of the working people who made the factories run. Covering four walls of the museum, his magnificent murals[†] are alive with color and movement as men of clearly different races toil before a glowing furnace that was meant, at certain times of day, to catch and mirror light. Completed in an astonishing eight months, the murals are much more than realistic depictions of daily life in a factory. Rivera carefully imbued his figures and forms with symbolic meanings that are woven together into a coherent whole stressing the connections between industry and nature, while compelling the viewer's eye from beginning to end.

Tone   a. neutral

b. ironic

c. impressed

d. judgmental

WEB QUEST   **The Response to Rivera's Frescoes**

What was the reaction to *Detroit Industry*?

_____

_____

_____

_____

     REVIEWING THROUGH WRITING

The writer of the following passage employs a neutral tone. Rewrite it using a different tone.

   In April 2010, a German shepherd dog was found locked in a garage, and he might have starved to death had a passerby not heard the dog and brought him to an

---

[†]murals: paintings done on a wall.

emergency veterinary clinic. The adult dog, named Bosco, weighed only thirty-seven pounds. He was weak from hunger and could neither walk nor lift his head. When alerted of his condition, the German Shepherd Rescue of Orange County, California (GSROC), offered to care for the dog, who was renamed Courage. Courage required emergency care, which included blood and plasma transfusions, along with antibiotics and a complete flushing of his intestinal tract. The dog survived and gained thirty pounds. By May he was behaving like a normal dog, and a member of the GSROC had adopted him. The dog's owner was arrested for animal cruelty, and she faces up to four years in jail.

Tone and Figurative Language

"Metaphor is the energy charge that leaps between images revealing their connections."

—Robin Morgan, writer

Figurative language relies on implicit or explicit comparisons of two seemingly unlike people, things, events, or ideas that when examined more closely share an underlying similarity. Writers use figurative language as a way of making their explanations clearer and their writing more engaging for the reader. The more figurative language present in a piece of writing, the more vivid or striking the tone is. If there is a lot of figurative language present in a reading, you can count on the writer's purpose being persuasive even if the writing appears in a context where readers would expect a more informative purpose. Along with allusions, similes and metaphors are the most common kinds of figurative language used to create tone.

Similes

A writer who uses a simile makes an overt comparison by using the word *like* or *as.*[†] Here, for instance, is how one writer, the *New Yorker*'s James Wood, uses a simile to describe the sex appeal of actor Timothy Olyphant

---

[†]The use of similes is more complicated in poetry. Fortunately, this book is dealing with prose, where the simile is used to explain an idea that might otherwise remain unclear.

in the television series *Justified*: "Olyphant is perfectly cast as Raylan, the skeptical cowboy who attracts ladies like refrigerator magnets."

Similes were also a part of what made mystery writer Raymond Chandler such a terrific stylist. In one famous simile, he said a character was "as crazy as two waltzing mice." In another well-known comparison, he described a huge hulk of a man called Moose Malloy, as being "about as inconspicuous as a tarantula on a slice of angel food cake."

Metaphors

Like similes, metaphors make comparisons. They aren't, however, quite as easy to spot because they don't use the words *like* or *as*. But you won't miss them if you stay alert to implicit comparisons like the one shown here:

> Life is a journey and you should expect the ride to get really bumpy at times.

In this sentence, the comparison is twofold. There is a comparison of life to a long journey or trip and a comparison between the hard knocks life can deal out and the bumps you can expect to encounter on a long journey. The point of the metaphor is that no one should expect life to be without difficulties. Having analyzed that example, see if you can identify the two things compared in this next sentence and explain the metaphor's point: "Love is always a wild card."

The comparison is fairly straightforward. Love is like a wild card in a card game. The point of the comparison takes a little more thought. Since a wild card is one that can have any suit, value, or color in a game, the quote about love being a wild card suggests that love can take many different forms. Thus, when love comes into your life, you can never know what to expect.

Implicit and explicit comparisons are central to persuasive writing. They help writers clarify their ideas and establish the tone of their writing. Readers who want to understand an author's message and identify the tone used to create it keep a sharp eye out for the similes and metaphors used by the author.

◆ EXERCISE 7   Creating Figurative Language

DIRECTIONS Comparisons underlie all figurative language. For each experience described, choose the best comparison.

1. If you wanted to say that time was passing by too quickly, would you compare it to

   a. a witch?

   b. a thief?

   c. a turtle?

   Please explain why you chose this comparison.

   _____

   _____

2. If you wanted to say that a speech was hard to follow because the speaker contradicted herself so often, would you compare it to

   a. a beach?

   b. a maze?

   c. a box of candy?

   Please explain why you chose this comparison.

   _____

   _____

3. If you wanted to describe someone who seemed not to have a care in the world, would you compare him or her to

   a. a cat staring fixedly at a mouse?

   b. a dog out for a walk with its owner?

   c. a goat in a corral eating a tin can?

   Please explain why you chose this comparison.

   _____

   _____

4. If you wanted to describe someone who quite suddenly refused to talk, would you compare it to

a. a gurgling stream?

b. a bird suddenly taking flight into the air?

c. a door slamming shut?

Please explain why you chose this comparison.

_____

_____

Tone and Bias

Tone is a dead giveaway to bias. If an attitude or emotion comes through in the author's words, you can pretty much assume the author has a bias, or is promoting a particular point of view. In persuasive writing, that's not a bad thing. We expect a strong point of view when the writer's intention is to persuade. It's informative writing that requires the writer to attempt to eliminate all personal opinion.

It's also important to realize that bias doesn't always come through in the author's tone. Even a writer who uses a cool, reasonable tone and acknowledges opposing points of view can have a strong bias. For instance, an author who describes one point of view in minute detail while dismissing the opposing perspective in a few general sentences is also conveying a bias. There are times, too, when bias is revealed by what the author doesn't say more than by what she does.

◆ EXERCISE 8   Recognizing Tone and Bias

DIRECTIONS Read each passage. Circle the letter that best describes your sense of the author's tone. Then describe what you think is the author's bias.

1. **Lowell, Robert (1917–1977)** American poet from a famous aristocratic family; regarded by most critics as the best English-language poet of his generation and by certain readers as beyond criticism altogether. For better or for worse, Lowell was the modern poet as film star; his private affairs were apparently carried out mainly in public (this is called "confessionalism"): his themes included the personalities and behavior of his relatives, his various marriages and affairs,

the presumably affective disorder[†] which landed him in the hospital many times, and so on. Lowell was extremely gifted, but the conventional view of his development—even here it judges the most recent poems as failures—is not quite correct, for it mistakes potential for achievement, and overrates him. (Adapted from Martin Seymour-Smith, *Who's Who in Twentieth Century Literature*, McGraw-Hill, 1977, p. 216.)

Tone   a. admiring

b. belittling

c. neutral

d. cautious

Which statement best describes the author's bias?

a. The author really likes Lowell's work.

b. The author thinks Lowell wasn't especially talented.

c. There is no evidence of any bias.

 2. At the height of World War I, Josephus Daniels, the deeply religious Secretary of the Navy, actually believed that having authority over so many young men was a God-given opportunity to improve their morals. He called navy ships "floating universities" of moral reform. Daniels gave orders to the navy to clear out the red light districts that had been a fixture near every base. The army did the same in towns near its training camps, most famously Storyville, across the river from New Orleans.

Prostitution no more disappeared than people stopped drinking alcohol. But the flush of excitement in the reformers' short-term victories confirmed their belief that, among its horrors, the war had transformed society into a laboratory where it could be reshaped for the better, (Adapted from Joseph Conlin, *The American Past* 9e, Vol. II, © Cengage Learning.)

Tone   a. disbelieving

b. critical

c. neutral

d. admiring

[†]affective disorder: any mental disorder in which the emotions are involved.

Which statement best describes the author's bias?

a. The author admires the reformers' accomplishments.

b. The author thinks the reformers accomplished next to nothing.

c. There is no evidence of any bias.

3. Overshadowed in her lifetime by the fame of her much more talented husband, the artist Frida Kahlo (1907–1954) managed to overtake him in death. Her name, in fact, has become better known than his, mainly because she has been embraced by feminists always eager to identify forgotten female geniuses wherever they can. Yet in comparing the works of the two artists, serious art critics have a key question: Does Kahlo's fame rest on the quality of her work or the fact that she was a female artist whose work was overshadowed by a more talented husband? Kahlo did have some minor ability but neither her gender nor her marital relationship makes her a great artist. To evaluate it fairly, one needs to look at her work objectively, without taking pity on her because of her personal misery.

Tone

a. admiring

b. neutral

c. skeptical

d. enthusiastic

Which statement best describes the author's bias?

a. The author is pleased that feminists rediscovered Kahlo's work.

b. The author thinks feminists are too eager to celebrate Kahlo for the wrong reasons.

c. There is no evidence of any bias.

4. **Jefferson's Bible**

While serving as third president of the United States, Thomas Jefferson began a project to revise the Bible. Jefferson studied the scriptures every day and selected what he considered to be the Bible's best and most authentic material. Concentrating on the New Testament—especially the Gospels of Matthew, Mark, and Luke—Jefferson literally cut out his favorite passages (which he said were like "diamonds in a dunghill") with a razor and pasted them together to create his own version of the Bible. In doing so, he censored any mention of Jesus as God or the Son of God. He also eliminated all miracles and supernatural events.

Jefferson never intended for anyone to see his personal version of the Bible. However, it was discovered in 1886 and published by the Government Printing Office from 1904 to 1957. In 2001, Jefferson's Bible was distributed by Beacon Press, and there was an immediate public outcry from those who thought Jefferson had committed sacrilege.

Sacrilege seems a strong word in this case because Jefferson never intended the Bible to be published. He never even intended it to be seen by anyone except himself. What Jefferson did was not especially different from people who underline or highlight favorite passages, something many devout Christians have done for years without anyone accusing them of sacrilege. Instead of attacking Jefferson for being sacrilegious, we should view his Bible as an important historical document that helps us better understand the religious outlook of one of our most important founding fathers.

Tone
a. neutral

b. approving

c. mistrustful

d. outraged

Which statement best describes the author's bias?

a. The author thinks Jefferson's creation of his personal Bible was an achievement.

b. The author thinks that Jefferson should have left the Bible as it was and not presumed he had the right to edit.

c. There is no evidence of any bias.

✔ CHECK YOUR UNDERSTANDING

1. What ingredients go into creating tone in writing?

   _____

   _____

2. Why do readers need to pay attention to tone?

   _____

   _____

   _____

3. How would you describe an ironic tone?

   _____

4. When readers recognize a distinct tone in a piece of writing, they know immediately

   that _____.

5. What does figurative language do?

   _____

   _____

6. What's the central difference between a simile and a metaphor?

   _____

   _____

7. Explain the point of the simile in the following sentence: "Many parents complain
   that bringing home a first baby is like walking around with a dozen eggs on their
   head."

   _____

8. What two things was Thomas Jefferson comparing in the following metaphor and what does the metaphor imply? "Slavery is a wolf America holds by the ears."

_____

_____

_____

WORD CHECK

The following words were introduced and defined in pages 550–577. See how well you can match the words with the meanings. When you finish, make sure to check the meanings of any words you missed because the same words will turn up in tests at the end of the chapter.

1. progressive (p. 550) _____

2. messianic (p. 550) _____

3. vile (p. 551) _____

4. forage (p. 552) _____

5. compulsory (p. 556) _____

6. debilitating (p. 557) _____

7. crux (p. 561) _____

8. vested interest (p. 563) _____

9. status quo (p. 563) _____

10. archaic (p. 567) _____

11. methodology (p. 567) _____

12. magnitude (p. 572) _____

13. stodgy (p. 576) _____

14. immersion (p. 576) _____

15. maligned (p. 577) _____

a. core, heart, key point

b. having a zealous devotion to a cause

c. weakening, causing loss of energy

d. disgusting, despicable

e. ancient, obsolete

f. existing or given state of affairs

g. a special reason to promote or protect that which gives one a personal advantage

h. advanced, forward-thinking, open to change

i. mandatory, binding, required or commanded by authority

j. a system for getting something accomplished, procedure, set of rules

k. great size or extent, importance

l. deep involvement, concentration; the physical act of sinking into water

m. criticized in an unfair and spiteful manner

n. dull, uninspired, lacking in imagination

o. looking for food over a wide area

◆ **EXERCISE 9**   **More About Form and Meaning**

DIRECTIONS Fill in the blanks with one of the words listed below.

progressive	vile	debilitating	crux	status quo
vested interest	messianic	compulsory	maligned	archaic
forage	methodology	magnitude	stodgy	immersion

1. Many car fans believe that the much _____ Corvair was a better car than the media, or consumer advocate Ralph Nader, made it out to be.

2. Telling someone to get to the point is a less formal way of asking for the _____ of an issue.

3. Writers have a(n) _____ in encouraging a passion for language.

4. Helmets should be _____ for everyone who rides a motorcycle.

5. After the art critic fell in love, he abandoned his _____ and unfashionable clothing, in favor of stylish and trendy new apparel.

6. In the deep snows, the deer had to travel longer and longer distances to _____ for food.

7. It's not surprising when people who have all their needs and wants met are happy with the _____; why would they want anything to change?

8. Making fun of people with disabilities, abusing one's pets, and profiting from the misfortune of others are all examples of _____ behavior.

9. It's wonderful for people to have a cause they believe in, but if they become _____ about it, they can be so annoying.

10. Many professional athletes suffer so many _____ injuries in the course of their careers that their bodies never quite recover.

11. The _____ of the earthquake was way beyond anything that had happened before in that area of the world.

12. To evaluate the results of a study, you first need to understand the _____ that was used to obtain them.

13. A(n) _____ thinker, Henry Wallace irritated members of the Democratic Party, who saw to it that he was bypassed as a vice presidential candidate in 1944.

14. No one uses the word *thou* anymore; the usage is considered _____ .

15. To experience complete cultural _____, you probably need to live with a family from another culture; just visiting a new place or country isn't enough to understand the customs and norms that govern the lives of the inhabitants.

TAKING STOCK More Guns = More Killing

Looking Ahead Elisabeth Rosenthal is a physician and a science reporter for the *New York Times*. In this reading, she offers an answer to those who say that the way to stop violence is for more guns to be readily available to ordinary citizens.

1   In the wake of the tragic shooting deaths at Sandy Hook Elementary School in Newtown, Conn., last month [December 14, 2012], the National Rifle Association (N.R.A.) proposed that the best way to protect schoolchildren was to place a guard—a "good guy with a gun"—in every school, part of a so-called National School Shield Emergency Response Program. Indeed, the N.R.A.'s solution to the expansion of gun violence in America has been generally to advocate for the more widespread deployment and carrying of guns.

2   I recently visited some Latin American countries that mesh with the N.R.A.'s vision of the promised land, where guards with guns grace every office lobby, storefront, A.T.M., restaurant and gas station. It has not made those countries safer or saner. Despite the ubiquitous presence of "good guys" with guns, countries like Guatemala, Honduras, El Salvador, Colombia and Venezuela have some of the highest homicide rates in the world.

3   "A society that is relying on guys with guns to stop violence is a sign of a society where institutions have broken down," said Rebecca Peters, former director of the International Action Network on Small Arms. "It's shocking to hear anyone in the United States considering a solution that would make it seem more like Colombia." As guns proliferate, legally and illegally, innocent people often seem more terrorized than protected.

4   In Guatemala, riding a public bus is a risky business. More than 500 bus drivers have been killed in robberies since 2007, leading InSight Crime, which tracks organized crime in the Americas, to call it "the most dangerous profession on the planet." And when bullets start flying, everyone is vulnerable: in 2010 the onboard tally included 155 drivers, 54 bus assistants, 71 passengers and 14 presumed criminals. Some were killed by the robbers' bullets and some by gun-carrying passengers.

5   Scientific studies have consistently found that places with more guns have more violent deaths, both homicides and suicides. Women and children are more likely to die if there's a gun in the house. The more guns in an area, the higher the local suicide rates. "Generally, if you live in a civilized society, more guns mean more death," said David Hemenway, director of the Harvard Injury Control Research Center. "There is no evidence that having more guns reduces crime. None at all."

6   After a gruesome mass murder in 1996 provoked public outrage, Australia enacted stricter gun laws, including a 28-day waiting period before purchase and a ban on semiautomatic weapons. Before then, Australia had averaged one mass shooting a year. Since, rates of both homicide and suicide have dropped 50 percent, and there have been no mass killings, said Ms. Peters, who lobbied for the legislation.

7   Distinctive factors contribute to the high rates of violent crime in Latin America. Many countries in the region had recent civil wars, resulting in a large number of weapons in circulation. Drug- and gang-related violence is widespread. "It's dangerous to make too tight a link between the availability of weapons and homicide rates," said Jeremy McDermott, a co-director of InSight Crime who is based in Medellín, Colombia. "There are lots of other variables."

8   Still, he said that the recent sharp increase in homicides in Venezuela could be in part explained by the abundance of arms there. Although the government last spring imposed a one-year ban on importing weapons, there had previously been a plentiful influx from Russia. There is a Kalashnikov plant in the country.

9   In 2011, according to the United Nations Office on Drugs and Crime, Honduras led the world in homicides, with 91.6 per 100,000 people. But rates were also alarmingly high in El Salvador (69.1), Jamaica (40.9), Colombia (31.4) and Guatemala (38.5). Venezuela's was 45.1 in 2010 but is expected to be close to 80 this year. The United States' rate is about 5.

10   Though many of these countries have restrictions on gun ownership, enforcement is lax. According to research by Flacso, the Guatemalan Social Science Academy, illegal guns far outnumber legal weapons in Central America. All that has spawned a thriving security industry—the good guys with guns that grace every street corner—though experts say it is often unclear if their presence is making crime better or worse. In many countries, the armed guards have only six weeks of training.

11   Guatemala, with approximately 20,000 police officers, has 41,000 registered private security guards and an estimated 80,000 who are working without authorization. "To put people with guns who are not accountable or trained in places where there are lots of innocent people is just dangerous," Ms. Peters said, noting that lethal force is used to deter minor crimes like shoplifting.

12   Indeed, even as some Americans propose expanding our gun culture into elementary schools, some Latin American cities are trying to rein in theirs. Bogotá's new mayor, Gustavo Petro, has forbidden residents to carry weapons on streets, in cars or in any public space since last February, and

the murder rate has dropped 50 percent to a 27-year low. He said, "Guns are not a defense, they are a risk."

13   William Godnick, coordinator of the Public Security Program at the United Nations Regional Center for Peace, Disarmament and Development in Latin America and the Caribbean, said that United Nations studies in Central America showed that people who used a gun to defend against an armed assault were far more likely to be injured or killed than if they had no weapon.

14   Post–Sandy Hook, gun groups in the United States are now offering teachers firearms training. But do I really want my kid's teachers packing a weapon? "If you're living in a 'Mad Max' world, where criminals have free rein and there's no government to stop them, then I'd want to be armed," said Dr. Hemenway of Harvard. "But we're not in that circumstance. We're a developed, stable country." ("More Guns = More Killing" by Elisabeth Rosenthal from *The New York Times*, January 5, 2013. Copyright © 2013 The New York Times. All rights reserved. Used by permission and protected by the Copyright Laws of the United States. The printing, copying, redistribution, or retransmission of this Content without express written permission is prohibited.)

Sharpening Your Skills

DIRECTIONS Answer the following questions by circling the letter of the correct response or filling in the blanks.

Making Predictions 1. Based on the title, which of the following predictions would make the most sense?

a. The reading will support the idea that citizens who arm themselves are safer than citizens who don't.

b. The reading will support the idea that school guards need to be armed.

c. The reading will oppose the idea that citizens who carry firearms are ensuring their safety.

Using Context Clues

2. Based on the context, which of the following definitions would you choose for the word *deployment* as it appears in this sentence? "Indeed, the N.R.A.'s solution to the expansion of gun violence in America has been generally to advocate for the more widespread *deployment* and carrying of guns."

a. discussion

b. distribution

c. improvement

d. elimination

3. Based on the context, which of the following definitions would you choose for the word *ubiquitous* as it appears in this sentence? "Despite the *ubiquitous* presence of 'good guys' with guns, countries like Guatemala, Honduras, El Salvador, Colombia and Venezuela have some of the highest homicide rates in the world."

a. hidden

b. mysterious

c. constant

d. unusual

4. Based on the context, what would be a good synonym for *proliferate* in the following sentence? "As guns *proliferate*, legally and illegally, innocent people often seem more terrorized than protected."

_____

Identifying the Controlling Main Idea

5. Which paragraph introduces the overall main idea of the reading?

a. paragraph 1

b. paragraph 2

c. paragraph 3

6. In your own words, what's the main idea of the entire reading?

_____

_____

Identifying the
Author's Purpose

7. Which statement best describes the author's purpose?

   a. The author wants to tell readers about the countries where people protect themselves by carrying weapons.

   b. The author wants to rebut the N.R.A.'s argument that the world gets less dangerous when the "good guys" carry guns.

Analyzing
Arguments

8. What question would critical readers ask about the scientific studies mentioned in paragraph 5?

   _____

9. Are the homicide statistics in paragraph 9 relevant or irrelevant to the author's main idea? _____ Please explain.

   _____

   _____

10. In paragraph 13, William Godnick provides expert opinion for what point of view?

    _____

11. Does Godnick's affiliation suggest he might have a bias? _____ Please explain.

    _____

12. Which statement best describes Jeremy McDermott's role in the reading?

    a. He is an expert mentioned to support the author's opinion that arming citizens leads to greater violence.

    b. He is an expert who does not fully agree with the author's point of view.

    c. He is an expert who supports the N.R.A.'s position that ordinary citizens need to be armed if they want to be safe.

Paraphrasing 13. Which statement best paraphrases McDermott's point of view?

    a. In Latin America, drug running is the real source of violence; it's not citizens who carry firearms to protect themselves.

    b. It's probably a mistake to insist that the homicide rate is solely the result of gun availability; there are other issues involved.

    c. The availability of guns is not the reason that the homicide rates are so high in Latin American countries.

Drawing Personal 14. How do you think the author would react if her daughter came
Conclusions home and told her that the teachers in her school were getting training in firearms to better protect their students?

_____

_____

Recognizing Bias 15. Which statement best describes the presence of bias in the reading?

    a. The author is extremely opposed to the idea that citizens who are well-armed are safer from harm.

    b. The author is opposed to assault rifles but believes that hand-guns might keep the general population safer from harm.

    c. There is no evidence of the author's personal opinion.

▶ TEST 1   Analyzing Arguments

DIRECTIONS   Read each argument and answer the questions that follow by filling in the blanks or circling the letter of the correct response. *Note*: The author may or may not respond to opposition, and the argument may or may not include an error.

1. Kids and Sports

1   For many parents, competitive team sports like Little League Baseball and pee wee football are an essential part of childhood. Thus they are anxious for their kids to try out for and "make the team." Supposedly, competitive sports build physical strength. Even more important—or so the argument goes—playing competitive sports early on in childhood builds character. Still, parents intent on making sure their kids learn how to compete might want to rethink the notion that sports in which somebody has to win or lose are important to a young child's development. Competitive sports for pre-teens have some important disadvantages; these disadvantages need to be considered before parents push kids onto a playing field where the winner takes all.

2   Here's one thing that should be considered: Competitive sports can unduly stress a child's still-developing body. Football, basketball, baseball, and even tennis are physically demanding. They put a very heavy strain on the body. This is particularly true if muscles or bones are still developing. Now, a ten-year-old who is just playing for the fun of it will probably not repeat a movement or motion that hurts, but what if that same child is playing for a trophy? Is he or she going to stop throwing that tough-to-hit curve ball just because there is a little pain involved? It's not likely. Unfortunately, the end result can be lifelong damage to a shoulder or an arm. Thomas Tutko, author of *Winning Is Everything and Other American Myths*, argues that kids should not be playing physically demanding sports before the age of fourteen. From Tutko's perspective, playing competitive sports before that age is simply too "traumatic," both physically and psychologically.

3   In his book *No Contest: The Case Against Competition*, author and researcher Alfie Kohn emphasizes that the psychological effects of competitive sports on those still too young to play them may be worse than the physical injuries that can ensue. Kohn's book summarizes the results of several hundred studies focusing on the effects of competition both on and off the playing field. Whether in the context of sports or the classroom, Kohn contends in his book that competition "undermines self-esteem, poisons our relationships, and holds us back from doing our best." Clearly, Kohn would not support the notion of competition as a character builder for children. If anything, he sees it as a character destroyer, even if those competing are grown-ups.

4   To be fair to those who insist there's no point to playing basketball, football, or baseball unless you keep score, these are games where the score counts. However, the position argued here is not that competitive sports should be abandoned; rather, they should be postponed until the child is ready to be not just a winner but a loser as well. A fifteen-year-old is probably able to accept the simple fact that, at some time in life, everyone loses at something. But does a nine-year-old have to learn this lesson? In their early years, kids should concentrate on achieving their personal best. Are they running faster, jumping higher, or throwing farther than they did the last time around? Those are the questions they should be asking themselves, not who won and who lost.

1. What is the author's point?

   _____

   _____

2. Identify the two reasons used to support that point.

   a. _____

   _____

   b. _____

   _____

3. Does the author include any of the following?

   a. examples or illustrations

   b. research results

   c. expert opinion

4. Does the author respond to any opposing point of view? _____
   If so, fill in the blanks that follow.

Opposition   _____

              _____

Response   _____

              _____

5. How would you describe the author's tone?

    a. irritated

    b. light-hearted

    c. concerned

    d. neutral

2. Opening Up Adoption Files

1   Children who were adopted may or may not have access to their adoption records. It all depends on the state where the adoption took place, and there are no blanket laws guaranteeing adoptees access to their records when they come of age as adults. In some states, adoptees are allowed no information. In others, they have access to "non-identifying information." This information is limited to age, physical characteristics, talents, hobbies, and basic medical data of the biological parent or parents. But even that amount of information depends on the agency or institution involved in the original adoption procedure. Some may offer detailed reports, others keep the details to a bare minimum.

2   Over the years, many adoptees have rightly protested this situation, causing some states to modify their rules for access. For instance, even the most restrictive state laws now allow for the opening of sealed files via court order. But the decision about access to adoption records should *not* be left to the individual states. Instead, Congress should step in and enact legislation that gives adopted children the blanket right to discover their parents and their history, both personal and medical. As many adoptees have pointed out, the sealed records policy may serve adopted children but becomes counterproductive when those children grow up and become adults who want or, in the case of medical emergency, need information.

3   After all, restricting access to adoption files makes the search more difficult, without stopping adoptees—and less frequently birth parents—from searching. Those men and women desperate for information will, if they can afford it, hire a detective to find out what they are driven to know.

4   The truth is that many adoptees feel guilty about being put up for adoption. They assume that they did something wrong, something that made them so unlovable their parents were forced to give them up. These people need to know the real causes for their adoption. It helps an adoptee to know, for example, that his mother gave him up for adoption because she was too young to support a child, not because she didn't love her baby.

Such knowledge helps relieve the burden of guilt some adoptees carry around their entire lives.

5   There are also physical—rather than psychological—reasons why adoptees need access to their files. To take proper care of their health, they need to know what diseases they might have inherited and if it's possible to avoid them. They also need to know about any inherited diseases they might be passing on to their own children. When it comes to managing their health care, adoptees who know nothing about their parents are at a terrible disadvantage—one that could cost them their lives or bring heartbreak to their children.

6   Some parents who have given up their children for adoption resent the idea of opening adoption files. They feel that their right to privacy will be threatened. Yet this objection is based on the assumption that adopted children want to hunt down their parents and intrude on their lives. But, as study after study shows, adoptees only want to know who their biological parents are. In some cases, they may even want to meet them, but they do not want to push their way into the lives of people who will not accept them. Giving the adopted person access to files does not mean that the parent or parents forsake all rights to privacy. It only means that the adopted child can attempt to make contact if he or she wishes, and the parents can refuse or accept as they see fit.

1. What is the author's point?

_____

_____

_____

2. Identify the three reasons used to support that point.

a. _____

_____

b. _____

c. _____

_____

3. Which of the following does the author include?

    a. examples or illustrations

    b. research results

    c. expert opinion

4. Does the author respond to any opposing point of view? _____ If so, fill in the blanks that follow.

Opposition   _____

                  _____

Response   _____

                  _____

5. How would you describe the author's tone?

    a. reasonable

    b. angry

    c. comical

    d. neutral

▶ TEST 2   Analyzing Arguments

DIRECTIONS Read each argument and answer the questions that follow by filling in the blanks or circling the letter of the correct response. *Note*: The author may or may not respond to opposition and the argument may or may not include an error.

1. Banning Peanuts

1   There was a time when the peanut butter and jelly sandwich was a staple of the school lunchbox. Often it was the one food that fussy children would willingly eat, and parents were grateful it existed, even if they personally found the combination distasteful. The popularity of peanut butter and jelly sandwiches, however, is a thing of the past as schools from New York to California have stopped serving them in the cafeteria. Many school officials have also asked parents not to put peanut products of any kind into their kids' lunches.

2   If the ban on peanuts sounds silly to you, then you obviously don't know an important fact: The Food Allergy and Anaphylaxis[†] Network (FAAN) estimated that 1 in every 125 children is affected by a peanut allergy. Studies like the one published by the Centers for Disease Control in 2013 also indicate that the number of children with food allergies is increasing at alarming rates, with peanut allergies at the top of the list. The need for a ban on peanuts in the schools is not a trivial issue. It's a matter of life or death.

3   In May 2010, seventeen-year-old Yia Aquino of California died after she unknowingly ate peanut butter at her senior prom. She is not the first young person to die as a result of ingesting the nuts her body could not tolerate. The volunteer group Washington Feast, which is devoted to disseminating information about food allergies, formed after ten-year-old Kristine Kastner of Mercer Island, Washington, died from anaphylactic shock, the result of eating a chocolate chip cookie that had finely minced peanuts in it. The reality is that children can and do die if they unwittingly ingest peanut products, and neither parents nor educators can afford to take the chance that this might happen.

4   Critics of the ban, among them some members of FAAN, worry that the peanut ban pits parent against parent, especially when desperate parents reduce the issue to "My kid's life or your kid's peanut butter sandwich." Opponents of the ban argue that there are other ways to handle the problem.

[†]anaphylaxis: hypersensitivity to a foreign substance that, in some cases, can result in death.

They emphasize self-management on the part of the child along with special lunch zones where peanuts are, or are not, allowed.

5   Such suggestions, however, overlook several crucial points. Labels don't always make it easy to discover exactly what's in the food being consumed. Then, too, kids will be kids. Tell them to stay in one area of the cafeteria while avoiding another and they will do the exact opposite. Thus if peanuts in any form are allowed in school, there's always the possibility that a child with an allergy will ingest a snack that might prove deadly. Naturally, a child allergic to peanuts is not going to bite into a peanut butter and jelly sandwich, but that same child might well munch on a chocolate chip cookie containing peanuts, not realizing that nuts are in the cookie.

6   Parents of children allergic to peanuts are aware that many do not want peanut products banned from schools. One of those parents is Mark LoPresti of Grand Island, a suburb in Buffalo, New York. LoPresti's son Vincent is allergic to peanuts and almost died after eating them by mistake. While the father acknowledges the ban can create problems, he is fiercely committed to banning them from schools. As he put it, "I'm not going to sacrifice my son's life for the right to have a peanut butter sandwich." It's hard not to sympathize with this point of view. When it comes to the ban on peanut products in schools, an old adage seems to apply: "It's better to be safe than sorry." (Source of quotation: Carrie Hedges, "Peanut Ban Spreads to Cafeteria," *USA Today*, December 3, 1998, p. 17a)

1. What is the author's point?

_____

_____

2. Identify the reason used to support that point.

_____

_____

3. Does the author respond to any opposing point of view? _____
If so, fill in the blanks that follow.

Opposition   _____

_____

_____

Response _____

_____

_____

4. How would you describe the author's tone?

_____

_____

2. Protecting Our Children from Pornography

1   The Children's Internet Protection Act (CIPA) requires schools and libraries to have in place software filters that block computer access to sites featuring obscenity or pornography and considered harmful to minors. Libraries or schools that do not have such filters in place cannot participate in the federal E-rate program, which offers affordable technology for schools and libraries.

2   This legislation appears so eminently sensible. It seems almost impossible that anyone would quarrel with it. Yet, in fact, when CIPA was first proposed there was immediate opposition from the American Civil Liberties Union and, in particular, the American Library Association. Stranger still, a lower court actually sided with the American Library Association in a suit challenging the constitutionality of applying CIPA to libraries.

3   Fortunately, on June 23, 2003, the Supreme Court struck down the lower court's ruling. But even though the issue has come to a legal resolution, and CIPA is now the law of the land, the question remains: How is it that sensible people in the past, and in the present, can challenge legislation that does nothing more than protect innocent children?

4   Practically all of our nation's public libraries now offer Internet access. Thanks to that access, any twelve-year-old—unless filters are in place—can reach sites featuring hardcore sex scenes. Even worse, kids can access chatrooms where they could make contact with sex offenders or child molesters. Children should not be exposed to such websites or chatrooms.

5   Opponents of the filters on library computers argue that they also block access to constitutionally protected free speech and unfairly infringe on the right of adults to access information not considered illegal in any way. But this complaint is sheer nonsense. Adults who want access to sites filtered out by the software can ask that it be temporarily disabled. This is a right that is actually guaranteed by the CIPA legislation.

6   Libraries routinely act the role of censor when they refuse to stock their shelves with pornographic books, magazines, or videos, and you won't find copies of *Hustler* or *Penthouse* tucked away in the magazine rack of your local library. Nor for that matter will you find a copy of *Deep Throat*[†] in the movie and media section. Yet no one claims that this act of censorship infringes on the right to free speech. Why shouldn't the same principle apply to the Internet? Libraries don't stock pornography; therefore, why shouldn't they exclude pornographic sites from their offerings to the public?

7   Our libraries need to be open to everyone. But by allowing children access to any website available on the Internet, we are turning our libraries into adult bookstores and doing what real adult bookstores cannot do for fear of legal retribution. Libraries that don't use software filters are exposing vulnerable children to pornographic material that might well do them terrible, even deadly, harm.

1. What is the author's point?

_____

_____

2. Identify the two reasons used to support that point.

a. _____

_____

b. _____

_____

3. Does the author respond to any opposing point of view? _____ If so, fill in the blanks that follow.

Opposition _____

Response _____

4. How would you describe the author's tone?

_____

_____

[†]*Deep Throat*: A 1972 pornographic film that created a huge public stir because it was extremely graphic sexually.

▶ **TEST 3** **Reviewing New Vocabulary**

DIRECTIONS Fill in the blanks with one of the words listed below.

debilitating	stodgy	crux	immersed	vile
archaic	compulsory	messianic	vested interest	status quo
malign	foraging	progressives	methodology	magnitude

1. **When a Group Becomes a Mob**

In one of his most famous books, *Group Psychology and the Analysis of the Ego*, Sigmund Freud tried to explain how seemingly independent individuals can sometimes be transformed into an unthinking, uninhibited mob. For Freud, people in groups were inclined to give over their free will to a

_____ leader who says that he alone can provide safety from harm in exchange for complete obedience. It was, Freud claimed, as

if individual identity became _____ in the larger group identity as it was defined by the powerful leader.

Despite his lack of any convincing _____—Freud worked largely through insight and intuition—Freud's theory may be accurate because people in groups do seem to lose their independence and defer to the person who is most outspoken and aggressive. The more strong-willed the leader seems to be, the less inclined group

members are to assert their individuality. It's as if they had reverted to

some _____, stone age mentality, where safety could only be achieved by remaining part of a group. People who give themselves over to groupthink also become less willing to question the

_____ because to do so might get them ejected from the community that provides their identity. In fact, they would often pre-

fer to _____ anyone who challenges the group's actions or beliefs rather than consider that the group might actually be in error. Although it would be hard to test Freud's theory empirically, it may well account for the often barbaric behavior of people in groups.

2. _____ drug testing for certain professions, like police, pilots, and firefighters, arouses understandable controversy. At the

_____ of the controversy is, to a large degree, the method

of testing. After all, it does seem _____ for an employer to
ask employees to submit urine samples. But employers and the public at

large have a _____ in being sure that those responsible

for the public's safety are not under the influence of _____
drugs that might interfere with performance. The public might also be
more willing to trust organizations whose rules and regulations suggest a
desire for complete openness, especially during a time when prescription

and illegal drug use is a problem of great _____.

3. More and more people are determined to leave behind modern culture
and do what's called "living off the land." They have revived farming prac-

tices like plowing the fields with oxen or horses and roam the country-

side _____ for wild mushrooms and edible ferns. They
take pleasure in being traditionalists who cherish the past rather than

_____ who look toward the future. They consider being

called _____ and out of fashion compliments rather than
criticisms.

Evaluating Arguments

"Arguments, like men, are often pretenders."
—Plato

As Chapter 9 explains, writers who want to convince you to share their point of view often mount an argument. They tell you, that is, why their opinion should also be yours. But, for any number of reasons—over-confidence, lack of time, or a stubborn unwillingness to admit they might be wrong—writers occasionally provide readers with support that only seems convincing. In other words, it only makes sense if you don't analyze it. Thus, the goal of this chapter is to make sure that you look closely at the support writers use to promote their ideas and recognize when that support is lacking in substance or riddled with errors.

Support That Gets a Failing Grade

In this section, you'll learn about some of the most common mistakes writers can make when providing support for an opinion. Familiarize yourself with these errors so that you can readily spot them when they appear in writing, yours or someone else's.

Circular Reasoning

Solid arguments follow opinions with relevant reasons. But writers confident of their own rightness don't always give much thought to what will make their opinion convincing to others. Instead, they engage in **circular reasoning**: They offer an opinion and follow it with a reason that says the same thing. Only the language is different, not the idea.

In the following passage, for example, the writer believes that the U.S. system of food inspection needs to be overhauled because the food supply is contaminated. But instead of offering reasons for that opinion, the author merely repeats it in different words.

> Currently, our food supply is in danger of being contaminated from many different sources. When the very food we put into our mouths endangers our health, it is clear that we need to institute strict and regular inspections of food raised or grown in the United States. These inspections should also apply to food imported from other countries. People should be able to sit down to a meal and not worry that the food they eat will make them sick. However, we won't have that sense of security about our food supply unless we improve our current system of inspections.

The author of this paragraph doesn't acknowledge that other people might not share the belief that the U.S. food supply is in danger of contamination from "many different sources." The writer simply presents the idea as a fact accepted by everyone. Then she calls for more food inspections based on a threat in her mind so obvious, no proof needs to be supplied.

Hasty Generalizations

Generalizations are broad statements that summarize a number of different but related events. The following are all examples of generalizations:

1. The American military has not done enough to eliminate the sexual abuse of enlisted women.

2. The more people text in order to communicate the more likely they are to suffer from phone phobia.

3. In the past, Google has had no problem with invasion of privacy—consider Google Maps—and Google Glass will only further erode personal privacy.

Because generalizations cover a lot of territory, the rule of thumb for using them effectively is this: The broader and more wide-ranging the generalization, the more examples writers need to supply in order to be convincing. If an author generalizes about a large group on the basis of one or even two examples, critical readers think twice before making the author's opinion their own.

In the following passage, the author offers a generalization about how insurance companies treat women who get breast cancer. Unfortunately, that statement is based on one lone example. That makes it a **hasty generalization**, or a generalization based on too few examples to be immediately believable:

> Insurance companies routinely find ways to get rid of patients diagnosed with breast cancer. The companies use sophisticated software to identify women who have contracted the disease and then find some technical reason to drop them from their list of insured. It doesn't matter if the women have been paying their premiums on time or have never filed a previous claim; their insurance gets canceled. Patricia Relling, a successful art gallery owner from Louisville, Kentucky, found out the hard way what happens to insurance coverage when women who think their insurance will pay for medical treatment get breast cancer. Like so many others, her policy was canceled on a technicality once her insurer discovered she had breast cancer. (Source of information: www .reuters.com/article/2010/04/23/us-wellpoint-breastcancer-idUSTRE63M5D420100423.)

What the author says about insurance companies and women with breast cancer may be accurate. But this paragraph should not convince anyone that it is. One example to illustrate such a broad generalization is not enough to be convincing.

ALLUSION ALERT

The Great Gatsby

The Great Gatsby by F. Scott Fitzgerald is an American classic. It tells the story of Jay Gatsby, a poor young man who amasses a huge fortune in an attempt to win Daisy Buchanan, the young woman he loves. In telling the story of Daisy and Jay, Fitzgerald also describes a world where the very rich live by their own rules while casually destroying the lives of others in the process. Allusions to the book have come to suggest the pursuit of wealth, excessive spending, and a longing for the American dream, defined as financial success—for example, "Except for Fitzgerald's Gatsby, few people have spent so much money to win so little."

Irrelevant Reasons

As Chapter 8 explains, authors sometimes include facts that aren't relevant to their opinion or claim. Here, for example, is an argument that gets off track and includes an **irrelevant reason**:

Between April and May of 2012 ten people died in an attempt to ascend Mount Everest, the world's tallest mountain. Unlike the tragedy of 1996,[†] when twelve climbers died on the mountain, these deaths were not triggered by an unexpected storm that left inexperienced, snow-blinded climbers struggling to find their way on their own. The 2012 deaths were a tragic and all too predictable result of over-confidence and inexperience. Those who died ignored obvious symptoms of altitude sickness. They climbed too slowly and fell behind, failing to turn back even when it became clear to more experienced climbers that the newcomers were growing physically and mentally weaker. Because inexperience and over-confidence had also contributed to the deaths in 1996, attempts had been made over the years to make climbing Mount Everest subject to regulation, both for climbers and expedition outfitters. But the deaths in the spring of 2012 are evidence that those attempts did not succeed. Scores of untrained, unfit people—perhaps triple the number that arrived in 1996—still turn up at the mountain's base camp eager to begin their climbing career on the world's tallest mountain. While respectable climbing outfitters would, and do, turn inexperienced climbers away, there are plenty of others who accept anyone who comes up with the price of the climb, a staggering $30,000 to $100,000. Given the dangers the inexperienced climbers create both for themselves and others, this should not be allowed. It's also true that rich people shouldn't be encouraged to think money buys everything. As F. Scott Fitzgerald so powerfully showed in his masterpiece *The Great Gatsby*, that attitude can lead to tragedy and death.

[†]Jon Krakauer, who participated in the 1996 climb, wrote a best-selling book, *Into Thin Air*, about the experience.

The point of this passage is clear: Beginning climbers should not try to ascend Mount Everest. If they don't have the common sense to stay off the mountain, then regulations need to be in place to prevent them, because their lack of preparation can lead to fatal mistakes. But tucked away at the end of the passage is a less relevant reason: Rich people should not be allowed to think money buys everything. Well, maybe they shouldn't. Yet that reason, along with the allusion to *The Great Gatsby*, is not related to the author's claim. Nor for that matter is it clear that people who can pay the price of the climb are automatically rich. Some people, possessed by the dream of scaling Mount Everest, sell all their possessions to take their chances on the mountain. In any case, neither the last reason nor the closing allusion clarifies why climbing novices should be prevented from scaling Mount Everest. This is the point that needs to be argued with relevant reasons.

Unidentified or Inappropriate Experts

In the cloning passage on page 553, it makes sense for the author to quote a bioethicist as support for her opinion. Bioethicists specialize in the study of moral and ethical issues that result from or apply to medical and biological discoveries and procedures. However, critical readers are rightly suspicious of references to unidentified experts, who may or may not be qualified to offer an opinion. Consider, for example, the "expert" cited in the following passage:

> Despite the doom-and-gloom sayers who voice their alarm about the state of the environment, Earth is actually in pretty good shape. As Dr. Paula Benjamin recently pointed out, "Nature is perfectly capable of taking care of herself; she's been doing it for hundreds of years." Benjamin is in good company. Her sentiments were echoed by an even more eloquent expert, Michael S. Berliner, co-chairman of the board of directors of the Ayn Rand Institute in Irvine, California. In an opinion piece posted on the Ayn Rand Center of Individual Rights website, Mr. Berliner said, "Earth Day approaches, and with it a grave danger faces mankind. The danger is not from acid rain, global warming, smog, or the logging of rain forests, as environmentalists would have us believe. The danger to mankind is from environmentalism."

The author starts off by using Dr. Paula Benjamin to support the claim that environmentalists anxious about the earth's future are dead wrong. Earth is in fine shape. Yet for all we know, Dr. Benjamin might be a dentist. A dental degree does not qualify her as an environmental expert. Without some knowledge of Dr. Benjamin's credentials, or qualifications, we shouldn't be swayed by her opinion. It also would help to know more about Dr. Benjamin's personal background and biases. If, for example, she's worked for a company cited for abuses to the environment, her ability to stay objective, or neutral, is suspect.

The second supporting expert in the paragraph is Michael Berliner, whose lack of a scientific title should already arouse your suspicions. Mr. Berliner also believes that environmentalists worried about the hazards facing the earth are nervous Nellies, whose concerns get too much attention. But before taking that notion to heart, critical readers need to realize that Mr. Berliner does not have the scientific background to judge. The institute he co-chairs promotes the philosophy of novelist Ayn Rand, who insisted that individuals should have unfettered freedom to do whatever they want. While his background helps explain Mr. Berliner's point of view, it shouldn't encourage readers to share it.

Unidentified Research

To be convincing as support, scientific research needs **attribution**. Readers need to know, that is, who conducted the research. In the following passage, the author relies on some "studies" to convince readers that pornography should be more strictly censored. What's missing from the passage is information about who performed the studies.

> Because pornography puts women's lives in danger, it should be more strictly censored. Studies have repeatedly shown that pornography is directly related to rapes and assaults on women, making porn a key cause of rape in the United States and the rest of the world. As if the studies weren't enough, common sense should tell us that pornography, by reducing women to pure sexual objects, encourages men to think of them as not quite human. The less men think of women as fully human, the more likely they are to engage in rape. Actually this is yet another cause and effect relationship noted by several prominent researchers.

Unnamed studies like those referred to in the previous passage should arouse readers' skepticism. Anytime a writer tells you what "studies have repeatedly shown" without saying who did the studies, your critical warning system should light up.

Where authors identify a study is not especially important. Some identify the names of researchers in parentheses within the text itself and then provide full source information at the article or book's end. Some identify the study or studies in a footnote that refers readers to a list of sources at the back of the book. Either method is fine as long as the writer tells you who performed the studies being cited.

Be Wary of Appeals to Common Sense

Be careful of authors who tell you to let "common sense" be your guide when evaluating their statements. It's not just that "common sense is not so common," as the writer and philosopher Voltaire claimed, but also that writers sometimes use this expression to intimidate their readers into agreement. Appeals to common sense suggest that anyone with common sense would share the author's point of view, and a reader who doesn't is an oddball.

Dated Research

It's also important to know *when* the study was conducted; a writer who uses out-of-date studies rightfully risks losing readers' confidence. Take, for example, the following passage:

> The threat of radon gas is not as serious as we have been led to believe. In 1954, a team of government researchers studying the effects of radon in the home found no relationship between high levels of the gas in private dwellings and the incidence of lung cancer. Over thirty years later in 1986, researchers agreed that radon was a risk factor in lung cancer. However, they could not agree on how high the level of radon in the home had to be in order to be a serious threat.

Here we have an author trying to prove a point about radon gas with a more than half-century-old study and another one that's decades old. To make matters worse, neither reference indicates who performed the research. To be considered effective evidence for an opinion, references to research should be considerably more up-to-date (as witnessed by the fact that scientists have now determined the figure at which radon is considered dangerous), and they should indicate what group or institution was involved in the study.

CHECK YOUR UNDERSTANDING

Complete the following chart by defining each error.

Type of Support	Possible Error	Definition of Error
Reasons	Irrelevant reasons	
	Circular reasoning	
Examples and illustrations	Hasty generalizations	
Expert opinion	Unidentified experts	
	Inappropriate experts	
Research results	Unidentified research	
	Dated research	

◆ EXERCISE 1   Recognizing Support That Fails

DIRECTIONS   Circle the appropriate letter to identify the author's error. *Note*: The example below shows two errors in reasoning. The paragraphs in the exercise don't necessarily include two errors, although some do.

EXAMPLE

Eat French Fries at Your Peril

1   These days it's difficult to avoid the fact that the United States is in the grip of a serious health problem: More than 60 percent of the population is overweight. As a result, many men and women are at increased risk of

The phrase "without a doubt" suggests the author may not be able to prove the opening claim, and the rhetorical question doesn't help matters.

Cooking methods may increase profits, but that reason isn't linked to weight gain.

serious diseases, ranging from colon cancer to diabetes. Without a doubt, the chief culprits behind the looming health disaster are the makers of fast food. If you count up the calories in, say, an oversized cheeseburger or a slice of double-cheese pizza, is it any wonder that obesity is a growing problem?

2   Fast food companies arose to meet a real need: Americans were pressed for time and often needed to eat their meals on the run. But instead of making those meals healthy as well as profitable, the fast food industry decided it was better to use cooking methods that shortened preparation time and, not incidentally, increased profits. Thus Americans were consuming, without their knowledge, high-calorie meals that didn't cost all that much in dollars but were actually very expensive in terms of health risks. No wonder people have sued fast food companies for obesity-related health problems. As Professor James Darwin has pointed out, when it comes to America's health problems, the fast food industry has a lot to answer for.

(a.) irrelevant reason

b. circular reasoning

c. hasty generalization

(d.) unidentified or inappropriate expert

e. unidentified or dated research

EXPLANATION   While the cooking methods of fast food may, in some way, contribute to weight gain and health problems, we'd need to know more about those methods and how they contribute before considering that supporting detail a relevant reason, making *a* the first correct answer. Although the author uses the words of Professor James Darwin for supporting evidence, we know nothing about Professor Darwin's area of expertise. Without knowing about Darwin's background, we cannot tell if he is qualified to decide what the fast food industry does or does not have to answer for, making *d* the second correct answer.

1. If you have a grass lawn surrounding your house, you are contributing to this country's environmental problems. For one thing, you could be using fertilizers and pesticides that can damage the soil structure, pollute wells, and kill wildlife. Homeowners with lawns actually use more fertilizers annually than the entire country of India puts on its crops. They also apply up to ten times more pesticides than U.S. farmers do. Unfortunately, research has proven

that these chemicals wash off yards and pollute water supplies, thus contaminating the food chain. Lawn mowers cause another environmental problem. They produce as much air pollution in one hour as a car produces in a 350-mile drive. In addition, grass clippings are choking already overflowing landfills. Yard waste, most of which is cut grass, is the second-largest component of the 160 million tons of solid waste we dump into landfills every year. If that weren't enough, your lawn may be contributing to the destruction of plant and animal species. When developers building new houses bulldoze complex habitats and replace them with houses and grass, many plants and animals are killed or starved out.

a. irrelevant reason

b. circular reasoning

c. hasty generalization

d. unidentified or inappropriate expert

e. unidentified or dated research

2. The U.S. government needs to invest more money to improve and expand this country's rail service. In particular, Congress should commit to developing a national intercity network of high-speed trains. An intermodal transportation system (one that includes rail along with highways and airlines) is essential to keeping Americans moving in the event of a crisis. During a national emergency that disrupts one mode of transportation, the others should be able to absorb the traffic and allow people to continue to travel. For example, when airplanes were grounded for several days following terrorist attacks in September 2001, people relied on Amtrak passenger trains to get them where they needed to be. Without the trains, our nation would have been paralyzed. Furthermore, European countries such as France and Germany have excellent rail systems. Railroad transportation is an important public service, and it needs to be kept efficient and up to date.

a. irrelevant reason

b. circular reasoning

c. hasty generalization

d. unidentified or inappropriate expert

e. unidentified or dated research

3. The British mathematician Alan Turing (1912–1954) was a certified genius who enormously enriched the world during his relatively brief lifetime. Had he not lived, the world would be a very different place today. We would probably be decades behind our current level of technology expertise. Yet how did the British government and the general public repay him for his many contributions? They hounded him into suicide, and to this day the level of his accomplishments has never been adequately acknowledged. Arrested in March of 1952 for the crime of being homosexual, Turing was given a harsh choice: go to prison for a year or take estrogen injections to eliminate his sex drive. Humiliated and desperate, Turing chose the injections. But the forced injections weren't all he suffered. Turing was also depressed at being denied government security clearance, a standard policy concerning homosexuals. By 1954, he had given in to despair and died by his own hand after eating an apple laced with cyanide. Turing shows how we treat genius in this world. We ignore and deride it. For the lucky few, fame and recognition might come after death. Turing, unfortunately, was not one of those few, and he still hasn't gotten the recognition he deserves.

a. irrelevant reason

b. circular reasoning

c. hasty generalization

d. unidentified or inappropriate expert

e. unidentified or dated research

4. It just may be nature itself—not humans burning fossil fuels—that is causing global warming. Naturally occurring gases, such as water vapor, methane, nitrous oxide, and ozone, contribute to the so-called greenhouse effect that has raised Earth's temperature 30 degrees since the "Little Ice Age" of the seventeenth and eighteenth centuries. The oceans, too, seem to be partly responsible for the overall increase in our planet's temperature. From 1958 to 1978, Dane Chang and his colleagues at Hill Laboratories carefully studied the correlation between ocean temperatures and levels of carbon dioxide, the gas that causes global warming. These researchers found that increases in ocean temperature follow a rise in the atmosphere's carbon dioxide level. Such studies would seem to indicate that natural factors are producing our warmer climate.

a. irrelevant reason

b. circular reasoning

c. hasty generalization

d. unidentified or inappropriate expert

e. unidentified or dated research

5. A growing number of school districts are banning the childhood game of dodgeball from physical education classes, and rightly so. The game is simply too aggressive and causes serious injuries. In one California incident, a child playing dodgeball was knocked to the ground by the ball's impact and suffered a concussion. Dodgeball is also not especially good exercise, particularly for those who are overweight. The slowest and heaviest children usually get knocked out of the game quickly. They then spend the rest of the game on the sidelines while the more athletic kids keep playing. It doesn't take a highly trained psychologist to realize that this experience cannot be good for an overweight child's self-esteem or self-image.

a. irrelevant reason

b. circular reasoning

c. hasty generalization

d. unidentified or inappropriate expert

e. unidentified or dated research

Responding to Bias in Persuasive Writing

We don't expect to find bias in informative writing. When we do, it comes as a surprise because we are aware that writers with an informative purpose generally try to avoid conveying their personal opinion. But we have different expectations for persuasive writing. We expect writers to be personally engaged and to tell us why we should share their opinion and reject the opposing point of view. In short, we expect persuasive writing to reveal a bias in favor of one point of view over another. Consequently, we don't immediately mistrust a writer who speaks frankly about his or her preferences for a particular idea or position.

Here, for instance, is educational historian Diane Ravitch, in her 2011 book *The Death and Life of the Great American School System.*

Ravitch gives readers her opinion on how poorly state officials did in 2000 when they tried to create nationwide educational standards. Note, in particular, the italicized language.

> The Clinton administration's Goals 2000 program gave the states federal money to write their own academic standards, but most of the state standards *were vague* when it came to any curriculum content. It seemed that *the states had learned from the battle over the history standards*[†] that *it was better to say nothing than to provoke controversy by setting out any real curriculum standards. Most state standards were windy rhetoric** devoid of concrete descriptions* of what students should be expected to know and be able to do. A few examples will suffice. (Diane Ravitch, *The Death and Life of the Great American School System*, 2011, Basic Books, p.19.)

As you can probably tell, Ravitch didn't think much of the state standards developed in 2000, and she isn't pretending to be neutral. But then she doesn't have to be. She is writing with a persuasive intent and is more than willing to show her bias because, as the last sentence of the passage indicates, she thinks she has the facts to back it up.

She also openly acknowledges, throughout her book, points of view that she might not share but still respects. Ravitch expresses then what is an **acceptable bias** because it (1) appears in writing with a clearly persuasive intent, (2) acknowledges opposing points of view with respect, and (3) is backed up by supporting evidence.

When Bias Goes Overboard

The previous paragraph by the highly respected Diane Ravitch illustrates a key point about bias: It's only bad when it becomes excessive. Writers blinded by **excessive bias** often forget that they need to supply evidence for their position. Since they are completely convinced their view is the right one, they think everyone else must feel the same way.

Blinkered by bias, they are also inclined to ignore opposing points of view, describe them simplistically, or treat them with contempt. Sometimes they do all three. Because excessively biased writers can, consciously or unconsciously, misrepresent or ignore opposing points of view, experienced

---

[†]In the early nineties, Gary Nash, a professor from UCLA, led an effort to create standards for what students in high school should learn from history. The results of this attempt aroused such furious controversy that the idea of having standards for history teaching was abandoned.
*rhetoric: language used more to impress than to communicate; the art of effective or persuasive speaking or writing.

readers always try to determine when an author's bias has gone overboard, making him or her unable to treat other points of view fairly.

To improve your ability to evaluate the bias of an argument meant to persuade, review the four questions below. Anytime you read an argument and can answer *yes* to one or more of these questions, you are dealing with an author whose bias has gone overboard and you should look elsewhere for information on your topic.

> 1. Does the author use a tone that is heavy with outrage, sarcasm, or irony?
>
> 2. Does the author insist that an opposing point of view is not possible for anyone who has common sense?
>
> 3. Does the author claim that the opposing point of view has no merit without explaining *why* the opposition does not have a leg to stand on?
>
> 4. Does the author spend more time insulting the opposition than supporting his or her point of view?

Evaluating Bias

Read each of the following passages. Put an *A* for acceptable or an *E* for excessive at the end of each paragraph.

Paragraph 1   After reading about instructors who encourage the use of social media in the classroom, I continue to be appalled by some of the idiocy that abounds on college campuses today. After all, what else should instructors do if they discover their students aren't completing their homework assignments but are, instead, wasting time on Facebook, Twitter, or Instagram? Why, the answer is simple. See to it that students spend even more time on these and similar sites by bringing social media right into the classroom. It makes perfect sense. That way teachers can avoid making demands on students and, at the same time, avoid having to prepare for class. The students can sit in the classroom and read Facebook posts while the teacher claims to be enhancing their social media skills. It's a win-win situation for both students and teachers, and nobody has to do any serious work.

———

Paragraph 2   I must admit to being puzzled by instructors who believe that the topic of social media should be addressed in the classroom. While it's clear that social media can be a valuable professional tool that helps students network and make the right career connections, it's not at all clear that students are lacking in social media skills. As Jakob Nielsen, who has been conducting studies of computer literacy and usability for over two decades, pointed out in his February 2013 *Alertbox* newsletter, young people are very good at using social media. They excel, in fact. What they don't do especially well is use the Internet for serious academic research. If that is the case—and Nielsen is one of the most respected voices in the field of technology studies—it seems pointless to have students polish their social media skills in the classroom when what they really need to learn is how to use the Internet for research.

———

The author of the first passage expresses a strong bias against social media in the classroom. The author, however, doesn't make any attempt to explain or defend the opinion expressed. What readers get is a tone of outraged irony. The writer seems to be working under the assumption that personal outrage is all it takes to convince readers social media should be kept out of the classroom. This is an example of excessive bias, the kind that should make readers look at the work of other people writing on the subject of social media and education, because this author is too biased to be fair.

The second passage also reveals a bias. But note the difference. This writer doesn't think personal outrage equals an argument. Instead, the author admits that social media can be useful professionally but goes on to cite evidence indicating students probably don't need to spend class time learning how to use it. It's important, too, that the evidence comes from a study completed by a well-known expert, whose credentials can be checked.

CHECK YOUR UNDERSTANDING

1. What are the characteristics of acceptable bias?

_____

_____

2. Identify the three different ways excessively biased writers respond to opposing points of view:

_____

3. In your own words what are the four questions that can help you decide if an author's bias is excessive?

_____

_____

_____

_____

_____

_____

_____

REVIEWING THROUGH WRITING

Here is a passage where every attempt has been made to eliminate any bias on the author's part. Rewrite it, first, to illustrate a passage in which the bias has gone overboard. Then rewrite it again to make the bias more appropriate for persuasive writing.

According to his mother, Jeremy Hammond is a genius with a high IQ but no wisdom. Hammond was arrested in 2012 for allegedly hacking the server of the global intelligence company Stratfor and making off with 200 gigabytes of data as well as a number of incriminating emails. Hammond was arrested largely on the basis of testimony from a friend and fellow hacker who was secretly working under cover with the FBI. At the time of his arrest, Hammond had already served two years in jail for hacking into the credit card database of ProtestWarrior.com, a conservative* website. Considered by many to be a "hacktavist,"[†] Hammond has dubbed himself an electronic Robin Hood, dedicated to the defeat of corporate and government corruption. He is also the man behind the popular website Hackthissite.org. His attorney is Elizabeth Fink, who represented the former Attica inmates who filed a class action suit against the state of New York (see p. 632) and eventually won an $8 million settlement for her clients. According to the judge in his trial, Hammond could face life in prison if convicted

Distracting the Reader

Writers whose bias is so strong it keeps them from seriously considering opposing points of view often try to distract the reader from noticing any holes in their argument. Writers try to distract readers from an argument's weakness in many ways; here are four of the most common.

Making Personal Character Attacks

"Putting the focus on the arguer or person being discussed can distract us from the issues that matter."

—Yvonne Raley, journalist

Be wary of writers who respond to opposing points of view by attacking the actions, background, or associations of those they disagree with. In the following passage, note how the author attacks her opponent's past actions rather than his point of view.

On his talk show "Viewpoint," former New York governor Eliot Spitzer criticized the Justice Department for refusing to prosecute Goldman Sachs for stock-trading practices that allegedly contributed to the country's 2008 financial meltdown. According to Spitzer, "the Justice

---

*conservative: sharing a political ideology that encourages the preservation of the past and the right of individuals to do as they please without government interference; more inclined to be pro- rather than anti-capitalism.

[†]hacktavist: The meaning of the word changes depending on whom you talk to. However, the German group the Cult of the Dead Cow claims to have coined the term and insists that hacktavism was meant to help political dissidents communicate anonymously and avoid being imprisoned. It was never meant to break the law.

Department has simply not been there for the American public. . . ." Spitzer has been much applauded for taking such a public and tough stand against the activities of both Goldman Sachs and the Justice Department, which shows what a short memory the public has. This is the man who in March of 2008 had to resign as governor because of his relationships with high-priced call girls. Yet only a few years later, he has the nerve to criticize the behavior of others. Given his scandalous actions, he has no business airing his opinions on television, and he certainly should not be criticizing the Justice Department.

There's no doubt that Eliot Spitzer has some scandals in his past. But that doesn't mean his opinion on how Goldman Sachs should have been treated by the Justice Department is worthless. It might be. It might not. But to discredit it, the writer needs to evaluate Spitzer's argument, not his personal past.

Sliding Down the Slippery Slope

Writers whose bias has gotten out of hand are also inclined to engage in **slippery slope** thinking. Using this approach, the writer insists that taking even one step in a particular direction will *invariably* lead to a series of steps ending in disaster. Here's an example:

> Congress has listened to the voices of the country's citizens. Attempts to ban military assault weapons have once again been defeated, and rightly so. If we ban assault weapons, the next step will be the banning of rifles, and then people who hunt for food will no longer be able to feed their families.

Writers who use the slippery slope approach, like the one shown here, ignore the fact that attitudes and events usually arise in response to, or as a result of, specific circumstances. Those who want to ban military style assault rifles for civilians believe that a ban would reduce the chances of one or two individuals going on a killing spree and taking many lives in a matter of minutes. However, those arguing for a ban don't view hunting and assault rifles in the same light. They know that the two kinds of rifles have different capabilities and different purposes. It does not follow, therefore, that a desire to ban assault rifles leads automatically to a desire to ban all rifles, even those that cannot cause the carnage* assault rifles can.

---

*carnage: massacre, slaughter, butchery.

Playing on the Reader's Emotions

Writers who have a weak argument to begin with often try to sidestep reason altogether. Instead, they rely totally on shared cultural symbols and allusions, carefully selected to elicit an emotional response that short-circuits the reader's willingness to think critically. Here's an example:

> A recent letter to the editor argued against the invasion of Iran, claiming that an attack on Iran would only harden the country's resolve to obtain and use nuclear weapons. The reasoning here is appalling and shameful. When has this great country ever responded to a threat by sitting on its hands and waiting to see what the other side would do? From the days of the Revolutionary War, this has been a country of action and Americans are not afraid to fight for what they believe in.

The letter that produced this impassioned response may be "appalling." But we can't assume that based on this writer's argument. Although the author's disagreement is clearly stated, there is no attempt to challenge the reasoning in the letter. What the reader gets instead is a celebration of America's fighting spirit and an allusion to one of the country's proudest moments, the Revolutionary War.[†] Both are meant to stir up readers' emotions and distract them from thinking about how empty the author's argument truly is. References to taking pride in our country, motherhood, our founding fathers, innocent children, love of animals, and the American flag are all likely staples in this writer's bag of tricks.

No Comment Is Proof Enough

During World War II, a number of spurious, or fake, arguments were used to make the imprisonment of Japanese-Americans seem acceptable even though they hadn't committed any crime. In addition to the argument that no proof of spying was proof of how clever the spies were, the additional "reason" was given that the general public supported internment by its silence. This is an error in logic called the *fallacy*[*] *of*

[†]Revolutionary War (1775–1783): The war in which American colonists fought and won their independence from England.
[*]fallacy: error, mistake.

tacit* agreement. It argues that no comment or no protest is proof of agreement. Here's an example:

> Executive Order 9066 has excluded Japanese-Americans from living in specific areas and put into motion the process of transferring Japanese-Americans to internment camps, where they can do no harm to their adopted country. Those who oppose internment, largely those who are of Japanese origin themselves, have insisted that there is no evidence that any Japanese-Americans have acted as spies for Japan. Since it's common sense that Japanese-Americans would feel attached to the country of their forebears,* the lack of evidence is only proof of how clever they have been in their secret activities. What's also clear is that Americans, in general, support Executive Order 9066. They have, after all, given their silent assent. They realize that some Japanese-Americans must be biased in favor of Japan's winning the war, and they understand that internment is the only way to eliminate this threat to the war effort.

If you have ever kept quiet because you did not want to call attention to yourself and get in trouble with, say, your teacher, manager, or drill sergeant, then you know that there are plenty of reasons why people do not speak up in the face of an authority behaving in a way they consider harsh or unfair. It's impossible to know why there wasn't more widespread protest over the internment of the Japanese. Yet this author pretends a talent for mind reading, which none of us possess. No comment is precisely that, no comment. A writer can't be allowed to interpret silence to mean anything he or she pleases.

CHECK YOUR UNDERSTANDING

In your own words, explain each of the four ways writers try to keep readers from noticing that an argument is weak.

1. Making personal character attacks:

   _____

   _____

---

*tacit: implied but not stated.
*forebears: ancestors.

2. Slippery slope reasoning:

_____

_____

3. Playing on the reader's emotions:

_____

_____

4. The fallacy of tacit agreement:

_____

◆ **EXERCISE 2** **Looking for Errors in Reasoning**

DIRECTIONS Circle the appropriate letter to identify any errors in reasoning.

1. **No Sexual Harassment Equals No Soldiers**

1   Over the years, there's been a good deal of attention focused on sexual harassment in the military, and rightly so. No one wants to see officers in charge of young female recruits abuse their power by sexually harassing those in their care. However, supporters of women in the military are making a crucial mistake when they try to eliminate sexism in the military and at the same time insist that women deserve to be in combat alongside men.

2   To be a warrior means that a soldier has to revert to a more primitive mode of behavior and thought. It means that one has to assume a kill-or-be-killed mentality that allows little room for compassion or thought. It is very difficult, perhaps impossible, to encourage a more sensitive mindset in men and still expect them to engage in the savagery that war requires. As Fred C. Iklé, an undersecretary of defense in the Reagan administration, expressed it, "You can't cultivate the necessary commitment to physical

violence and fully protect against the risk of harassment. Military life may . . . foster the attitudes that tend toward rape, such as aggression and single-minded assertion."[†]

3   Viewed from this perspective, efforts to eliminate sexual harassment could have disastrous consequences during wartime, particularly now that women are being allowed into combat. Committed to being respectful toward women, male soldiers will also feel that they must rein in their aggression in the presence of women. As a result, they will hold back during combat training. In time, they will hold back during combat itself. In the end, our country will lose its military strength and be forced to give up its position as a world power.

a. The author engages in a character attack.

b. The author uses slippery slope reasoning.

c. The author appeals to the reader's emotions.

d. The author suggests that no comment is proof enough.

2. Egg Donation May Not Be Such a Miracle for Donors

1   Because so many couples desperately want a child and can't have one, the search for women willing to donate their eggs for in vitro fertilization[†] has become a big business. Although many people consider in vitro fertilization a wondrous miracle, I must admit to being skeptical about the use of egg donors. The couple who gains a child, thanks to a donor, may be rightly jubilant;[*] the donor, however, may be taking more risks than she realizes.

2   For starters, the egg-donation process is not particularly pleasant. To prepare, women take daily hormone injections, which force the maturation of ten to twenty eggs instead of the normal one or two. As a result of fertility drug injections, donors often experience cramping and mood swings. Some women also experience ovarian hyperstimulation syndrome (OHSS), which in most causes a feeling of bloated discomfort that resolves itself. A few women who have received fertility injections get a more severe form of OHSS that requires hospitalization.

3   Early on in the use of fertility drugs, there was some evidence that the injections might increase the risk of ovarian cancer. But more recent studies have not confirmed that link. Yet the truth is, no one really knows for

[†]This line of reasoning was used by Richard Rayner, "The Warrior Besieged," *New York Times*, June 22, 1997, p. 29.

[†]in vitro fertilization: *in vitro* literally means "in glass"; the term refers to the process of creating life in an artificial setting outside the human body.

[*]jubilant: overjoyed, thrilled.

sure what the long-term effects are mainly because in vitro fertilization hasn't been around that long. Asked about the possible long-term risks of in vitro fertilization, the doctors involved in both the research and the practice of in vitro fertilization have had little to say, which is a sure sign that they are worried about what the future will bring for women who have undergone fertility treatments. (Source of information: American Society for Reproductive Medicine Fact Sheet.)

a. The author engages in a character attack.

b. The author uses slippery slope reasoning.

c. The author appeals to the reader's emotions.

d. The author suggests that no comment is proof enough.

3. Attica Still Haunts Us

1   The worst prison insurrection* in U.S. history occurred at the Attica Correctional Facility near Buffalo, New York, in September 1971. Armed with baseball bats, pipes, chairs, and knives, inmates seized control of an exercise yard and took forty guards hostage. They demanded, among other things, better conditions and amnesty for crimes committed during the revolt. They also insisted that New York's governor, Nelson Rockefeller, come to the prison to address the problem. Governor Rockefeller refused. Three days after the riot began, he authorized state police to regain control of the facility by force if necessary.

2   On September 13, police armed with tear gas and shotguns stormed the prison, firing more than 2,000 rounds of ammunition in six minutes. As a direct result of the attack, 10 hostages and 33 inmates were killed. Once the prison guards regained control, they stripped, beat, and tortured inmates. They were especially brutal with the riot's leaders. In the first hours after regaining control of the prison, police also denied medical care to the wounded. As a result, in 1974, lawyers filed a class-action lawsuit on behalf of the 1,281 prisoners who were harassed during the attack.

3   But it took twenty-six years for the State of New York to settle the suit filed on behalf of the 1,281 prisoners who rioted and survived the Attica rebellion. Those men still alive in 2000 received a group settlement of $8 million for the suffering they endured as a result of the prison insurrection. These men deserve every penny of that settlement, and a good

---

*insurrection: a violent uprising against authority or government.

deal more. Prior to the revolt, inmates had endured appallingly inhumane conditions at the facility. But their treatment following the revolt was truly barbaric, as those who surrendered were stripped naked and forced to run a gauntlet of guards armed with ax handles and clubs.

4   Given what happened to the men of Attica before and after the rebellion, it's difficult to understand the mindset of those like Texas district attorney Alma Wertmuller, who thinks the Attica settlement was an example of liberal guilt run amok,[†] dispensing money and mercy where none was due. Ms. Wertmuller's opinion may be based on the fact that she has so little knowledge of prison conditions. During her long career, she amassed enough wealth to keep herself out of jail when she was arrested two years ago for drinking while driving and leaving the scene of an accident.

a. The author engages in a character attack.

b. The author uses slippery slope reasoning.

c. The author appeals to the reader's emotions.

d. The author suggests that no comment is proof enough.

4. Of Power and Prosecutors

1   In April 2007, the attorney general of North Carolina, Roy A. Cooper III, announced that he was dismissing all charges against three Duke University lacrosse players. The three young men had been accused of raping a young woman who performed at one of their parties. At the same time that he announced the dismissal of the charges, Cooper also rebuked Michael B. Nifong, the district attorney of Durham County, for rushing to accuse the young men while failing to thoroughly investigate the woman's allegations.

2   Cooper's public rebuke highlights a point made by Angela J. Davis in her 2007 book, *Arbitrary Justice: The Power of the American Prosecutor*. Davis, a professor of law at American University Washington College of Law, argues that prosecutors all over the country have the power to direct and control the outcome of criminal cases, often with serious, even disastrous, consequences.

3   According to Professor Davis, Nifong, who has been accused of withholding exculpatory evidence[†] favorable to the defense, is the rule rather

---

[†]run amok: The phrase comes from the Malay word *amuk* meaning to "attack furiously." In English, we use "to run amok" to suggest something being done without thought and in a wild and thoughtless manner.
[†]exculpatory evidence: evidence that would help the accused be proven innocent.

than the exception. She insists that prosecutors intent on winning withhold evidence all the time, without oversight or penalty for their actions, and that our current judicial system, with its lack of transparency,* has no system in place for checking prosecutorial power. If anything, Davis argues, state legislatures have routinely passed laws that increase the power of prosecutors without worrying about the possibility that prosecutors might, unconsciously or intentionally, be corrupted by the extent of their authority. Victims of prosecutorial excess, she insists, are usually poor people who do not have the resources to mount a defense against prosecutorial injustice. Her hope is that the Duke case will shine a much-needed light on this problem in the American justice system and force a change.

4   Despite Professor Davis's detailed and often eloquent analysis of the failings in the current judicial system, those ready to agree with her and demand a change in our justice system should remember that Professor Davis was once intimately acquainted with the criminal justice system. Angela Davis first came to the public's attention when she was linked to the murder of Judge Harold Haley during an attempt to free a Black Panther defendant in a courtroom in 1970. Davis went underground, becoming the subject of an intense manhunt. After eighteen months as a fugitive, she was captured, arrested, tried, and eventually acquitted in one of the most famous trials in recent U.S. history. Is it any wonder that she doesn't like prosecutors? (Source of information on Professor Davis's new book: Evan R. Goldstein, "The Power of the Prosecutor," *Chronicle of Higher Education*, May 11, 2007, p. B2.)

a. The author engages in a character attack.

b. The author uses slippery slope reasoning.

c. The author appeals to the reader's emotions.

d. The author suggests that no comment is proof enough.

5. Dress Codes Are So Yesterday

1   Unlike teenagers of a generation ago, many of today's kids have a more relaxed attitude about gender identity. In contrast to their parents, they don't feel compelled to follow the unspoken rules of their gender. This is particularly true concerning their appearance, and teenagers all over the country are challenging the boundaries of appropriate male or female dress and demeanor.* Unfortunately the response of many school

---

*transparency: openness, ease of visibility.
*demeanor: behavior in relation to others.

administrators to this more relaxed attitude is not quite so progressive. Some administrators seem to believe they are living in the 1960s when gender roles were strictly defined and girls wearing pants to school were subject to suspension.

2   In Houston, Texas, for instance, a cross-dressing senior was sent home when his wig violated school rules about hair length for males. A similar fate met a teenager in Cobb County, Georgia, after he arrived at school in full makeup and skinny jeans. A Mississippi teen found her photo eliminated from her yearbook because she had posed in a man's tux instead of the girls' traditional black drape around the shoulders.

5   For teenagers, dress is a form of self-expression and social experimentation. It's a way of trying on and testing personal and sexual identity to determine the right fit, even if that fit doesn't follow traditional patterns of behavior. If kids can't try out different modes of being in high school, when can they do it? They certainly can't do it when their job might be at stake. School administrators who try to limit teenagers' self-expression are completely out of touch with reality. They don't seem to know that the reign of stodgy Queen Victoria[†] ended more than a century ago. Anyone living or working with kids today needs to leave the stone age behind and enter the twenty-first century. If they don't, they risk being regarded in much the way ancient fossils are, as relics of a bygone age that have nothing to tell us about modern times.

a. The author engages in a character attack.

b. The author uses slippery slope reasoning.

c. The author appeals to the reader's emotions.

d. The author suggests that no comment is proof enough.

[‡] The reign of Queen Victoria of England (1819–1901) is associated with rigid standards of male and female behavior.

WORD CHECK

The following words were introduced and defined in pages 622–634. See how well you can match the words with the meanings. When you finish, make sure to check the meanings of any words you missed because the same words will turn up in tests at the end of the chapter.

1. rhetoric (p. 622)	_____	a. massacre, slaughter, butchery
2. conservative (p. 626)	_____	b. openness, ease of visibility
3. carnage (p. 627)	_____	c. language used more to impress than to communicate; the art of speaking and writing well
4. fallacy (p. 628)	_____	
5. tacit (p. 629)	_____	d. outward behavior, conduct
6. forebears (p. 629)	_____	e. sharing a political ideology that encourages the preservation of the past and the right of individuals to do as they please without government interference; more inclined to be pro- rather than anti-capitalism.
7. jubilant (p. 631)	_____	
8. insurrection (p. 362)	_____	
9. transparency (p. 634)	_____	f. overjoyed, thrilled
10. demeanor (p. 634)	_____	g. error in reasoning, mistake, unfounded belief
		h. ancestors
		i. implied but not stated directly
		j. armed and violent uprising against authority or government

◆ **EXERCISE 3**   **More About Form and Meaning**

DIRECTIONS Fill in the blanks with one of the words listed below.

demeanor	carnage	insurrection	tacit	conservatives
transparent	jubilant	forebears	fallacies	rhetoric

1. The United Nations should have done more to stop the bloody

_____ that occurred in the African country of Rwanda in 1994 when civil war broke out.

2. The Baltimore Ravens were _____ when they won the Super Bowl.

3. Neither England nor France was able to put down the _____ on the island that would one day be called Haiti.

4. The group used revolutionary _____ to disguise that what they were doing was enriching themselves at the expense of the poor.

5. The broker's argument was so filled with _____, the disgusted clients just stood up and left, leaving him sitting there with his mouth open.

6. When Charles Darwin first published his revolutionary work *On the Origin of Species* in 1859, many were furious at the idea that their _____ might be members of the animal kingdom.

7. Julian Assange, the founder of Wikileaks, the group that hacked government files and published them on the Internet, believes that governments should be completely _____ in all of their dealings.

8. "_____ —and I count myself as one—succeed when we attract new supporters to timeless traditions."—Ken Mehlman, former Republican National Committee chair, quoted in the *New York Times*.

9. The babysitter did not think she had anything to worry about because the child's _____ was so shy and timid. Then the parents left, and the child underwent a startling transformation.

10. *Gentleman's Agreement* was a 1947 film directed by Elia Kazan that focused on the _____ agreement to discriminate against Jews in almost every area of society.

TAKING STOCK

Use Your Own Words

Looking Ahead

What follows is a reading about spelling. The author, Anne Trubek, a professor from Oberlin College, thinks traditional spelling rules need to be more open to interpretation. In short, she argues that we don't need to be consistent about how we spell. We can, she says, just make up our own rules.

1   A misspelled tweet describing a crush as adorable is changed to say she is "affordable." The text message "I like himm" is changed to "I like Himmler."[†] Damn you, autocorrect! By now most of us have had unfortunate experiences with autocorrection software—innocuous messages turned anatomical or lunch plans morphed into love notes. (Pro tip: Don't ever abbreviate Wednesday.) Damn You Autocorrect! is even the name of a popular website that collates hilariously obtuse examples of texts perverted by software assistants.

2   Our supposedly helpful correction software isn't doing us any favors, and not just because it routinely turns easily decipherable errors into bizarre non sequiturs.[†] And definitely not for any of the reasons your third-grade English teacher might cite: that it makes us lazy or robs us of our ability to spell. No, autocorrect and spellcheckers are wrongheaded because they reinforce a traditional spelling standard. Consistent spelling was a great way to ensure clarity in the print era. But with new technologies, the way that we write and read (and search and data-mine) is changing, and so must spelling.

3   English spelling is a terrible mess anyway, full of arbitrary contrivances and exceptions that outnumber rules. Why receipt but deceit? Water but daughter? Daughter but laughter? What is the logic behind the *ough* in through, dough, and cough? Instead of trying to get the letters right with imperfect tools, it would be far better to loosen our idea of correct spelling.

4   The notion that words can and should be spelled only one way is a fairly recent invention. "The phrase 'bad speller' rarely appears in English-language books before the 1770s," Jack Lynch notes in his book *The Lexicographer's Dilemma*. Until William Caxton used a printing press in 1475, English words were reproduced by scribes in scriptoria.[†] There were no dictionaries (or Google) to check for "proper" spelling. Most words were spelled several different ways—there were at least 114 variants of *through*. (Even the

---

[†]Heinrich Himmler (1900–1945): Himmler was head of Hitler's feared security forces, notorious for their barbarous brutality.

[†]non sequitur: Latin for "it does not follow." Non sequiturs are statements that don't seem to follow from or fit with what was said before.

[†]scriptoria: the rooms where monks in the Middle Ages wrote their manuscripts by hand.

spelling of something as personal as a name was inconsistent; there are six surviving instances of Shakespeare's signature, and they're all spelled differently.) Even after the advent of print, variant spellings were the rule. Typesetters would alter spellings to help them justify type (perhaps this is how deceit lost its *p*?).

5   And it's not like things are set in stone—in fact, advocating for a more sensible English spelling system is a noble American tradition. In 1768, Benjamin Franklin published "A Scheme for a New Alphabet and Reformed Mode of Spelling," a treatise that laid out a detailed plan for making spelling sensible. He invented three new vowels and removed *c, j, q, w, x*, and *y* from our alphabet. Noah Webster (of *Webster's Dictionary*) agreed with many of Franklin's suggestions and came up with more of his own, some of which were accepted: Webster is why the American spelling of *color* has no *u*. Mark Twain placed the blame for spelling errors on "this present silly alphabet, which I fancy was invented by a drunken thief," and proposed a "sane, determinate" alternative with "a system of accents, giving to each vowel its own soul and value."

6   So who shud tell us how to spel? Ourselves. Language is not static—or constantly degenerating, as many claim. It is ever evolving, and spelling evolves, too, as we create new words, styles, and guidelines (rules governing use of the semicolon date to the 18th century, meaning they're a more recent innovation than the steam engine). The most widely used American word in the world, OK, was invented during the age of the telegraph because it was concise. No one considers it, or abbreviations like ASAP and IOU, a sign of corruption. More recent textisms signal a similarly creative, bottom-up play with language: "won" becomes "1," "later" becomes "l8r." After all, new technology creates new inertia for change: The apostrophe requires an additional step on an iPhone, so we send text messages using "your" (or "UR") instead of "you're." And it doesn't matter—the messagee will still understand our message.

7   Standardized spelling enables readers to understand writing, to aid communication and ensure clarity. Period. There is no additional reason, other than snobbery, for spelling rules. Computers, smartphones, and tablets are speeding the adoption of more casual forms of communication—texting is closer to speech than letter writing. But the distinction between the oral and the written is only going to become more blurry, and the future isn't autocorrect, it's Siri. We need a new set of tools that recognize more variations instead of rigidly enforcing outdated dogma. Let's make our own rules. It's not like the English language has many good ones **anyway.** ("Use Your Own Words." Copyright © 2012 Conde Nast. *Wired* magazine. All rights reserved. Article by Ann Trubek. Reprinted by permission.)

Sharpening Your Skills

DIRECTIONS Answer the following questions by filling in the blanks or circling the letter of the correct response.

Making Predictions 1. What does the title suggest the author will say about spelling?

_____

Using Context Clues 2. Which of the following is an example of an "innocuous message turned anatomical" (paragraph 1)?

a. He wondered why the baseball was getting bigger. Then it hit him.

b. I didn't remember how to throw a boomerang until it came back to me.

c. Please keep me a breast of the changes.

3. Based on the context, what would be good synonyms for *variations* and *dogma* in the following sentence from paragraph 7? "We need a new set of tools that recognize more *variations* instead of rigidly enforcing outdated *dogma*."

_____

_____

4. Based on the context, which of its two meanings does the word *static* have in this sentence from paragraph 6: "Language is not *static*—or constantly *degenerating*, as many claim."

a. crackling or hissing sound

b. unchanging

Based on the context, which meaning for *degenerating* makes more sense?

a. characterized by density or thickness

b. declining in quality

Using the Web for Definitions

5. What's a quick web definition for the word *innocuous*?

_____

Identifying Opinion Statements and Analyzing Arguments

6. What type of opinion statement or statements drive this argument?

_____

Paraphrase the opinion that holds the argument together.

_____

_____

Identifying Sentence Functions

7. In paragraph 3, the author tells us that the English language is in a terrible mess and then poses some questions. Are these questions rhetorical? _____

What's the relationship between the questions and the opening statement?

_____

_____

Paraphrasing

8. Which statement best paraphrases the topic sentence of paragraph 5?

a. People have been trying to enforce spelling rules for centuries, and it's time they gave up.

b. Spelling rules are not fixed in stone; we can change them if we want to.

c. There is no law against changing the rules for spelling; over the course of time, some notable people have suggested such changes.

Recognizing Tone

9. How would you describe the author's tone?

_____

_____

10. In these two sentences from paragraph 7, what effect is the word *period* supposed to have on the statement that precedes it? "Standardized spelling enables readers to understand writing, to aid communication and ensure clarity. Period."

    a. It suggests that the reader could not ask standardized spelling to do more than that.

    b. It suggests that standardized spelling is not as important as punctuation.

    c. It suggests that what standardized spelling accomplishes isn't all that much.

Evaluating Arguments

11. Is the word *period* meant to provide support for the author's argument? _____ Please explain.

    _____

    _____

12. Who are some of the people the author cites in support of her point of view?

    _____

13. Do these people qualify as experts who should convince readers that the author is correct? _____ Please explain.

    _____

    _____

    _____

    _____

    _____

14. What would a critical reader ask about this statement?

"Language is not static—or constantly degenerating, as many claim."

_____

_____

Drawing Personal Conclusions **15.** Based on what the author says in this reading, do you think she would correct student papers that failed to use *who* and *whom* correctly?

_____

_____

ALLUSION ALERT

Rip Van Winkle

Rip Van Winkle is a character in a short story of the same name. Written by nineteenth-century American writer Washington Irving, "Rip Van Winkle" describes how Rip meets some mysterious strangers in the woods. They give him a drink that puts him to sleep for twenty years. When he wakes up and tries to find his old house and old life, Rip is stunned by all the changes that occurred. When allusions are now made to Rip Van Winkle, they suggest that someone feels completely out of synch with a world grown very different from whatever he or she once knew, for instance: "Returning to school after twenty years as a corporate executive, Karen felt like Rip Van Winkle returning to a world completely transformed by educational technology."

▶ **TEST 1**   **Identifying Opinions and Evaluating Support**

DIRECTIONS   Read each argument through. Then paraphrase the opinion being argued and circle the letter of any error you spot in the supporting details.

1. Mothers Gone Mad

1 We've all read about those horrific cases in which a mother either abandons or kills her newborn child. Such acts seem so vicious and so heartless we are quick to condemn the mothers involved as monsters worthy of the severest punishment. That instinctive reaction is understandable. Yet a convincing case can be made for a different response, one based more on compassion than fury, because women who commit such crimes are extremely ill and not conscious of what they are doing.

2   As Michel Delcroix, a former gynecologist and trial expert on the subject points out, the women who murder their children following pregnancy are in a "psychotic[†] state and no more responsible for their actions than a schizophrenic[†] who kills" under the delusion that he or she is being attacked. Those sentiments are echoed by Felix Navarro, a doctor and president of the French Association for the Recognition of Pregnancy Denial. According to Navarro, "The judgment of the women is altered; they're not aware of what they're doing. Legally, they should not be tried. They are in a sort of state of temporary insanity."

3   Dr. Navarro's point is well taken. In a study of women who gave birth out of wedlock, conducted in 1890, at least 50 percent of the one hundred women included in the study showed symptoms of insanity. (Source of quotations: Tracy Clark-Flory, "Defending Mothers Who Kill," Salon.com, July 30, 2010.)

1. In your own words, what is the point of the author's argument?

_____

_____

[†]psychotic state: showing a loss of contact with reality and the consequences of one's actions.

[†]schizophrenic: a person suffering from disrupted thought processes, which are often characterized by irrational delusions.

2. What error in reasoning appears in the support?

a. irrelevant reason or example

b. circular reasoning

c. hasty generalization

d. unidentified or inappropriate expert

e. unidentified or dated research

2. The Legacy of *Silent Spring*

1 For more than four decades, ecologists and environmentalists have revered Rachel Carson, author of the 1962 book *Silent Spring*, for alerting the world to the dangers of chemical pesticides. Arguing that pesticides such as DDT upset the balance of nature, kill wildlife, and cause cancer in humans, Carson created widespread "chemophobia" that culminated in a ban on DDT's use. Unfortunately, though, Carson's impassioned and vividly written plea for protecting nature and human health has left generations of readers with a skewed view of pesticides.

2   According to Dr. I. L. Baldwin, Carson greatly exaggerated the risks. Using questionable statistics and anecdotes, such as the doubtful tale of a woman who immediately developed cancer after spraying her basement with DDT, Carson pronounced this pesticide to be a human carcinogen[†] even though most scientists disagreed. Carson was also irresponsible in her refusal to acknowledge the pesticide's benefits, which far outweighed their potential for harm. As Dr. Baldwin pointed out, pesticides have dramatically improved human health and welfare by getting rid of insects and parasites that destroy crops and transmit deadly diseases. Today, mosquito-borne malaria is still a leading cause of death and illness worldwide because Carson's devotees won't allow DDT to be restored as a weapon in the battle against this disease. (Source of information: John Tierney, "Fateful Voice of a Generation Still Drowns Out Real Science," *New York Times*, June 5, 2007.)

1. In your own words, what is the point of the author's argument?

_____

_____

_____

[†]carcinogen: cause of cancer.

2. What error in reasoning appears in the support?

   a. irrelevant reason or example

   b. circular reasoning

   c. hasty generalization

   d. unidentified or inappropriate expert

   e. unidentified or dated research

3. Plagiarism Should Not Be the Wave of the Future

1   Only a modern-day Rip Van Winkle could have missed the fact that digital technology has made it much easier to plagiarize. As the *New York Times* expressed it in the title of a 2010 article on the subject, "Plagiarism Lines Blur for Students in Digital Age." The article goes on to say what many instructors on college campuses have noted: A disturbing number of students seem to think it is acceptable to "write" a paper by pulling up several websites on the same topic and then cutting and pasting together sentences or entire paragraphs drawn from the various sites. Even worse, there are signs that this trend is on the rise across the country.

2   A recent article in the *Arkansas Bee* reported on an entire class that failed an exam after it was discovered that the students in the class had all cheated on a science test. While many parents protested the school's re-sponse, the school board refused to let the children officially graduate and move on to middle school until they had taken a brand new test especially created for them.

1. In your own words, what is the point of the author's argument?

_____

_____

2. What error in reasoning appears in the support?

   a. irrelevant reason or example

   b. circular reasoning

   c. hasty generalization

   d. unidentified or inappropriate expert

   e. unidentified or dated research

4. Women and the Draft

1   Two years after repealing the ban on homosexuals in the United States military, Defense Secretary Leon Panetta announced the lifting of the ban on women in combat. For the many women who have served unofficially in combat, the ground-breaking decision of the Joint Chiefs of Staff to formally allow women into combat serves as formal proof that women have finally been fully accepted as soldiers the equal of men. Panetta himself acknowledged that women have long been willing and capable of serving combat roles and said they should now be formally recognized for their contributions in combat.

2   Now, however, that the Pentagon is allowing women to serve in combat, women ages eighteen to twenty-five also should have to register for the Selective Service. True, there has been no draft since 1973. But men aged eighteen to twenty-five are still required to register, so women should have to do so as well. As retired Col. Peter Mansoor, a professor of military history at the Ohio State University in Columbus and a former U.S. Army brigade commander who served two tours in Iraq, says, "If we open up combat arms to women, even on a voluntary basis, if there is a draft, we should be able to force women into those positions." Colonel Mansoor illustrates the viewpoint of the entire military establishment: As long as the Pentagon views women as capable of serving in combat, it would not be fair to continue requiring only men to register for the Selective Service. How can we justify allowing women to serve in combat without requiring them to be conscripted into service in the event of an emergency? Now that women will be able to serve in combat, it stands to reason that they should also be eligible for the draft. (Adapted from www.csmonitor.com/USA/Military/2013/0123/Women-in-combat-Will-they-have-to-register-for-the-draft.)

1. In your own words, what is the point of the author's argument?

_____

_____

2. What error in reasoning appears in the support?

   a. irrelevant reason or example

   b. circular reasoning

   c. hasty generalization

   d. unidentified or inappropriate expert

   e. unidentified or dated research

▶ **TEST 2** **Recognizing Errors in Reasoning**

DIRECTIONS Paraphrase the opinion being expressed. Then circle the appropriate letters to identify any errors in reasoning and evaluate the author's degree of bias.

1. Looking for Another Fifteen Minutes of Fame

1   Dr. David A. Kessler, a pediatrician and former commissioner of the U.S. Food and Drug Administration, is on record claiming that "Our food safety system is broken." Kessler also wrote a 2009 book titled *The End of Overeating*,[†] in which he claims that fat, sugar, and salt dominate the American diet, thereby encouraging both obesity and the diseases that come with being overweight. In a 2013 editorial in the *New York Times*, titled "Antibiotics, Farm Animals and You," he railed about antibiotics in meat and the supposed threat they pose to consumer health.

2   With all due respect to the good doctor, the question that has to be asked is this: If the food safety system was in such a bad way, why didn't Dr. Kessler fix it when he was FDA commissioner under presidents Bush and Clinton? Why did he save all of his outrage for the years when he had no way to implement his theories?

3   All too often, political officials, once they are out of the limelight, look for causes that will help them recover the public's attention, and that's what David Kessler is doing. Besides, why would anyone listen to a man famous for his lack of self-control? David Kessler's binge eating has made his weight fluctuate wildly from 160 to 230 pounds. He should reform himself before he starts trying to fix our food system.

1. In your own words, what is the point of the author's argument?

———————————————————————————

———————————————————————————

[†]Dr. Kessler also published an adapted version of this book for teenagers. It's titled *Your Food Is Fooling You.*

2. Which of the following applies to the author's argument?

   a. The author engages in a character attack.

   b. The author uses slippery slope reasoning.

   c. The author appeals to the reader's emotions.

   d. The author suggests that no comment is proof enough.

   e. The author's argument contains no errors in reasoning.

3. Which statement accurately describes the bias in this piece of writing?

   a. The author expresses an acceptable degree of bias for a persuasive piece of writing.

   b. The author's bias is excessive even within the context of persuasive writing.

2. Saying No to Physician-Assisted Suicide

1   Oregon, Montana, and Washington are currently the three states that allow physician-assisted suicide in the United States. In 2012, Massachusetts almost became the fourth. Somehow advocates of assisted suicide managed to gather enough signatures to get it on the November 2012 ballot, and it was narrowly defeated 51 percent to 49 percent.

2   What this narrow defeat in Massachusetts suggests is that the legalizing of physician-assisted suicide should never be decided by a ballot initiative.[†] Otherwise the practice may spread as intentional misinformation and emotional manipulation encourage voters to sign a petition in favor of putting legalization on the ballot. In turn, many of those same petitioners will cast their votes to enact legislation they are bound to regret.

3   Once allowing doctors to help the terminally ill end their lives becomes legal state by state, thanks, in part, due to ballot initiatives, a host of unintended consequences are bound to follow. The time will quickly come when children who want to take elderly parents off life support will be allowed to do so without their parents' permission. In an era when the spiraling costs of health care are of great concern, health care providers may be inclined to end the lives of those who cannot pay for more sophisticated medical treatment. As Paul Longmore, professor of history and

---

[†]ballot initiative: a form of participatory democracy, where citizens get a fixed number of signatures to put a piece of legislation before the voters and bypass established officeholders or lawmakers.

a disability advocate, expressed it, "Poor people, people of color, elderly people with chronic or progressive conditions or disabilities, and anyone who is, in fact, terminally ill, will find themselves at serious risk."

4   Longmore is correct in his predictions about what would happen should physician-assisted suicide become the law of the land. Yet this is not how Americans treat the weak and the helpless. This great country grew strong because of its willingness to take in the poor and the suffering. We cannot now abandon that great tradition in favor of ending the lives of those in pain because caring for them would be too expensive. (Source of quotation: http://dredf.org/assisted_suicide/assistedsuicide.html.)

1. In your own words, what is the point of the author's argument?

   _____

   _____

2. Which of the following applies to the author's argument?
   a. The author engages in a character attack.
   b. The author uses slippery slope reasoning.
   c. The author appeals to the reader's emotions.
   d. The author suggests that no comment is proof enough.
   e. The author's argument contains no errors in reasoning.

3. Which statement accurately describes the bias in this piece of writing?
   a. The author expresses an acceptable degree of bias for a persuasive piece of writing.
   b. The author's bias is excessive even within the context of persuasive writing.

3. Parents Approve Block Scheduling

1 Our school board has decided to implement block scheduling at our local high school starting in the next school year. Students will work with a three-day rotating schedule that will include ninety-minute blocks for instruction in the core subjects, such as math, science, English, and foreign languages. With block scheduling, teachers work with fewer students each day, which allows them more opportunities to individualize instruction according to students' needs. Because of the increased amount of time

spent on each subject, students have the opportunity to explore topics in greater depth than they do with traditional scheduling. Teachers also have the freedom to develop longer lessons that can be completed in one or two class periods instead of over the course of a week or more.

2   Because parental cooperation is so important in the success of this venture, the school committee recently held a public forum at which parents and teachers were invited to ask questions and comment on the proposed changes. As we had hoped, the parents are solidly behind our plan. After viewing a presentation that explained how their children would benefit from the new system, the parents had numerous questions but voiced no complaints or criticisms. Thus we in the administration know we can move forward with the full support of our students' parents. This is a crucial ingredient in making the program succeed.

1. In your own words, what is the point of the author's argument?

_____

_____

2. Which of the following applies to the author's argument?

   a. The author engages in a character attack.

   b. The author uses slippery slope reasoning.

   c. The author appeals to the reader's emotions.

   d. The author suggests that no comment is proof enough.

   e. The author's argument contains no errors in reasoning.

3. Which statement accurately describes the bias in this piece of writing?

   a. The author expresses an acceptable degree of bias for a persuasive piece of writing.

   b. The author's bias is excessive even within the context of persuasive writing.

▶ **TEST 3** **Reviewing New Vocabulary**

DIRECTIONS Fill in the blanks with one of the words listed below.

fallacy	conservative	forebears	transparent	jubilant
demeanor	insurrection	carnage	rhetoric	tacit

Britain's Big Mistake

1   Many of America's colonists had British _____, which may have been one reason why the British crown thought the Americans would never rebel. But that faith in some long lost family connection

was a major _____ when it came to Britain's understanding of the colonists across the sea. While some of the wealthier American merchants did cultivate British traditions and even adopted a

British _____ and accent, most Americans were far less

_____ in their thinking.

2   They were looking toward the future, not the past, and dreaming of political independence even if that dream led to the _____ of war. Those favoring independence from Britain didn't need a crystal ball

to know that an armed _____ was practically unavoidable if the British continued to tax the colonies without bothering to make their

motives _____ to the people they arrogantly burdened with tax after tax.

3   The British government, however, took no notice of its struggling subjects. Instead, it kept levying taxes and fines without indicating how, in the long run, they might help the colonies. But then, the taxes and fines were

never meant to help the colonists. While Britain's _____ about its colonies oozed concern for its subjects, the reality was altogether different. As it did with all of its colonies, the British Empire sought to pay its debts by squeezing its far-flung subjects for treasure and natural resources.

4   Ironically, the British officials who actually lived on American soil and saw the colonists face to face were even more in the dark about what was happening in the country than their leaders back home. The lack of insight

was due to the _____ agreement Britain's colonial officials

had with wealthier members of the colonies. The more monied colonists, most of them merchants, would be kept in comfort and privilege as long as they undermined or reported any signs of rebellion and refused to participate in any boycotts of British goods. Comfortable with their protected position, most wealthy Americans neither had nor wanted information about the movement for independence.

5   But merchants weren't the rebels in colonial America. The lawyers were. Men with legal training like James Otis, Thomas Jefferson, and John Adams were smart, articulate, and determined to throw off British rule. It's no surprise, then, that of the fifty-six signers of the Declaration of Independence, twenty-eight were lawyers. By 1783, the Americans had defeated their Brit-

ish rulers. While the Americans were _____ in victory, the British were mystified in defeat. They were left wondering how they had managed to so underestimate the American colonists they thought could so easily be ruled and exploited.

Putting It All Together

© Ulrich Flemming

The readings that follow let you apply everything you have learned about understanding and evaluating a writer's explanation or argument. However, these readings are meant to serve another purpose as well. Because they explore issues of past and current importance for our culture, you should try to determine your own personal perspective on the issues discussed. As the preface of *Reading for Thinking* points out, the goal of this textbook was always twofold: to help you analyze the thoughts of others while hammering out your own position on topics relevant to your life, if not right now, then very soon.

◆ **READING 1** ## Living in a Digital World

Samuel Greengard

Looking Ahead The author of the following reading is a journalist writing for *Communications of the ACM* (Association for Computing Machinery) magazine. Greengard explores the ways in which technology may be changing behavior.

Getting Focused The title provides the basis for questions to focus your reading: According to the author, what effect does living in a digital world have upon its inhabitants? Does the author describe mainly positive or mainly negative effects? Does he include a description of both? As you read, try to determine whether or not it's possible to generalize about the effects of living in a digital world.

Word Watch The following words may be difficult to define from context. Read the definitions and say them aloud. Watch for the words as you read. They will be marked with an asterisk.

> **seductive (6):** tempting, compelling by being attractive
>
> **velocity (7):** speed, quickness
>
> **paradox (7):** a statement that seems to be contradictory and absurd but when studied more closely makes sense and fits the situation or behavior it describes
>
> **staccato (8):** marked by brevity and abruptness
>
> **gibberish (9):** unintelligible or meaningless speech
>
> **tethered (12):** fastened, restrained, connected; also describes one device connected to another

Where in paragraph 1 do you see the author shifting away from the opening point of view?

1 It is no secret that humans have an innate urge to connect with one another. In fact, research shows that well-adjusted people spend more time engaged in social interaction and activities. However, in the age of always-on digital technology, the notion of connectedness—and the definition of friendship—are changing radically. Increasingly, the route to human interaction is through a digital device.

2   Approximately two billion people now tap into the Internet. About five billion people use mobile phones and a growing number of those devices offer sophisticated computing and communications capabilities. There's cell service atop Mt. Everest and in remote South Pacific atolls. Incredibly,

the average 13- to 17-year-old in the U.S. sends about 110 messages per day. In fact, it's become increasingly difficult to go anywhere without getting caught in the tractor beam of digital technology.

Is the writer talking literally or figuratively about a new frontier?

What's your guess? Is the author going to focus on the new ways to connect or the potential problems?

3   Not surprisingly, as people use these devices more frequently—and for more hours each day—researchers are studying the effects with growing interest. Add to this the extreme multitasking we increasingly engage in, either by choice or by necessity, and it is clear that society is venturing into a brave new frontier. "We're seeing people so absorbed in digital media that it's becoming their primary reference point for life," observes Clifford Nass a communications professor at Stanford University and author of *The Man Who Lied to His Laptop: What Machines Teach Us About Human Relationships.*

4   What is the impact of digital immersion? How is it changing people's thinking and behavior? And how does it affect the way we view the world and interact with others? It's a complex equation that researchers are only now beginning to understand. "Digital technology brings people together," says Michael Suman, research director at the Center for the Digital Future at the University of Southern California. "It allows people to connect in ways that were never before possible. But it also creates new sets of questions and potential problems."

Net Losses

5   There's no disputing that digital technology has thoroughly invaded our lives. A 2011 study conducted by telecommunications giant Ericsson found that 35% of iPhone and Android users check their email or Facebook account before getting out of bed in the morning. In addition, 40% use their phones in bed before they go to sleep at night. The average American is digitally connected between 2.5 to 3.5 hours a day. Nielsen reports that social networking, online games and email are the biggest attractions.

Is there any indication that the author agrees or disagrees with Turkle?

6   Few people have examined the topic more closely than Sherry Turkle, a professor of social studies of science and technology at Massachusetts Institute of Technology and author of *Alone Together: Why We Expect More from Technology and Less from Each Other.* She believes that digital immersion is seductive* because it seemingly addresses our human vulnerabilities. "As it turns out, we are very vulnerable," she says. "We are lonely but fearful of intimacy. Constant connectivity offers the illusion of companionship without the demands of friendship. We can't get enough of each other, if we can have each other at a distance and in amounts that we can control."

7   The heavy use of digital technology trains society to have less patience for the particular skills, pace, and sensitivities of face-to-face interaction. We have become used to the volume and velocity* of the digital medium, explains Turkle. "We adapt to it and, over time, become more comfortable with its simplifications." The upshot? "People complain that they are too busy communicating to think, too busy communicating to create, and in a final paradox,* too busy communicating to fully connect with people who matter. We are in continual contact but we are alone together."

What are we dealing with here, fact or opinion?

8   The ripples of digital technology also make it easier to hide. Turkle says many people admit they are relieved to leave a voicemail message rather than reach the intended person. Some say the texting lets them avoid the time commitment of phone calls. "We are using technology to dial down human contact," she says. "People are comforted by being in touch with a lot of people that they keep at bay. The result? We imagine that email and texting will give us more control over our time and emotional exposure," but eventually "anything but staccato* texts seems too exhausting."

Master or Slave?

What cause and effect relationship is described in paragraph 9?

9   The allure of digital technology impacts people in other ways. Suman says the students he teaches have more trouble than ever focusing on lectures and learning: Text messages and emails arrive in gibberish* he says, and students end up asking the same questions over and over. Even when they have switched off their devices they are too often unable to think through concepts and ideas. "They are increasingly challenged to engage in deep and meaningful thought," he says. "Sequential, logical rational thinking seems to be severely compromised."

Does paragraph 10 describe an additional cause or effect?

10   A breakdown of social etiquette—if not outright rudeness—is also more pervasive, Nass says. "Today people think it's okay to text in the middle of dinner, at a meeting, in class, wherever. They text while you are talking to them and then they look and say, 'What?'" Humans he says aren't good at multitasking. In fact, studies show that multitasking doesn't exist. We simply switch back and forth from one task to another very quickly. The heaviest "multitaskers" show signs of diminished short-term memory. In other words, they're forgetful.

11   Yair Amichai-Hamburger, director of the Research Center for Internet Psychology at the Sammy Ofer School of Communications, says it's time to consider whether we are served or enslaved by today's technology. "For many of us, it is becoming increasingly difficult to control the impulse to check the inbox yet again." Worse, he says, we're constantly surrounded

by advertisements urging us to find fulfillment through the acquisition of material goods. The latest acquisition of a shiny new gadget gives us a quick fix but does nothing to feed the soul.

12　For many, the next effect is an always-on digital lifestyle. In a world where time is often equated to money, society increasingly buys into the notion that being technologically tethered* is essential and even unavoidable. What's more, as employers require individuals to check digital devices and respond 24/7, there's no clear separation between home and work. These pressures, Amichai-Hamburger says, put modern society at danger of "swapping standard of living for quality of life."

What's the relationship between the first sentence and the second?

13　In fact, studies show that heavy technology use can result in higher levels of loneliness and depression—and the U.S. and other countries are trending upward. Irena Stepanikova, an assistant professor of sociology at the University of South Carolina, examined various digital tools in a 2010 study, "Time on the Internet at Home, Loneliness and Life Satisfaction." Researchers found that people who spent more time at home browsing the Web and using instant messaging, chat rooms, and newsgroups felt lonelier and less satisfied. Email, on the other hand, neither increased nor decreased mental well-being.

14　The thing that's easy to overlook, Stepanikova says, is that we frequently use digital tools in isolation as a way to connect with others. While digital technology can connect families and friends over geographic distances, it's critical to recognize that Facebook pokes and postings aren't equal to actual conversation. Too often, "we use the Internet alone and even if others are present, we do not actively interact with them," she says. Consequently, "the solitude of these activities may counter some of the potential social benefits." It's no small problem. "The more time people spend at home on the Internet," says Stepanikova, "the less time they spend on social activities, parties, conversation, attending sports, and cultural events—and essentially on any activities performed together with family members and with friends."

Switching Off

Given how the paragraph opens, what should you be asking at this point?

15　A growing number of researchers and social scientists believe it is important to take steps to regain control of the technology and our lives. One approach that is gaining popularity is the concept of switching off electronics and taking clearly defined breaks. In 2010, the Sabbath Manifesto project emerged. It promotes the idea of unplugging every seventh day, "deadlines and paperwork be damned" and creating more defined boundaries in order to avoid "destroying the fabric of your life."

16 Amichai-Hamburger says that being unplugged at least one day a week "gives you a chance to be with those you care about." No less important: It changes the flow of life and provides perspective about what's really important. "It reminds us that we have to lead technology and not be led by it. It gives us space to think."

17 Turkle also believes that venturing offline can be refreshing. "It can be a reminder of the importance of solitude that refreshes and sustains." Nevertheless, she believes that "unplugging" is not the way of the future and that we've only begun the process of adapting to digital technology and learning how to manage our actions and reactions effectively.

18 "We must begin to make corrections," says Turkle. "We are not doing justice to the complexity of the problems we face, just as we are not doing justice to each other. We need to learn how to be on a digital diet so that we can make healthy choices about the kind of life we want to lead, the kind of life that will make us productive, and how we can be content and fulfilled individually and in relationships." (Samuel Greengard, "Living in a Digital World," *Communications of the ACM* 54, no. 10 (October 2011): 17–19. Copyright © 2011. Reprinted by permission.)

TAKING A CLOSER LOOK This set of questions focuses on your understanding of the text, both its content and the language used to convey that content.

DIRECTIONS Answer the following questions by circling the letter of the correct response or filling in the blanks.

Recognizing
the Controlling
Main Idea

1. Which statement best sums up the overall main idea of this reading?

   a. Thanks to digital devices, people are finding new ways to make and maintain friendships.

   b. Digital devices have given us new ways to connect to other people, but our current dependence on these devices may be costing too high a price.

   c. Digital technology may have increased our opportunities to make friends but it has also allowed work to invade our personal lives to an unhealthy degree.

   d. Given that so much research indicates our dependence on digital technology has become unhealthy, there is a growing movement to unplug altogether.

2. The controlling main idea is

    a. stated.

    b. implied.

Tracing Repetition and Reference

3. At the end of paragraph 3, the quote from Clifford Nass is used to define what phrase from the previous sentence?

_____

Understanding Supporting Details

4. In paragraph 5, the statistics used are

    a. major details.

    b. minor details.

Please explain why you chose that answer.

_____

5. In paragraph 8, the major supporting details all provide examples of what cause and effect relationship?

_____

6. In paragraph 9, what word in the topic sentence is a clue to the major details?

_____

Using Context Clues

7. Based on the context, how would you define *pervasive* in the following sentence from paragraph 10: "A breakdown of social etiquette— if not outright rudeness—is also more *pervasive*"?

_____

Understanding Supporting Details

8. Clifford Nass is also quoted in paragraph 10. Why does the author mention him again?

_____

_____

Recognizing Transitions

9. In paragraph 13, what key opening phrase tells readers that the author is continuing the same train of thought begun in the previous paragraph?

_____

In paragraph 17, the paragraph opens with Turkle agreeing to the point of the previous paragraph. What word announces a change in her point of view?

_____

Outlining and Summarizing

10. If you were outlining or summarizing this reading, would you need to include the information about Mount Everest and the South Pacific? _____ Please explain.

_____

_____

READING WITH A CRITICAL EYE   Your goal here is not to be critical in the negative sense, but rather to evaluate how effectively the author explains an idea or argues an opinion.

Identifying the Author's Purpose

1. Which statement do you think best describes the author's purpose?

   a. The author wants to convey to readers some of the concerns being expressed about living in a digital world.

   b. The author wants to sum up for readers what Sherry Turkle says about the effect of technology on our lives.

   c. The author wants to persuade readers that they should share the concerns about technology voiced by the people he quotes.

Identifying Tone

2. Which tone does the author use throughout?

   a. casual

   b. humorous

   c. neutral

   d. concerned

3. When the author opens paragraph 5 with the phrase "There's no disputing," what should critical readers immediately think?

_____

_____

Distinguishing Between Fact and Opinion

4. In paragraph 7, the author makes this claim: "The heavy use of digital technology trains society to have less patience for the particular skills, pace, and sensitivities of face-to-face interaction." How can you tell it's an opinion as opposed to a fact?

_____

Which statement best describes the relationship between fact and opinion in this reading?

a. The author includes facts and opinions in equal amount.

b. The author reports more facts than opinions.

c. The author relies more on opinions than facts.

Evaluating Arguments

5. Do you think the author makes effective use of expert opinion to persuade his readers? _____ Please explain.

_____

6. Which statement best describes the author's handling of an opposing point of view?

a. The author briefly mentions those who do not fear the effects of heavy technology use.

b. The author doesn't mention that there is an opposing point of view.

c. The author is rude and dismissive toward those who are not concerned about the effects of heavy technology use.

7. In paragraph 13, the author says this: "In fact, studies show that heavy technology use can result in higher levels of loneliness and depression." Would you say that there is adequate support for this claim? _____ Please explain.

_____

_____

8. To accept the significance of Professor Stepanikova's study, referred to in paragraph 13, do we need to know anything more than the paragraph tells us? _____ Please explain.

_____

_____

Understanding Figurative Language

9. In paragraph 18, Sherry Turkle says, "We need to learn how to be on a digital diet, so that we can make healthy choices about the kind of life we want to lead." That statement contains a _____

that compares heavy technology use to _____.

Synthesizing

10. What follows below is a brief reading on how technology affects the life of one specific person, twenty-five-year-old Canadian Keith Knight. Once you finish reading it, look over the three thesis statements below and decide which *one* does *not* effectively synthesize the two readings.

a. The author of "Living in a Digital World" illustrates what is often the case with writing on technology—people don't have moderate positions. They tend to be either deeply concerned about technology's drawbacks or celebrating its possibilities. The experience of Keith Knight, the subject of "Gaming with the Best of Them," suggests, however, what is probably true about living in a digital world. There is no one generalization that covers everyone.

b. Five years ago, descriptions of the wonders that technology could perform were everywhere, but times have changed, and these days celebration of technology are a good deal rarer. Far more typical are articles like Samuel Greengard's "Living in a Digital World," which warns of the dangers that lie ahead if we don't regularly unplug our digital devices and get more in touch with flesh-and-blood people.

c. While the kind of concerns outlined in "Living in a Digital World" should not be ignored—we do need to keep in touch with flesh-and-blood people—we shouldn't lose sight of the profound and positive ways technology can also improve our lives, and the story of Canadian Keith Knight is a good illustration of that point.

Gaming with the Best of Them

Keith Knight is a young Canadian who loves playing video games. You can find him on Twitch.tv, which live streams video game matches. Knight favors the popular PC games *League of Legends* and *Guild Wars 2*. Currently, Knight is streaming his games to raise money for his favorite cause, finding a cure for muscular dystrophy, a degenerative disease that progressively cripples the body. Knight has a particularly acute form of the disease called Amyoplasia Arthrogryposis. As a result of his illness, which has left him without the use of his limbs, he plays video games lying belly down on his bed with a pen in his mouth and a computer mouse pressing against his cheek.

Knight is forced to rely solely on his face and head to do just about everything and games are no exception. He started out as a kid playing video games on the Nintendo 64, but as console game controllers got more complex and more difficult to use, Knight had to move on to PC games. Similarly, as those friends he played with in his youth moved on and moved away, Knight had to find other ways to play the games that excited his mind and imagination. Fortunately, the multiplayer, online game *World of Warcraft* and its newer competitor, the team-based *League of Legends*, provided brand new outlets for Knight's fiercely competitive nature. This time around, there is little chance that he will run out of people to play with. Subscribers for these games number in the millions. In 2012, Knight raised $5,000 by playing under the name "Aieron" on Twitch.tv, and he plans to continue raising money to fight the disease that has ravaged his body without managing to damage his fighting spirit.

What Do You Think? By the time you finished "Living in a Digital World" did you feel you had had solid answers to the questions that opened paragraph 4? Did the author convince you that digital devices have become so much a part of our lives that they are changing people's thinking and behavior?

Thinking Through Writing Using search terms like *technology* and *disability*, do some research on the way technology has helped people who have lost the full use of their body participate more fully in life. Then write a paper that opens with this quotation from wheelchair racer Anne Wafula Strike: "When you have a disability, knowing that you are not defined by it is the sweetest feeling." Follow the quotation with an introductory or transitional sentence that paves the way for a controlling main idea like this: "For people with disabilities, new computer technology has been a godsend." Use examples from your research to make your point convincing.

◆ **READING 2**   # Necessary Conversations

Sherry Turkle

Looking Ahead   Sherry Turkle was quoted extensively in reading 1. Now here's an excerpt from her book *Alone Together*, in which she further explains why she has concerns about how we are currently living in a digital world.

Getting Focused   The title of the selection should focus your reading, suggesting questions like, What are these conversations about and why are they necessary? Who needs to be involved in them?

Word Watch   The following words may be difficult to define from context. Read the definitions and say them aloud. Watch for the words as you read. They will be marked with an asterisk.

> **reductive (4):** using a simplistic explanation to explain a complex idea or process
>
> **genres (4):** different categories or kinds of writing
>
> **sensibilities (8):** feelings of mental awareness and responsiveness to the world
>
> **inanimate (8):** not alive, lacking in life
>
> **dictum (9):** short statement that expresses a general truth; a statement made by someone in authority
>
> **affordances (10):** qualities or properties of an object upon which one can act; physical features that afford the user control over a function, e.g., "Web browsers are an affordance that allows us access to the Web."
>
> **curtailed (12):** limited, restricted
>
> **cautionary (12):** warning
>
> **benchmarks (12):** standards of assessment

When the author starts off with a discussion of what she/he thought over thirty years ago, what do you expect will happen?

1   During my earliest days at MIT,[†] I met the idea (at that time altogether novel to me) that part of my job would be to think of ways to keep technology busy. In the fall of 1978, Michael Dertouzos, director of the Laboratory for Computer Science, held a two-day retreat at MIT's Endicott House on the future of personal computers, at the time widely called "home computers." It was clear that "everyday people," as Dertouzos put it, would soon be

[†]MIT (Massachusetts Institute of Technology): a university famous for its work in engineering, mathematics, and computer programming.

able to have their own computers. The first of these—the first that could be bought and didn't have to be built—were just coming on the market. But what could people do with them?

Why does the author tell us what was in her notes?

2 There was technological potential, but it needed to be put to work. Some of the most brilliant computer scientists in the world—such pioneers of information processing as Robert Fano, J. C. R. Licklider, Marvin Minsky, and Seymour Papert—were asked to brainstorm on the question. My notes from this meeting show suggestions on tax preparation and teaching children to program. No one thought that anyone except academics would really want to write on computers. Several people suggested a calendar; others thought that was a dumb idea. There would be games.

What does the word *now* signal to readers?

3 Now we know that once computers connected us to each other, once we became tethered to the network, we really didn't need to keep computers busy. *They keep us busy.* It is as though we have become their killer app. "We don't do our email; our email does us." We talk about spending hours on email, but, we too, are being spent. Niels Bohr[†] suggests that the opposite of a "deep truth" is a truth no less profound. As we contemplate online life, it helps to keep this in mind.

4 Online, we easily find "company" but are exhausted by the pressures of performance. We enjoy continual connection but rarely have each other's full attention. We can have instant audiences but flatten out what we say to each other in new reductive* genres* of abbreviation. We like it that the Web knows us, but this is only possible because we compromise our privacy, leaving electronic breadcrumbs that can be easily exploited both politically and commercially.

5 We have many new encounters but have come to experience them as tentative, to be put on hold if better ones come along. Indeed, new encounters need not be better to get our attention. We are wired to respond positively to their simply being new. We can work from home, but our work bleeds into our private lives until we can barely discern the boundaries between them. We like being able to reach each other almost instantaneously but have to hide our phones to force ourselves to take a quiet moment.

6 Overwhelmed by the pace that technology makes possible, we think about how new, more efficient technologies might help dig us out. But new devices encourage even greater volume and velocity. In this escalation of demands, one of the things that comes to feel safe is using technology to connect to people at a distance or, more precisely, to a lot of people from a distance. But even a lot of people from a distance can turn out to be

---

[†]Niels Bohr (1885–1962): Danish physicist, whose work on the structure of the atom won him a Pulitzer Prize in 1922.

not enough people at all. We brag about how many we have "friended" on Facebook, yet Americans say they have fewer friends than before.[1] When asked in whom they can confide and to whom they turn in an emergency, more and more say their only resource is their family.

7   The ties that we form through the Internet are not, in the end, the ties that bind. But they are the ties that preoccupy. We text each other at family dinners, while we jog, while we drive, and as we push our children on swings in the park. We don't want to intrude on each other, so instead we constantly intrude on each other, but not in "real time." When we misplace our mobile devices, we become anxious—impossible really. We have heard teenagers insist that even when their cell phones are not on their person, they can feel them vibrate. "I know when I am being called," says a sixteen-year-old. "I just do." Sentiments of dependency echo across generations. "I never am without my cell phone," says a fifty-two-year-old father. "It is my protection."

8   In the evening, when sensibilities* such as these come together, they are likely to form what have been called "postfamilial families." Their members are alone together each in their own rooms, each on a networked computer. We go online because we are busy but end up spending more time with technology and less time with each other. We defend connectivity as a way to be close, even as we effectively hide from each other. At the limit, we will settle for the inanimate,* if that's what it takes.

9   Bohr's dictum* is equally true in the area of sociable robotics, where things are no less tangled. Roboticists insist that robotic emotions are made up of the same ultimate particles as human ones (because mind is ultimately made of matter), but it is also true that robots' claims to emotion derive from programs designed to get an emotional rise out of us.

10   Roboticists present, as though it were a first principle, the idea that as our population ages, we simply won't have enough people to take care of our human needs, and so, as a companion, a sociable robot is "better than nothing." But what are our first principles? We know that we warm to machines when they seem to show an interest in us, when their affordances* speak to our vulnerabilities. But we don't have to say yes to everything that speaks to us in this way. Even if, as adults, we are intrigued by the idea that a sociable robot will distract our aging parents, our children ask, "Don't we have people for these jobs?" We should attend to their hesitations. Sorting

---

[1]One study comparing data from 1985 and 2004 found that the mean number of people with whom Americans can discuss matters important to them dropped by nearly one-third. Researchers also found that the number of people who said they had no one with whom to discuss such matters more than doubled.

all this out will not be easy. But we are at a crossroads—at a time and place to initiate new conversations.

11   As I was working on this book, I discussed its themes with a former colleague, Richard, who has been left severely disabled by an automobile accident. He is now confined to a wheelchair in his home and needs nearly full-time nursing care. Richard is interested in robots being developed to provide practical help and companionship to people in his situation, but his reaction to the idea is complex. He begins by saying, "Show me a person in my shoes who is looking for a robot, and I'll show you someone who is looking for a person and can't find one," but then he makes the best possible case for robotic helpers when he turns the conversation to *human* cruelty. "Some of the aides and nurses at the rehab center hurt you because they are unskilled, and some hurt you because they mean to. I had both. One of them, she pulled me by the hair. One dragged me by my tubes. A robot would never do that," he says. And then he adds, "But you know, in the end, that person who dragged me by my tubes had a story. I could find out about it. She had a story."

12   For Richard, being with a person, even an unpleasant, sadistic person, makes him feel that he is still alive. It signifies that his way of being in the world has a certain dignity, even if his activities are radically curtailed.* For him, dignity requires a feeling of authenticity, a sense of being connected to the human narrative. Although he would not want his life endangered, he prefers the sadist to the robot. Richard's perspective is a cautionary* tale to those who would speak in too simple terms of pure technical benchmarks* for human and machine interactions. ("Necessary Conversations" from *Alone Together* by Sherry Turkle. Copyright © 2011 Sherry Turkle. Reprinted by permission of Basic Books, a member of the Perseus Books Group.)

Marginal notes:

What does Richard's comment suggest to you?

What do you think Richard means when he says, "She had a story"?

Do you agree with the author's interpretation of Richard's story?

TAKING A CLOSER LOOK   This set of questions focuses on your understanding of the text, both its content and the language used to convey that content.

DIRECTIONS   Answer the following questions by circling the letter of the correct response or filling in the blanks.

Recognizing the Controlling Main Idea

1. Which statement best expresses the overall main idea of this reading?

   a. When computers first entered our lives, no one really knew what to do with them, but we quickly found numerous ways to integrate them into every aspect of our daily lives.

b. Personal computers have connected us to each other in a way that was completely unexpected in 1978 when the notion of personal computers started to become a reality. At the time, the question was, How do we use them? Now the question is, How do we stop using them before they take over every aspect of our lives?

c. Despite the initial inability of technology experts to figure out how personal computers could be used in our daily lives, they have become an essential part of how we live, producing consequences that have not been completely positive, and it's time to rethink how we should use them.

d. The effect of personal computers on our daily lives just goes to show how little experts really know. When computers first came on the market, the experts could barely imagine the things personal computers could accomplish, and they thought only academics would want to use them. In other words, the experts, as usual, were dead wrong.

Drawing Inferences 2. What's the implied main idea of paragraph 4?

_____

_____

Paraphrasing 3. Which sentence best paraphrases this statement from paragraph 4: "We can have instant audiences but flatten out what we say to each other in new reductive genres of abbreviation."

a. Thanks to technology, we can quickly find new people to talk to, but everything we say is so abbreviated, we seldom say anything very complex or interesting.

b. We can always find new people to talk to but we are in such a hurry we don't follow the rule against using abbreviations in writing.

c. When texting, we use so many abbreviations, it's as if we were using a language other than English.

Recognizing Transitions and Identifying Main Ideas 4. In paragraph 6, the author starts out with this sentence: "Overwhelmed by the pace that technology makes possible, we think about how new, more efficient technologies might help dig us out." What word in the paragraph then signals that the author's train of thought will be revised? _____

5. In your own words, then, what is the main idea of paragraph 6?

_____

_____

Tracing Repetition and Reference

6. In paragraph 7, the following quotations are both examples of what phrase in the paragraph? (1) "'I know when I am being called,' says a sixteen-year-old. 'I just do.'" (2) "'I never am without my cell phone,' says a fifty-two-year-old father. 'It is my protection.'"

_____

7. In paragraph 8, the phrase "sensibilities such as these" refers to who or what from the previous paragraph?

_____

_____

Paraphrasing

8. In paragraph 10, the author opens with a claim about what roboticists think. How would you paraphrase their thinking?

_____

_____

Understanding Supporting Details

9. The author uses the story of her friend Richard in paragraph 11 to support what claim?

_____

_____

Recognizing Organizational Patterns

10. What's the primary pattern organizing this reading?

a. cause and effect

b. comparison and contrast

c. classification

d. sequence of dates and events

READING WITH A CRITICAL EYE   Your goal here is not to be critical in the negative sense, but rather to evaluate how effectively the author explains an idea or argues an opinion.

Identifying the Author's Purpose

1. How would you describe the author's purpose?

   a. She wants to describe for readers some concerns people have about the role technology plays in our lives.

   b. She wants to tell readers what it was like in the early days of computer use before people quite knew what the new technology could do.

   c. She wants to persuade readers that technology plays too big a role in our lives and is having a negative effect on human interaction.

   d. She wants to persuade readers that robotics is not the answer to social problems.

Identifying Tone

2. Which answer best describes the tone of the author's writing?

   a. ironically skeptical

   b. concerned and serious

   c. humorous and critical

   d. distant and objective

3. Why do you think the author uses *we* when she talks about the effect of technology on our lives?

   _____

   _____

Distinguishing Between Fact and Opinion

4. How would you describe the following statement from paragraph 4? "Online, we easily find 'company' but are exhausted by the pressures of performance. We enjoy continual connection but rarely have each other's full attention."

   a. fact

   b. opinion

   c. a mix of fact and opinion

5. How would you describe the following statement from paragraph 5? "Indeed, new encounters need not be better to get our attention. We are wired to respond positively to their simply being new."

    a. fact

    b. opinion

    c. a mix of fact and opinion

Overall, which statement most accurately describes the author's use of fact and opinion?

    a. The reading is extremely factual.

    b. There is a balance between fact and opinion.

    c. The reading is based almost purely on opinion.

Understanding Figurative Language   6. In paragraph 10, the author says, "But we are at a crossroads—at a time and place to initiate new conversations." Is she speaking literally or figuratively?

_____

In your own words, what is the point of that statement?

_____

_____

Evaluating Bias   7. Which statement best describes the writer's level of bias?

    a. The author shows no evidence of bias.

    b. The author is biased in favor of heavy technology use, but the bias is not excessive.

    c. The author is biased against heavy technology use, but the bias is not excessive.

    d. The author's bias is excessive and makes her unable to fairly evaluate opposing points of view.

Evaluating Arguments   8. In paragraph 6, the author says, "We brag about how many we have 'friended' on Facebook, yet Americans say they have fewer friends than before."

What is the basis for this generalization?

_____

Drawing Personal Conclusions

9. Since 2009 the world's most widely used search engine, Google, has been customizing its search results based on a user's past history of interests and preferences.[†] In other words, if you are a conservative who types in the name Sarah Palin, you are likely to get a number of websites that say positive things about the former governor of Alaska. If you are liberal, your search engine will include more websites that do not portray Palin in a positive light. What do you think Turkle would have to say about this feature?

_____

_____

_____

_____

_____

Synthesizing

10. The following excerpt comes from Don Tapscott's book *Grown Up Digital: How the Net Generation Is Changing Your World*. After you read it, write a synthesis statement that combines the main ideas of readings 1 and 2 with Tapscott's point of view.

_____

_____

_____

_____

_____

_____

[†]For a discussion of this customization, see Eli Pariser, *The Filter Bubble*, 2011, Penguin Press, pp. 1–20.

Freedom

When my generation graduated from college, we were grateful for that first job. We hung onto it like a life preserver. But times have changed. Kids see no reason to commit, at least not to the first job. High performers are on their fifth job by the time they are 27 and their average tenure at a job is 2.6 years. They revel in their freedom. My son Alex, for instance, is thinking about getting an MBA or a law degree. But when I asked him about his immediate plans for a job, he put it this way: "A commitment of three years or more would make me hesitate. I don't want to get locked in to something I may not enjoy 10 years down the road. I want to have the freedom to try new and different things. If I like what I'm doing, if it challenges me and is fun, then I would definitely commit to it. I guess, I think about the time I reach age 30, I would settle on something. I view my twenties as a period of self-discovery and self-realization."

Alex is typical of his generation. The Internet has given them the freedom to choose what to buy, where to work, when to do things like buy a book or talk to friends, and even who they want to be. Politicians like Barack Obama have tapped into it. Obama's iconic line, "Yes we can," has spawned a music video by Will.i.am of the Black Eyed Peas, plus the spoofs—proof positive that it went viral. These three words speak volumes about the Net Gen's belief that they can do anything, that no one can tell them not to. "Yes we can" was perfectly tuned to this generation, just as the peace sign was for mine. They're on a quest for freedom, and it's setting up expectations that may surprise and infuriate their elders.

(Don Tapscott, *Grown Up Digital*, 2009, McGraw-Hill, pp. 74–75.)

What Do You Think? Do you agree that the twenties should be "a period of self-discovery and self-realization"? Why or why not? If you are or plan on being a parent, would you encourage your child to view the twenties as a time for exploration rather than a time to get started earning a living? Why or why not?

Thinking Through Writing Write a paper on what you see technology doing to your life. Has it improved the way you live or made it worse in some ways? Or do you see it as having both positive and negative effects?

Start your paper with the synthesis statement you created for question 10. Then use an introductory and/or transitional sentence to lead into your controlling main idea. Follow that main idea with some very specific examples of how you use technology on a regular basis, making sure that the examples support your overall main idea. If possible, use quotations from Turkle, Greengard, or Tapscott to support your point or challenge an opposing point of view.

◆ **READING 3**   **Are Today's Students Lacking in Empathy?**

Laraine Flemming

Looking Ahead Don Tapscott, the author of the excerpt *Freedom* on pages 674–675, calls today's generation of young people the Net Generation, or Net Geners. He's not the only one summing up an entire generation with a label. Labeling and analyzing young adults in their teens and twenties is something of a spectator sport among writers and reporters. Every generation seems to get a nickname, from Bobby Soxers[†] to Generation X to the current Me Generation (also known as the Millennials). Now there's even a study that allegedly proves what the label Me Generation implies: Today's young people have little interest in anyone except themselves.

Getting Focused Any time the title is a question, reading for the answer is absolutely essential to getting the most out of the chapter section, article, or essay.

Word Watch The following words may be difficult to define from context. Read the definitions and say them aloud. Watch for the words as you read. They will be marked with an asterisk.

> **narcissism (1):** self-absorption, an intense focus on the self to the exclusion of everyone else
>
> **posited (6):** put forth, suggested
>
> **complemented (7):** fit with, made complete, added to
>
> **intangible (11):** not capable of being touched, not having a physical presence

Whenever you see a study cited in a reading, how should you respond?

1 According to a study presented at the 2010 meeting of the Association for Psychological Science, today's college students are not as empathetic as college students of the 1980s and 1990s. The lead researcher on the study, Dr. Sara Konrath, who specializes in issues related to self-esteem and narcissism,* says that "college kids today are about 40 percent lower in empathy than their counterparts of twenty or thirty years ago, as measured by standard tests of the personality trait."

2   Konrath and two University of Michigan students, graduate student Edward O'Brien and undergraduate Courtney Hsing, conducted what is called a *meta-analysis*—that is, they looked at 72 different studies of

---

[†]Bobby Soxers was the nickname for teenagers in the 1940s.

14,000 American college students carried out between 1979 and 2009. The trio also looked at representative samples of the population queried about their views concerning young people of college age. Their goal in this separate but related study was to determine how others viewed today's young people. The results of the group's analysis were not especially heartening from either perspective.

3   In contrast to students in the late 1970s, today's college students were much less likely to agree with statements like the following: "I sometimes try to understand my friends better by imagining how things look from their perspective"; "I often have tender, concerned feelings for people less fortunate than I"; and "I try to look at everybody's side of a disagreement before I make a decision." Based on negative responses to these and similar statements, Konrath concluded that empathy among college-age kids was on the decline.

When the opening sentence refers to "multiple theories," you should expect the major details to do what?

4   The researchers had multiple theories as to why this apparent drop in empathy might be occurring. One researcher, Edward O'Brien, pointed to the possibility that social media might be having an effect. "The ease of having friends online might make people more likely to just tune out when they don't feel like responding to others' problems, a behavior that could carry over online." O'Brien also suggested that "college students today may be so busy worrying about themselves and their own issues, they don't have time to spend empathizing with others."

5   Another culprit from O'Brien's point of view was students' "over-inflated expectations of success, borne of celebrity 'reality shows.'" College students who see themselves engaged in a no-holds-barred fight for the most exciting jobs available—which is the theme of numerous reality shows—are unlikely to spend much time thinking about others, except to figure out how they can beat out those others in their pursuit of success.

6   Like O'Brien, Dr. Konrath also posited* a reason. But she didn't finger social media or reality shows as much as video games, with their emphasis on murder and mayhem. As she expressed it, "This generation grew up with video games, and a growing body of research, including work done by my colleagues at Michigan, is establishing that exposure to violent media numbs people to the pain of others."

7   As for how the current crop of college students is seen by others, the results of the researchers' analysis complemented* the studies of the students themselves. Konrath explained that people in general did not consider today's college students to be members of the helpful generation: "Many people see the current group of college students—sometimes

called Generation Me—as one of the most self-centered, narcissistic, competitive, confident, and individualistic in recent history." Exactly how people arrived at this determination of youthful character was not clear from accounts of the study results.

How does the author direct the reader's attention in the opening of paragraph 8?

8   What was clear, though, was that the media response to the empathy study resembled trout spotting a juicy worm: They swallowed it whole. Just about every account treated the study as empirical proof, or hard evidence, of kids' selfishness. In fact, when the study first came out, no one in the traditional media raised any critical questions about its methodology. For instance, might kids who grew up watching the ironic humor of *Seinfeld* be less inclined to say *yes* to questions that so obviously patted on the back those who said *yes*, questions like "I often have tender, concerned feelings for people less fortunate than I"?

How does the author want readers to respond to the question opening paragraph 9?

9   Might the results have been different if today's students were asked, "In the last week, have you posted on your Facebook page any websites that offer help for people being confronted by tragedy?" or "When was the last time you 'tweeted' an article or 'pinned' a video describing a social cause or issue you think others should know about?" More to the point, did it occur to anyone conducting or promoting this study to consider the language of the twenty-year-old questions rather than the character of the twenty-year-old kids?

10   Then there is the larger question of how easy it is to study empathy through questionnaires. Unfortunately, the people who actually posed this question were not among those working for mainstream publications. The mainstream news outlets generally quoted one another and uniformly portrayed today's young people as navel-gazing narcissists.

11   Bloggers, however, were less inclined to accept the study's findings as fact. One online critic, for instance, posting on the blog *Perverse Egalitarianism*, made a point other traditional news outlets forgot to mention: Measuring an intangible* feeling like empathy is not an easy matter. As the post cleverly expressed it, "These efforts to study empathy as though it was a chemical element are quite comical to me. I wonder if someone is working on a precise instrument to measure it—*empathometer*—and whether this technology could be used to assess, for example, full-of-himself-ness?"

12   Yes, social media, video games, and reality shows may well have had an effect on young people's ability to empathize with others. But as of yet, there isn't enough hard evidence to make that claim while there is plenty of evidence suggesting the opposite. Just look at the many people on Twitter, Digg, Pinterest, Reddit, and Facebook posting links to websites

and videos about social causes they care about and want others to discuss or contribute to. Don't tell me they were all born before 1985. (Source of quotations and study description: http://health.usnews.com/health-news/family-health/brain-and-behavior/articles/2010/05/28/todays-college-students-more-likely-to-lack-empathy.html; www.sciencecentric.com/news/10052932-empathy-college.)

TAKING A CLOSER LOOK This set of questions focuses on your understanding of the text, both its content and the language used to convey that content.

DIRECTIONS Answer the following questions by circling the letter of the correct response or filling in the blanks.

Recognizing the Controlling Main Idea

1. Which statement best paraphrases the overall main idea of this reading?

   a. A study suggesting that today's college students may be less empathetic than college students of an earlier generation has been too easily accepted by the mainstream media.

   b. Today's college students are much less empathetic than they were two decades ago, and the rise of social media is to blame.

   c. A new study has provided scientific proof for what everyone knows: Today's college students are completely focused on themselves and their own concerns.

   d. The media like studies that encourage the tendency to label entire generations.

Using Context Clues and Paraphrasing

2. Based on the context and the definition in the reading, what, in your own words, is a meta-analysis (paragraph 2)?

   _____

   _____

Tracing Repetition and Reference

3. In sentence 2 of paragraph 2, what word or phrase stands in for the names of the researchers? _____

Recognizing Organizational Patterns

4. The topic sentence in paragraph 4 suggests what pattern of development?

_____

Understanding Supporting Details

5. The allusion to the comedy *Seinfeld* in paragraph 8 is used to support what point?

_____

_____

Spotting Transitional Signals

6. Paragraph 8 opens with a phrase that signals

a. the previous train of thought will be continued.

b. the previous train of thought is being revised.

c. the author is introducing a point of comparison.

d. the author is ready to describe the effect of the cause previously described.

Drawing Inferences

7. Which statement best expresses the implied main idea of paragraph 9?

a. The responses from students would have been altogether different if the questionnaire had been posted on Facebook.

b. Maybe the researchers should have paid more attention to how dated the language of the questions was rather than jumping to conclusions about how today's students function in relation to others.

c. Students today have a variety of ways to express their interest in social causes, from Facebook to Pinterest; however, they have no interest in social causes.

Making Organizational Patterns

8. Paragraphs 4 through 6 are united by which kind of relationship?

a. comparison and contrast

b. cause and effect

c. classification

d. sequence of dates and events

Spotting Transitional Signals

9. What is the transitional sentence from paragraph 12?

_____

Drawing Inferences

10. In paragraph 10, the author raises the "larger question" of how easy it is to measure empathy. What's the implied answer?

_____

READING WITH A CRITICAL EYE   Your goal here is not to be critical in the negative sense, but rather to evaluate how effectively the author explains an idea or argues an opinion.

DIRECTIONS   Answer the following questions by filling in the blanks or circling the letter of the correct response.

Identifying the Author's Purpose

1. How would you describe the author's purpose?

a. The author wants to report on a new study of empathy among college students.

b. The author wants to convince readers not to take the study of declining empathy among college students too seriously.

Drawing Personal Conclusions

2. Based on the following quotation from reading 3, should readers assume that there is definitely a cause and effect relationship between watching a lot of video-game violence and developing emotional numbness to the suffering of others? "This generation grew up with video games, and a growing body of research, including work done by my colleagues at Michigan, is establishing that exposure to violent media numbs people to the pain of others" (paragraph 6). _____

Please explain your answer.

_____

_____

_____

_____

3. For this statement and the study itself to be considered as evidence, what word or phrase should be more clearly defined or described,

"College kids today are about 40 percent lower in empathy than their counterparts of twenty or thirty years ago, as measured by standard tests of the personality trait" ? (paragraph 1).

_____

Why would this word or phrase need to be more clearly defined?

_____

Understanding 4. What figure of speech do you see at work in the following sentence:
Figurative "What was clear, though, was that the media response to the empa-
Language thy study resembled trout spotting bait: They swallowed it whole"

(paragraph 8)? _____

What point does the figure of speech make?

_____

_____

What figure of speech is used in the following sentence from paragraph 11: "These efforts to study empathy as though it was a chemi-

cal element are quite comical to me"? _____

What point does the author make with that figure of speech?

_____

Recognizing Bias 5. Which statement best describes the author's bias?

a. The author is inclined to strongly agree with the study results about students' lack of empathy.

b. The author is inclined to be suspicious of the study results.

c. It's impossible to find any evidence of bias in either direction.

6. Which statement more accurately describes the author's point of view?

a. The author favors bloggers over mainstream media as a source of news.

b. When it comes to how the empathy study was reported, the author favors bloggers over mainstream media.

c. The author reveals no preference.

Evaluating Arguments

7. In paragraph 11, the author says, "Bloggers, however, were less inclined to accept the study's findings as fact." What evidence does the author offer to support that generalization? _____

Is the support adequate? _____ Please explain your answer.

_____

_____

_____

Identifying Tone

8. How would you describe the author's tone?

a. puzzled

b. neutral

c. cautious

d. skeptical

The author's tone

a. remains the same throughout the reading.

b. shifts from neutral to skeptical.

c. shifts from neutral to puzzled.

9. What tone does the blogger assume in this quotation from paragraph 11?

"As the post on Perverse Egalitarianism cleverly expressed it, 'These efforts to study empathy as though it was a chemical element are quite comical to me. I wonder if someone is working on a precise instrument to measure it—*empathometer*—and whether this technology could be used to assess, for example, full-of-himself-ness?'"

_____

Synthesizing

10. What follows below is a brief reading on the attitudes of recent college graduates toward work. Read it and then decide which of the following synthesis statements most effectively combines the points of both readings into a synthesis statement with a persuasive purpose.

a. What "Finding the Perfect Job" and "Are Today's Students Lacking in Empathy?" both suggest is that today's college students consider themselves to be at the center of the universe. It's precisely this attitude that makes them unable to consider the feelings of others and equally unable to develop financial independence from their parents.

b. In contrast to "Finding the Perfect Job," which paints a depressing portrait of how college students view their future, "Are Today's Students Lacking in Empathy?" suggests that young adults today do not necessarily deserve the labels bestowed on them by the media.

c. The readings "Finding the Perfect Job" and "Are Today's Students Lacking in Empathy?" suggest that the attitudes of today's college students cannot be easily pigeonholed as right or wrong, good and bad. How those attitudes or behaviors are viewed depends on who's doing the viewing.

Finding the Perfect Job

Jeffrey Jensen Arnett is a psychology professor from Clark University who's written a book entitled *Emerging Adulthood: The Winding Road from the Late Teens Through the Twenties*. Part of Arnett's work on the book involved interviewing hundreds of college students who have graduated or are getting ready to graduate. In those interviews, Arnett discovered that college students are supremely confident about what the future holds for them despite entering a job market in the worst economic downturn since the 1930s. Arnett says that today's graduates believe they are going to get "not just a job but an expression of their identity, a form of self-fulfillment," and they are not about to settle for anything less. From Arnett's perspective, college students are "extraordinarily optimistic" that "bright days are ahead and eventually they will find that terrific job."

So convinced are college graduates that their professional future is bright, they are willing to turn down jobs that don't suit their desires. According to the National Association of Colleges and Employers, which annually surveys thousands of college students about their work attitudes and prospects, 41 percent of the job seekers interviewing in 2010 turned down jobs they felt didn't suit them. Instead of taking a job they didn't like, they moved back home with their parents, where they could wait for the right job offer to come along.

To their critics, these supremely confident young people are a textbook case of overconfidence, and that may be what will get them into trouble in the long run. Jean Twenge, a professor of psychology at San Diego State University and the author of *Generation Me*, argues that such over-confidence is bound to come smack up against life's hard knocks and falter, at which point the confident generation will slide straight into a well of depression and lack the emotional resources to climb out again.

Judith Warner, the author of the best-selling book *Perfect Madness: Motherhood in the Age of Anxiety,* has a different take. She believes that the current generation of young people has an emotional resilience that may armor them against the anxiety and fear that dogged other generations faced with life's difficult realities and choices. As she expressed it in an article for the *New York Times Magazine*, today's college students are "not maladapted. . . . On the contrary with their seemingly inexhaustible well of positive self-regard, their refusal to have their horizons be defined by the limitations of our era, they just may bear witness to the precise sort of resilience that all parents, educators and pop psychologists now say they view as proof of a successful upbringing." Could be, and then again maybe not. Only time will tell how this generation will fare in the years ahead. (Source of quotations: Judith Warner, "The Why-Worry Generation," *New York Times Magazine*, May 30, 2010, pp. 11–12.)

What Do You Think? Is empathy among the younger generation declining? Please explain your answer.

Thinking Through Writing Write a few paragraphs in which you explain why young adults *should* leave home after college and make their own way rather than burdening their parents. Or argue the opposite, that young people who move back in with parents after graduating to wait for the right job to come along are doing the right thing. You can also come up with your own point of view on this topic. Just make sure you mount an argument for it by providing evidence for your point of view and responding to the opposition.

◆ READING 4   **Society Makes Us Human**

Jim Henslin

Looking Ahead This reading speaks with more depth to a question addressed earlier (pp. 324–325) in this text: Which influences us more, our biological inheritance or our upbringing?

Getting Focused The title provides the basis for an excellent focus question: What does the author mean when he says that society makes us human? Put a check mark next to any paragraph that you think offers an answer. When you finish the reading, you should be able to provide some specific examples of how society makes us human.

Word Watch The following words may be difficult to define from context. Read the definitions and say them aloud. Watch for the words as you read. They will be marked with an asterisk.

> **apt (3):** fitting, appropriate
> **skittering (5):** jerky
> **gait (5):** manner of walking
> **garbled (18):** confused, not making sense
> **extrapolating (24):** drawing additional conclusions based on conclusions already drawn, applying conclusions drawn in one situation to a different situation

1   "What do you mean, society makes us human?" is probably what you are asking. "That sounds ridiculous. I was born a human." Well, maybe. As we explore this idea, perhaps the meaning of the title will become more apparent—and change your ideas, or at least challenge them slightly.

2   Let's start by considering what is human about human nature. How much of a person's characteristics comes from "nature" (heredity) and how much from "nurture" (the social environment, contact with others)? One way that experts are trying to answer the nature-nurture question is by studying children who have had little human contact.

Feral Children

The naked child was found in the forest, walking on all fours, eating grass and lapping water from the river. When he saw a small animal, he pounced on it. Growling, he ripped at it with his teeth. Tearing chunks from the body, he chewed them ravenously.

Based on the previous sentence and this description, how would you define the word *feral* in the heading?

Is the first sentence in paragraph 3 an opinion or a fact?

3 This is an apt* description of reports that have come in over the centuries. Supposedly, these *feral* (wild) *children* could not speak; they bit, scratched, growled, and walked on all fours. They drank by lapping water, ate grass, tore eagerly at raw meat, and showed insensitivity to pain and cold.

4 Why am I even mentioning stories that sound so exaggerated? Consider what happened in 1798. In that year, such a child was found in the forests of Aveyron, France. "The wild boy of Aveyron," as he became known, would have been written off as another folk myth, except that French scientists took the child to a laboratory and studied him. Like the feral children in the earlier informal reports, this child, too, gave no indication of feeling the cold. Most startling, though, the boy would growl when he saw a small animal, pounce on it, and devour it uncooked. Even today, the French scientists' detailed reports make fascinating reading (Itard 1962).

What is the purpose of this insert?

> Ever since I read Itard's† account of this boy, I've been fascinated by the seemingly fantastic possibility that animals could rear human children. But 1798 was a long time ago, and I knew I would never have the chance to see or talk to a feral child. Then came an exciting report from a contact in Cambodia that a feral child had been found in the jungle. Supposedly, he had been raised by monkeys. I grabbed the opportunity to visit the child and interview his caregivers. When I arrived at the remote location where the boy was living, I found that the story was true, but only in a limited sense. When the infant, now a boy of about ten years, was about two months old, the Khmer Rouge† had killed his parents. After they abandoned the baby to die, monkeys took the infant. Months later (I never could pin anyone down on the exact time), villagers spotted a female monkey that was carrying a human baby. They shot the monkey and took the baby from her clutched hands. The account was fascinating, but there were few details for me to learn and no generalizable information to pass on. My visit, though, did confirm that there are real feral children, and that they can even appear in our day and age.

How do you think the author will answer this question?

5 The basic sociological question we face is this: If we were untouched by society, would we be like the feral child documented in France? By nature, would our behavior be like that of wild animals? Unable to study feral children, today's sociologists have studied isolated children. Let's see what we can learn from them.

---

†Jean-Marc Gaspard Itard: a French physician who worked with a feral child, who came to be known as the Wild Boy of Aveyron. The boy had been found in the woods by hunters.
†Khmer Rouge: Cambodian communists notorious for their brutality under leader Pol Pot, who ruled from 1963 until his death in 1998.

> ### Isolated Children
>
> Isabelle was discovered in Ohio in 1938 when she was about 6½ years old, living in a dark room with her deaf-mute mother. Isabelle couldn't talk, but she did use gestures to communicate with her mother. An inadequate diet and lack of sunshine had given Isabelle a disease called rickets. Sociologist Kingsley Davis who investigated this case said
>
> "[Her legs] were so bowed that as she stood erect the soles of her shoes came nearly flat together, and she got about with a skittering* gait.* Her behavior toward strangers, especially men, was almost that of a wild animal, manifesting much fear and hostility. In lieu of speech she made only a strange croaking sound." (Davis 1940/2007:156–157)

6   What can isolated children tell us about human nature? We can first conclude that isolated children like Isabelle have no natural language.

7   But maybe Isabelle was mentally impaired, unable to progress through children's usual stages of development. It certainly looked that way—she scored practically zero on her first intelligence test. But after a few months of language training, Isabelle was able to speak in short sentences. In just a year, she could write a few words, do simple addition, and retell stories after hearing them. Seven months later, she had a vocabulary of almost 2,000 words. In just two years, Isabelle reached the intellectual level that is normal for her age. She then went on to school, where she was "bright, cheerful, energetic . . . and participated in all school activities as normally as other children" (Davis 1940/2007).

8   Language is the key to human development. Without language, people have no mechanism for developing thought and communicating their experiences. Unlike animals, humans have no instincts that take the place of language. If an individual lacks language, he or she lives in a world of internal silence, without shared ideas, lacking connections to others.

Why did the author put this sentence in italics?

9   *Without language, there can be no culture—no shared way of life—and culture is the key to what people become.* Each of us possesses a biological heritage, but this heritage does not determine specific behaviors, attitudes, or values. It is our culture that superimposes the specifics of what we become onto our biological heritage.

Institutionalized Children

10   Other than language, what else is required for a child to develop into what we consider a healthy, balanced, intelligent human being? We find part of the answer in an intriguing experiment.

If an author uses a heading to introduce a study or experiment, how should the reader respond?

11 **The Skeels/Dye Experiment** Back in the 1930s, orphanages were common because parents were more likely than now to die before their children were grown. Children reared in orphanages tended to have low IQs. "Common sense" (which we depend on to make sense out of our experiences in life, but which can be remarkably unreliable) made it seem obvious to everyone that the orphans' low intelligence was because of their poor brains. ("They're just born that way," everyone thought.) Then came two psychologists, H. M. Skeels and H. B. Dye (1939), who began to suspect a social cause.

12   Skeels (1966) provides this account of a "good" orphanage in Iowa, one where he and Dye were consultants:

> Until about six months, they were cared for in the infant nursery. The babies were kept in standard hospital cribs that often had protective sheeting on the sides, thus effectively limiting visual stimulation; no toys or other objects were hung in the infants' line of vision. Human interactions were limited to busy nurses who, with the speed born of practice and necessity, changed diapers or bedding, bathed and medicated the infants, and fed them efficiently with propped bottles.

13   Perhaps, thought Skeels and Dye, the problem was not the children's brains, but, instead, the absence of stimulating social interaction. This was a controversial idea. To test it, they selected thirteen infants who were so slow mentally that no one wanted to adopt them. They placed the infants, then about 19 months old, in an institution for mentally retarded women. They assigned each infant to a separate ward of women ranging in mental age from 5 to 12 and in chronological age from 18 to 50. The women were pleased. They enjoyed taking care of the infants' physical needs—diapering, feeding, and so on. And they also loved to play with the children. They cuddled them and showered them with attention. They even competed to see which ward would have "its baby" walking or talking first. In each ward, one woman became particularly attached to the child and figuratively adopted him or her:

> As a consequence, an intense one-to-one adult–child relationship developed, which was supplemented by the less intense but frequent interactions with the other adults in the environment. Each child had some one person with whom he [or she] was identified and who was particularly interested in him [or her] and his [or her] achievements. (Skeels 1966)

14   The researchers left a control group of twelve infants at the orphanage. These infants received the usual care. They also had low IQs, but they were considered somewhat higher in intelligence than the thirteen in the experimental group. Two and a half years later, Skeels and Dye tested all the children's intelligence. Their findings are startling: Those cared for by

the women in the institution gained an average of 28 IQ points while those who remained in the orphanage lost 30 points.

Within the context of this reading, do you think the differences will matter?

15   What happened after these children were grown? Did these initial differences matter? Twenty-one years later, Skeels and Dye did a follow-up study. The twelve in the control group, those who had remained in the orphanage, averaged less than a third-grade education. Four still lived in state institutions, and the others held low-level jobs. Only two had married. The thirteen in the experimental group, those cared for by the institution-alized women, had an average education of twelve grades (about normal for that period). Five had completed one or more years of college. One had even gone to graduate school. Eleven had married. All thirteen were self-supporting or were homemakers (Skeels 1966). Apparently, "high intel-ligence" depends on early, close relations with other humans.

Based on what's gone before, what will be the topic of the research?

16   **Current Research in India** Researchers in India have confirmed the Skeels/Dye findings. Life is shorter in India, and, unfortunately, many children are abandoned by parents who don't have enough food to feed them. Some of India's orphanages are like those that Skeels and Dye studied—dismal places where unattended children lie in bed all day. When Indian researchers added stimulating play and interaction to the children's activities, not only did the children's motor skills improve, but so did their IQs (Taneja et al. 2002).

17   The longer that children lack stimulating interaction, though, the more difficulty they have recovering intellectually and socially (Meese 2005). From another heart-wrenching case, that of Genie, you can see how important timing is in the development of "human" characteristics.

18   **Timing and Human Development** Genie was discovered when she was 13 years old. She had been locked in a small room and tied to a chair since she was 20 months old:

> Apparently Genie's father (70 years old when Genie was discovered in 1970) hated children. He probably had caused the death of two of Genie's siblings. Her 50-year-old mother was partially blind and fright-ened of her husband. Genie could not speak, did not know how to chew, was unable to stand upright, and could not straighten her hands and legs. On intelligence tests, she scored at the level of a 1-year-old. After intensive training, Genie learned to walk and to say simple sentences (although they were garbled*). Genie's language remained primitive as she grew up. She would take anyone's property if it appealed to her, and she would pee and defecate wherever she wanted. At the age of 21, she was sent to a home for adults who cannot live alone. (Pines 1981)

When the author uses *we* in the first sentence, what effect does that have on the reader's response?

19   From Genie's pathetic story and from the research on institutionalized children, we can conclude that the basic human traits of intelligence and the ability to establish close bonds with others depend on early interaction with other humans. In addition, there seems to be a period prior to age 13 in which children must learn language and experience human bonding if they are to develop normal intelligence and the ability to be sociable and follow social norms.

Deprived Animals

20   Finally, let's consider animals that have been deprived of normal interaction. In a series of experiments with rhesus monkeys, psychologists Harry and Margaret Harlow demonstrated the importance of early learning. The Harlows (1962) raised baby monkeys in isolation. They gave each monkey two artificial mothers. One "mother" was only a wire frame with a wooden head, but it did have a nipple from which the baby could nurse. The frame of the other "mother," which had no bottle, was covered with soft terry-cloth. To obtain food, the baby monkeys nursed at the wire frame.

21   When the Harlows (1965) frightened the baby monkeys with a mechanical bear or dog, the babies did not run to the wire frame "mother." Instead, they would cling pathetically to their terrycloth "mother." The Harlows concluded that infant–mother bonding is not the result of feeding but, rather, of what they termed "intimate physical contact." To most of us, this phrase means cuddling.

22   The monkeys raised in isolation could not adjust to monkey life. Placed with other monkeys when they were grown, they didn't know how to participate in "monkey interaction"—to play and to engage in pretend fights—and the other monkeys rejected them. Despite their futile attempts, they didn't even know how to have sexual intercourse. The experimenters designed a special device, which allowed some females to become pregnant. Their isolation, however, made them "ineffective, inadequate, and brutal mothers." They "struck their babies, kicked them, or crushed the babies against the cage floor." (It is quite likely that many of the "ineffective, inadequate, and brutal" mothers that you hear about on the evening news—those who have brutalized or killed their children—had isolating experiences of various sorts in early childhood.)

23   In one of their many experiments, the Harlows isolated baby monkeys for different lengths of time and then put them in with the other monkeys. Monkeys that had been isolated for shorter periods (about three months) were able to adjust to normal monkey life. They learned to play and engage in pretend fights. Those isolated for six months or more, however,

couldn't make the adjustment, and the other monkeys rejected them. In other words, the longer the period of isolation, the more difficult its effects are to overcome. In addition, there seems to be a critical learning stage: If this stage is missed, it may be impossible to compensate for what has been lost. This may have been the case with Genie.

24   Because humans are not monkeys, we must be careful about ex-trapolating* from animal studies to human behavior. The Harlow experiments, however, support what we know about children who are reared in isolation.

At this point in the reading and given the heading, what do you expect the author to do?

25   **In Sum** Let's look again at that phrase, *society makes us human*. Babies do not develop "naturally" into social adults. If children are reared in isolation, their bodies grow, but they become little more than big animals. Without the concepts that language provides, they can't grasp relationships between people (the "connections" we call brother, sister, parent, friend, teacher, and so on). And without warm, friendly interactions, they can't bond with others. They don't become "friendly" or cooperate with others, and they are stunted intellectually. In short, it is through human contact that people learn to be members of the human community. This process by which we learn the ways of society (or of particular groups), called *socialization*, is what sociologists have in mind when they say "Society makes us human." ("Society Makes Us Human," © 2013 by Jim Henslin. Reprinted by permission of the author. Professor Emeritus, Department of Sociology, Southern Illinois University, Edwardsville, Illinois.)

TAKING A CLOSER LOOK   This set of questions focuses on your understanding of the text, both its content and the language used to convey that content.

DIRECTIONS   Answer the following questions by circling the letter of the correct response or filling in the blanks.

Recognizing the Controlling Main Idea

1. In which paragraph does the author directly answer this question posed in the beginning of the reading: "How much of a person's characteristics comes from 'nature' (heredity) and how much from 'nurture' (the social environment, contact with others)?"

    a. paragraph 1

    b. paragraph 5

    c. paragraph 8

    d. paragraph 9

Paraphrasing **2.** Which statement best paraphrases the overall or controlling main idea of this reading?

    a. Language is what makes us human and without the presence of other human beings during childhood, we would never learn to speak.

    b. Studies on monkeys have shown that bonding between mother and infant is critical to the development of normal human behavior; without it, human beings remain little more than large, clumsy animals.

    c. Human behavior is a product of our culture; our human nature depends on how we are raised and the presence or absence of other human beings with whom we can communicate and bond.

    d. Children reared in isolation are never able to recover from the trauma of their early experiences.

Understanding **3.** In relation to the overall main idea, is the discussion of feral children
Supporting Details a major or a minor detail? _____ Please explain.

_____

_____

Identifying **4.** What is the function of paragraph 5?
Paragraph
Functions   a. It sums up the overall main idea.

    b. It provides a major supporting detail.

    c. It provides a minor supporting detail.

    d. It provides a transition.

Spotting **5.** What word in paragraph 7 announces that the author is shifting
Transitional Signals away from his opening train of thought? _____

Drawing **6.** What is the implied main idea of paragraph 7?
Inferences

_____

_____

Identifying Paragraph Functions

7. What is the function of paragraph 10?

   a. It sums up the overall main idea.

   b. It provides a major supporting detail.

   c. It provides a minor supporting detail.

   d. It provides a transition.

Understanding Supporting Details and Drawing Inferences

8. The author recounts the Skeels and Dye experiment to make a point that is directly expressed in paragraph

   a. 11.

   b. 13.

   c. 14.

   d. 15.

Tracing Repetition and Reference

9. In paragraph 24, the author says, "The Harlow experiments, however, support what we know about children who are reared in isolation."

   Based on the reading, what is it we know about children reared in isolation?

   _____

Recognizing Organizational Patterns

10. What are the two key aspects of society that the author says make us human?

    a. _____

    b. _____

    Because the author describes what makes us become humans rather than especially clumsy animals, it's clear that the reading has to rely on what organizational pattern?

    _____

READING WITH A CRITICAL EYE   Your goal here is not to be critical in the negative sense, but rather to evaluate how effectively the author explains an idea or argues an opinion.

DIRECTIONS   Answer the following questions by filling in the blanks or circling the letter of the correct response.

Identifying the Author's Purpose

1. Which statement most accurately identifies the author's purpose?

   a. The author wants to tell readers about children raised either in the wild or in isolation.

   b. The author wants to describe studies suggesting that children who appear to be mentally deficient may, in reality, have been denied affection.

   c. The author wants to convince readers that the most powerful influence on our development is the environment we grow up in.

   d. The author wants to persuade readers that children raised in isolation can never recover what they have lost.

Synthesizing

2. The headings identify three categories of children. What do all three have in common and why is that similarity important to the author's controlling idea?

   _____

   _____

   _____

Identifying Tone

3. Which words best describe the author's tone?

   a. confident and direct

   b. cool and neutral

   c. skeptical but open

   d. bossy and overbearing

4. How does the author's use of the first person *I* contribute to the author's tone?

   _____

   _____

   _____

5. When the author uses *we*, what does he imply about his readers?

   _____

6. What relationship with his readers does the author suggest in this sentence? "From another heart-wrenching case, that of Genie, you can see how important timing is in the development of 'human' characteristics."

   _____

   _____

7. In terms of both tone and the overall main idea, why does the author tell readers about his trip to Cambodia?

   _____

   _____

Distinguishing Between Fact and Opinion   8. Is the following statement a fact or an opinion? "The basic sociological question we face is this: If we were untouched by society, would we be like the feral child documented in France?" (paragraph 5)

   _____

   _____

Drawing Personal Conclusions   9. In his book *Intelligence and How to Get It*, Richard Nisbett argues that studies using identical twins to prove genes are the deciding factor in intelligence have a big flaw: Identical twins who are adopted and live apart often get adopted by people of the same economic status. Thus their similar scores on IQ tests have as much to do with their environment as their genetics. Is this an idea that the author of the reading would support?

   _____

   _____

Synthesizing **10.** Reread the excerpt on pages 512–513 about Richard Nisbett's book. Then read the selection that follows. Write a synthesis statement that, in some way, combines all three points of view.

_____

_____

_____

_____

When It Comes to Nature or Nurture, Money Matters

For decades, studies of identical twins seemed to show that intelligence was a matter of good genes. When identical twins were adopted and lived miles apart, their IQ scores were still very similar, suggesting that IQ was a product of genetic inheritance rather than environment. After all, the separated twins had received very different upbringings; yet their IQ tests showed the same or similar results. The conclusion was obvious: Intelligence was a matter of biology, not background.

But then along came a professor of psychology named Eric Turkheimer, a researcher respected for his original mind and his dedication to careful scientific methodology. Turkheimer thought the twins studies told "too simple a story." Above all, he noticed, what should have been noted long ago, that most adoptions involve affluent families. It's far less common for working class families, let alone poor ones, to adopt. Thus identical twin studies weren't doing what they're supposed to do: studying how siblings with the same genetic equipment function in altogether different environments. The environments into which twins were adopted were actually more similar than different.

Turkheimer's analysis of existing studies showed that, in the few instances where identical twins were adopted by families with altogether different financial backgrounds, i.e., high income versus low income, the twins did not perform equally well on tests of intelligence. On the contrary, the twin adopted by the wealthy family did far better than the twin from the poorer one. As Turkheimer put it,

"If you have a chaotic environment [one where things like shelter and parental attention are not always stable], a kid's genetic potential doesn't have a chance to be expressed. Well-off families can provide the mental stimulation needed for genes to build the brain circuitry for intelligence." Since 2003, when Turkheimer first started thinking in public about potential flaws in existing studies of intelligence based on twins, additional research has confirmed his findings. The good news in all this, however, is that, unlike one's genetic inheritance, a person's background or environment can be altered or improved over time. (Source of quotations: http://economistsview.typepad.com/economistsview/2006/07/nature_vs_nurtu.html; http://oscar.virginia.edu/x5701.xml.)

Thinking Through Writing   Richard Nisbett, the author of *Intelligence and How to Get It*, says that parents should encourage self-discipline in their kids. He bases his claim on studies performed by psychologist Walter Mischel in the 1960s (his most famous study is often referred to as the "Marshmallow Test") and a more recent one carried out by the psychologists Martin Seligman and Angela Duckworth.

Use these names to create search terms that bring up several different accounts of the studies. Then read at least two newspaper or magazine accounts for Mischel's "Marshmallow Test" and at least two for the research carried out by Duckworth and Seligman. Your goal is to write a paper in which you use summaries of the studies to explain or prove that self-discipline plays a key role in academic success.

After you finish reading in preparation, get started writing by making a rough draft of your thesis statement. Then, concentrate on paraphrasing the accounts of the studies in your own words, making careful use of transitions to take the reader smoothly from one study to the next. It's up to you to decide how you want to order the studies.

Once you think the studies are summarized with enough detail to make your point clear and convincing, work on the introduction, making use of this quotation from Richard Nisbett, "If you had to choose for your child a high IQ or strong self-discipline, you might be wise to pick the latter."

If you want a model for your paper, the reading by Jim Henslin is a perfect—albeit more extended—example. Henslin does a great job telling us what he thinks and how he arrived at his conclusions.

◆ **READING 5** ## Raising Successful Children

Madeline Levine

Looking Ahead Reading 4 was concerned with what happens to children who have too little contact with any caretaker. This reading looks at what happens when they get too much.

Getting Focused As it so often does, the title provides the foundation for a focus question: What do parents have to do to raise successful children? And as questions so often do, this one leads to another: How does the author define the word *successful*?

Word Watch The following words may be difficult to define from context. Read the definitions and say them aloud. Watch for the words as you read. They will be marked with an asterisk.

> **optimal (2):** best, most effective
>
> **autonomy (2):** independence
>
> **counterintuitive (4):** to go against what seems natural
>
> **in thrall (6):** in a state of complete absorption or fascination
>
> **chastise (6):** punish or reprimand
>
> **dire (6):** dreadful, awful
>
> **breach (15):** make a gap or poke a hole and break through

Within the context of the paragraph, what must the opening terms "tiger mom" and "helicopter parent" refer to?

1 Phrases like "tiger mom" and "helicopter parent" have made their way into everyday language. But does over-parenting hurt, or help? While parents who are clearly and embarrassingly inappropriate come in for ridicule, many of us find ourselves drawn to the idea that with just a bit more parental elbow grease, we might turn out children with great talents and assured futures. Is there really anything wrong with a kind of "over-parenting lite"?

When a writer tells you that an issue has a long history of being studied, what would you expect the writer to do next?

2 Parental involvement has a long and rich history of being studied. Decades of studies, many of them by Diana Baumrind, a clinical and developmental psychologist at the University of California, Berkeley, have found that the optimal* parent is one who is involved and responsive, who sets high expectations but respects her child's autonomy.* These "authoritative parents" appear to hit the sweet spot of parental involvement and generally raise children who do better academically, psychologically and socially than children whose parents are either permissive and less involved, or controlling and more involved. Why is this particular parenting style so successful, and what does it tell us about over-parenting?

3   For one thing, authoritative parents actually help cultivate motivation in their children. Carol Dweck, a social and developmental psychologist at Stanford University, has done research that indicates why authoritative parents raise more motivated, and thus more successful, children. In a typical experiment, Dr. Dweck takes young children into a room and asks them to solve a simple puzzle. Most do so with little difficulty. But then Dr. Dweck tells some, but not all, of the kids how very bright and capable they are. As it turns out, the children who are not told they're smart are more motivated to tackle increasingly difficult puzzles. They also exhibit higher levels of confidence and show greater overall progress in puzzle-solving.

4   This may seem counterintuitive,* but praising children's talents and abilities seems to rattle their confidence. Tackling more difficult puzzles carries the risk of losing one's status as "smart" and deprives kids of the thrill of choosing to work simply for its own sake, regardless of outcomes. Dr. Dweck's work aligns nicely with that of Dr. Baumrind, who also found that reasonably supporting a child's autonomy and limiting interference results in better academic and emotional outcomes. Their research confirms what I've seen in more than 25 years of clinical work, treating children in Marin County, an affluent suburb of San Francisco. The happiest, most successful children have parents who do not do for them what they are capable of doing, or almost capable of doing; and their parents do not do things for them that satisfy their own needs rather than the needs of the child.

After the author announces what the central task of growing up is, what should you be looking for?

5   The central task of growing up is to develop a sense of self that is autonomous, confident and generally in accord with reality. If you treat your walking toddler as if she can't walk, you diminish her confidence and distort reality. Ditto nightly "reviews" of homework, repetitive phone calls to "just check if you're O.K." and "editing" (read: writing) your child's college application essay. Once your child is capable of doing something, congratulate yourself on a job well done and move on. Continued, unnecessary intervention makes your child feel bad about himself (if he's young) or angry at you (if he's a teenager).

6   But isn't it a parent's job to help with those things that are just beyond your child's reach? Why is it over-parenting to do for your child what he or she is almost capable of? Think back to when your toddler learned to walk. She would take a weaving step or two, collapse and immediately look to you for your reaction. You were in thrall* to those early attempts and would do everything possible to encourage her to get up again. You certainly didn't chastise* her for failing or utter dire* predictions about flipping burgers for the rest of her life if she fell again. You were present, alert and available to guide if necessary. But you didn't pick her up every time.

Why do you think writers sometimes include one-sentence paragraphs?

What's the key word in the first sentence that is likely to be repeated or referred to throughout the paragraph?

7   You knew she had to get it wrong many times before she could get it right.

8   Hanging back and allowing children to make mistakes is one of the greatest challenges of parenting. It's easier when they're young—tolerating a stumbling toddler is far different from allowing a preteenager to meet her friends at the mall. The potential mistakes carry greater risks, and part of being a parent is minimizing risk for our children.

9   What kinds of risks should we tolerate? If there's a predator loose in the neighborhood, your daughter doesn't get to go to the mall. But under normal circumstances an 11-year-old girl is quite capable of taking care of herself for a few hours in the company of her friends. She may forget a package, overpay for an item or forget that she was supposed to call home at noon. Mastery of the world is an expanding geography for our kids, for toddlers, it's the backyard; for preteens, the neighborhood, for teens the wider world. But it is in the small daily risks—the taller slide, the bike ride around the block, the invitation extended to a new classmate that growth takes place. In this gray area of just beyond the comfortable is where resilience is born.

10   So if children are able to live with mistakes and even failing, why does it drive us crazy? So many parents have said to me, "I can't stand to see my child unhappy." If you can't stand to see your child unhappy, you are in the wrong business. The small challenges that start in infancy (the first whimper that doesn't bring you running) present the opportunity for "successful failures," that is, failures your child can live with and grow from. To rush in too quickly, to shield them, to deprive them of those challenges is to deprive them of the tools they will need to handle the inevitable, difficult, challenging and sometimes devastating demands of life.

11   While doing things for your child unnecessarily or prematurely can reduce motivation and increase dependency, it is the inability to maintain parental boundaries that most damages child development. When we do things for our children out of our own needs rather than theirs, it forces them to circumvent the most critical task of childhood: to develop a robust sense of self.

12   There is an important distinction between good and bad parental involvement. For example, a young child doesn't want to sit and do his math homework. Good parents insist on compliance, not because they need their child to be a perfect student but because the child needs to learn the fundamentals of math and develop a good work ethic. Compare this with the parent who spends weeks "helping" his or her child fill out college applications with the clear expectation that if they both work hard enough, a "gotta get into" school is a certainty. (While most

of my parent patients have graduated from college, it is always a telltale sign of over-parenting when they talk about how "we're applying to Columbia.")

13   In both situations parents are using control, in the first case behavioral (sit down, do your math) and in the second psychological ("we're applying"). It is psychological control that carries with it a textbook's worth of damage to a child's developing identity. If pushing, direction, motivation and reward always come from the outside, the child never has the opportunity to craft an inside. Having tutors prep your anxious 3-year-old for a preschool interview because all your friends' children are going to this particular school or pushing your exhausted child to take one more advanced-placement course because it will ensure her spot as class valedictorian is not involved parenting but toxic over-parenting aimed at meeting the parents' need for status or affirmation and not the child's needs.

<aside>How does the author answer this opening question?</aside>

14   So how do parents find the courage to discard the malpractice of over-parenting? It's hard to swim upstream, to resist peer pressure. But we must remember that children thrive best in an environment that is reliable, available, consistent and noninterfering.

15   A loving parent is warm, willing to set limits and unwilling to breach* a child's psychological boundaries by invoking shame or guilt. Parents must acknowledge their own anxiety. Your job is to know your child well enough to make a good call about whether he can manage a particular situation. Will you stay up worrying? Probably, but the child's job is to grow, yours is to control your anxiety so it doesn't get in the way of his reasonable moves toward autonomy.

16   Parents also have to be clear about their own values. Children watch us closely. If you want your children to be able to stand up for their values, you have to do the same. If you believe that a summer spent reading, taking creek walks and playing is better than a specialized camp, then stick to your guns. Parents also have to make sure their own lives are fulfilling. There is no parent more vulnerable to the excesses of over-parenting than an unhappy parent. One of the most important things we do for our children is to present them with a version of adult life that is appealing and worth striving for. ("Raising Successful Children" by Madeline Levine from *The New York Times*, August 4, 2012. Copyright © 2013 The New York Times. All rights reserved. Used by permission and protected by the Copyright Laws of the United States. The printing, copying, redistribution, or retransmission of this Content without express written permission is prohibited.)

TAKING A CLOSER LOOK This set of questions focuses on your understanding of the text, both its content and the language used to convey that content.

DIRECTIONS Answer the following questions by circling the letter of the correct response or filling in the blanks.

Recognizing the Controlling Main Idea 1. In your own words, what's the overall main idea of the entire reading?

_____

_____

_____

_____

Is that main idea

a. stated?

b. implied?

Spotting Transitional Signals 2. What word or phrase in paragraph 3 makes it clear that the author is starting to answer the question that ends paragraph 2?

_____

Drawing Inferences 3. What's the implied main idea of paragraph 5?

a. If your toddler falls down while learning to walk, don't pick her up.

b. Over-protective parents interfere with one of the key tasks of becoming an adult: developing an independent, realistic, and confident sense of self.

c. If a child does something well, the over-protective parent is likely to take credit for the accomplishment, and that behavior damages the child's self-esteem.

Outlining and Summarizing 4. In paragraph 9, the author gives an example of a risk you would not take with a daughter. Is that a detail that should go into an outline or a summary? _____ Please explain.

_____

Paraphrasing 5. In your own words, what is a "successful failure," a term introduced in paragraph 10?

_____

_____

Does the term "successful failure" fit the definition of a paradox, introduced on page 655? _____ Please explain.

_____

_____

Using Context 6. Based on the context, what do you think _circumvent_ means in the
Clues and Word following sentence in paragraph 11: "When we do things for our
Analysis children out of our own needs rather than theirs, it forces them to
circumvent the most critical task of childhood: to develop a robust
sense of self"?

_____

If you weren't completely sure about the meaning you derived from context, could word analysis be of help? _____ Please explain.

_____

_____

Drawing 7. What is the implied answer to the question posed at the start of
Inferences paragraph 14?

_____

_____

Paraphrasing 8. Which statement best paraphrases the author's description of the most damaging thing a parent can do when raising a child (paragraph 11)?

    a. Being over-protective is the most damaging thing a parent can do when raising a child.

    b. The biggest mistake a parent can make in child-rearing is to confuse his or her own needs with the needs of the child.

    c. Parents who don't wait to see if their child can accomplish a new task before leaping in to do it for them are harming the child's sense of self-confidence and self-sufficiency.

Recognizing Organizational Patterns 9. What's the primary pattern organizing the information in paragraph 12?

    a. comparison and contrast

    b. classification

    c. simple listing

    d. process

What word in the topic sentence offers a clue to the pattern?

_____

10. Which pair of patterns is essential to this reading?

    a. process and classification

    b. simple listing and definition

    c. cause and effect and classification

    d. cause and effect and comparison and contrast

READING WITH A CRITICAL EYE   Your goal here is not to be critical in the negative sense, but rather to evaluate how effectively the author explains an idea or argues an opinion.

DIRECTIONS Answer the following questions by filling in the blanks or circling the letter of the correct response.

Identifying the Author's Purpose

1. Which statement best describes the author's purpose?

    a. The author wants to describe for readers some of the research that has been done on how to raise children.

    b. The author wants to tell readers what experts have discovered about child-rearing methods.

    c. The author wants to persuade parents to guide their children through life's ups and downs rather than over-protecting them.

    d. The author wants to convince readers that over-protective parents are becoming far too common, causing their children to feel both entitled yet lacking in a strong sense of self-worth.

2. Why does the author mention in paragraph 4 that she has been treating children for twenty-five years?

    _____

    _____

Identifying Tone and Evaluating Bias

3. How would you describe the author's tone?

    a. serious and critical

    b. authoritative

    c. light-hearted and relaxed

    d. neutral

    Which statement accurately describes the bias revealed in the author's tone?

    a. The author expresses an acceptable bias.

    b. The author expresses an unacceptable degree of bias.

4. When the author uses pronouns such as *you* and *us*, what effect is that meant to have on her audience?

_____

_____

Understanding Figurative Language

5. When the author says in paragraph 1 that many of us are drawn to the idea that a "bit more parental elbow grease" would produce children with great futures, what type of figurative language is she using?

_____

How would you paraphrase the point of that figurative language?

_____

_____

Does the reading as a whole agree with that point? _____

Distinguishing Between Fact and Opinion

6. How would you label this statement from paragraph 11, as a fact or an opinion? "While doing things for your child unnecessarily or prematurely can reduce motivation and increase dependency, it is the inability to maintain parental boundaries that most damages child development." _____ Please explain.

_____

_____

_____

Drawing Personal Conclusions

7. Based on this reading, do you think the author would agree with Richard Nisbett's idea that attitude may outweigh IQ when it comes to achievement? _____

Please explain the basis for your conclusion, making sure to be as specific as possible.

_____

_____

_____

8. Based on this reading, do you think the author believes children benefit from getting rewarded for their efforts with presents or money? _____ Please explain the basis for your conclusion, making sure to be as specific as possible.

_____

_____

Evaluating Arguments

9. The author uses studies as evidence. How would you rate her use of them as support for her opinion? _____ Please explain your answer.

_____

_____

_____

Synthesizing

10. The reading that follows is another view on why children grow up as they do. When you finish the reading, write two synthesis statements that sum up both points of view, that of Madeline Levine and Judith Rich Harris. Make one statement informative and the other persuasive.

Informative: _____

_____

_____

_____

Persuasive: _____

_____

_____

_____

Who Counts More: Peers or Parents?

Many psychologists would prefer *not* to take Judith Rich Harris seriously. She is, after all, not a trained psychologist. She is the author of a psychology textbook and has no Ph.D. after her name. What Harris does have, though, is an analytical mind sharp enough to attract the attention of the famed experimental psychologist Steven Pinker, who has publicly praised her work. Pinker even wrote a foreword for her book *The Nurture Assumption: Why Children Turn Out the Way They Do,* which raised the hackles of many in the academic and medical communities.

What Harris argues in painstaking and sometimes mind-numbing detail is that established thinking about the overwhelming role of parental influence in a child's life was dead wrong. While Harris definitely believed that nature provided children with a genetic package of talents and abilities that environment could either nurture or obstruct, she was no longer convinced that parents constituted the environment that really mattered. As she eloquently expresses it in the opening chapter of her book:

> The use of *nurture* as a *synonym* for environment is based on the assumption that what influences children's development apart from their genes, is the way their parents bring them up. I call this the *nurture assumption.* Only after rearing two children of my own and co-authoring three editions of a college textbook on child development did I begin to question this assumption. Only recently did I come to the conclusion that it was wrong.

From Harris's perspective, most traditional psychologists had, for too long, equated environment with the parental home and failed to look at the role of peers in shaping personality. She argued, instead, that for children their peers and popular culture were far more influential on their sense of self than parents were. She insisted, too, that the influence of peers and popular culture came at a time when children were consciously shaping their sense of identity, making it more powerful than parental authority figures.

For Harris, this broader vision of environmental influence explained why children of immigrant parents almost always adopted not the accent of their parents but the accents of their friends and classmates. It also clarified why the hearing children of deaf parents who did not speak seemed to have no problem mastering spoken language. Harris's theory also offered an explanation of why siblings raised by the same parents with similar rules and attitudes could be as different as day from night, with one becoming a model student and the other an indifferent dropout.

While many established psychologists like the famed Jerome Kagan ridiculed Harris for her lack of scientific understanding, Harris was lauded by other equally famous researchers like neuroscientist Robert Sapolsky, who called her work a breakthrough in the history of psychology. In what must have been for her a delicious irony, Harris ended up receiving the prestigious George A. Miller award for her work, bestowed upon her by the American Psychological Association. In the sixties, Harris had been booted out of a doctoral program for showing a lack of interest in the research possibilities suggested by her advisers. The dean of the psychology program at the time was none other than the legendary George A. Miller, who wrote: "I hesitate to say that you lack originality and independence, because in many areas of life you obviously possess both of those traits in abundance. But for some reason you have not been able to bring them to bear on the kind of problems in psychology to which this department is dedicated. . . . We are in considerable doubt that you will develop into our professional stereotype of what an experimental psychologist should be." (The first chapter of *The Nurture Assumption* is available here: www.nytimes.com/books/first/h/harris-nurture.html. The quotation from George A. Miller comes from Malcolm Gladwell's article "Do Parents Matter?" August 17, 1998, available online in the archives of the *New Yorker*.)

What Do You Think? Are you more inclined to agree with Levine or Harris? Can you explain why one makes more sense than the other, or do you think they both do?

Thinking Through Writing Come up with a synthesis statement—you can use the one you already created if you wish—that favors one point of view or the other, or else argues in favor of a mixture of both. Then use evidence from your own experience to show why you believe that your thesis statement is an opinion that should be shared by others. Once you have used your own experience, use two studies from a psychology text to illustrate that you are not alone in your point of view. Some experts, in fact, agree with you.

Index

academic vocabulary development, 70–74.
  See also vocabulary development
addition transitions, 131–32
Allusion Alerts, 91
  bread and circuses, 280
  Dionysus, 494
  fountain of youth, 360
  Garden of Eden, 195
  The Great Gatsby, 612–13
  hedonism, 456
  Impressionism, 298
  A Man for All Seasons, 394
  Pygmalion, 152
  Rip Van Winkle, 643
  Tweedledee and Tweedledum, 513–14
allusions, 66, 89–93, 582
  common knowledge and, 90–91
  for government and history, 91–93
  varying for audience, 90
anecdotes, for persuasive writing, 150, 545
annotating
  example of, 19–20
  paraphrasing in, 16, 22
  pointers for, 16–17
  as reading strategy, 15–20
  summary writing and, 282, 283, 284
  symbols for, 17–19
antecedents, 349–52
antonyms
  as contrast clues, 78
  as recall clues, 76
approximate meanings, 77
arguments
  bias in, 585, 621–24
  common introductions for, 545–46
  common types of support in, 549–55
  examples and illustrations in, 551–52
  expert opinions in, 552–53, 614–15
  opinion statements in, 538–42
  opposing points of view in, 537, 562–64
  personal experience in, 550
  reasons in, 551
  research results in, 553–55, 615–16
  tone in, 537, 571–75, 582–83
  See also persuasive writing
arguments, flawed, 610–17
  appeals to common sense, 616
  bandwagon appeal, 38
  circular reasoning, 611
  excessive bias, 622–24
  hasty generalizations, 611–12
  irrelevant reasons, 613–14
  no evidence or comment as proof, 37, 628–29

personal character attacks, 626–27
playing on reader's emotions, 628
rhetorical questions, 37
slippery slope thinking, 627
tactic agreement, 629
unidentified or dated research, 36, 615–16
unidentified or inappropriate experts,
  614–15
author's purpose. *See* purpose, author's

background knowledge
  in introductory sentences, 117–18
  reading comprehension and, 28
  Web searches for, 28–40
bandwagon appeal, 38
bias
  acceptable, 622
  errors in logic and, 626–29
  excessive, 622–24
  personal character attacks, 626–27
  in persuasive writing, 621–24
  question for evaluating, 623
  tone and, 585, 623, 624
  on websites, 34, 38
  See also arguments, flawed; opinions;
    persuasive writing
boldface, for key terms, 3, 67, 70, 72, 182
bridging inferences, 375–76, 502

Carr, Nicholas, 47
category words, 157–58, 200
cause and effect pattern, 219–22
  chains of cause and effect in, 221–22
  characteristics of, 219
  common connectives in, 220–21
  pointers for, 222
  topic sentences in, 219
  transitions and verbs signaling, 220
chains of repetition and reference, 349–53
circular reasoning, 611, 617
classification pattern, 206–8
  characteristics of, 206
  pointers for, 207–8
  topic sentences in, 207
collaboration, between readers and writers, 377
common knowledge, allusions and, 90–91
common sense, appeals to, 616
comparison and contrast pattern, 211–15
  characteristics of, 211–13
  diagrams for, 212, 213, 215
  pointers for, 215
  topic sentences in, 213–14
  transitions indicating, 214

concept maps
  for definitions, 183
  for reviewing, 10
  for simple listing pattern, 201
conclusions
  compared with inferences, 398
  drawing personal, 398–99
  thesis statements as, 258
connotative language, 495–96
context, 77
  in definition pattern, 182
  specialized vocabulary and, 68
context clues, 77–79
continuation transitions, 131–32
contrast. *See* comparison and contrast pattern
contrast clues, 78
controlling main idea, 257. *See also* main idea

dates and events pattern. *See* sequence
  of dates and events pattern
definition pattern, 181–83
  characteristics of, 181–82
  pointers for, 183
  topic sentences in, 182–83
definitions
  concept maps for, 183
  for key terms, 67–68, 70, 71–72, 182
denotative language, 150, 495
details. *See* supporting details
dictionaries, 68–69, 77
differences, transitions indicating, 214

elaborative encoding, 52, 75
errors in reasoning. *See* arguments, flawed
evidence
  absence of, as proof, 37
  vague references to, 36
example clues, 78–79
examples
  in arguments, 551–52
  supporting details as, 151
expert opinions
  in arguments, 552–53
  in flawed arguments, 614–15, 617
  on websites, 36
explanatory patterns, 5, 6

facts
  blending opinions and, 495–96
  changing, 488–89
  characteristics of, 489
  in informative writing, 266
  informed opinions and, 501, 516

711